A HISTORY
OF RELIGIOUS
IDEAS

Translated from the French by Willard R. Trask

MIRCEA ELIADE

A HISTORY OF RELIGIOUS IDEAS

The University of Chicago Press

The University of Chicago Press, Chicago 60637
William Collins Sons & Co Ltd, London

Library of Congress Cataloging in Publication Data
Eliade, Mircea, 1907–
　　A History of religious ideas.
　　Translation of Histoire des croyances et des idées
religieuses.
　　CONTENTS:　1.　From the stone age to the Eleusinian
mysteries.
　　1. Religion—History. 2. Religions—History.
I. Title.
BL48.E3813　　　　291　　　　77-16784
ISBN 0-226-20400-6　(cloth)　　ISBN 0-226-20401-4　(paper)

Originally published in French under the
title *Histoire des croyances et des idées
religieuses*. Vol. 1: *De l'âge de la pierre
aux mystères d'Éleusis*. © Payot, Paris, 1976.

For Christinel

Contents

Preface

For the historian of religions, *every* manifestation of the sacred is important: every rite, every myth, every belief or divine figure reflects the experience of the sacred and hence implies the notions of *being*, of *meaning*, and of *truth*. As I observed on another occasion, "it is difficult to imagine how the human mind could function without the conviction that there is something irreducibly *real* in the world; and it is impossible to imagine how consciousness could appear without conferring a *meaning* on man's impulses and experiences. Consciousness of a real and meaningful world is intimately connected with the discovery of the sacred. Through experience of the sacred, the human mind has perceived the difference between what reveals itself as being real, powerful, rich, and meaningful and what lacks these qualities, that is, the chaotic and dangerous flux of things, their fortuitous and senseless appearances and disappearances" (preface to *The Quest: History and Meaning in Religion* [1969]). In short, the "sacred" is an element in the structure of consciousness and not a stage in the history of consciousness. On the most archaic levels of culture, *living, considered as being human*, is in itself a *religious act*, for food-getting, sexual life, and work have a sacramental value. In other words, to be—or, rather, to become—*a man* signifies being "religious" (ibid.).

I have discussed the dialectic of the sacred and its morphology in earlier publications, from my *Patterns in Comparative Religion* (1958) to my little book devoted to Australian religions (*Australian Religions: An Introduction* [1973]). The present work was conceived and executed from a different point of view. On the one hand, I have analyzed the manifestations of the sacred in chronological order (but it is important not to confuse the "age" of a religious conception with the date of the earliest document that attests to it!); on the other hand—and insofar as the documentation makes it possible—I have emphasized the crises in depth and, above all, the creative moments of the different traditions. In short, I have attempted to elucidate the major contributions to the history of religious ideas and beliefs.

Every manifestation of the sacred is important to the historian of religions; but it is no less obvious that the structure of the god Anu, for example, or the theogony and cosmogony handed down in the *Enuma elish*, or the saga of Gilgamesh, reveal the religious creativity and originality of the Mesopotamians more effectively than, let us say, the apotropaic rites against Lamashtu or the mythology of the god Nusku. Sometimes the importance of a religious creation is revealed by its later valorizations. Very little is known about the Eleusinian Mysteries and the earliest manifestations of Orphism; yet the fascination that they have exercised over the best minds of Europe for more than twenty centuries constitutes a *religious fact* that is highly significant and whose consequences have not yet been properly understood. Certainly, the Eleusinian initiation and the secret Orphic rites, extolled by certain late authors, reflect mythologizing Gnosticism and Greco-Oriental syncretism. But it is precisely *this* conception of the Mysteries and of Orphism that influenced medieval Hermeticism, the Italian Renaissance, the "occultist" traditions of the eighteenth century, and Romanticism; and the Mysteries and the Orpheus that inspired modern European poetry, from Rilke to T. S. Eliot and Pierre Emmanuel, are still the Mysteries and the Orpheus of the scholars and mystics and theologians of Alexandria.

The validity of the criterion chosen to define the great contributions to the history of religious ideas is, of course, open to discussion. Yet the development of many religions confirms it; for it is because of crises in depth and the creations that result from them that religious traditions are able to renew themselves. It is enough to cite the case of India, where the tension and despair brought on by the religious devalorization of the Brahmanic sacrifice produced a series of outstanding creations (the Upanishads, the codification of Yogic techniques, the message of Gautama Buddha, mystical devotion, etc.), each one of them constituting a different and daring resolution of the same crisis (see chapters 9, 17, 18, and 19).

For years I have had in mind a short, concise work, which could be read in a few days. For continuous reading reveals above all the *fundamental unity* of religious phenomena and at the same time the inexhaustible *newness* of their expressions. The reader of such a book would be given access to the Vedic hymns, the *Brāhmaṇas*, and the Upanishads a few hours after he had reviewed the ideas and beliefs of the Paleolithics, of Mesopotamia, and of Egypt; he would discover Sankara, Tantrism and Milarepa, Islam, Gioachino da Fiore or Paracelsus, the day after he had meditated on Zarathustra, Gautama Buddha, and Taoism, on the Hellenistic Mysteries, the rise of Christianity, Gnosticism, alchemy, or the mythology of the Grail; he would encounter the German illuminists and Romantics, Hegel, Max Müller, Freud, Jung, and Bonhoeffer, soon after discovering Quetzalcoatl and Viracocha, the twelve Alvârs and Gregory Palamas, the earliest Cabalists, Avicenna or Eisai.

Alas, that short, concise book has not yet been written. For the moment, I have resigned myself to presenting a work in three volumes, in the hope of eventually reducing it to one volume of some 400 pages. I have chosen this compromise formula for two reasons in particular: on the one hand, I considered it advisable to quote a certain number of texts that are both important and insufficiently known; on the other hand, I wanted to provide the student with comparatively full critical bibliographies. So I have reduced footnotes to the text to the absolute minimum and have brought together, in a separate section, the bibliographies and the discussion of certain matters either not referred to at all or treated too summarily in the text. Hence the work can be read continuously, without the interruptions necessitated by discussions of sources and summaries of the present position of studies on particular points. Books presenting a general view of a subject and intended for an audience of other than specialists usually provide a list of titles at the end of each chapter. The structure of this *History of Religious Ideas* demanded a more complex critical apparatus. So I have divided the chapters into numbered sections, each with its own title. The student can thus easily consult the bibliographies and the summaries of the present position of studies in the second part of the book as he pursues his reading of the text. For each section I have tried to provide the essential recent critical bibliography, not omitting works whose methodological orientation I do not share. With very few exceptions, I have not mentioned contributions published in the Scandinavian, Slavic, or

Balkan languages. To facilitate reading, I have simplified the trans-
literation of Oriental terms and proper names.

Except for a few chapters, this book reproduces the substance of the
courses in the History of Religions that I have given at the University
of Bucharest from 1933 to 1938, at the Ecole des Hautes Études in
1946 and 1948, and, since 1956, at the University of Chicago. I
belong to the category of historians of religions who, whatever their
"specialty" may be, make every effort to keep up with the progress
achieved in neighboring domains and do not hesitate to keep their
students informed concerning the various problems raised by their
discipline. I hold, in short, that any historical study implies a certain
familiarity with universal history; hence the strictest specialization
does not absolve the scholar from situating his researches in the
perspective of universal history. I also share the conviction of those
who think that the study of Dante or Shakespeare, and even of
Dostoevski or Proust, is illuminated by a knowledge of Kalidasa, the
Noh plays, or the *Pilgrim Monkey*. This is not a matter of a vain and,
in the end, sterile pseudo-encyclopedism. It is simply a matter of not
losing sight of the profound and indivisible unity of the history of the
human mind.

   Consciousness of this unity of the spiritual history of humanity is
a recent discovery, which has not yet been sufficiently assimilated.
Its importance for the future of our discipline will become manifest
in the last chapter of the third volume. It is also in this final chapter,
in the course of a discussion of the crises brought on by the masters
of reductionism—from Marx and Nietzsche to Freud—and of the
contributions made by anthropology, the history of religions, phe-
nomenology, and the new hermeneutics, that the reader will be able
to judge the sole, but important, religious creation of the modern
Western world. I refer to the ultimate stage of desacralization. The
process is of considerable interest to the historian of religions, for it
illustrates the complete camouflage of the "sacred"—more precisely,
its identification with the "profane."

In the course of fifty years of work, I have learned a great deal from
my masters, my colleagues, and my students. To all of them, whether
dead or living, I continue to feel the most sincere gratitude. Like
everything else that I have written since 1950, this book could not

have been brought to completion without the presence, the affection, and the devotion of my wife. It is with joy and gratitude that I inscribe her name on the first page of what will probably be my last contribution to a discipline that is dear to us.

M. E.

University of Chicago
September 1975

A HISTORY
OF RELIGIOUS
IDEAS

1 In the Beginning...: Magico-Religious Behavior of the Paleanthropians

1. *Orientatio*. Tools to make tools. The "domestication" of fire

Despite its importance for an understanding of the religious phenomenon, we shall not here discuss the problem of "hominization." It is sufficient to recall that the vertical posture already marks a transcending of the condition typical of the primates. Uprightness cannot be maintained except in a state of wakefulness. It is because of man's vertical posture that space is organized in a structure inaccessible to the prehominians: in four horizontal directions radiating from an "up"-"down" central axis. In other words, space can be organized around the human body as extending forward, backward, to right, to left, upward, and downward. It is from this original and originating experience—feeling oneself "thrown" into the middle of an apparently limitless, unknown, and threatening extension—that the different methods of *orientatio* are developed; for it is impossible to survive for any length of time in the vertigo brought on by disorientation. This experience of space oriented around a "center" explains the importance of the paradigmatic divisions and distributions of territories, agglomerations, and habitations and their cosmological symbolism (cf. § 12).[1]

An equally decisive difference from the mode of existence of the primates is clearly shown by the use of tools. The Paleanthropians not only use tools, they are also able to manufacture them. It is true that certain monkeys use objects as if they were tools, and are even known to make them in certain cases. But the Paleanthropians also produce tools to make tools. In addition, their use of tools is much

1. Though he is no longer conscious of its "existential" value, the experience of oriented space is still familiar to the man of modern societies.

more complex; they keep them accessible, ready for use in the future. In short, their use of tools is not confined to a particular situation or a specific moment, as is the case with monkeys. It is also important to note that tools do not serve as extensions of the human body, for the earliest-known worked stones were shaped to perform a function not prefigured in the body's structure, namely, the function of cutting (an action completely different from tearing with the teeth or scratching with the nails).[2] The very slow progress made in technology does not imply a similar development of intelligence. We know that the extraordinary upsurge in technology during the past two centuries has not found expression in a comparable development of Western man's intelligence. Besides, as has been said, "every innovation brought with it the danger of collective death" (André Varagnac). Their technical immobility insured the survival of the Paleanthropians.

The domestication of fire—that is, the possibility of producing, preserving, and transporting it—marks, we might say, the definitive separation of the Paleanthropians from their zoological predecessors. The most ancient "document" for the use of fire dates from Choukoutien (about 600,000 B.C.), but its domestication probably took place much earlier and in several places.

These few well-known facts needed to be repeated so that the reader of the following analyses will bear in mind that prehistoric man already behaved in the manner of a being endowed with intelligence and imagination. As for the activity of the unconscious— dreams, fantasies, visions, fabulization, and so on—it is presumed not to have differed in intensity and scope from what is found among our contemporaries. But the terms "intensity" and "scope" must be understood in their strongest and most dramatic sense. For man is the final product of a decision made "at the beginnings of Time": the decision to kill in order to live. In short, the hominians succeeded in outstripping their ancestors by becoming flesh-eaters. For some two million years, the Paleanthropians lived by hunting; fruits, roots, mollusks, and so on, gathered by the women and children, did not suffice to insure the survival of the species. Hunting determined the division of labor in accordance with sex, thus reinforcing "hominization"; for among the carnivora, and in the entire animal world, no such difference exists.

2. See Karl Narr, "Approaches to the Social Life of Earliest Man," pp. 605 ff.

But the ceaseless pursuit and killing of game ended by creating a unique system of relationships between the hunter and the slain animals. We shall return to this problem. For the moment, we merely state that the "mystical solidarity" between the hunter and his victims is revealed by the mere act of killing: the shed blood is similar in every respect to human blood. In the last analysis, this "mystical solidarity" with the game reveals the kinship between human societies and the animal world. To kill the hunted beast or, later, the domestic animal is equivalent to a "sacrifice" in which the victims are interchangeable.[3] We must add that all these concepts came into existence during the last phases of the process of hominization. They are still active—altered, revalorized, camouflaged—millennia after the disappearance of the Paleolithic civilizations.

2. The "opaqueness" of prehistoric documents

If the Paleanthropians are regarded as complete men, it follows that they also possessed a certain number of beliefs and practiced certain rites. For, as we stated before, the experience of the sacred constitutes an element in the structure of consciousness. In other words, if the question of the religiosity or nonreligiosity of prehistoric men is raised, it falls to the defenders of nonreligiosity to adduce proofs in support of their hypothesis. Probably the theory of the nonreligiosity of the Paleanthropians was conceived and generally accepted during the heyday of evolutionism, when similarities to the primates had just been discovered. But a misconception is involved here, for what matters is not the anatomico-osteological structure of the Paleanthropians (which is similar, to be sure, to that of the primates) but their *works*; and these demonstrate the activity of an intelligence that cannot be defined otherwise than as "human."

But if today there is agreement on the fact that the Paleanthropians had a religion, in practice it is difficult, if not impossible, to determine what its content was. The investigators, however, have not cried defeat; for there remain a certain number of testimonial "documents" for the life of the Paleanthropians, and it is hoped that their religious

3. This extremely archaic idea still survived into Mediterranean antiquity; not only were animals substituted for human victims (a custom universally disseminated), but men were sacrificed in the place of animals. See Walter Burkert, *Homo Necans*, p. 29, n. 34.

meaning will one day be deciphered. In other words, it is hoped that these "documents" can constitute a "language," just as, thanks to the genius of Freud, the creations of the unconscious, which until his time were regarded as absurd or meaningless—dreams, waking dreams, phantasms, and so on—have revealed the existence of a language that is extremely precious for a knowledge of man.

These documents are, in fact, comparatively numerous, but they are "opaque" and not very various: human bones, especially skulls, stone tools, pigments (most abundantly red ocher, hematite), various objects found in burials. It is only from the late Paleolithic that we have rock paintings and engravings, painted pebbles, and bone and stone statuettes. In certain cases (burials, works of art) and within the limits that we shall examine, there is at least the certainty of a religious intention, but the majority of the documents from before the Aurignacian (30,000 B.C.)—that is, tools—reveal nothing beyond their utilitarian value.

Yet it is inconceivable that tools were not charged with a certain sacrality and did not inspire numerous mythological episodes. The first technological discoveries—the transformation of stone into instruments for attack and defense, the mastery over fire—not only insured the survival and development of the human species; they also produced a universe of mythico-religious values and inspired and fed the creative imagination. It is enough to examine the role of tools in the religious life and mythology of the primitives who still remain at the hunting and fishing stage. The magico-religious value of a weapon—be it made of wood or stone or metal—still survives among the rural populations of Europe, and not only in their folklore. We shall not here consider the kratophanies and hierophanies of stone, of rocks, of pebbles; the reader will find examples of these in a chapter of our *Patterns in Comparative Religion*.

It is, above all, mastery over distance, gained by the projectile weapon, which gave rise to countless beliefs, myths, and legends. We need only think of the mythologies built up around lances that pierce the vault of the sky and thus make an ascent to heaven possible, of arrows that fly through clouds, transfix demons, or form a chain reaching to heaven, and so on. It is necessary to cite at least some of the beliefs and mythologies that surround tools and implements— and especially weapons—in order better to estimate all that the worked stones of the Paleanthropians *can no longer communicate to us*.

The semantic opaqueness of these prehistoric documents is not peculiar to them. Every document, even of our own time, is spiritually opaque as long as it has not been successfully deciphered by being integrated into a system of meanings. A tool, be it prehistoric or contemporary, can reveal only its technological intention; all that its producer or its owners thought, felt, dreamed, hoped in relation to it escapes us. But we must at least try to imagine the nonmaterial values of prehistoric tools. Otherwise, this semantic opaqueness may well force us to entertain a completely erroneous conception of the history of culture. We are in danger, for example, of confusing the appearance of a belief with the date at which it is clearly documented for the first time.[4] When, in the age of metals, certain traditions refer to craft secrets in respect to mining, metallurgy, and the making of weapons, it would be rash to believe that we are in the presence of an unprecedented invention, for these traditions continue, at least in part, an inheritance from the Stone Age.

For some two million years, the Paleanthropians lived chiefly by hunting, fishing, and gathering. But the first archeological indications in respect to the religious universe of the Paleolithic hunter go back only to Franco-Cantabrian rock art (30,000 B.C.). What is more, if we examine the religious beliefs and behavior of contemporary hunting peoples, we realize the almost complete impossibility of *proving the existence or the absence* of similar beliefs among the Paleanthropians. Primitive hunters[5] regard animals as similar to men but endowed with supernatural powers; they believe that a man can change into an animal and vice versa; that the souls of the dead can enter animals; finally, that mysterious relations exist between a certain person and a certain animal (this used to be termed "nagualism"). As for the supernatural beings documented in the religions of hunting peoples, we find that they are of various kinds: theriomorphic companions or guardian spirits—divinities of the type Supreme Being–Lord of Wild Beasts—which protect both the game and the hunters; spirits of the bush; and spirits of the different species of animals.

In addition, certain patterns of religious behavior are peculiar to

4. Strictly applied, this method would have led to dating the German folktales at 1812–22, the date of their publication by the brothers Grimm.

5. For the sake of simplicity, we use the synthetic account by J. Haeckel, "Jäger und Jagdriten," *Religion in Geschichte und Gegenwart*, 3d ed. (1959), vol. 3, cols. 511–13.

hunting civilizations. For example, killing the animal constitutes a ritual, which implies the belief that the Lord of Wild Beasts takes care that the hunter kills only what he needs as food and that food is not wasted. Then, too, the bones, especially the skull, have a marked ritual value (probably because of the belief that they contain the "soul" or the "life" of the animal and that it is from the skeleton that the Lord of Wild Beasts will cause a new flesh to grow); this is why the skull and the long bones are exposed on branches or on high places. Finally, among certain peoples the soul of the slain animal is sent to its spiritual home (cf. the "bear festival" among the Ainus and the Giliaks); the custom of offering the Supreme Beings a piece of each slain animal (Pygmies, Philippine Negritos, and others) or the skull and the long bones (Samoyeds and others) also exists; and among certain Sudanese peoples the young man, after bringing down his first game animal, smears the walls of a cave with its blood.

How many of these beliefs and ceremonies can be identified in the archeological documents in our possession? At most, the offerings of skulls and long bones. The richness and complexity of the religious ideology of hunting peoples must never be underestimated—and likewise the almost complete impossibility of proving or denying its existence among the Paleanthropians. As has often been said: beliefs and ideas cannot be fossilized. Hence certain scholars have preferred to say nothing about the ideas and beliefs of the Paleanthropians, instead of reconstructing them by the help of comparisons with the hunting civilizations. This radical methodological position is not without its dangers. To leave an immense part of the history of the human mind a blank runs the risk of encouraging the idea that during all those millennia the activity of the mind was confined to the preservation and transmission of technology. Such an opinion is not only erroneous, it is fatal to a knowledge of man. *Homo faber* was at the same time *Homo ludens*, *sapiens*, and *religiosus*. Since we cannot reconstruct his religious beliefs and practices, we must at least point out certain analogies that can illuminate them, if only indirectly.

3. Symbolic meanings of burials

The earliest and most numerous "documents" are, obviously, bones. From the Mousterian (70,000–50,000 B.C.), we can speak with certainty of burials. But skulls and lower mandibles have been found at much earlier sites, for example at Choukoutien (at a level datable at 400,000–300,000 B.C.), and their presence has raised problems. Since there is no question of burials here, the preservation of these skulls could be explained as due to religious reasons. The Abbé Breuil and Wilhelm Schmidt have referred to the custom, documented among the Australians and other primitive peoples,[6] of preserving the skulls of dead relatives and carrying them along when the tribe travels. Though credible, the hypothesis has not been accepted by most scholars. The same facts have also been interpreted as proof of cannibalism, whether ritual or profane. It is in this way that A. C. Blanc has explained the mutilation of a Neanderthal skull found in a cave at Monte Circeo: the man would have been killed by a blow that broke his right eye-socket and the hole would later have been enlarged so that the brain could be extracted through it and eaten ritually. But this explanation has not been unanimously accepted either.[7]

Belief in a survival after death seems to be demonstrated, from the earliest times, by the use of red ocher as a ritual substitute for blood, hence as a symbol of life. The custom of dusting corpses with ocher is universally disseminated in both time and space, from Choukoutien to the western shores of Europe, in Africa as far as the Cape of Good Hope, in Australia, in Tasmania, in America as far as Tierra del Fuego. As to the religious meaning of burials, it has been the subject of vigorous controversy. There can be no doubt that the burial of the dead *should* have a justification—but which one? To begin with, it must not be forgotten that "pure and simple abandonment of the corpse in some thicket, dismemberment, leaving it to be devoured by birds, instant flight from the habitation, leaving the corpse inside it, did not signify the absence of ideas of survival."[8] A fortiori, belief in survival is confirmed by burials; otherwise there would be no understanding the effort expended in interring the body. This survival

6. J. Maringer, *The Gods of Prehistoric Man*, pp. 18 ff.
7. Leroi-Gourhan is not convinced that the man was killed and eaten (*Les religions de la préhistoire*, p. 44). Maringer, who had refused to recognize anthropophagy at Choukoutien (*Gods of Prehistoric Man*, p. 20), also rejects Blanc's explanation (ibid., pp. 31 ff.). See, however, Müller-Karpe, *Altsteinzeit*, pp. 230 ff., 240, and M. K. Roper, "A Survey of Evidence for Intrahuman Killing in the Pleistocene."
8. Leroi-Gourhan, p. 54.

could be purely spiritual, that is, conceived as a postexistence of the soul, a belief corroborated by the appearance of the dead in dreams. But certain burials can equally well be interpreted as a precaution against the possible return of the deceased; in these cases the corpses were bent and perhaps tied. On the other hand, nothing makes it impossible that the bent position of the dead body, far from expressing fear of "living corpses" (a fear documented among certain peoples), on the contrary signifies the hope of a rebirth; for we know of a number of cases of intentional burial in the fetal position.

Among the best examples of burials with a magico-religious signification we will mention the one at Teshik Tash, in Uzbekistan (a child surrounded by an arrangement of ibex horns); the one at La Chapelle-aux-Saints, in Corrèze (several flint tools and some pieces of red ocher[9] were found in the excavation in which the body lay); and the one at Farrassie, in Dordogne (several grave mounds, with deposits of flint tools). The cemetery in a cave on Mount Carmel, with ten burials, should be added. The authenticity and the meaning of food offerings or objects placed in graves are still the subject of discussion; the most familiar example is that of the woman's skull at Mas-d'Azil, fitted with artificial eyes and placed on the lower jaw and antler of a reindeer.[10]

During the Upper Paleolithic, the practice of inhumation appears to have become general. Corpses sprinkled with red ocher are buried in graves in which a certain number of objects intended for personal adornment (shells, pendants, necklaces) have been found. It is probable that the animal skulls and bones discovered near graves are the remains of ritual feasts, if not of offerings. Leroi-Gourhan holds that "funerary chattels," that is, the personal objects of the deceased, are "very questionable" (*Les religions de la préhistoire*, p. 62). The problem is important, for the presence of such objects implies not only belief in a personal survival but also the certainty that the

9. Recent archeological discoveries have shown that hematite was extracted from a mine in Swaziland 29,000 years ago and, in Rhodesia, 43,000 years ago. The extraction of hematite from these African mines continued for millennia. The discovery of a similar operation near Lake Baraton, in Hungary, occurring about 24,000 B.C., illustrates the technical capabilities of the Paleolithics and the extent of their communications. See R. A. Dart, "The Multimillennial Prehistory of Ochre Mining" and "The Birth of Symbology," pp. 21 ff.

10. According to Leroi-Gourhan, this find represents a "heap of culinary detritus on which a probably secularized and certainly displaced human relic lay" (p. 57).

deceased will continue his particular activity in the other world. Similar ideas are abundantly documented, and on various levels of culture. In any case, Leroi-Gourhan (p. 63) recognizes the authenticity of an Aurignacian grave in Liguria, where the skeleton is accompanied by four of those mysterious objects called *bâtons de commandement*. Hence at least certain graves undoubtedly indicate belief in a postmortem continuation of a particular activity.[11]

To sum up, we may conclude that the burials confirm the belief in survival (already indicated by the use of red ocher) and furnish some additional details: burials oriented toward the East, showing an intention to connect the fate of the soul with the course of the sun, hence the hope of a rebirth, that is, of a postexistence in another world; belief in the continuation of a specific activity; certain funeral rites, indicated by offerings of objects of personal adornment and by the remains of meals.

But an examination of burial as practiced by an archaic people of our own time is enough to demonstrate the richness and depth of the religious symbolism implied in a ceremony that appears to be so simple. Reichel-Dolmatoff has given a detailed description of a contemporary (1966) burial of a girl among the Kogi Indians, a tribe speaking the Chibcha language and inhabiting the Sierra Nevada de Santa Maria in Colombia.[12] After choosing the site for the grave, the shaman (*máma*) performs a series of ritual gestures and declares: "Here is the village of Death; here is the ceremonial house of Death; here is the womb. I will open the house. The house is shut, and I will open it." After this he announces, "The house is open," shows the men the place where they are to dig the grave, and withdraws. The dead girl is wrapped in white cloth, and her father sews the shroud. During all this time her mother and grandmother chant a slow, almost wordless song. Small green stones, shells of shellfish, and the shell of a gastropod are placed in the bottom of the grave. Then the shaman tries to lift the body, giving the impression that it is too heavy; he does not succeed until the ninth attempt. The body is laid with its head toward the East, and ".the house is closed," that is, the excavation is filled up. Other ritual movements around the grave

11. It should be noted that other scholars hold that the number of authentic "documents" found in graves is much larger.

12. C. Reichel-Dolmatoff, "Notas sobre el simbolismo religioso de los Indios de la Sierra Nevada de Santa Maria," *Razon y Fabula, Revista de la Universidad de los Andes*, no. 1 (1967), pp. 55–72.

follow, and finally all withdraw. The ceremony has continued for two hours.

As Reichel-Dolmatoff observes, a future archeologist, excavating the grave, will find only a skeleton with its head toward the East and some stones and shells. The rites, and especially the implied religious ideology, are no longer recoverable on the basis of these remains.[13] In addition, the symbolism will remain inaccessible even to a contemporary observer who does not know the religion of the Kogi. For, as Reichel-Dolmatoff writes, what is involved is verbalization of the cemetery as "village of Death" and "ceremonial house of Death," and verbalization of the grave as "house" and "womb" (which explains the fetal position of the corpse, laid on its left side), followed by verbalization of the offerings as "food for Death," and by the ritual of the "opening" and "closing" of the "house-womb." A final purification by a ritual circumvallation completes the ceremony.

On the other hand, the Kogi identify the world—womb of the Universal Mother—with each village, each cult house, each habitation, and each grave. When the shaman lifts the corpse nine times, he indicates the return of the body to the fetal state by going through the nine months of gestation in reverse order. And since the grave is assimilated to the world, the funerary offerings acquire a cosmic meaning. In addition, the offerings, "food for Death," also have a sexual meaning (in the myths, dreams, and marriage regulations of the Kogi the act of eating symbolizes the sexual act) and consequently constitute a "semen" that fertilizes the Mother. The shellfish shells carry a quite complex symbolism, which is not only sexual: they represent the living members of the family. On the other hand, the gastropod shell symbolizes the dead girl's "husband," for if it is not present in the grave, the girl, as soon as she reaches the other world, "will demand a husband," and this will cause the death of a young man of the tribe.[14]

Here we end our analysis of the religious symbolism contained in a Kogi burial. But it is important to emphasize that, *approached solely on the archeological level*, this symbolism is as inaccessible to us as that of a Paleolithic interment. It is the particular modality of

13. It was, in fact, almost unknown before Reichel-Dolmatoff's observations.
14. This custom is extremely widespread, and it still survives in eastern Europe, where those who die young are "married" to a fir tree.

archeological documents that limits and impoverishes the "messages" that they can transmit. This fact must always be kept in mind when we are confronted by the poverty and opaqueness of our sources.

4.   The controversy concerning deposits of bones

Deposits of bones of cave bears, discovered in the Alps and the surrounding regions, constitute the most numerous, but also the most hotly debated, "documents" concerning the religious ideas of the last interglacial period. In the Drachenloch cave (Switzerland) Emil Bächler found deposits of bones, principally of skulls and long bones; they were grouped together and placed along the cave wall, or in natural niches in the rock, or in a sort of stone coffer. From 1923 to 1925, Bächler explored another cave, the Wildenmannlisloch; here he found several bear skulls without mandibles, with long bones placed among them. Similar discoveries were made by other prehistorians in various caves in the Alps; the most important were in the Drachenhoetli, in Styria, and in the Petershoehle, in Franconia, where K. Hoermann discovered bear skulls in niches 1.20 meters above the cave floor. Similarly, in 1950, K. Ehrenberg found in the Salzofenhoehle (Austrian Alps) three bear skulls in natural niches in the cave wall and associated with long bones oriented from East to West.

Since these deposits appeared to be intentional, scholars set themselves to decipher their meaning. A. Gahs compared them to the offering of first fruits (*Primitialopfer*) made by certain Arctic peoples to a supreme being. This consisted in exposing the skull and long bones of the slain animal on platforms; the divinity was offered the animal's brain and marrow, that is, the parts most relished by the hunter. This interpretation was accepted by Wilhelm Schmidt and W. Koppers, among others; for these ethnologists, here was proof that the cave-bear hunters of the last interglacial period believed in a Supreme Being or a Lord of Wild Beasts. Other authors compared the deposits of skulls with the bear cult as it is—or was, until the nineteenth century—practiced in the Northern Hemisphere. This cult involves preserving the skull and long bones of the slain bear so that the Lord of Wild Beasts can resuscitate it the following year. Karl Meuli saw in it only a particular form of the "interment of animals," which he regarded as the earliest of hunting rites. For the

Swiss scholar, the rite showed a direct relation between hunter and game; the former interred the remains of the latter in order to permit its reincarnation. No divine being was implied.

All these interpretations were questioned by a scholar from Basel, F. E. Koby, according to whom many "deposits" of skulls result from chance and from the bears themselves moving and scratching among the bones. Leroi-Gourhan has declared that he is in complete agreement with this radical critique: the skulls contained in stone "coffers," grouped along the walls, or suspended in niches and surrounded by long bones are explained by geological facts and by the behavior of the bears themselves (*Les religions de la préhistoire*, pp. 31 ff.). This critique of the intentionality of the deposits appears to be convincing, all the more so since the earliest excavations of the caves left much to be desired; nevertheless, it is surprising that the same type of deposit should be found in a number of caves, especially in niches more than a meter above the cave floor. In addition, Leroi-Gourhan recognizes that "rehandling by man is probable in some instances" (p. 31).

In any case, the interpretation of deposits as offerings to supreme beings has been discarded, even by the supporters of Wilhelm Schmidt and W. Koppers. In a recent study of sacrifices among the Paleanthropians, Johannes Maringer came to the following conclusions: (1) on the level of the Lower Paleolithic (Torralba, Choukoutien, Lehringen), *sacrifices* are not documented; (2) the documents from the Middle Paleolithic (Drachenloch, Petershoehle, etc.) can be interpreted in various ways, but their *religious* character (i.e., as sacrifices to supernatural beings) is not evident; (3) it is not until the Upper Paleolithic (Willendorf, Meiendorf, Stellmoor, Montespan, etc.) that it is possible to speak, "with more or less certainty," of sacrifices.[15]

As might be expected, the investigator is confronted either by the *absence* of irrefutable documents or by the *semantic opaqueness* of those documents whose authenticity appears to be certain. The spiritual activity of the Paleanthropians—like that, be it added, of the "primitives" of our day—left fragile traces. To give only one example, the arguments adduced by Koby and Leroi-Gourhan can equally well be used to invalidate their own conclusions: the geological facts and the behavior of cave bears suffice to explain the *absence* of

15. J. Maringer, "Die Opfer der paläolithischen Menschen," p. 271.

ritual deposits. As to the *semantic opacity* of the bone deposits whose authenticity is certain, parallels are found among contemporary Arctic hunters. In itself, the deposit is simply the *expression of a magico-religious intentionality*; the particular meanings of the act become accessible to us only through the information communicated by members of the respective societies. We then learn whether the skulls and long bones represent offerings to a Supreme Being or a Lord of Wild Beasts, or whether, on the contrary, they are preserved in the hope that they will be covered with flesh again. Even this last belief can be interpreted in various ways: the animal is reborn by virtue either of the Lord of Wild Beasts or of the soul that resides in its bones or, finally, by virtue of the fact that the hunter has provided it with a burial (to keep its bones from being devoured by dogs).

We must always take into consideration the multiplicity of possible interpretations of a document whose magico-religious intentionality is probable. On the other hand, we must not forget that, whatever the difference between the Arctic hunters and the Paleolithics may be, they all share the same economy and very probably the same religious ideology, both of which are specific characteristics of hunting civilizations. Hence, comparison of prehistoric documents with ethnological facts is justified.

It has been proposed to interpret from this point of view the discovery in Silesia of the fossil skull of a young brown bear belonging to a level of the early Aurignacian; while the incisors and canines had been sawed or filed, the molars were still in excellent condition. W. Koppers has referred this find to the bear festival among the Giliaks of the island of Sakhalin and the Ainus of the island of Yezo; here, before it is slaughtered, the canines and incisors of the young bear are cut with a sort of saw, so that it can no longer wound the participants in the ceremony.[16] And since, during the same ceremony, the children shoot showers of arrows into the bound animal, the same interpretation has been proposed for certain parietal engravings in the Trois Frères cave, which show bears struck by arrows and stones and apparently vomiting a stream of blood.[17] But such scenes can be interpreted in various ways.

16. This is an extremely important ritual: the bear's soul is sent as a messenger from men to the guardian divinity, so that the latter will insure the success of future hunts.

17. Cf. J. Maringer, *The Gods of Prehistoric Man*, pp. 103 ff. and fig. 14.

The importance of an archaic religious idea is likewise confirmed by its ability to survive into later periods. Thus the belief that an animal can be reborn from its bones is found in a considerable number of cultures.[18] That is why it is forbidden to break the bones of animals whose flesh has been eaten. This is an idea which is proper to the civilizations of hunters and herders but which has survived in more complex religions and mythologies. A well-known example is that of Thor's goats, which had their throats cut and were eaten in the evening but which the god resuscitated from their bones the next day (*Gylfaginning*, chap. 26). Equally well known is a vision seen by Ezekiel (37:1–8 ff.): the prophet was transported into a "valley full of bones" and, obeying the Lord's command, he spoke to them: "Dry bones, hear the word of Yahweh. The Lord Yahweh says this to these bones: I am now going to make the breath enter you, and you will live. . . . There was a noise, a sound of clattering; and the bones joined together. I looked, and saw that they were covered with sinews; flesh was growing on them."[19]

5.   Rock paintings: Images or symbols?

The most important and most numerous figurative documents have been provided by the exploration of decorated caves. These treasures of Paleolithic art are disseminated over a comparatively restricted territory, between the Urals and the Atlantic. Objects of mobiliary art have been found in much of western and central Europe and in Russia as far as the Don. But parietal art is confined to Spain, France, and southern Italy (with the exception of a painted cave in the Urals, discovered in 1961). What strikes us first of all, as Leroi-Gourhan remarks, is the "extraordinary unity of the artistic content: the apparent import of the images seems not to have varied from 30,000 B.C. to 9000 B.C. and remains the same in Asturias and on the Don."[20] According to Leroi-Gourhan (p. 84), we here have a

---

18. See Eliade, *Shamanism: Archaic Techniques of Ecstasy*, pp. 160 ff., with the bibliographies cited in the notes, and especially Joseph Henninger, "Neuere Forschungen zum Verbot des Knochenzerbrechens," passim.

19. Unless otherwise specified, this and all other quotations from the Bible are from *The Jerusalem Bible*, ed. A. Jones et al. (Garden City, N.Y.: Doubleday, 1966).

20. Leroi-Gourhan, *Les religions de la préhistoire*, p. 83.

dissemination by contact of a single ideological system—notably, the system that marks the "religion of the caves."[21]

Since the paintings are found at a considerable distance from the entrance, investigators agree in regarding the caves as a sort of sanctuary. Besides, many of these caves were uninhabitable, and difficulties of access reinforced their numinous character. To reach the decorated walls it is necessary to proceed for hundreds of meters, as in the case of the Niaux and Trois Frères caves. The Cabarets cave is a real labyrinth, a journey through which takes several hours. At Lascaux, access to the lower gallery, which contains one of the masterpieces of Paleolithic art, is obtained by descending a rope ladder through a shaft 6.30 meters deep. The intentionality of these painted or engraved works seems to be beyond doubt. To interpret them, the majority of investigators appealed to ethnological parallels. Certain comparisons were not convincing, especially when an insistent attempt was made to "complete" the Paleolithic document in order to increase its likeness to some ethnological analogue. But such risky explanations impugn only their authors, not the method which they claimed to use.

The bears, lions, and other wild animals riddled with arrows, or the clay figures found in the Montespan cave and representing a bear and several lions pierced by deep round holes, have been interpreted as proofs of "hunting magic."[22] The hypothesis is plausible, but some of these works could as well be interpreted as the reactualization of a primordial hunt. It is also probable that rites were performed in the deepest parts of the "sanctuaries," perhaps before a hunting expedition or on the occasion of what could be termed the "initiation" of adolescents.[23] A scene in the Trois Frères cave has been

21. Leroi-Gourhan has established the chronology and morphology of Paleolithic works of art, which he divides into five epochs, beginning with the Prefigurative period (50,000 B.C.), followed by the Primitive period (30,000 B.C.), in which strongly stylized figures appear; the Archaic period (ca. 20,000–15,000 B.C.), characterized by great technical mastery; the Classic period (during the Magdalenian, ca. 15,000–11,000 B.C.), with a realism of forms that is carried very far, only to decline and end in the Late period (ca. 10,000 B.C.).

22. Bégouen and Casteret have reconstructed a whole ritual on the basis of the Montespan figure of a bear modeled in clay; see the critique of this reconstruction by P. Graziosi, *Palaeolithic Art*, p. 152, and cf. Peter J. Ucko and André Rosenfeld, *Paleolithic Cave Art*, pp. 188–89, for a discussion of Bégouen and Casteret's publications.

23. Charet has interpreted the prints of human feet in the Tuc d'Aubert cave as a proof of the initiation of boys; the hypothesis has been accepted by

explained as representing a dancer masked as a bison and playing an instrument that might be a flute. The interpretation seems convincing, since we know, in Paleolithic art, some fifty-five representations of men dressed in skins, often in a dancing posture.[24] In addition, this is a characteristic ritual behavior of contemporary hunting peoples.

The Abbé Breuil has given celebrity to the "Great Magician" of the Trois Frères cave, an engraving 75 centimeters high cut into the wall. Breuil's drawing of it shows a figure with the head of a stag bearing large antlers, but with the face of an owl, the ears of a wolf, and the beard of a chamois. Its arms end in bear paws, and it has a long horse's tail. Only the lower limbs, the sex, and the dancing posture indicate that the figure is that of a human being. But recent photographs taken in the cave do not show all the elements carefully described by Breuil.[25] It is possible that certain details have been damaged since the discovery of the engraving (for example, the second antler), but it is not impossible that the Abbé Breuil made his sketch incorrectly. As it appears in recent photographs, the "Great Magician" is less impressive. However, the figure can be interpreted as a Lord of Wild Beasts or as a sorcerer personifying him. In addition, a slate slab recently discovered at Lourdes shows a man wrapped in a deerskin, with a horse's tail and with his head surmounted by antlers.

No less celebrated, and no less the subject of controversy, is the famous composition recently discovered at Lascaux, in a lower gallery to which access is extremely difficult. It shows a wounded bison thrusting its horns toward a man who is apparently dead and who lies on the ground; his weapon, a sort of pike with a hook, is pressed against the animal's belly; near the man (whose head ends in a beak) is a bird on a perch. The scene has generally been interpreted as representing a hunting accident. In 1950 Horst Kirchner proposed seeing in it a shamanic séance; in this case, the man would not be dead but in a trance before the sacrificed bison, while his soul would be traveling in the beyond. The perched bird, a motif typical of Siberian shamanism, would be his guardian spirit. According to Kirchner, the séance was undertaken to enable the shaman to travel,

---

some scholars but is rejected by Ucko and Rosenfeld, *Paleolithic Cave Art*, pp. 177–78.

24. Maringer, *The Gods of Prehistoric Man*, p. 145.

25. Ucko and Rosenfeld, fig. 89 and pp. 204, 206.

in ecstasy, into the presence of the gods to ask for their blessing, that is, for success in the hunt. The same author considers that the mysterious *bâtons de commandement* are drumsticks. If this interpretation is accepted, it would mean that the Paleolithic sorcerers used drums comparable to those of the Siberian shamans.[26]

Kirchner's explanation has been disputed, and we do not consider ourselves competent to pronounce on it. However, the existence of a certain type of shamanism during the Paleolithic period seems to be certain. On the one hand, shamanism still dominates the religious ideology of hunters and pastoralists in our day. On the other hand, the ecstatic experience as such, as an original phenomenon, is a constitutive element of the human condition; it is impossible to imagine a period in which man did not have dreams and waking reveries and did not enter into "trance"—a loss of consciousness that was interpreted as the soul's traveling into the beyond. What was modified and changed with the different forms of culture and religion was the interpretation and evaluation of the ecstatic experience. Since the spiritual universe of the Paleolithics was dominated by the mystical relations between man and animal, it is not difficult to divine the functions of a specialist in ecstasy.

The so-called X-ray drawings, that is, drawings showing the skeleton and internal organs of the animal, have also been referred to shamanism. These drawings, documented in France during the Magdalenian (13,000–6000 B.C.) and in Norway between 6000 and 2000 B.C., are also found in eastern Siberia, among the Eskimos, in America (among the Ojibways, the Pueblos, and others), but also in India, Malaysia, New Guinea, and northwestern Australia.[27] It is an art specifically characteristic of hunting cultures, but the religious ideology with which it is saturated is shamanic. For it is only the shaman who, by virtue of his supernatural vision, is able to "see his own skeleton."[28] In other words, he is able to penetrate even into the source of animal life, the bony element. That we here have an experience fundamental for a certain type of mystic is proved, among other things, by the fact that it is still cultivated in Tibetan Buddhism.

26. H. Kirchner, "Ein archäologischer Beitrag zur Urgeschichte des Schamanismus," pp. 244 ff., 279 ff. In this connection we may cite the fact that bone drumsticks have been found on the island of Oleny in the Barents Sea, in a site dated ca. 500 B.C.; cf. Eliade, *Shamanism*, p. 503.
27. Andreas Lommel, *Shamanism: The Beginnings of Art*, pp. 129 ff.
28. Eliade, *Shamanism*, pp. 62 ff.

6. The presence of woman

The discovery of feminine representations in the last Ice Age has raised problems that are still being discussed. Their distribution is quite extensive, from southwestern France to Lake Baikal in Siberia, and from northern Italy to the Rhine. The statuettes, which range from 5 to 25 centimeters in height, are carved in stone, bone, and ivory. They have been called, quite unjustifiably, "Venuses," the most celebrated being the Venuses of Lespuges, Willendorf (Austria), and Laussel (Dordogne).[29] However, especially because of the scrupulousness of the excavations, the most instructive examples are the ones discovered at Gagarino and Mezine in the Ukraine. They come from levels of habitation and hence seem to be related to domestic religion. Gagarino has yielded, close to the walls of the habitation, six figurines carved from bones of the mammoth. They are carved summarily, with an abdomen of exaggerated size and a head without features. The examples discovered at Mezine are strongly stylized; some of them can be interpreted as female forms reduced to geometric elements (this type is documented elsewhere in central Europe); others very probably represent birds. The figurines are decorated with various geometric designs, among others the swastika. To explain their possible religious function, Hančar has cited the fact that certain hunting tribes of northern Asia make small anthropomorphic sculptures called *dzuli*. In the tribes in which the *dzuli* are female, these "idols" represent the mythical ancestress from whom all members of the tribe are presumed to descend; they protect the tribal families and habitations, and upon the return from great hunts they are given offerings of wheat flour and fat.

Still more significant is Gerasimov's discovery, at Mal'ta, in Siberia, of a "village" whose rectangular houses were divided into two halves, the right half reserved for men (only objects of masculine use were found), and the left half belonging to the women; the female statuettes come only from this section. Their homologues in the male quarters represent birds, but some of them have been interpreted as phalluses.[30]

29. Franz Hančar, "Zum Problem der Venusstatuetten in eurasiatischen Jungpaläolithikum," pp. 90 ff., 150 ff.
30. M. M. Gerasimov, "Paleolithischeskaja stojanka Mal'ta," p. 40, summarized by Karl Jettmar in *Les religions arctiques et finnoises*, p. 292.

It is impossible to determine the religious function of these figurines. Presumably they in some sort represent feminine sacrality and hence the magico-religious powers of the goddesses. The "mystery" constituted by woman's particular mode of existence has played an important part in numerous religions, both primitive and historical. We owe it to Leroi-Gourhan to have illuminated the central function of the polarity masculine/feminine in the ensemble of Paleolithic art, i.e., rock paintings and reliefs, stone statuettes or slabs. He has further been able to show the unity of this symbolic language, from the Franco-Cantabrian region to Siberia. By making use of topographical and statistical analysis, Leroi-Gourhan has concluded that the *figures* (forms, faces, etc.) and the *signs* are interchangeable; for example, the image of a bison has the same ("female") value as "wounds" or other geometrical signs. He then observed that there is a pairing of male-female values, for example, bison (female) and horse (male). Deciphered in the light of this symbolism, the cave proves to be a world both organized and laden with meanings.

For Leroi-Gourhan, there is no doubt that the cave is a sanctuary and that the stone slabs and the figurines constitute portable sanctuaries possessing the same symbolic structure as the decorated caves. However, the same author admits that the synthesis he believes he has reconstructed does not teach us the *language* of Paleolithic religion. His method forbids him to recognize the "events" suggested in certain rock paintings. In the celebrated "scene" at Lascaux, interpreted by other investigators as a hunting accident or a shamanic séance, Leroi-Gourhan sees only a bird belonging to a certain "topographical group" and "symbolically equivalent to the man or the rhinoceros which are in fact its neighbors on the wall" (*Les religions de la préhistoire*, p. 148). Except for the pairing of symbols of different sexual values (which perhaps expresses the religious importance attributed to this complementarity), all that Leroi-Gourhan can put forward is that "the representations cover an extremely complex and rich system, a system far richer and more complex than had been previously imagined" (p. 151).

Leroi-Gourhan's theory has been criticized from various points of view. He has been especially reproached with a certain inconsistency in his "readings" of figures and signs and with the fact that he did not connect the rites performed in the caves with his newly established symbolic system.[31] However this may be, Leroi-Gourhan's contribution is important: he has demonstrated the stylistic and ideological unity of Paleolithic art and has illuminated the complementarity of the religious values camouflaged under the signs "male" and "female." An analogous symbolism characterized the village of Mal'ta, with its two completely separate halves destined for the two sexes. Systems implying the complementarity of the two sexual and cosmological principles still abound in primitive societies, and we shall also find them in the archaic religions. It is probable that this principle of complementarity was called upon both to organize the world and to explain the mystery of its periodical creation and regeneration.

7. Rites, thought, and imagination among the Paleolithic hunters

The recent discoveries of paleontology have it in common that they continually push the beginnings of man and of culture backward in time. Man proves to be more ancient and his psychomental activity more complex than they were thought to be a few decades ago. Alexander Marshak has recently been able to demonstrate the existence, in the Upper Paleolithic, of a symbolic system of temporal notations, based on observation of the moon's phases. These notations, which the author terms "time-factored," that is, accumulated continuously over a long period, permit the supposition that certain seasonal or periodic ceremonies were fixed long in advance, as is the case in our day among Siberians and North American Indians. This system of notations remained in force for more than 25,000 years, from the early Aurignacian to the late Magdalenian. According to Marshak, writing, arithmetic, and the calendar properly speaking, which make their appearance in the first civilizations, are probably connected with the symbolism with which the system of notations used during the Paleolithic is impregnated.[32]

31. Ucko and Rosenfeld, *Paleolithic Cave Art*, p. 220; 195 ff. Similar criticisms have been made by Henri Lhote.
32. Alexander Marshak, *The Roots of Civilization*, pp. 81 ff. Equally significant is the ability of the Paleolithics accurately to observe and draw the phases of plant life (see Marshak, *Roots*, pp. 172 ff., and his "Le bâton de commandement de Montgaudier (Charente)," pp. 329 ff.

Whatever may be thought of Marshak's general theory concerning the development of civilization, the fact remains that the lunar cycle was analyzed, memorized, and used for practical purposes some 15,000 years before the discovery of agriculture. This makes more comprehensible the considerable role of the moon in archaic mythologies, and especially the fact that lunar symbolism was integrated into a single system comprising such different realities as woman, the waters, vegetation, the serpent, fertility, death, "rebirth," etc.[33]

From analyzing the meanders engraved on objects or painted on the walls of caves, Marshak concludes that these designs constitute a system because they present a succession and express an intentionality. This structure is already documented in the designs engraved on a bone excavated at Pech de l'Azé (Dordogne) and belonging to the Acheulian level (ca. 135,000 B.C.), that is, at least 100,000 years before the meanders of the Upper Paleolithic. What is more, the meanders are represented around and upon designs of animals, indicating a certain ritual ("individual act of participation," as Marshak terms it). It is difficult to determine their meaning, but from a certain moment on (for example, the design at Petersfeld, Baden), the meanders are presented in "running angles" and are accompanied by fish. In this case, the aquatic symbolism is obvious. But, according to the author, we are not presented with a simple image of water; the countless traces left by fingers and various tools denote an "individual act of participation" in which aquatic symbolism or mythology played a part.[34]

Such analyses confirm the *ritual function* of Paleolithic signs and figures. It now seems evident that these images and symbols refer to certain "stories," that is, to events related to the seasons, the habits of game, sexuality, death, the mysterious powers of certain supernatural beings and certain persons ("specialists in the sacred"). We may regard the Paleolithic representations as a code that signifies the *symbolic* (hence magico-religious) *value* of the images and at the same time their *function* in the ceremonies connected with various "stories." But the "systems" in which the different symbols take

33. Eliade, *Patterns in Comparative Religion*, chap. 4.
34. A. Marshak, "The Meander as System." The author holds that the tradition of meanders cannot be explained by hunting magic or by sexual symbolism. The complex Serpent–Water–Rain–Storm Cloud is found in Neolithic Eurasia, Australia, Africa, and the two Americas.

their place permit us at least to divine their importance in the magico-religious practices of the Paleolithics—and the more so because a number of these "systems" are shared by the hunting societies.

As we observed above (§ 4), it is permissible to reconstruct certain aspects of the religions of prehistory by considering the rites and beliefs typical of primitive hunters. It is not simply a matter of ethnographic parallels, a method which has been used, more or less successfully, by all investigators except Leroi-Gourhan and Laming-Emperair.[35] But, taking into consideration all the differences that separate a prehistoric from a primitive culture, it is still possible to circumscribe certain fundamental configurations. For a number of archaic civilizations based on hunting, fishing, and gathering have survived until recent times on the margin of the ecumene (in Tierra del Fuego, in Africa among the Hottentots and the Bushmen, in the Arctic, in Australia, etc.) or in the great tropical forests (the Bambuti Pygmies, etc.). Despite influences from the neighboring agricultural civilizations (at least in certain cases), the original structures were still intact at the end of the nineteenth century. These civilizations, arrested at a stage similar to the Upper Paleolithic, thus constitute a sort of living fossils.[36]

Of course, there is no attempt to transpose the religious practices and mythologies of the "primitives" to the men of the Old Stone Age. However, as we have already observed, ecstasy of the shamanic type appears to be documented in the Paleolithic. This implies, on the one hand, belief in a "soul," able to leave the body and travel freely through the world, and, on the other hand, the conviction that, during such a journey, the soul can meet certain superhuman beings and ask them for help or a blessing. The shamanic ecstasy also implies the possibility of possessing, that is, entering, the bodies of

35. Their failure to use this method has provoked criticism from Ucko (*Paleolithic Cave Art*, pp. 140 ff.), who, after citing some examples in which ethnographic comparison has illuminated certain aspects of prehistoric societies (pp. 151 ff.), offers an analysis of Paleolithic rock art in the light of Australian and African facts (pp. 191 ff.).

36. The concept of "living fossils" has been successfully employed in several branches of biology, especially in speleology. The troglobionts that today inhabit caves belong to a fauna that has long since been transcended. "They are veritable living fossils and often represent very ancient stages in the history of life—Tertiary or even Secondary" (Dr. Racovitza). Thus caves preserve an archaic fauna, of great importance for an understanding of the primitive zoomorphic groups *that are not fossilizable*.

human beings, and also of being possessed by the soul of a dead person or by a spirit or a god.

To recall another example, the separation of the sexes (§6) permits us to suppose the existence of secret rites in which only men may take part and that are performed before hunting expeditions. Similar rites are the prerogative of groups of adults similar to the "men's societies" (*Männerbünde*); the "secrets" are revealed to adolescents by means of initiation rites. Some authors consider that they have found proof of such an initiation in the Montespan cave, but this interpretation has been contested. However, the archaism of initiation rites is beyond doubt. The analogies between a number of ceremonies documented at the farthest regions of the ecumene (Australia, South and North America)[37] bear witness to a common tradition already developed during the Paleolithic.

As for the "circular dance" at Montespan (whatever interpretation is given to the marks left by the feet of young men on the clay floor of the cave), Curt Sachs has no doubt that this ritual choreography was well known to the Paleolithics.[38] But the circular dance is extremely widespread (throughout Eurasia, in eastern Europe, in Melanesia, among the Indians of California, etc.). It is practiced everywhere by hunters, whether to pacify the soul of the slain animal or to insure the multiplication of game.[39] In either case, the continuity with the religious ideology of the Paleolithic hunters is obvious. In addition, the mystical solidarity between the group of hunters and the game supports the presumption of various trade secrets known only to men; now, such "secrets" are imparted to adolescents by means of initiations.

The circular dance admirably illustrates the persistence of pre-historic rites and beliefs in the contemporary archaic cultures. We shall come upon other examples. For the moment, we will repeat that what made it possible to "decipher" certain rock paintings of the Hoggar and the Tassili was an initiatory myth of the Peul shepherds, a myth communicated by an educated Malian to the Africanist Germaine Dieterlen, who published it.[40] For his part,

37. See Eliade, *Birth and Rebirth*, pp. 28 ff.
38. Curt Sachs, *World History of the Dance* (1937), pp. 124, 208.
39. See the abundant documentation in Evel Gasparini, *Il Matriarcato Slavo*, pp. 667 ff.
40. G. Dieterlen, *Koumen*; cf. Henri Lhote, "Les gravures et les peintures rupestres du Sahara," pp. 282 ff.

H. von Sicard, in a monograph on Luwe and his onomastic analogues, came to the conclusion that this African god represents the earliest religious belief of the Euro-African hunters, at a period which the Swedish scholar dates before 8000 B.C.[41]

In short, it seems plausible to state that a certain number of myths were familiar to the Paleolithic populations, first of all the cosmogonic myths and the myths of origin (origin of man, of game, of death, etc.). To give only one example, a cosmogonic myth brings on the stage the primordial Waters and the Creator, the latter either as anthropomorphic or in the form of an aquatic animal, descending to the bottom of the ocean to bring back the material necessary for the creation of the world. The immense dissemination of this cosmogony and its archaic structure point to a tradition inherited from earliest prehistory.[42] Similarly, myths, legends, and rites related to ascent to the sky and "magical flight" (wings, feathers of birds of prey— eagle, falcon) are universally documented, on all the continents, from Australia and South America to the Arctic.[43] Now these myths are bound up with certain oneiric and ecstatic experiences specifically characteristic of shamanism, and their archaism is indubitable.

Equally widespread are the myths and symbols of the rainbow and its terrestrial counterpart the bridge, the preeminent means of connection with the otherworld. It is also permissible to suppose the existence of a cosmological "system" built up on the basis of the fundamental experience of a Center of the World, around which space is organized. As early as 1914, W. Gaerte had collected a large number of prehistoric signs and images that could be interpreted as cosmic mountains, navels of the earth, and paradigmatic rivers dividing the "world" in four directions.[44]

As for myths of the origin of animals and the religious relations among the hunter, the game, and the Lord of Wild Beasts, it is probable that they are very often mentioned, in cryptographic codes, in the iconographic repertory of the Paleolithics. It is equally

41. H. von Sicard, "*Luwe* und verwandte mythische Gestalten," pp. 720 ff.
42. See the comparative analysis of all its variants in our book *Zalmoxis: The Vanishing God*, pp. 76–130.
43. See Eliade, *Myths, Dreams, and Mysteries*, pp. 121–22, *Shamanism*, pp. 403 ff., 448 ff., 477 ff., and *Australian Religions*, pp. 137 ff.
44. W. Gaerte, "Kosmische Vorstellungen im Bilde prähistorischer Zeit: Erdberg, Himmelsberg, Erdnabel und Weltströme." It should be noted that most of the examples cited by Gaerte belong to the more recent prehistoric cultures.

difficult for us to imagine a society of hunters without myths of the origin of fire, and the more so since the majority of these myths give a leading role to sexual activity. Finally, we must always take into consideration the primary experience of the sacrality of the sky and of celestial and atmospheric phenomena. This is one of the few experiences that spontaneously reveal transcendence and majesty. In addition, the ecstatic ascents of shamans, the symbolism of flight, the imaginary experience of altitude as a deliverance from weight, contribute to consecrating the celestial space as supremely the source and dwelling place of superhuman beings: gods, spirits, civilizing heroes. But equally important and significant are the "revelations" of night and darkness, of the killing of game and the death of a member of the family, of cosmic catastrophes, of the occasional crises of enthusiasm, madness, or homicidal ferocity among members of the tribe.

A decisive part is played by the magico-religious valorizations of language. Certain gestures could already indicate the epiphany of a sacred power or of a cosmic "mystery." It is probable that the gestures of the anthropomorphic figures of prehistoric art were laden not only with meaning but also with power. The religious meaning of "gestures-epiphanies" were still known to certain primitive societies toward the end of the nineteenth century.[45] A fortiori, phonetic inventiveness must have constituted an inexhaustible source of magico-religious powers. Even before articulate language, the human voice was able not only to transmit information, orders, or desires but also to bring into being a whole imaginary universe by its sonorous explosions, its phonic innovations. It is enough to think of the fictional creations, not only paramythological and parapoetic but also iconographic, brought into existence by the preliminary exercises of shamans preparing for their ecstatic journeys or by the repetition of mantras during certain yogic meditations, which involve both the rhythm of respiration (*prāṇāyāma*) and at the same time the visualization of the "mystical syllables."

45. Among certain tribes of northern Australia the principal rite in the initiation of a girl consists in solemnly presenting her before the community. She is *shown* to be an adult—in other words, ready to assume the behavior proper to women. Now to show something ritually, be it a sign, an object, or an animal, is to declare a sacred presence, to acclaim the miracle of a hierophany; see Eliade, *Australian Religions*, pp. 116–17; for other examples see *Birth and Rebirth*, pp. 43 ff.

In proportion as it was perfected, language increased its magico-religious abilities. The uttered word loosed a force difficult, if not impossible, to annul. Similar beliefs still survive in a number of primitive and folk cultures. They are also found in the ritual function of the magical formulas of panegyric, satire, execration, and anathema in the most complex societies. The exalting experience of the word as magico-religious force has sometimes led to the certainty that language is able to insure the results obtained by ritual action.

To conclude, it is also necessary to take into consideration the difference between the various types of personality. One hunter was distinguished by his prowess or his craftiness, another by the intensity of his ecstatic trances. These characterological differences imply a certain variety in the valorization and interpretation of religious experiences. In the last analysis, despite the few fundamental ideas common to it, the religious heritage of the Paleolithic already displayed a complex configuration.

2 The Longest Revolution: The Discovery of Agriculture—Mesolithic and Neolithic

8. A lost paradise

The end of the Ice Age, about 8000 B.C., radically changed the climate and landscape, and hence the flora and fauna, of Europe north of the Alps. The retreat of the glaciers brought on a migration of the fauna toward the northern regions. Gradually, forest replaced the arctic steppes. The hunters followed the game, especially the herds of reindeer, but the diminishing stock of game animals obliged them to settle on the banks of lakes and at the seashore and to live by fishing. The new cultures that developed during the following millennia have been termed Mesolithic. In western Europe they are distinctly poorer than the grandiose creations of the Upper Paleoiithic. By contrast, in Southwest Asia, and especially in Palestine, the Mesolithic constitutes an axial period: it is the time of the domestication of the first animals and the beginnings of agriculture.

Little is known concerning the religious practices of the hunters who had followed the reindeer herds into northern Europe. In the deposit of silt in a pool at Stellmoor, near Hamburg, A. Rust found the remains of twelve entire reindeer, submerged with stones in their thoracic cages or abdomens. Rust and other authors have interpreted this as a first-fruits offering presented to a divinity, probably the Lord of Wild Beasts. But H. Pohlhausen has cited the fact that the Eskimos preserve supplies of meat in the icy water of lakes and rivers.[1] However, as Pohlhausen himself admits, this empirical explanation does not exclude the religious intention of certain

---

1. A. Rust, *Die alt- und mittelsteinzeitliche Funde von Stellmoor;* H. Müller-Karpe, *Handbuch der Vorgeschichte,* vol. 1, pp. 224 ff.; H. Pohlhausen, "Zum Motiv der Renntierversenkung," pp. 988–89; J. Maringer, "Die Opfer der paläolitischen Menschen," pp. 266 ff.

deposits. For sacrifice by immersion is amply documented, and at different periods, from northern Europe to India.[2]

The lake of Stellmoor was probably considered a sacred place by the Mesolithic hunters. Rust collected various objects from the deposit: wooden arrows, bone tools, axes made from reindeer antlers. In all likelihood they represent offerings, as is the case with objects from the Bronze Age and the Iron Age found in certain ponds and lakes in western Europe. To be sure, more than five millennia separate the two groups of objects, but the continuity of this type of religious practice is beyond doubt. Discoveries at the Saint-Sauveur spring (Forest of Compiègne) have included flints from the Neolithic period (intentionally broken to signify that they were *ex votos*), objects from the time of the Gauls and the Gallo-Romans, and from the Middle Ages to our own day.[3] It must also be taken into consideration that, in this last instance, the practice remained in force despite the cultural influence of imperial Rome and, above all, in spite of repeated prohibitions by the Church. In addition to its intrinsic interest, this example has a paradigmatic value: it admirably illustrates the continuity of "sacred places" and of certain religious practices.

Still in the Mesolithic stratum at Stellmoor, Rust discovered a pinewood post with a reindeer skull set at its summit. According to Maringer, this cult post probably indicates ritual meals: the flesh of reindeer was eaten and their heads were offered to a divine being. Not far from Ahrensburg-Hopfenbach, in a Mesolithic station dated at 10,000 B.C., Rust brought up from the bottom of a pond the trunk of a willow 3.50 meters in length, crudely sculptured; it is possible to make out a head, a long neck, and deeply incised lines that, according to the maker of the discovery, represent arms. This "idol" had been set up in the pond, but neither bones nor any other objects were found around it. In all probability it represents the image of a supernatural being, though it is impossible to determine the structure of the latter.[4]

2. Cf. A. Closs, "Das Versenkungsopfer," passim.

3. Eliade, *Patterns in Comparative Religion*, p. 200 (1958 Sheed & Ward edition).

4. A. Rust, *Die jungpaläolitischen Zeltanlagen von Ahrensburg*, pp. 141 ff.; J. Maringer, "Die Opfer der paläolitischen Menschen," pp. 267 ff. H. Müller-Karpe, *Handbuch d. Vorgeschichte*, vol. 2, pp. 496–97 (no. 347), hesitates to see an idol in this object.

In comparison with the poverty of these few documents of the reindeer-hunters, the rock art of eastern Spain offers the historian of religions a large quantity of data. The naturalistic rock painting of the Upper Paleolithic was transformed, in the "Spanish Levant," into a rigid and formalistic geometrical art. The rock walls of the Sierra Morena are covered with anthropomorphic and theriomorphic figures (principally of stags and ibexes), reduced to a few lines, and with various signs (undulating ribbons, circles, points, suns). Hugo Obermeier has shown that these anthropomorphic figures bear a resemblance to the painted pebbles of the Azilian.[5] Since that civilization derives from Spain, the anthropomorphic representations inscribed on the rock walls and on pebbles must have similar meanings. They have been explained as phallic symbols, as elements of a system of writing, or as magical signs. The comparison with the Australian *tjurungas* seems more convincing. These ritual objects, most often of stone and decorated with various geometrical designs, are known to represent the mystical body of the ancestors. The *tjurungas* are hidden in caves or buried in certain sacred places and are communicated to the young men only at the end of their initiation. Among the Aranda, the father addresses his son as follows: "Here is your own body, from which you came forth by a new birth," or "This is your own body. It is the ancestor whom you were when, during your former existence, you traveled. Then you went down into the sacred cave to rest."[6]

Even if the painted pebbles from Mas d'Azil had, as is probable, a function similar to that of the *tjurungas*, it is impossible to know if their makers held ideas similar to those of the Australians. Yet there can be no doubt of the religious significance of the Azilian pebbles.

In the Birsek cave, in Switzerland, 133 painted pebbles were found, almost all of them broken. It seems plausible that they were broken by enemies or by later occupants of the cave. In either case, what was sought was annihilation of the magico-religious force present in these objects. In all probability the caves and other sites decorated with

5. A civilization of hunters and fishers, so named from the station of Mas d'Azil, a cave in the French Pyrenees.

6. Eliade, *Australian Religions*, pp. 95 ff., esp. p. 98 (quote). It is clear that, according to the beliefs of the Australians, the ancestor exists simultaneously in his mystical body, the *tjurunga*, and in the man in whom he has become reincarnated. It should be added that he also exists underground and in the form of "spirit children" (ibid., p. 49).

rock paintings in the Spanish Levant constituted holy places. As for the suns and other geometrical signs that accompany the anthropomorphic representations, their meaning remains mysterious.[7]

We have no means of determining the origin and development of the belief in ancestors during prehistory. To judge by the ethnographic parallels, this religious complex is able to coexist with belief in supernatural beings or Lords of Wild Beasts. There seems to be no reason why the idea of mythical ancestors should not form part of the religious system of the Paleolithics: it is bound up with the mythology of origins—origin of the world, of game, of man, of death—that is typical of hunting civilizations. In addition, it is a religious idea that is universally disseminated and mythologically fertile, for it has survived in all religions, even the most complex (with the exception of Hināyāna Buddhism). It can happen that an archaic religious idea will develop in an unexpected way in certain periods and following upon particular circumstances. If it is true that the idea of the mythical ancestor and the cult of ancestors dominate the European Mesolithic, it is probable, as Maringer believes (*The Gods of Prehistoric Man*, p. 183), that the importance of this religious complex is explained by the memory of the Ice Age, when the distant ancestors lived in a sort of hunters' paradise. And in fact the Australians consider that their mythical ancestors lived during a golden age, in an earthly paradise in which game abounded and the notions of good and evil were practically unknown.[8] It is this paradisal world that the Australians attempt to reactualize during certain festivals, when laws and prohibitions are suspended.

9. Work, technology, and imaginary worlds

As we said: in the Near East, and especially in Palestine, the Mesolithic represents a creative period, though at the same time it retains the character of transition between two types of civilizations, the one based on hunting and gathering, the other on cultivation of cereals. In Palestine the hunters of the Upper Paleolithic seem to

7. We mention that the Australians, as well as a number of South American tribes, believe that their mythical ancestors were either changed into stars or ascended into the sky to inhabit the sun and stars.
8. Eliade, *Australian Religions*, p. 46.

have lived in caves for long periods. But it was especially the bearers of the Natufian culture[9] who chose a definitely sedentary existence. They inhabited caves as well as open-air sites (as at Einan, where excavation has revealed a village made up of circular huts with fire-places). The Natufians had discovered the importance of wild cereals as foodstuffs, and they harvested them with stone sickles and ground the seeds in a mortar with the help of a pestle.[10] It was a great step forward toward agriculture. The domestication of animals also began during the Mesolithic (though it did not become general until the beginning of the Neolithic): the sheep at Zawi Chemi-Shanidar, about 8000 B.C.; the goat at Jericho, in Jordania, about 7000 B.C., and the pig about 6500 B.C.; and the dog at Stan Carr, in England, about 7500 B.C.[11] The immediate results of the domesti-cation of Graminaceae appear in the expansion of the population and the development of commerce, phenomena already characteristic of the Natufians.

Unlike the geometrical schematism typical of the designs and paintings of the European Mesolithic, the art of the Natufians is naturalistic; excavations have yielded small sculptures of animals and human figurines, sometimes in erotic postures.[12] The sexual symbolism of pestles sculptured in the shape of a phallus is so obvious that their magico-religious meaning cannot be doubted.

The two types of Natufian burial—(a) inhumation of the entire body in a bent position and (b) burial of skulls—were known in the Paleolithic and will continue into the Neolithic. In regard to the skeletons excavated at Einan,[13] it has been supposed that a human

9. The designation "Natufian" derives from Wadi en-Natuf, where this Mesolithic population was recognized for the first time.

10. Emmanuel Anati, *Palestine before the Hebrews*, pp. 49 ff.; Müller-Karpe, *Handbuch*, vol. 2, pp. 245 ff.; R. de Vaux, *Histoire ancienne d'Israël*, vol. 1, pp. 41 ff.

11. All these dates have been obtained by radiocarbon analyses. On the domestication of animals, see Müller-Karpe, *Handbuch*, vol. 2, pp. 250 ff. A recent discovery in the valley of the Upper Nile has revealed a pre-Neolithic alimentary complex based on cereal and dated 13,000 B.C.; see Fred Wendorf, S. Rushdi, and R. Schild, "Egyptian Prehistory: Some New Concepts," *Science* 169 (1970): 1161–71.

12. See, for example, the figurine found at Ain Sakhri (Anati, *Palestine*, p. 160). Now see Jacques Cauvin, *Religions néolithiques*, pp. 21 ff.

13. One of these tombs can be regarded as the earliest megalithic monument in the world (Anati, *Palestine*, p. 172). On Einan, see Müller-Karpe, *Handbuch*, vol. 2, p. 349.

victim was sacrificed in connection with the burial, but the meaning of the ritual remains unknown. As for the deposits of skulls, the Natufian documents have been compared with the deposits discovered at Offnet, in Bavaria, and in the Höhlenstein cave in Württemberg; all these skulls belonged to individuals who had been massacred, perhaps by headhunters or cannibals.[14]

In both cases we may presume a magico-religious act, since the head (i.e., the brain) was considered to be the seat of the "soul." As the result of dreams and ecstatic and paraecstatic experiences, there had long been a recognition of the existence of an element independent of the body, which modern languages designate by the terms "soul," "spirit," "breath," "life," "double," etc. This spiritual element (as it must be called, since it was apprehended as image, vision, apparition, etc.) was present in the entire body; it constituted in some sort its "double." But localizing the "soul" or "spirit" in the brain had marked consequences;[15] on the one hand, it was believed that the victim's spiritual element could be assimilated by eating his brain; on the other hand, the brain, the source of power, became the object of a cult.

In addition to agriculture, other inventions took place during the Mesolithic, the most important being the bow and the manufacture of cords, nets, hooks, and boats able to make fairly long voyages. Like the other earlier inventions (stone tools, various objects made from bone and antlers, clothes and tents made from skins, etc.), and like those that will be achieved during the Neolithic (first and foremost, pottery), all these discoveries gave rise to mythologies and paramythological fictions and sometimes became the basis for various ritual behaviors. The empirical value of these inventions is evident. What is less so is *the importance of the imaginative activity inspired by familiarity with the different modalities of matter.* In working with a piece of flint or a primitive needle, in joining together animal hides or wooden planks, in preparing a fishhook or an arrowhead, in shaping a clay statuette, the imagination discovers unsuspected analogies among the different levels of the real; tools and

14. Anati, *Palestine*, p. 175; Maringer, *The Gods of Prehistoric Man*, pp. 184 ff. See also Müller-Karpe, *Handbuch*, vol. 1, pp. 239 ff.

15. And not only for the beliefs accepted during prehistory. The Greeks, too, had localized the soul (and later, with Alcmaeon of Crotona, the sperm) in the head. Cf. Onians, *Origins of European Thought*, pp. 107–8, 115, 134–36, etc.

objects are laden with countless symbolisms, the world of work—the microuniverse that absorbs the artisan's attention for long hours— becomes a mysterious and sacred center, rich in meanings.

The imaginary world created and continually enriched by intimacy with matter can be only inadequately grasped in the figurative or geometric creations of the various prehistoric cultures, but it is still accessible to us in the experiences of our own imagination. It is above all this continuity on the plane of imaginative activity that permits us to comprehend the existence of men living in those distant periods. But, unlike the man of modern societies, the imaginative activity of prehistoric man also possessed a mythological dimension. A considerable number of supernatural figures and mythological episodes, which we shall encounter again in later religious traditions, very probably represent discoveries of the Stone Age.

10. The heritage of the Paleolithic hunters

The various kinds of progress effected during the Mesolithic put an end to the cultural unity of the Paleolithic populations and launch the variety and divergences that will thereafter become the chief characteristic of civilizations. The remnants of the Paleolithic hunting societies begin to make their way into the marginal regions or those to which access is difficult: the desert, the great forests, the mountains. But this increasing remoteness and isolation of the Paleolithic societies does not imply the disappearance of the behavior and spirituality typical of the hunter. Hunting as means of sub- sistence continues in the societies of agriculturalists. Probably a certain number of hunters who refused to take an active part in the economy of the cultivators were employed as guardians of the villages—first against the wild beasts that harassed the sedentary populations and damaged the cultivated fields, later against bands of marauders. Probably, too, the first military organizations took shape from these groups of hunters acting as guardians. As we shall soon see, warriors, conquerors, and military aristocracies carry on the symbolism and ideology of the paradigmatic hunter.

On the other hand, blood sacrifices, which were practiced by both cultivators and pastoralists, in the last analysis repeat the killing of game by the hunter. A type of behavior that, for one or two million years, had been inseparable from the human (or at least the masculine) mode is not easily abolished.

Several millennia after the triumph of the agricultural economy, the *Weltanschauung* of the primitive hunter will again have repercussions on history. For the invasions and conquests of the Indo-Europeans and the Turko-Mongols will be undertaken under the sign of the supreme hunter, the carnivore. The members of the Indo-European military confraternities (*Männerbünde*) and the nomadic horsemen of Central Asia behaved toward the sedentary populations that they attacked like carnivores hunting, strangling, and devouring the herbivores of the steppe or the farmers' cattle. Numerous Indo-European and Turko-Mongol tribes had eponyms of beasts of prey (primarily the wolf) and regarded themselves as descended from a theriomorphic mythical ancestor. The military initiations of the Indo-Europeans involved a ritual transformation into a wolf: the paradigmatic warrior appropriated the behavior of a carnivore.

On the other hand, the pursuit and killing of a wild animal becomes the mythical model for the conquest of a territory (*Landnáma*) and the founding of a state.[16] Among the Assyrians, the Iranians, and the Turko-Mongols the techniques of hunting and war are so much alike as to be hardly separable. Everywhere in the Eurasian world, from the appearance of the Assyrians to the beginnings of the modern period, hunting constitutes at once the typical school and training ground, and the favorite sport, of sovereigns and military aristocracies. In addition, the fabled prestige of the hunter's existence, in comparison with that of the sedentary cultivators, is still maintained among numerous primitive peoples.[17] The hundreds of thousands of years spent in a sort of mystical symbiosis with the animal world have left indelible traces. What is more, orgiastic ecstasy is able to reactualize the religious behavior of the earliest Paleohominians, when the game was eaten raw; this happened in Greece, among the worshipers of Dionysus (§124), or, still at the beginning of the twentieth century, among the Aissawa of Morocco.

16. In Africa and elsewhere the ritual hunt is performed on the occasion of initiations and at the installation of a new chief.

17. A characteristic example: the Desana of Colombia call themselves hunters, even though 75 percent of their food comes from fishing and horticulture. In their view, only the hunter's life is worth living.

11. The domestication of food plants: Origin myths

Since 1960 it has been known that villages preceded the discovery of
agriculture. What Gordon Childe called the "Neolithic Revolution"
took place gradually between 9000 and 7000 B.C. It is also known
that, contrary to what was thought until quite recently, the cultivation
of Graminaceae and the domestication of animals preceded the
making of pottery. Agriculture properly speaking—that is, the
cultivation of cereals—developed in Southwest Asia and Central
America. "Vegeculture," which depends upon the vegetative reproduction of tubers, roots, or rhizomes, seems to have originated in the
humid tropical plains of America and Southeast Asia.

The antiquity of vegeculture and its relations with "cerealiculture"
have not yet been adequately worked out. Some ethnologists are
inclined to consider vegeculture earlier than the cultivation of grains;
others, on the contrary, hold that it represents an impoverished
imitation of agriculture. One of the few clear indications was furnished
by excavations made in South America. In the plains of Rancho
Peludo, in Venezuela, and Momil, in Colombia, vestiges of a
cultivation of cassava were found below the level of the cultivation
of maize, which signifies the priority of vegeculture.[18] A new proof
of the antiquity of vegeculture was recently brought to light in
Thailand, where excavation in a cave (the "Cave of Phantoms")
yielded cultivated peas, beans, and roots of tropical plants; radiocarbon analysis indicates dates of about 9000 B.C.[19]

It is unnecessary to emphasize the importance of the discovery of
agriculture for the history of civilization. By becoming the *producer*
of his food, man was obliged to alter his ancestral behavior. Above
all, he had to perfect his technique for calculating time, the first
discovery of which had already been made in the Paleolithic. It was
no longer enough for him to ascertain certain future dates correctly
by means of a rudimentary lunar calendar. From now on, the
cultivator had to make his plans several months before they were to
be implemented, had to perform, in an exact order, a series of
complex activities in view of a distant and, especially in the beginning,

18. David R. Harris, "Agricultural Systems, Ecosystems, and the Origins
of Agriculture," in *The Domestication and Exploitation of Plants and Animals*,
p. 12.
19. William Solhein, "Relics from Two Diggings Indicate Thais Were the
First Agrarians," *New York Times*, 12 January 1970.

always uncertain result: the harvest. In addition, the cultivation of plants imposed a differently oriented division of labor from that which had earlier been in force, for thenceforth the chief responsibility for assuring the means of subsistence fell upon women.

The consequences of the discovery of agriculture were no less important for the religious history of mankind. The domestication of plants gave rise to an existential situation that had previously been inaccessible; hence it inspired creations of values and reversals of them that radically altered the spiritual universe of pre-Neolithic man. We shall soon analyze this religious revolution whose beginnings followed on the triumph of the cultivation of cereals. For the moment, we will cite some of the myths that explain the origin of the two types of agriculture. In learning how the cultivators explained the appearance of food plants, we at the same time learn the religious justification for various aspects of their behavior.

The majority of origin myths have been collected among primitive populations practicing either vegeculture or cereal culture. (Such myths are scarcer, and sometimes radically reinterpreted, in developed cultures.) A rather widely disseminated theme explains that edible tubers and fruit trees (coconut, banana, etc.) were born from an immolated divinity. The most famous example comes from Ceram, one of the islands off New Guinea: from the dismembered and buried body of a semidivine maiden, Hainuwele, spring plants until then unknown, especially tubers. This primordial murder radically changed the human condition, for it introduced sexuality and death and first established the religious and social institutions that are still in force. Hainuwele's violent death is not only a "creative" death, it permits the goddess to be continually present in the life of human beings and even in their death. Obtaining nourishment from plants that have sprung from her own body is, in reality, to obtain it from the actual substance of the goddess.

We shall not expand upon the importance of this origin myth for the religious life and culture of the paleocultivators. It is enough to say that all responsible activities (puberty ceremonies, animal or human sacrifices, cannibalism, funerary ceremonies, etc.) properly speaking constitute a recalling, a "remembrance," of the primordial murder.[20] It is significant that the cultivator associates with a murder the essentially peaceful labor that insures his existence, whereas in

20. Eliade, *Myth and Reality*, pp. 105 ff.

societies of hunters the responsibility for slaughter is attributed to *another*, to a "stranger." It is easy to understand the hunter: he fears the vengeance of the slain animal (more precisely, of its "soul") or he justifies himself before the Lord of Wild Beasts. As for the paleocultivators, the myth of the primordial murder certainly justifies such sanguinary rites as human sacrifice and cannibalism, but it is difficult to determine its initial religious context.

A similar mythical theme explains the origin of food plants—both tubers and cereals—as arising from the excreta or the sweat of a divinity or mythical ancestor. When the beneficiaries discover the repulsive source of their foodstuffs, they kill the author; but, following his advice, they dismember his body and bury the pieces. Food plants and other elements of culture (agricultural implements, silkworms, etc.) spring from his corpse.[21]

The meaning of these myths is obvious: food plants are sacred, since they are derived from the body of a divinity (for the excreta and the sweat are also part of the divine substance). By feeding himself, man, in the last analysis, eats a divine being. *The food plant is not "given" in the world,* as the animal is. It is the result of a primitive dramatic event; in this case it is the *product of a murder.* We shall later see the consequences of these alimentary theologies.

The German ethnologist A. E. Jensen held that the myth of Hainuwele is peculiar to the paleocultivators of tubers. As for the myths concerning the origin of cereal culture, they feature a primordial theft: cereals exist, but in the sky, jealously guarded by the gods; a civilizing hero ascends into the sky, makes off with a few seeds, and bestows them on mankind. Jensen called these two types of mythologies "Hainuwele" and "Prometheus" and connected them respectively with the civilization of the paleocultivators (vegeculture) and that of the agriculturalists properly speaking (cereal culture).[22] The distinction is certainly real. However, in respect to the two types of origin myths, it is less rigid than Jensen thought, for a number of myths explain the appearance of *cereals* from an immolated primitive being. We should add that in the religions of agriculturalists the origin of cereals is also divine; the bestowal of cereals on human

---

21. See most recently Atsuhiko Yoshida, "Les excrétions de la Déesse et l'origine de l'agriculture."

22. See A. E. Jensen, *Das religiöse Weltbild einer frühen Kultur*, pp. 35 ff., and *Myth and Cult among Primitive Peoples*, pp. 166 ff.

beings is sometimes connected with a hierogamy between the god of the sky (or of the atmosphere) and Mother Earth or with a mythical drama involving sexual union, death, and resurrection.

12. Woman and vegetation. Sacred space and periodical renewal of the world

The first, and perhaps the most important, consequence of the discovery of agriculture precipitates a crisis in the values of the Paleolithic hunters: religious relations with the animal world are supplanted by what may be called *the mystical solidarity between man and vegetation*. If the bone and the blood until then represented the essence and the sacrality of life, from then on it is the sperm and the blood that incarnate them. In addition, woman and feminine sacrality are raised to the first rank. Since women played a decisive part in the domestication of plants, they become the owners of the cultivated fields, which raises their social position and creates characteristic institutions, such as, for example, matrilocation, the husband being obliged to live in his wife's house.

The fertility of the earth is bound up with feminine fecundity; hence women become responsible for the abundance of harvests, for they know the "mystery" of creation. It is a religious mystery, for it governs the origin of life, the food supply, and death. The soil is assimilated to woman. Later, after the discovery of the plow, agricultural work is assimilated to the sexual act.[23] But for millennia Mother Earth gave birth by herself, through parthenogenesis. The memory of this "mystery" still survived in the Olympian mythology (Hera conceives alone and gives birth to Hephaestus and Ares) and can be read in numerous myths and popular beliefs concerning the birth of men from the Earth, giving birth on the ground, depositing the newborn infant on the ground, etc.[24] Born of the Earth, man, when he dies, returns to his mother. "Crawl toward the earth, thy mother," the Vedic poet exclaims (Rig Veda 10. 18. 10).

To be sure, feminine and maternal sacrality was not unknown in the Paleolithic (§ 6), but the discovery of agriculture markedly increases its power. The sacrality of sexual life, and first of all of

23. For some examples see *Patterns in Comparative Religion*, §§ 91 ff.
24. See ibid., §§ 86 ff., and *Myths, Dreams, and Mysteries*, pp. 165 ff.

feminine sexuality, becomes inseparable from the miraculous enigma of creation. Parthenogenesis, the *hieros gamos*, and the ritual orgy express, on different planes, the religious character of sexuality. A complex symbolism, anthropocosmic in structure, associates woman and sexuality with the lunar rhythms, with the earth (assimilated to the womb), and with what must be called the "mystery" of vegetation. It is a mystery that demands the "death" of the seed in order to insure it a new birth, a birth all the more marvelous because accompanied by an astonishing multiplication. The assimilation of human existence to vegetable life finds expression in images and metaphors drawn from the drama of vegetation (life is like the flower of the field, etc.). This imagery nourished poetry and philosophical reflection for millennia, and it still remains "true" for contemporary man.

All these religious values that followed upon the invention of agriculture were progressively articulated in the course of time. We have, however, cited them now to bring out the specific character of the Mesolithic and Neolithic creations. We shall constantly encounter religious ideas, mythologies, and ritual scenarios that are bound up with the "mystery" of vegetable life. For religious creativity was stimulated, not *by the empirical phenomenon of agriculture*, but *by the mystery of birth, death, and rebirth* identified in the rhythm of vegetation. In order to be understood, accepted, and mastered, the crises that threaten the harvest (floods, droughts, etc.) will be translated into mythological dramas. These mythologies and the ritual scenarios that depend on them will dominate the religions of the Near East for millennia. The mythical theme of gods who die and return to life is among the most important. In certain cases, these archaic scenarios will give birth to new religious creations (for example, Eleusis, the Greco-Oriental mysteries; see § 96).

The agrarian cultures develop what may be called a *cosmic religion*, since religious activity is concentrated around the central mystery: *the periodical renewal of the world*. Like human existence, the cosmic rhythms are expressed in terms drawn from vegetable life. The mystery of cosmic sacrality is symbolized in the World Tree. The universe is conceived as an organism that must be renewed periodically—in other words, each year. "Absolute reality," rejuvenation, immortality, are accessible to certain privileged persons through the power residing in a certain fruit or in a spring near a tree.[25] The Cosmic Tree is held to be at the center of the world, and it unites the three cosmic regions, for it sends its roots down into the underworld, and its top touches the sky.[26]

Since the world must be renewed periodically, the cosmogony will be ritually reiterated at each New Year. This mythico-ritual scenario is documented in the Near East and among the Indo-Iranians. But it is also found in the societies of the primitive cultivators, who in some sense prolong the religious conceptions of the Neolithic. The fundamental idea—renewal of the world by repetition of the cosmogony—is certainly earlier, preagricultural. It is found, with the inevitable variations, among the Australians and a number of North American tribes.[27] Among both the paleocultivators and the agriculturalists the mythico-ritual scenario of the New Year includes the return of the dead, and similar ceremonies survive in classical Greece, among the ancient Germans, in Japan, etc.

The experience of cosmic time, especially in the framework of agricultural labors, ends by imposing the idea of *circular time* and the *cosmic cycle*. Since the world and human existence are valorized in terms of vegetable life, the cosmic cycle is conceived as the indefinite repetition of the same rhythm: birth, death, rebirth. In post-Vedic India this conception will be elaborated in two intertwined doctrines: that of cycles (*yugas*), repeated to infinity, and that of the transmigration of souls. In addition, the archaic ideas articulated around the periodic renewal of the world will be taken up again, reinterpreted, and made part of several religious systems of the Near East. The cosmologies, eschatologies, and messianisms that will dominate the East and the Mediterranean world for two millennia have their deepest roots in the conceptions of the Neolithics.

The *religious valorizations of space*—primarily of the habitation and the village—were equally important. A sedentary existence organizes the "world" differently from a nomadic life. For the agriculturalist, the "true world" is the space in which he lives:

25. See *Patterns*, §§ 99 ff.
26. The Cosmic Tree is the most widespread expression of the *axis mundi*; but the symbolism of the cosmic axis probably precedes—or is independent of —the agricultural civilizations, since it is found in certain arctic cultures.
27. See some examples in Eliade, *Myth and Reality*, pp. 43 ff. Properly speaking, the Australians do not know a cosmogony, but the "formation of the world" by superhuman beings is equivalent to its "creation"; see *Australian Religions*, pp. 44 ff.

house, village, cultivated fields. The "center of the world" is the place consecrated by rituals and prayers, for it is there that communication with the superhuman beings is effected. We do not know what religious meanings the Neolithics of the Near East attributed to their houses and villages; we know only that, from a certain moment, they built altars and sanctuaries. But in China it is possible to reconstruct the symbolism of the Neolithic house, since there is continuity or analogy with certain types of habitations found in North Asia and Tibet. In the Neolithic culture of Yang-chao there were small circular constructions (ca. 5 meters in diameter) with pillars supporting the roof and spaced around a central hole that served as hearth. Possibly the roof was pierced by a smoke hole above the hearth. This house would have had, in lasting materials, the same structure as the Mongol yurt of our day.[28] Now the cosmological symbolism that pervades the yurt and the tents of the North Asian populations is well known; the sky is conceived as an immense tent held up by a central pillar: the tent pole, or the aperture above for the escape of smoke, are assimilated to the World Pillar or to the "Hole in the Sky," the North Star.[29] This opening is also called the "Sky Window." The Tibetans call the opening in the roof of their houses "Fortune of the Sky" or "Gate of the Sky."

The cosmological symbolism of the habitation is documented in numerous primitive societies. In ways more or less manifest, the habitation is considered an *imago mundi*. Since examples of this are found at all levels of culture, there seems to be no reason why the Neolithics of the Near East should have been an exception, the more so since it is in this region that the cosmological symbolism of architecture will attain its richest development. The division of the habitation between the two sexes (a custom already documented in the Paleolithic; see § 6) probably had a cosmological meaning. The divisions exhibited by the villages of cultivators correspond in general to a dichotomy that is at once classificatory and ritual (sky and earth, masculine and feminine, etc.) but also to two ritually antagonistic groups. Now, as we shall see on many occasions, ritual combats

28. R. Stein, "Architecture et pensée religieuse en Extrême-Orient," p. 168. See also Stein's description of another type of Chinese Neolithic habitation, square or rectangular in construction, half underground, with steps leading down to it.

29. See Eliade, *Shamanism*, p. 262.

between two opposing groups play an important part, especially in the New Year scenarios. Whether it is the repetition of a mythical combat, as in Mesopotamia (§ 22) or simply the confrontation between two cosmogonic principles (winter/summer; day/night; life/death), the deep meaning is always the same: confrontation, jousts, combats awaken, stimulate, or increase the creative forces of life.[30] This biocosmological conception, probably elaborated by the Neolithic agriculturalists, will undergo many reinterpretations, and even deformations, in the course of time. It is recognizable only with difficulty, for example in certain types of religious dualism.

We do not claim to have enumerated all the religious creations inspired by the discovery of agriculture. We have considered it enough to show the common source, in the Neolithic, of certain ideas that will sometimes reach their full flowering only millennia later. We will add that the dissemination of the religiosity whose structure is agrarian resulted, despite countless variations and innovations, in the constitution of a certain fundamental unity that, even in our day, still underlies certain common traits in peasant societies as far apart as those of the Mediterranean, India, and China.

13. Neolithic religions of the Near East

It could be said that, from the Neolithic to the Iron Age, the history of religious ideas and beliefs is one with the history of civilization. Each technological discovery, each economic and social innovation, is, it would seem, "doubled" by a religious meaning and value. When, in the following pages, we shall mention certain innovations of the Neolithic, their religious echo must be taken into consideration too. However, in order not to break the unity of our exposition, we shall not always emphasize these echoes.

Thus, for example, all the aspects of the culture of Jericho would deserve a religious commentary. It is perhaps the most ancient city on earth (ca. 6850, 6770 B.C.),[31] though it is ignorant of ceramics.

---

30. See Eliade, "Prolegomenon to Religious Dualism: Dyads and Polarities," in *The Quest*, pp. 127–75, esp. pp. 163 ff.

31. K. M. Kenyon, *Archaeology in the Holy Land*, pp. 39 ff. The formula "the first city in the world" has been criticized by Gordon Childe and R. J. Braidwood. According to Kathleen Kenyon, the earliest Natufians had built a sanctuary near the great spring; it was burned before 7800 B.C.

However, the fortifications, the massive tower, the large public edifices—at least one of which seems to have been built for ritual ceremonies—denote a social integration and an economic organization that are the prelude to the future city-states of Mesopotamia. The Garstangs and Kathleen Kenyon have brought to light several buildings of unusual structure, which they have called "temples" and a "family chapel." Among the clearly religious documents, two feminine statuettes and a few others representing animals indicate a fertility cult. Some authors have attributed especial significance to the remains of three plaster images discovered by the Garstangs in the 1930s: they are thought to represent a bearded male, a woman, and a child. The eyes are marked by shells. The Garstangs thought it possible to identify in these remains the earliest-known divine triad, probably bound up with a mythology similar to those that will later dominate the Near East. But this interpretation is still disputed.[32]

The dead were buried under the floors of the houses. Some skulls exhumed by Kathleen Kenyon[33] show a strange preparation: the lower parts are molded in plaster, and the eyes are represented by shells, to the point that they have been compared to actual portraits. All this undoubtedly indicates a cult of skulls.[34] But it almost seems that an attempt was made to preserve the memory of the living individual.

The cult of skulls is also found at Tell Ramad (in Syria, near Damascus), where excavations have brought to light craniums with the forehead painted red and the face filled out with modeled clay.[35] Still from Syria (Tell Ramad and Byblos), more precisely from levels dated to the fifth millennium, come some anthropomorphic figurines in clay. The one found at Byblos is bisexual.[36] Other feminine statuettes, found in Palestine and dated about 4500 B.C., show the Mother Goddess in a terrifying and demonic aspect.[37]

32. See Anati, *Palestine before the Hebrews*, p. 256, who accepts the Garstangs' interpretation (*The Story of Jericho*). Against it: J. Cauvin, *Religions néolithiques de Syro-Palestine*, p. 51.
33. Kenyon, *Archaeology in the Holy Land*, p. 50.
34. Kenyon, *Digging up Jericho*, pp. 53 ff, 84 ff. See also Müller-Karpe, *Handbuch*, vol. 2, pp. 380–81; Cauvin, *Religions néolithiques*, pp. 44 ff.
35. Excavations by Contenson, summarized by Cauvin, pp. 59 ff. and fig. 18.
36. Excavations by Contenson (Tell Ramad) and Dunand (Byblos), summarized by Cauvin, pp. 79 ff. and figs. 29–30.
37. See the figurines found at Munhata, Tel-Aviv, and Shaar-Ha-Golan, reproduced in Cauvin, figs. 29–30.

The fertility cult and the cult of the dead seem, then, to be bound together. Indeed, the cultures of Hacilar and of Çatal Hüyük (7000 B.C.) in Anatolia, which preceded—and probably influenced—the preceramic culture of Jericho, indicate the existence of similar beliefs. The cult of skulls is well documented at Hacilar. At Çatal Hüyük the skeletons were buried under the floors of houses, accompanied by funeral gifts: jewels, semiprecious stones, weapons, textiles, wooden vessels, etc.[38] In the forty sanctuaries excavated up to 1965, numerous stone and clay statuettes were found. The principal divinity is the goddess, presented under three aspects: young woman, mother giving birth to a child (or to a bull), and old crone (sometimes accompanied by a bird of prey). The masculine divinity appears in the form of a boy or youth—the goddess's child or lover—and of a bearded adult, occasionally mounted on his sacred animal, the bull. The variety of paintings on the walls is astonishing; no two sanctuaries are alike. Reliefs of the goddess, sometimes 2 meters high, modeled in plaster, wood, or clay, and heads of bulls (the epiphany of the god) were fastened to the walls. Sexual imagery is absent, but a woman's bust and a bull's horn—symbols of life—are sometimes combined. A sanctuary (ca. 6200 B.C.) contained four men's skulls deposited under the bulls' heads fastened to the walls. One wall is decorated with paintings depicting vultures with anthropomorphic legs attacking a decapitated man. This must certainly represent an important mythico-ritual complex, the meaning of which unfortunately escapes us.

At Hacilar, at a level dated 5700 B.C., the goddess is shown seated on a leopard, or standing and holding a leopard cub, but also alone, standing, seated, kneeling, resting, or accompanied by a child. Sometimes she is naked or has a tiny *cache-sexe*. Here, too, she is represented sometimes as young, sometimes as older. On a more recent level (between 5435 and 5200 B.C.) the figurines of the goddess, accompanied by a child or an animal, disappear, as do the masculine statues. However, the last phases of the Hacilar culture are characterized by admirable ceramics, richly ornamented with geometrical designs.[39]

38. James Mellaart, *Çatal Hüyük: A Neolithic Town of Anatolia*, pp. 60 ff., and *Earliest Civilizations of the Near East*, pp. 87 ff.
39. Mellaart, "Hacilar: A Neolithic Village Site," pp. 94 ff., and *Earliest Civilizations of the Near East*, pp. 102 ff.

The Tell Halaf culture, as it is called,[40] appears at the time when the Anatolian cultures disappear. It knows copper and seems to be the creation of a population coming down from the North, perhaps as refugees from Hacilar and Çatal Hüyük. The Tell Halaf religious complex is not very different from the cultures we have so far considered. The dead were buried with gifts, among them clay figurines. The wild bull was venerated as an epiphany of male fertility. Images of bulls, bucrania, ram's heads, and the double ax certainly had a cult role, related to the storm god, so important in all the religions of the ancient Near East. However, no masculine figurines have been found, whereas images of the goddess are abundant; often in a crouching position, accompanied by doves and with exaggerated breasts, it is difficult not to recognize in them the paradigmatic image of the Mother Goddess.[41]

The Halafian culture was destroyed or disappeared about 4400–4300 B.C., while the culture of Obeid, which originated in southern Iraq, was being disseminated throughout Mesopotamia. It is already documented at Warka (Sumerian Uruk, Semitic Erech) about 4325 B.C. No other prehistoric culture exercised a comparable influence. Progress in metalworking is considerable (copper axes, various objects of gold). Wealth accumulates through the progress of agriculture and through commerce. An almost life-size head of a man and animal heads in marble certainly have a religious meaning. Some seals of the Gawra type represent various cult scenes (persons around an altar decorated with bucrania; ritual dances; emblematic animals, etc.). The human figures are strongly schematized. In fact, a nonfigurative tendency characterizes the entire Obeid culture. The sanctuaries depicted on amulets are not copies of particular edifices but represent a sort of paradigmatic image of the temple.

Some human statuettes in chalk probably represent priests. For in fact the most significant novelty of the Obeid period is precisely the appearance of monumental temples.[42] One of the most remarkable

40. From the name of the site, Tell Halaf, in the village of Arpachiyah, near Mosul.

41. For a general presentation and bibliography see Müller-Karpe, *Handbuch*, vol. 2, pp. 59 ff. For the religious symbolism of the Halafian figurines and iconographic motifs, see B. L. Goff, *Symbols of Prehistoric Mesopotamia*, pp. 11 ff.

42. See Müller-Karpe, *Handbuch*, vol. 2, pp. 61 ff., 339, 351, 423; M. E. L. Mallowan, *Early Mesopotamia and Iran*, pp. 40 ff. (the White Temple).

is the White Temple (3100 B.C.), 22.3 × 17.5 meters, raised on a
platform 70 meters long, 66 meters wide, and 13 meters high. This
platform incorporates the remains of ancient sanctuaries and constitutes a ziggurat, a sacred "mountain," whose symbolism we shall
investigate later (§ 54).

14. The spiritual edifice of the Neolithic

For our purpose it would be useless to follow the dissemination of
agriculture and, later, of metallurgy through the Aegean and the
eastern Mediterranean—to Greece and the Balkans—and thence
through the Danubian regions and the rest of Europe; it would be
equally unnecessary to follow its spread into India, China, and
Southeast Asia. We will merely mention that, in the beginning,
agriculture made its way only slowly into some regions of Europe.
On the one hand, the postglacial climate permitted the Mesolithic
societies of central and western Europe to subsist on the products of
hunting and fishing. On the other hand, the cultivation of cereals had
to be adapted to a temperate and forest-covered zone. The earliest
agricultural communities develop along watercourses and on the
edges of the great forests. Nevertheless, the propagation of Neolithic
agriculture, begun in the Near East about 8000 B.C., proves to be an
inescapable process. Despite the resistance of certain populations,
especially after the crystallization of pastoralism, the dissemination
of the cultivation of food plants was approaching Australia and
Patagonia when the effects of European colonization and the
Industrial Revolution were beginning to be felt.

The propagation of cereal culture carries with it rites, myths, and
religious ideas peculiar to that mode of life. But this is by no means a
mechanical process. Even reduced, as we are, to archeological
documents—in other words, ignorant of their religious meanings and,
above all, of the concomitant myths and rituals—we still observe
differences, sometimes of great importance, between the Neolithic
cultures of Europe and their Eastern sources. It is certain, for
example, that the cult of the bull, documented by numerous images
in the Danubian regions, comes from the Near East. Yet there is no
proof of the sacrifice of bulls, such as was practiced in Crete or in the
Neolithic cultures of the Indus. So, too, idols of the gods, or the

iconographic ensemble of Mother Goddess and Child, idols so common in the East, are comparatively scarce in the Danubian regions. What is more, such statuettes have never been found in burials.

Some recent discoveries have brilliantly confirmed the originality of the archaic cultures of southeastern Europe, that is, of the complex that Marija Gimbutas calls "Old European civilization." For in fact a civilization that includes the cultivation of wheat and barley and the domestication of sheep, cattle, and the pig is manifested simultaneously, about 7000 B.C. or earlier, on the coasts of Greece and Italy, in Crete, in southern Anatolia, in Syria and Palestine, and in the Fertile Crescent. Now on the basis of radiocarbon dates it is impossible to say that this cultural complex made its appearance in Greece *later* than in the Fertile Crescent, Syria, Cilicia, or Palestine. We still do not know what the "initial impulse" for this culture was.[43] But there is no archeological proof indicating an influx of immigrants arriving in Greece from Asia Minor and possessing cultivated plants and domesticated animals.[44]

Whatever its origin may have been, the "Old European civilization" developed in an original way, one that distinguishes it both from the cultures of the Near East and from those of central and northern Europe. Between 6500 and 5300 B.C. there was a powerful upsurge of culture in the Balkan Peninsula and in central Anatolia. A large number of objects (seals with ideograms, human and animal figures, theriomorphic vessels, images of divine masks) indicate ritual activities. Toward the middle of the sixth millennium there is a multiplication of villages defended by ditches or walls and able to contain up to a thousand inhabitants.[45] A large number of altars and sanctuaries, as well as various cult objects, bear witness to a well-organized religion. In the Aeneolithic station of Căscioarele, 60 kilometers south of Bucharest, excavation has revealed a temple whose walls were painted with magnificent spirals in red and green on a yellowish-white ground. No statuettes were found, but a column 2 meters high and also a smaller one indicate a cult of the sacred

43. Marija Gimbutas, "Old Europe, c. 7000–3500 B.C.," p. 5.
44. In addition, cattle, the pig, and a species of wheat (einkorn wheat) have indigenous ancestors in Europe (Gimbutas, p. 5).
45. In comparison, groups of habitations like those of the Swiss lakes seem to be hamlets (Gimbutas, p. 6).

pillar, symbol of the *axis mundi*.[46] Above this temple another, of later date, was found, which yielded a terra-cotta model of a sanctuary. The model represents a decidedly impressive architectonic complex: four temples set on a high pedestal.[47]

Several models of temples have been found in the Balkan Peninsula. Added to countless other documents (figurines, masks, various non-figurative symbols, etc.), they indicate the richness and complexity of a religion whose content still remains inaccessible.[48]

It is unnecessary to enumerate all the Neolithic documents that can support a religious interpretation. We will sometimes refer to them when we discuss the religious prehistory of certain nuclear zones (the Mediterranean, India, China, Southeast Asia, Central America). At this point we will say that, reduced solely to the archeological documents, and without the light thrown by the texts or traditions of certain agricultural societies (traditions that were still alive at the beginning of this century), the Neolithic religions run the risk of appearing simplistic and monotonous. But the archeological documents present us with a fragmentary, and indeed mutilated, vision of religious life and thought. We have just seen what the religious documents of the earliest Neolithic cultures reveal: cults of the dead and of fertility, indicated by statuettes of goddesses and of the storm god (with his epiphanies: the bull, the bucranium); beliefs and rituals connected with the "mystery" of vegetation; the assimilation woman/cultivated soil/plant, implying the homology birth/rebirth (initiation); very probably the hope of a postexistence; a cosmology including the symbolism of a "center of the world" and inhabited space as an *imago mundi*. It is enough to consider a

46. Vladimir Dumitrescu, "Edifice destiné au culte découvert à Căscioarele," p. 21. The two columns are hollow, which means that they were modeled around tree trunks (ibid., pp. 14, 21). The symbolism of the *axis mundi* assimilates the Cosmic Tree to the Cosmic Pillar (*columna universalis*). The radiocarbon dates given by Dumitrescu vary between 4035 and 3620 B.C. (see ibid., p. 24, n. 25); Marija Gimbutas says "about 5000 B.C." ("Old Europe," p. 11).

47. Hortensia Dumitrescu, "Un modèle de sanctuaire découvert à Căscioarele," figs. 1 and 4 (the latter is reproduced by Gimbutas, fig. 1, p. 12).

48. According to Gimbutas, the "Old European civilization" had also developed a writing (see figs. 2 and 3) as early as ca. 5300–5200 B.C., that is, 2,000 years before Sumer (p. 12). The disintegration of this civilization begins after 3500 B.C., subsequent to the invasion by the populations of the Pontic steppe (p. 13).

contemporary society of primitive cultivators to realize the complexity and richness of a religion articulated around ideas of chthonian fertility and the cycle life-death-postexistence.[49]

In addition, as soon as the earliest texts come to supplement the archeological documents of the Near East, we see how greatly they reveal a universe of meanings that are not only complex and profound but that have long been meditated on and reinterpreted and, indeed, are sometimes on the way to becoming obscure and almost unintelligible. In some cases the earliest texts available to us represent an approximate recollection of immemorial religious creations that have become outdated or half-forgotten. We must not lose sight of the fact that the grandiose Neolithic spirituality is not "transparent" through the documentation at our disposal. The semantic possibilities of archeological documents are limited, and the earliest texts express a vision of the world that is strongly influenced by the religious ideas bound up with metallurgy, urban civilization, royalty, and an organized priesthood.

But if the spiritual edifice of the Neolithic[50] is no longer accessible to us in its entirety, scattered fragments have been preserved in the traditions of peasant societies. The continuity of "sacred places" (cf. § 8) and of certain agricultural and funerary rituals is no longer in need of proof. In twentieth-century Egypt, the ritual sheaf is still tied exactly as we see it on the ancient monuments—where, be it added, a custom inherited from prehistory is reproduced. In Arabia Petraea, the last sheaf is buried under the name of "the Old Man," which is the same name that it bore in the Egypt of the pharaohs. The grain gruel that is offered at funerals and festivals of the dead in Romania and the Balkans is called *coliva*. The name (*kollyba*) and the offering are documented in ancient Greece, but the custom is certainly more archaic (it is believed to have been represented in the Dipylon burials). Leopold Schmidt has shown that certain mythico-ritual scenarios, still in use among the peasants of central and south-eastern Europe at the beginning of the twentieth century, preserve mythological fragments and rituals that had disappeared, in ancient

49. A comparative analysis of the iconography and symbolism of the ornamental motifs found on vessels and bronze objects can sometimes markedly increase our knowledge of a prehistoric religion; but this is possible only from the time of painted ceramics and, above all, from the Age of Metals.

50. We refer, of course, to the archeological Neolithic of the Near East and Europe.

Greece, before Homer. There is no use extending the list. We would only emphasize that such rites maintained themselves for a period of 4,000 to 5,000 years, of which the last 1,000 to 1,500 were under the vigilant scrutiny of two monotheisms famous for their vigor, Christianity and Islam.

15. Religious context of metallurgy: Mythology of the Iron Age

The "mythology of polished stone" was succeeded by a "mythology of metals"; the richest and most characteristic was developed around iron. It is known that the archaic preliterate peoples, as well as the prehistoric populations, worked meteoric iron long before they learned to use the ferrous ores occurring on the earth's surface. They treated certain ores like stones, that is, they regarded them as raw material for the manufacture of lithic tools.[51] When Cortez asked the Aztec chieftains where they got their knives, they pointed to the sky. And in fact excavations have revealed no trace of terrestrial iron in the prehistoric deposits of the New World.[52] The paleo-Oriental peoples presumably held similar ideas. The Sumerian word AN.BAR, the earliest vocable designating iron, is written with the signs "sky" and "fire." It is generally translated as "celestial metal" or "star-metal." For a long period the Egyptians knew only meteoric iron. The same is true of the Hittites: a text of the fourteenth century states that the Hittite kings used "the black iron of the sky."[53]

Iron, therefore, was scarce (it was as precious as gold), and its use was principally ritual. It required the discovery of the smelting of ores to inaugurate a new stage in the history of mankind. Unlike copper and bronze, the metallurgy of iron very soon became industrial. Once the secret of smelting magnetite or hematite was discovered, there was no more difficulty in obtaining large quantities of iron, for the deposits were very rich and easy to work. But the treatment of terrestrial ore was not like that of meteoric iron, and it also differed from the smelting of copper and bronze. It was only after the discovery of furnaces, and especially after the perfecting of

51. See Eliade, *The Forge and the Crucible*, p. 21.
52. R. C. Forbes, *Metallurgy in Antiquity*, p. 401.
53. T. A. Richard, *Man and Metals*, vol. 1, p. 149.

the technique of "hardening" metal brought to the white-hot point, that iron achieved its predominant position. It was the metallurgy of terrestrial iron that made this metal fit for everyday use.

This fact had important religious consequences. Beside the celestial sacredness of the sky, immanent in meteorites, there is now the telluric sacredness of the earth, in which mines and ores share. Metals "grow" in the bosom of the earth.[54] Caves and mines are assimilated to the womb of Mother Earth. The ores extracted from mines are in some sort "embryos." They grow slowly, as if they obey a different temporal rhythm from the life of vegetable and animal organisms; nevertheless, they grow, they "ripen" in the telluric darkness. Hence their extraction from the bosom of Mother Earth is an operation performed prematurely. If they had been given the time to develop (that is, in the *geological rhythm* of time), ores would have become ripe, "perfect" metals.

All over the world miners practice rites involving a state of purity, fasting, meditation, prayers, and cult acts. The rites are governed by the nature of the intended operation, for the performer of them is to introduce himself into a sacred zone, supposedly inviolable; he enters into contact with a sacrality that does not participate in the familiar religious universe, for it is a deeper and also more dangerous sacrality. He has the feeling that he risks entering a domain that does not rightfully belong to man: the underground world with its mysteries of the slow mineralogical gestation that takes place in the womb of Mother Earth. All the mythologies of mines and mountains, the countless fairies, genii, elves, phantoms, and spirits, are the multiple epiphanies of the *sacred presence* that the individual confronts when he penetrates into the geological levels of Life.

Laden with this dark sacrality, the ores are taken to the furnaces. Then begins the most difficult and the riskiest operation. The artisan takes the place of Mother Earth in order to hasten and perfect the "growth" of the ores. The furnaces are in some sort a new, artificial womb, in which the ore completes its gestation. Hence the countless precautions, taboos, and rituals that accompany smelting.[55]

54. See *The Forge and the Crucible*, pp. 43 ff.
55. Ibid., pp. 57 ff. Certain African populations divide ores into "male" and "female"; in ancient China, Yu the Great, the primordial Smelter, distinguished male metals and female metals (ibid., p. 37). In Africa the work of smelting is assimilated to the sexual act (ibid., p. 57).

The metallurgist, like the blacksmith and, before him, the potter, is a "master of fire." It is by means of fire that he brings about the passage of the material from one state to another. As for the metallurgist, he accelerates the "growth" of ores, he makes them "ripe" in a miraculously short time. Smelting proves to be the means of "acting faster" but also of acting to make *a different thing* from what already existed in nature. This is why, in archaic societies, smelters and smiths are held to be masters of fire, along with shamans, medicine men, and magicians. But the ambivalent character of metal —laden with powers at once sacred and demonic—is transferred to metallurgists and smiths: they are highly esteemed but are also feared, segregated, or even scorned.[56]

In many mythologies the divine smiths forge the weapons of the gods, thus insuring them victory over dragons or other monstrous beings. In the Canaanite myth, Koshar-wa-Hasis (literally, "Adroit-and-Clever") forges for Baal the two clubs with which he will kill Yam, lord of the seas and underground waters (see § 49). In the Egyptian version of the myth, Ptah (the potter god) forges the weapons that enable Horus to conquer Seth. Similarly, the divine smith Tvaṣṭṛ makes Indra's weapons for his battle with Vṛtra; Hephaestus forges the thunderbolt that will enable Zeus to triumph over Typhon (see § 84). But the cooperation between the divine smith and the gods is not confined to his help in the final combat for sovereignty over the world. The smith is also the architect and artisan of the gods, supervises the construction of Baal's palace, and equips the sanctuaries of the other divinities. In addition, this god-smith has connections with music and song, just as in a number of societies the smiths and braziers are also musicians, poets, healers, and magicians.[57] It seems, then, that on different levels of culture (an indication of great antiquity) there is an intimate connection between the art of the smith, occult techniques (shamanism, magic, healing, etc.), and the arts of song, of the dance, and of poetry.

All these ideas and beliefs articulated around the trades of miners, metallurgists, and smiths have markedly enriched the mythology of *Homo faber* inherited from the Stone Age. But the wish to collaborate in the perfecting of matter had important consequences. In assuming the responsibility for changing nature, man took the place of time;

56. On the ambivalent situation of smiths in Africa, see ibid., pp. 89 ff.
57. Ibid., pp. 97 ff.

what would have required eons to ripen in the subterranean depths, the artisan believes he can obtain in a few weeks; for the furnace replaces the telluric womb.

Millennia later, the alchemist will not think differently. A character in Ben Jonson's play *The Alchemist* declares: "lead and other metals . . . would be gold *if they had had time*" to become so. And another alchemist adds: "And that our art doth further."[58] The struggle for mastery over time—which will enjoy its greatest success with synthetic products obtained by organic chemistry, a decisive stage in the synthetic preparation of life itself (the homunculus, the old dream of the alchemists)—the struggle to take the place of time that characterizes the man of the modern technological societies, had already begun in the Iron Age. We shall later estimate its religious meanings.

58. See ibid., pp. 51 ff., 171 ff. See also the chapters on Occidental alchemy and on the religious implications of "scientific progress" in the third volume of the present work.

3 The Mesopotamian Religions

16. "History begins at Sumer"

This is the well-known title of a book by S. N. Kramer. In it, the eminent American Orientalist showed that our earliest information concerning a number of religious institutions, techniques, and conceptions is preserved in Sumerian texts. That is, they represent the earliest *written* documents, whose originals go back to the third millennium. But these documents certainly reflect more archaic religious beliefs.

The origin and early history of Sumerian civilizations are still imperfectly known. It is supposed that a population speaking Sumerian, a language that is not Semitic and cannot be explained by any other known linguistic family, came down from the northern regions and settled in Lower Mesopotamia. Very probably the Sumerians conquered the autochthonous inhabitants, whose ethnic component is still unknown (culturally, they shared in the Obeid civilization; see § 13). Not long afterward, groups of nomads coming from the Syrian desert and speaking a Semitic language, Akkadian, began entering the territories north of Sumer, at the same time infiltrating the Sumerian cities in successive waves. Toward the middle of the third millennium, under a leader who became legendary, Sargon, the Akkadians imposed their supremacy on the Sumerian cities. Yet, even before the conquest, a Sumero-Akkadian symbiosis developed, which was greatly increased by the unification of the two countries. Thirty or forty years ago scholars referred to a single culture, the Babylonian, the result of the fusion of these two ethnic stocks. It is now generally agreed that the Sumerian and Akkadian contributions should be studied separately, for, despite the fact that the invaders had assimilated the culture of the defeated people, the creative genius of the two was different.

It is especially in the religious domain that these differences are perceptible. From the most remote antiquity, the characteristic emblem of divine beings was a *horned* tiara. At Sumer, then, as everywhere in the Near East, the religious symbolism of the bull, documented from the Neolithic, had been handed down uninterruptedly. In other words, the divine modality was defined by the power and the "transcendence" of *space*, i.e., the stormy sky in which thunder sounds (for thunder was assimilated to the bellowing of bulls). The "transcendent," celestial structure of divine beings is confirmed by the determinative sign that precedes their ideograms and that originally represented a star. According to the vocabularies, the proper meaning of this determinative is "sky." Hence every divinity was imagined as a celestial being; this is why the gods and goddesses radiated a very bright light.

The earliest Sumerian texts reflect the work of classification and systematization accomplished by the priests. First of all is the triad of the great gods, followed by the triad of the planetary gods. We have also been left lengthy lists of divinities of all kinds, concerning whom we very often know nothing but their names. At the dawn of its *history*, the Sumerian religion already proves to be ancient. To be sure, the texts so far discovered are fragmentary and peculiarly difficult to interpret. However, even on the basis of this sparse information, we can understand that certain religious traditions were in the course of losing their original meanings. The process is perceptible even in the triad of the great gods, made up of An, En-lil, and En-ki. As his name shows (*an* = sky), the first is a uranian god. He must have been the supreme sovereign god, the most important in the pantheon; but An already presents the syndrome of a *deus otiosus*. More active and more "actual" are En-lil, god of the atmosphere (also called the "Great Mount"), and En-ki, "Lord of the Earth," god of the "foundations," who has wrongly been taken by modern scholars to be the god of the primordial waters because, in the Sumerian view, the earth was supposed to rest on the ocean.

So far, no cosmogonic text properly speaking has been discovered, but some allusions permit us to reconstruct the decisive moments of creation, as the Sumerians conceived it. The goddess Nammu (whose name is written with the pictograph representing the primordial sea) is presented as "the mother who gave birth to the Sky and the Earth" and the "ancestress who brought forth all the gods." The theme of the primordial waters, imagined as a totality at once cosmic and divine, is quite frequent in archaic cosmogonies. In this case too, the watery mass is identified with the original Mother, who, by parthenogenesis, gave birth to the first couple, the Sky (An) and the Earth (Ki), incarnating the male and female principles. This first couple was united, to the point of merging, in the *hieros gamos*. From their union was born En-lil, the god of the atmosphere. Another fragment informs us that the latter separated his parents: the god An carried the sky upward, and En-lil took his mother, the Earth, with him.[1] The cosmogonic theme of the separation of sky and earth is also widely disseminated. It is found, indeed, at different levels of culture. But probably the version recorded in the Near East and the Mediterranean derive, in the last analysis, from the Sumerian tradition.

Certain texts describe the perfection and bliss of the "beginnings": "the ancient days when each thing was created perfect," etc.[2] However, the true Paradise seems to be Dilmun, a country in which neither illness nor death exists. There "no lion kills, no wolf carries off a lamb. . . . No man with eye disease repeats: 'My eyes are sick.' . . . No night watchman walks about his post."[3] Yet, all in all, this perfection was a stagnation. For the god En-ki, the Lord of Dilmun, lay asleep beside his wife, who was still a virgin, as the earth itself was virgin. When he woke, En-ki united with the goddess Nin-gur-sag, then with the daughter whom the latter bore, and finally with the daughter's daughter—for this is a theogony that must be completed in this paradisal land. But an apparently insignificant incident occasions the first divine drama. The god eats certain plants that had just been created; but he was supposed to "determine their destiny," that is, to settle their mode of being and their function. Outraged by this senseless act, Nin-gur-sag declares that she will no longer look on En-ki with the "look of life," and thus he will die. And in fact

1. See S. N. Kramer, *From the Tablets of Sumer*, pp. 77 ff., and *The Sumerians*, p. 145.

2. See a new translation of the poem "Gilgamesh, Enkidu, and the Underworld" in Giorgio R. Castellino, *Mitologia sumerico-accadia*, pp. 176–81. On the Egyptian conception of initial perfection, see § 25.

3. After the translation of Maurice Lambert, in *La Naissance du Monde*, p. 106.

unknown ills afflict the god, and his increasing weakness presages his speedy death. Finally, it is his wife who cures him.[4]

As it has been possible to reconstruct it, this myth shows instances of rehandling, the purpose of which cannot be determined. The paradisal theme, completed by a theogony, ends in a drama that reveals the crime and punishment of a creator god, followed by an increasing weakness that portends his death. Certainly, a fatal fault is involved, for En-ki *did not behave in accordance with the principle that he incarnated.* This fault came near to compromising the structure of his own creation. Other texts have preserved the lamentations of the gods when they fall victims to fate. And we shall later see the risks run by Inanna in going beyond the frontiers of her sovereignty. What is surprising in the drama of En-ki is not the mortal nature of the gods but the mythological context in which it is proclaimed.

17. Man before his gods

There are at least four Sumerian narratives that explain the origin of man. They are so different that we must assume a plurality of traditions. One myth relates that the first human beings sprouted from the ground like the plants. According to another version, man was fashioned from clay by certain divine artisans; then the goddess Nammu modeled a heart for him, and En-ki gave him life. Other texts name the goddess Aruru as the creator of human beings. Finally, according to the fourth version, man was formed from the blood of two Lăgma gods immolated for the purpose. This last theme will be revived and reinterpreted in the famous Babylonian cosmogonic poem, *Enuma elish* (§ 21).

All these motifs, with numerous variants, are documented more or less throughout the world. According to two of the Sumerian versions, the primitive man shared in a way in the divine substance: in En-ki's vital breath or in the blood of the Lăgma gods. This means that there was no impassable distance between the divine mode of being and the human condition. It is true that man was created in order to serve the gods, who, first of all, needed to be fed and clothed.[5]

4. We follow the interpretation given by R. Jestin, "La religion sumérienne," p. 170.

5. On the cult, see Kramer, *The Sumerians*, pp. 140 ff.; A. L. Oppenheim, *Ancient Mesopotamia*, pp. 183 ff.

The cult was conceived of as service to the gods. However, if men are the gods' servants, they are not their slaves. The sacrifice consisted primarily in offerings and homage. As for the great collective festivals of the city—celebrated at the New Year or at the building of a temple —they have a cosmological structure.

Raymond Jestin emphasizes the fact that the notion of sin, the expiatory element, and the idea of the scapegoat are not documented in the texts.[6] This implies that men are not only servants of the gods but are also their imitators and hence their collaborators. Since the gods are responsible for the cosmic order, men must obey their commands, for these are based on the norms—the "decrees," *me*— which insure the functioning both of the world and of human society.[7] These decrees establish, that is, *determine*, the destiny of every being, of every form of life, of every divine or human enterprise. The determination of the decrees is accomplished by the act of *nam-tar*, which constitutes, and proclaims, the decision taken. At each New Year the gods fix the destiny of the following twelve months. This, to be sure, is an old idea, found elsewhere in the Near East; but the first strictly articulated expression of it is Sumerian and shows the deep work of investigation and systematization performed by the theologians.

The cosmic order is continually troubled, first of all by the Great Serpent, which threatens to reduce the world to chaos, and then by men's crimes, faults, and errors, which must be expiated and purged by the help of various rites. But the world is periodically regenerated, i.e., re-created, by the festival of the New Year. "The Sumerian name of this festival, *à-ki-til*, means 'power making the world live again' (*til* means 'live' and 'live again'; thus a sick man 'lives [again],' that is, is cured); the whole cycle of the law of eternal return is evoked."[8] More or less similar mythico-ritual scenarios of the New Year are

6. Jestin, "La religion sumérienne," p. 184. "'Penitential psalms' appear in the late literature, but the increasing Semitic influence that is discernible in them no longer permits them to be considered genuine expressions of Sumerian consciousness" (ibid.).

7. On the *me* of the different trades, vocations, and institutions, see Kramer, *From the Tablets*, pp. 89 ff.; *The Sumerians*, pp. 117 ff. The term *me* has been translated by "being" (Jacobsen) or "divine power" (Landsberger and Falkenstein) and has been interpreted as a "divine immanence in dead and living matter, unchangeable, subsistent, but impersonal, to which only the gods have access" (J. van Dijk).

8. Jestin, "La religion sumérienne," p. 181.

documented in countless cultures. We shall have occasion to gauge their importance when we analyze the Babylonian festival *akitu* (§ 22). The scenario involves the *hieros gamos* between two patron divinities of the city, represented by their statues or by the sovereign (who received the title of husband of the goddess Inanna and incarnated Dumuzi)[9] and a hierodule. This *hieros gamos* actualized the communion between the gods and men—a momentary communion, to be sure, but with considerable consequences. For the divine energy flowed directly upon the city (that is, upon the Earth), sanctified it, and insured its prosperity and happiness for the beginning year.

Still more important than the New Year festival was the one associated with the building of a temple. It was no less a reiteration of the cosmogony, for the temple—the "palace" of the god—represented the most perfect *imago mundi*. The idea is archaic and widely disseminated. (We shall find it in the myth of Baal, § 50.) According to the Sumerian tradition, after the creation of man, one of the gods founded the five cities; he built them "in pure places, called their names, apportioned them as cult centers."[10] Since that time the gods have contented themselves with imparting the plans of cities and sanctuaries directly to the sovereigns. In a dream King Gudea sees both the goddess Nidaba showing him a placard on which the beneficent stars are named and a god revealing the plan of the temple to him.[11] The models of the temple and the city are, we might say, "transcendental," for they preexist in the sky. The Babylonian cities had their archetypes in the constellations: Sippar in Cancer, Niniveh in the Great Bear, Assur in Arcturus, etc.[12] This concept is general in the ancient East.

The institution of kingship was similarly "lowered from the sky," together with its emblems, the tiara and the throne.[13] After the flood, it was brought down to earth for the second time. The belief in the preexistence of words and institutions will have considerable importance for archaic ontology and will find its most famous

9. See S. N. Kramer, "Le Rite de Mariage sacré Dumuzi-Inanna," p. 129, and his *The Sacred Marriage Rite*, pp. 49 ff.

10. See the text translated by Kramer, *From the Tablets*, p. 177.

11. E. Burrows, "Some Cosmological Patterns in Babylonian Religion," pp. 65 ff.

12. See ibid., pp. 60 ff.

13. See the "Sumerian King List," translated by Kramer, *The Sumerians*, pp. 328 ff.

expression in the Platonic doctrine of Ideas. It is attested for the first time in Sumerian documents, but its roots presumably reach down into prehistory. Indeed, the theory of celestial models continues and develops the universally disseminated archaic conception that man's acts are only the repetition (imitation) of acts revealed by divine beings.

18. The first myth of the flood

Royalty had to be brought down from the sky again after the flood, for the diluvial catastrophe was equivalent to the end of the world. In fact, only a single human being, named Zisudra in the Sumerian version and Utnapishtim in the Akkadian, was saved. But, unlike Noah, he was not allowed to live on in the new earth that emerged from the waters. More or less divinized, but in any case enjoying immortality, the survivor is transported to the land of Dilmun (Zisudra) or to the "mouth of the rivers" (Utnapishtim). From the few fragments of the Sumerian version that have come down to us we learn that, despite the reluctance or the opposition of some members of the pantheon, the great gods decide to destroy humanity by the flood. Someone mentions the merits of King Zisudra, "humble, obedient, pious." Informed by his protector, Zisudra learns of the decision reached by An and En-lil. The text is here interrupted by a long lacuna. Probably Zisudra received exact instructions for building the ark. After seven days and seven nights the sun comes out again, and Zisudra prostrates himself before the sun god, Utu. In the last fragment that has been preserved, An and En-lil confer on him "the life of a god" and the "eternal breath" of the gods and send him to live in the fabulous land of Dilmun.[14]

The same theme of the Deluge is found in the *Epic of Gilgamesh*. This famous work, which has been fairly well preserved, casts still greater light on the similarities to the biblical narrative. In all probability, we may assume the existence of a common, and quite archaic, source. As has been well known since the compilations made by R. Andree, H. Usener, and J. G. Frazer, the deluge myth is almost universally disseminated; it is documented in all the continents

14. See Kramer, *From the Tablets*, pp. 177 ff.; Kramer, *Sumerian Mythology*, pp. 97 ff.; and G. R. Castellino, *Mitologia*, pp. 140–43.

(though very rarely in Africa) and on various cultural levels. A certain number of variants seem to be the result of dissemination, first from Mesopotamia and then from India. It is equally possible that one or several diluvial catastrophes gave rise to fabulous narratives. But it would be risky to explain so widespread a myth by phenomena of which no geological traces have been found. The majority of the flood myths seem in some sense to form part of the cosmic rhythm: the old world, peopled by a fallen humanity, is submerged under the waters, and some time later a new world emerges from the aquatic "chaos."[15]

In a large number of variants, the flood is the result of the sins (or ritual faults) of human beings: sometimes it results simply from the wish of a divine being to put an end to mankind. It is difficult to determine the cause of the flood in the Mesopotamian tradition. Some allusions suggest that the gods reached the decision because of "sinners." According to another, En-lil's anger was aroused by the intolerable "uproar" made by human beings.[16] However, if we examine the myths that, in other cultures, announce the coming flood, we find that the chief causes lie *at once in the sins of men and the decrepitude of the world.* By the mere fact that it exists—that is, that it *lives* and *produces*—the cosmos gradually deteriorates and ends by falling into decay. This is the reason why it has to be re-created. In other words, the flood *realizes*, on the macrocosmic scale, what is symbolically effected during the New Year festival: the "end of the world" and the end of a sinful humanity in order to make a new creation possible.[17]

19. Descent to the underworld: Inanna and Dumuzi

The triad of Sumerian planetary gods was made up of Nanna-Suen (the Moor), Utu (the Sun), and Inanna, goddess of the planet Venus

15. On the symbolism implicit in certain flood myths, see Eliade, *Patterns in Comparative Religion*, pp. 210 ff.

16. We shall see (§ 21) that it is always the "noise"—on this occasion, the uproar made by the young gods, preventing him from sleeping—that decides Apsu to exterminate them (see *Enuma elish*, tab. I, lines 21 ff.).

17. See *Myth and Reality*, pp. 54 ff. According to the version preserved in the *Epic of Atrahasis*, after the flood Ea decided to create seven men and seven women; see Heidel, *The Gilgamesh Epic*, pp. 259–60.

and of love. The gods of the Moon and the Sun will have their apogee during the Babylonian period. As for Inanna, homologized with the Akkadian Ishtar and later with Ashtarte, she will enjoy an "actuality" in both cult and mythology never approached by any other goddess of the Near East. At her apogee, Inanna-Ishtar was the goddess at once of love and of war, that is, she governed life and death; to indicate the fullness of her powers, she was called hermaphroditic (*Ishtar barbata*). Her personality was already fully outlined in the Sumerian period, and her central myth constitutes one of the most significant creations of the ancient world. The myth begins with a love story: Inanna, the tutelary goddess of Erech, marries the shepherd Dumuzi,[18] who thus becomes sovereign of the city. Inanna proclaims her passion and her happiness aloud: "I, in joy I walk! ... My Lord is seemly for the sacred lap." Yet she has a presentiment of the tragic fate that awaits her husband: "My beloved, my man of the heart ... thee, I have brought about an evil for you ... you have touched your mouth to mine, you have pressed my lips to your head, that is why you have been decreed an evil fate" (Kramer, "Le rite de mariage sacré," p. 141).

This "evil fate" was decided on the day when the ambitious Inanna determined to go down into the underworld to supplant her "elder sister," Ereshkigal. Sovereign of the Great Above, Inanna aspires also to reign over the World Below. She manages to enter Ereshkigal's palace, but, as she successively passes through the Seven Gates, the gatekeepers strip her of her clothes and ornaments. Inanna arrives stark naked—that is, stripped of all "power"—in her sister's presence. Ereshkigal fixes the "look of death" on her, and "her body became inert." After three days, her devoted friend Ninshubur, obeying the instructions that Inanna had given her before setting out, informs the gods En-lil and Nanna-Sin. But they decline to intervene, because Inanna, they say, by entering a domain—the Land of the Dead—which is governed by inviolable decrees, "sought to meddle with forbidden things." However, En-lil finds a solution: he creates two messengers and sends them to the underworld carrying "the

18. According to another version, she first preferred the farmer Enkimdu, but her brother, the sun god Utu, makes her change her mind; see Kramer, *The Sacred Marriage Rite*, pp. 69 ff., and his "Le Rite de Mariage Sacré Dumuzi-Inanna," pp. 124 ff. Except where otherwise specified, we use the translations by Kramer published in the latter article.

food of life" and "the water of life." By a trick, they succeed in reviving "the corpse, which was hanging from a nail." Inanna was preparing to ascend, when the Seven Judges of the Underworld (the Anunaki) held her back, saying: "Who, having descended into the underworld, has ever ascended from the underworld again unharmed? If Inanna wishes to ascend out of the underworld, let her furnish a replacement!"[19]

Inanna returns to earth escorted by a troop of demons, the *gallas*; they are to bring her back if she does not furnish them with another divine being. The demons first try to seize Ninshubur, but Inanna stops them. Next they all go to the cities of Umma and Bad-Tibira; terrified, their tutelary divinities crawl in the dust at Inanna's feet, and the goddess pities them and decides to search elsewhere. Finally they arrive at Erech. In surprise and indignation, Inanna discovers that, instead of lamenting, Dumuzi was sitting on his throne, richly clad—satisfied, it almost seemed, to be sole sovereign of the city. "She fixed an eye on him: the eye of death! She spoke a word against him: the word of despair! She cried out against him: the cry of damnation! 'This one (she said to the demons), carry him away.'"[20]

Dumuzi implores his brother-in-law, the sun god Utu, to change him into a snake, and flees to the house of his sister, Geshtinanna, then to his sheepfold. There the demons seize him, torture him, and lead him to the underworld. A lacuna in the text prevents us from reading the epilogue. "In all probability, it is Ereshkigal who, softened by Dumuzi's tears, lightens his sad fate by deciding that he should spend only half the year in the netherworld and that his sister, Geshtinanna, should replace him during the other half" (Kramer, "Le rite de mariage sacré," p. 144).

The same myth, but with some significant differences, is narrated in the Akkadian version of the *Descent of Ishtar to the Underworld.* Before the publication and translation of the Sumerian texts, it was possible to believe that the goddess journeyed to the "Land without return" *after* the "death" of Tammuz and precisely in order to bring him back. Certain elements that are absent in the Sumerian version

19. After the translation by Jean Bottéro, *Annuaire de l'Ecole des Hautes Etudes*, sec. 4 (1971–72), p. 85.

20. After the translation by Bottéro, ibid., p. 91. In another version, it is fear that seems to explain Inanna's action. When the demons seized her and were threatening to take her back, "Terrified, she abandons Dumuzi to them! 'This young man' (she says to them), 'chain his feet' " (ibid.).

seemed to support this interpretation—in the first place, the disastrous consequences of Ishtar's captivity, which are emphasized in the Akkadian version: human and animal reproduction ended entirely after the goddess's disappearance. This calamity was understandable as following upon the interruption of the *hieros gamos* between the goddess of love and fertility and Tammuz, her beloved husband. The catastrophe was of cosmic proportions, and, in the Akkadian version, it is the great gods who, terrified by the imminent disappearance of life, had to intervene to free Ishtar.

What is surprising in the Sumerian version is the "psychological," that is, human, justification for the condemnation of Dumuzi: everything seems to be explained by Inanna's anger at finding her husband proudly seated on his throne. This romantic explanation appears to overlie a more archaic idea: "death"—ritual and therefore reversible—inevitably follows every act of creation or procreation. The kings of Sumer, like the Akkadian kings later, incarnate Dumuzi in the *hieros gamos* with Inanna.[21] This, to a greater or lesser degree, implies acceptance of the ritual "death" of the king. In this case, we must suppose, behind the story transmitted by the Sumerian text, a "mystery" established by Inanna to insure the cycle of universal fertility. It is possible to perceive an allusion to this "mystery" in Gilgamesh's scornful answer when Ishtar invites him to become her husband: he reminds her that it is she who decreed the yearly lamentations for Tammuz.[22] But these lamentations were ritual: the young god's descent to the underworld was bewailed on the eighteenth of the month of Tammuz (June–July), though everyone knew that he would rise again six months later.

The cult of Tammuz is disseminated more or less everywhere in the Middle East. In the sixth century, Ezekiel (8:14) cried out against the women who wept for him even at the gates of the Temple. Tammuz ends by taking on the dramatic and elegiac figure of the young gods who die and are resurrected annually. But his Sumerian prototype probably had a more complex structure: the kings who incarnated him, and who therefore shared his fate, annually celebrated the re-creation of the world. But in order to be re-created

21. See Kramer, *The Sacred Marriage Rite*, pp. 63 ff., and "Le Rite de Mariage Sacré," pp. 131 ff.

22. Tablet VI, lines 46–47. Bottéro (p. 83) renders: "Tammuz, thy first husband, it is thou who didst establish universal mourning for him."

anew, the world had to be annihilated; the precosmogonic chaos also implied the ritual death of the king, his descent to the underworld. In short, the two cosmic modalities—life/death, chaos/cosmos, sterility/fertility—constituted the two moments of a single process. This "mystery," perceived after the discovery of agriculture, becomes the principle of a unified explanation of the world, of life, and of human existence; it transcends the vegetable drama, since it also governs the cosmic rhythms, human destiny, and relations with the gods. The myth relates *the defeat of the goddess of love* and fertility in her attempt to conquer the kingdom of Ereshkigal, that is, *to abolish death*. In consequence, men, as well as certain gods, have to accept the alternation life/death. Dumuzi-Tammuz disappears, to reappear six months later. This alternation—periodical presence and absence of the god—was able to institute "mysteries" concerning the salvation of men, their destiny after death. The role of Dumuzi-Tammuz, ritually incarnated by the Sumero-Akkadian kings, was considerable, for it effected a connection between the divine and human modalities. Eventually, every human being could hope to enjoy this privilege, previously reserved for kings.

20. The Sumero-Akkadian synthesis

The majority of the Sumerian city-temples were united by Lugalzaggisi, the sovereign of Umma, about 2375 B.C. This is the first manifestation of the imperial idea of which we have any knowledge. A generation later the attempt was repeated, with greater success, by Sargon, king of Akkad. But Sumerian civilization preserved all its structures. The change concerned only the kings of the city-temples: they acknowledged themselves to be tributaries to the Akkadian conqueror. Sargon's empire collapsed after a century, as the result of attacks by the Gutians, barbarians who led a nomadic existence in the region of the Upper Tigris. Thereafter, the history of Mesopotamia seems to repeat itself: the political unity of Sumer and Akkad is destroyed by barbarians from without; in their turn, these are overthrown by internal revolts.

Thus, the domination of the Gutians lasted only a century, and was replaced, for another century (ca. 2050–1950 B.C.), by the kings of the third dynasty of Ur. It is during this period that Sumerian civilization attained its culminating point. But it was also the last manifestation of Sumerian political power. Harassed by the Elamites on the east and, on the west, by the Amorites, who came from the Syro-Arabian desert, the empire fell. For more than two centuries Mesopotamia remained divided into several states. It was not until about 1700 B.C. that Hammurabi, the Amorite sovereign of Babylon, succeeded in imposing unity. He fixed the center of the empire farther north, in the city of which he was the sovereign. The dynasty founded by Hammurabi, which appeared to be all-powerful, reigned for less than a century. Other barbarians, the Kassites, come down from the north and begin to harass the Amorites. Finally, about 1525 B.C., they triumph. They will remain the masters of Mesopotamia for four centuries.

The transformation of the city-temples to city-states and then to the empire represents a phenomenon of considerable importance in the history of the Near East.[23] For our purpose, it is important to cite the fact that the Sumerian language, though it ceased to be spoken about 2000 B.C., retained its function as the liturgical language and, indeed, as the language of knowledge for fifteen more centuries. Other liturgical languages will have a similar destiny: Sanskrit, Hebrew, Latin, Old Slavic. Sumerian religious conservatism is carried on in the Akkadian structures. The supreme triad remained the same: An, En-lil, Ea (= En-ki). The astral triad partly takes over the Semitic names of the respective divinities: the Moon, Sin (which derives from the Sumerian Suen); the Sun, Shamash; the planet Venus, Ishtar (= Inanna). The underworld continued to be governed by Ereshkigal and her husband, Nergal. The few changes, imposed by the needs of the empire—for example, the transfer of religious primacy to Babylon and the replacement of En-lil by Marduk— "took centuries to come about."[24] As for the temple, "nothing essential changed in its general plan . . . from the Sumerian phase on, except perhaps the size and number of buildings."[25]

Nevertheless, the contributions of the Semitic religious genius are added to the earlier structures. A first example is that of the two "national" gods—Marduk of Babylon and, later, the Assyrian

---

23. New institutions (such as the professional army and the bureaucracy) are first documented; in the course of time they will be adopted by other states.

24. Jean Nougayrol, "La religion babylonienne," p. 217.

25. Ibid., p. 236.

Assur—who are raised to the rank of universal divinities. Equally significant is the importance assumed in the cult by personal prayers and penitential psalms. One of the most beautiful Babylonian prayers is addressed to all the gods, even to those whom the speaker of the prayer admits that he does not know: "O Lord, . . . great are my sins. O god whom I do not know, great are my sins. . . . O goddess whom I do not know, great are my sins. . . . Man knows nothing; whether he is committing sin or doing good, he does not even know. . . . O my Lord, do not cast thy servant down. My transgressions are seven times seven; remove my transgressions."[26] In the penitential psalms the speaker acknowledges his guilt and confesses his sins aloud. The confession is accompanied by precise liturgical gestures: kneeling, prostration, and "flattening the nose."

The great gods—An, En-lil, and Ea—gradually lose their supremacy in the cult. The worshipers address themselves rather to Marduk or to the astral divinities, Ishtar and especially Shamash. In the course of time the latter will become the unrivaled universal divinity. A hymn proclaims that the sun god is revered everywhere, even among foreigners; Shamash defends justice, he punishes the wrongdoer and rewards the just.[27] The numinous character of the gods increases: they inspire a holy fear, especially by their terrifying brightness. Light is considered to be the particular attribute of divinity, and, insofar as the king shares in the divine condition, he himself emanates rays of light.[28]

Another creation of Akkadian religious thought is divination. We also note a multiplication of magical practices and the development of the occult disciplines (especially astrology), which will later become popular throughout the Asiatic and Mediterranean world.

In short, the Semitic contribution is characterized by the importance accorded to the personal element in religious experience and by the exaltation of certain divinities to a supreme rank. Yet this new and grandiose Mesopotamian synthesis presents a tragic view of human existence.

26. Translation condensed from F. J. Stevens, in *ANET*, pp. 391–92. The lines cited are 21–26, 51–53, and 59–60.

27. See the translation in *ANET*, pp. 387–89.

28. A. Leo Oppenheim, *Ancient Mesopotamia*, p. 176; E. Cassin, *La splendeur divine*, pp. 26 ff., 65 ff., and passim.

21. Creation of the world

The cosmogonic poem known as the *Enuma elish* (after its *incipit*: "When on high") constitutes, with the *Epic of Gilgamesh*, the most important creation of the Akkadian religion. Nothing comparable in greatness, in dramatic tension, in its effort to connect the theogony, the cosmogony, and the creation of man, is to be found in Sumerian literature. The *Enuma elish* narrates the origin of the world in order to exalt Marduk. Despite their being reinterpreted, the themes are ancient: first of all, the primordial image of an undifferentiated aquatic totality, in which the first couple, Apsu and Tiamat, can be discerned. (Other sources specify that Tiamat represents the sea, and Apsu the mass of fresh water on which the earth floats.) Like so many other original divinities, Tiamat is conceived of as at once woman and bisexual. From the mixture of fresh and salt waters other divine couples are born. Almost nothing is known about the second couple, Lakhmu and Lakhamu (according to one tradition they were sacrificed in order to create man). As for the third couple, Anshar and Kishar, their names in Sumerian mean "totality of the upper elements" and "totality of the lower elements."

Time passes ("the days stretched out, the years multiplied").[29] From the *hieros gamos* of these two complementary "totalities" is born the god of the sky, Anu, who in his turn engenders Nudimmud (= Ea).[30] By their play and their cries these young gods trouble Apsu's repose. He complains to Tiamat: "Unbearable to me is their behavior. By day, I cannot rest; by night, I cannot sleep. I want to annihilate them, in order to put an end to their doings. And let silence reign for us, at last we can sleep!" (tablet 1, lines 37–39). We can read in these lines the nostalgia of matter (that is, of a mode of being corresponding to the inertia and unconsciousness of substance) for the primordial immobility, the resistance to all movement—the preliminary condition for the cosmogony. Tiamat "began to cry out against her husband. She gave a cry of pain . . . : 'What! We shall ourselves destroy what we have created! Painful, to be sure, is their

29. Tablet I, line 13. Unless otherwise indicated, we follow the translation by Paul Garelli and Marcel Leibovici, "La naissance du monde selon Akkad," pp. 133–45. We have also used the translations by Labat, Heidel, Speiser, and Castellino.

30. Of the divinities of the great Sumerian triad, En-lil is missing; his place was taken by Marduk, son of Ea.

behavior, but let us be patient and mild'" (1. 41–46). But Apsu would not be persuaded.

When the young gods learned of their ancestor's decision, "they were left speechless" (58). But the "all-knowing Ea" set to work. With his magical incantations, he makes Apsu sink into a deep sleep, he takes away "his brightness and clothes himself in it," and, after binding him, kills him. Ea thus became the god of the Waters, which he thenceforth named *apsu*. It is in the depths of the *apsu*, "in the chamber of destinies, the sanctuary of archetypes" (79), that his wife, Damkina, gave birth to Marduk. The text exalts the gigantic majesty, the wisdom, and the omnipotence of this last-born of the gods. It is then that Anu resumes the attack on his ancestors. He caused the four winds to rise and "created the waves to trouble Tiamat" (108). The gods, deprived of rest, turn to their mother: "When they killed Apsu, thy spouse, far from walking at his side, thou didst remain apart without a word" (113–14).

This time, Tiamat decided to react. She formed monsters, snakes, the "great lion," "raging demons," and yet others, "pitiless bearers of arms, unafraid of battle" (144). And "among the gods, her first-born, . . . she exalted Kingu" (147 f.). Tiamat fastened to Kingu's chest the tablet of Destinies and bestowed the supreme power on him (144 ff.). Faced with these preparations, the young gods lose courage. Neither Anu nor Ea dares to confront Kingu. It is only Marduk who accepts the battle, but on condition that he should first be proclaimed supreme god, which the gods hasten to grant. The battle between the two troops is decided by a single combat between Tiamat and Marduk. "When Tiamat opened her maw to swallow him" (4. 97), Marduk hurled the raging winds, which "dilated her body. She was left with her belly swollen and her mouth gaping. He then loosed an arrow, which perforated her belly, tore her entrails, and pierced her heart. Having thus overcome her, he took her life, threw the corpse on the ground, and stood on it" (100–104). Tiamat's partisans tried to escape, but Marduk "bound them and broke their weapons" (111); he then chained Kingu, snatched the tablet of Destinies from him, and fastened it to his own chest (120 ff.). Finally, he returned to Tiamat, split her skull, and cut the corpse in two, "like a dried fish" (137); one half became the vault of the sky, the other half the earth. Marduk set up in the sky a replica of the palace of the *apsu* and fixed the courses of the stars. The fifth tablet reports the organization of the planetary universe, the determination of time, and the configuration of the earth from Tiamat's organs (from her eyes flow the Euphrates and the Tigris, "from a loop of her tail he created the link between sky and earth" [5. 59]; etc.).

Finally, Marduk decides to create man, so that "on him shall rest the service of the gods, for their relief" (6. 8). The conquered and chained gods were still awaiting their punishment. Ea suggests that only one of them shall be sacrificed. Asked who "fomented war, incited Tiamat to revolt, and began the battle" (23–24), all give but one name: Kingu. His veins are cut, and from his blood Ea creates mankind (30).[31] The poem then relates the building of a sanctuary (i.e., his palace) in honor of Marduk.

While using traditional mythological themes, the *Enuma elish* presents a rather somber cosmogony and a pessimistic anthropology. To exalt the young champion, Marduk, the gods of the primordial epoch, and most of all Tiamat, are charged with demonic values. Tiamat is no longer merely the primitive chaotic totality that precedes any cosmogony; she ends by proving to be the producer of countless monsters. Her "creativity" is thus wholly negative. As it is described in the *Enuma elish*, the creative process is very soon endangered by Apsu's wish to annihilate the young gods, that is, in the last analysis, to stop the creation of the universe in the bud. (A certain "world" already existed, since the gods were multiplying and had "dwellings"; but it was a purely formal mode of being.) The killing of Apsu opens the series of "creative murders," for Ea not only takes his place but also begins a first organization in the aquatic mass ("in this place he established his dwelling place . . . he determined the sanctuaries"). The cosmogony is the result of a conflict between two groups of gods, but Tiamat's troop also includes her monstrous and demonic creatures. In other words, "primordiality" as such is presented as the source of "negative creations." It is from Tiamat's remains that Marduk forms the sky and the earth. This theme, which is also documented in other traditions, can be variously interpreted. The universe, made from the body of an original divinity, shares in its substance. But, after the "demonization" of Tiamat, can one still speak of a substance that is divine?

Hence the cosmos has a double nature; it consists of an ambivalent,

31. We will add that other parallel traditions concerning the cosmology and the creation of man also exist.

if not frankly demonic, matter and a divine form, for it is the work of Marduk. The celestial vault is formed from one half of Tiamat's body, but the stars and constellations become "dwellings" or images of the gods. The earth itself comprises the other half of Tiamat and her various organs, but it is sanctified by the cities and temples. In the last analysis, the world proves to be the result of a mingling of chaotic and demonic primordiality on the one hand with divine creativity, presence, and wisdom on the other. This is perhaps the most complex cosmogonic formula arrived at by Mesopotamian speculation, for it combines in a daring synthesis all the structures of a divine society, some of which had become incomprehensible or unusable.

As for the creation of man, it continues the Sumerian tradition (man is created to serve the gods), particularly the version that explains his origin from the two sacrificed Lăgma gods. But it adds this aggravating element: Kingu, despite his having been one of the first gods, became the archdemon, the leader of the troop of monsters and demons created by Tiamat. Hence man is made from a demonic substance: the blood of Kingu. The difference from the Sumerian versions is significant. We can speak of a tragic pessimism, for man seems to be already condemned by his own origin. His only hope lies in the fact that it is Ea who fashioned him; hence he possesses a form created by a great god. From this point of view, there is a symmetry between the creation of man and the origin of the world. In both cases, the raw material is constituted by the substance of a fallen primordial divinity, demonized and put to death by the victorious young gods.

22. Sacrality of the Mesopotamian sovereign

At Babylon the *Enuma elish* was recited in the temple on the fourth day of the New Year festival. This festival, named *zagmuk* ("beginning of the year") in Sumerian and *akitu* in Akkadian, took place during the first twelve days of the month of Nisan. It comprised several sequences, of which we will mention the most important: (1) a day of expiation for the king, corresponding to Marduk's "captivity"; (2) the freeing of Marduk; (3) ritual combats and a triumphal procession, led by the king, to the Bit Akitu (the house of the New Year festival), where a banquet was held; (4) the *hieros gamos* of the king with a hierodule personifying the goddess; and (5) the determination of destinies by the gods.

The first sequence of this mythico-ritual scenario—the king's humiliation and Marduk's captivity—indicates the regression of the world to the precosmogonic chaos. In the sanctuary of Marduk the high priest stripped the king of his emblems (scepter, ring, scimitar, and crown) and struck him in the face. Then, on his knees, the king uttered a declaration of innocence: "I have not sinned, O lord of the lands, I have not been negligent regarding thy divinity." The high priest, speaking in Marduk's name, replied: "Do not fear. . . . Marduk will hear thy prayer. He will increase thy dominion."[32]

During this time the people sought for Marduk, supposed to be "shut up in the mountain" (a formula indicating the "death" of a divinity). As we saw in the case of Inanna-Ishtar, this "death" was not final; yet she had to be redeemed from the lower world. Similarly, Marduk was made to descend "far from the sun and light."[33] Finally, he was delivered, and the gods assembled (that is, their statues were brought together) to determine the destinies. (This episode corresponds, in the *Enuma elish*, to Marduk's advancement to the rank of supreme god.) The king led the procession to the Bit Akitu, a building situated outside of the city. The procession represented the army of the gods advancing against Tiamat. According to an inscription of Sennacherib, we may suppose that the primordial battle was mimed, the king personifying Assur (the god who had replaced Marduk).[34] The *hieros gamos* took place after the return from the banquet at the Bit Akitu. The last act consisted in the determination of the destinies[35] for each month of the year. By "determining" it, the year was ritually *created*, that is, the good fortune, fertility, and richness of the new world that had just been born were insured.

The *akitu* represents the Mesopotamian version of a quite wide-

32. Texts cited by H. Frankfort, *Kingship and the Gods*, p. 320.

33. The classic authors refer to the "tomb of Bel" (= Marduk) at Babylon. This was in all probability the ziggurat of the Etemenanki temple, considered the god's momentary burial place.

34. Some allusions imply that there were mimed combats between two groups of actors.

35. Just as, in the *Enuma elish*, Marduk had determined the laws governing the universe that he had just created.

spread mythico-ritual scenario, specifically of the New Year festival considered as a repetition of the cosmogony.[36] Since the periodic regeneration of the cosmos constitutes the great hope of traditional societies, we shall often refer to New Year festivals. We will mention at this point that various episodes of the *akitu* are found (to confine ourselves to the Near East) in Egypt, among the Hittites, at Ugarit, in Iran, and among the Mandaeans. Thus, for example, "chaos," ritually actualized during the last days of the year, was signified by orgiastic excesses of the Saturnalia type, by the reversal of all social order, by the extinguishing of fires, and by the return of the dead (represented by maskers). Combats between two groups of actors are documented in Egypt, among the Hittites, and at Ugarit. The custom of "fixing the fates" of the twelve months during the twelve inter-calary days still persists in the Near East and in eastern Europe.[37]

The role of the king in the *akitu* is inadequately known. His "humiliation" corresponds to the regression of the world to chaos and to Marduk's captivity in the mountain. The king personifies the god in the battle against Tiamat and in the *hieros gamos* with a hierodule. But identification with the god is not always indicated; as we have seen, during his "humiliation" the king addresses Marduk. Nevertheless, the sacrality of the Mesopotamian sovereign is amply documented. We have mentioned the sacred marriage of the Sumerian king, representing Dumuzi, to the goddess Inanna; this *hieros gamos* took place during the New Year festival (§ 19). For the Sumerians, royalty was held to have descended from the sky; its origin was divine, and this conception remained in force until the disappearance of the Assyro-Babylonian civilization.

The sovereign's sacrality was proclaimed in many ways. He was called "king of the land" (that is, of the world) or "of the four regions of the universe," titles originally appertaining to the gods alone.[38] Just as in the case of the gods, a supernatural light shone from his head.[39] Even before his birth, the gods had predestined him to sovereignty. Though the king recognized his earthly begetting, he was considered a "son of god" (Hammurabi declares that he was

36. See Eliade, *Cosmos and History*, pp. 49 ff.; *Myth and Reality*, pp. 41 ff.
37. See *Cosmos and History*, pp. 65 ff.
38. See Frankfort, *Kingship*, pp. 227 ff.
39. This light, named *melammû* in Akkadian, corresponds to the *xvarenah* of the Iranians; see Oppenheim, *Ancient Mesopotamia*, p. 206; Cassin, *La splendeur divine*, pp. 65 ff.

begotten by Sin, and Lipitishtar by En-lil). This twofold descent made him supremely the intermediary between gods and men. The sovereign represented the people before the gods, and it was he who expiated the sins of his subjects. Sometimes he had to suffer death for his people's crimes; this is why the Assyrians had a "substitute for the king."[40] The texts proclaim that the king had lived in fellowship with the gods in the fabulous garden that contains the Tree of Life and the Water of Life.[41] (Actually, it is he and his courtiers who eat the food offered daily to the statues of the gods.) The king is the "envoy" of the gods, the "shepherd of the people," named by god to establish justice and peace on earth.[42] "When Anu and En-lil called Lipit-Ishtar to the government of the land in order to establish justice in the land . . . , then I, Lipit-Ishtar, the humble shepherd of Nippur . . . , established justice in Sumer and Akkad, in accordance with the word of En-lil."[43]

It could be said that the king shared in the divine modality, but without becoming a god. He *represented* the god, and this, on the archaic levels of culture, also implied that he *was* in a way he whom he personified. In any case, as mediator between the world of men and the world of the gods, the Mesopotamian king effected, in his own person, a ritual union between the two modalities of existence, the divine and the human. It was by virtue of this twofold nature that the king was considered, at least metaphorically, to be the creator of life and fertility. *But he was not a god, a new member of the pantheon* (as the Egyptian pharaoh was; cf. § 27). Prayers were not addressed to him; on the contrary, the gods were implored to protect him. For the sovereigns, despite their intimacy with the divine world, despite the *hieros gamos* with certain goddesses, did not reach the point of transmuting the human condition. In the last analysis, they remained mortals. It was never forgotten that even the fabled king of Uruk, Gilgamesh, failed in his attempt to gain immortality.

40. Labat, *Le caractère religieux de la royauté assyro-babylonienne*, pp. 352 ff.; Frankfort, *Kingship*, pp. 262 ff.

41. It is the king who, in the role of gardener, took care of the Tree of Life; see Widengren, *The King and the Tree of Life in Ancient Near Eastern Religion*, esp. pp. 22 ff., 59 ff.

42. See the introduction to the "Code of Hammurabi" (I. 50), in *ANET*, p. 164.

43. Prologue to the "Lipit-Ishtar Lawcode," *ANET*, p. 159. See the texts cited and translated by J. Zandee, "Le Messie," pp. 13, 14, 16.

23. Gilgamesh in quest of immortality

The *Epic of Gilgamesh* is certainly the best known and most popular of Babylonian creations. Its hero, Gilgamesh, king of Uruk, was already famous in the archaic period, and the Sumerian version of several episodes from his legendary life has been found. Despite these antecedents, however, the *Epic of Gilgamesh* is a product of the Semitic genius. It is in the Akkadian version in which it was composed on the basis of various isolated episodes that we may read one of the most moving tales of the quest for immortality or, more precisely, of the final failure of an undertaking that seemed to have every possibility of succeeding. This saga, which begins with the erotic excesses of a hero who is at the same time a tyrant, reveals, in the last analysis, the inability of purely "heroic" virtues radically to transcend the human condition.

And yet Gilgamesh was two-thirds a divine being, son of the goddess Ninsun and a mortal.[44] At the outset the text praises his omniscience and the grandiose works of construction that he had undertaken. But immediately afterward we are presented with a tyrant who violates women and girls and wears men out in forced labor. The inhabitants pray to the gods, and the gods decide to create a being of gigantic size who can confront Gilgamesh. This half-savage creature, who receives the name of Enkidu, lives in peace with the wild beasts; they all drink together at the same springs. Gilgamesh obtains knowledge of his existence first in a dream and then from a hunter who had come upon him. He sends a courtesan to bewitch him by her charms and lead him to Uruk. As the gods had foreseen, the two champions compete as soon as they meet each other. Gilgamesh emerges victorious, but he conceives an affection for Enkidu and makes him his companion. In the last analysis, the gods' plan was not foiled; henceforth Gilgamesh will expend his strength on heroic adventures.

Accompanied by Enkidu, he sets out for the distant and fabulous forest of cedars, which is guarded by a monstrous and all-powerful being, Huwawa. After cutting down his sacred cedar, the two heroes kill him. On his way back to Uruk, Ishtar sees Gilgamesh. The goddess invites him to marry her, but he returns an insolent refusal.

44. A high priest of the city of Uruk, according to Sumerian tradition; see A. Heidel, *The Gilgamesh Epic*, p. 4.

Humiliated, Ishtar begs her father, Anu, to create the Bull of Heaven to destroy Gilgamesh and his city. Anu at first refuses, but he gives in when Ishtar threatens to bring the dead back from the underworld. The Bull of Heaven charges at Uruk, and its bellowings make the king's men drop dead by hundreds. However, Enkidu succeeds in catching it by the tail, and Gilgamesh thrusts his sword into its neck. Furious, Ishtar mounts the city walls and curses the king. Intoxicated by their victory, Enkidu tears a thigh from the Bull of Heaven and throws it at the goddess's feet, at the same time assailing her with insults. This is the culminating moment in the career of the two heroes, but it is also the prologue to a tragedy. That same night Enkidu dreams that he has been condemned by the gods. The next day he falls ill, and, twelve days later, he dies.

An unexpected change makes Gilgamesh unrecognizable. For seven days and seven nights he mourns for his friend and refuses to let him be buried. He hopes that his laments will finally bring him back to life. It is not until the body shows the first signs of decomposition that Gilgamesh yields, and Enkidu is given a magnificent funeral. The king leaves the city and wanders through the desert, complaining: "Shall not I, too, die like Enkidu?" (tablet 9, column 1, line 4).[45] He is terrified by the thought of death. Heroic exploits do not console him. Henceforth his only purpose is to escape from the human condition, to gain immortality. He knows that the famous Utnapishtim, survivor of the flood, is still alive, and he decides to search for him.

His journey is full of ordeals of the initiatory type. He comes to the mountains of Mashu and finds the gate through which the Sun passes daily. The gate is guarded by a scorpion-man and his wife, "whose glance is death" (9. 2. 7). The invincible hero is paralyzed by fear and prostrates himself humbly. But the scorpion-man and his wife recognize the divine part of Gilgamesh and allow him to enter the tunnel. After walking for twelve hours in darkness, Gilgamesh comes to a marvelous garden on the other side of the mountains. Some distance away, by the seaside, he meets the nymph Siduri and asks her where he can find Utnapishtim. Siduri tries to make him change his mind: "When the gods made men, they saw death for men; they kept life for themselves. Thou, Gilgamesh, fill thy belly and make merry

45. Except as otherwise indicated, we follow the translation by Contenau, *L'épopée de Gilgamesh.*

by day and night. On each day make a feast, and dance and play, day and night."[46]

But Gilgamesh holds to his decision, and then Siduri sends him to Urshanabi, Utnapishtim's boatman, who happened to be nearby. They cross the Waters of Death and reach the shore on which Utnapishtim lived. Gilgamesh asks him how he had gained immortality. He thus learns the story of the flood and the gods' decision to make Utnapishtim and his wife their "kin," establishing them "at the mouths of the rivers." "But," Utnapishtim asks Gilgamesh, "as for thee, which of the gods will unite thee to their assembly, that thou mayest obtain the life that thou seekest?" (11. 198). However, what he goes on to say is unexpected: "Up, try not to sleep for six days and seven nights!" (199). What we have here is, undoubtedly, the most difficult of initiatory ordeals: conquering sleep, remaining "awake," is equivalent to a transmutation of the human condition.[47] Are we to take it that Utnapishtim, knowing that the gods will not grant Gilgamesh immortality, suggests that he conquer it by means of an initiation? The hero has already successfully gone through several ordeals: the journey through the tunnel, the "temptation" by Siduri, crossing the Waters of Death. These were in some sense ordeals of the heroic type. This time, however, the ordeal is "spiritual," for only an unusual power of concentration can enable a human being to remain awake for six days and seven nights. But Gilgamesh at once falls asleep, and Utnapishtim exclaims sarcastically: "Look at the strong man who desires immortality: sleep has come over him like a violent wind!" (203–4). He sleeps without a break for six days and seven nights; and, when Utnapishtim wakes him, Gilgamesh reproaches him for waking him when he had only just fallen asleep. However, he has to accept the evidence, and he falls to lamenting again: "What shall I do, Utnapishtim, where shall I go? a demon has taken possession of my body; in the room in which I sleep, death lives, and wherever I go, death is there!" (230–34).

Gilgamesh now makes ready to leave, but at the last moment Utnapishtim, at his wife's suggestion, reveals a "secret of the gods" to him: the place where he can find the plant that brings back youth.

46. Tablet X, column III, lines 6–9; after the translation by Jean Nougayrol, *Histoire des religions*, vol. 1, p. 222.
47. See Eliade, *Birth and Rebirth*, pp. 14 ff.

Gilgamesh goes down to the bottom of the sea, gathers it,[48] and starts back rejoicing. After traveling for a few days, he sees a spring of fresh water and hurries to bathe. Attracted by the odor of the plant, a snake comes out of the spring, carries off the plant, and sheds its skin.[49] Sobbing, Gilgamesh complains to Urshanabi of his bad fortune. This episode may be read as a failure in another initiatory ordeal: the hero failed to profit from an unexpected gift; in short, he was lacking in wisdom. The text ends abruptly: arrived at Uruk, Gilgamesh invites Urshanabi to go up on the city walls and admire its foundations.[50]

The *Epic of Gilgamesh* has been seen as a dramatized illustration of the human condition, defined by the inevitability of death. Yet this first masterpiece of universal literature can also be understood as illustrating the belief that certain beings are capable, even without help from the gods, of obtaining immortality, on the condition that they successfully pass through a series of initiatory ordeals. Seen from this point of view, the story of Gilgamesh would prove to be the dramatized account of a failed initiation.

24. Destiny and the gods

Unfortunately, we do not know the ritual context of Mesopotamian initiation, always supposing that such a thing existed. The initiatory meaning of the quest for immortality can be deciphered in the particular structure of the ordeals undergone by Gilgamesh. The Arthurian romances present a similar situation; they, too, are filled with initiatory symbols and motifs, but it is impossible to decide whether these belong to a ritual scenario, represent recollections of Celtic mythology or Hermetic gnosticism, or are merely products of the imagination. In the case of the Arthurian romances, we at least know the initiatory traditions that preceded their composition, whereas we

48. We may wonder why Gilgamesh did not eat it as soon as he had gathered it, but he was saving it for later; see Heidel, *The Gilgamesh Epic*, p. 62, n. 211.

49. This is a well-known folklore theme: by shedding its old skin, the snake renews its life.

50. Tablet XII, composed in Sumerian, was added later; the incidents narrated in it have no direct relation to the narrative we have summarized.

know nothing of the protohistory of the initiatory scenario possibly implied in Gilgamesh's adventures.

It has been emphasized, and rightly, that Akkadian religious thought puts the accent on man. In the last analysis, the story of Gilgamesh becomes paradigmatic: it proclaims the precariousness of the human condition, the impossibility—even for a hero—of gaining immortality. Man was created mortal, and he was created solely to serve the gods. This pessimistic anthropology was already formulated in the *Enuma elish*. It is also found in other important religious texts. The "Dialogue between Master and Servant" seems to be the product of nihilism exacerbated by a neurosis: the master does not even know what he wants. He is obsessed by the vanity of all human effort: "Climb the mounds of ancient ruins and walk about: look at these skulls of late and early men; who among them is an evildoer, who a public benefactor?"[51]

Another celebrated text, the "Dialogue about Human Misery," which has been called the "Babylonian Ecclesiastes," is even more despairing. "Does the fierce lion, who eats the best of meat, / Present his dough-and-incense offering to appease his goddess' displeasure? / ... [As for me,] have I withheld the meal-oblation? [No], I have prayed to the gods, / I have presented the prescribed sacrifices to the goddess" (lines 50 ff.). From his childhood, this just man has striven to understand the god's thought, he has sought the goddess humbly and piously. Yet "the god brought me scarcity instead of wealth" (lines 71 ff.). On the contrary, it is the scoundrel, the godless, who has acquired wealth (line 236). People "extol the word of a prominent man, expert in murder, / But they abase the humble, who has committed no violence." The evildoer is justified, the righteous man is driven away. It is the bandit who receives gold, while the weak are left to hunger. The wicked man is strengthened, the feeble are cast down (lines 267 ff.).[52]

This despair arises, not from a meditation on the vanity of human existence, but from the experience of general injustice: the wicked triumph, prayers are not answered; the gods seem indifferent to human affairs. From the second millennium, similar spiritual crises will make themselves felt elsewhere (Egypt, Israel, Iran, India,

51. "A Pessimistic Dialogue between Master and Servant," line 84; trans. R. H. Pfeiffer, *ANET*, p. 438.
52. "A Dialogue about Human Misery," trans. Pfeiffer, *ANET*, pp. 439–40.

Greece), with various consequences; for the responses to this type of nihilistic experience were made in accordance with the religious genius characteristic of each culture. But in the Mesopotamian wisdom literature the gods do not always prove to be indifferent. One text presents the physical and mental sufferings of an innocent man who has been compared to Job. He is the very pattern of the just man suffering, for no divinity seems to help him. Countless sicknesses have reduced him to being "soaked in his own excrement," and he is already bewailed as dead by his relatives when a series of dreams reveals to him that Marduk will save him. As in an ecstatic trance, he sees the god destroying the demons of sickness and then extracting his pains from his body as one uproots a plant. Finally, his health restored, the just man gives thanks to Marduk by ritually passing through the twelve gates of his temple at Babylon.[53]

In the last analysis, by putting the accent on man, Akkadian religious thought brings out the limits of human possibilities. The distance between men and the gods proves to be impossible to cross. Yet man is not isolated in his own solitude. First of all, he shares in a spiritual element that can be regarded as divine: it is his "spirit," *ilu* (literally, "god").[54] Secondly, through rites and prayers he hopes to obtain the blessing of the gods. Above all, he knows that he forms part of a universe that is unified by homologies: he lives in a city that constitutes an *imago mundi* and whose temples and ziggurats represent "centers of the world" and, in consequence, insure communication with heaven and the gods. Babylon was a Bab-il-ani, a "Gate of the Gods," for it is there that the gods came down to earth. A number of cities and sanctuaries were named "Link between Heaven and Earth."[55] In other words, man does not live in a closed world, separated from the gods, completely isolated from the cosmic rhythms. In addition, a complex system of correspondences between heaven and earth made it possible for terrestrial realities to be understood and at the same time to be "influenced" by their respective celestial prototypes. An example: Since each planet had its corresponding metal and color, everything colored was under the

53. "I Will Praise the Lord of Wisdom," trans. Pfeiffer, *ANET*, pp. 434–37.

54. The spirit (*ilu*) is the most important element of a personality. The others are *ištaru* (its destiny), *lamassu* (its individuality; resembles a statue), and *šēdu* (comparable to Lat. *genius*); see A. L. Oppenheimer, *Ancient Mesopotamia*, pp. 198–206.

55. Eliade, *Cosmos and History*, pp. 14 ff.

influence of a planet. But each planet belonged to a god, who, by that fact, was represented by the respective metal.[56] In consequence, one who ritually manipulated a certain metallic object or a semiprecious stone of a particular color felt that he was under the protection of a god.

Finally, numerous techniques of divination, most of them developed during the Akkadian period, made it possible to know the future. So it was believed that certain misadventures could be avoided. The variety of techniques and the large number of written documents that have come down to us prove the high esteem in which the mantic art was held on all levels of society. The most elaborate method was extispicy, that is, examining the entrails of a victim; the least costly, lecanomancy, consisted in pouring a little oil on water, or vice versa, and interpreting the signs that could be read in the shapes produced by the two liquids. Astrology, developed later than the other techniques, was principally practiced by the royal entourage. As for the interpretation of dreams, it was complemented, from the beginning of the second millennium, by methods of offsetting unfavorable omens.[57]

All the techniques of divination pursued the discovery of "signs," whose hidden meanings were interpreted in accordance with certain traditional rules. *The world, then, revealed itself to be structured and governed by laws.* If the signs were deciphered, the future could be known; in other words, *time was "mastered,"* for events that were to occur only after a certain interval of time were foreseen. The attention paid to signs led to discoveries of genuine scientific value. Some of these discoveries were later taken over and perfected by the Greeks. But Babylonian science remained a "traditional" science, in the sense that scientific knowledge preserved a totalitarian structure, that is, a structure that involved cosmological, ethical, and existential presuppositions.[58]

Toward 1500 B.C. the creative period of Mesopotamian thought seems definitely to have ended. During the ten following centuries, intellectual activity appears to spend itself in erudition and compilation. But the influence of Mesopotamian culture, documented from

56. Gold corresponded to En-lil, silver to Anu, bronze to Ea. When Shamash took En-lil's place, he became the "patron" of gold; see B. Meissner, *Babylonien und Assyrien*, vol. 2, pp. 130 ff., 254.

57. J. Nougayrol, "La divination babylonienne," esp. pp. 39 ff.

58. As did, for example, medicine and alchemy in China.

the most ancient times, continues and increases. Ideas, beliefs, and techniques of Mesopotamian origin circulate from the western Mediterranean to the Hindu Kush. It is significant that the Babylonian discoveries that were destined to become popular imply, whether more or less directly, correspondences between heaven and earth, or macrocosm-microcosm.

4 Religious Ideas and Political Crises in Ancient Egypt

25. The unforgettable miracle: The "First Time"

The birth of Egyptian civilization has never failed to inspire wonder and admiration in one historian after another. During the two millennia that preceded the formation of the United Kingdom, the Neolithic cultures continued to develop, but without any profound changes. However, from the fourth millennium, contacts with the civilization of Sumeria bring about nothing short of a mutation. Egypt borrows the cylinder seal, the art of construction in brick, the technique of boat-building, a number of artistic motifs, and, above all, writing, which appears suddenly, with no antecedents, at the beginning of the First Dynasty (ca. 3000 B.C.).[1]

But Egyptian civilization very quickly elaborated a characteristic style, manifest in all its creations. To be sure, the geography of the country itself imposed a development different from that of the Sumero-Akkadian cultures. For, unlike Mesopotamia, vulnerable to invasions from every direction, Egypt—more precisely, the Nile Valley—was not only isolated but also defended by the desert, the Red Sea, and the Mediterranean. Until the invasion by the Hyksos (1674 B.C.), Egypt experienced no danger coming from without. On the other hand, the navigability of the Nile enabled the sovereign to govern the country by an increasingly centralized administration. In addition, Egypt had no great cities of the Mesopotamian type. It could be said that the country was constituted by a rural mass ruled by representatives of an incarnate god, the pharaoh.

But it is religion, and especially the dogma of the pharaoh's

1. H. Frankfort, *The Birth of Civilization in the Near East*, pp. 100–11; E. J. Baumgartel, *The Culture of Prehistoric Egypt*, pp. 48 ff.

divinity, which, from the beginning, contributed to shaping the structure of Egyptian civilization. According to tradition, the unification of the country and the founding of the state were the work of the first sovereign, known by the name of Menes. A native of the South, Menes built the new capital for this united Egypt at Memphis, near the present city of Cairo. It was there that, for the first time, he celebrated the ceremony of coronation. Later, and for more than three thousand years, the pharaohs were crowned at Memphis; in all probability, the culminating ceremony represented the one inaugurated by Menes. It was not a commemoration of Menes' exploits but *the renewal of the creative source present in the original event.*[2]

The founding of the united state was the equivalent of a cosmogony. The pharaoh, incarnate god, established a new world, a civilization infinitely more complex, and far higher, than that of the Neolithic villages. It was supremely important to insure the permanence of this work, accomplished in accordance with a divine model—in other words, to avoid crises that could shake the foundations of the new world. The divinity of the pharaoh constituted the most potent guarantee. Since he was immortal, his death meant no more than his translation to heaven. The continuity from one incarnate god to another incarnate god, and hence the continuity of the cosmic order, was insured.

It is remarkable that the most important sociopolitical and cultural creations took place during the earliest dynasties. It is these creations that established the models for the following fifteen centuries. After the Fifth Dynasty (2500–2300 B.C.) almost nothing of importance was added to the cultural patrimony. This "immobilism," which is characteristic of Egyptian civilization but which is also found in the myths and nostalgias of other traditional societies, is religious in origin. The stability of hieratic forms, the repetition of gestures and exploits performed at the dawn of time, are the logical consequence of a theology that considered the cosmic order to be supremely the divine work and saw in all change the danger of a regression to chaos and hence the triumph of demonic forces.

The tendency that European scholars have termed "immobilism" made the utmost effort to maintain the original creation intact, for it was perfect from every point of view—cosmological, religious, social, ethical. The successive phases of the cosmogony are vividly

2. H. Frankfort, *Kingship and the Gods*, p. 23.

recalled in the various mythological traditions. Indeed, the myths refer exclusively to the events that took place in the fabled time of the beginnings. This period, called *Tep zepi*, the "First Time," lasted from the appearance of the creating god above the primordial waters down to the enthronement of Horus. All existing things, from natural phenomena to religious and cultural realities (plans of temples, the calendar, writing, rituals, royal emblems, etc.), owe their validity and their justification to the fact that they were created during the initial period. Clearly, the First Time constitutes the Golden Age of absolute perfection, "before anger, or noise, or conflict, or disorder made their appearance." Neither death nor disease were known during this marvelous period, called "the time of Re" (or Osiris or Horus).[3] At a certain moment, as a result of the intrusion of evil, disorder appeared, putting an end to the Golden Age. But the fabled period of the First Time was not relegated to the relics of a past that had finitely run its course. Since it constitutes the sum of the models that are to be imitated, this period is continually reactualized. In short, it could be said that the rites, pursuing the defeat of the demonic forces, have as their purpose restoring the initial perfection.

26. Theogonies and cosmogonies

As in all the traditional religions, the cosmogony and the origin myths (origin of man, of royalty, of social institutions, of rituals, etc.) constituted the essence of the science of sacred things. Naturally, there were several cosmogonic myths, featuring different gods and localizing the beginning of Creation in a multitude of religious centers. Their themes belong among the most archaic: the emergence of a mound, a lotus, or an egg above the primordial waters. As for the creator-gods, each important city gave the leading role to its own. Dynastic changes were often followed by a change of capital. Such events obliged the theologians of the new capital to combine several cosmogonic traditions, identifying their chief local god with the demiurge. When creator-gods were involved, assimilation was made easy by their structural similarity. But the theologians also elaborated

3. See Rundle Clark, *Myth and Symbol in Ancient Egypt*, pp. 263–64. "The perfection of the beginnings" is a widespread mythical motif.

daring syntheses by assimilating heterogeneous religious systems and associating definitely antagonistic divine figures.[4]

Like so many other traditions, the Egyptian cosmogony begins with the emergence of a mound in the primordial waters. The appearance of this "First Place" above the aquatic immensity signifies the emergence of the earth, but also the beginning of light, life, and consciousness.[5] At Heliopolis, the place named the "Hill of Sand," which formed part of the temple of the sun, was identified with the primordial hill. Hermopolis was famous for its lake, from which the cosmogonic lotus emerged. But other localities took advantage of the same privilege.[6] Indeed, each city, each sanctuary, was considered to be a "center of the world," the place where the Creation had begun. The initial mound sometimes became the cosmic mountain up which the pharaoh climbed to meet the sun god.

Other versions tell of the primordial egg, which contained the "Bird of Light" (*Coffin Texts*, vol. 4, 181c ff.), or of the original lotus that bore the Child Sun,[7] or, finally, of the primitive serpent, first and last image of the god Atum. (And in fact chapter 175 of the *Book of the Dead* prophesies that when the world returns to the state of chaos, Atum will become the new serpent. In Atum we may recognize the supreme and hidden God, whereas Re, the Sun, is above all the manifest God; see § 32.) The stages of creation— cosmogony, theogony, creation of living beings, etc.—are variously presented. According to the solar theology of Heliopolis, a city situated at the apex of the Delta, the god Re-Atum-Khepri[8] created a first divine couple, Shu (the Atmosphere) and Tefnut, who became parents of the god Geb (the Earth) and of the goddess Nut (the Sky). The demiurge performed the act of creation by masturbating himself or by spitting. The expressions are naively coarse, but their meaning

---

4. The myths were not related in a continuous and consistent way in order to constitute, as it were, "canonical versions." Consequently we have to reconstruct them from episodes and allusions found in the earliest collections, especially in the *Pyramid Texts* (ca. 2500–2300 B.C.), the *Coffin Texts* (ca. 2300–2000 B.C.), and the *Book of the Dead* (after 1500 B.C.).

5. See Rundle Clark, *Myth and Symbol in Ancient Egypt*, p. 36.

6. See the texts cited and commented on by Frankfort, *Kingship*, pp. 151 ff.

7. Sauneron and Yoyotte, in *La Naissance du Monde*, p. 37, and the references given in S. Morenz, *La religion égyptienne*, pp. 234 ff. (Eng. trans., pp. 325 ff.).

8. The trinomial represents three forms of the sun: Khepri, the rising sun; Re, the sun at the zenith; and Atum, the setting sun.

is clear: the divinities are born from the very substance of the supreme god. Just as in the Sumerian tradition (§16), Sky and Earth were united in an uninterrupted *hieros gamos* until the moment when they were separated by Shu, the god of the atmosphere.[9] From their union were born Osiris and Isis, Seth and Nephthys, protagonists of a touching drama that will engage our attention further on.

At Hermopolis, in Middle Egypt, the theologians elaborated a complex doctrine around the Ogdoad, the group of eight gods, later joined by Ptah. In the primordial lake of Hermopolis there emerged a lotus, from which came the "sacrosanct child, the perfect heir engendered by the Ogdoad, divine seed of the very first Anterior Gods," "he who knotted the seeds of gods and men."[10]

But it is in Memphis, capital of the pharaohs of the First Dynasty, that the most systematic theology was articulated, around the god Ptah. The principal text of what has been called the "Memphite theology" was engraved on stone in the time of the Pharaoh Shakaba (ca. 700 B.C.), but the original was composed some two thousand years earlier. It is surprising that the earliest Egyptian cosmogony yet known is also the most philosophical. For Ptah creates by his mind (his "heart") and his word (his "tongue"). "He who manifested himself as the heart (= mind), he who manifested himself as the tongue (= word), under the appearance of Atum, he is Ptah the most ancient." Ptah is proclaimed the greatest god, Atum being considered only the author of the first divine couple. It is Ptah "who made the gods exist." Afterward, the gods assumed their visible bodies, entering into "every kind of plant, every kind of stone, every kind of clay, into everything that sprouts on its surface (i.e., of the earth) and by which they can manifest themselves."[11]

In short, the theogony and the cosmogony are effected by the

9. See the texts cited by Sauneron and Yoyotte, *La Naissance du Monde*, pp. 46–47. We add that the role of separator is not given exclusively to Shu; see the texts cited by Morenz, *La religion égyptienne*, p. 228 (Eng. trans., p. 174), where the agent of the separation is Ptah.

10. Texts cited by Sauneron and Yoyotte, *La Naissance du Monde*, p. 59. See other texts translated, with commentaries, by Morenz and Schubert in *Der Gott auf der Blume*, pp. 32 ff.; cf. also Morenz, *La religion égyptienne*, pp. 229 ff. (Eng. trans., pp. 174 ff.).

11. After the translation by Sauneron and Yoyotte, *Naissance*, pp. 63–64. See the commentary by Morenz, *Rel. égyptienne*, pp. 216 ff. (Eng. trans., pp. 163 ff.) and, especially, Frankfort, *Kingship*, pp. 24–35.

creative power of the thought and word of a single god. We here certainly have the highest expression of Egyptian metaphysical speculation. As John Wilson observes (*ANET*, p. 4), it is *at the beginning* of Egyptian history that we find a doctrine that can be compared with the Christian theology of the Logos.

In comparison with the theogony and the cosmogony, the myths concerning the origin of man prove to be rather summary. Men (*erme*) are born from the tears (*erme*) of the solar god, Re. In a text composed later (ca. 2000 B.C.), during a period of crisis, it is written: "Men, the cattle of God, have been well provided for. He (i.e., the sun god) made the sky and the earth for their benefit. . . . He made the air to vivify their nostrils, for they are his images, issued from his flesh. He shines in the sky, he makes plants and animals for them, birds and fish to feed them."[12]

However, when Re discovers that men have plotted against him, he decides to destroy them. It is Hathor who undertakes to carry out the slaughter. But when she threatens to destroy the human race completely, Re has recourse to a subterfuge and manages to get her drunk.[13] The revolt of men and its consequences took place during the mythical age. Obviously, "men" were the earliest inhabitants of Egypt, since Egypt was the first country formed, hence the center of the world.[14] The Egyptians were its only rightful inhabitants; this explains the prohibition against foreigners entering sanctuaries, which were microcosmic images of the country.[15] Certain late texts reflect the tendency toward universalism. The gods (Horus, Sekhmet) protect not only the Egyptians but also the Palestinians, the Nubians, and the Libyans.[16] However, the mythical history of the first men does not play an important role. During the prodigious period of the First Time, the two decisive moments were the *cosmogony* and the *advent of the pharaoh*.

12. Passage from *The Instruction of King Meri-ka-Re*, after the translation by Sauneron and Yoyotte, *Naissance*, pp. 75–76. See the complete translation by Wilson, *ANET*, pp. 414–18.

13. See the text translated by Wilson, *ANET*, pp. 10–11. The Canaanite tradition includes a similar myth; see § 50.

14. See the examples cited by Morenz, *Rel. égyptienne*, pp. 70 ff. (Eng. trans., pp. 43 ff.). The conception is one that is typical of the traditional civilizations; cf. Eliade, *Cosmos and History*, pp. 12 ff.

15. See the examples in Morenz, *Rel. égyptienne*, pp. 78 ff.

16. *The Book of Gates*, portion translated by Sauneron and Yoyotte, *Naissance*, pp. 76–77. See other references in Morenz, p. 80 (Eng. trans., p. 51).

27. The responsibilities of an incarnate god

As Henri Frankfort observes,[17] the cosmogony is the most important of events because it represents the *only real change*: the emergence of the world. Thenceforth only the changes involved in the rhythms of cosmic life have any meaning. But, in this case, we are dealing with successive moments expressed in different cycles and insuring their periodicity: the motions of the heavenly bodies, the circle of the seasons, the phases of the moon, the rhythm of vegetation, the flux and reflux of the Nile, etc. Now it is precisely this periodicity of the cosmic rhythms that constitutes the perfection established in the age of the "First Time." Disorder implies a useless, and therefore harmful, change in the paradigmatic cycle of perfectly ordered changes.

Since the social order represents an aspect of the cosmic order, royalty is held to have existed from the beginning of the world. The Creator was the first king;[18] he transmits this function to his son and successor, the first pharaoh. This delegation consecrated royalty as a divine institution. And indeed the pharaoh's gestures and deeds are described in the same terms as those used to describe the acts of the god Re or of the solar epiphanies. To give only two examples: Re's creation is sometimes summarized in a precise formula: "He put order (*ma^c at*) in the place of Chaos." And it is these same terms that are used of Tut-ankh-Amon when he restored order after the "heresy" of Akh-en-Aton (cf. § 32), or of Pepi II: "He put *ma^c at* in the place of falsehood (of disorder)." Similarly, the verb *khay*, "to shine," is used indifferently to depict the emergence of the sun at the moment of creation or at each dawn and the appearance of the pharaoh at the coronation ceremony, at festivals, or at the privy council.[19]

The pharaoh is the incarnation of *ma^c at*, a term translated by "truth" but whose general meaning is "good order" and hence "right," "justice." *Ma^c at* belongs to the original creation; hence it reflects the perfection of the Golden Age. Since it constitutes the

17. Frankfort, *Ancient Egyptian Religion*, pp. 49 ff.

18. In the *Book of the Dead* (chap. 17) the God proclaims: "I am Atum, when I was alone in Num (the primeval ocean). I am Re in his first appearance, when he began to rule that which he had made." A gloss adds the following explanation: "This means that Re began to appear *as a king*, as one who existed before Shu had even lifted heaven from earth" (Frankfort, *Ancient Egyptian Religion*, pp. 54–55).

19. Frankfort, ibid., pp. 54 ff. See other examples in *Kingship*, pp. 148 ff.

very foundation of the cosmos and life, *ma^cat* can be known by each individual separately. In texts of different origins and periods, there are such declarations as these: "Incite your heart to know *ma^cat*"; "I make thee to know the thing of *ma^cat* in thy heart; mayest thou do what is right for thee!" Or: "I was a man who loved *ma^cat* and hated sin. For I knew that (sin) is an abomination to God." And in fact it is God who bestows the necessary knowledge. A prince is defined as "one who knows truth (*ma^cat*) and whom God teaches." The author of a prayer to Re cries: "Mayest Thou give me *ma^cat* in my heart!"[20]

As incarnating *ma^cat*, the pharaoh constitutes the paradigmatic example for all his subjects. As the vizier Rekh-mi-Re expresses it: "He is a god who makes us live by his acts."[21] The work of the pharaoh insures the stability of the cosmos and the state and hence the continuity of life. And indeed the cosmogony is repeated every morning, when the solar god "repels" the serpent Apophis, though without being able to destroy him; for chaos (= the original darkness) represents virtuality; hence it is indestructible. The pharaoh's political activity repeats Re's exploit: he too "repels" Apophis, in other words he sees to it that the world does not return to chaos. When enemies appear at the frontiers, they will be assimilated to Apophis, and the pharaoh's victory will reproduce Re's triumph. (This tendency to interpret life and history in terms of categories and paradigmatic models is characteristic of the traditional cultures.)[22] Certainly, the pharaoh was the only protagonist of particular, non-repeatable historical events: military campaigns in various countries, victories over various peoples, etc. Yet when Ramses III builds his tomb, he repeats the names of the conquered cities inscribed on the funerary temple of Ramses II. Even in the period of the Old Kingdom, the Libyans who "appear as the victims of Pepi II's conquests bear the same personal names as those who appear in the temple reliefs of Sahure, two centuries earlier."[23]

20. Texts translated in Morenz, *Rel. égyptienne*, pp. 167–70 (Eng. trans., pp. 122–24).
21. According to Frankfort, such a conception explains the complete absence of popular uprisings. During the political troubles of the Intermediate periods (ca. 2250–2040 and 1730–1562) the institution of the monarchy was not called into question (*Ancient Egyptian Religion*, p. 43).
22. See *Cosmos and History*, chap. 1.
23. H. Frankfort, *Kingship*, p. 347.

It is impossible to recognize the individual features of the pharaohs as they are depicted on the monuments and in the texts. In many characteristic details—for example, the initiative and courage of Thut-mose III during the battle of Megiddo—A. de Buck has recognized the conventional elements of the portrait of an ideal sovereign. The same tendency toward impersonality is observable in the representation of the gods. Except for Osiris and Isis, all the gods, despite their distinct forms and functions, are evoked in the hymns and prayers in almost the same terms.[24]

In principle, the cult was to be celebrated by the pharaoh, but he delegated his functions to the priests of the different temples. Directly or indirectly, the purpose of the rituals was the defense, hence the stability, of the "original creation." At each New Year the cosmogony was reiterated,[25] and even more paradigmatically than Re's daily victory, for a vaster temporal cycle was involved. The enthronement of the pharaoh reproduced the episodes of the *gesta* of Menes: the unification of the two lands. In short, the founding of the state was ritually repeated (cf. § 25). The coronation ceremony was reenacted on the occasion of the *sed* festival, performed thirty years after the enthronement and intended to renew the sovereign's divine energy.[26] As for the periodical festivals of certain gods (Horus, Min, Anubis, etc.), we have only scanty information. The priests, walking in procession, carried on their shoulders the statue of the god or the sacred boat; the procession included songs, music, and dances and took place amid the plaudits of the worshiping crowd.

The great festival of Min, one of the most popular in all Egypt, is better known to us by virtue of the fact that it was later associated with the royal cult. Originally it was the harvest festival; the king, the queen, and a white bull took part in the procession. The king cut

24. See the comparison between Min and Sobek in Frankfort, *Ancient Egyptian Religion*, pp. 25–26. Recognizing the importance of the static vision of the universe, interpreted as a rhythmical movement within an immutable totality, Frankfort has proposed an ingenious explanation for the manifestations of the gods in animal forms: whereas among human beings individual characteristics outbalance morphological structure, animals are unchanging; they always reproduce their species. Thus, in the eyes of the Egyptians, animal life appeared superhuman, since it shared in the static life of the universe (ibid., pp. 13–14).

25. Cf. *Cosmos and History*, pp. 51 ff.; Frankfort, *Kingship*, pp. 155 ff.

26. Cf. Frankfort, *Kingship*, pp. 82 ff.; Vandier, *La Religion égyptienne*, pp. 200–201.

a sheaf of grain and offered it to the bull; the remainder of the rites is obscure.[27] The ceremonies of the foundation and inauguration of temples were presided over by the pharaoh. Unfortunately, we know only certain symbolic gestures: in the trench opened on the site of a future temple the king placed the "foundation deposits" (a brick molded by the sovereign, gold ingots, etc.); at the inauguration, he consecrated the building by raising his right arm, etc.

The daily divine cult was addressed to the statue of the god kept in the naos. Once the ritual purification was accomplished, the officiant approached the naos, broke the clay seal, and opened the door. He prostrated himself before the statue, declaring that he had entered heaven (the naos) to contemplate the god. The statue was then purified with natron to "open the mouth" of the god. Finally, the officiant shut the door again, sealed the bolt, and withdrew, walking backward.[28]

Our information concerning the funerary cult is very much fuller. Death and the beyond preoccupied the Egyptians more than they did the other Near Eastern peoples. For the pharaoh, death constituted the point of departure for his celestial journey and his "immortalization." In addition, death directly involved one of the most popular Egyptian gods: Osiris.

28. The pharaoh's ascent to heaven

So far as they can be reconstructed, the earliest Egyptian beliefs concerning existence after death resembled the two traditions that are amply documented throughout the world: the dwelling place of the dead was either underground or else in the sky—more precisely, among the stars. After death, souls made their way to the stars and shared in their eternity. The sky was imagined as a Mother Goddess, and death was equivalent to a new birth, in other words to a rebirth in the sidereal world. The maternity of the sky implied the idea that the dead person had to be engendered a second time; after his

27. According to Gardiner, the service also included a ceremonial union of the royal couple (see Frankfort, *Kingship*, p. 390).

28. A. Moret, *Le rituel du culte divin journalier en Égypte*, passim; Vandier, *Relig. égyptienne*, pp. 164 ff.

celestial rebirth he was fed on the milk of the Mother Goddess (represented in the form of a cow).[29]

The subterranean localization of the otherworld was a predominant belief in the Neolithic cultures. Already as early as the predynastic period (i.e., at the beginning of the fourth millennium), certain religious traditions bound up with agriculture found expression in the mythico-ritual Osirian complex. Now, Osiris, the only Egyptian god who suffered a violent death, also figured in the royal cult. We shall later examine the consequences of this encounter between a god who dies and the solar theology that defined and validated the immortalization of the pharaoh.

The *Pyramid Texts* express almost exclusively conceptions concerning the postmortem destiny of the king. Despite the efforts of the theologians, the doctrine was not perfectly systematized. We find a certain opposition between parallel and sometimes antagonistic conceptions. The majority of the formulas forcefully repeat that the pharaoh, son of Atum (= Re), engendered by the Great God before the creation of the world, cannot die; but other texts assure the king that his body will not suffer decomposition. Here, certainly, there are two different religious ideologies that are not yet adequately integrated.[30] However, the majority of the formulas refer to the pharaoh's celestial journey. He flies away in the form of a bird—a falcon, heron, wild goose (*Pyr.* 461–63, 890–91, 913, 1048), a scarabaeus (366), or a grasshopper (890–91), etc. The winds, the clouds, the gods are bound to help him. Sometimes the king ascends to the sky by a ladder (365, 390, 971 ff., 2083). During his ascent the king is already a god, totally different in essence from the race of human beings (650, 809).[31]

Nevertheless, before arriving at the celestial abode in the East, named the Field of Offerings, the pharaoh had to undergo certain ordeals. The entrance was defended by a lake "with winding shores"

29. This idea justifies the incestuous union of the dead pharaoh, called the "Bull Who Makes His Mother Fertile." See Frankfort, *Kingship*, pp. 177 ff.

30. Certain texts (*Pyr.* 2007–9) give instructions that the king's bones shall be reassembled and his limbs freed from their wrappings to insure his ascension; Vandier has shown that this belongs to an Osirian mythico-ritual complex (*Relig. égyptienne*, p. 81).

31. Texts cited by Vandier, p. 78. See also the passages translated by Breasted (*Development of Religion and Thought in Ancient Egypt*, pp. 109–15, 118–20, 122, 136) and reproduced in our anthology *From Primitives to Zen*, pp. 353–55.

(*Pyr.* 2061), and the ferryman had the power of a judge. To be admitted into the boat, the pharaoh must have accomplished all the ritual purifications (*Pyr.* 519, 1116) and, above all, must answer an interrogation of the initiatory type, that is to say, must answer by stereotyped formulas that served as passwords. Sometimes the king has recourse to pleading (1188–89), or to magic (492 ff.), or even to threats. He implores the gods (especially Re, Thoth, and Horus), or begs the two sycamore trees between which the sun rises every day, to let him pass on into the "Field of Reeds."[32]

Arrived in heaven, the pharaoh is received in triumph by the Sun God, and messengers are sent to the four quarters of the world to announce his victory over death. In heaven, the king continues his earthly existence: seated on the throne, he receives the homage of his subjects and still judges and gives orders.[33] For though he alone enjoys solar immortality, the pharaoh is surrounded by a number of his subjects, principally the members of his family and high officials.[34] These are identified with the stars and are called "the glorified." According to Vandier (*Religion égyptienne*, p. 80): "The stellar passages of the *Pyramid Texts* are suffused with a poetry of exceptional quality: in them we find the simple and spontaneous imagination of a primitive people that moves easily in the realm of mystery."

As we observed, the soteriological doctrine of the *Pyramid Texts* is not always consistent. By identifying him with Re, the solar theology stressed the privileged role of the pharaoh: he did not fall under the jurisdiction of Osiris, the ruler of the dead. "Thou openest thy place in Heaven among the stars of Heaven, for thou art a star. . . . Thou

32. Vandier, *Relig. égyptienne*, p. 72. A more detailed discussion is to be found in Breasted, *Development*, pp. 103 ff., and in R. Weill, *Le champ des roseaux et le champ des offrandes*, pp. 16 ff. Such ordeals are known in many archaic traditions. They presuppose a preparatory initiation, including certain rituals and teachings (funerary mythology and geography, secret formulas, etc.). The few allusions found in the *Pyramid Texts* constitute the earliest written documents having to do with obtaining a privileged destiny by virtue of certain secret kinds of knowledge. We here undoubtedly have an immemorial heritage, also shared by the predynastic Neolithic cultures. In the royal Egyptian ideology, these initiatory allusions more nearly represent a useless relic; as son of god and god incarnate, the pharaoh did not need initiatory ordeals in order to gain the right to enter the celestial paradise.

33. *Pyr.* 1301, 1721; 134–35, 712–13, 1774–76, cited by Vandier, *Relig. égyptienne*, p. 79. See other texts translated, with commentaries, by Breasted, *Development*, pp. 118 ff.

34. That is, those who were buried in the vicinity of the royal tombs.

lookest over Osiris, thou commandest the dead, thou keepest thyself apart from them, thou art not of them" (*Pyr.* 251). "Re-Atum does not deliver thee to Osiris, who judges not thy heart and has not power over thy heart. . . . Osiris, thou shalt not lay hold on him, thy son (Horus) shall not lay hold on him" (*Pyr.* 145–46; after the translation by R. Weill, p. 116). Other texts are even aggressive; they affirm that Osiris is a dead god, for he was murdered and thrown into the water. Certain passages, however, allude to the pharaoh's identification with Osiris. We find such formulas as this: "Even as Osiris lives, this king Unis lives; even as Osiris does not die, so this king Unis does not die" (*Pyr.* 167 f.).

29. Osiris, the murdered god

To grasp the meaning of such formulas, we must briefly present the myths and the religious function of Osiris. To begin, we mention that the most complete version of the Osiris myth is the one transmitted by Plutarch (second century A.D.) in his treatise *De Iside et Osiride*. For as we observed in regard to the cosmogony (§ 26), the Egyptian texts refer only to isolated episodes. Despite certain inconsistencies and contradictions, which can be explained by the tensions and syncretisms that preceded the final victory of Osiris, his central myth can easily be reconstructed. According to all the traditions, he was a legendary king, famous for the energy and justice with which he governed Egypt. Seth, his brother, set a snare for him and succeeded in murdering him. His wife, Isis, a "great magician," manages to become pregnant by the dead Osiris. After burying his body, she takes refuge in the Delta; there, hidden in the papyrus thickets, she gives birth to a son, Horus. Grown up, Horus first makes the gods of the Ennead recognize his rights, then he attacks his uncle.

At first, Seth is able to tear out one of his eyes (*Pyr.* 1463), but the combat continues, and Horus finally triumphs. He recovers his eye and offers it to Osiris. (It was thus that Osiris returned to life; see *Pyr.* 609 ff., etc.) The gods condemn Seth to carry his victim (for example, Seth is transformed into the boat that carries Osiris on the Nile).[35] But, like Apophis, Seth cannot be finally destroyed, for he

35. *Pyr.* 626–27, 651–52, etc. According to a variant that Plutarch emphasizes, Seth dismembered Osiris' corpse (cf. *Pyr.* 1867) into fourteen pieces and

too incarnates an irreducible force. After his victory, Horus goes down to the land of the dead and announces the good news: recognized as his father's legitimate successor, he is crowned king. It is thus that he "awakens" Osiris; according to the texts, "he sets his soul in motion."

It is especially this last act of the drama that throws light on the mode of being characteristic of Osiris. Horus finds him in a state of unconscious torpor and is able to reanimate him. "Osiris! look! Osiris! listen! Arise! Live again!" (*Pyr.* 258 ff.). Osiris is never represented as in motion; he is always shown as powerless and passive.[36] After his coronation—that is, after he has put an end to the period of crisis ("chaos")—Horus reanimates him: "Osiris! thou wert gone, but thou hast returned; thou didst sleep, but thou hast been awakened; thou didst die, but thou livest again!" (*Pyr.* 1004 ff.). However, Osiris is resuscitated as "spiritual person" (= soul) and vital energy. It is he who will henceforth insure vegetable fertility and all the powers of reproduction. He is described as being the entire Earth or is compared to the Ocean that encircles the world. Already by about 2750 Osiris symbolizes the sources of fecundity and growth.[37] In other words, Osiris, the murdered king (= the deceased pharaoh), insures the prosperity of the kingdom ruled by his son, Horus (represented by the newly installed pharaoh).

We can perceive the general outline of the relations among Re, the pharaoh, and the pair Osiris-Horus. The sun and the royal tombs constituted the two principal sources of sacrality. According to the solar theology, the pharaoh was the son of Re; but since he succeeded to the deceased sovereign (= Osiris), the reigning pharaoh was also Horus. The tension between these two orientations of the Egyptian religious spirit, "solarization" and "Osirianization,"[38] appears in

---

scattered them. But Isis found them all (except the sexual organ, which had been swallowed by a fish) and buried them where they had been scattered; this explains the fact that numerous sanctuaries were supposed to possess a tomb of Osiris. See A. Brunner, "Zum Raumbegriff der Aegypter," p. 615.

36. It is only in texts from the Ninth and Tenth dynasties that Osiris begins to speak in his own name; see Rundle Clark, *Myth and Symbol in Ancient Egypt*, p. 110.

37. See Frankfort, *Kingship*, pp. 195 ff. (Osiris in the grain and in the Nile).

38. From a certain viewpoint it is possible to speak of the rivalry between a dead god, Osiris, and a dying god, Re; for the sun, too, "died" every evening but was reborn at dawn the next day.

the function of royalty. As we have seen, Egyptian civilization is the result of the union of Upper and Lower Egypt in a single kingdom. In the beginning Re was regarded as sovereign of the Golden Age; but from the time of the Middle Kingdom (ca. 2040–1730 B.C.), this role was transferred to Osiris. In the royal ideology, the Osirian formula ended by imposing itself, for the filiation Osiris-Horus guaranteed the continuity of the dynasty and, in addition, insured the prosperity of the country. As source of universal fertility, Osiris made the reign of his son and successor flourish.

A text from the Middle Kingdom admirably expresses the exaltation of Osiris as source and foundation of all creation: "Whether I live or die, I am Osiris; I enter in and reappear through you, I decay in you, I grow in you. . . . The gods are living in me, for I live and grow in the corn that sustains the Honoured Ones. I cover the earth; whether I live or die I am Barley. I am not destroyed. I have entered the Order. . . . I become Master of Order, I emerge in the Order."[39]

We here have a daring valorization of death, henceforth accepted as a sort of exalting transmutation of incarnate existence. Death accomplishes passage from the sphere of the meaningless to the sphere of the meaningful. The tomb is the place where man's transfiguration (*sakh*) is accomplished, for the dead person becomes an *Akh*, a "transfigured spirit."[40] What is important for our purpose is the fact that Osiris increasingly becomes the paradigmatic model, not only for the sovereigns but for every individual. To be sure, his cult was already popular under the Old Kingdom; this explains his presence in the *Pyramid Texts* despite the resistance of the Heliopolitan theologians. But a first serious crisis, which we shall soon recount, had suddenly put an end to the classic period of Egyptian civilization. Once order was reestablished, Osiris is found to be at the center of ethical preoccupations and religious hopes. It is the begin-

39. *Coffin Texts* 330, trans. Rundle Clark, *Myth and Symbol in Ancient Egypt*, p. 142.

40. Frankfort, *Ancient Egyptian Religion*, pp. 96, 101. It should be borne in mind that laying the deceased in his coffin meant placing him in the arms of his mother, the sky goddess Nut: "Thou art given to thy mother Nut under her name of Coffin" (*Pyr.* 616). Another text compares Nut to a bed in which the deceased sleeps, waiting to wake to a new life (*Pyr.* 741). The four sides of the coffin are personified as Isis, Nephthys, Horus, and Thoth; its floor is identified with Geb, the earth god, and its cover with the sky goddess. Thus the deceased in his coffin was surrounded by personifications of the entire cosmos; cf. A. Piankoff, *The Shrines of Tut-Ankh-Amon*, pp. 21–22.

ning of a process that has been described as the "democratization" of Osiris.

And indeed, besides the pharaohs, many others profess their ritual participation in the drama and apotheosis of Osiris. The texts formerly inscribed on the walls of the hidden chambers in the pyramids erected for the pharaohs are now reproduced inside the coffins of the nobility and even of totally unprivileged people. Osiris becomes the model for all those who hope to conquer death. A *Coffin Text* (4. 276 ff.) proclaims: "Thou art now the son of a king, a prince, as long as thy heart (i.e., spirit) shall be with thee." Following Osiris' example, and with his help, the dead are able to transform themselves into "souls," that is, into perfectly integrated and hence indestructible spiritual beings. Murdered and dismembered, Osiris was "reconstituted" by Isis and reanimated by Horus. In this way he inaugurated a new mode of existence: from a powerless shade, he became a "person" who "knows," a duly initiated spiritual being. [41] It is probable that the Hellenistic mysteries of Isis and Osiris developed similar ideas. Osiris takes over from Re the function of judge of the dead; he becomes the Master of Justice, installed in a palace or on the Primordial Mound, that is, at the "center of the world." Meanwhile, as we shall see (§ 33), the tension Re-Osiris will find a solution during the Middle Kingdom and the Empire.

30. Syncope: Anarchy, despair, and "democratization" of the afterlife

Pepi II was the last pharaoh of the Sixth Dynasty. Soon after his death, about 2200 B.C., Egypt was seriously shaken by civil war, and the state collapsed. The weakness of the central power had encouraged the ambition of dynasts. For some time, anarchy ravaged the country. At a certain moment Egypt was divided into two kingdoms, that of the North, with its capital at Heracleopolis, and that of the South, whose capital was Thebes. The civil war ended with the victory of the Thebans, and the last kings of the Eleventh Dynasty were able to reunite the country. The period of anarchy, known to historians as

41. When Horus descended into the otherworld and resuscitated Osiris, he bestowed on him the power of "knowing." Osiris was an easy victim because he "did not know," he had no knowledge of Seth's true nature; see the text translated, with commentaries, by Rundle Clark, *Myth and Symbol*, pp. 114 ff.

the First Intermediate Period (or First Interregnum), ended in 2050 B.C. with the accession of the Twelfth Dynasty. The restoration of the central power marked the beginning of a veritable renaissance.

It was during the Intermediate Period that the "democratization" of life after death took place: the nobles copied on their coffins the *Pyramid Texts* that had been composed exclusively for the pharaohs. This is also the only period in Egyptian history when the pharaoh was accused of weakness and even of immorality. By the aid of several extremely interesting literary compositions we can follow the profound transformations that took place during the crisis. The most important texts are known by the titles *The Instruction for King Meri-ka-Re; The Admonitions of Ipu-wer; A Song of the Harper;* and *The Dispute of a Man Weary of Life with His Soul.* Their authors describe the disasters brought on by the collapse of traditional authority, and especially the injustices and crimes that encourage skepticism and despair, even suicide. But these documents at the same time indicate a change of an inward kind. At least certain dignitaries question themselves as to their responsibility in the catastrophe and do not hesitate to pronounce themselves guilty.

A certain Ipu-wer comes before the pharaoh to report the extent of the disaster to him. "Behold now, it has come to a point where the land is despoiled of the kingship by a few irresponsible men! . . . Behold now, it has come to a point where men rebel against the royal uraeus, . . . which makes the Two Lands peaceful. . . . The royal residence may be razed within an hour!" Provinces and temples no longer pay taxes because of the civil war. The tombs of the pyramids have been savagely pillaged. "The king has been taken away by poor men. Behold, he who was buried as a (divine) falcon (now lies) on a (mere) bier; what the pyramid hid has become empty." Yet, as he went on speaking, the "prophet" Ipu-wer became bolder and ended by blaming the pharaoh for the general anarchy. For the king should be the shepherd of his people, yet his reign enthroned death. "Authority and justice are with thee, (but) it is confusion which thou wouldst set throughout the land, together with the voice of contention. Behold, one thrusts against another. Men conform to that which thou hast commanded. This really means that thou hast acted to bring such (a situation) into being, and thou hast spoken lies." [42]

42. *The Admonitions of Ipu-wer*, translated by Wilson, *ANET*, pp. 441–44; Erman-Blackman, *The Ancient Egyptians*, pp. 92 ff.

One of the kings of the same period composed a treatise for his son Meri-ka-Re. He humbly admits his sins: "Egypt fights even in the necropolis . . . I did the same!" The misfortunes of the country "happened through what I had done, and I knew of it only after I had done it!" He recommends to his son "to do justice (*ma^cat*) whilst thou endurest upon earth." "Do not trust in length of years, for the judges (who will judge thee after death) regard a lifetime as (but) an hour." Only a man's acts remain with him. Hence, "do not evil." Instead of erecting a monument of stone, "make thy memorial to last through the love of thee." "Love all men!" For the gods esteem justice more than offerings. "Quiet the weeper; do not oppress the widow; supplant no man in the property of his father. . . . Be on thy guard against punishing unjustly. Do not slaughter!"[43]

One kind of vandalism had particularly horrified the Egyptians: men destroyed the ancestral tombs, threw out the bodies, and carried off the stones for their own tombs. As Ipu-wer said: "Many dead are buried in the river. The stream is a tomb." And the king advised his son Meri-ka-Re: "Harm not the tomb of another. . . . Build not thy tomb from ruins!" The *Song of the Harper* describes the pillage and destruction of tombs, but for entirely different reasons. "The gods who lived formerly (i.e., the kings) rest in their pyramids, the beatified dead (i.e., the nobles) also, buried in their pyramids—their places are not. See what has been made of them! . . . Their walls are broken apart, and their places are not—as though they had never been!" For the author of the poem, however, these iniquities only confirm once more the impenetrable mystery of death. "There is none who comes back from (over) there, that he may tell their state, that he may tell their needs, that he may still our hearts until we too (may) travel to the place where they have gone." And so the Harper concludes: "Make holiday, and weary not therein!"[44]

The downfall of all the traditional institutions finds expression at once in agnosticism and pessimism and in an exaltation of joy that cannot hide a profound despair. The syncope of the divine royalty inevitably brings on the religious devalorization of death. If the pharaoh no longer behaves like an incarnate god, everything becomes doubtful again, first of all the meaning of life and hence the reality

43. Trans. Wilson, *ANET*, pp. 414–18; Erman-Blackman, pp. 72 ff.
44. Trans. Wilson, *ANET*, p. 467; see also Breasted, *Development of Religion and Thought*, p. 183; Erman-Blackman, pp. 132 ff.

of a postexistence beyond the grave. The *Song of the Harper* is reminiscent of other crises of despair—in Israel, in Greece, in ancient India—crises brought on by the collapse of traditional values.

The most moving text is certainly the *Dispute of a Man Weary of Life*. It is a dialogue between a man overwhelmed by despair and his soul (*ba*). The man tries to convince his soul of the expedience of suicide. "To whom can I speak today? One's fellows are evil; the friends of today do not love. . . . Hearts are rapacious: every man seizes his fellow's goods. . . . There are no righteous; the land is left to those who do wrong. . . . The sin which treads the earth, it has no end." Called to mind amid these evils, death seems to him more than desirable: it fills him with forgotten or seldom-known blessings. "Death is in my sight today (like) the recovery of a sick man . . . like the odor of myrrh . . . like the odor of lotus blossoms . . . like the scent (of fields) after rain . . . like the longing of a man to see his house again after he has spent many years held in captivity." His soul (*ba*) reminds him that suicide will forbid him burial and funeral services; it then tries to persuade him to forget his troubles by seeking for sensual pleasures. Finally the soul assures him that it will remain with him even if he decides to kill himself.[45]

The literary compositions of the Intermediate Period continued to be read and copied long after the restoration of political unity under the pharaohs of the Middle Kingdom (2040–1730 B.C.). These texts represented not only incomparable testimonies to the great crisis; they also illustrated a tendency of the Egyptian religious spirit that did not cease to increase from that time on. It is a current of thought that it is difficult to describe briefly, but whose chief characteristic is the importance accorded to the human person as a virtual replica of the paradigmatic model, the person of the pharaoh.

31. Theology and politics of "solarization"

The Middle Kingdom was ruled by a series of excellent sovereigns, almost all of them belonging to the Twelfth Dynasty. Under their reign Egypt experienced a period of economic expansion and great

45. Trans. Wilson, *ANET*, pp. 405–7; cf. Breasted, *Development*, pp. 189 ff.; Erman-Blackman, pp. 86 ff.

international prestige.[46] The names chosen by the pharaohs at their coronation express their will to conduct themselves justly (*ma^cat*) toward men and gods.[47] It is during the Twelfth Dynasty that Amon, one of the eight gods worshiped at Hermopolis, rose to the supreme rank under the title Amon-Re. (The founder of the dynasty was named Amen-em-het, "Amon is at the head.") The "hidden" god (cf. § 26) was identified with the sun, the supremely "manifested" god. It was due to "solarization" that Amon became the universal god of the Empire, which succeeded to the defunct Old and Middle kingdoms.

Paradoxically, this empire was the consequence, delayed but inevitable, of a second crisis that arose after the extinction of the Twelfth Dynasty. A large number of sovereigns followed one another in rapid succession until the invasion by the Hyksos in 1674 B.C. The causes of the disintegration of the state, which began as early as two generations before the Hyksos attacked, are not known, but in any case the Egyptians could not long have resisted the assault of these redoubtable warriors, who used the horse, the chariot, armor, and the composite bow. The history of the Hyksos is inadequately known;[48] however, their thrust toward Egypt was certainly the result of the migrations that had shaken the Near East during the seventeenth century.

After their victory, the conquerors settled in the Delta. From their capital, Avaris, and through the agency of vassals, they governed the greater part of Lower Egypt; but they made the mistake of tolerating, in exchange for a tribute, the succession of the pharaohs in Upper Egypt. The Hyksos imported certain Syrian gods, most importantly

46. A result all the more creditable in view of the fact that the governors of the various regions had kept their local sovereignty intact.

47. See the examples cited by Wilson, *The Culture of Ancient Egypt*, p. 133. It is true that the Egyptians still regarded themselves as the only *really* human beings; foreigners were assimilated to animals, and in certain cases they could be sacrificed (see Wilson, ibid., p. 140).

48. The etymological source of the term Hyksos is Egyptian: *hikau khasut*, "governor of foreign lands." The majority of the known names are of Semitic origin, but Hurrian words have also been identified. The Hyksos are not mentioned in any contemporary Egyptian document. A reference to their fortified town, Tanis, occurs in a text of the Nineteenth Dynasty and in a popular tale composed at about the same period. As was to be expected, the conquerors ("barbarians" in Egyptian eyes) were assimilated to the serpent Apophis, symbol of primordial chaos.

Baal and Teshub, whom they identified with Seth. The advancement of the murderer of Osiris to the supreme rank certainly constituted a cruel humiliation. It must, however, be borne in mind that the cult of Seth was already practiced in the Delta in the days of the Fourth Dynasty.

For the Egyptians, the Hyksos invasion represented a catastrophe difficult to comprehend. Confidence in their privileged position, predetermined by the gods, was severely shaken. In addition, while the Delta was colonized by Asiatics, the conquerors, withdrawn into their fortified fields, scornfully ignored Egyptian civilization. But the Egyptians understood the lesson. They learned more and more to handle the arms of their conquerors. A century after the collapse (i.e., ca. 1600 B.C.), Thebes, where a pharaoh of the Seventeenth Dynasty was ruling, began the war of liberation. The final victory coincides with the accession of the Eighteenth Dynasty (1562–1308 B.C.) and the founding of the Empire.[49]

The liberation found expression in the rise of nationalism and xenophobia. It took at least a century to quench the thirst for revenge against the Hyksos. At first the sovereigns launched punitive raids. But in 1470 B.C. Thut-mose III opened the series of military campaigns in Asia by an expedition against the former fortified places of the Hyksos. The feeling of insecurity produced by the foreign occupation was long in disappearing. It was in order to make Egypt invulnerable to external aggression that Thut-mose III proceeded to a series of conquests that ended in the Empire. Very probably, the frustrations undergone during the first twenty-two years of his reign increased his military ambitions. For during all that time the actual sovereign was his aunt and mother-in-law, Hat-shepsut. This singularly gifted queen preferred cultural and commercial expansion to wars of conquest. But two weeks after her fall from power, Thut-mose was on his way to Palestine and Syria—to reduce the "rebels." Not long afterward he triumphed at Megiddo. Fortunately for the future of the Empire, Thut-mose proved to be generous to the vanquished.

It was the end of Egyptian isolationism, but it also marked the

49. No official document records the expulsion of the Hyksos. The only testimony occurs in the short autobiography of a minor participant in the war of liberation; the text was translated by Breasted, *Ancient Records of Egypt*, vol. 2, pp. 1 ff.; see also Wilson, *The Culture of Ancient Egypt*, pp. 164–65.

decline of the traditional Egyptian culture. Despite the comparatively short life of the Empire, its repercussions were irreversible. As the result of its international policy, Egypt increasingly opened itself to a cosmopolitan culture. A century after the victory at Megiddo the massive presence of "Asiatics" is documented everywhere, even in the administration and the royal residences.[50] A number of foreign divinities were not only tolerated but were assimilated to national divinities. What is more, the Egyptian gods began to be worshiped in foreign lands, and Amon-Re became a universal god.

The solarization of Amon had facilitated both religious syncretism and the restoration of the solar god to the first rank. For the sun was the only universally accessible god.[51] The most beautiful hymns to Amon-Re, exalting him as the universal creator and cosmocrator, were composed at the beginning of the imperial period. Then too, the worship of the solar god as *the* supreme god prepared a certain religious unity: the supremacy of one and the same divine principle imposed itself progressively, from the Nile Valley to Syria and Anatolia. In Egypt this solar theology, with its universalist tendency, was fatefully involved in the existence of political tensions. During the Eighteenth Dynasty the temples of Amon-Re were considerably enlarged, and their revenues were increased tenfold. As the result of the Hyksos occupation, and above all of the liberation of Egypt by a Theban pharaoh, the gods were led to govern the business of the state more directly. This meant that the gods—and first of all Amon-Re—communicated their advice through the priests. The high priest of Amon acquired considerable authority; his place was directly below the pharaoh. Egypt was in the course of becoming a theocracy; yet this did not diminish the struggle for power between the high priest and the pharaohs. It was this excessive politicization of the priestly hierarchy that stiffened the tension between different theological orientations into sometimes irreducible antagonisms.

32. Akh-en-Aton, or the unsuccessful reform

What has been called the "Amarna Revolution" (1375–1350), that is, the advancement of Aton, the solar disk, as sole supreme divinity,

50. See Wilson, *Culture*, pp. 189 ff.
51. For reasons that we have examined elsewhere (§ 20; see also *Patterns in Comparative Religion*, §§ 14, 30), the celestial gods had become *dii otiosi*.

is partly explained by the determination of the Pharaoh Amen-hotep IV to free himself from the domination of the high priest. In fact, soon after his enthronement the young sovereign deprived the high priest of Amon of the administration of the god's properties, thus taking away the source of his power. Next, the pharaoh changed his name ("Amon-is-satisfied") to Akh-en-Aton ("He-who-serves-Aton"), abandoned the old capital, Thebes, the "city of Amon," and built another, 500 kilometers farther north, which he called Akhet-Aton (now Tell el-Amarna) and where he built palaces and temples of Aton. Unlike Amon's sanctuaries, Aton's were not roofed; the Sun could be worshiped in all his glory. This was not Akh-en-Aton's only innovation. In the figurative arts he encouraged the style later called Amarnan "naturalism," and, for the first time, the popular language was introduced into royal inscriptions and official decrees; in addition, the pharaoh renounced the strict conventionality imposed by etiquette and allowed spontaneity to govern relations with the members of his family and his intimates.

All these innovations were justified by the religious value that Akh-en-Aton accorded to "truth" (*ma°at*), hence to all that was "natural," in conformity with the rhythms of life. For this sickly and almost deformed pharaoh, who was to die very young, had discovered the religious significance of the "joy of life," the bliss of enjoying Aton's inexhaustible creation, first of all, divine light. To impose his "reform," Akh-en-Aton ousted Amon and all the other gods[52] in favor of Aton, the Supreme God, identified with the solar disk, universal source of life: he was represented with his rays ending in hands, bringing his worshipers the symbol of life (the *ankh*). The essence of Akh-en-Aton's theology is found in two hymns addressed to Aton, the only ones that have been preserved. Beyond any doubt they represent one of the noblest Egyptian religious expressions. The Sun "is the beginning of life," his rays "embrace all lands." "Though thou art very far away, thy rays are on the earth; even though thou art on the faces of men, thy traces are invisible."[53] Aton is "the creator of the seed in woman," and it is he who gives life to the

52. In principle, for he retained Re, Ma°at, and Har-akhti.
53. "When thou settest . . . the Earth is in darkness, like unto death." It is during the night that wild beasts and snakes move about, and then "the world sinks into silence." Akh-en-Aton describes, with details that are surprisingly fresh, the miracle of dawn, the bliss shared by trees, flowers, birds, fish.

embryo and guards the birth and growth of the child—even as he also gives breath to the chick in the egg and later protects it. "How diverse are thy works! They are hidden before men, O! sole God, than whom there is not another."[54] It is Aton who created all the lands, and men and women, and put each created thing in its proper place, supplying its needs. "The world subsists by thee!" "Each has his food."

This hymn has rightly been compared to Psalm 104. There has even been discussion of the "monotheistic" character of Akh-en-Aton's reform. The originality and importance of this "first individual in history," as Breasted called him, are still disputed, but there can be no doubt of his religious fervor. The prayer found in his coffin contained these lines: "I go to breathe the sweet breath of thy mouth. Every day, I shall behold thy beauty. . . . Give me thy hands, laden with thy spirit, so that I may receive thee and live by it. Call my name for all eternity: it will never fail to answer thy summons!" After thirty-three centuries, this prayer still keeps its power to move.

During Akh-en-Aton's reign, and precisely because of his political and military passivity, Egypt had lost her Asiatic empire. His successor, Tut-ankh-Amon (1357–1349 B.C.), resumed relations with the high priest of Amon and returned to Thebes. The traces of the "Atonist reform" were largely obliterated. Soon afterward the last pharaoh of the long and glorious Eighteenth Dynasty died.

According to the view generally accepted among scholars, the extinction of the Eighteenth Dynasty also marks the end of the creativity of the Egyptian genius. As for religious creations, we may wonder if their unpretentiousness until the foundation of the Mysteries of Isis and Osiris is not explained by the greatness and effectiveness of the syntheses worked out during the New Empire.[55] For, from a certain point of view, these syntheses represent the high point of Egyptian religious thought: they constitute a perfectly articulated system that encourages only stylistic innovations.

The better to grasp the importance of these theological syntheses, let us return for a moment to "Atonist monotheism." To begin, it

54. "Thou didst create the Earth . . . when thou wert alone." "Thou madest the sky distant, so that thou mightest rise thither and look upon all that thou hast made!"
55. We are thinking, of course, of the religious elites to whom the deep meanings of these syntheses were accessible.

must be made clear that the expression used by Akh-en-Aton in his hymn—the "sole God, than whom there is not another"—had already been applied, a thousand years before the Amarna reform, to Amon, to Re, to Atum, and to other gods. In other words, as John Wilson observes, there were at least *two* gods, for Akh-en-Aton was himself worshiped as a divinity.[56] The prayers of the faithful (that is, of the small group of court functionaries and dignitaries) were addressed not to Aton but directly to Akh-en-Aton. In his admirable hymn, the pharaoh declares that Aton is his *personal god*: "Thou art in my heart, and no one else knows thee except thy son (i.e., Akh-en-Aton) whom thou hast initiated into thy plans and thy power!" This explains the almost instantaneous disappearance of "Atonism" after Akh-en-Aton's death. In the last analysis, it was a devotion confined to the royal family and the courtiers.

We must add that Aton was known and worshiped long before the Amarna reform.[57] In *The Book of What Is in the Beyond*, Re is called "Lord of the Disk (Aton)." In other texts of the Eighteenth Dynasty, Amon (the "hidden god") is overlooked, while Re is described as the god whose "face is covered" and who "hides in the other world." In other words, Re's mysterious character and invisibility are declared to be complementary aspects of Aton, the god fully manifested in the solar disk.[58]

33. Final synthesis: The association Re-Osiris

The theologians of the New Empire stress the complementarity of opposed, or even antagonistic, gods. In the *Litany of Re*, the solar god is called "The One-joined-together"; he is represented in the form of an Osiris mummy, wearing the crown of Upper Egypt. In other words, Osiris is imbued with the soul of Re.[59] The identification of the two gods takes place in the person of the dead pharaoh: after the process of Osirification, the king revives as the young Re. For the sun's course represents the paradigmatic model of man's destiny: passage from one mode of being to another, from life to death and,

56. Wilson, *Culture of Ancient Egypt*, pp. 223 ff.
57. See ibid., pp. 210 ff.; A. Piankoff, *The Shrines of Tut-Ankh-Amon*, pp. 5 ff.
58. Piankoff, *Shrines*, p. 2.
59. Piankoff, *The Litany of Re*, p. 11.

after that, to a new birth. Re's descent into the underworld signifies
at once his death and his resurrection. A certain text speaks of "Re
who goes to rest in Osiris, and Osiris who goes to rest in Re."[60]
Numerous mythological allusions emphasize the twofold aspect of
Re: solar and Osirian. By descending into the otherworld, the king
becomes the equivalent of the binomial Osiris-Re.

According to one of the texts cited above, Re "hides himself in the
other world." Several invocations in the *Litany* (lines 20–23) emphasize the watery nature of Re and identify the solar god with the
primordial ocean. But the union of contraries is principally expressed
by the occult solidarity between Re and Osiris or between Horus and
Seth.[61] To use a brilliant formula of Rundle Clark (*Myth and Symbol*,
p. 158), *Re as transcendent and Osiris as emergent are the complementary forms of deity*. In the last analysis, both represent the same
"mystery," and especially the multiplicity of forms emanated by the
one God.[62] According to the theogony and cosmogony accomplished
by Atum (§ 26), the divinity is *at the same time* one and multiple; the
creation consists in the multiplication of his names and forms.

The association and coalescence of the gods were operations
familiar to Egyptian religious thought from the most remote antiquity. What makes the originality of the theology of the Empire is,
on the one hand, the postulate of the twofold process of the Osirification of Re and the solarization of Osiris and, on the other hand, the
conviction that this twofold process reveals the secret meaning of
human existence: *the complementarity between life and death*.[63] From
a certain point of view, this theological synthesis confirms the victory
of Osiris at the same time that it gives him a new meaning. The
triumph of the murdered god was already complete at the beginning
of the Middle Kingdom. From the Eighteenth Dynasty, Osiris
becomes the judge of the dead. The two acts of the after-death drama
—the "trial" and the "weighing of the heart"—take place in the

60. Piankoff, *Ramesses VI*, p. 35.
61. See the examples cited by Piankoff, *Litany*, p. 49, n. 3.
62. Already in the *Pyramid Texts*, Atum causes the gods to emanate from his
own being. In his primordial-serpent form (see § 26) Atum has also been identified with Osiris (which implies that he, too, can "die") and, consequently,
with Horus; see the texts cited and commented on by Piankoff, *Litany*, p. 11,
n. 2.
63. A similar effort, though in pursuit of different ends, was made in India
from the period of the *Brāhmaṇas*; see chapter 9.

presence of Osiris. Separate in the *Coffin Texts*, the "trial" and the "weighing of the soul" tend to become amalgamated in the *Book of the Dead*.[64] These funerary texts, published during the Empire but containing earlier material, will enjoy an unequaled popularity until the end of Egyptian civilization. The *Book of the Dead* is the supreme guide of the soul in the beyond. The prayers and magical formulas that it contains are intended to facilitate the soul's journey and, above all, to insure its success in the ordeals of the "trial" and the "weighing of the heart."

Among the archaic elements in the *Book of the Dead*, mention must be made of the danger of a "second death" (chaps. 44, 130, 135–36, 175–76) and the importance of preserving one's memory (chap. 90) and remembering one's name (chap. 25)—beliefs that are amply documented among the "primitives" but also in Greece and in ancient India. The work, however, reflects the theological syntheses of the Empire. A hymn to Re (chap. 15) describes the sun's daily journey; when he enters the world underground, he spreads joy. The dead "rejoice when thou shinest there for the great god Osiris, the master of eternity." No less significant is the dead person's desire to identify himself with a divinity: Re, Horus, Osiris, Anubis, Ptah, etc. This does not exclude the use of magical formulas. And indeed, to know the name of a god is equivalent to obtaining a certain power over him. The magical value of names, and of words in general, was certainly known from prehistory. For the Egyptians, magic was a weapon created by the gods for the defense of men. In the period of the Empire, magic is personified by a god who accompanies Re in his boat as an attribute of the solar god.[65] In the last analysis, Re's nightly journey through the subterranean world, a dangerous descent, strewn with obstacles, constitutes the paradigmatic model of the journey of each dead person to the place of judgment.[66]

One of the most important chapters in the *Book of the Dead*,

64. Yoyotte, "Le jugement des morts dans l'Egypte ancienne," p. 45. It should be made clear that the judgment of the dead and the notion of a celestial justice "occurring after the death of all, men and kings," are clearly documented from the Ninth Dynasty (ibid., p. 64).

65. But the role of magical formulas finally becomes supreme, especially among the common people.

66. Other funerary collections—*The Book of What Is in the Beyond, The Book of Gates*, etc.—systematically describe the kingdom of the dead, through which Re travels in his boat during the twelve hours of night.

chapter 125, is devoted to the judgment of the soul in the great hall called "Of the Two *Ma^cats*." [67] The deceased's heart is suspended on one pan of the scales; on the other is a feather or an eye, symbols of *ma^cat*. During the operation, the deceased recites a prayer, imploring his heart not to bear witness against him. Then he must utter a declaration of innocence, erroneously termed the "negative confession":

I have not committed evil against men. . . .
I have not blasphemed a god.
I have not done violence to a poor man. . . .
I have not killed. . . .
I have not caused anyone suffering.
I have not cut down on the food(-income) in the temples, . . .
I am pure. I am pure. I am pure. I am pure.

The deceased addresses the forty-two gods who make up the tribunal: "Hail to you, ye gods who are here! I know you, I know your names. I shall not fall under your blows. You will not report that I am wicked to the god whose suite you form. . . . You will say that *ma^cat* is my due, in the presence of the Universal Master; for I have practiced *ma^cat* in Egypt." He utters his own eulogy: "I have satisfied God by that which he loves (to see done). I have given bread to him who was hungry, water to him who was thirsty, clothing to him who was naked, a boat to him who had none. . . . Save me then, protect me then! Make no report against me in the presence of the great god!" Finally he turns to Osiris: "O god who art high on thy support . . . mayest thou protect me from these messengers who sow evil and raise up troubles . . . for I have practiced *ma^cat* for the sake of the Master of *ma^cat*. I am pure." [68] The deceased must also undergo an interrogation of the initiatory type. He must prove that he knows the secret names of the different parts of the door and the threshold, or the gatekeeper of the hall, and of the gods.[69]

It is by meditating on the mystery of death that the Egyptian genius realized the last religious synthesis, the only one that maintained its supremacy until the end of Egyptian civilization. It is, of

67. On the meaning of this expression, see Yoyotte, "Jugement des morts," pp. 61 ff.
68. After the translation by Yoyotte, ibid., pp. 52–56.
69. Ibid., pp. 56–57. During the Old Kingdom, the pharaoh too had to undergo an initiatory interrogation; see § 28.

course, a creation susceptible of many interpretations and applications. The deep meaning of the binomial Re-Osiris or of the continuity life-death-transfiguration was not necessarily accessible to those believers who were convinced of the infallibility of magical formulas; nevertheless, these reflected the same eschatological gnosis. By developing the old conception of death as spiritual transmutation, the theologians of the Empire identified the models of this "mystery" at once in Re's daily exploits and in the primordial drama of Osiris. In this way they articulated in a single system what seemed the supreme example of the eternal and invulnerable (the course of the sun), what was only a tragic episode but, in the last analysis, a fortuitous one (the murder of Osiris), and what would seem by definition to be ephemeral and meaningless (human existence). In the articulation of this soteriology, the role of Osiris was essential. By virtue of him, every mortal could henceforth hope for a "royal destiny" in the other world. In the last analysis, the pharaoh constituted the universal model.

The tension among "privilege," "initiatory wisdom," and "good works" is resolved in a way that can sometimes be deceptive. For if "justice" was always assured, "initiatory wisdom" could be reduced to the possession of magical formulas. Everything depended on the point of view assumed in respect to the eschatological summa, awkwardly connected in the *Book of the Dead* and other similar works. These texts were open to various "readings," performed on different levels. The magical reading was, of course, the easiest: it implied only faith in the omnipotence of the word. In proportion as, by virtue of the new eschatology, the "royal destiny" becomes universally accessible, the prestige of magic will not fail to increase. The twilight of Egyptian civilization will be dominated by magical beliefs and practices.[70] But it is only right to remember that, in the "Memphite Theology" (cf. § 26), Ptah had created the gods and the world by the power of the Word.

70. See the second volume of the present work.

5 Megaliths, Temples, Ceremonial Centers: Occident, Mediterranean, Indus Valley

34. Stone and banana

The megalithic constructions of western and northern Europe have fascinated investigators for over a century. Indeed, it is impossible to look at a good photograph of the alignments at Carnac or the gigantic trilithons of Stonehenge without wondering what their purpose and meaning could have been. The technological ability of these farmers of the Age of Polished Stone arouses astonishment. How did thay manage to set 300-ton blocks in an upright position and lift 100-ton slabs? Then, too, such monuments are not isolated. They form part of a whole megalithic complex, which extends from the Mediterranean coast of Spain, covers Portugal, half of France, the western seaboard of England, and continues into Ireland, Denmark, and the southern coast of Sweden. To be sure, there are significant morphological variations. But two generations of prehistorians have made every effort to demonstrate the continuity of all the European megalithic cultures—a continuity that could be explained only by dissemination of the megalithic complex from a center situated at Los Millares, in the province of Almeria.

The megalithic complex comprises three categories of structures: (1) the menhir (from Breton *men* = "stone" and *hir* = "long") is a large stone, sometimes of considerable height,[1] set vertically into the ground; (2) the cromlech (from *crom* = "circle, curve," and *lech* = "place"), which designates a group of menhirs, set in a circle or half-circle (the most monumental is the cromlech of Stonehenge, near Salisbury); sometimes the menhirs are aligned in several parallel

1. The menhir located near Locmariaquer measured more than 20 meters in height. In Brittany certain isolated menhirs are associated with burials.

rows, as at Carnac in Brittany;[2] (3) the dolmen (*dol* = "table" and *men* = "stone") is made up of an immense capstone supported by several upright stones arranged to form a sort of enclosure or chamber. Originally the dolmen was covered by a mound.

Strictly speaking, dolmens are burial places. Later and in certain regions—western Europe, Sweden—the dolmen was transformed into a covered passage by the addition of a sort of vestibule in the form of a long corridor covered with capstones. Some dolmens are gigantic; the one at Soto (near Seville), for example, is 21 meters long and has as pediment a granite block 3.40 meters high, 3.10 meters wide, and 0.72 meters thick and weighing 21 tons. At Los Millares a necropolis of about a hundred covered passages has been excavated. Most of the graves are under enormous mounds. Certain burials contain as many as a hundred dead, representing several generations of the same *gens*. Sometimes the burial chambers have a central pillar, and remains of painting can still be discerned on the walls. Dolmens are found along the Atlantic, especially in Brittany, and as far as the Netherlands. In Ireland the funerary chambers, which are comparatively high, have walls decorated with sculptures.

All this undoubtedly testifies to a very important cult of the dead. Whereas the houses of the Neolithic peasants who raised these monuments were modest and ephemeral (and in fact have left almost no traces), the dwellings for the dead were built of stone. It is obvious that there was an intention to construct imposing and solid works, capable of resisting time. The complexity of lithic symbolism and the religious valences of stones and rocks are well known.[3] The rock, the slab, the granite block reveal duration without end, permanence, incorruptibility—in the last analysis a modality of *existing* independently of temporal becoming.

When we contemplate the grandiose megalithic monuments of the earliest agriculturalists of western Europe, we cannot but call to mind a certain Indonesian myth. In the beginning, when the sky was very near to the earth, God hung his gifts on a cord in order to bestow them on the primordial couple. One day he sent them a stone, but the ancestors, surprised and indignant, refused it. Some days later God let the cord down again, this time with a banana, which

2. The alignments at Carnac comprise 2,935 menhirs on a terrain 3,900 meters long.
3. See our *Patterns in Comparative Religion*, §§ 74 ff.

was immediately accepted. Then the ancestors heard the creator's voice: "Since you have chosen the banana, your life shall be like the life of that fruit. If you had chosen the stone, your life would have been like the existence of stone, unchangeable and immortal."[4]

As we have seen (§ 12), the discovery of agriculture radically changed the conception of human existence: it proved to be as frail and ephemeral as the life of plants. Yet, on the other hand, man shared in the cyclical destiny of vegetation: birth, life, death, rebirth. The megalithic monuments could be interpreted as a response to our Indonesian myth: since man's life is like the life of cereals, strength and perenniality become accessible *through death*. The dead return to the bosom of Mother Earth, with the hope of sharing the destiny of sown seed; but they are also mystically associated with the stone blocks of the burial chambers and consequently become as strong and indestructible as rocks.

For the megalithic cult of the dead appears to include not only a certainty of the soul's survival but, above all, confidence in the power of the ancestors and the hope that they will protect and help the living. Such a confidence differs radically from the concepts documented among other peoples of antiquity (Mesopotamians, Hittites, Hebrews, Greeks, etc.), for whom the dead were pitiable shades, unhappy and powerless. What is more: whereas for the megalith-builders, from Ireland to Malta and the Aegean islands, *ritual communion with the ancestors* constituted the keystone of their religious activity, in the protohistorical cultures of central Europe, as n the ancient Near East, *separation between the dead and the living* was strictly prescribed.

In addition to various ceremonies (processions, dances, etc.), the megalithic cult of the dead involved offerings (food, beverages, etc.), sacrifices performed in the vicinity of the monuments, and ritual meals on the burial places. A certain number of menhirs were erected independently of burials. In all probability, these stones constituted a sort of "substitute body," in which the souls of the dead were incorporated.[5] In the last analysis, *a stone "substitute" was a body*

---

4. A. C. Kruijt, cited by J. G. Frazer, *The Belief in Immortality* (1913), vol. 1, pp. 74–75. We have commented on this myth in "Mythologies of Death" (chap. 3 of *Occultism, Witchcraft, and Cultural Fashions*).

5. Horst Kirchner, "Die Menhire in Mitteleuropa und der Menhirgedanke," pp. 698 ff. (pp. 90 ff. of the offprint).

built for eternity. Menhirs are sometimes found decorated with human figures; in other words, they are the "dwelling," the "body" of the dead. Similarly, the stylized figures depicted on the walls of dolmens, together with the small idols excavated from the megalithic burial places of Spain, probably represented the ancestors. In certain cases a parallel belief can be discerned: the ancestor's soul is able to leave the tomb from time to time.[6] The perforated stones that close certain megalithic tombs, and which, furthermore, are called "soul holes," allowed communication with the living.

The sexual meaning of menhirs must also be taken into consideration, for it is universally documented, and on various levels of culture. Jeremiah (2:27) refers to those "who say to a piece of wood, 'You are my father,' to a stone, 'You have begotten me.'"[7] Belief in the fertilizing virtues of menhirs was still common among European peasants at the beginning of this century. In France, in order to have children, young women performed the *glissade* (letting themselves slide along a stone) and the *friction* (sitting on monoliths or rubbing their abdomens against certain rocks).[8]

This generative function must not be explained by the phallic symbolism of the menhir, though such a symbolism is documented in certain cultures. The original, and fundamental, idea was the "transmutation" of the ancestors into stone, either by the device of a menhir as "substitute body" or by incorporating an essential element of the dead person—skeleton, ashes, "soul"—into the actual structure of the monument. In either case the dead person

6. Certain Breton menhirs, set up in front of the galleries of dolmens, have been explained by the Egyptian belief that the souls of the dead, transformed into birds, left their tombs to perch on a pillar in full sunlight. "This notion appears to have been entertained throughout the Mediterranean area and also in western Europe" (Maringer, *The Gods of Prehistoric Man*, p. 235). Carl Schuchhardt put forward the same interpretation for the obelisks painted on the sarcophagus of Hagia Triada (see § 41), on which birds are perched. But see the critique by Kirchner, "Die Menhire," p. 706 (offprint, p. 98). In the megalithic cultures of Southeast Asia, the menhir serves as "seat" for souls (cf. § 36).

7. Nevertheless, even such a vigorously Yahwistic treatise as Deuteronomy still uses the ontological metaphor of stone when it proclaims the absolute reality of God as sole source of creativity: "You forget the Rock who begot you, unmindful now of the God who fathered you" (Deut. 32:18).

8. See some examples and the bibliography in *Patterns in Comparative Religion*, § 77, to which Kirchner, "Die Menhire," pp. 650 ff. (offprint, p. 42) should be added.

"animated" the stone; he inhabited a new body that, being mineral, was imperishable. Hence the menhir or the megalithic tomb constituted an inexhaustible reservoir of vitality and power. By virtue of their projection into the structures of the funerary stones, the dead became masters of fertility and prosperity. In the language of the Indonesian myth, they had succeeded in taking possession of both the stone and the banana.

35. Ceremonial centers and megalithic constructions

Certain megalithic complexes, such as the one at Carnac or the one at Ashdown, in Berkshire (containing 800 megaliths in a parallelogram 250 by 500 meters), undoubtedly constituted important ceremonial centers. The festivals included sacrifices and, it may be presumed, dances and processions. Indeed, thousands of men could move in procession along the great avenue at Carnac. Probably most of the festivals were connected with the cult of the dead. Like other similar English monuments,[9] the Stonehenge cromlech was situated in the middle of a field of funeral barrows. This famous ceremonial center constituted, at least in its primitive form,[10] a sanctuary built to insure relations with the ancestors. In terms of structure, Stonehenge can be compared with certain megalithic complexes developed, in other cultures, from a sacred area: temples or cities. We have the same valorization of the sacred space as "center of the world," the privileged place that affords communication with heaven and the underworld, that is, with the gods, the chthonian goddesses, and the spirits of the dead.

In certain parts of France, in the Iberian Peninsula, and elsewhere, traces have been found of a cult of the Goddess, the guardian divinity of the dead. Yet nowhere else did megalithic architecture, the cult of the dead, and worship of a Great Goddess find such spectacular expression as on Malta. Excavations have brought to light very few houses; but up to now seventeen temples have been

9. For example, Woodhenge, Avebury, Arminghall, and Arbor Low; see Maringer, *The Gods of Prehistoric Man*, p. 247.
10. Stonehenge was not all built at once. It is now known that the original work underwent several rehandlings. See Colin Renfrew, *Before Civilization*, pp. 214 ff.

discovered, and their number is thought to be still greater, which justifies the opinion of certain scholars that during the Neolithic period Malta was an *isola sacra*.[11] The vast elliptical terraces that stretched before the sanctuaries or between them certainly served for processional and ritual choreography. The temple walls are decorated with admirable spirals in low relief, and a number of stone sculptures representing women lying on one side have been excavated. But the most sensational discovery is the enormous statue of a woman—certainly a goddess—in a seated position.

The excavations have revealed an elaborate cult, with animal sacrifices, food offerings and libations, and rites of incubation and divination, indicating the existence of an important and well-organized sacerdotal body. The cult of the dead probably played the central role. In the remarkable necropolis at Hal Saflieni, now called the Hypogeum and comprising several chambers cut into the rock, the bones of some 7,000 persons have been exhumed. It is the Hypogeum that has yielded the statues of recumbent women, suggesting an incubation rite. Just as in other megalithic monuments, the inner rooms have their walls sculptured and painted. These large chambers served for certain religious ceremonies reserved for priests and initiates, for they were isolated by carved screens.[12]

Whereas the Hypogeum was at once necropolis and chapel, no burials have been found in the temples. The curvilinear structure of the Maltese sanctuaries seems to be unique; the archeologists describe it as "kidney-shaped," but according to Zuntz their structure more nearly suggests that of the womb. Since the temples were covered by a roof and the rooms were without windows and rather dark, entering a sanctuary was equivalent to entering the "bowels of the earth," i.e., the womb of the chthonian Goddess. But the rock-cut tombs are also womb-shaped. One would say that the dead person is placed in the bosom of the earth for a new life. "The temples reproduce the same model on a large scale. The living who enter them enter the body of the goddess." Indeed, Zuntz concludes, these monuments constitute the stage for "a mystery-cult in the exact sense of the word."[13]

11. Gunther Zuntz, *Persephone*, p. 4, n. 1.
12. J. D. Evans, *Malta*, p. 139; Glyn Daniel and J. D. Evans, *The Western Mediterranean*, p. 20.
13. Zuntz, *Persephone*, pp. 8, 25.

We will add that the surfaces of the dolmens and menhirs of
Iberia and western Europe also display other magico-religious signs
and symbols—for example, the image of a sun with rays, the sign of
the ax (peculiar to storm gods), the snake, symbol of life, associated
with figures of the ancestors, the stag, etc. To be sure, these figures
have been discovered in different regions and belong to cultures of
different ages, but they have in common the fact that they are bound
up with the same megalithic complex. This may be explained either
by the variety of religious ideas held by the different "megalithic"
peoples or by the fact that the cult of ancestors, despite its importance,
was associated with different religious complexes.

36. The "enigma of the megaliths"

A decade ago archeologists explained the megalithic cultures by
influences from colonizers arrived from the eastern Mediterranean,
where, in fact, collective burials are already documented in the third
millennium.[14] In the course of its dissemination into the West, the
construction of dolmens ("chamber tombs") was transformed into
cyclopean architecture. According to Glyn Daniel, this transformation took place on Malta, in the Iberian Peninsula, and in southern
France. The same writer compares the dissemination of megalithic
architecture with the Greek and Phoenician colonization in the
Mediterranean or the expansion of Islam into Spain. "It was a
powerful, compelling, Aegean-inspired religion that made them
build their tombs (or their tomb temples?) with such labor and
preserve . . . the image of their tutelary and funerary goddess.
The goddess figure, the axe, the horns, and other symbols take us
back from the Paris Basin, from Gavrinnis, from Anghelu Raju to
Crete, the Aegean, even Troy. It cannot be disputed that a powerful
religion of east Mediterranean origin informed and inspired the
builders of the megalithic tombs as they spread through western
Europe."[15] But religion was not the primary cause of their migrations;
religion was only "the solace of their exile in the far west and the

14. The Minoan collective tombs were either natural caves or circular
enclosures, usually called *tholoi*; see Glyn Daniel, *The Megalithic Builders of
Western Europe*, 2d ed. (1962), p. 129.
15. Ibid., p. 136.

north of Europe." The emigrants were seeking new countries to live in and ores for their trade.[16]

In his last book, Gordon Childe discussed a "megalithic religion," disseminated by Mediterranean prospectors and colonizers. Once accepted, the idea of building megalithic tombs was adapted by the various societies, without, however, affecting their specific structures. Each tomb probably belonged to a nobleman or to the head of a family; the labor was supplied by his companions. "A megalithic tomb should be compared to a church rather than a castle, and its occupants to Celtic saints rather than to Norman barons."[17] The "missionaries" of the megalithic faith, a religion above all of the Mother Goddess, attracted a large number of agriculturalists to their communities. And in fact the dolmens and cromlechs are located in the regions most suitable for Neolithic agriculture.[18]

Similar explanations of the megalithic complex have been proposed by other eminent prehistorians.[19] However, these explanations were invalidated by the discovery of dating by the radioactivity of carbon and by dendrochronology.[20] It has been possible to show that the megalithic sepulchers ("chamber tombs") of Brittany were built before 4000 B.C. and that in England and Denmark stone tombs were being built before 3000 B.C.[21] As for the gigantic complex of Stonehenge, it was thought to be contemporary with the Wessex culture, which was linked with the Mycenaean civilization. But

16. Ibid., pp. 136–37.

17. Gordon Childe, *The Prehistory of European Society*, pp. 126 ff. The author (p. 128) compares the megalithic tombs with the little chapels founded by the Welsh and Irish saints in the same parts of the British Isles.

18. Ibid., p. 129.

19. Stuart Piggott derives the megalithic monuments from the eastern Mediterranean and compares them with Christian churches or mosques; see his *Ancient Europe*, p. 60. For Grahame Clark, the Aegean rite of collective burials, associated with the cult of the Mother Goddess, was disseminated in the West by prospectors and explorers for mines; see his *World Prehistory*, pp. 138–39.

20. For this "tree-ring calibration of radiocarbon," see a clear exposition in Colin Renfrew, *Before Civilization*, pp. 48–83. As is well known, the two "revolutions"—dating by carbon 14 and by dendrochronology—radically altered the chronology of European prehistory.

21. It should be born in mind that in Egypt the earliest stone pyramids were erected about 2700 B.C. It is true that these pyramids had predecessors of brick, but the fact remains that, before 3000 B.C., we know of no Egyptian stone monument comparable to the megaliths of western Europe; see Renfrew, *Before Civilization*, p. 123.

analyses based on the recent methods prove that Stonehenge was finished before Mycenae; its last rebuilding (Stonehenge III) dates from 2100–1900 B.C.[22] So too on Malta, the period represented by the Tarxien temples and the necropolis of Hal Saflieni had ended before 2000 B.C.; hence certain of its characteristic features cannot be explained by an influence from the Minoan Bronze Age.[23] So the conclusion is inescapable that *the European megalithic complex precedes the Aegean contribution.* We are dealing with a series of original autochthonous creations.

However, the chronological "upset" and the demonstration of the originality of the western populations have not advanced the interpretation of the megalithic monuments. There has been much discussion concerning Stonehenge, but, despite some noteworthy contributions,[24] the religious function and the symbolism of the monument are still disputed. Furthermore, in reaction against certain risky hypotheses (for example, that of Sir Grafton Elliot Smith, who derived all the megalithic constructions from the one source of pharaonic Egypt), investigators no longer dare to attack the problem as a whole. But this timidity is regrettable, for "megalithism" is an exemplary, and probably unique, subject of study. Indeed, comparative research should be able to show to what extent the analysis of the numerous megalithic cultures that were still flourishing in the nineteenth century can contribute to an understanding of the religious concepts held by the originators of the prehistoric monuments.

37. Ethnography and prehistory

It is well known that, outside of the Mediterranean and western and northern Europe, megaliths of prehistoric and protohistoric origin are spread over a vast area: Algeria, Palestine, Abyssinia, the Deccan,

22. See the documentation ibid., pp. 214 ff.

23. Ibid., p. 152. See also Daniel and Evans, *The Western Mediterranean*, p. 21. Zuntz, however, thinks of an Egyptian or Sumerian influence (*Persephone*, pp. 10 ff.).

24. Since the tectonic structure of Stonehenge seems also to imply the function of an astronomical observatory, it is probable that the chief festivals were related to the changes of the seasons, as among the Hopis and the Cherokees; see Renfrew, *Before Civilization*, pp. 239 ff.

Assam, Ceylon, Tibet, and Korea. As for the megalithic cultures that were still alive at the beginning of the twentieth century, the most notable are documented in Indonesia and Melanesia. Robert Heine-Geldern, who devoted part of his life to studying this problem, held that the two groups of megalithic cultures—those of prehistory and those of cultures at the ethnographic stage—are historically connected, for in his view the megalithic complex was disseminated from a single center, very probably the eastern Mediterranean.

We shall later return to Heine-Geldern's hypothesis. For the moment, we may appropriately summarize his conclusions regarding the beliefs typical of the living megalithic societies. Megaliths have a relation to certain ideas concerning existence after death. The majority of them are built in the course of ceremonies intended to defend the soul during its journey into the beyond; but they also insure an eternal postexistence, both to those who raise them during their own lifetime and to those for whom they are built after death. In addition, megaliths constitute the unrivaled connection between the living and the dead; they are believed to perpetuate the magical virtues of those who constructed them or for whom they were constructed, thus insuring the fertility of men, cattle, and harvests. In all the megalithic cultures that still flourish, the cult of ancestors plays an important part.[25]

The monuments serve as the seat of the souls of the dead when they come back to visit the village, but they are also used by the living. The place where the megaliths stand is at once the outstanding cult site (ceremonial choreography, sacrifices, etc.) and the center of social activity. In the megalithic-type cult of the dead, genealogies play an important part. According to Heine-Geldern, it is probable that the genealogies of the ancestors—that is, of the founders of villages and of certain families—were ritually recited. It is important to emphasize this fact: *man hopes that his name will be remembered through the agency of stone;* in other words, connection with the ancestors is insured by memory of their names and exploits, a memory "fixed" in the megaliths.

As we have just observed, Heine-Geldern claims for the megalithic civilizations a continuity extending from the fifth millennium down to the contemporary "primitive" societies. However, he rejects G.

25. R. Heine-Geldern, "Prehistoric Research in the Netherlands Indies," p. 149, and "Das Megalithproblem," pp. 167 ff.

Elliot Smith's and J. W. Perry's pan-Egyptian hypothesis. In addition, he denies the existence of a "megalithic religion," for the simple reason that certain "megalithic" beliefs and concepts are documented in connection with many religious forms, both elementary and higher. The Austrian scholar compares the megalithic complex with certain "mystical" movements—for example, Tantrism, which can be indifferently either Hindu or Buddhist. He also denies the existence of a "megalithic cultural circle," made up, according to certain authors, of particular myths and characteristic social or economic institutions; and in fact megalithic ideas and practices are documented among populations that possess a great variety of social forms, economic structures, and cultural institutions.[26]

The analysis of the megalithic complex accomplished by Heine-Geldern still has value. But his hypotheses concerning the unity of ancient and contemporary megalithic cultures are today disputed, or simply ignored, by many investigators. The problem of the "continuity" of the megalithic complex is substantial and must remain open. For, as a certain author put it recently, it represents "the greatest enigma of prehistory." In any case—and whatever hypothesis is adopted, whether continuity or convergence—it is impossible to speak of *one* megalithic culture. For our purpose, it should be noted that, in the megalithic religions, the sacrality of stone is chiefly valorized in relation to postexistence. The attempt is made to "found" a particular mode of existence after death by means of the ontophany peculiar to stones. In the megalithic cultures of western Europe, the fascination exercised by stone in masses is obvious; but it is a fascination aroused by the desire to transform collective burials into spectacular and indestructible monuments. By virtue of the megalithic constructions the dead enjoy an exceptional power; however, since communication with the ancestors is ritually assured, this power can be shared by the living. To be sure, other forms of the cult of ancestors exist. What characterizes the megalithic religions is the fact that the ideas of *perenniality* and of *continuity between life and death* are apprehended through the *exaltation of the ancestors as identified, or associated, with the stones.* We will add, however, that these religious ideas were not fully realized and perfectly expressed except in a few privileged creations.

26. See "Das Megalithproblem," pp. 164 ff.

38. The first cities of India

Recent researches into the prehistory of Indian civilization have opened perspectives that were unforeseeable a few decades ago. They also raised problems that have not yet received satisfactory solutions. The excavation of the two cities, Harappa and Mohenjo-daro, brought to light a quite advanced urban civilization, at once mercantile and theocratic. The chronology is still in dispute, but it appears certain that the Indus civilization was fully developed about 2500 B.C. What most struck the directors of the earliest excavations was the uniformity and stagnation of the Harappan civilization. No change, no innovation, could be discerned in the thousand years of its history. The two towns were probably the capitals of the "empire." This uniformity and continuity can be explained only by supposing a regime based on some kind of religious authority.[27]

Today this culture is known to have extended far beyond the Indus Valley, and it everywhere presented the same uniformity. Gordon Childe considered Harappan technology to be equal to those of Egypt and Mesopotamia. However, the majority of its products lack imagination, "suggesting that the people of Harappa had their eyes on things not of this world."[28]

As for the origin of this earliest urban civilization to develop in India, scholars are agreed in looking for it in Baluchistan. According to Fairservis, the ancestors of the Harappans were descended from the pre-Āryan agriculturalists of Iran. Certain phases of the pre-Harappan culture are beginning to be better known as a result of the excavations made in southern Baluchistan. It is noteworthy that the earliest important agglomerations were built near structures that had a ceremonial function. In the important archeological complex excavated in the region of the Porali River and known as the "Edith Shahr Complex," a mound 7 to 12 meters high has been brought to light, together with a number of structures surrounded by walls. At its summit the mound rose in the form of a ziggurat; several stairways led to the platform. The structures in stone seem to have been seldom and sporadically inhabited, which indicates that the function of the entire edifice was ceremonial. The second phase of the same complex (phase B) is characterized by the presence of great stone circles, by

27. Cf. M. Eliade, *Yoga: Immortality and Freedom*, pp. 353 ff.
28. B. and R. Allchin, *The Birth of Indian Civilization*, p. 136.

more than a hundred buildings, 3 to 8 meters wide, and by "avenues" of white stones. These structures, too, appear to have served only religious objectives.[29]

Fairservis compares these sacred sites, and in general the structures excavated in the Quetta Valley (representing the pre-Harappan phases of Sind and Baluchistan), with Mohenjo-daro and Harappa, cities that he considers were originally built for cult ceremonies. This hypothesis is still disputed, though there is no doubt concerning the religious function of the "citadel," a platform comprising characteristic structures, which are the same in the two cities. For our purpose the controversy is of little interest. For, on the one hand, the cult origin of the pre-Harappan agglomerations (hence, of the earliest cities!) is certain, and, on the other hand, scholars today agree in seeing ceremonial complexes in the most ancient urban centers. Paul Wheatley has brilliantly demonstrated the religious intention and function of the earliest cities in China, Mesopotamia, Egypt, Central America, and elsewhere.[30] The most ancient cities were built around sanctuaries, that is, close to a sacred space, a "center of the world," where communication between earth, heaven, and the subterranean regions was deemed possible.[31] If it could be shown that the two capital cities of the Indus are clearly different from their pre-Harappan prototypes (and from other ancient cities), Harappa and Mohenjo-daro would have to be considered the first examples of the secularization of an urban structure, which is an essentially modern phenomenon.

What needs to be emphasized for the moment is the morphological diversity of the sacred space and the cult center. In the megalithic cultures of the Mediterranean and western Europe, the ceremonial center, bound up with the cult of the dead, was consecrated by menhirs and dolmens, seldom by sanctuaries, and the agglomerations did not exceed the dimensions of villages.[32] As we have seen, the real

29. W. A. Fairservis, *The Roots of Ancient India*, pp. 195 ff., 362 ff. On the relations between this phase of pre-Harappan culture and the megaliths of southern India, see ibid., pp. 375 ff.

30. Paul Wheatley, *The Pivot of the Four Quarters*, esp. pp. 20 ff., 107 ff., 225 ff.

31. Eliade, *Cosmos and History*, chap. 1, and "Centre du Monde, Temple, Maison."

32. The earliest cities built in these regions were likewise "sacred cities," that is, "centers of the world"; cf. Werner Müller, *Die heilige Stadt*, passim.

megalithic "cities" in the West were built for the dead: they were necropolises.

39. Protohistorical religious concepts and their parallels in Hinduism

The Harappan religion—that is, the religion of the first urban civilization of India—is also important for another reason: its relationship with Hinduism. Despite the skepticism of some authors, the religious life of Mohenjo-daro and Harappa is accessible to us, at least in its general outlines. Thus, for example, a great number of figurines and certain designs inscribed on seals indicate cults of a Mother Goddess. In addition, as Sir John Marshall had already recognized, an ithyphallic figure seated in a "yogic" position and surrounded by wild animals represents a Great God, probably a prototype of Śiva.[33] Fairservis has called attention to the large number of scenes of worship or sacrifice depicted on the seals. The most famous one shows a figure seated (or dancing) on a platform between two kneeling suppliants, each accompanied by a cobra. Other seals feature a personage immobilizing two tigers, in the manner of Gilgamesh, or a horned god with the legs and tail of a bull, suggesting the Mesopotamian Enkidu; there are also various tree spirits, to which sacrifices are being brought, processions of people carrying "standards," etc.[34] In the scenes painted on certain urns excavated at Harappa, Vats believed that he could identify the souls of the dead preparing to cross a stream.[35]

Since Sir John Marshall, scholars have emphasized the "Hindu-istic" character of the Harappan religion. Aside from the examples already cited—the Great Goddess, a proto-Śiva in "yogic" position, the ritual value of trees and snakes and the *lingam*—we may mention the "Grand Bath" at Mohenjo-daro, which resembles the bathing pools of modern Hindu temples, the *pipal* tree, the use of the turban (unknown in the Vedic texts, documented only after the period of the

33. Sir John Marshall, *Mohenjo-daro*, vol. 1, p. 52; Eliade, *Yoga*, p. 355. Stones in the form of the *lingam* have also been found in these cities; see Allchin, *Birth of Indian Civilization*, p. 312.
34. Fairservis, *Roots of Ancient India*, pp. 274 ff.
35. Allchin, p. 314 and fig. 75.

Brāhmaṇas), nasal ornaments, the ivory comb, etc.[36] The historical process that insured the transmission of a part of the Harappan heritage and its absorption into Hinduism is inadequately known. Scholars are still discussing the causes for the decadence and ultimate ruin of the two capital cities. The catastrophic floods of the Indus have been suggested, as have the consequences of desiccation, seismic movements,[37] and the attacks of the Āryan invaders. It would seem probable that the decline had multiple causes. In any case, about 1750 B.C. the Indus civilization was on its deathbed, and the Indo-Āryans only gave it its mortal blow (cf. § 64). But it must be made clear, on the one hand, that the invasion by the Āryan tribes took place progressively, during several centuries, and, on the other hand, that in the South, in the region formerly known as Saurashtra, a culture derived from the nuclear Harappan complex continued its development after the Āryan thrust.[38]

Twenty years ago we wrote concerning the destruction of the Indus culture:

The collapse of an urban civilization is not equivalent to the simple extinction of its culture, but merely to that culture's regression to rural, larval, "popular" forms. (This phenomenon was amply demonstrated in Europe during and after the great barbarian invasions.) But before very long the Āryanization of the Punjab launched the great movement of synthesis that was one day to become Hinduism. The considerable number of "Harappan" elements found in Hinduism can be explained only by a contact, begun quite early, between the Indo-European conquerors and the representatives of the Indus culture. These representatives were not necessarily the authors of the Indus culture or their direct descendants; they might be tributaries, by dissemination, of certain Harappan cultural forms, which they had preserved in eccentric regions, spared by the first waves of Āryanization. This would explain the following apparently strange fact: the cult of the Great Goddess and of Śiva, phallism and tree worship, asceticism and Yoga, etc., appear for the first time in India as the religious

36. See Eliade, *Yoga*, p. 356; Piggott, *Prehistoric India*, pp. 268 ff.; Allchin, *Birth of Indian Civilization*, pp. 310 ff.; Sir Mortimer Wheeler, *The Indus Civilization*, p. 135.

37. See the discussion of these hypotheses in Wheeler, pp. 127 ff., Allchin, pp. 143 ff., and Fairservis, pp. 302 ff.

38. Wheeler, pp. 133 ff., Allchin, pp. 179 ff., Fairservis, pp. 293, 295.

expression of a high urban civilization, that of the Indus—whereas, in medieval and modern India, these religious elements are characteristic of "popular" cultures. To be sure, from the Harappan period on, there was certainly a synthesis between the spirituality of the Australoid aborigines and that of the "masters," the authors of the urban civilization. But we must presume that it was not only this synthesis that was preserved, but also the specific and almost exclusive contribution of the "masters" (a contribution related especially to their theocratic conceptions). Otherwise it would be impossible to explain the considerable importance assumed by the Brāhmans after the Vedic period. Very probably all these Harappan religious conceptions (which strongly contrast with those of the Indo-Europeans) were preserved, with inevitable regressions, among the "popular" strata, in the margin of the society and civilization of the new Āryan-speaking masters. Very probably it is from there that they welled up, in successive waves, during the later synthesis that ended in the formation of Hinduism.[39]

Since that was published (1954), other proofs of continuity have been adduced.[40] What is more, similar processes are documented elsewhere, notably in Crete, in continental Greece, and in the Aegean region as a whole, where the Hellenic culture and religion are the result of a symbiosis between the Mediterranean substratum and the Indo-European conquerors from the north. Here, just as in India, the religious ideas and beliefs of the autochthonous inhabitants are accessible chiefly through the *archeological* data, whereas the earliest *texts*—Homer and Hesiod first of all—largely reflect the traditions of the Āryan-speaking invaders. It must be made clear, however, that Homer and Hesiod already represent the first phases of the Hellenic synthesis.

40. Crete: Sacred caves, labyrinths, goddesses

On Crete the Neolithic culture, documented from the fifth millennium, came to an end when, about the third millennium, the island was colonized by immigrants arriving from the south and the east. The

39. *Yoga*, p. 358.
40. They will be found in the works by Wheeler, Allchin, and Fairservis. See also Mario Cappiori, "Ist die Indus-Kultur und ihre Bevölkerung wirklich verschwunden?"; W. Koppers, "Zentralindische Fruchtbarkeitsriten und ihre Beziehungen zur Induskultur"; J. Haekel, " 'Adonisgärtchen' im Zeremonielwesen der Rathwa in Gujerat (Zentralindien). Vergleich und Problematik."

newcomers were masters of the metallurgical techniques of copper and bronze. Sir Arthur Evans called their culture "Minoan," after the legendary King Minos, and divided it into three periods: Early Minoan (about the end of the third millennium); Middle Minoan (from the building of the palaces of Cnossus and Mallia, 2000 B.C.–1580 B.C.); and Late Minoan (1580–1150 B.C.).[41] During the Middle Minoan the Cretans used a hieroglyphic script, followed, about 1700 B.C., by a linear script (Linear A); neither has yet been deciphered. It is during this period (between 2000 and 1900 B.C.) that the first Greeks, the Minyans, entered continental Greece. They represent the advance guard of the Indo-European groups that, in successive waves, will come to settle in Hellas, in the islands, and on the littoral of Asia Minor. The first phase of Late Minoan (1580–1450 B.C.) constitutes the apogee of the Minoan civilization. This is the period during which, in the Peloponnesus, the Āryan-speaking invaders build Mycenae and maintain relations with Crete. Not long afterward (1450–1400 B.C.) the Mycenaeans (or Achaeans) settle at Cnossus and introduce the type of script known as Linear B. The last phase of Late Minoan, called the Mycenaean Period (1400–1150 B.C.), ends with the invasion by the Dorians and the final destruction of the Cretan civilization.

Until Ventris deciphered Linear B in 1952, the only documents for Minoan culture and religion came from archeological excavations. They are still the most important. The first indications of acts having a religious intention were discovered in caves. In Crete, as everywhere else in the Mediterranean, caves long served as dwelling places, but also, especially since the Neolithic, as cemeteries (a custom that has survived down to modern times). However, a considerable number of caves were consecrated to various autochthonous divinities. Certain rites, myths, and legends associated with these power-haunted caves were later incorporated into the religious traditions of the Greeks. Thus, one of the most celebrated, the cave at Amnisos, near Cnossus, was consecrated to Eileithyia, a pre-Hellenic goddess of childbirth. Another, on Mount Dicte,[42] was famous for having

41. On these periods, see R. W. Hutchinson, *Prehistoric Crete*, pp. 137–98, 267–316; R. F. Willetts, *Cretan Cults and Festivals*, pp. 8–37.

42. On sacred caves, see M. P. Nilsson, *The Minoan-Mycenaean Religion*, pp. 53 ff.; Charles Picard, *Les religions préhelléniques*, pp. 58 ff., 130–31; Willetts, *Cretan Cults and Festivals*, pp. 141 ff.

sheltered the infant Zeus; it was there that the future master of Olympus came into the world, and the nursling's cries were smothered under the clashing of the Curetes' shields. The armed dance of the Curetes probably constituted an initiation ceremony, performed by the young men's brotherhoods (cf. § 83). For certain caves were used by the brotherhoods for their secret rites—for example, the cave on Mount Ida, which was the scene of the assemblies of the Dactyls, the mythological personification of a brotherhood of master metallurgists.

As is well known, caves played a religious role from the Paleolithic. The labyrinth takes over and enlarges this role; entering a cave or a labyrinth was equivalent to a descent into Hades, in other words, to a ritual death of the initiatory type. The mythology of the famous labyrinth of Minos is obscure and fragmentary, but its most dramatic episodes are connected with an initiation. The original meaning of this mythico-ritual scenario was probably forgotten long before the first written documents that attest to it. The saga of Theseus, and especially his entrance into the labyrinth and his victorious fight with the Minotaur, will engage our attention later (§ 94). But it is appropriate at this point to mention the ritual function of the labyrinth as initiatory ordeal.

The excavations at Cnossus have revealed no trace of Daedalus' fabulous handiwork. Nevertheless, the labyrinth appears on Cretan coins of the classic period, and labyrinths are mentioned in connection with other cities. As for its etymology, the word had been explained as meaning "house of the double ax" (*labrys*), in other words, designating the royal palace of Cnossus. But the Achaean word for "ax" was *pelekys* (cf. Mesopotamian *pilakku*). More probably the term derives from the Asiatic *labra/laura*, "stone," "cave." Hence "labyrinth" designated an underground quarry, hewn out by human hands. And in fact the cave of Ampelusia, near Gortyna, is still called a "labyrinth" in our day.[43] For the moment, we will point out the archaism of the ritual role of caves. We shall return to the persistence of this role, for it admirably illustrates the continuity of certain religious ideas and initiatory scenarios, from prehistory down into modern times (§ 92).

Feminine figurines increase in number during the Neolithic; they are characterized by their bell-shaped skirt, which leaves the breasts

43. P. Faure, "Spéléologie crétoise et humanisme," p. 47.

bare, and their arms, raised in a gesture of worship. Whether they represent *ex votos* or "idols," these figurines indicate the religious preeminence of woman and, above all, the primacy of the Goddess. Later documents confirm and define this primacy. If we judge by the representations of processions, palace festivals, and scenes of sacrifice, women played a large part in all these activities.[44] The goddesses are represented veiled or partly naked, pressing their breasts or raising their arms in token of benediction.[45] Other images represent them as Mistress of Wild Beasts (*potnia therōn*). A seal from Cnossus shows the Lady of the Mountains pointing her scepter down toward a male worshiper, who covers his eyes.[46] On the intaglios, the goddess is seen preceded by a lion, or grasping a doe or a ram, or standing between two animals, etc. As we shall see, the Mistress of Wild Beasts survives in Greek mythology and religion (cf. § 92).

The cult was celebrated on the summits of mountains as well as in palace chapels or private houses. And everywhere the goddesses are found at the center of religious activity. The beginning of the Middle Minoan (2100–1900 B.C.) furnishes our earliest evidence for sanctuaries on high places. At first these are only modest enclosures; later they are small edifices. In the sanctuaries at Petsofa, as on Mount Juktas, the thick layer of ashes has yielded a number of human and animal figures in terra cotta. Nilsson holds that a goddess of nature was worshiped there, with casting of votive figurines into fires that were periodically ignited.[47] More complex, and still enigmatic, are the so-called agrarian or vegetation cults. Of rural origin, they were incorporated, at least symbolically, into the palace services. But they were chiefly celebrated in the sacred enclosures. To judge from intaglios and the paintings and reliefs on vases, these cults comprised dances, processions of sacred objects, and lustrations.

Trees played a central role. The iconographic documents show various personages in the act of touching leaves, worshiping the goddess of vegetation, or performing ritual dances. Certain scenes

44. Picard, *Les religions préhistoriques*, pp. 71, 159 ff.
45. Evans, *Palace of Minos*, vol. 2, pp. 277 ff.; Picard, *Religions préhistoriques*, pp. 74 ff.; Nilsson, *Minoan-Mycenaean Religion*, pp. 296 ff. The goddesses are sometimes replaced by columns and pillars; see Picard, p. 77; Nilsson, pp. 250 ff.
46. Picard, p. 63. But Nilsson considers this impression to be comparatively late, and Hutchinson makes it Mycenaean (*Prehistoric Crete*, p. 206).
47. Nilsson, *Minoan-Mycenaean Religion*, p. 75.

stress the extravagant, not to say ecstatic, nature of the rite: a naked woman passionately clasps the trunk of a tree; an officiant pulls the tree away with averted face, while his companion appears to be weeping on a tomb.[48] Such scenes have been rightly viewed as depicting not only the yearly drama of vegetation but also the religious experience inspired by discovering the mystical solidarity between man and plant (cf. §§ 12, 14).[49]

41. Characteristic features of Minoan religion

According to Picard, "as yet, we have no proof of the existence of an adult male god."[50] The goddess is sometimes escorted by an armed acolyte, but his role is obscure. Nevertheless, certain vegetation gods were undoubtedly known, for the Greek myths refer to hierogamies that took place in Crete, hierogamies characteristic of the agrarian religions. Persson has attempted, on the basis of iconographic representations, to reconstruct the ritual scenario of the periodical death and resurrection of vegetation. The Swedish scholar believed that he could place the different scenes of the cult in the seasons of the agrarian cycle: spring (epiphany of the goddess of nature and her worship by officiants, etc.); summer (epiphany of the god of vegetation, etc.); winter (ritual laments; scenes representing the departure of the divinities, etc.).[51] Some of these interpretations are persuasive, but the reconstruction of the whole scenario is disputed.

What seems to be certain is that the majority of the iconographic documents had a religious meaning and that the cult was centered on the "mysteries" of life, death, and rebirth; hence it included initiation rites, funerary laments, orgiastic and ecstatic ceremonies. As Francis Vian rightly emphasizes:

> It would be a mistake to conclude, from the smallness of the places devoted to it, that religion played little part in the princely dwellings. The fact is that it is the palace in its entirety that is sacred, for

48. Evans, *Palace of Minos*, vol. 2, pp. 838 ff.; Nilsson, *Minoan-Mycenaean Religion*, pp. 268 ff.; Axel W. Persson, *The Religion of Greece in Prehistoric Times*, pp. 38–39.

49. Picard, *Religions préhistoriques*, p. 152.

50. Ibid., p. 80. The masculine figures represent worshipers (ibid., p. 154).

51. Persson, *Religion of Greece in Prehistoric Times*, pp. 25–104.

it is the residence of the divine patroness and of the priest-king
who serves as intercessor between her and men. The dance floors
surrounded by tiers of steps, the inner courts in which altars stand,
the storerooms themselves, are religious installations. The throne
was an object of veneration, as is proved by the symbolic griffons
that flank it at Cnossus and Pylos; possibly it was even reserved
for the epiphany of the goddess rather than for the sovereign.[52]

It is important to emphasize the function of the palace as ceremonial center. The sacred bullfights, in which the bull was not killed,
were performed in the spaces surrounded by tiers of steps, the so-
called theatrical areas of the palaces. Paintings at Cnossus show us
acrobats of both sexes vaulting over bulls. Despite Nilsson's skepticism, the religious meaning of "acrobats" is indubitable: passing
across the running bull constitutes a perfect initiatory ordeal.[53] Very
probably the legend of Theseus' companions, seven youths and seven
maidens "offered" to the Minotaur, reflects the memory of such an
initiatory ordeal. Unfortunately, we know nothing of the mythology
of the divine bull and his role in the cult. Probably the specifically
Cretan cult object known as "horns of consecration" represents the
stylization of the frontal aspect of a bull. Its omnipresence confirms
the importance of its religious function: the horns served to consecrate objects placed between them.

The religious meaning and the symbolism of a certain number of
cult objects are still in dispute. The double ax was certainly used in
sacrifices. It is found in an area of considerable extent outside of
Crete. In Asia Minor, as symbol of the thunderbolt, it is the emblem
of the storm god. But as early as the Paleolithic, it is also found
beside a naked goddess in Iraq, at Tell Arpachiyah. In Crete, too, the
double ax is seen in the hands of women—priestesses or goddesses—
or on their heads. Taking into consideration its double cutting edge,
Evans explained it as an emblem symbolizing the union of the
complementary masculine and feminine principles.

Columns and pillars probably shared in the cosmological symbolism of the *axis mundi*, already documented from prehistory on

52. F. Vian, "La religion de la Crète minoenne et de la Grèce achéenne,"
in Henri-Charles Puech, ed., *Histoire des religions*, vol. 1, p. 475. Evans had
already called the king of Cnossus a priest-king, a term accepted by Nilsson
(pp. 486 ff.) and Picard (pp. 70 ff.). See also Willetts, *Cretan Cults*, pp. 84 ff.
53. Evans, *Palace of Minos*, vol. 3, p. 220, fig. 154; Picard, pp. 144, 199;
Persson, pp. 93 ff.; J. W. Graham, *The Palaces of Crete*, pp. 73 ff.

(cf. §12). The colonnettes surmounted by birds can be variously interpreted, since the bird can represent the soul as well as the epiphany of a goddess. In any case, columns and pillars replace the goddess, "for they are sometimes seen, like her, flanked by lions or griffons heraldically attached." [54]

The cult of the dead played a considerable part. Corpses were introduced from above into the deep chambers of the ossuaries. As elsewhere in Asia Minor and the Mediterranean, underground libations were bestowed on the dead. The living could go down into certain chambers, furnished with benches for the cult. Probably the funeral service was performed under the auspices of the Goddess (cf. § 35). In fact, the rock-cut tomb of a priest-king of Cnossus comprised a pillared crypt, whose blue-painted ceiling represented the celestial vault; above, a chapel resembling the palace sanctuaries of the Mother Goddess had been built. [55]

The most precious, but also the most enigmatic, document concerning Cretan religion is constituted by the two decorated panels of a sarcophagus excavated at Hagia Triada. To be sure, this document reflects the religious ideas of its period (thirteenth to twelfth centuries), when the Mycenaeans were already established in Crete. Nevertheless, insofar as the scenes depicted on the panels are susceptible of a coherent interpretation, they evoke Minoan and Oriental beliefs and customs. One of the panels depicts the sacrifice of a bull: three priestesses advance toward it in procession; on the other side of the victim, whose throat has been cut, a blood sacrifice before a sacred tree is shown. On the second panel we see the completion of the funeral libation: a priestess pours the red liquid into a large urn. The last scene is the most mysterious: in front of his tomb, the dead man, in a long robe, lends his presence to the funerary offering; three male sacrificers bring him a small boat and two calves. [56]

54. Picard, p. 77.
55. Evans, *Palace of Minos*, vol. 4, pt. 2, pp. 962 ff. Picard cites the tradition transmitted by Diodorus (4. 76–80; 16. 9), according to which Minos was buried in a crypt-tomb over which a temple dedicated to Aphrodite, who inherited the role of the Aegean Goddess, was built (*Religions préhistoriques*, p. 173).
56. See the reproductions in Paribeni, "Il sarcofago dipinto . . . ," pls. I–III, and J. Harrison, *Themis*, figs. 31–38. See also Nilsson, pp. 426 ff.; Picard, pp. 168 ff. The marine voyage to the afterlife left traces in the Greek conception of the Isles of the Blessed; see Hesiod, *Works and Days* 167 ff.; Pindar, *Second Olympian* 67 ff.

A number of scholars, judging from his appearance (according to Picard, "one would say a mummy"), hold that the dead man is deified. The hypothesis is plausible. The representation would then be of a privileged person, such as the priest-king of Cnossus or one of the Greek heroes (Heracles, Achilles, Menelaus). However, it seems more likely that the scenes suggest, not the dead man's *divinization*, but the accomplishment of his *initiation*, a ceremony of the mystery-religion type, able to insure him a happy postexistence. And in fact Diodorus (first century B.C.) had already noted the similarity between the Cretan religion and the mystery religions. Now this type of religion will later be suppressed in so-called Dorian Greece and will live on only within certain closed societies, the *thiasoi* (perhaps a pre-Hellenic word).[57]

The tradition transmitted by Diodorus is of the highest interest, for it indicates the limits of the process of assimilation of Oriental and Mediterranean religious ideas by the Āryan-speaking conquerors.

42. Continuity of the pre-Hellenic religious structures

The deciphering of Linear B has proved that, about 1400 B.C., Greek was spoken and written at Cnossus. It follows, therefore, that the Mycenaean invaders played a decisive part not only in the destruction of the Minoan civilization but also in its final period; in other words, during its last phase Cretan civilization also included continental Greece. If we consider the fact that, before the invasion by the Mycenaeans, influences from Egypt and Asia Minor[58] had resulted in an Asianic-Mediterranean synthesis, we can gauge the antiquity and complexity of the Greek cultural phenomenon. Hellenism sends its roots into Egypt and Asia; but it is the contribution of the Mycenaean conquerors that will produce the "Greek miracle."

The tablets unearthed at Cnossus, Pylos, and Mycenae mention the Homeric gods under their classical names: Zeus, Hera, Athena, Poseidon, and Dionysus. Unfortunately, the information they afford regarding mythology and cult is rather meager; mention is

57. Picard, p. 142. See also § 99.
58. It should be noted that the influences were also exercised in the opposite direction.

made of Zeus Dictaeus and of Daedalus, of "slaves of the god," of the "slave of Athena," of names of priestesses, etc. Decidedly more significant is the fame of Crete in the mythology and religion of classical Greece. It is in Crete that Zeus was held to have had his birth and death; Dionysus, Apollo, Heracles performed their childhood exploits in Crete; it is there that Demeter loved Iasion and that Minos received the laws and, with Rhadamanthys, became judge in Hades. And it was still from Crete that, at the height of the classical period, accredited purifiers were summoned.[59] The island was endowed with the fabulous virtues of the period of the *primordium*: for classical Greece, Minoan Crete shared in the prodigies of "origins" and of "autochthony."

There can be no doubt that the religious traditions of the Greeks were modified by symbiosis with the autochthonous inhabitants, in Crete as well as elsewhere in the Aegean zone. Nilsson had pointed out that, of the four religious centers of classical Greece—Delphi, Delos, Eleusis, and Olympia—the first three were inherited from the Mycenaeans. The persistence of certain Minoan religious structures has been aptly brought out. It has been possible to show the prolongation of the Minoan-Mycenaean chapel in the Greek sanctuary and the continuity between the Cretan cult of the hearth and that of the Mycenaean palaces. The image of the *psychē*-butterfly was familiar to the Minoans. The origins of the cult of Demeter are documented in Crete, and the oldest sanctuary at Eleusis dates from Mycenaean times. "Certain architectural and other dispositions of the mystery temples of classical times appear to derive, more or less, from installations recorded in pre-Hellenic Crete."[60]

As in pre-Āryan India, it is above all the cults of the Goddesses, and the rites and beliefs related to fertility, death, and the soul's survival, which persisted. In certain cases the continuity is found from prehistory down to modern times. To cite only one example, the cave of Skoteino, "one of the most grandiose and picturesque in all Crete," is 60 meters deep and has four levels; at the end of the second level are two "cult idols, set up above, and in front of, a stone altar" —a woman and "a beardless bust with a sardonic smile." In front of these two statues "the fragments of vessels reach a height of several meters; others litter the floor of the third underground level.

59. Picard, p. 73.
60. Ibid., p. 142.

... Chronologically, they follow one another without a break from the beginning of the second millennium B.C. to the end of the Roman period."[61] The sanctity of the cave has persisted down to our day. Very near by is a small white chapel dedicated to the Parasceve (Good Friday). On July 26 there is an assemblage at the entrance to the cave. It consists of "the entire population of the valley of the Aposelemi and of the Chersonese region; there is dancing in two areas under the vault and heavy drinking, and love songs are sung as ritually as mass was heard in the near-by chapel."[62]

Continuity is also demonstrated in respect to other specific expressions of archaic Cretan religiosity. Sir Arthur Evans emphasized the solidarity between the tree cult and the veneration of sacred stones. A similar solidarity is found in the cult of Athena Parthenos at Athens: a pillar associated with the sacred tree (the olive) and with the owl, the goddess's emblematic bird. Evans also showed the survival of the pillar cult down to modern times; for example, the sacred pillar at Tekekioi, near Skoplje, a replica of the Minoan column, venerated by both Christians and Muslims. The belief that sacred springs are associated with goddesses is found again in classical Greece, where springs were worshiped as Nereids; it persists in our day: fairies are still called *Neraides*.

There is no need to multiply examples. It should be remembered that a similar process of continuity of archaic religious structures is characteristic of all folk cultures, from western Europe and the Mediterranean to the plain of the Ganges and China (cf. §14). For our purpose, it is important to emphasize the fact that this religious complex, linking goddesses of fertility and death with rites and beliefs concerning initiation and the survival of the soul, was not incorporated into the Homeric religion. Despite symbiosis with the countless pre-Hellenic traditions, the Āryan-speaking conquerors succeeded in imposing their pantheon and in maintaining their specific religious style (see chapters 10–11).

61. P. Faure, "Spéléologie crétoise et humanisme," p. 40.
62. Ibid., p. 40. Numerous caves are dedicated to saints, and more than a hundred chapels are located in caves (ibid., p. 45).

6 The Religions of The Hittites and The Canaanites

43. Anatolian symbiosis and Hittite syncretism

The surprising religious continuity that existed in Anatolia, from the seventh millennium to the introduction of Christianity, has been remarked upon. "Indeed, there is no solution of continuity between the shapeless statuettes of a masculine divinity standing on a bull, like the ones found at Çatal Hüyük on level VI (ca. 6000 B.C.), the representations of the storm god from the Hittite period, and the statues of Jupiter Dolichenus, worshiped by the soldiers of the Roman legions; nor between the goddess with leopards from Çatal Hüyük, the Hittite goddess Hebat, and the Cybele of the classical period."[1]

At least in part, this continuity is the consequence of an astonishing vocation for religious syncretism. The Indo-European ethnic group that modern historiography designates by the name Hittites dominated Anatolia during the second millennium (the Old Kingdom, ca. 1740–1460 B.C., and the Empire, ca. 1460–1200 B.C.). By subjugating the Hattians—the earliest Anatolian population whose language is known—the Āryan-speaking invaders began a process of cultural symbiosis that continued long after the collapse of their political creations. Soon after entering Anatolia, the Hittites underwent Babylonian influences. Later, and especially during the Empire, they assimilated the essentials of the culture of the Hurrians, a non-Indo-European population inhabiting the northern regions of Mesopotamia and Syria. Hence, in the Hittite pantheon, divinities of Sumero-Akkadian stock stood side by side with Anatolian and

1. Maurice Vieyra, "La religion de l'Anatolie antique," in *Histoire des religions*, vol. 1, p. 258.

Hurrian divinities. The greater part of the Hittite myths and rituals so far known have parallels, and even models, in the Hattian or Hurrian religious traditions. The Indo-European heritage proves to be the least significant. Nevertheless, despite the heterogeneity of their sources, the creations of the Hittite genius—first of all, its religious art—do not lack originality.

The divinities were distinguished by the terrifying and luminous force that emanated from them (cf. "the divine splendor," *melammu*, § 20). The pantheon was very large, but of certain gods nothing is known except their names. Each important town was the principal residence of a deity, who was, however, surrounded by other divine personages. As everywhere in the ancient Near East, the divinities "lived in" the temples; the priests and their acolytes had the duty of bathing, dressing, and feeding them and entertaining them with dances and music. From time to time the gods left their temples and went traveling; sometimes these absences could be used to explain failures in the answering of requests.

The pantheon was conceived as a large family, having as its head the first couple, the patrons of the Hittite country: the storm god and a Great Goddess. The storm god was known principally by his Hurrian name, Teshub, the name that we shall adopt. His wife was named, in the Hurrian language, Hebat. Their sacred animals—the bull and, for Hebat, the lion (or the panther)—confirm the continuity from prehistory (cf. §13). The most famous Great Goddess was known by the name "sun" goddess of Arinna (in the Hattian language, Wurusema). In fact, she was an epiphany of the *same* Mother Goddess,[2] since she is praised as "queen of the land, queen of Earth and Heaven, protectress of the kings and queens of the Hatti land," etc. Probably the "solarization" represents an act of homage, performed when the goddess of Arinna became the patroness of the Hittite kingdom.

The Babylonian ideogram "Ishtar" was used to designate the numerous local goddesses, whose Anatolian names are unknown. The Hurrian name was Shanshka. But it must be borne in mind that

2. In a beautiful prayer, Queen Pudu-hepas identifies the goddess of Arinna with Hebat (see the translation by A. Goetze, *ANET*, p. 393). However, this is the only document that points in this direction. In the rituals and lists of offerings the names of the two goddesses are given one after the other. This fact may be explained by the importance obtained, under the Hittite sovereigns, by the two famous epiphanies of the Mother Goddess.

the Babylonian Ishtar, goddess of love and war, was known in Anatolia; hence in certain cases we have an Anatolian-Babylonian syncretism. The sun god, son of Teshub, was considered, like Shamash, the defender of right and justice. No less popular was Telepinus, also a son of Teshub, whose myth we shall soon consider.

As for religious life, the sources inform us only about the official cult. The prayers whose texts have been preserved belong to the royal milieu. In other words, we know nothing of the beliefs and rituals of the people. However, there can be no doubt of the roles attributed to the goddesses of fecundity and the god of storms. The seasonal festivals, especially the New Year festival (*purulli*), were celebrated by the king, representative of the Āryan-speaking conquerors; but similar ceremonies had been performed in the country from Neolithic times.

Black magic was forbidden by the law code; those guilty of it were executed. This indirectly confirms the extraordinary repute that certain archaic practices enjoyed in popular circles. On the other hand, the considerable number of texts so far discovered proves that white magic was openly and frequently practiced; it chiefly involved rituals of purification and the banishment of evil.

The prestige and the religious role of the king are considerable. Sovereignty is a gift of the gods. "To me, the King, have the gods— Sun God and Storm God—entrusted the land and my house. . . . (The gods) have taken care of the kings. They have renewed his strength and set no limit to his years."[3] The king is "loved" by a great god. (However, fictitious divine descent, of the Mesopotamian type, is not documented.) His prosperity is identified with that of the whole people. The sovereign is the vicar of the gods on earth, but he also represents the people before the pantheon.

No text describing the ceremonial of the king's consecration has been found, but it is known that the sovereign was anointed with oil, clothed in a special dress, and crowned; finally, he received a royal name. The sovereign was also a high priest, and, alone or with the queen, he celebrated the most important festivals of the year. After their death the kings were deified. In speaking of the death of a king, the phrase "he has become a god" was used. His statue was placed in the temple, and the reigning sovereigns brought him offerings.

3. Ritual for the erection of a new palace, trans. Goetze, *ANET*, p. 357.

According to certain texts, the king, during his lifetime, was considered to be the incarnation of his deified ancestors.[4]

44. The "god who disappears"

The originality of "Hittite"[5] religious thought is seen especially in the reinterpretation of some important myths. One of the most notable themes is that of the "god who disappears." In the best-known version, the protagonist is Telepinus. Other texts give the role to his father, the storm god, to the sun god, or to certain goddesses. The background, like the name Telepinus, is Hattian. The Hittite versions were composed in connection with various rituals; in other words, the recitation of the myth played a fundamental part in the cult.

Since the beginning of the narrative[6] is lost, we do not know why Telepinus decides to "disappear." Perhaps it is because men have angered him. But the consequences of his disappearance immediately make themselves felt. Fires go out on hearths, gods and men feel "stifled"; the ewe neglects her lamb, the cow her calf; "grain and spelt thrive no longer"; animals and men do not copulate; the pastures dry up, the springs fail. (This is, perhaps, the earliest literary version of the well-known mythological motif of the "waste land," made famous by the Grail romances.) Then the sun god sends messengers—first the eagle, then the storm god himself—to look for Telepinus, but without success. Finally, the Mother Goddess sends the bee; it finds the god asleep in a grove, and, by stinging him, wakes him. Furious, Telepinus brings down such calamities on the land that the gods take fright and, to calm him, have recourse to magic. By magical ceremonies and formulas, Telepinus is purged of his anger and of "evil."[7] Pacified, he finally returns to his place among the gods—and life resumes its rhythms.

4. O. R. Gurney, "Hittite Kingship," p. 115.
5. We have added the quotation marks to indicate that, in many cases, the myths are originally Hattian or Hurrian, translated or adapted into the Hittite language.
6. We use the translations by A. Goetze, *ANET*, pp. 126–28, by Güterbock, *Mythologies of the Ancient World*, pp. 144 ff., and by Vieyra in R. Labat, ed., *Les religions du Proche-Orient*, pp. 532 ff. See also Theodor Gaster, *Thespis*, pp. 302–9.
7. Similar pacification rites are performed by the priest; see the text translated by Gaster, *Thespis*, pp. 311–12.

Telepinus is a god who, angered, hides—that is to say, disappears from the world around him. He does not belong to the category of vegetation gods, who die and return to life periodically. Nevertheless, his disappearance has the same disastrous consequences on all levels of cosmic life. Furthermore, "disappearance" and "epiphany" signify both descent to the underworld and return to earth (cf. Dionysus, § 122). But what distinguishes Telepinus from the vegetation gods is the fact that his discovery and reanimation by the bee make the situation worse; it is purgation rituals that succeed in pacifying him.

The specific characteristic of Telepinus is his demonic rage, which threatened to ruin the entire country. What we have here is the capricious and irrational fury of a fertility god against his own creation, *life* in all its forms. Similar conceptions of divine ambivalence are found elsewhere; they will be elaborated especially in Hinduism (cf. Śiva, Kālī). The fact that the role of Telepinus was also given to the gods of the storm and the sun and to certain goddesses—that is, in general, to divinities governing various sectors of *cosmic life*—proves that the myth refers to a more complex drama than that of vegetation; in fact, it illustrates the incomprehensible mystery of the destruction of the Creation *by its own creators*.

45. Conquering the Dragon

On the occasion of the New Year festival, *purulli*, the myth of the battle between the storm god and the dragon (*illuyankas*)[8] was ritually recited. In a first encounter, the storm god is vanquished and begs for the help of the other divinities. The goddess Inaras makes ready a banquet and invites the Dragon. Before this, she had asked the help of a mortal, Hupasiyas. He accepted, on condition that she would sleep with him; the goddess consented. The Dragon eats and drinks so voraciously that he cannot descend to his lair again, and Hupasiyas binds him with a rope. Enter the storm god, who kills the Dragon without a fight. This version of the myth ends with an incident well known in fairy tales: Hupasiyas comes to live in Inaras' house but does not heed the goddess's warning not to look out the window

8. Illuyankas, literally "dragon," "serpent," is also a proper name.

during her absence. He sees his wife and children and begs Inaras to let him go home. The rest of the text is lost, but Hupasiyas is presumably killed.

The second version gives this detail: the Dragon conquers the storm god and takes his heart and eyes. Then the storm god marries the daughter of a poor man and has a son by her. When he grows up, the son decides to marry the Dragon's daughter. Instructed by his father, the young man has no sooner entered his wife's house than he asks for the storm god's heart and eyes; he obtains them and gives them to his father. In possession of his "forces," the storm god again meets the Dragon, "near the sea," and succeeds in vanquishing him. But, by marrying his daughter, the son has obliged himself to be loyal to the Dragon, and he asks his father not to spare him. "So the storm god killed the Dragon and his own son too." [9]

The fight between a god and a dragon is a well-known mythico-ritual theme. A first defeat of the god and his mutilation have their parallels in the fight between Zeus and the giant Typhon. The latter succeeded in cutting the tendons out of Zeus's hands and feet, took him on his shoulders, and carried him to a cave in Cilicia. Typhon hid the tendons in the pelt of a bear, but Hermes and Aegipan finally managed to steal them. Zeus recovered his power and overthrew the giant.[10] The motif of the theft of a vital organ is well known. But in the Hittite version the Dragon is no longer the terrifying monster that appears in a number of cosmogonic myths or myths of combats for the sovereignty of the world (cf. Tiamat, Leviathan, Typhon, etc.). Illuyankas already represents certain characteristics of the dragons of folktales, for he lacks intelligence and is a glutton.[11]

The storm god, vanquished a first time (theme documented elsewhere), ends by triumphing not by virtue of his own heroism but with the help of a human being (Hupasiyas or the storm god's son by a mortal woman). It is true that, in both versions, this human personage has previously been equipped with a force of divine origin: he is the lover of the goddess Inaras or the son of the storm god. In both cases, though for different reasons, the helper is done away with by the very author of his quasi-divinization. After sleeping

9. Trans. Goetze, *ANET*, pp. 125–26; Vieyra, in Labat, *Les religions du Proche-Orient*, pp. 526 ff.
10. Apollodorus, *Bibliotheca* 1. 6. 3.
11. See Gaster, *Thespis*, pp. 259–60.

with Inaras, Hupasiyas no longer has the right to rejoin his family—that is, human society—for, having shared in the divine condition, he could transmit it to other human beings.

Despite this partial folklorization, the myth of Illuyankas played a central role: it was ritually recited in the setting of the New Year festival. Certain texts show the existence of a ritual combat between two opposing groups,[12] comparable to the Babylonian *akitu* ceremony. The cosmogonic meaning of the myth, evident in the struggle between Marduk and Tiamat, is replaced by the competition for the sovereignty of the world (cf. Zeus-Typhon). The god's victory insures the stability and prosperity of the country. We may presume that, before its folklorization, the myth presented the reign of the Dragon as a "chaotic" period, endangering the very sources of life (the Dragon symbolizes not only "virtuality" (potentiality) and darkness, but also drought, the suspension of norms, and death).

46. Kumarbi and sovereignty

Exceptional interest attaches to what has been called the Hurrito-Hittite "theogony,"[13] that is, the sequence of mythical events whose protagonist is Kumarbi, the father of the gods. The initial episode, "Kingship in Heaven," explains the succession of the first gods. In the beginning, Alalu was king, and Anu, the most important of the gods, bowed before him and served him. But after nine years Anu attacked and vanquished him. Then Alalu took refuge in the subterranean world, and Kumarbi became the new sovereign's servant. Nine years passed, and Kumarbi in his turn attacked Anu. The latter fled, flying into the sky, but Kumarbi pursued him, caught him by the feet, and threw him to the ground, after biting his "loins."[14] Since he was laughing and rejoicing over his exploit, Anu told him that he had been impregnated. Kumarbi spat out what was still in his mouth,

12. See the text (KUB XVII 95, III 9–17) translated by Gaster, *Thespis*, pp. 267 ff. See also O. R. Gurney, *The Hittites*, p. 155. Another text refers to the "fixing of the destinies" by the assembly of the gods (see Gurney, *The Hittites*, p. 152, and his "Hittite Kingship," pp. 107 ff.).

13. The reference is to Hittite translations from Hurrian texts, made ca. 1300 B.C. The Hurrian "theogony" reflects syncretism with the earlier Sumerian and North Syrian traditions.

14. The first translators proposed "knees." The two terms are euphemisms for the male genital organ.

but a part of Anu's virility entered his body, and he became big with three gods. The rest of the text is badly mutilated, but it is presumed that Anu's "children," with Teshub, the storm god leading them, make war on Kumarbi and dethrone him.

The following episode, the "Song of Ullikummi," relates the effort made by Kumarbi to recover the royalty that Teshub had taken from him. In order to create a rival able to conquer Teshub, he impregnated a rock with his semen. The product of this union was Ullikummi, an anthropomorphic being made of stone. Placed on the shoulder of the giant Ubelluri, who, with half his body emerging from the sea, supports heaven and earth (this is the Hurrian analogue of Atlas), Ullikummi grew so fast that he reached the sky. Teshub went to the seaside and attacked the diorite giant but was vanquished. The text presents considerable lacunae, but the sequence of events can be reconstructed. Ullikummi threatens to destroy all mankind, and the gods, in alarm, assemble and decide to appeal to Ea. The latter at once goes to Ellil and then to Ubelluri and asks them if they have learned that a stone giant has resolved to overthrow Teshub. Ellil's answer is lost. As for Ubelluri, he reports a detail of great importance. "When they built heaven and earth upon me, I did not know anything. When they came and separated the heaven from the earth with a cleaver, I did not know that either. Now my right shoulder is a little sore. But I do not know who that god is." Ea then asks the "olden gods" to "open the ancient storehouses of the fathers and forefathers" and to bring the old knife with which they had separated heaven from earth. Ullikummi's feet are sawed, thus crippling him, but the diorite man still boasts that the celestial kingship was assigned to him by his father, Kumarbi. Finally, he is overthrown by Teshub.

This myth is remarkable in several respects. First, it contains certain archaic elements: Kumarbi's self-fecundation by swallowing the sexual organ of the god whom he has dethroned; the sexual union of a divine being with a mass of rock, resulting in the birth of an anthropomorphic mineral monster; the relations between this diorite giant and the Hurrian Atlas, Ubelluri. The first episode can be interpreted as an allusion to the bisexuality of Kumarbi, a characteristic of primordial divinities (cf., for example, Tiamat, Zurvan). In this case, Teshub, who irrevocably obtains the sovereignty, is the son of a celestial god (Anu) by an androgynous divinity.[15] As for the fecundation of a rock by a superhuman being, a similar myth is found in Phrygia: Papas (= Zeus) fertilizes a stone named Agdos, and it engenders a hermaphroditic monster, Agditis; but the gods castrate Agditis, thus transforming him into the goddess Cybele (Pausanias 7. 17. 10–12).

Much more widespread are the myths that recount the birth of men from stones; these are found in Asia Minor, in the Far East, and in Polynesia. Probably what is involved is the mythical theme of the autochthony of the first men; they are engendered by a chthonian Great Goddess. Certain gods (Mithra, for example) are also imagined as emerging from a rock, like the sun, whose light shines out every morning above the mountains. But this mythical theme cannot be reduced to a solar epiphany.[16] It could be said that the *petra genetrix* reinforces the sacrality of Mother Earth with the prodigious virtues with which stones were held to be imbued. As we have seen (§ 34), the sacredness of massive rock was nowhere more exalted than in the megalithic religions. It is not by chance that Ullikummi is set on the shoulder of the giant who holds up the heavens; the "diorite man" is himself also preparing to become a *columna universalis*. However, this motif, specifically characteristic of the megalithic religions, is integrated into a larger context: the struggle for succession to the divine sovereignty.

47. Conflicts between divine generations

From the first translation of the Hurrian/Hittite text, analogies were noted between it and the Phoenician theogony, as presented by Philo of Byblos, and, on the other hand, between it and the tradition transmitted by Hesiod. According to Philo,[17] the first sovereign god

15. According to certain mythological fragments, it seems that the gods who were "inside" Kumarbi discussed with him through what apertures of his body they were to emerge (Güterbock, *Mythologies of the Ancient World*, pp. 157–58).

16. In fact, Mithra's first combat, when he had only just emerged from the rock, is with the Sun. Victorious, he takes away the Sun's radiant crown. But soon afterward the two gods pledge friendship by shaking hands.

17. Some fragments of his *Phoenician History* have been preserved by Eusebius and Porphyry. Philo states that he summarizes the writings of Sanchoniaton, a Phoenician scholar who was supposed to have lived "before the Trojan War." See Clemen, *Die phönikische Religion*, p. 28.

was Elioun (in Greek, Hypsistos, "The Most High"), corresponding in the Hurrian/Hittite mythology to Alalu. From his union with Bruth there came into the world Uranus (corresponding to Anu) and Ge (Gaea). In their turn, these two engendered four sons, the first of whom, El (or Kronos), corresponds to Kumarbi. As the result of a quarrel with his wife, Uranus tries to destroy his progeny, but El forges a saw (or lance?) for himself, drives out his father, and becomes the sovereign.[18] Finally, Baal (representing the fourth generation and corresponding to Teshub and Zeus) obtains the sovereignty; exceptionally, he obtains it without a combat.

Until the discovery of Ugaritic literature there was doubt concerning the genuineness of this tradition transmitted by Philo. But the succession of divine generations is documented in Canaanite mythology (see § 49). The fact that Hesiod (§ 83) mentions only three generations—represented by Uranus, Kronos, and Zeus—reconfirms the genuineness of the Philo ("Sanchoniaton") version, for the latter mentions, before Uranus (= Anu), the reign of Elioun (= Alalu). It is probable that the Phoenician version of the myth of divine sovereignty derives from, or was strongly influenced by, the Hurrian myth. We may presume that Hesiod made use of the same tradition, known in Greece either through the Phoenicians or directly from the Hittites.

It is important to emphasize at once the "specialized" and at the same time syncretistic character of this myth, and not only in its Hurrian/Hittite version (in which, besides, there are a number of Sumero-Akkadian elements).[19] The *Enuma elish* likewise presents (1) a series of divine generations, (2) the battle of the young gods against the old gods, and (3) the victory of Marduk, who thus assumes the sovereignty. But in the Mesopotamian myth the victorious combat ends with a cosmogony, more precisely with the creation of the universe as men will know it. This myth takes its place in the series of cosmogonies that involve a combat between a god and the Dragon, followed by the dismemberment of the con-

18. It is not until thirty-two years later that El succeeds in castrating Uranus. The two acts, castration of the father and conquest of the sovereignty, which go together in the Hurrian/Hittite and Greek myths, are here separated.

19. Cf. the names of the divinities Anu, Ishtar, and perhaps Alalu; a god Alala appears in a Babylonian list as one of the ancestors of Anu (Güterbock, *Mythologies of the Ancient World*, p. 160).

quered foe. In Hesiod's *Theogony* the cosmogonic act—i.e., the separation of Heaven (Uranus) from Earth (Gaea) by the castration of Uranus—takes place at the beginning of the drama and in fact precipitates the struggle for sovereignty. The same situation obtains in the Hurrian/Hittite myth: the cosmogony—that is, the separation of Heaven and Earth—took place long before, during the period of the "olden gods."

To sum up, all the myths that recount the conflicts between successive generations of gods for the conquest of universal sovereignty justify, on the one hand, the exalted position of the last conquering god and, on the other hand, explain the present structure of the world and the actual condition of humanity.

48. A Canaanite pantheon: Ugarit

Shortly before 3000 B.C. a new civilization, that of the Early Bronze Age, appears in Palestine: *it marks the first establishment of the Semites.* Following the usage of the Bible, we may call them "Canaanites," but the name is merely conventional.[20] The invaders become sedentary, practice agriculture, and develop an urban civilization. During the next several centuries, other immigrants filter into the region, and exchanges with the neighboring countries, especially with Egypt, increase. About 2200 B.C. the Early Bronze civilization is ruined by the irruption of a new Semitic population, the Amorites, seminomadic warriors, occasional agriculturalists, but principally herders. The end of this civilization, however, constitutes the beginning of a new era. The invasion of Syria and Palestine by the Amorites (MAR.TU in Sumerian, Amurru in Akkadian) is only an episode in a much larger movement, documented, at about the same period, in Mesopotamia and Egypt. There is a constant series of attacks by impetuous and "savage" nomads,[21] hurrying on, wave after wave, from the Syrian desert, at once fascinated and exasperated

20. Canaan is not mentioned in the texts before the middle of the second millennium; see R. de Vaux, *Histoire ancienne d'Israël*, vol. 1, p. 58.

21. In the Mesopotamian literary texts of the end of the third millennium, the MAR.TU are designated as "mountain rustics," "who do not know wheat," "who know neither house not city" (texts cited by de Vaux, *Histoire ancienne d'Israël*, p. 64).

by the opulence of the cities and the cultivated fields. But, in the course of conquering them, they adopt the life style of the aborigines and become civilized. After a certain length of time their descendants will be obliged to defend themselves against the armed incursions of other barbarians leading a nomadic life on the outskirts of the cultivated areas. The process will be repeated during the last centuries of the second millennium, when the Israelites will begin to enter Canaan.

The tension and the symbiosis between the cults of agrarian fertility that flourished on the Syro-Palestinian coast and the religious ideology of the nomadic pastoralists, which was dominated by celestial and astral divinities, will reach a new intensity with the settling of the Hebrews in Canaan. It could be said that this tension, which often finally led to symbiosis, will be raised to the rank of a paradigmatic model, for it is here, in Palestine, that a new type of religious experience came into conflict with the old and venerable traditions of cosmic religiosity.

Until 1929 the available data concerning the Syro-Canaanite religion came from the Old Testament, Phoenician inscriptions, and certain Greek authors—especially Philo of Byblos (first/second centuries A.D.) but also Lucian of Samosata (second century A.D.) and Nonnus of Panopolis (fifth century). However, the Old Testament reflects the polemic against paganism, and the other sources are either late or too fragmentary. Since 1929 a large number of mytho-logical texts have been brought to light by the excavations at Ras Shamra, the ancient Ugarit, a port city on the northern coast of Syria. They are texts composed in the fourteenth to twelfth centuries but containing mythico-religious conceptions that are earlier. The documents so far deciphered and translated still do not suffice to give us a comprehensive view of Ugaritic religion and mythology. Unfortunately lacunae interrupt the narratives; the beginnings and ends of columns having been broken, there is not even general agree-ment concerning the order of the mythological episodes. Despite this fragmentary condition, the Ugaritic literature is of inestimable value. But the fact must be borne in mind that *the religion of Ugarit was never that of all Canaan.*

The interest of the Ugaritic documents lies above all in the fact that they illustrate the phases of the passage from one religious ideology to another. El is the head of the pantheon. His name means "god" in Semitic, but among the West Semites he is a personal god. He is called "Powerful," "Bull," "Father of Gods and Men,"[22] "King," "Father of the Years." He is "holy," "merciful," "very wise." On a stela of the fourteenth century he is represented enthroned, majestic, bearded, clad in a long robe, and wearing a tiara crowned by horns.[23] Up to the present, no cosmogonic text has been found.[24] However, the creation of the stars by hierogamy can be interpreted as reflecting Canaanite cosmogonic conceptions. And indeed text number 52 ("The birth of the gracious and beautiful gods") describes El impregnating his two wives, Asherah and Anath, with the Morning Star and the Evening Star.[25] Asherah, herself "engendered by El," is named "Mother of the Gods" (text number 51); she bore seventy divine sons. Except for Baal, all the gods descend from the first couple, El-Asherah.

Yet, despite the epithets that present him as a powerful god, true "Lord of the Earth," despite the fact that in the sacrificial lists his name is always mentioned first, El appears in the myths as physically weak, indecisive, senile, resigned. Certain gods treat him with scorn. Finally, his two wives, Asherah and Anath, are taken from him by Baal. We must conclude that the laudatory epithets reflect an earlier situation, when El was in fact the head of the pantheon. The replacement of an old creator and cosmocrator god by a more dynamic young god, "specialized" in cosmic fertility, is a rather frequent phenomenon. Often the creator becomes a *deus otiosus* and withdraws farther and farther from his creation. Sometimes his replacement is the result of a conflict between divine generations or between their representatives. Insofar as it is possible to reconstruct the essential themes of Ugaritic mythology, we may say that the texts show us the advancement of Baal to the supreme rank. But it is an

22. The title *ab*, "father," is one of the most frequent epithets; cf. also *ab adm*, "father of humanity" (see M. H. Pope, *El in the Ugaritic Texts*, pp. 47 ff.).

23. F. A. Schaeffer, *The Cuneiform Texts of Ras Shamra-Ugarit*, pl. XXXI, pp. 60, 62.

24. In the West Semitic inscriptions, however, El is called "Creator of the Earth"; see Pope, *WdM*, vol. 1, p. 280.

25. This myth is the model for a ritual performed at the beginning of a new cycle of seven years, which proves that at an early date El was still regarded as the author of the fertility of the earth, an eminence that will later fall to Baal. See Cyrus H. Gordon, "Canaanite Mythology," pp. 185 ff.; Ulf Oldenburg, *The Conflict between El and Baal in Canaanite Religion*, pp. 19 ff.; and Cross, *Canaanite Myth*, pp. 21 ff.

advancement obtained by force and cleverness, and it does not lack a certain ambiguity.

Baal is the only god who, while reckoned among the sons of El (since the latter was the father of all the gods), is called "Son of Dagan." This god, whose name signifies "grain," was venerated in the third millennium in the Upper and Middle Euphrates regions.[26] However, Dagan plays no part in the mythological texts from Ugarit, where Baal is the chief protagonist. The common noun *baal* ("master") became his personal name. He also has a proper name, Haddu, that is, Hadad. He is called "Rider of the Clouds," "Prince, Master of the Earth." One of his epithets is Aliyan, the "Powerful," the "Sovereign." He is the source and principle of fertility but is also a warrior, as his sister and wife Anath is at once the goddess of love and war. Beside them, the most important mythological personages are Yam, "Prince Sea, River Regent," and Mot, "Death," who challenge the young god for the supreme power. In fact, a great part of Ugaritic mythology is devoted to the conflict between El and Baal and to Baal's combats with Yam and Mot to impose and maintain his sovereignty.

49. Baal captures the sovereignty and triumphs over the Dragon

According to a badly mutilated text,[27] Baal and his confederates attack El by surprise in his palace on Mount Sapan and succeed in tying him up and wounding him. Apparently "something" falls to the ground, which can be interpreted as the castration of the father of the gods. The hypothesis is plausible, not only because, in similar conflicts for the sovereignty, Uranus and the Hurrian/Hittite god

26. The name Anath is also documented in the same regions. It is possible that Baal son of Dagan was introduced by the Amorites; see, most recently, Oldenburg, *The Conflict between El and Baal*, pp. 151 ff. In this case he must have been agglutinated with a local "Baal" = Hadad, for it is impossible to conceive of the old Canaanite religion without that famous Semitic god of the storm and hence of fertility. See also Cross, *Canaanite Myth and Hebrew Epic*, pp. 112 ff.

27. The reference is to tablet VI AB, first published by C. Virolleaud; see the translation by Oldenburg, *The Conflict between El and Baal*, pp. 185–86. The text has been interpreted by Cassuto, Pope, and Oldenburg (p. 123) as referring to Baal's attack and El's fall from his throne.

Anu are castrated, but also because, despite the hostility he shows to Baal, El will never attempt to recover his supreme position, not even when he learns that Baal has been killed by Mot.[28] For in the ancient East, such a mutilation excludes the victim of it from sovereignty. Besides, except for text number 56, in which El proves his virility by engendering the planetary gods, the Ugaritic documents seem to make him impotent. This explains his submissive and hesitant attitude and also the fact that Baal carries off his wife.

By usurping his throne on Mount Sapan, Baal forces El to take refuge at the end of the world, "at the source of the Rivers, in the hollow of the Abysses," which will henceforth be his dwelling place.[29] El laments and implores the help of his family. Yam is the first to hear him, and offers him a strong drink. El blesses him, gives him a new name, and proclaims him his successor. He further promises to build a palace for him; but he also urges him to drive Baal from the throne.

The text that describes the combat between Yam and Baal is interrupted by lacunae. Though Yam now appears to be the sovereign, El is seen, with the majority of the gods, on a mountain that is obviously no longer Mount Sapan. Since Baal has insulted Yam, by declaring that he has presumptuously raised himself to his position and that he will be destroyed, Yam sends messengers and demands that Baal surrender. The gods are frightened, and Baal reprimands them: "Raise your heads, gods, from your knees, and I myself will frighten Yam's messengers!"[30] But El receives the messengers and declares that Baal is their slave and will pay a tribute to Yam. And since it appears that Baal will prove to be threatening, El adds that the messengers can easily subdue him. However, helped by Anath, Baal prepares to confront Yam. (According to another tablet, Yam drove Baal from his throne, and it was Anath who vanquished him.)[31]

28. He addresses Asherah: "Give one of thy sons, that I may make him king" (Cyrus Gordon, *Ugaritic Manual*, 49:I:16–18; Oldenburg, p. 112).

29. Since the mountain is a celestial symbol, for a sovereign god its loss is equivalent to his fall.

30. G. R. Driver, *Canaanite Myths and Legends*, p. 79. See also Vieyra, in Labat, *Les religions du Proche-Orient*, p. 386, and Cross, *Canaanite Myths and Hebrew Epic*, pp. 114 ff.

31. "Did I not destroy the beloved of El, Yam? Did I not annihilate Nahar, the great god? Did I not muzzle Tannin (= the Dragon)? I muzzled him! I destroyed the crooked Serpent, the Powerful One with seven heads!" (trans. Oldenburg, p. 198; cf. *ANET*, p. 137). Hence this text alludes to a first

The divine blacksmith, Koshar-wa-Hasis ("Adroit and Skillful"), brings him two magical cudgels, which have the ability to hurl themselves like arrows from the hands of the user. The first cudgel strikes Yam on the shoulder, but he does not fall. The second strikes his forehead, and "Prince Sea" crashes to the ground. Baal finishes him off, and the goddess Athtart asks him to dismember and scatter his corpse.[32]

Yam is portrayed as at once god and demon. He is the son "loved by El," and, as a god, he receives sacrifices like the other members of the pantheon. On the other hand, he is an aquatic monster, a seven-headed dragon, "Prince Sea," principle and epiphany of the subterranean waters. The mythological meaning of the combat is manifold. On the one hand, on the plane of seasonal and agricultural imagery, Baal's victory signifies the triumph of rain over the sea and the subterranean waters; the rhythm of rain, representing the cosmic norm, replaces the chaotic and sterile immensity of the sea and catastrophic floods. Baal's victory marks the triumph of confidence in order and in the stability of the seasons. On the other hand, the battle with the aquatic Dragon illustrates the emergence of a young god as champion, and hence as new sovereign, of the pantheon. Finally, we can read in this episode the vengeance of the firstborn (Yam) against the usurper who has castrated and dethroned his father (El).[33]

Such combats are paradigmatic, that is, can be repeated indefinitely. It is for this reason that Yam, though "killed" by Baal, will reappear in the texts. Nor is he alone in enjoying a "circular existence." As we shall see, Baal and Mot have a similar mode of being.

50.   The palace of Baal

In order to celebrate the victory over the Dragon, Anath gives a banquet in Baal's honor. Soon after, the goddess shuts the doors of the palace and, succumbing to homicidal fury, falls to killing the

---

victory of Yam over Baal, followed by his defeat (in this case, by Anath), which corresponds to a well-known mythological theme: the god's defeat by, and triumphant revenge over, an ophidian monster.

32. Gordon, *Ugaritic Manual*, § 68:28–31, trans. Caquot and Sznycer, in Labat, ed., *Les religions du Proche-Orient*, p. 389.

33. On this motif, see Oldenburg, *Conflict*, pp. 130 ff.

guards, the soldiers, the old; in the blood that rises to her knees she girdles herself with the heads and hands of her victims. The episode is significant.[34] Parallels to it have been found in Egypt and especially in the mythology and iconography of the Indian goddess Durgā.[35] Carnage and cannibalism are characteristic features of archaic fertility goddesses. From this point of view, the myth of Anath can be classed among the elements common to the ancient agricultural civilization that extended from the eastern Mediterranean to the plain of the Ganges. In another episode, Anath threatens her own father, El: she will cover his hair and his beard with blood (text ʿnt:V: Oldenburg, p. 26). When she found Baal's lifeless body, Anath began to lament, "eating his flesh without a knife and drinking his blood without a cup."[36] It is because of her brutal and sanguinary behavior that Anath, like other goddesses of love and war, was given male attributes and hence was regarded as bisexual.

After another lacuna the text shows Baal sending messengers bearing gifts to Anath. He informs her that war is hateful to him; so let her lay down her arms and make offerings for peace and the fecundity of the fields. He tells her that he is about to create thunder and lightning so that gods and men may know that rain is coming. Anath assures him that she will follow his advice.

However, although he is sovereign, Baal has neither a palace nor a chapel, whereas the other gods have them. In other words, Baal does not own a temple sufficiently grandiose to proclaim his sovereignty. A series of episodes relates the building of the palace. Contradictions are not lacking. Indeed, though he has dethroned El, Baal needs his authorization; he sends Asherah to plead his cause, and the mother of the gods lauds the fact that henceforth Baal "will give abundance of rain" and will "send forth his voice in the clouds." El consents, and Baal instructs Koshar-wa-Hasis to build him the

34. Blood being regarded as the essence of life, it has been proposed to see in this slaughter a rite whose purpose was passage from the sterility of the Syrian late summer to the fertility of the new season; see Gray, *The Legacy of Canaan*, p. 36. The text is translated by Caquot and Sznycer in *Les religions du Proche-Orient*, pp. 393–94.

35. As it has been transmitted to us, the Egyptian myth no longer presents the primitive stage; see above, § 26. The comparison with Durgā, which Marvin Pope has emphasized (see, most recently, *WdM*, vol. 1, p. 239), had already been made by Walter Dostal, "Ein Beitrag," pp. 74 ff.

36. Text published by Virolleaud, "Un nouvel épisode du mythe ugaritique de Baal," pp. 182 ff.; cf. Albright, *Yahweh and the Gods of Canaan*, pp. 131 ff.

palace. At first Baal refuses to have his dwelling fitted with windows, for fear that Yam may enter it. But he finally agrees.[37]

The building of a temple-palace after the god's victory over the Dragon proclaims his advancement to the supreme rank. The gods build the temple-palace in honor of Marduk after the defeat of Tiamat and the creation of the world (cf. § 21). But the cosmogonic symbolism is also present in the myth of Baal. The temple-palace being an *imago mundi*, its building corresponds in a certain way to a cosmogony. In fact, by triumphing over the aquatic "chaos," by regulating the rhythm of the rains, Baal "forms" the world as it is today.[38]

51. Baal confronts Mot: Death and return to life

When the palace is finished, Baal prepares to confront Mot, "Death." The latter is a highly interesting god. He is, of course, a son of El and reigns over the subterranean world; but he represents the only known Near Eastern example of a personification (which is also a deification) of Death. Baal sends him messengers to inform him that henceforth Baal alone is king of gods and men, "so that the gods may grow fat, and human beings, the multitudes on earth, may be filled with food" (Gordon, *Ugaritic Manual*, VII:50 2; Driver, *Canaanite Myths and Legends*, p. 101). Baal orders his messengers to travel to the two mountains that mark the limits of the world, to lift them up, and to descend under the earth. They will find Mot seated on his throne in the mud, in a region covered with ordure. But they must not approach him too closely, otherwise Mot will swallow them down his enormous throat. Nor must they forget, Baal adds, that Mot is responsible for the deaths caused by torrid heat.

Mot sends back the messengers, bidding Baal come to him. For, he explains, Baal killed Yam; it is now his turn to descend to the

37. The windows might symbolize the opening in the clouds through which Baal sends rain. His temple at Ugarit was built with an opening in the roof, so that the rain fell on the god's face represented on a stela; see Schaeffer, *Cuneiform Texts*, p. 6, pl. XXXII, fig. 2. But the symbolism and function of roof apertures are more complex; see, among others, A. K. Coomaraswamy, "The Symbolism of the Dome."

38. Loren R. Fisher uses the term "creation of the Baal type" and distinguishes it from "creation of the El type"; see his "Creation at Ugarit," pp. 320 ff.

underworld.[39] This is enough to confound Baal. "Hail, Mot, son of El," he tells his messengers to say, "I am thy slave, thine forever." Exultant, Mot declares that, once he is in the underworld, Baal will lose his strength and be destroyed. He orders him to bring his sons and his suite of winds, clouds, and rain with him—and Baal consents. But before going down into the underworld, he couples with a heifer and conceives a son. Baal clothes the child in his own garment and entrusts him to El. It would seem that, at the moment of extreme danger, Baal recovers his first form, that of the cosmic bull; at the same time, he makes sure that he will have a successor in case he does not return to earth.

We do not know how Baal dies, whether he was vanquished in combat or simply succumbed to the terrifying presence of Mot. The interest of the Ugaritic myth lies in the fact that Baal, young god of the storm and fecundity and recently head of the pantheon, goes down to the underworld and perishes like Tammuz and the other vegetation gods. No other "Baal-Hadad" undergoes a like fate, neither the Adad revered in Mesopotamia nor the Hurrian Teshub. (However, at a late date, Marduk "disappeared" too, annually, "shut up in the mountain.") We divine in this *descensus ad inferos* the will to bestow manifold and complementary qualities on Baal; he is the champion, who triumphs over the aquatic "chaos" and hence is a cosmocratic, even cosmogonic, god; he is god of the storm and agrarian fertility (we must remember that he is the son of Dagan, "Grain"); but he is also the sovereign god, determined to extend his sovereignty over the entire world (hence also over the underworld).

In any case, after this last undertaking the relations between El and Baal change. In addition, the structure and rhythms of the universe receive their present form. When the text resumes after another lacuna, two messengers are reporting to El that they have found Baal's corpse. El sits down on the ground, tears his garments, beats his breast, and gashes his face; in short, he proclaims the ritual mourning that was practiced at Ugarit. "Baal is dead!" he cries. "What will become of the multitudes of men?"[40] Suddenly, El seems to be freed from his resentment and his desire for revenge.

39. Gordon, *Ugaritic Manual*, § 67:I:1–8; translation by Oldenburg, *The Conflict between El and Baal*, p. 133.
40. Driver, *Canaanite Myths and Legends*, p. 109; Caquot and Sznycer, in Labat, ed., *Religions du Proche-Orient*, pp. 424–25.

He behaves like a true cosmocrator god; he realizes that universal life is endangered by Baal's death. El asks his wife to name one of his sons king in Baal's stead. Asherah chooses Athar, "the Terrible," but when he seats himself on the throne he discovers that he is not big enough to occupy it and admits that he cannot be king.

In the meanwhile, Anath goes to search for the corpse. When she finds it, she lifts it on her shoulder and sets out northward. Having buried it, she sacrifices a large number of cattle for the funerary banquet. After a certain time Anath meets with Mot. She seizes him, and "with a blade she cuts him; with the winnowing basket she winnows him; with fire she roasts him; with the mill she crushes him; in the fields she sows him, and the birds eat him."[41] Anath performs a sort of ritual murder, treating Mot like an ear of grain. In general, this kind of death is specifically characteristic of vegetation gods and spirits.[42] We may wonder if it is not precisely because of this type of agrarian death that Mot will later return to life.

However this may be, the killing of Mot is not without connections with the destiny of Baal. El dreams that Baal is alive and that "fat rained down from heaven, and honey ran in the wadies" (which recalls biblical images; cf. Ezekiel 32:14; Job 20:17). He bursts out laughing and declares that he will sit down and rest, for "the victorious Baal is alive, the Prince of the Earth exists" (Driver, p. 113). But, just as Yam returns to life, Mot reappears after seven years and complains of the treatment he has received from Anath. He also complains of Baal's having robbed him of the sovereignty, and the two adversaries begin the combat again. They confront each other, striking with their heads and feet like wild oxen, bite each other like snakes, until they both crash to the ground, Baal on top of Mot. But Shapash, the goddess of the sun, gives Mot a warning from El that it is useless to continue the battle, and Mot surrenders, recognizing Baal's sovereignty. After some other episodes that are only partially comprehensible, Anath is informed that Baal will be king forever, inaugurating an era of peace, when "the ox shall have the voice of the gazelle and the falcon the voice of the sparrow."[43]

41. Driver, p. 111; Caquot and Sznycer, p. 430.
42. It has been proposed to see in Mot a "spirit of the harvest," but his funerary characteristics are too evident: he lives in the underground world or the desert, and everything that he touches turns to desolation.
43. Driver, p. 119.

52. Canaanite religious vision

Certain authors claim to have seen in this myth a reflection of the annual death and reappearance of vegetation. But in Syria and Palestine summer does not bring the "death" of vegetable life: on the contrary, it is the season of fruits. It is not torrid heat that frightens the farmer but a prolonged drought. So it seems plausible that Mot's victory refers to the cycle of seven dry years, of which there are echoes in the Old Testament (Genesis 41; 2 Samuel 24:12 ff.).[44]

But the interest of the myth goes beyond its possible connections with the rhythm of vegetation. In fact, these touching and sometimes spectacular events reveal to us a specific mode of divine existence, particularly a mode of being that includes defeat and "death," "disappearance" by burial (Baal) or by dismemberment (Mot), followed by more or less periodical "reappearances." This type of existence, at once intermittent and circular, recalls the modality of the gods who govern the cycle of vegetation. However, this is a new religious creation, which aims at integrating certain negative aspects of life into a unified system of antagonistic rhythms.

In the last analysis, Baal's combats, with his defeats and his victories, insure him the sovereignty of heaven and earth; but Yam continues to reign over the sea and Mot remains lord over the subterranean world of the dead. The myths bring out the primacy of Baal and hence the perenniality of life and the norms that rule the cosmos and human society. By this very fact the negative aspects represented by Yam and Mot find their justification. The fact that Mot is a son of El, and, above all, that Baal is unable to destroy him, proclaims the normality of death. In the last analysis, death proves to be the condition *sine qua non* of life.[45]

It is probable that the myth that relates the combat between Baal and Yam was recited during the New Year festival and the myth of the Baal-Mot conflict at the harvest season; but no text so far known mentions these facts. So, too, we may suppose that the king—of

44. See Cyrus Gordon, "Canaanite Mythology," pp. 184, 195 ff.; M. Pope, in *WdM*, vol. 1, pp. 262–64.

45. It is only in Buddhist mythology that we find another great god of death, Māra, who owes his immense power precisely to the blind love of life felt by human beings. But obviously, from the post-Upanishadic Indian point of view, the cycle life–sexuality–death–return-to-life is the greatest obstacle on the path to deliverance (see the second volume of the present work).

whom we know that he played an important part in the cult—represented Baal in these mythico-ritual scenarios; but this is still the subject of controversy. The sacrifices were regarded as food offered to the gods. The sacrificial system appears to resemble that of the Old Testament: it included the holocaust, the sacrifice or offering of "peace" and "communion," and the expiatory sacrifice.

The priests (*khnm*) had the same name as in Hebrew (*kōhēn*). With the priests, there is also mention of priestesses (*khnt*) and *qadešim*, "consecrated" persons. (In the Bible this term designates sacred prostitution, but the Ugaritic texts indicate nothing of the kind.) Finally, there is mention of the oracular priests or prophets. The temples were furnished with altars and decorated with images of the gods and divine symbols. Aside from the blood sacrifices, the cult included dances and many orgiastic acts and gestures, which later aroused the wrath of the prophets. But it must be remembered that the documentary lacunae allow us only an approximate supposition as to Canaanite religious life. We do not have a single prayer. We know that life is a divine gift, but we do not know the myth of the creation of man.

Such a religious vision was not exclusively Canaanite. But its importance and significance were increased by the fact that the Israelites, when they entered Canaan, were confronted with this type of cosmic sacrality, which inspired a complex cult activity and which, despite its orgiastic excesses, was not without a certain grandeur. Since belief in the sacredness of life was also shared by the Israelites, a problem immediately arose: how would it be possible to preserve such a belief without accepting other elements of the Canaanite religious ideology, of which it was an integral part? This ideology implied, as we have just seen, a particular theology centered on the intermittent and circular modality of the chief god, Baal, symbol of the totality of life. Now Yahweh did not share in this mode of being. (Nor, indeed, did El, but El had undergone other humiliating changes.) In addition, though his cult involved a certain number of sacrifices, Yahweh did not allow himself to be constrained by cult acts: he demanded the inner transformation of his worshipers through obedience and trust (§114).

As we shall see (§ 60), many Canaanite religious elements were assimilated by the Israelites.

But these borrowings were themselves an aspect of the conflict: Baal was combated with his own arms. If we consider that all the foreign groups, even such non-Semites as the Hurrians and later the Philistines, completely forgot their own religion very soon after they arrived in Canaan, we must consider it humanly extraordinary that this struggle between Yahweh and Baal continued for so long and that, despite certain compromises and many lapses into infidelity, it concluded with the victory of Yahwism.[46]

46. R. de Vaux, *Histoire ancienne d'Israël*, vol. 1, pp. 147–48.

7 "When Israel Was a Child..."

53. The first two chapters of Genesis

The religion of Israel is supremely the religion of the Book. This scriptural corpus is made up of texts of different ages and orientations, representing, to be sure, oral traditions of considerable antiquity but reinterpreted, corrected, and redacted in the course of several centuries and in different milieus.[1] Modern authors begin the history of the religion of Israel with Abraham. And in fact, according to the tradition, it is he who was chosen by God to become the ancestor of the people of Israel and to take possession of Canaan. But the first eleven chapters of Genesis recount the fabulous events that preceded Abraham's election, from the creation to the flood and the Tower of Babel. The redaction of these chapters is well known to be more recent than that of many other texts of the Pentateuch. Then, too, certain authors, and by no means the least respected, have maintained that cosmogony and origin myths (creation of man, origin of death, etc.) played a secondary part in the religious consciousness of Israel. In short, the Hebrews were more interested in "sacred history," that is, in their relations with God, than in the history of origins narrating the fabulous and mythical events of the *primordium*.

1. The problems raised by the sources and redaction of the Pentateuch, that is, the first five books of the law (*tôrâh*) are considerable. For our purpose it is enough to say that the sources have been designated by the following terms: *Yahwistic* (because this source, which is the earliest—tenth or ninth century—calls God Yahweh); *Elohistic* (a little later; it uses the name Elohim, "God"); *Sacerdotal* (the latest; the work of the priests, it stresses the cult and the Law); and *Deuteronomic* (this source occurs almost exclusively in the Book of Deuteronomy). We add, however, that for contemporary Old Testament criticism, textual analysis is more complex and more subtle. Except where otherwise indicated, we quote from the Jerusalem Bible.

This may be true from a certain period on and, above all, for a
certain religious elite. But there are no reasons for concluding that
the ancestors of the Israelites were indifferent to the questions in
which all archaic societies were intensely interested, notably the
cosmogony, the creation of man, the origin of death, and certain
other grandiose episodes. Even in our day, after 2,500 years of
"reforms," the events reported in the first chapters of Genesis
continue to feed the imagination and the religious thought of the
heirs of Abraham. Hence, following the premodern tradition, we
begin our exposition with the first chapters of Genesis. The late date
of their redaction does not constitute a difficulty, for their content is
archaic; in fact, it reflects conceptions much older than the saga of
Abraham.

Genesis opens with a famous passage: "In the beginning God
(Elohim) created the heavens and the earth. Now the earth was a
formless void, there was darkness over the deep, and God's spirit
hovered over the water" (1:1–2). The image of the primordial ocean,
over which there hovers a creator god, is extremely archaic.[2] However, the theme of the god flying over the watery abyss is not documented in the Mesopotamian cosmogony, though the myth narrated
in the *Enuma elish* was probably familiar to the author of the biblical
text. (And in fact the primordial ocean is called in Hebrew *tehôm*, a
word etymologically closely connected with the Babylonian *tiāmat*).
The creation properly speaking, that is, the organization of "chaos"
(*tôhû wâ bôhû*), is effected by the power of the word of God. He said:
"Let there be light," and there was light (1:3). The successive stages
of the creation are all accomplished by the divine word. The aquatic
chaos is not personified (cf. Tiamat) and hence is not "conquered" in
a cosmogonic combat.

This biblical account presents a specific structure: (1) creation by
the Word;[3] (2) of a world that is "good"; and (3) of life (animal and
vegetable) that is "good" and that God blesses (1:10, 21, 31); (4)
finally, the cosmogonic work is crowned by the creation of man. On

2. In a number of traditions the Creator is imagined in the form of a bird.
But this is a "hardening" of the original symbol: the divine spirit transcends
the aquatic mass, it is free to move; hence it "flies" like a bird. The bird is, of
course, one of the archetypal images of spirit.

3. We add that the creative word of the god is documented in other traditions, not only in Egyptian theology but also among the Polynesians. See
Eliade, *Myth and Reality*, pp. 31 ff.

the sixth and last day, God says: "Let us make man in our own image, in the likeness of ourselves, and let them be masters of the fish of the sea, the birds of heaven, the cattle," etc. (1:26). There is no spectacular exploit (combat of the Tiamat-Marduk type),[4] no "pessimistic" element in the cosmogony or the anthropogony (the world formed from a "demonic" primordial being, Tiamat; man modeled from the blood of an archdemon, Kingu). The world is "good" and man is an *imago dei*; he lives, like his creator and model, in paradise. However, as Genesis is not slow to emphasize, life is painful, even though it was blessed by God, and men no longer inhabit paradise. But all that is the result of a series of errors and sins on the part of the ancestors. It is they who changed the human condition. God has no responsibility in this deterioration of his masterpiece. As he is for post-Upaniṣadic Indian thought, man— more precisely, the human species—*is the result of his own acts.*

The other, Yahwistic, account (2:5 ff.) is older and differs markedly from the sacerdotal text we have just summarized. There is no longer any question of the creation of heaven and earth but rather of a desert that God (Yahweh) made fertile by a flood that rose from the ground. Yahweh modeled man (*âdâm*) from loam and animated him by breathing "into his nostrils a breath of life." Then Yahweh "planted a garden in Eden," made every kind of "good tree" grow (2:8 ff.), and set man in the garden to "cultivate and take care of it" (2:15). Then Yahweh fashioned the animals and birds, still from the soil, and brought them to Adam, and Adam gave them names.[5] Finally, after putting him to sleep, God took one of Adam's ribs and formed a woman, who received the name of Eve (Heb. *hawwâh*, a word etymologically closely connected with the term meaning "life").

The exegetes have observed that the Yahwistic account, which is simpler, does not oppose the aquatic "chaos" to the world of "forms" but rather the desert and dryness to life and vegetation. So it seems plausible that this origin myth came into existence in a

4. But there are other texts that refer to a victory over an ophidian monster, called dragon (*tannin*) or Rahab or Leviathan, and that are reminiscent of the Mesopotamian and Canaanite traditions (cf., for example, Psalm 74:13 ff.; Job 26:12 ff.).

5. This is a feature peculiar to the archaic ontologies: animals and plants begin really to exist from the moment when they are given names (cf. the example of an Australian tribe in Eliade, *Myths, Dreams, and Mysteries*, p. 194).

desert region. As for the creation of the first man from loam, the theme was known, as we have seen (§17), at Sumer. Similar myths are documented more or less throughout the world, from ancient Egypt and Greece to the "primitive" peoples. The basic idea seems to be the same: man was formed from a primal substance (earth, wood, bone) and was animated by the creator's breath. In a number of cases his form is that of his originator. In other words, as we have already observed in regard to a Sumerian myth, by his "form" and his "life" man in some way shares in the condition of the creator. It is only his body that belongs to "matter." [6]

The creation of woman from a rib taken from Adam can be interpreted as indicating the androgyny of the primordial man. Similar conceptions are documented in other traditions, including those transmitted by certain *midrashim*. The myth of the androgyne illustrates a comparatively widespread belief: human perfection, identified in the mythical ancestor, comprises a unity that is at the same time a *totality*. We shall gauge the importance of androgyny when we come to discuss certain Gnostic and Hermetic speculations. We should note that human androgyny has as its model divine bisexuality, a conception shared by a number of cultures. [7]

54. Paradise lost. Cain and Abel

The Garden of Eden, with its river that divided into four branches, and its trees that Adam was to guard and cultivate, is reminiscent of Mesopotamian imagery. Probably, in this case too, the biblical narrative makes use of a particular Babylonian tradition. But the myth of an original paradise, inhabited by the primordial man, and

6. We add that, according to many traditions, at death the "spirit" returns to the presence of its celestial creator and the body is restored to the earth. But this anthropological "dualism" was rejected by the biblical authors, as it was, furthermore, by the majority of their Near Eastern contemporaries. It is only comparatively late that new anthropological conceptions proposed a more daring solution.

7. Divine bisexuality is one of the many formulas for the totality/unity signified by the union of opposed pairs: feminine-masculine, visible-invisible, heaven-earth, light-darkness, but also goodness-wickedness, creation-destruction, etc. Meditation on these pairs of opposites led, in various regions, to daring conclusions concerning both the paradoxical condition of the divinity and the revalorization of the human condition.

the myth of a paradisal place whose access is difficult for human beings, were known beyond the Euphrates and the Mediterranean. Like all "paradises," Eden[8] is situated at the "center of the world," where the four-branched river emerges. In the middle of the garden stood the Tree of Life and the Tree of the Knowledge of Good and Evil (2:9). Yahweh gave man this commandment: "You may eat indeed of all the trees in the garden. Nevertheless the tree of the knowledge of good and evil, you are not to eat, for on the day you eat of it you shall most surely die" (2:16–17). An idea that is unknown elsewhere emerges from this prohibition: *the existential value of knowledge*. In other words, *knowing* can radically alter the structure of human *existence*.

However, the serpent succeeds in tempting Eve. "No! You will not die," it says to her. "God knows in fact that on the day you eat it your eyes will be opened, and you will be like gods, knowing good and evil" (3:4–5). This rather mysterious episode has given rise to countless interpretations. The background suggests a well-known mythological emblem: the naked goddess, the miraculous tree, and its guardian, the serpent. But instead of a hero who triumphs and wins a share in the symbol of life (miraculous fruit, fountain of youth, treasure, etc.), the biblical narrative gives us Adam, ingenuous victim of the serpent's perfidy. In short, we are dealing with a failed "immortalization," like that of Gilgamesh (§ 23). For, once omniscient, equal to the "gods," Adam could discover the Tree of Life (of which Yahweh had not spoken to him) and become immortal. The text is clear and categorical: "Yahweh God said, See, the man has become like one of us, with his knowledge of good and evil. He must not be allowed to stretch his hand out next and pick from the tree of life also and eat some and live forever" (3:22). And God banished the couple from paradise and condemned them to work for a living.

If we return to the scenario mentioned a moment ago, of the naked goddess and the miraculous tree, guarded by a dragon, we can see that the serpent of Genesis succeeded, all things considered, in its role as guardian of a symbol of life or of youth. But this archaic myth was

---

8. The Hebrews connected the world with ᶜ*eden*, "delights." The term "paradise," of Iranian origin (*pairi-daeza*), is later. Parallel images, chiefly familiar in the Near East and the Aegean world, present a Great Goddess beside a Tree of Life and a vivifying spring, or a Tree of Life guarded by monsters and griffins; see Eliade, *Patterns in Comparative Religion*, §§ 104–8.

radically altered by the author of the biblical accounts. Adam's "initiatory failure" was reinterpreted as a well-justified punishment: his disobedience betrayed his Luciferian pride, the desire to be like God. It was the greatest sin that the creature could commit against his creator. It was the "original sin," a notion pregnant with consequences for the Hebrew and Christian theologies. Such a vision of the "fall" could command recognition only in a religion centered on the omnipotence and jealousy of God. As it has been handed down to us, the biblical narrative indicates the increasing authority of Yahwistic monotheism.[9]

According to the redactors of chapters 4–7 of Genesis, this first sin not only brought about the loss of paradise and the transformation of the human condition; it became in some sense the source of all the evils that burdened humanity. Eve gave birth to Cain, who "tilled the soil," and Abel, a "shepherd." When the brothers made their thank offering—Cain of the products of the soil, and Abel of the firstborn of his flock—Yahweh accepted the latter's offering, but not Cain's. Angry, Cain "set on his brother Abel and killed him" (4:8). "Now," spake Yahweh, "be accursed and driven from the ground. . . . When you till the ground, it shall no longer yield you any of its produce. You shall be a fugitive and a wanderer over the earth" (4:11–12).

It is possible to find in this episode an opposition between cultivators and herders and, implicitly, an apologia for the latter. Yet, if the name Abel means "shepherd," Cain means "smith." Their conflict reflects the ambivalent position of the smith in certain societies of pastoralists, where he is either scorned or respected but is always feared.[10] As we saw (§15), the smith is regarded as the "master of fire" and possesses redoubtable magical powers. In any case, the tradition preserved in the biblical narrative reflects the idealization of the "simple and pure" existence of the nomadic herders and the resistance against the sedentary life of agriculturalists and dwellers in towns. Cain became "builder of a town" (4:17),

9. It must be added, however, that the myth of the "fall" has not always been understood in accordance with its biblical interpretation. Especially from the Hellenistic period and down to the time of illuminism, countless speculations have sought to elaborate a more daring, and often more original, Adamic mythology.

10. See Eliade, *The Forge and the Crucible*, pp. 89 ff.

and one of his descendants is Tubal-cain, "the ancestor of all metal-workers in bronze or iron" (4:22). So the first murder is performed by him who in some sort incarnates the symbol of technology and urban civilization. Implicitly, all techniques are suspected of magic.

55. Before and after the flood

It would serve no purpose to enumerate the descendants of Cain and of Seth, Adam's third son. In conformity with the tradition documented in Mesopotamia, according to which the earliest ancestors attain a fabulous age, Adam engendered Seth at the age of 130 and died 800 years later (5:3 ff.). All the descendants of Seth and Cain enjoyed lives 800 to 900 years in length. A curious episode marks this prediluvial period: the union of certain celestial beings, "sons of God," with the daughters of men, who gave them children, "the heroes of days gone by, the famous men" (6:1–4). These "sons of God" are probably "fallen angels." Their story will be told in full in a late book (Enoch 6–11), which does not necessarily imply that the myth was previously unknown. And in fact similar beliefs are found in ancient Greece and in India: it is the period of the heroes, semi-divine figures whose activity took place just before the beginning of the present age ("at the dawn of history"), that is, at the time when the institutions peculiar to each culture were being established. To return to the biblical narrative, it was after these unions between the fallen angels and the daughters of mortals that God resolved to limit man's lifetime to 120 years. Whatever the origin of these mythical themes may be (Cain and Abel, the patriarchs of the time before the flood, the descent of the "sons of God," the birth of the heroes), it is significant that the redactors maintained them in the final text of Genesis, and this despite certain anthropomorphic characteristics with which they burden Yahweh.

The greatest event of this period was the flood. "Yahweh saw that the wickedness of man was great on the earth, and that the thoughts of his heart fashioned nothing but wickedness all day long" (6:5). God repented of having created man and decided to destroy him. Only Noah, his wife, and his sons (Shem, Ham, and Japheth), with their wives, were saved. For "Noah was a good man . . . and he walked with God" (6:10). Following Yahweh's detailed instructions,

Noah built the ark and filled it with representatives of all the animal species. "In the six hundredth year of Noah's life, in the second month, and on the seventeenth day of that month, that very day all the springs of the great deep broke through, and the sluices of heaven opened. It rained on the earth forty days and forty nights" (7:11–12). When the waters withdrew, the ark stopped on Mount Ararat. Noah went out of the ark and offered a sacrifice. "Yahweh smelt the appeasing fragrance" and, pacified, promised himself that he would not "curse the earth again because of man" (8:21). And he made a covenant with Noah and his descendants, and the sign of the covenant was the rainbow (9:13).

The biblical account has a certain number of elements in common with the account of the flood in the *Epic of Gilgamesh*. It is possible that the redactor knew the Mesopotamian version or, what seems still more probable, used an archaic source, preserved from time immemorial in the Near East. Flood myths, as we observed before (§18), are extremely widespread, and they all share in essentially the same symbolism: the need to radically destroy a degenerate world and humanity so that they can be recreated, that is, restored to their initial integrity. But this cyclical cosmology proves to be already modified in the Sumerian and Akkadian versions. The redactor of the biblical narrative returns to and carries on the reinterpretation of the catastrophe of the flood: he raises it to the rank of an episode in sacred history. Yahweh punishes man's depravity and does not regret the victims of the cataclysm (as the gods do in the Babylonian version; cf. the *Epic of Gilgamesh*, tablet 11, lines 116–25, 136–37). The importance that he accords to moral purity and to obedience anticipates the Law that will be revealed to Moses. Like so many other fabulous events, the flood was later continually reinterpreted and revalorized from different points of view.

The sons of Noah became the ancestors of a new humanity. In that period everyone spoke the same language. But one day men decided to build "a tower with its top reaching heaven" (11:14). This was the last Luciferian exploit. Yahweh "came down to see the town and the tower" and realized that, henceforth, "there will be nothing too hard for them to do" (11:5–6). Then he confused their language, and men no longer understood one another. After that, Yahweh scattered them "over the whole face of the earth, and they stopped building the town" (11:7–8), which later was known by the name of Babel.

In this case, too, we are dealing with an old mythical theme reinterpreted from the viewpoint of Yahwism. We have, first of all, the archaic tradition according to which certain privileged beings (ancestors, heroes, legendary kings, shamans) mounted to the sky by the help of a tree, a lance, a rope, or a chain of arrows. But ascent to the sky *in concreto* was interrupted at the end of the primordial mythical period.[11] Other myths report the failure of later attempts to climb to heaven by means of various scaffoldings. It is impossible to know if the redactor of the biblical narrative knew of these immemorial beliefs. In any case, he was familiar with the Babylonian ziggurats, which had a similar symbolism. Indeed, the ziggurat was considered to have its base at the navel of the earth and its summit in the sky. By climbing the ziggurat, the king or the priest arrived ritually (that is, symbolically) in heaven. Now, for the redactor of the biblical narrative, this belief, which he took literally, was at once simplistic and sacrilegious, so it was radically reinterpreted; more precisely, it was desacralized and demythicized.

It is important to emphasize the following fact: despite a long and complex labor of selection, elimination, and devalorization of the archaic materials, whether inherited or borrowed, the last redactors of Genesis preserved a whole mythology of the traditional type. It begins with the cosmogony and the creation of man, paints the "paradisal" existence of the ancestors, relates the drama of the "fall," with its fatal consequences (mortality, need to work in order to live, etc.), describes the progressive degeneration of the first humanity, which justifies the flood, and concludes with a last fabulous episode: the loss of linguistic unity and the dispersal of the second, postdiluvial humanity, the consequence of a new Luciferian project. As in the archaic and traditional cultures, this mythology, all things considered, constitutes a "sacred history": it explains the origin of the world and at the same time the actual human condition. To be sure, for the Hebrews this "sacred history" became paradigmatic after Abraham and, above all, with Moses; but this does not invalidate the mythological structure and function of the first eleven chapters of Genesis.

A number of authors have dwelt on the fact that the religion of Israel did not invent even one myth. Yet if the term "invent" is

11. In our day shamans undertake this celestial journey "in spirit," that is, in an ecstatic trance.

understood to mean a spiritual creation, the work of selection and criticism of the immemorial mythological traditions is equivalent to the emergence of a new myth, in other words, of a new religious vision of the world which can become paradigmatic. Now the religious genius of Israel transformed the relations of God with the chosen people into a sacred history of a type previously unknown. After a certain moment, this "sacred history," seemingly exclusively national, proves to be a paradigmatic model for all humanity.

56. The religion of the patriarchs

The twelfth chapter of Genesis introduces us into a new religious world. Yahweh[12] says to Abraham: "Leave your country, your family, and your father's house for a land I will show you. I will make you a great nation; I will bless you and make your name so famous that it will be used as a blessing. I will bless those who bless you: I will curse those who slight you. All the tribes of the earth shall bless themselves in you" (12:1–3).

In its present form this text was certainly redacted centuries after the event that it relates. But the religious conception implicit in the "election" of Abraham continues beliefs and customs well known in the Near East of the second millennium. What distinguishes the biblical narrative is God's personal message and its consequences. Without being first invoked, God reveals himself to a human being and, after laying a series of injunctions on him, makes him a series of prodigious promises. According to the tradition, Abraham obeys him, as he will obey him later, when God will demand that he sacrifice Isaac. We are here in the presence of a new type of religious experience—"Abrahamic faith," as it was understood after Moses— which, in the course of time, will become the religious experience peculiar to Judaism and to Christianity.

So Abraham left Ur of the Chaldaeans and arrived at Haran, in the northwest part of Mesopotamia. Later he traveled south and settled for a time at Shechem; after that he led his caravans between Palestine and Egypt (Gen. 13:1–3). The history of Abraham and the

12. Obviously, "Yahweh" is an anachronism, here and in all the other passages previously cited, for the name was revealed later, to Moses.

adventures of his son Isaac, of his grandson Jacob, and of Joseph, constitute the period known as the Age of the Patriarchs. For a long time, criticism held the patriarchs to be legendary figures. But for the past half-century, especially in the light of archeological discoveries, some authors have been inclined to accept, at least in part, the historicity of the patriarchal traditions. To be sure, this does not mean that chapters 11–50 of Genesis represent "historical documents."

For our purpose it is of little significance to know if the ancestors of the Hebrews, the *Ápiru,* were donkey-breeders and merchant caravaners[13] or if they were herders of lesser cattle on the way to becoming sedentary.[14] It is enough to remember that there are a certain number of analogies between the customs of the patriarchs and the social and juridical institutions of the Near East. It is also admitted that many mythological traditions were known to, and adapted by, the patriarchs during their stay in Mesopotamia. As for the religion of the patriarchs, it is characterized by the cult of the "god of the father."[15] He is invoked, or manifests himself, as "the god of my/thy/his father" (Gen. 31:5; etc.). Other formulas include a proper name, sometimes preceded by the word "father": "the god of Abraham" (Gen. 31:53), "the god of thy father Abraham" (26:24; etc.), "the god of Isaac" (28:13), "the god of my/his father Isaac" (32:10; etc.), or "god of Abraham, of Isaac, and of Jacob" (32:24, etc.). These formulas have parallels in the ancient East.[16]

The "god of the father" is primitively the god of the immediate ancestor, whom his sons recognize. By revealing himself to the ancestor, he certified a sort of kinship. He is a god of nomads, not tied to a sanctuary but to a group of men, whom he accompanies and protects. He "binds himself to those who believe in him by

13. As Albright maintained in several works; see most recently his *Yahweh and the Gods of Canaan,* pp. 62–64 and passim.

14. This is the thesis maintained by, among others, R. de Vaux, *Histoire ancienne d'Israël,* vol. 1, pp. 220–22.

15. Albrecht Alt was the first to call attention to this particular characteristic; see his *Der Gott der Väter* (1929).

16. In the nineteenth century B.C. the Assyrians of Cappadocia called to witness "the god of my father" (or of thy/his father). See the sources cited by Ringgren, *La religion d'Israël,* p. 32 (Eng. trans., p. 20); Fohrer, *History of Israelite Religion,* p. 37; de Vaux, *Histoire ancienne d'Israël,* vol. 1, pp. 257–58. For a more subtle interpretation, see Cross, *Canaanite Myth and Hebrew Epic,* pp. 12 ff.

promises."[17] Other names, perhaps even more ancient, are *pahad yiṣḥâk*, which has been translated "fear of Isaac" but which rather means "kinsman of Isaac," and *ᶜabhir yaᶜ aqobh*, which means "fortress (or defender) of Jacob" (Gen. 31:42, 53).

On entering Canaan the patriarchs were confronted by the cult of the god El, and the "god of the father" ended by being identified with him.[18] This assimilation allows us to suppose that there was a certain structural resemblance between the two types of divinity. In any case, once he was identified with El, the "god of the father" obtained the cosmic dimension that he could not have as the divinity of families and clans. This is the first historically documented example of a synthesis that enriches the patriarchal heritage. It will not be the only one.

A number of passages describe, though rather summarily, the religious practices of the patriarchs. Some of these passages, how-ever, reflect a later situation. Hence it is advisable to compare the biblical data with the practices typical of archaic pastoral cultures and, first of all, those of the pre-Islamic Arabs. According to Genesis, the patriarchs offered sacrifices, built altars, and set up stones, which they anointed with oil. But it is probable that only the blood sacrifice (*zèbah*) of the pastoral type, without priests and, according to some, without altars, was practiced: "Each sacrificer immolated his own victim, chosen from the flock; it was not burned, it was eaten in common by the sacrificer and his family."[19]

It is difficult to determine the original meaning of standing stones (*massebah*), for their religious context differs. A stone can bear witness to a compact (Gen. 31:45, 51–52), serve as a tomb (35:20),

---

17. De Vaux, p. 261: "The theme of the promise recurs often in Genesis. It appears there in different forms: promise of a posterity, or of land, or of both together."

18. The patriarchal narratives mention names made up of the element *ᶜel* followed by a substantive: El Roi, "El of the vision" (Gen. 16:13); El Shaddaï, "He of the Mountain" (18:1; etc.); El ᶜOlam, "El of Eternity" (21:33); El Bethel (31:13; etc.). See de Vaux, pp. 262 ff.; Ringgren, pp. 33 ff. (Eng. trans., pp. 20 ff.); Cross, pp. 44 ff.

19. De Vaux, p. 271: "In Central Arabia, the victim was immolated before a standing stone, symbol of the divine presence; the blood was poured over the stone or into a trench dug at the foot of it. Such sacrifices were offered espe-cially at the festivals that the nomadic Arabs celebrated in the first spring month to insure the fertility and prosperity of the herd. It is probable that the an-cestors of Israel, seminomadic herders, already celebrated a similar festival."

or indicate a theophany, as in the episode of Jacob. Jacob fell asleep with his head on a stone and saw a ladder whose top reached heaven, and "Yahweh was there, standing over him," and promised him that country. When he woke, Jacob set up the stone on which he had slept, and he called the place *bêth-el*, the "house of God" (Gen. 28:10–22). Standing stones played a role in the Canaanite cult; this is why they were later condemned by Yahwism. But the custom existed among the pre-Islamic Arabs (cf. note 19), so it is probable that it was also practiced by the ancestors of the Israelites.[20]

57. Abraham, "Father of the Faith"

However, the two rituals that played a considerable part in the religious history of Israel are the sacrifice marking the covenant and the sacrifice of Isaac. The first (Gen. 15:9 ff.) was directly prescribed to Abraham by God. It included dividing a heifer, a goat, and a ram in two, a rite that has analogies elsewhere (for example, among the Hittites; cf. § 43). But the decisive element is a nocturnal theophany: "When the sun had set . . . there appeared a smoking furnace and a firebrand that went between the halves (of the sacrificed animals)" (15:17). "That day (God) made a covenant with Abraham" (15:18). This covenant is not a contract. God laid no obligation on Abraham: it is only he who engages himself. The ritual, of which no other example is found in the Old Testament, was practiced until the time of Jeremiah. A number of authors deny that it was known in the days of the patriarchs. To be sure, the sacrifice is presented in a Yahwistic context, but its theological interpretation could not destroy its primitive character.

In Genesis only one sacrifice is described in detail: the sacrifice of Isaac (22:1–19). God had demanded of Abraham that he sacrifice his son to him as a burnt offering (*°olah*), and Abraham was preparing to sacrifice Isaac when a ram was substituted for him. This episode has given rise to countless controversies. For one thing, it has been

20. The patriarchal narratives mention certain sacred trees, for example the Oak of Moreh (Gen. 12:6) and the Oak of Mamre (13:18; etc.). These trees of the patriarchs, the veneration of which became embarrassing, were later forbidden, when condemnations were issued against the Canaanite cult sites ("on hills, under any spreading tree"—Deut. 12:2).

observed that the term "burnt offering" is repeated six times. Now this type of sacrifice appears to have been borrowed from the Canaanites after the definitive settlement of the tribes.[21] The term "idealization of the past" has also been used. However, it must not be forgotten that Genesis contains a number of sordid stories, "which shows that the writers were more concerned with the *faithful transmission of tradition than with idealization.*"[22] (The italics are ours.)

Whatever its origin may be, the episode illustrates, more forcefully than any other in the Old Testament, the deep meaning of "Abrahamic" faith. Abraham did not prepare to sacrifice his son in pursuit of a definite purpose, as Mesha, king of the Moabites, did when he sacrificed his eldest in order to wrest victory from Israel (2 Kings 3:27), or as Jephthah did, who vowed to Yahweh that he would sacrifice the first person he met after the victory as a burnt offering to him, never imagining that it would be his own daughter, his only child (Judges 11:30 ff.). This is not a sacrifice of the firstborn, a ritual that, in any case, was not known until later and that never became common among the Israelites. Abraham felt that he was bound to his God by "faith." He did not "understand" the meaning of the act that God had demanded of him, whereas those who offered their firstborn to a divinity were perfectly well aware of the meaning and the magico-religious power of the ritual. On the other hand, Abraham never doubted the sanctity, perfection, and omnipotence of his God. Consequently, if the prescribed act had every appearance of being an infanticide, it was because of the powerlessness of human understanding. God alone knew the meaning and the value of a gesture that, for all others, was indistinguishable from a crime.

Here we are confronted by a special case of the dialectic of the sacred: not only is the "profane" transmuted into the "sacred," at the same time retaining its original structure (a *sacred* stone does not cease to be a *stone*), but its "sacralization" is not even comprehensible

21. De Vaux, *Histoire ancienne d'Israël*, p. 270: "The first mentions in the unquestionably ancient texts date from the period of the Judges."

22. H. H. Rowley, *Worship in Ancient Israel*, p. 27. And indeed the text teaches us very little about the cult practiced by some of Jacob's sons, but we are told many stories that are dishonorable to him, for example the story of Simeon and Levi at Shechem (Gen. 34) or of Judah and Tamar (Gen. 38).

by the mind: infanticide is not transformed into a ritual intended to produce a particular effect (as was the case with those who sacrificed their firstborn). Abraham did not perform a ritual (since he pursued no objective and did not understand the meaning of his act); on the other hand, his "faith" assured him that he was not committing a crime. One would say that Abraham did not doubt the "sacrality" of his gesture, but it was "irrecognizable" and hence unknowable.

Meditation on this impossibility of recognizing the sacred (since the sacred is completely identified with the profane) will have marked consequences. As we shall see, Abrahamic faith will enable the Jewish people, after the destruction of the Temple and the disappearance of the state, to bear all the ordeals of their tragic history. And it is equally by meditating on the example of Abraham that, even at such a late date as the nineteenth and twentieth centuries, certain Christian thinkers have grasped the paradoxical and, in the last analysis, "irrecognizable" nature of their faith. Kierkegaard renounced his fiancée in the hope that, in some way impossible to imagine, she would be restored to him. And when Leon Chestov affirmed that true faith implies only one certainty—that "for God all is possible"—he was only restating, in simpler terms, the experience of Abraham.

58. Moses and the departure from Egypt

The beginnings of the religion of Israel are related in Genesis, chapters 46–50, in Exodus, and in the Book of Numbers. Their content is a series of events, most of which were directly caused by God. We list the most important: the settling of Jacob and his sons in Egypt; the persecution launched some centuries later by a pharaoh who ordered the extermination of the firstborn of the Israelites; the vicissitudes of Moses (miraculously saved from the massacre and brought up at the pharaoh's court) after killing an Egyptian soldier who was beating a Hebrew, especially his flight into the desert of Midian, the appearance of the "burning bush" (his first encounter with Yahweh), the mission laid upon him by God, to bring his people out of Egypt, and the revelation of the divine name; the ten plagues sent by God to force the pharaoh to consent; the departure of the Israelites and their crossing the Sea of Reeds, whose waters overwhelmed the Egyptian chariots and soldiers that were pursuing them; the theophany on Mount Sinai and Yahweh's covenant with his people, followed by instructions concerning the content of the revelation and the cult; finally, the forty years of journeying in the desert, the death of Moses, and the conquest of Canaan under the leadership of Joshua.

For more than a century criticism has made every effort to separate the "probable," and hence "historical," elements of these biblical narratives from the mass of "mythological" and "folkloric" excrescences and sedimentations.[23] Use has also been made of the philological and archeological documents relating to the political, cultural, and religious history of the Egyptians, the Canaanites, and other peoples of the Near East. With the help of such documents, there was hope of illuminating and clarifying, perhaps even of reconstructing, the history of the different groups of Hebrews, from Jacob's settling in Egypt (eighteenth to seventeenth centuries) down to the events that are echoed in the traditions of the Exodus and the entry into Canaan, events that a number of authors place in the twelfth century.[24] The extrabiblical documents have certainly contributed to fitting the Exodus and the conquest of Canaan at least partially into a historical context. Quite definite dates have, for example, been proposed for the departure from Egypt, on the basis of data concerning the military and political situation of certain pharaohs of the Nineteenth Dynasty; the stages of the conquest of Canaan have been identified by taking into consideration the results of excavations, first of all the dates of the successive destructions of certain Canaanite cities. But a number of these chronological correlations and concordances are still in dispute.

It is not for us to take a position in a controversy in which few specialists are in agreement. It is enough to cite the fact that it has not been possible, as it had been hoped, to recover the historicity of

23. The work of "demythicization" was comparatively easy (for such "miracles" as the ten plagues or the crossing of the Sea of Reeds could not be regarded as "historical" events). On the other hand, the interpretation of the possible historicity of the biblical texts proved to be extremely delicate. Analysis had distinguished several redactions, made at different periods and from different theological viewpoints. In addition, the influence of several literary genres had been detected. The seeming historicity of an episode became subject to doubt when it was found that the redactor used the clichés of a particular literary genre (saga, novella, proverb, etc.).

24. According to Exodus 12:40, the Israelites remained in Egypt for 430 years.

certain events of the utmost importance for the religion of Israel. This, of course, in no way proves their nonhistoricity. But the historical events and personages have been so much modeled on paradigmatic categories that in most cases it is no longer possible to detect their original "reality." There are no reasons for doubting the reality of the personage known by the name of Moses, but his biography and the specific traits of his personality escape us. By the mere fact that he has become a charismatic and fabulous figure, his life, beginning with his miraculous preservation in a papyrus basket left among the reeds of the Nile, follows the model of many other heroes (Theseus, Perseus, Sargon of Agade, Romulus, Cyrus, etc.).

The name of Moses, like that of other members of his family, is Egyptian. It contains the element *mśy*, "born, son," comparable to Ahmosis or Rameses (Ra-messes, "son of Ra"). The name of one of Levi's sons, Merari, is the Egyptian *Mrry*, "Well-loved"; Pinhas, Aaron's grandson, is *Pᶜ-nḥsy*, "the Negro." It is not impossible that the young Moses knew the "reform" of Akh-en-Aton (ca. 1375–1350), who had replaced the cult of Amon by the solar "monotheism" of Aton. Some scholars have noted[25] the analogy between the two religions: Aton, too, is proclaimed "the only god"; like Yahweh, he is the god "who creates everything that exists"; finally, the importance that Akh-en-Aton's "reform" accords to "instruction" is comparable to the role of the Torah in Yahwism. On the other hand, the Ramesside society, in which Moses was brought up two generations after Akh-en-Aton's "reform" had been suppressed, could not attract him. Its cosmopolitanism, religious syncretism (especially between Egyptian and Canaanite cults), certain orgiastic practices (prostitution of both sexes), the "cult" of animals, were so many abominations for anyone brought up in the "religion of the Fathers."

As for the departure from Egypt, it seems certainly to reflect a historical event. However, it does not involve the exodus of the whole people, but only of a group, and precisely of the group led by Moses. Other groups had already begun their more or less peaceful entrance into Canaan. Later, the Exodus was claimed by all the

25. See, for example, Albright, *From the Stone Age to Christianity*, pp. 218 ff., 269 ff., and his *The Biblical Period from Abraham to Ezra*, pp. 15 ff. But for other authors the analogies do not seem convincing; see Ringgren, *La religion d'Israël*, p. 51 (Eng. trans., p. 39); Fohrer, *History of Israelite Religion*, p. 79.

Israelite tribes as an episode of their sacred history. What is important for our purpose is that the departure from Egypt was put into relation with the celebration of the Passover. In other words, an archaic sacrifice peculiar to nomad herders and practiced for millennia by the ancestors of the Israelites was revalorized and incorporated into the sacred history of Yahwism. A ritual belonging to cosmic religiosity (the pastoral festival of spring) was interpreted as the commemoration of a historical event. *The transformation of religious structures of the cosmic type into events of sacred history* is characteristic of Yahwistic monotheism and will be taken up again and continued by Christianity.

59. "I Am Who I Am"

While he is keeping sheep for his father-in-law Jethro, the priest of Midian, Moses crosses the desert and comes to the "mountain of God," Horeb. There he sees a "flame of fire coming from the middle of a bush" and hears himself called by name. A few moments later the voice of God comes to him, saying, "I am the God of your father, the God of Abraham, the God of Isaac, and the God of Jacob" (Exodus 3:6). Nevertheless, Moses senses that he is in the presence of an unknown aspect of the divinity, or even of a new god. He accepts the order to go to the children of Israel and say to them, "The God of your fathers has sent me to you"; but, if they ask what God's name is, "what am I to tell them?" (3:13). "And God said to Moses, I Am Who I am (*'eyèh 'ăšèr 'ehyèh*)." And he teaches him to address the children of Israel in these terms: "I Am has sent me to you" (3:14).

This name has given rise to an immense amount of discussion.[26] God's answer is mysterious enough: he refers to his mode of being but does not reveal his person. All that can be said is that the divine name suggests, to use a modern expression, the totality of being and of the existent. Yet Yahweh declares that he is the god of Abraham and the other patriarchs, and this identity is still accepted today by all those who lay claim to the Abrahamic inheritance. And in fact

26. See the recent bibliographies given in Ringgren, pp. 43 ff. (Eng. trans., pp. 31 ff.), Fohrer, pp. 75 ff., de Vaux, *Histoire ancienne d'Israël*, pp. 321 ff., and Cross, *Canaanite Myth and Hebrew Epic*, pp. 60 ff.

it is possible to discover a certain continuity between the god of the father and the god who reveals himself to Moses. As has been said, "to begin with, there is the fact that Yahwism is born in a milieu of herders and develops in the desert. The return to pure Yahwism will be presented as a return to the desert situation: it will be the 'nomadic ideal' of the prophets."[27] Exactly like the god of the father, Yahweh is not attached to a particular place; in addition, he has a special relation to Moses as leader of a group.

But the differences are significant. While the god of the father was anonymous, Yahweh is a proper name that indicates his mystery and his transcendence. The relations between the divinity and his worshipers have changed: instead of the former "*god* of the father," we now hear of the "*people* of Yahweh." The idea of divine election, present in the promises made to Abraham (Gen. 12:1–3), becomes more definite: Yahweh calls the descendants of the patriarchs "my people"; they are—to use R. de Vaux's expression—his "personal property." As the assimilation of the god of the father with El proceeded, Yahweh was also identified with him. He took El's cosmic structure as well as his title of king. "From the religion of El, Yahwism also took the idea of the divine court formed by the *benê 'ĕlohîm*."[28] On the other hand, Yahweh's warlike character carries on the role of the god of the father, supremely the protector of his worshipers.

The essence of the revelation is concentrated in the Decalogue (Exod. 20:3–17; cf. Exod. 34:10–27). In its present form the text cannot date from the time of Moses, but the most important commandments certainly reflect the spirit of primitive Yahwism. The first article of the Decalogue, "You shall have no gods except me," shows that what is involved is not monotheism in the strict sense. The existence of other gods is not denied. In the song of victory chanted after the passage of the Sea of Reeds, Moses exclaims: "Who among the gods is your like, Yahweh?" (Exod. 15:11). But absolute fidelity is demanded, for Yahweh is a "jealous God" (Exod. 20:5). The struggle against the false gods begins immediately after the

27. De Vaux, p. 424. In what follows, we make use of his analyses, pp. 424–31.
28. De Vaux, p. 428. "But it seems more correct to say that El gave his mildness and his compassion to Yahweh, who would primitively have been a fierce and violent god. In the probably ancient text of Exodus 34:6, Yahweh defines himself as 'tender and compassionate'" (ibid., p. 429).

escape from the desert, at Baal-peor. It is there that the daughters of the Moabites invite the Israelites to the sacrifices to their gods. "And the people ate and bowed down before their gods" (Numbers 25:2 ff.), thus arousing Yahweh's wrath. For Israel, this struggle, begun at Baal-peor, still continues.

The meaning of the Second Commandment, "You shall not make yourself a carved image . . ." is difficult to perceive. It is not a prohibition against the cult of idols. Images, familiar to the pagan cults, were well known to be only receptacles of the divinity. Probably the underlying idea of this commandment implied a prohibition against representing Yahweh by a cult object. Just as he had no name, Yahweh should have no image. God permitted himself to be seen, by certain privileged persons, face to face; for the rest of mankind he was manifest only through his acts. Unlike the other Near Eastern divinities, who manifested themselves indifferently in human, animal, or cosmic form, Yahweh is conceived as exclusively anthropomorphic. But he also has recourse to cosmic epiphanies, for the whole world is his creation.

Yahweh's anthropomorphism has a twofold aspect. On the one hand, Yahweh displays qualities and faults that are specifically human: compassion and hate, joy and grief, forgiveness and vengeance. (However, he does not show the weaknesses and faults of the Homeric gods, and he will not tolerate being ridiculed, as certain Olympians do.)[29] On the other hand, unlike the majority of divinities, Yahweh does not reflect the human situation; he does not have a family, but only a celestial court: Yahweh is alone. Are we to see another anthropomorphic characteristic in the fact that he demands absolute obedience from his worshipers, like an Oriental despot? This seems rather to be an inhuman desire for absolute perfection and purity. The intolerance and fanaticism that are characteristic of the prophets and missionaries of the three monotheisms have their model and their justification in Yahweh's example.

So, too, Yahweh's violence exceeds the bounds of anthropomorphism. His "wrath" sometimes proves to be so irrational that it has been possible to refer to his "demonism." To be sure, some of these negative characteristics will become indurated later, after the occupation of Canaan. But the "negative characteristics" belong to

29. See Fohrer, *History of Israelite Religion*, pp. 78 ff.

Yahweh's original structure. What is in fact involved is a new, and the most impressive, expression of the deity as absolutely different from his creation, the "utterly other" (the *ganz andere* of Rudoph Otto). The coexistence of these contradictory attributes, the irrationality of some of his acts, distinguish Yahweh from an ideal of perfection on the human scale. From this point of view, Yahweh resembles certain divinities of Hinduism, Śiva, for example, or Kālī-Durgā. But there is a difference, and a substantial one: these Indian divinities take their place beyond morality, and since their mode of being constitutes a paradigmatic model, their worshipers do not hesitate to imitate them. Yahweh, on the contrary, accords the greatest importance to ethical principles and practical morality: at least five commandments of the Decalogue refer to them.

According to the biblical narrative, it was three months after the departure from Egypt, and in the Sinai Desert, that the theophany took place. " The mountain of Sinai was entirely wrapped in smoke, because Yahweh had descended on it in the form of fire. Like smoke from a furnace the smoke went up, and the whole mountain shook violently. Louder and louder grew the sound of the trumpet, Moses spoke, and God answered him in peals of thunder" (Exod. 19:18–19). Then Yahweh appeared to the Israelites, who had remained at the foot of the mountain, and made a covenant with them, dictating the Laws of the Covenant, which begins with the Decalogue and includes a number of prescriptions for the cult (Exod. 20:22–26 and chaps. 24–26).[30] Later, Moses had another conversation with God and received the "two tablets of the Testimony, tablets of stone inscribed by the finger of God" (31:18; cf. another version, 34:1–28). Mendenhall has observed that the stylistic form of the Laws of the Covenant is reminiscent of the treaties of the Hittite sovereigns of the second millennium with their vassals in Asia Minor.[31] But the similarities between the two formulas, though real, do not appear to be decisive.

Nothing definite is known concerning the cult practiced by the Israelites during the forty years they spent in the desert. Exodus 26

30. It is unnecessary to state that all these texts were composed, or edited, later.

31. C. E. Mendenhall, *Law and Covenant in Israel and the Ancient East* (1935). Among others, Albright has accepted the hypothesis, in his *Yahveh and the Gods of Canaan*, pp. 107 ff.

and 38:8–38 give a detailed description of the desert sanctuary; it consists of the Tent of Meeting, which shelters the ark of the Testimony or ark of the Covenant, a wooden coffer containing—according to a late tradition—the tables of the Laws (Deut. 10:1–5; etc.). Very probably this tradition reflects a real situation. Cult tents or palanquins, in which stone idols were carried, are documented among the Arabs before Islam. The texts do not mention the ark and the tent together, but it is probable that, as among the Arabs, the tent covered the ark. As the god of the father had done earlier, Yahweh led his people. The ark symbolized that invisible presence, but it is impossible to know what it contained.

According to tradition, Moses died in the Plain of Moab, opposite Jericho. Yahweh showed him the land of Canaan: "I have let you see it with your own eyes, but you shall not cross into it" (Deut. 34:4; cf. Num. 27:12–14). This death, too, corresponds to the legendary and paradigmatic personage of Moses. All that can be said concerning the person known by that name is that he was distinguished by his repeated and dramatic encounters with Yahweh. The revelation of which Moses was the intermediary made him at once an ecstatic and oracular prophet and a "magician"—the model of the Levite priests and the supremely charismatic leader who succeeded in transforming a group of clans into the nucleus of a nation, the people of Israel.

60. Religion under the judges: The first phase of syncretism

The period between 1200 B.C., when the group that had been led by Moses entered Canaan under the leadership of Joshua, and 1020 B.C., when Saul was proclaimed king, is, by common consent, known as the Age of the Judges. The judges were military leaders, councillors, and magistrates. It is during this period that other tribes accept Yahwism, especially after certain brilliant victories. For Yahweh directly intervenes in battle. He assures Joshua: "Do not be afraid of these men; I have delivered them into your power" (Josh. 10:8). And in fact Yahweh caused "huge hailstones" to fall from heaven, killing the enemy by thousands (Josh. 10:11). After the victory over Jabin, king of Canaan, Deborah and Barak hymn the divine fury: "Yahweh, when you set out from Seir . . . earth shook, the heavens quaked, the clouds dissolved into water" (Judg. 5:4). In short, Yahweh proves to be stronger than the gods of the Canaanites. War waged in his name is a holy war:[32] the men are consecrated (*qiddeš*, "to sanctify") and must preserve ritual purity. As for booty, it is "forbidden," that is, it is entirely destroyed, offered as a holocaust to Yahweh.

But in adapting itself to a new style of existence, Yahwism evolves and changes. We first notice a reaction against the values most esteemed by every society of herders. The law of hospitality, the sacrosanct law among nomads, is traitorously broken by Jael: she invites the Canaanite chief, Sisera, who was fleeing after the defeat, into her tent and kills him in his sleep (Judg. 4:17 ff.). The portable sanctuary of Moses' day falls into disuse. The cult is now practiced in sanctuaries and sacred sites.

But, as was to be expected, it is above all the confrontation with the Canaanite religion that will have marked consequences. Indeed, this confrontation continues until the seventh century B.C. In consequence of the association Yahweh-El, the pre-Yahwistic sanctuaries belonging to the cult of El, together with a number of Canaanite sanctuaries, are consecrated to Yahweh.[33] More surprising is the confusion that existed, during the Age of the Judges, between Yahweh and Baal. Names with *baal* as an element are found even in families known for their Yahwistic faith. The famous Gideon is also named Jerubbaal, "Baal fights" (Judg. 6:32). This presupposes that the word *baal*, "Lord," was understood as an epithet of Yahweh or that Baal was venerated side by side with Yahweh.[34] In the beginning Baal must have been accepted as "god of the land," the supreme specialist in fecundity. It is only later that his cult was execrated and became the paradigmatic proof of apostasy.

32. G. von Rad, *Der heilige Krieg im alten Israel* (1951), summarized by Ringgren, *La religion d'Israël*, pp. 66–67 (Eng. trans., pp. 53–54). The term "forbidden," *hérèm*, derives from a root meaning "sacred." Ringgren considers the phenomenon typically Israelite; but A. Lods and Albright cite other examples, and not only among the Semites; cf. Rowley, *Worship in Ancient Israel*, p. 56 and note 7.

33. See the list of these sanctuaries in Fohrer, *History of Israelite Religion*, pp. 111–13. On the syncretism of the cults, see G. W. Ahlström, *Aspects of Syncretism in Israelite Religion*, pp. 11 ff.; Rowley, *Worship in Ancient Israel*, pp. 58 ff.

34. See Ringgren, p. 56 (Eng. trans., p. 44); Fohrer, p. 105.

A large part of the Canaanite sacrificial system was adopted. The simplest form of sacrifice consisted in the offering, on a consecrated site, of different gifts or in libations of oil or water. The offerings were regarded as food for the divinity (Judg. 6:19). It is at this time that the Israelites begin to practice the burnt offering (*ʿolah*), which they interpret as an oblation offered to Yahweh. In addition, they take over a number of Canaanite practices, related to agriculture, and even certain orgiastic rituals.[35] The process of assimilation is intensified later, under the monarchy, when there is mention of sacred prostitution of both sexes.

Sánctuaries are built after Canaanite models. They include an altar, *massebahs* (standing stones), *asherahs* (wooden posts symbolizing the Canaanite goddess Asherah), and vessels for libations. Among the ritual objects, we mention the most important: *teraphim* (images or masks) and *ephods* (originally garments put on the image). The personnel of the cult is organized around the sanctuaries of which it is the guardian. Of chief importance are the priests and Levites: they offer sacrifices and seek to determine Yahweh's will by lots and the *ephod*. Next to the priests and Levites we find diviners or seers (*rōʾêh*), but we have little information about their functions. The seers were not attached to sanctuaries, as the prophets (*nâbîim*) were. The most famous example is Balaam (Num. 22–24): he sees Yahweh in a dream or waking; he has to *see* the Israelites in order to be able to curse them. This type of ecstatic is documented in other nomadic societies (for example, the *kāhin* among the Arabs).[36]

Far more important was the function of the "prophet" (*nâbî*); we shall return to him later (§116). For the moment, we add that Israelite ecstatic prophecy has its deep roots in the Canaanite religion.[37] And in fact the cult of Baal included *nâbîim* (see 1 Kings 18:19 ff.; 2 Kings 10:19). But this is a type of ecstatic experience that is comparatively common in the ancient Near East, with the exception of Egypt. The Sumerians knew the "man who enters heaven," a designation that indicates an ecstatic journey comparable to that of the shamans. At Mari, texts of the eighteenth century speak of the

35. Fohrer, p. 106; Ahlström, pp. 14 ff.

36. J. Pedersen, "The Role Played by Inspired Persons among the Israelites and the Arabs"; J. Lindblom, *Prophecy in Ancient Israel*, pp. 86 ff.

37. See A. Haldar, *Association of Cult Prophets among the Ancient Semites*, pp. 91 ff., with bibliography.

āpilum ("he who responds") or of the *muhhûm* and *muhhûtum*, men or women who receive the oracles of the gods in dreams or visions. These *āpilum* and *muhhûm* correspond to the *nâbîim*. Like the prophets of Israel, they use oracular phrases that tend to be short and send their messages to kings, even when they contain bad news or criticize certain acts of the sovereign.[38]

Even in the first centuries of the conquest and colonization, we note a Canaanite influence that is profound and takes many forms. Indeed, the ritual system, the sacred sites and sanctuaries are taken over from the Canaanites; the priestly class is organized after Canaanite models; finally, even the prophets, who will soon react against the supremacy of the priests and against syncretism with the fertility cults, are also the product of a Canaanite influence. Yet the prophets lay claim to the purest Yahwism. From a certain point of view, they are right; but the Yahwism that they proclaim has already assimilated the most creative elements of Canaanite religion and culture, so savagely execrated by the prophets.

38. See Lindblom, pp. 29 ff., 85 ff., and Fohrer, pp. 225 ff., who cite other examples from Babylonia and Assyria.

8 The Religion of the Indo-Europeans: The Vedic Gods

61. Protohistory of the Indo-Europeans

The irruption of the Indo-Europeans into history is marked by terrible destruction. Between 2300 and 1900 B.C. in Greece and Asia Minor many cities are sacked and burned; for example, Troy (about 2300 B.C.), Beycesultan, Tarsus, and some three hundred cities and villages in Anatolia. The documents mention ethnic groups named Hittites, Luwians, and Mitanni. But Āryan-speaking elements are also attested in other bodies of invaders. The dispersal of the Indo-European peoples had begun some centuries earlier, and it continued for two millennia. By about 1200 B.C. the Āryans had made their way into the Indo-Gangetic plain, the Iranians were firmly established in Persia, and Greece and the islands were Indo-Europeanized. Some centuries later, the Indo-Europeanization of India, the Italian Peninsula, the Balkan Peninsula, the Carpatho-Danubian regions, and central, northern, and western Europe—from the Vistula to the Baltic Sea and the Atlantic—was either completed or well advanced. This characteristic process—migration, conquest of new territories, submission of the inhabitants, followed by their assimilation—did not end until the nineteenth century of our era. Such an example of linguistic and cultural expansion is otherwise unknown.

For more than a century, scholars have made every effort to identify the original homeland of the Indo-Europeans, to decipher their protohistory, and to clarify the phases of their migrations. Their land of origin has been sought in northern and central Europe, in the Russian steppes, in central Asia, in Anatolia, etc. It is generally agreed today to localize the home of the Indo-Europeans in the regions north of the Black Sea, between the Carpathians and the

Caucasus.[1] Between the fifth and third millennia these regions saw the development of the so-called Tumuli (*kurgan*) Culture. About 4000–3500 B.C. it expanded westward, as far as Tisza. During the following millennium the representatives of the Kurgan Culture made their way into central Europe, the Balkan Peninsula, Transcaucasia, Anatolia, and northern Iran (ca. 3500–3000 B.C.); in the third millennium they reached northern Europe, the Aegean zone (Greece and the coasts of Anatolia), and the eastern Mediterranean. According to Marija Gimbutas, the peoples who developed and disseminated the Kurgan Culture can only have been the Proto-Indo-Europeans and, in the last phases of their dispersal, the Indo-Europeans.

However this may be, it is certain that the origins of the Indo-European culture are rooted in the Neolithic, perhaps even in the Mesolithic. On the other hand, it is equally certain that during its formative period this culture was influenced by the more developed civilizations of the Near East. The use of the chariot and of metal[2] was transmitted by an Anatolian culture (the so-called Kuro-Araxas Culture). In the fourth millennium there appear, borrowed from the peoples of the Balkano-Mediterranean zone, clay, marble, or alabaster statues representing a seated goddess.

The common vocabulary shows that the Indo-Europeans practiced agriculture, raised cattle (but also the pig and probably the sheep), and knew the horse, either as wild or domesticated. Though they were never able to renounce agricultural products, the Indo-European peoples preferred to develop a pastoral economy. Pastoral nomadism, the patriarchal structure of the family, a proclivity for raids, and a military organization designed for conquest are characteristic features of the Indo-European societies. A more or less radical social differentiation is indicated by the contrast between the tumuli (tombs built in the form of a house and richly furnished) and the far poorer burials. Very probably the tumuli (*kurgan*) were reserved for the corpses of chiefs.

For our purpose it is important to determine to what an extent this mode of existence—pastoral nomadism, vigorously reorganized for

1. The common vocabulary for certain animals (wolf, bear, goose, freshwater salmon, wasp, bee) and trees (birch, beech, oak, and willow) indicates a temperate zone.

2. The terms for "copper" and "ax" are Sumerian; they were borrowed before the separation of the European linguistic groups (Germanic, Italic and Celtic, Illyrian and Thracian, Greek and Slavic).

war and conquest—encouraged and facilitated the emergence of specific religious values. Obviously, the creations of agricultural societies do not completely correspond to the religious aspirations of a pastoral society. On the other hand, no pastoral society can exist in complete independence from the economy and religion of the cultivators. What is more, in their migrations and conquests the Indo-Europeans continually brought into subjection and assimilated sedentary agricultural populations. In other words, quite early in their history the Indo-Europeans must have known the spiritual tensions produced by the symbiosis of heterogeneous—and even antithetical—religious orientations.

62. The first pantheon and the common religious vocabulary

It is possible to reconstitute certain structures of the common Indo-European religion. To begin with, there are the brief but valuable indications furnished by the religious vocabulary. The earliest studies already recognized the Indo-European root *deiwos*, "sky," in the terms designating the "god" (Lat. *deus*, Skr. *deva*, Iran. *div*, Lith. *diewas*, Old Ger. *tivar*) and in the names of the principal gods: Dyaus, Zeus, Jupiter. The idea of god proves to be bound up with celestial sacrality, that is, with light and "transcendence" (height) and, by extension, with the idea of sovereignty and with creativity in its immediate meaning: cosmogony and paternity. The (god of the) sky is supremely the father: cf. Indian Dyauspitar, Greek Zeus Pater, Illyrian Daipatūres, Latin Jupiter, Scythian Zeus-Papaios, Thraco-Phrygian Zeus-Pappos.[3]

Since celestial and atmospheric hierophanies play a cardinal role, it is not surprising that a certain number of gods are designated by the name of thunder: German Donar, Thôrr; Celtic Taranis (Tanaros); Baltic Perkûnas; Proto-Slavic Perun; etc. It is probable that in the Indo-European period the sky god (the supreme god as creator of the world and cosmocrator) was already yielding place to

3. The Greek vocable *theos* does not belong to the same series. It derives from a root designating the "soul," the "spirit of the deceased"; cf. Lith. *dwesiu*, "to breathe," Old Slavic *duch*, "breathing," *duša*, "soul." Hence it may be supposed that *theos*, "god," develops from the idea of the deified dead.

the storm gods—a phenomenon comparatively frequent in the history of religions. Similarly, fire, kindled by lightning, is regarded as of celestial origin. The cult of fire is a characteristic element of the Indo-European religions; the name of the important Vedic god Agni occurs in Latin *ignis*, Lithuanian *ugnis*, Old Slavic *ogni*.[4] It may also be supposed that the solar god held a preponderant place even from protohistory (cf. Vedic Sūrya, Greek Helios, Old German *sauil*, Old Slavic *solnce*, all designating the sun). But the solar gods had a checkered history among the different Indo-European peoples, especially after their contact with the Near Eastern religions.[5] As for the earth (*GHᶜEM), it was regarded as a vital energy opposed to the sky; but the religious idea of Mother Earth is more recent among the Indo-Europeans and occurs in a limited area.[6] We find another cosmic element, the wind, deified in Lithuanian Wejopatis, "Master of the Wind," and in Iranian Vayu and Indian Vāyu. But in the case of these last two we have more than cosmic epiphanies, for they show, especially Iranian Vayu, the characteristic features of sovereign gods.

The Indo-Europeans had elaborated a specific mythology and theology. They practiced sacrifices and knew the magico-religious value of the word and of chanting (*KAN). They possessed concepts and rituals that enabled them to consecrate space and to "cosmicize" the territories in which they settled (this mythico-ritual scenario is documented in ancient India, at Rome, and among the Celts), and this also enabled them periodically to renew the world (by ritual combat between two groups of celebrants, a rite of which vestiges still remain in India and Iran). The gods were regarded as being present at the festivals, side by side with men, and offerings to them were burned. The Indo-Europeans built no sanctuaries; very probably the cult was celebrated in a consecrated enclosure, under the open sky. Another characteristic feature is oral transmission of the

4. In Iran the name of the divinity of fire is Ātar; but there are indications that, in an earlier terminology of the cult, fire was called *agni*, not *ātar*: see Stig Wikander, *Der arische Männerbund*, pp. 77 ff.

5. In addition, in the period of Greco-Oriental syncretism, the sacrality represented by the sun gave scope for a daring theological and philosophical reelaboration, so that the solar god could be said to have been the last cosmic theophany to disappear before the expansion of Judeo-Christian monotheism.

6. We add that man, as a terrestrial being (GHᵉ MON), is later opposed in the West to celestial beings, whereas in the East we find the concept man, rational creature (Mᵉ NU), opposed to the animals; see Devoto, *Origini indo-europee*, pp. 264 ff.

tradition and, after their encounter with the Near Eastern civilizations, the prohibition against using writing.

But, as could be expected in view of the many centuries that separate the earliest Indo-European migrations (Hittites, Indo-Iranians, Greeks, Italics) from the latest (Germans, Balto-Slavs), the common heritage is not always recognizable in the vocabulary or the theologies and mythologies of the historical period. On the one hand, the different cultural contacts that occurred during the migrations must be taken into consideration; on the other hand, it must not be forgotten that no religious tradition continues to exist indefinitely without changes produced either by new spiritual creations or by borrowings, symbiosis, or elimination.

The vocabulary reflects this process of differentiation and innovation, which probably began even in protohistory. The most significant example is the absence in common Indo-European of a specific term designating the "sacred." On the other hand, in Iranian, Latin, and Greek two terms are available: Avestan *spenta/yaoždāta* (cf. also Gothic *hails/weih*); Latin *sacer/sanctus*; Greek *hieros/hagios*. "Study of each of these attested pairs ... leads to supposing, in prehistory, a biaspectual notion: positive, 'what is charged with divine presence,' and negative, 'what it is forbidden to men to touch.'"[7] Similarly, according to Benveniste, there was no common term to designate "sacrifice." But this absence "has as its counterpart, in the various languages and often within each of them, a great diversity of designations corresponding to the various forms of the sacrificial act: libation (Skr. *juhoti*, Gk. *spendō*), solemn verbal engagement (Lat. *voveo*, Gk. *euchomai*), ritual feast (Lat. *daps*), fumigation (Gk. *thuō*), rite of light (Lat. *lustro*)."[8] As for "prayer," the terminology was built up from two different roots.[9] In short,

---

7. E. Benveniste, *Le vocabulaire des institutions indo-européennes*, vol. 2, p. 179. As for *religion*, "not conceiving this omnipresent reality as a separate institution, the Indo-Europeans had no term to designate it" (ibid., p. 265). Georges Dumézil has several times analyzed the Indo-European vocabulary of the sacred; see, most recently, his *La religion romaine archaïque*, 2d ed. (1974), pp. 131–46 (Eng. trans. by Philip Krapp, *Archaic Roman Religion*, 2 vols. [Chicago, 1970], 1:129–38).

8. Benveniste, *Le vocabulaire*, p. 223. However, Erich Hamp has recently reconstructed the common term for "sacrifice"; see *JIES* 1 (1973): 320–22.

9. The original Hittite-Slavic-Baltic-Armenian (-Germanic?) dialectal grouping attests forms related to Hittite *maltāi-*, "to pray," whereas Iranian, Celtic, and Greek present terms derived from the root **ghwedh*—"to pray, to desire" (Benveniste, *Le vocabulaire*, p. 245).

from their common protohistory the different Indo-European peoples showed a marked tendency continually to reinterpret their religious traditions. This process was intensified in the course of the migrations.

63. The Indo-European tripartite ideology

The fragments of the various Indo-European mythologies constitute an important source. To be sure, these fragments are of different ages and have come down to us in heterogeneous documents of unequal value: hymns, ritual texts, epic poetry, theological commentaries, popular legends, historiographies, and late traditions recorded by Christian authors after the conversion of the peoples of central and northern Europe. Nevertheless, all these documents are valuable, for they preserve or reflect (even in distorted form) a number of original religious conceptions. The exaggerations and errors of "comparative mythology," as it was understood by Max Müller and his followers, must not be allowed to deny us the use of these materials. It is enough not to mistake their documentary value. A myth documented in the Rig Veda cannot be later than the second millennium B.C., whereas the traditions preserved by Livy, by the Irish epic, or by Snorri Sturluson are, from the chronological point of view, considerably more recent. But if such traditions agree in every point with the Vedic myth, it is difficult to doubt their common Indo-European character, especially if the coincidence is not isolated but falls into place in a system.

This is what Georges Dumézil has demonstrated in a series of works that have radically renewed the comparative study of Indo-European mythologies and religions. There is no need to summarize them here. Suffice it to say that the French scholar's researches have disclosed the fundamental structure of Indo-European society and ideology. To the division of society into three classes—priests, warriors, stock-breeders and farmers—corresponded a trifunctional religious ideology: the function of magical and juridical sovereignty, the function of the gods of martial force, and, finally, the function of the divinities of fecundity and economic prosperity. It is among the Indo-Iranians that we best perceive this tripartite division of the gods and society. And indeed, in ancient India, to the social classes of the *brāhmanas* (priests, sacrificers), *kṣatriya* (soldiers, protectors of the community), and *vaiśya* (producers), there correspond the gods Varuṇa and Mitra, Indra, and the twin Nāsatyas (or the Aśvins). The same gods appear, named in the same order, in the treaty concluded, about 1380, between a Hittite king and the chief of the para-Indians (Mitanni) in Asia Minor: Mitra-(V)aruṇa (variant Uruvana), Indara, the two Nāsatyas. Similarly, the Avesta distinguishes priests (*āthra.van*), warriors (fighting in chariots, *rathaē-štar*), stock-breeders and farmers (*vāstryō.fšuyant*)—with the difference that, in Iran, this social division did not harden into a caste system. According to Herodotus (4. 5–6), the Iranian Scythians also knew the division into three classes, and the tradition persisted into the nineteenth century among the Ossets of the Caucasus, direct descendants of the Scythians.

The Celts distributed society into druids (priests, jurists), military aristocracy (*flaith*, literally "power," the equivalent of Sanskrit *kṣatrā*), and *bó airig*, free men (*airig*) owning cows (*bó*). According to Dumézil, a similar social division can be discerned in the mythical, but strongly historicized, traditions of the founding of Rome: King Romulus, protected by Jupiter; the Etruscan Lucumon, technician of war; Tatius and the Sabines, who bring women and wealth. The Capitoline triad—Jupiter, Mars, Quirinus—in a way constitutes the divine, celestial model of Roman society. Finally, a similar triad dominates Scandinavian religion and mythology: Odin, the sovereign god, Thor, the champion, and Frey, patron of fecundity.

The division of the first function into two complementary parts or tendencies—magical sovereignty and juridical sovereignty—is clearly illustrated by the pair Varuṇa and Mitra. For the ancient Indians, Mitra is the sovereign god "in his reasoning, clear, ordered, calm, benevolent, sacerdotal aspect, and Varuṇa the sovereign in his attacking, somber, inspired, violent, terrible, warlike aspect."[10] Now the same diptych is found again, especially at Rome, with the same oppositions and the same alternations; on the one hand, there is the opposition between the Luperci—young men running naked through the city, striking women with a goatskin thong to make them fertile— and the priests proper, the Flamens; in another area, there are the different behaviors of the two first kings of Rome: Romulus, who founds the two cults of the terrible Jupiter, and Numa, who founds a

10. G. Dumézil, *Mitra-Varuna*, 2d ed. (1948), p. 85.

sanctuary of Fides Publica and professes a particular devotion to that goddess, who guarantees good faith and registers vows. In principle, the opposition Romulus-Numa coincides with the opposition Luperci-Flamens; it also corresponds exactly with the polarity Varuṇa-Mitra.

In his analysis of the two aspects of divine sovereignty among the Indians and the Romans, Dumézil has aptly emphasized the differences. In Vedic India as in Rome, the same Indo-European structure is recognizable, but the two "ideological fields" are not homogeneous. "The Romans think *historically*, whereas the Indians think *in fable*. The Romans think *nationally*, and the Indians *cosmically*." Over against the empirical, relativistic, political, juridical thought of the Romans stands the philosophical, absolute, dogmatic, moral, and mystical thought of the Indians.[11] Similar differences are discernible in the "ideological fields" of other Indo-European peoples. As we have already observed, the documents at our disposal constitute specific expressions of the different Āryan-speaking peoples in the course of history. In short, it is only the *general structure* of the Indo-European ideology that we can grasp, not the thought and religious practices of the original community. But this structure informs us concerning the type of religious experience and speculation peculiar to the Indo-Europeans. It allows us, furthermore, to appreciate the particular creativity of each of the Āryan-speaking peoples.

As was to be foreseen, the greatest morphological diversity is documented on the plane of the third function, for religious expressions related to abundance, peace, or fecundity are necessarily connected with the geography, economy, and historical situation of each group. As for the second function, physical force, and especially the use of force in combat, Dumézil has brought out a certain number of correspondences between India (already among the Indo-Europeans), Rome, and the Germanic world. Thus the supreme initiatory ordeal very probably consisted in the young warrior's fighting against three adversaries or against a three-headed monster (represented by a puppet?). And in fact such a scenario can be deciphered in the story of the victorious fight of the Irish hero Cuchulainn against three brothers, in the fight of Horatius against the three

11. Dumézil, *Servius et la Fortune*, pp. 190–92.

Curiatii, as well as in the myths of Indra and the Iranian hero Thraētaona, each of whom kills a monster with three heads. Victory produces in Cuchulainn and Horatius a "fury" (*furor*, Celtic *ferg*) that is dangerous to society and must be ritually exorcised. In addition, the mythical theme of the "three sins" of Indra finds homologues, in Scandinavia, in the tale of the hero Starcatherus, and, in Greece, in the mythology of Heracles.[12] Very probably these mythico-ritual themes did not exhaust the mythology and techniques of the warrior in the common Indo-European period. But it is important to note that they were preserved at the two extremes of the dispersal, India and Ireland.

So far as we can judge, the tripartite ideology constituted a consistent but flexible system, variously completed by a multitude of divine forms and religious ideas and practices. We shall have occasion to gauge their number and importance in studying the different Indo-European religions separately. There are reasons for believing that the tripartite ideology, though elaborated during the common period, had driven out or radically reinterpreted equally venerable conceptions, for example, that of the sky god as creator, sovereign, and father. The eviction of Dyauspitar for the benefit of Varuṇa, traces of which are found in the Rig Veda, seems to reflect, or to carry on, a process begun much earlier.

64. The Āryans in India

In their common period the Indo-Iranian tribes called themselves by a significant name, "noble (man)" (*airya* in Avestan, *ārya* in Sanskrit). The Āryans had begun their advance into northwestern India at the beginning of the second millennium; four or five centuries later they occupied the region of the "Seven Rivers," *sapta sindhavah*,[13] that is, the basin of the Upper Indus, the Punjab. As we remarked (§ 39), it is possible that the invaders attacked and ruined

12. These three sins are committed in respect to the three functions, taking place respectively in the domains of religious order, the warrior ideal, and fertility—which confirms the trifunctional hypothesis. We add that the identification of a common Indo-European motif in the mythology of Heracles is significant, for in Greece the tripartite ideology was early broken down as the result of symbiosis with Aegean culture.

13. The name is also known in the Avesta: *Haptahindu*.

certain Harappan cities. The Vedic texts recount the battles against the *dāsa* or *dasyu*, in whom we may recognize the continuers or survivors of the Indus civilization. They are described as having black skins, being "noseless," speaking a barbarian language, and professing the cult of the phallus (*śiśna deva*). They are rich in herds and live in fortified settlements (*pur*). It is these "forts" that Indra—surnamed *purandara*, "destroyer of fortifications"—attacked and ruined by the hundreds. The battles occurred before the composition of the hymns, for the memory of them is strongly mythologized. The Rig Veda also mentions another hostile population, the Pani, who steal cows and reject the Vedic cult. It is probable that Hari-yūpīyā, on the banks of the river Ravi, is identical with Harappa. In addition, the Vedic texts refer to the ruins (*arma, armaka*) inhabited by "witches"; this shows that the Āryans associated the ruined cities with the former inhabitants of the region.[14]

Nevertheless, symbiosis with the aborigines begins comparatively soon. If in the late books of the Rig Veda the word *dāsa* means "slave," indicating the fate of the conquered Dāsa, other members of the subjected population seem to be duly integrated into the Āryan society; for example, the chief Dāsa, praised because he protects the Brahmans (Rig Veda 8. 46. 32). Marriage with the autochthons leaves traces in the language. Vedic Sanskrit possesses a series of phonemes, especially the cerebral consonants, which are found in no other Indo-European idiom, not even in Iranian. Very probably these consonants reflect the pronunciation of the aborigines trying to learn the language of their masters. Similarly, the Vedic vocabulary preserves a large number of non-Āryan words. What is more, certain myths are of autochthonous origin.[15] This process of racial, cultural, and religious symbiosis, documented from the earliest period, will increase as the Āryans advance toward the plain of the Ganges.

The Vedic Indians practiced agriculture, but their economy was chiefly pastoral. Cattle performed the function of money. Milk and its products were eaten, but also the flesh of bovines. The horse was highly esteemed, but it was reserved exclusively for war, for raids,

---

14. B. and R. Allchin, *The Birth of Indian Civilization*, p. 155. The transformation of earthly enemies into demons, phantoms, or magicians is a comparatively frequent phenomenon; see Eliade, *Cosmos and History*, pp. 37 ff.

15. See Eliade, *Yoga*, pp. 352 ff., 429 ff.

and for the royal ritual (see § 73). The Āryans had no cities and knew nothing of writing. Despite the simplicity of their material culture, carpenters and bronzesmiths enjoyed great prestige.[16] Iron began to be used only about 1050 B.C.

The tribes were governed by military chiefs, *rājās*. The power of these kinglets was balanced by popular councils (*sabhā* and *samiti*). Toward the end of the Vedic period the organization of society into four classes had been completed. The term *varna*, designating the social classes, means "color," an indication of the ethnic multiplicity that was at the base of Indian society.

The hymns reveal only certain aspects of life during the Vedic period. Their representation is on the summary side: the Āryans love music and dancing: they play the flute, the lute, and the harp. They are fond of intoxicating drinks, *soma* and *surā*, the latter having no religious meaning. The game of dice was popular; an entire hymn of the Rig Veda (RV 10. 34) is devoted to it. A number of hymns refer to conflicts between different Āryan tribes. The most famous, the tribe of the Bharatas, had triumphed, under its king, Sudas, over a confederation of ten princes. But the historical data supplied by the Rig Veda are scanty enough. Certain names of Vedic tribes—for example, that of the Bharatas—reappear in later literature. The *Mahābhārata*, composed at least five or six centuries after the Vedic period, recounts the great war between the Kurus and their cousins, the Pāndavas. According to the tradition preserved by the Purāṇas, this war took place about 1400 B.C. in the Madhyadeśa, in the center of the peninsula, which indicates that the Āryans had advanced beyond the Ganges. At the time when the great theological treatise *Śatapatha Brāhmaṇa* was composed, between 1000 and 800 B.C., the provinces of Kosala and Videha were Āryanized. For its part, the *Rāmāyāna* shows that Āryan influence extended into the south.

Just as the adversaries of the Āryans were mythologized, metamorphosed into demons and sorcerers, the battles fought during the conquest of the territory were transfigured or, more precisely, assimilated to Indra's combats against Vṛtra and other demonic beings. We shall later discuss the cosmological implications of such paradigmatic combats (§ 68). For the moment, we will point out that

16. Naturally, this description of the material culture must be supplemented by the parallel world of the magico-religious values of tools and their respective mythologies (§ 9).

the occupation of a new territory became legitimate by the building of an altar (*gārhapatya*) dedicated to Agni.[17] "One says that one is settled (*avasyati*) when one has built a *gārhapatya*, and all those who build the fire altar are established" (*Śatapatha Br.* 7. 1. 1. 1–4). But the building of an altar dedicated to Agni is simply a ritual imitation of the creation. In other words, the occupied territory is first of all transformed from chaos to cosmos; by the effect of the rite, it receives a form and becomes *real*.

As we shall see in a moment, the Vedic pantheon is dominated by the gods. The few goddesses whose names we know play a more or less shadowy role: the enigmatic Aditi, the mother of the gods; Uśas, the goddess of dawn; Rātri, Night, to whom a beautiful hymn is devoted (Rig Veda 10. 127). All the more significant, then, is the dominant position of the Great Goddess in Hinduism; to be sure, she illustrates the triumph of extra-Brahmanic religiosity, but she also illustrates the creative power of the Indian spirit. Obviously, we must take it into account that the Vedic texts represent the religious system of a priestly elite which served a military aristocracy; the rest of the society—that is, the majority, the *vaiśyas* and the *sudras*— probably held ideas and beliefs similar to those that we find, two thousand years later, in Hinduism.[18] The hymns do not reflect the whole of the Vedic religion; they were composed for an audience primarily occupied with earthly goods: health, long life, many sons, abundant cattle, wealth.[19] So it is plausible to think that certain religious conceptions that will become popular later were already formulated in the Vedic period.

The creative power of the Indian spirit that we have just suggested appears especially in the process of symbiosis, assimilation, and revalorization that leads to the Āryanization of India and, later, to its Hinduization. For this process, which occupied several millennia, takes place in dialogue with the religious system elaborated by the Brahmans on the basis of the Vedic "revelation" (*śruti*). In the last

17. Cf. A. K. Coomaraswamy, *The Rigveda as Land-náma-bók*, p. 16; Eliade, *Cosmos and History*, p. 11.
18. Cf. Louis Renou, *Religions of Ancient India*, p. 6.
19. This is reminiscent of the situation of Greek religion in the time of Homer, whose poems were addressed to a military elite, little or not at all concerned with the mysteries of cosmic fertility and the postexistence of the soul—mysteries that, however, governed the religious activity of their wives and subjects.

analysis, the religious and cultural unity of India was the result of a long series of syntheses, effected under the sign of the poet-philosophers and ritualists of the Vedic period.

65. Varuṇa, primordial divinity: Devas and Asuras

The hymns do not present the oldest form of the Vedic religion. Dyaus, the Indo-European sky god, has already disappeared from the cult. His name now designates the "sky" or the "day." The vocable indicating the personification of uranian *sacrality* ends by designating a natural *phenomenon*. This is a comparatively frequent process in the history of celestial gods: they fade before other divinities and become *dii otiosi*. It is only insofar as he is venerated as sovereign god that a celestial god succeeds in preserving his original prestige.[20] Yet the Vedic poets still remember the "Sky that Knows All" (Atharva Veda 1. 32. 4), and they invoke the "Sky Father," Dyauspitar (ibid. 6. 4. 3); above all, Dyaus is present in the primordial pair, Dyāvāprithivī, "Sky and Earth" (Rig Veda 1. 160).

The place of Dyaus is very soon taken by Varuṇa, supremely the sovereign god. The stages that led to his advancement to the rank of universal king, *samraj* (RV 7. 82. 2) are little known. Varuna is designated especially by the title *asura*, a title also possessed by other gods, for example Agni (e.g., Atharva Veda 1. 10. 1, etc.). Now the Asuras constituted the most ancient divine family (AV 6. 100. 3). The Vedic texts refer to the conflict that opposed the gods (*devas*) to the Asuras. This conflict will be related and commented upon at length during the post-Vedic period, in the *Brāhmaṇas*, treatises devoted to the mystery of sacrifice. Indeed, thc victory of the gods was decided when Agni, at Indra's invitation, abandoned the Asuras, who did not possess sacrifice (RV 10. 124; 5. 5); soon afterward the Devas took the sacrificial Word (Vāc) from the Asuras. It was then that Indra invited Varuṇa into his kingdom (RV 5. 5). The victory of the Devas over the Asuras was assimilatcd to Indra's triumph over the Dasyus, who were also hurled down into deepest darkness (AV 10. 2. 17; cf. RV 7. 99. 4; etc.).

This mythical conflict reflects the battle of the young gods, directed by Indra, against a group of primordial divinities. The fact

20. See Eliade, *Patterns in Comparative Religion*, pp. 66 ff.

that the Asuras are reputed to be unrivaled magicians (AV 3. 9. 4; 6. 72. 1) and were assimilated to the *sudras* does not necessarily mean that they represent the gods of the pre-Āryan autochthonous populations. In the Vedas the title *asura* is used as an epithet for any god, even for Dyaus and Indra (the latter is named "Sovereign of the Asuras" in AV 6. 83. 3). In other words, the term *asura* refers to the specific sacred powers belonging to a primordial situation, especially that which existed before the organization of the world. The young gods, the Devas, did not fail to take over these sacred powers; this is why they enjoy the epithet *asura*.

It is important to emphasize that the "time of the Asuras" precedes the present epoch, ruled by the Devas. In India as in a number of archaic and traditional religions, the passage from a primordial epoch to the present epoch is explained in cosmogonic terms: passage from a state of chaos to an organized world, a cosmos. We shall find this cosmogonic background again in Indra's mythical combat against the primordial dragon, Vṛtra (§ 68). Now Varuṇa, as a primordial divinity, the outstanding *asura*, was identified with Vrtra. This identification made possible a whole series of esoteric speculations on the mystery of the divine biunity.

66. Varuṇa, universal king and magician: *ṛta* and *māyā*

The Vedic texts present Varuṇa as sovereign god: he reigns over the world, the gods (*devas*), and men. He "stretched out the Earth as a butcher stretches a hide, so that it should be the carpet of the Sun." He put "milk in cows, intelligence in hearts, fire in the waters, in the sky the sun, *soma* on the mountain" (RV 5. 85. 1–2). Cosmocrator, he possesses certain attributes of the celestial gods: he is *viśvadarśata*, "visible everywhere" (RV 8. 41. 3), omniscient (AV 4. 16. 2–7), and infallible (RV 4. 16. 2–7). He is "thousand-eyed" (RV 7. 34. 10), the mythical formula for the stars. Since he "sees" everything, and no sin, however hidden, escapes him, men feel "like slaves" in his presence (RV 1. 25. 1). "Terrible sovereign," "master of bonds," he has the magical power of binding his victims at a distance, but also of setting them free. Numerous hymns and rituals have as their object protecting or liberating man from the "bonds of Varuṇa."[21]

21. Eliade, *Images and Symbols*, pp. 95 ff. H. Petersson has explained Varuṇa's name from the Indo-European root *uer*, "to bind."

He is represented with a rope in his hand, and, in the ceremonies, whatever he binds or ties, beginning with knots, is called "Varunian."

Despite these spectacular accomplishments, Varuṇa is already in decline in the Vedic period. He is far from enjoying the popularity of Indra, for example. But he is intimately connected with two religious notions that will have an exceptional future: *ṛta* and *māyā*. The word *ṛta*, past participle of the verb "to fit," designates the order of the world—an order that is at once cosmic, liturgical, and moral.[22] There is no hymn addressed to *ṛta*, but the term is frequently used (more than 300 times in the Rig Veda). The creation is proclaimed to have been effected in conformity with *ṛta*, it is repeatedly said that the gods act according to *ṛta*, that *ṛta* rules both the cosmic rhythms and moral conduct. The same principle also governs the cult. "The seat of *ṛta*" is in the highest sky or in the fire altar.

Now Varuṇa was brought up in the "house" of *ṛta*, and he is declared to love *ṛta* and bear witness to *ṛta*. He is called the "King of *ṛta*," and this universal norm, identified with truth, is said to be "founded" in him. He who breaks the law is responsible before Varuṇa, and it is always Varuṇa, and only Varuṇa, who reestablishes the order damaged by sin, error, or ignorance. The sinner hopes for absolution through sacrifices (which, furthermore, are prescribed by Varuṇa himself). All this brings out his structure as cosmocrator-god. In the course of time Varuṇa will become a *deus otiosus*, surviving principally in the erudition of the ritualists and in religious folklore. Yet his relations to the idea of universal order suffice to insure him an important place in the history of Indian spirituality.[23]

At first sight it seems paradoxical that the guardian of *ṛta* should at the same time be intimately connected with *māyā*. Yet the association is comprehensible if we take into account the fact that Varuṇa's cosmic creativity also has a "magical" aspect. It has been agreed to derive the term *māyā* from the root *māy*, "to change." In the Rig Veda, *māyā* designates "destructive change or change that negates

22. "Seeing the prominent place held by this notion, almost under the same vocable, both among the para-Indians of Mesopotamia and Syria and among Iranians of every obedience, assures us that it already furnished the basis for the reflections and explanations of the Indian Indo-Iranians" (G. Dumézil, "Ordre, fantaisie, changement," *Revue des Etudes Latines* 32 [1957]: 140).

23. In the classic language the term *ṛta* will be replaced by the vocable *dharma*, whose grandiose destiny we shall see later. In the Rig Veda, *dhāman* and *dhārman* are used, respectively, 96 and 54 times.

good mechanisms, demonic and deceitful change, and also alteration of alteration." [24] In other words, there are good and evil *māyās*. In the first case, we have "ruses" and "magics," chiefly transformation magics of the demonic type, like those of the serpent Vrtra, who is the *māyin*, that is, the magician, the "trickster" without a rival. Such a *māyā* impairs the cosmic order; for example, it halts the course of the sun or holds the waters captive, etc. As for the good *māyās*, they are of two kinds: (1) the *māyās* of combat, the "counter-*māyās*" used by Indra when he challenges demonic beings, [25] and (2) the *māyā* that creates forms and beings—the privilege of the sovereign gods, first of all of Varuṇa. This cosmological *māyā* can be regarded as equivalent to *ṛta*. And in fact numerous passages present the alternation of day and night, the course of the sun, the falling of rain, and other phenomena implying *ṛta*, as resulting from the creative *māyā*.

So it is in the Rig Veda, some 1500 years before classic Vedānta, that we perceive the first meaning of *māyā*: "intentional change," that is, alteration—creation or destruction—and "alteration of alteration." It is to be noted now that the origin of the philosophical concept of *māyā*—cosmic illusion, unreality, nonbeing—is found at once in the idea of "change," of alteration of the cosmic norm, hence of *magical or demonic transformation*, and in the idea of the *creative power* of Varuṇa, who, by virtue of his *māyā*, reestablishes the order of the universe. From this we understand why *māyā* came to mean *cosmic illusion*; it is because, from the beginning, the notion involved is ambiguous, not to say ambivalent, for it implies not only demonic alteration of the cosmic order but also divine creativity. Later the cosmos itself will become, for Vedānta, an illusory "transformation," in other words, a system of changes devoid of reality.

To return to Varuṇa, it is to be noted that his mode of being—terrible sovereign, magician, and master of bonds—admits of a surprising closeness to the dragon Vṛtra. Whatever may be thought of the etymological kinship of their names, [26] it is proper to point

24. See Dumézil, "Ordre, fantaisie, changement," pp. 142 ff., with bibliography.
25. "He triumphed over the *māyin* by means of *māyās*"; such is the leitmotiv of numerous texts (Bergaigne, *La religion védique*, vol. 3, p. 82). Among Indra's "magics," the first place is held by his power of transformation; see Eliade, *Images and Symbols*, pp. 100 ff.; Dumézil, "Ordre, fantaisie, changement," pp. 143–44.
26. See Eliade, *Images and Symbols*, pp. 98 ff.

out that both of them are related to the primordial waters, and first of all to the "waters withheld" ("the great Varuṇa has hidden the sea," RV 9. 73. 3). Night (the nonmanifested),[27] the waters (the virtual; germs), transcendence and nonaction (characteristics of the sovereign gods) have a solidarity, at once mythical and metaphysical, not only with bonds of every kind, but also with the dragon Vṛtra, who, as we shall see, "withheld," "stopped," or "chained" the waters.

What is more, Varuṇa is assimilated to the serpent Ahi and to Vṛtra.[28] In the Atharva Veda (12. 3. 57) he is termed a "viper." But it is especially in the *Mahābhārata* that Varuṇa is identified with serpents. There he is called "Lord of the Sea" and "King of *nāgas*," and the ocean is the "dwelling place of the *nāgas*."[29]

67. Serpents and gods. Mitra, Aryaman, Aditi

This ambiguity and ambivalence of Varuṇa is important in several respects. But it is especially the paradigmatic character of the *union of opposites* that must claim our attention. For it constitutes one of the characteristics of Indian religious thought long before it becomes the object of systematic philosophy. Ambivalence and the union of contraries are not peculiar to Varuṇa alone. The Rig Veda (1. 79. 1) already termed Agni a "furious serpent." The *Aitareya Brāhmaṇa* (3. 36) states that the serpent Ahi Budhnya is invisibly (*parokṣeṇa*) what Agni is visibly (*pratyakṣa*). In other words, the serpent is a virtuality of fire, whereas darkness is nonmanifested light. In the *Vājasaneyi Samhitā* (5. 33), Ahi Budhnya and the Sun (*Aja Ekapad*) are identified. When the Sun rises at dawn, he "frees himself from Night . . . just as Ahi frees himself from his skin" (*Śat. Br.* 2. 3; 1. 3 and 6). Similarly, the god Soma, "just like Ahi, crawls out of his old skin" (RV 9. 86. 44). The *Śatapatha Brāhmaṇa* identifies him

27. Certain passages of the Rig Veda saw in Varuṇa the nonmanifested, the virtual, and the eternal.

28. See the references assembled by Coomaraswamy, "Angel and Titan," p. 391, note.

29. *Mahābhārata* 1. 21. 6 and 25. 4. In other passages King Varuṇa is regarded as being among the most preeminent *nāgas*, and he is mentioned in association with mythical serpents already documented in the Vedic sources; see G. Johnsen, "Varuṇa and Dhrtarāṣṭra," pp. 260 ff.

with Vṛtra (3. 4. 3. 13; etc.). The Adityas are said to have been originally serpents. Having cast off their old skins—which means that they
acquired immortality ("they have conquered Death")—they became
gods, Devas (*Pancaviṁśa Br.* 25. 15. 4). Finally, the *Śatapatha
Brāhmaṇa* (13. 4. 3. 9) declares that "the knowledge of the Serpents
(*sarpa-vidyā*) is the Veda."[30] In other words, the divine doctrine is
paradoxically identified with a "knowledge" that, at least in the
beginning, had a "demonic" character.

To be sure, the assimilation of the gods to the serpents in some
sort prolongs the idea, documented in the *Bṛhadāranyaka Upaniṣad*
(1. 3. 1), that the Devas and the Asuras are the children of Prajāpati
and that the Asuras are the elder. The common descent of antagonistic figures constitutes one of the favorite themes to illustrate the
primordial unity-totality. We shall find a spectacular example of this
when we study the theological interpretations of the famous mythical
combat between Indra and Vṛtra.

As for Mitra, his role is secondary when he is isolated from
Varuṇa. In the Veda, only one hymn (RV 3. 59) is devoted to him.
But he shares with Varuṇa the attributes of sovereignty, incarnating
its pacific, benevolent, juridical, and sacerdotal aspects. As his name
indicates, he is "Contract" personified, just like the Avestan Mithra.
He facilitates agreements between men and makes them honor their
engagements. The sun is his eye (*Taitt. Brāh.* 3. 1. 5. 1); all-seeing,
nothing escapes him. His importance in religious activity and thought
is especially manifested when he is invoked together with Varuṇa, of
whom he is at once the antithesis and the complement. The binomial
Mitra-Varuṇa, which even in the earliest period played a considerable
role as supreme expression of divine sovereignty, was later used as a
paradigmatic formula for all kinds of antagonistic pairs and complementary oppositions.

With Mitra are associated Aryaman and Bhaga. The former
protects the society of the Āryans; he especially governs the obliga-
tions that establish hospitality and is concerned with marriages.
Bhaga, whose name means "share," insures the distribution of
wealth. Together with Mitra and Varuṇa (and sometimes with other
gods), Aryaman and Bhaga make up the group of the Adityas, or
sons of the goddess Aditi, the "Nonbound," that is, the Free. Since

30. On this theme, see Eliade, *The Two and the One*, pp. 88 ff.

the time of Max Müller the structure of this goddess has been widely discussed. The texts identify her with the earth or even with the universe; she represents extension, breadth, freedom.[31] Very probably, Aditi was a Great Mother who, without being completely forgotten, had transmitted her qualities and her functions to her sons, the Adityas.

68. Indra, champion and demiurge

In the Rig Veda, Indra is the most popular god. Some 250 hymns are addressed to him, in comparison with 10 addressed to Varuṇa, and 35 to Mitra, Varuṇa, and the Adityas together. He is the hero without rival, paradigmatic model of warriors, redoubtable foe of the Dāsyus or Dāsas. His acolytes, the Maruts, reflect, on the mythological plane, the Indo-Iranian societies of young warriors (*marya*). But Indra is also demiurge and fecundator, personification of the exuberance of life, of cosmic and biological energy. Tireless consumer of *soma*, archetype of generative forces, he looses hurricanes, pours down rain, and commands all forms of wetness.[32]

The central myth of Indra, which is, furthermore, the most important myth in the Rig Veda, narrates his victorious battle against Vṛtra, the gigantic dragon who held back the waters in the "hollow of the mountains." Strengthened by *soma*, Indra lays the serpent low with his *vajra* ("thunderbolt"), the weapon forged by Tvaṣṭṛ, splits open his head, and frees the waters, which pour into the sea "like bellowing cows" (RV 1. 32).

The battle of a god against an ophidian or marine monster is well known to constitute a widespread mythological theme. We need only remember the struggle between Re and Apophis, between the Sumerian god Ninurta and Asag, Marduk and Tiamat, the Hittite storm god and the serpent Illuyankas, Zeus and Typhon, the Iranian hero Thraētaona and the three-headed dragon Azhi-dahâka. In certain cases (Marduk-Tiamat, for example) the god's victory

---

31. J. Gonda, *Some Observations on the Relations between "Gods" and "Powers,"* pp. 75 ff.

32. Indra is called *sahasramuṣka*, "with a thousand testicles" (RV 6. 46. 3); he is "the master of the fields" (RV 8. 21. 3) and "master of the earth" (Atharva Veda 12. 1. 6), the fecundator of fields, animals, and women; see Eliade, *Patterns in Comparative Religion*, p. 85.

constitutes the preliminary condition for the cosmogony. In other cases the stake is the inauguration of a new era or the establishment of a new sovereignty (cf. Zeus-Typhon, Baal-Yam). In short, it is by the slaying of an ophidian monster—symbol of the virtual, of "chaos," but also of the "autochthonous"—that a new cosmic or institutional "situation" comes into existence. A characteristic feature, and one common to all these myths, is the fright, or a first defeat, of the champion (Marduk and Re hesitate before fighting; at the outset, the serpent Illuyankas succeeds in mutilating the god; Typhon succeeds in cutting and carrying off Zeus's tendons). According to the *Śatapatha Brāhmaṇa* (1. 6. 3–17), Indra, on first seeing Vṛtra, runs away as far as possible, and the *Mārkaṇḍeya Purāṇa* describes him as "sick with fear" and hoping for peace.[33]

It would serve no purpose to dwell on the naturalistic interpretations of this myth; the victory over Vṛtra has been seen either as rain brought on by a thunderstorm or as the freeing of the mountain waters (Oldenberg) or as the triumphs of the sun over the cold that had "imprisoned" the waters by freezing them (Hillebrandt). Certainly, naturalistic elements are present, since the myth is multivalent; Indra's victory is equivalent, among other things, to the triumph of life over the sterility and death resulting from the immobilization of the waters by Vrtra. But the structure of the myth is cosmogonic. In Rig Veda 1. 33. 4 it is said that, by his victory, the god created the sun, the sky, and dawn. According to another hymn (RV 10. 113. 4–6), Indra, as soon as he was born, separated the Sky from the Earth, fixed the celestial vault, and, hurling the *vajra*, tore apart Vṛtra, who was holding the waters captive in the darkness. Now, Sky and Earth are the parents of the gods (1. 185. 6); Indra is the youngest (3. 38. 1) and also the last god to be born, because he put an end to the hierogamy of Sky and Earth: "By his strength, he spread out these two worlds, Sky and Earth, and caused the sun to shine" (8. 3. 6). After this demiurgic feat, Indra appointed Varuṇa

33. In fact he sent him messengers, who established "friendship" and "a pact" between them. Indra, however, broke the agreement by killing Vṛtra by trickery, and this was his great sin; see Dumézil, *Heur et malheur du guerrier*, pp. 71 ff. (Eng. trans., *The Destiny of the Warrior*, pp. 74 ff.). Another feature peculiar to the Indian myth is that, after the murder, Indra is stricken with fear, flees to the ends of the earth, and, "assuming a minute form," hides in a lotus (*Mahābhārata* 5. 9. 2 ff.; this theme had already appeared in RV 1. 32. 14).

cosmocrator and guardian of *ṛta* (which had remained concealed in the world below; 1. 62. 1).

As we shall see (§ 75), there are other types of Indian cosmogonies that explain the creation of the world from a *materia prima*. This is not the case with the myth we have just summarized, for here a certain type of "world" already existed. For Sky and Earth were formed and had engendered the gods. Indra only separated the cosmic parents, and, by hurling the *vajra* at Vṛtra, he put an end to the immobility, or even the "virtuality," symbolized by the dragon's mode of being.³⁴ According to certain traditions, the "fashioner" of the gods, Tvaṣṭṛ, whose role is not clear in the Rig Veda, had built himself a house and created Vṛtra as a sort of roof, but also as walls, for his habitation. Inside this dwelling, encircled by Vṛtra, Sky, Earth, and the Waters existed.³⁵ Indra bursts asunder this primordial monad by breaking the "resistance" and inertia of Vṛtra. In other words, the world and life could not come to birth except by the slaying of an amorphous Being. In countless variants, this myth is quite widespread, and in India itself we shall find it again in the dismemberment of Puruṣa by the gods and in the self-sacrifice of Prajāpati. However, Indra does not perform a sacrifice but, as a warrior, kills the paradigmatic adversary, the primordial dragon, incarnation of resistance and inertia.

The myth is multivalent; side by side with its cosmogonic meaning there are naturalistic and historical valences. Indra's combat served as model for the battles that the Āryans had to sustain against the Dāsyus (also termed *vṛtāṇi*): "He who triumphs in a battle, he truly kills Vṛtra" (*Maitrāyaṇi-Saṃhitā* 2. 1. 3). It is probable that in the early period the fight between Indra and Vṛtra constituted the mythico-ritual scenario of the New Year festival, which insured the regeneration of the world.³⁶ If that god is at once tireless champion, demiurge, and epiphany of orgiastic forces and universal fertility, it

34. Indra encounters Vṛtra "not divided, not awake, plunged in the deepest sleep, stretched out" (RV 4. 19. 3).

35. It has been Norman W. Brown in particular who has attempted to reconstruct this cosmological conception.

36. Kuiper, "The Ancient Aryan Verbal Contest," p. 269. The oratorical contests in Vedic India also reiterated the primordial struggle against the forces of resistance (*vṛtāṇi*). The poet compares himself to Indra: "I am the murderer of my rivals, without wounds, safe and sound like Indra" (RV 10. 166. 2; cf. Kuiper, pp. 251 ff.).

is because violence makes life spring up, increases it and regenerates it; but Indian speculation will very soon use this myth as an illustration of the divine biunity and, consequently, as an example of a hermeneutics seeking to unveil the ultimate reality.

69. Agni, chaplain of the gods: Sacrificial fire, light, and intelligence

The cult role of the domestic fire was already important in the Indo-European period. It certainly goes back to a prehistoric custom, which is also amply documented in a number of primitive societies. In the Veda, the god Agni supremely represents the sacrality of fire, but he does not submit to be limited by these cosmic and ritual hierophanies. He is the son of Dyaus (RV 1. 26. 10), just as his Iranian homologue, Atar, is the son of Ahura Mazdā (*Yasna* 2. 12; etc.). He "is born" in the sky, from which he descends in the form of lightning, but he is also in water, in wood, in plants. He is further identified with the sun.

Agni is described at once by his fiery epiphanies and by divine attributes that are peculiar to him. There is mention of his "flaming hair," his "golden jaw," the noise and terror that he produces ("When thou descendest on the trees like an eager bull, thy trail is black," RV 1. 58. 4). He is the "messenger" between sky and earth, and it is through him that offerings reach the gods. But Agni is above all the archetype of the priest; he is called the sacrificer or the "chaplain" (*purohita*). This is why the hymns devoted to him are put at the beginning of the Rig Veda. The first hymn opens with this strophe: "I sing Agni, the chaplain, the god of sacrifice, the priest, the oblator who showers us with gifts" (after the translation by Jean Varenne). He is eternally young ("the god who does not grow old," RV 1. 52. 2), for he is reborn with every new fire. As "master of the house" (*grihaspati*), Agni dispels darkness, drives away demons, and defends against sickness and sorcery. This is why men's relations with Agni are more intimate than with the other gods. It is he who "justly dispenses desirable goods" (1. 58. 3). He is invoked confidently: "Lead us, Agni, to riches by the right road . . . spare us the fault that leads astray . . . spare us sicknesses. Protect us always, Agni, with thy tireless guards. . . . Do not abandon us to the wicked man, the destroyer, the liar, or to misfortune" (1. 187. 1–5; after the translation by Jean Varenne).[37]

Although omnipresent in religious life—for the sacrificial fire plays a large part—Agni has no considerable mythology. Among the few myths that directly concern him, the most famous is that of Mātariśvan, who had brought fire from the sky.[38] On the cosmological plane, his role is apparently confused but important. On the one hand, he is called the "embryo of the Waters" (*āpam garbhah*, RV 3. 1. 12–13), and he is invoked as springing from the womb of the Waters, the Mothers (10. 91. 6). On the other hand, he is held to have penetrated the primordial waters and to have fecundated them. This certainly involves an archaic cosmological conception: creation by the union of an igneous element (fire itself, heat, light, *semen virile*) with the aquatic principle (waters, virtualities, *soma*). Certain attributes of Agni (heat, golden color—for he is said to have a body of gold [RV 4. 3. 1]—spermatic and creative powers [10. 20. 9]) will be found again in the cosmogonic speculations elaborated around Hiraṇygarbha (the Golden Embryo) and Prajāpati (§ 75).

The hymns emphasize Agni's spiritual faculties: he is a *ṛṣi*, endowed with great intelligence and clairvoyance. To estimate such speculations at their true value, we must take into account the innumerable images and symbols revealed by the "creative imagination" and meditations on the subject of fire, flames, heat. All this, in any case, constituted an inheritance that came down from prehistory. The Indian genius only elaborated, articulated, and systematized these immemorial discoveries. In later philosophical speculations we shall again find some of these primordial images connected with fire, for example in the concept of divine creative play (*līlā*) explained on the basis of the "play" of flames. As for the assimilation fire-(light)-intelligence, it is universally disseminated.[39]

It is here that we best gauge the importance of Agni in Indian religion and spirituality: he gave rise to countless cosmobiological meditations and speculations, he facilitated syntheses seeking the

37. Because of his role in the cremation of corpses, Agni is called "devourer of flesh" and is sometimes compared to the dog and the jackal. This is his only sinister aspect.

38. In other texts Agni is himself the messenger of Mātariśvan; see J. Gonda, *Les religions de l'Inde*, vol. 1, p. 89.

39. Religious meditation on the sacrificial fire plays an important part in Zoroastrianism (see § 104).

reduction of multiple and different planes to a single fundamental principle. To be sure, Agni has not been the only Indian god to feed such reveries and reflections, but his place is in the first rank. As early as the Vedic period, he was already identified with *tejas*, "fiery energy, splendor, efficacy, majesty, supernatural power." In the hymns he is implored to bestow this power (AV 7. 89. 4).[40] But the series of identifications, assimilations, and solidarizations—a process characteristic of Indian thought—is much greater. Agni, or one of his homologues, the Sun, is involved in the *philosophoumena* that seek to identify light with the *ātman* and the *semen virile*. By virtue of the rites and asceticisms that pursue the increase of "inner heat," Agni is equally bound up, though sometimes indirectly, with the religious valorization of "ascetic heat" (*tapas*) and some of the practices of Yoga.

70. The god Soma and the drink of "nondeath"

With the 120 hymns devoted to him, Soma appears as third in the Vedic pantheon. The entire ninth book of the Rig Veda is dedicated to Soma *pavamāna*—*soma* "in the process of clarification." Even more than in the case of Agni, it is not easy to separate the ritual reality—the plant and the drink—from the god who bears the same name. The myths are negligible. The most important of them relates the celestial origin of *soma*. An eagle, "flying up to the sky," hurled itself "with the swiftness of thought and forced the bronze fortress" (RV 8. 100. 8). The bird seized the plant and brought it back to earth. But *soma* is held to grow in the mountains;[41] only a seeming contradiction is involved, however, for mountaintops belong to the transcendental world; they are already assimilated to the sky. Besides, other texts state that *soma* springs up "at the navel of the earth, on the mountains" (RV 10. 82. 3), that is, at the "center of the world," where passage between earth and sky becomes possible.[42]

40. See Gonda, "*Gods*" *and* "*Powers*," pp. 58 ff.

41. The epithet "Maujavata" indicates Mount Mūjavat as the domain of *soma* (RV 10. 34. 1). Iranian tradition similarly localizes the plant *haoma* in the mountains (*Yasna* 10. 4; *Yašt* 9. 17; etc.).

42. In the texts of the Yajur-Veda the sacrifice of Soma by the gods is frequently mentioned; only Mitra refused to take part in it, but he, too, was finally persuaded. Traces of an origin myth could be deciphered in this

Soma has no attributes except the usual ones that are conferred on gods: he is clairvoyant, intelligent, wise, victorious, generous, etc. He is proclaimed the friend and protector of the other gods; first and foremost, he is the friend of Indra. He is also called King Soma, doubtless because of his ritual importance. His identification with the moon, which is unknown in the Avesta, is clearly documented only in the post-Vedic period.

A number of details connected with the squeezing of the plant are described in terms that are at once cosmic and biological; the dull sound produced by the lower millstone is assimilated to thunder, the wool of the filter represents the clouds, the juice is the rain that makes vegetation come up, etc. The squeezing is also identified with sexual union. But all these symbols of biocosmic fertility finally depend on the "mystical" value of Soma.

The texts emphasize the ceremonies that precede and accompany the purchase of the plant and, above all, the preparation of the drink. From the time of the Rig Veda the *soma* sacrifice was the most popular, "the soul and center of sacrifice" (Gonda). Whatever plant was used by the Indo-Aryans in the early centuries, it is certain that it was later replaced by other botanical species. *Soma/haoma* is the Indo-Iranian formula for the drink of "nondeath" (*amṛta*); presumably it replaced the Indo-European drink *madhu*, "hydromel."

All the virtues of *soma* are bound up with the ecstatic experience brought on by its ingestion. "We have drunk *soma*," says a famous hymn (RV 8. 48), "we have become immortal; arrived at light, we have found the Gods. What can the impiety or the malice of mortals do to us now, O immortal?" (strophe 3). *Soma* is implored to lengthen "our time to live"; for it is "the guardian of our body," and "weaknesses, sicknesses, have taken flight" (after the translation by L. Renou). *Soma* stimulates thought, revives the warrior's courage, increases sexual vigor, cures diseases. Drunk in common by priests and gods, it brings Earth close to the Sky, reinforces and lengthens life, insures fecundity. And in fact the ecstatic experience reveals at once the fullness of life, the sense of a limitless freedom, the possession of almost unsuspected physical and spiritual powers. From this comes the feeling of community with the gods, even of

---

episode: the creation of the "immortalizing" drink by the sacrifice of a primordial being. This first murder, performed by the gods, is indefinitely repeated in the ritual squeezing of the plant *soma*.

belonging to the divine world, the certainty of "nondeath," that is, in the first place, of a plenitude of life that is indefinitely prolonged. Who is speaking in the famous hymn 10. 119, the god or the ecstatic who had just imbibed the sacred drink? "The five (human) tribes did not seem to me worth even a look—have I not drunk *soma*?" The personage enumerates his exploits: "I have dominated the sky with my stature, dominated the vast earth. . . . I shall strike this earth great blows. . . . I traced one of my wings in the sky, I traced the other here below. . . . I am great, great, I have propelled myself even up to the clouds—have I not drunk *soma*?" (after the translation by Renou).[43]

We will not stop to consider the surrogates and substitutes for the original plant in the cult. It is the role that these somic experiences play in Indian thought that is important. Very probably such experiences were confined to priests and a certain number of sacrificers. But they had considerable repercussions by virtue of the hymns that praised them and especially by virtue of the interpretations the hymns called forth. The revelation of a full and beatific existence, in communion with the gods, continued to haunt Indian spirituality long after the disappearance of the original drink. Hence the attempt was made to attain such an existence by the help of other means: asceticism or orgiastic excesses, meditation, the techniques of Yoga, mystical devotion. As we shall see (§ 79), archaic India knew several types of ecstatics. In addition, the quest for absolute freedom gave rise to a whole series of methods and *philosophoumena* that, in the last analysis, opened out into new perspectives and vistas, unsuspected in the Vedic period. In all these later developments, the *god* Soma played a not very prominent role; it is the cosmological and sacrificial *principle* that he signified which ended by preempting the attention of theologians and metaphysicians.

71. Two Great Gods in the Vedic period: Rudra-Śiva and Viṣṇu

The Vedic texts also mention a certain number of other divinities. Most of them will gradually lose their importance and end by being forgotten, while others will finally attain an unequaled position.

43. "It seems that the hymn should be put in the mouth of the god Agni, who, in the course of a sacrifice, would have been asked by the poet to express the effects he experiences after drinking the divine liquid" (L. Renou, *Hymnes spéculatifs du Véda*, p. 252).

Among the former we may mention the goddess of dawn, Uṣas, daughter of the Sky (Dyaus); Vāyu, god of the wind and of its homologues, "breath" and the "cosmic soul"; Parjanya, god of storms and of the rainy season; Sūrya and Saviṭr, solar divinities; Pūṣan, ancient pastoral god but on the way to disappearing (he has almost no cult), guardian of roads and guide of the dead, who has been compared to Hermes; the twin Aśvins (or Nāsatyas), sons of Dyaus, heroes of many myths and legends that have given them a preponderant place in later literature; the Maruts, sons of Rudra, a troop of young men (*marya*), whom Stig Wikander has interpreted as the mythical model for a "men's society" of the Indo-European type.

The second category is represented by Rudra-Śiva and Viṣṇu. They occupy a small place in the Vedic texts, but in the classic period they will become Great Gods. In the Rig Veda, Viṣṇu appears as a divinity kindly disposed toward men (1. 186. 10), friend and ally of Indra, whom he helps in his battle against Vṛtra, afterward stretching out the space between sky and earth (6. 69. 5). He crossed space in three strides, reaching, with the third, the abode of the gods (1. 155. 6). This myth inspires and justifies a rite in the *Brāhmaṇas*: Viṣṇu is identified with sacrifice (*Śatapatha Br.* 14. 1. 1. 6); and the sacrificer, by ritually imitating his three strides, is assimilated to the god and attains the sky (1. 9. 3. 9 ff.). Viṣṇu appears to symbolize at once limitless spatial extent (which makes the organization of the cosmos possible), the beneficient and omnipotent energy that exalts life, and the cosmic axis that steadies the world. The Rig Veda (7. 99. 2) states specifically that he supports the upper part of the universe.[44] The *Brāhmaṇas* emphasize his relations with Prajāpati, which are documented from the Vedic period. But it is not until later, in the Upanishads of the second category (contemporary with the *Bhagavad Gītā*, hence of about the fourth century B.C.), that Viṣṇu is exalted as a supreme god of monotheistic structure. We shall later dwell on this process, which is, furthermore, characteristic of Indian religious creativity.

Morphologically, Rudra represents a divinity of the opposite type. He has no friends among the gods, and he does not love men, whom he terrorizes by his demonic fury and decimates by sicknesses and

44. See J. Gonda, *Viṣṇuism and Śivaism*, pp. 10 ff. The sacrificial post, *yūpa*, belongs to him (the *yūpa* is a replica of the *axis mundi*). See also Gonda, *Aspects of Early Viṣṇuism*, pp. 81 ff.

disasters. Rudra wears his hair braided (RV 1. 114. 1. 5), and his color is dark brown (2. 33. 5); his belly is black and his back red. He is armed with bow and arrows, dressed in animal skins, and haunts the mountains, his favorite resort. He is associated with numerous demonic beings.

Post-Vedic literature accentuates the god's maleficent nature. Rudra lives in forests and jungles, is called "Lord of Wild Beasts" (*Śat. Br.* 12. 7. 3. 20), and protects those who shun the Āryan society. While the gods live in the East, Rudra lives in the North (i.e., the Himalayas). He is excluded from the *soma* sacrifice and receives only offerings of food thrown on the ground (*bali*) or the remains of oblations or spoiled sacrificial offerings (*Śat. Br.* 1. 7. 4. 9). Epithets multiply: he is called Śiva, "the gracious," Hara, "the destroyer," Shaṃkara, "the salutary," and Mahādeva, "the great god."

According to the Vedic texts and the *Brāhmaṇas*, Rudra-Śiva appears to be an epiphany of the demonic (or at least ambivalent) powers inhabiting wild, unpeopled places; he symbolizes all that is chaotic, dangerous, unforeseeable; he inspires fear, but his mysterious magic can also be directed toward beneficial ends (he is "physician of physicians"). There has been much discussion concerning the origin and original structure of Rudra-Śiva, considered by some to be the god of death but also of fertility (Arbman), laden with non-Āryan elements (Lommel), divinity of that mysterious class of ascetics, the *vrātyas* (Hauer). The stages of the transformation of the Vedic Rudra-Śiva into the Supreme God that he first proves to be in the *Śvetāśvatara-Upaniṣad* escape us. It seems certain that in the course of time Rudra-Śiva assimilated—like most of the other gods—a number of elements of "popular" religiosity, whether Āryan or non-Āryan. On the other hand, it would be risky to believe that the Vedic texts have brought us the "original structure" of Rudra-Śiva. We must always remember that the Vedic hymns and the Brahmanic treatises were composed for an elite, the aristocracy and the priests, and that a considerable part of the religious life of the Āryan society was strictly ignored. However, the advancement of Śiva to the rank of supreme god of Hinduism cannot be explained by his "origin," even if it was non-Āryan or popular. In him we have a creation whose originality we shall gauge when we analyze the Indian religious dialectic, as it appears in the continual reinterpretation and revalorization of myths, rites, and divine forms.

9 India before Gautama Buddha: From the Cosmic Sacrifice to the Supreme Identity Ātman-Brahman

72. Morphology of the Vedic rituals

The Vedic cult had no sanctuary; the rites were performed either in the sacrificer's house or on a nearby piece of grassy ground, on which the three fires were placed. The nonflesh offerings were milk, butter, cereals, and cakes. Also sacrificed were the goat, the cow, the bull, the ram, and the horse. But from the period of the Rig Veda the *soma* sacrifice was considered the most important one.

The rites fall into two classes: domestic (*gṛhya*) and solemn (*śrauta*). The former, performed by the master of the house (*gṛhapati*), are justified by tradition (*smṛti*, "memory"). In contrast, the solemn rites are usually performed by officiants.[1] Their authority is based on direct revelation ("auditory," *śruti*) of eternal truth. Among the private rituals, aside from keeping up the domestic fire and the agricultural festivals, the most important are the sacraments or consecrations (*saṃskāra*) in connection with the conception and birth of children; the introduction (*upanayana*) of the boy to his Brahmanic preceptor; marriage; and funerals. These are all comparatively simple ceremonies, involving nonflesh oblations and offerings[2] and,

1. The number of officiants varies. The most important is the *hotṛ* or "pourer of the oblation" (cf. Avestan *zaôtar*, "priest"); he later becomes the principal reciter. The *adhvaryu* bears the responsibility for the sacrifice: he moves about, keeps up the fires, manipulates the utensils, etc. The *brahman*, representative of the sacred power that his name designates (*brahman*, neuter), is the silent overseer of the cult; seated in the center of the area, true "physician of the sacrifice," he intervenes only if an error is made, when he performs the necessary expiation. The *brahman* receives half of the honorarium, which confirms his importance.

2. A part of the offerings, thrown into the fire, was transmitted to the gods by Agni. The rest was eaten by the officiants, who thus partook of a divine food.

for the sacraments, ritual gestures accompanied by formulas murmured by the master of the house.

Of all the sacraments, the *upanayana* is certainly the most important. This rite constitutes the homologue of the puberty initiations typical of archaic societies. Atharva Veda 11. 5. 3, where the *upanayana* is first documented, states that the preceptor transforms the boy into an embryo and keeps him for three nights in his belly. The *Śatapatha Brāhmaṇa* (11. 5. 4. 12–13) supplies the following details: the preceptor conceives at the moment when he puts his hand on the child's shoulder, and, on the third day, the child is reborn in the state of brahmanhood. The Atharva Veda (19. 17) calls him who has gone through the *upanayana* "twice-born" (*dvi-ja*), and this is the first appearance of the term, which is to enjoy an exceptional destiny.

The second birth is evidently of a spiritual order, and the later texts emphasize this essential point. According to the Laws of Manu (2. 144), he who communicates the word of the Veda—that is, the *brahman*—to the novice must be regarded as mother and father; indeed, as between a boy's biological father and his Brahmanic preceptor, it is the latter who is the true father (2. 146); the *true* birth[3] —in other words, birth to immortality—is given by the *sāvitrī* formula (2. 148). During his whole period of study with his preceptor, the pupil (the *brahmacārin*) is obliged to follow certain rules: to beg food for his master and himself, observe chastity, etc.

The solemn rites make up liturgical systems that are of great, yet monotonous, complexity. The detailed description of a single system would take several hundred pages. It would be useless to attempt to summarize all the *śrauta* sacrifices. The simplest, the *agnihotra* ("the oblation to fire"), takes place at dawn and twilight and consists in an offering of milk to Agni. There are also rites connected with the cosmic rhythms: the sacrifices called "of rain and of the new moon," seasonal ceremonies (*cāturmāsya*), and first-fruits rites (*āgrayaṇa*). But the essential sacrifices, specifically characteristic of the Vedic cult, are those of *soma*. The *agniṣṭoma* ("praise of Agni") is performed once a year, in spring, and consists, aside from the preliminary operations, in three days of "homage" (*upasad*). Among the prelimi-

3. This is a pan-Indian conception, and is taken up again by Buddhism. By giving up his family name the novice became a "son of Buddha" (*sakyaputto*); for examples see Eliade, *Birth and Rebirth*, pp. 53 ff.; Gonda, *Change and Continuity*, pp. 447 ff.

nary operations, the most important is the *dīkṣā*, which sanctifies the sacrificer by causing him to be reborn. The significance of this initiatory ritual will become clear further on. The *soma* is squeezed in the morning, at noon, and in the evening. At the midday squeezing there is a distribution of honorariums (*dākṣiṇā*): 7, 21, 60, or 1,000 cows, or, on occasion, the whole of the sacrificer's possessions. All the gods are invited, and they take part in the festival, first separately, then together.[4]

Other *soma* sacrifices are also known. Some are completed in a single day; others last for at least twelve days or, often, a year, and theoretically they can last for twelve years. In addition, there are ritual systems that were associated with the *soma* services, for example the *mahāvrata* ("great observance"), which includes music, dances, dramatic gestures, dialogues, and obscene scenes (one of the priests swings in a swing, a sexual union takes place, etc.). The *vajapeya* ("drink of victory") lasts from seventeen days to a year and constitutes an entire mythico-ritual scenario: a race between horses harnessed to seventeen chariots, the "ascent to the sun," performed by the sacrificer and his wife, who ceremonially climb the sacred post, etc. The royal consecration (*rājasūya*) was also incorporated into the somic sacrificial system. In this case, too, we find lively episodes (a simulated raid by the king on a herd of cows; the king plays dice with a priest and wins, etc.), but in essence the ritual is directed to the mystical rebirth of the sovereign (§ 74). Another ceremonial system was associated, though optionally, with the *soma* sacrifice: this is the *agnicayana*, the "piling up (of bricks for the altar) of fire." The texts state that "in former days" five victims were immolated, one of them a man. Their heads were then walled up in the first course of bricks. The preliminaries lasted for a year. The altar, built with 10,800 bricks piled up in five courses, sometimes took the form of a bird, symbol of the sacrificer's mystical ascent to heaven. The *agnicayana* gave rise to cosmogonic speculations that were decisive for Indian thought. The immolation of a man repeated the self-sacrifice of Prajāpati, and the building of the altar symbolized the creation of the universe (§ 75).

4. Another rite, *pravargya*, was early incorporated into the *agnistoma*, but it probably constituted an autonomous ceremony, the purpose of which was to strengthen the sun after the rainy season. The interest of the *pravargya* lies especially in its having the characteristics of a "mystery" and also in the fact

73. The supreme sacrifices: *aśvamedha* and *puruṣamedha*

The most important and most celebrated Vedic ritual was the "horse sacrifice," the *aśvamedha*. It could be performed only by a victorious king, who thus gained the dignity of "Universal Sovereign." But the results of the sacrifice radiated over the entire kingdom; in fact, the *aśvamedha* was held to cleanse pollutions and insure fecundity and prosperity throughout the country. The preliminary ceremonies were spaced out over a year, during which the stallion was left at liberty with a hundred other horses. Four hundred young men were on guard to keep it from approaching the mares. The ritual proper lasted for three days. On the second day, after some specific ceremonies (mares were shown to the stallion, it was harnessed to a chariot, the prince drove it to a pond, etc.), numerous domestic animals were immolated. Finally, the stallion, which thenceforth incarnated the god Prajāpati ready to sacrifice himself, was suffocated. The four queens, each accompanied by a hundred female attendants, walked around the body, and the principal wife lay down beside it; covered with a cloak, she simulated sexual union. During this time the priests and the women exchanged obscene pleasantries. As soon as the queen rose, the horse and the other victims were cut up. The third day included other rituals, and finally the honorariums (*dākṣiṇā*) were distributed to the priests; they also received the four queens or their attendants.

The horse sacrifice is certainly of Indo-European origin. Traces of it are found among the Germans, the Iranians, the Greeks, the Romans, the Armenians, the Massagetae, the Dalmatians. But it is only in India that this mythico-ritual scenario has obtained so considerable a place in religious life and theological speculation. Probably the *aśvamedha* was, in the beginning, a spring festival, more precisely a rite celebrated at the time of the New Year. Its structure includes cosmogonic elements. On the one hand, the horse is identified with the cosmos (= Prajāpati) and its sacrifice symbolizes (that is, *reproduces*) the act of creation. On the other hand, the Rigvedic and Brahmanic texts emphasize the relations between the horse and the primordial waters. Now in India the waters represent the cosmo-

---

that it offers the earliest illustration of *pūjā*, i.e., the worship of a divinity symbolized in an icon. See J. A. van Buitenen, *The Pravargya*, pp. 25 ff., 38, and passim.

gonic substance par excellence. But this complex rite also constitutes a "mystery" of the esoteric type. "Indeed, the *aśvamedha* is all, and he who, being a Brahman, knows nothing of the *aśvamedha*, knows nothing at all, he is not a Brahman, he deserves to be plundered" (*Śat. Br.* 13. 4. 2. 17). The sacrifice is intended to regenerate the entire cosmos and, at the same time, to reestablish all the social classes and all the vocations in their paradigmatic excellence.[5] The horse, representative of the royal power (*kṣatrā*), and further identified with Yama, Aditya (the sun), and Soma (that is, with the sovereign gods), is in a way a substitute for the king. Such processes of assimilation and substitution must be taken into account when we analyze a parallel scenario, the *puruṣamedha*; and in fact the "sacrifice of a man" closely follows the *aśvamedha*. In addition to the animal victims, a Brahman or a *kṣatrya*, bought for the price of 1,000 cows and 100 horses, was sacrificed. He, too, was left free for a year, and, as soon as he was killed, the queen lay down beside his corpse. The *puruṣamedha* was believed to obtain all that could be achieved by the *aśvamedha*.

It has been asked if such a sacrifice was ever practiced. The *puruṣamedha* is described in several *śrautasūtras*, but only the *Sānkhāyana* and the *Vaitāna* prescribe the killing of the victim. In the other liturgical treatises, the man is released at the last moment, and an animal is immolated in his stead. It is significant that during the *puruṣamedha* there is a recitation of the famous cosmogonic hymn *Puruṣasūkta* (Rig Veda 10. 90). The identification of the victim with Puruṣa-Prajāpati leads to the identification of the sacrificer with Prajāpati. It has been shown that the mythico-ritual scenario of the *puruṣamedha* has an astonishing parallel in Germanic tradition: wounded by a lance and hung on the World Tree for nine nights, Odin sacrifices "himself to himself" in order to obtain wisdom and to master magic (*Hávamál* 138).[6] According to Adam of Bremen,

5. During the sacrifice a priest recites: "May the Brahman be born in holiness! . . . May the prince be born in royal majesty, hero, archer, warrior with a strong bow, with invincible chariots. May the cow be born milk-giving, strong the draught bull, swift the horse, fecund the woman, victorious the soldier, eloquent the young man! May this sacrificer have a hero for his son! May Parjanya ever give us rain enough! May the wheat ripen abundantly for us!" (*Vājasaneyi Saṃhitā* 22. 22).

6. See James L. Sauvé, "The Divine Victim"; the author cites all the relevant passages from the Germanic and Sanskrit sources pertaining to human sacrifice.

who wrote in the eleventh century, this sacrifice was reactualized every nine years at Uppsala by hanging nine men and other animal victims. This Indo-European parallel gives plausibility to the hypothesis that the *puruṣamedha* was literally carried out. But in India, where the practice and theory of sacrifice have been continually reinterpreted, the immolation of human victims ended by illustrating a metaphysics of the soteriological type.

74. Initiatory structure of rituals: Initiation (*dīkṣā*), royal consecration (*rājasūya*)

For a better understanding of this process, it is important to clarify the initiatory presuppositions of the *śrauta* rituals. An initiation implies the "death" and "rebirth" of the novice, that is, his birth to a higher mode of being. Ritual "death" is obtained by immolation or by a *regressus ad uterum*, both symbolic. The equivalence of these two methods implies the assimilation of "sacrificial death" to a "procreation." As the *Śatapatha Brāhmaṇa* (11. 2. 1. 1) proclaims, "Man is born thrice: the first time of his parents, the second time when he sacrifices, . . . the third time when he dies and is put on the fire, and thereupon he comes into existence once again." In reality, what is involved is a great number of "deaths," for every "twice-born" performs a certain number of *śrauta* sacrifices in his lifetime.

Initiation, *dīkṣā*, constitutes the indispensable preliminary to every somic sacrifice, but it is also practiced on other occasions.[7] We repeat that the sacrificer who is receiving *dīkṣā* is already twice-born by virtue of his *upanayana*, when he underwent the initiatory *regressus ad uterum*. Now the same return to the embryonic condition takes place during the *dīkṣā*. In fact, "the priests transform into an embryo him to whom they give the *dīkṣā*. They sprinkle him with water; water is the male seed. . . . They make him enter a special shed: the special shed is the womb of him who performs the *dīkṣā*. They cover

7. Cf. Eliade, *Birth and Rebirth*, pp. 54 ff.; Gonda, *Change and Continuity*, pp. 315 ff. The Rig Veda appears to know nothing of the *dīkṣā*, but we must not forget that these liturgical texts do not represent the Vedic religion in its entirety (see Gonda, p. 349). The ceremony is documented in the Atharva Veda 11. 5. 6, where the *brahmacārin* is called *dīkṣita*, "he who performs the *dīkṣā*."

him with a garment: the garment is the amnion. . . . He has his fists closed; and indeed the embryo has its fists closed as long as it is in the womb" (*Aitareya Brāhmaṇa* 1. 3). The parallel texts emphasize the embryological and obstetric character of the rite: "The *dīkṣita* (i.e., he who performs the *dīkṣā*) is semen" (*Maitrāyanī-Saṃhitā* 3. 6. 1); "The *dīkṣita* is an embryo, his garment is the chorion" (*Taittīrya-Saṃ.* 1. 3. 2). The reason for this *regressus ad uterum* is continually recalled: "Man is in truth not born. It is through the sacrifice that he comes to birth" (*Mait.-Saṃ.* 3. 6. 7).[8]

This new, mystical birth, which is repeated at each sacrifice, makes possible the assimilation of the sacrificer to the gods. "The sacrificer is destined really to be born in the celestial world" (*Śat. Br.* 7. 3. 1. 12). "He who is initiated approaches the gods and becomes one of them" (ibid. 3. 1. 1. 8). The same treatise affirms that the sacrificer in the process of being born anew must stand facing the four directions of space, i.e., he must master the universe (7. 7. 2. 11 ff.). But the *dīkṣā* is also identified with death. "When he initiates himself, he (the sacrificer) dies for the second time" (*Jaim. Upaniṣad Brāh.* 3. 11. 3).[9] According to other sources, the "*dīkṣita* is the oblation" (*Taitt. Saṃhitā* 6. 1. 45), for "the victim is really the sacrificer himself" (*Ait. Brāh.* 2. 11). In short, "the initiate is the oblation offered to the gods" (*Śat. Br.* 3. 6. 3. 19).[10] The example was given by the gods: "O Agni, sacrifice thine own body!" (Rig Veda 6. 11. 2); "Sacrifice thyself, increasing thy body!" (10. 81. 5). For it is "by sacrifice that the gods offered the Sacrifice" (10. 90. 16).

A ritual death, then, is the preliminary condition for attaining to the presence of the gods and, at the same time, for obtaining a full life in this world. In the Vedic period, "divinization," which was obtained, though in any case only momentarily, through sacrifice, implied no devalorization of life and human existence. On the contrary, it was by such ritual ascents to heaven, and into the

8. All these initiation rites naturally have a mythical model: it is Indra who, to prevent the birth of a terrifying monster as the result of the union of the Word (*Vāc*) with Sacrifice (*Yajña*), changed himself into an embryo and entered Vāc's womb (*Śat. Br.* 3. 2. 1. 18 ff.).

9. Cf. also the texts cited by Gonda, *Change and Continuity*, p. 385.

10. The sacrificer "throws himself in the form of seed" (represented by grains of sand) into the domestic fire, in order to insure his rebirth here below on earth, and into the sacrificial altar in view of a rebirth in heaven; see the texts cited by A. Coomaraswamy, "Atmayajña: Self-Sacrifice," p. 360.

presence of the gods, that the sacrificer, together with both the whole society and nature, was blessed and regenerated. We have seen what results were obtained as the effect of an *aśvamedha* sacrifice (see above, note 5). Probably cosmic regeneration and reinforcement of the royal power were also the purpose of the human sacrifices practiced in pagan Uppsala. But all this was obtained by rites that, intending a repetition of the creation, included at once the "death," the "embryonic gestation," and the "rebirth" of the sacrificer.

The consecration of the Indian king—the *rājasūya*—comprised a similar scenario. The central ceremonies took place around the New Year. The anointing was preceded by a year of *dīkṣā* and was usually followed by another year of closing ceremonies. The *rājasūya* is in all likelihood a shortened version of a series of annual ceremonies intended to restore the universe. The king had a central role because, like the *śrauta* sacrificer, he in some sense incorporated the cosmos. The different phases of the rite successively brought about the future sovereign's regression to the embryonic state, his gestation for a year, and his mystical rebirth as cosmocrator, identified both with Prajā-pati and with the cosmos. The "embryonic period" of the future sovereign corresponded to the process of maturation of the universe and, very probably, was originally related to the maturing of crops. The second phase of the ritual completed the formation of the sovereign's new body: a symbolic body, which was obtained either as the result of the king's mystical marriage with the Brahman caste or with the people (a marriage that allowed him to be born from their womb) or as the result of the union of the male waters with the female waters or of the union of gold—signifying fire—with water.

The third phase was made up of a series of rites by virtue of which the king gained sovereignty over the three worlds; in other words, he incarnated the cosmos and, at the same time, established himself as cosmocrator. When the sovereign raises his arm, the gesture has a cosmogonic meaning: it symbolizes the erection of the *axis mundi*. When the king is anointed, he stands on the throne with his arms raised: he incarnates the cosmic axis fixed in the navel of the earth— that is, the throne, the "center of the world"—and touches heaven. The aspersion is connected with the primordial waters that descend from heaven along the *axis mundi*—represented by the king—to fertilize the earth. Then the king takes a step toward each of the four cardinal points and symbolically ascends to the zenith. In consequence of these rites the king acquires sovereignty over the four directions of space and over the seasons; in other words, he masters the whole of the spatiotemporal universe.[11]

The intimate connection between ritual death and ritual rebirth on the one hand, and between cosmogony and regeneration of the world on the other, has been noted. All these ideas are bound up with cosmogonic myths that we shall discuss in a moment. They will be elaborated and articulated by the authors of the *Brāhmaṇas* from their particular point of view, especially their inordinate exaltation of sacrifice.

75. Cosmogonies and metaphysics

Directly or by way of allusion, the Vedic hymns present serveral cosmogonies. These myths are more or less widespread and documented on various levels of culture. It would be useless to seek the origin of each of these cosmogonies. Even those that we may assume to have been brought by the Āryans have parallels in earlier or more primitive cultures. The cosmologies, like so many other religious ideas and beliefs, represent a heritage transmitted from prehistory everywhere in the ancient world. What is of importance for our purpose is the Indian interpretations and revalorizations of certain cosmogonic myths. It should be remembered that the antiquity of a cosmogony must not be judged from the earliest documents that present it. One of the most archaic and most widespread myths, the "cosmic dive," becomes popular in India comparatively late, especially in the Epic and the Purāṇas.

Essentially, four types of cosmogonies seem to have fascinated the Vedic poets and theologians. They may be designated as follows: (1) creation by fecundation of the original waters; (2) creation by the dismembering of a primordial giant, Puruṣa; (3) creation out of a unity-totality, at once being and nonbeing; (4) creation by the separation of heaven and earth.

In the celebrated hymn of the Rig Veda 10. 121, the god imagined as Hiraṇyagarbha (the Golden Embryo) hovers over the Waters; by entering them, he fecundates the Waters, which give birth to the god

11. See J. C. Heesterman, *The Ancient Indian Royal Consecration*, pp. 17 ff., 52 ff., 101 ff.

of fire, Agni (strophe 7). The Atharva Veda (10. 7. 28) identifies the Golden Embryo with the Cosmic Pillar, *skambha*. Rig Veda 10. 82. 5 relates the first germ that the Waters received to the Universal Artisan, Viśvakarman, but the image of the embryo is not congruous with this divine personage, the supreme jack-of-all-trades. In these examples we have to do with variants of an original myth, which presented the Golden Embryo as the seed of the creator god flying above the primitive Waters.[12]

The second cosmogonic theme, radically reinterpreted from a ritualistic point of view, is found in an equally famous hymn, the *Puruṣasūkta* (RV 10. 90). The primordial giant Puruṣa (the "Man") is represented at once as cosmic totality (strophes 1–4) and as an androgynous being. And indeed (strophe 5) Puruṣa engenders the creative female energy, Virāj, and then is borne by her.[13] Creation proper is the result of a cosmic sacrifice. The gods sacrifice the "Man": from his dismembered body proceed the animals, the liturgical elements, the social classes, the earth, the sky, the gods: "His mouth became the Brahman, the Warrior was the product of his arms, his thighs were the Artisan, from his feet was born the Servitor" (strophe 12, after the translation by Renou). The sky came from his head, the earth from his feet, the moon from his consciousness, the sun from his gaze, Indra and Agni from his mouth, the wind from his breath, etc. (strophes 13–14).

The paradigmatic function of this sacrifice is emphasized in the last strophe (16): "The gods sacrificed the sacrifice by the sacrifice"; in other words, Puruṣa was at once sacrificial victim and divinity of the sacrifice. The hymn clearly states that Puruṣa precedes and surpasses the creation, though the cosmos, life, and men proceed from his own body. In other words, Puruṣa is at once transcendent and immanent, a paradoxical mode of being but one that is typical of the Indian cosmogonic gods (cf. Prajāpati). The myth, parallels to which are found in China (P'an-ku), among the ancient Germans (Ymir), and in Mesopotamia (Tiamat), illustrates a cosmogony of an archaic type: creation by the sacrifice of an anthropomorphic divine being.

12. The image of the Golden Embryo will become, in classical India, the cosmic egg engendered by the waters (already in the Upanishads: *Kāṭha Up.* 4. 6; *Śvetāśvatara* 3. 4. 12).

13. Virāj is a kind of Śakti. In the *Bṛhadāraṇyaka Up.* 4. 2. 3 she marries Puruṣa.

The *Puruṣasūkta* has given rise to countless speculations. But just as, in archaic societies, the myth serves as the paradigmatic model for all kinds of creation, so this hymn is recited in one of the rites that follow the birth of a son, in the ceremonies for the foundation of a temple (built, furthermore, in the likeness of Puruṣa), and in the purificatory rites of renewal.[14]

In the most famous hymn of the Rig Veda (10. 129) the cosmogony is presented as a metaphysics. The poet asks himself how Being could have come out of non-Being, since, in the beginning, neither "non-Being existed, nor Being" (strophe 1. 1). "In that time there existed neither death nor nondeath" (that is, neither men nor gods). There was only the undifferentiated principle called "One" (neuter). "The One breathed from its own impulse, without there being any breath." Aside from that, "nothing else existed" (str. 2). "In the beginning, darkness was hidden by darkness," but heat (generated by asceticism, *tapas*) gave birth to the "One," "potential" (*ābhū*)— i.e., "embryo"—"covered with emptiness" (we may understand: surrounded by the primitive waters). From this germ ("potential") develops Desire (*kāma*), and it is this same Desire that "was the first seed (*retas*) of Consciousness (*manas*)," an astonishing assertion, which anticipates one of the chief theses of Indian philosophical thought. The poets, by their reflection, "were able to discover the place of Being in non-Being" (str. 4). The "first seed" then divided itself into "high" and "low," into a male principle and a female principle (cf. RV 10. 72. 4). But the enigma of the "secondary creation," that is, of the phenomenal creation, remains. The gods are born *afterward* (str. 6), hence they are not the authors of the creation of the world. The poet concludes with a question mark: "He who oversees this (world) in the highest firmament alone knows it (i.e., knows the origin of the 'secondary creation')—unless he does not know it?"

The hymn represents the highest point attained by Vedic speculation. The axiom of an unknowable supreme being—the "One,"[15] the "That"—transcending both the gods and creation, will be developed in the Upanishads and in certain philosophical systems.

14. See the references to the texts in Gonda, *Viṣṇuism and Śivaism*, p. 27.

15. In the Rig Veda a tendency is already observable to reduce the plurality of the gods to a single divine principle: "what is only One, the inspired poets call many" (1. 164. 46).

Like the Puruṣa of Rig Veda 10. 90, the One precedes the universe and creates the world by emanation from its own being, without thereby losing its transcendence. This idea should be kept firmly in mind, since it is fundamental for later Indian speculation: both *consciousness* and the *universe* are the product of procreative *desire* (*kāma*). One of the germs of the Sāṃkhya-Yoga philosophy and of Buddhism is to be seen here.

As for the fourth cosmogonic theme (the separation of heaven and earth, or the dissection of Vṛtra by Indra), this myth is related to the *Puruṣasūkta*; in both there is the violent division of a totality for the purpose of creating (or renewing) the world. The theme is archaic and capable of surprising reinterpretations and applications. As we have seen (§ 68), Indra's demiurgic act of striking down and dismembering the primordial dragon serves as the model for acts as different as building a house or an oratorical competition.

Finally, we will cite creation by a divine being, the Universal Artisan, Viśvakarman (RV 10. 81), who fashions the world like a sculptor, a smith, or a carpenter. But this mythical motif, famous in other religions, is connected by the Vedic poets with the theme, made famous by the *Puruṣasūkta*, of the creation-sacrifice.

The multiplicity of cosmogonies is paralleled by the manifold traditions concerning the theogony and the origin of man. According to the Rig Veda, the gods were engendered by the primordial couple Heaven and Earth, or they emerged from the original mass of the waters or from non-Being. In any case, they came into existence *after* the creation of the world. A late hymn (RV 10. 63. 2) relates that the gods were born of the goddess Aditi, the Waters, and the Earth. But they were not all immortal. The Rig Veda adds that they received this gift from Savitri (4. 54. 2) or from Agni (6. 7. 4) or from drinking *soma* (9. 106. 8). Indra obtained immortality by asceticism, *tapas* (10. 167. 1), and the Atharva Veda declares that all the other gods gained it in the same way (11. 5. 19; 4. 11. 6). According to the *Brāhmaṇas*, it was by performing certain sacrifices that the gods became immortal.

Men, too, descend from the primordial couple Heaven-Earth. Their mythical ancestor is Manu, son of the god Vivasvat, the first sacrificer and the first man (RV 10. 63. 7). Another version makes man's mythical parents the children of Vivasvat, Yama and his sister Yami (10. 10). Finally, as we have just seen, the *Puruṣasūkta* (10. 90.

12) explains the origin of men (that is, the four social classes) as being from the organs of the sacrificial primordial giant. In the beginning, men, too, could become immortal through sacrifice; but the gods decided that this immortality should be purely spiritual, that is, accessible to human beings only after death (*Śatapatha Br.* 10. 4. 3. 9). There are other mythological explanations for the origin of death. In the *Mahābhārata*, death is introduced by Brahmā in order to relieve the earth, burdened by a human mass that threatened to make it fall into the ocean (6. 52–54; 12. 256–58).

Some of these myths concerning the birth of the gods and men, the loss or conquest of immortality, are found among other Indo-European peoples. In any case, similar myths are documented in many traditional cultures. However, it is only in India that these myths have given rise to sacrificial techniques, contemplative methods, and speculations so decisive for the awakening of a new religious consciousness.

76. The doctrine of sacrifice in the *Brāhmaṇas*

The *Puruṣasūkta* is the point of departure and the doctrinal justification for the theory of sacrifice elaborated in the *Brāhmaṇas* (ca. 1000–800 B.C.). Just as Puruṣa gave himself to the gods and let himself be immolated so that the universe could be created, Prajāpati will suffer lethal "exhaustion" after his cosmogonic labor. As the *Brāhmaṇas* present him, Prajāpati appears to be a creation of learned speculation, but his structure is archaic. This Lord of Creatures is close to the cosmic Great Gods. He in a way resembles both the "One" of Rig Veda 10. 129 and Viśvakarman, but, especially, he continues Puruṣa. Besides, the identity Puruṣa-Prajāpati is documented by the texts: "Puruṣa is Prajāpati; Puruṣa is the Year" (*Jaim. Br.* 2. 56; cf. *Śatapatha Br.* 6. 1. 1. 5). In the beginning, Prajāpati was the nonmanifested Unity-Totality, a purely spiritual presence. But desire (*kāma*) incited him to multiply and reproduce himself (*Śat. Br.* 6. 1. 1). He "heated" himself to an extreme degree by asceticism (*tapas*, literally, "heat, ardor") and created by emanation;[16] we may understand this to mean by sweating, as in

16. The term used is *visṛj*, from the root *sṛj*, "to protect"; *vi-* indicates dispersal in all directions.

certain primitive cosmogonies, or by seminal emission. He first created the *brahman*, that is, the Threefold Knowledge (the three Vedas); then he created the Waters from the Word. Desiring to reproduce himself by the Waters, he penetrated them; an egg developed, whose shell became the earth. Then the gods were created to people the heavens and the Asuras to people the earth, etc. (ibid. 11. 1. 6. 1 ff.).[17]

Prajāpati thought: "Truly, I have created a pendant to myself, that is, the Year." This is why it is said: "Prajāpati is the Year" (ibid. 11. 1. 6. 13). By giving his own self (*ātman*) to the gods, he created another pendant to himself, that is, sacrifice, and that is why people say: "Sacrifice is Prajāpati." It is further stated that the joints (*parvam*) of Prajāpati's cosmic body are the five seasons of the year and the five courses of the fire altar (ibid. 6. 1. 2).

This triple identification of Prajāpati with the *universe*, with *cyclic time* (the year), and with the *fire altar* constitutes the great novelty of the Brahmanic theory of sacrifice. It marks the decline of the conception that was the informing spirit of the Vedic ritual and prepares the discoveries achieved by the authors of the Upanishads. The fundamental idea is that, in creating by "heating" and by repeated "emissions," Prajāpati consumes himself and ends by becoming exhausted. The two key terms—*tapas* (ascetic ardor) and *visṛj* (dispersed emission)—can have indirect or implied sexual connotations, for asceticism and sexuality are intimately connected in Indian religious thought. The myth and its images translate the cosmogony into biological terms; their own mode of being brings it about that the world and life exhaust themselves by their very duration.[18] Prajāpati's exhaustion is expressed in striking images: "After Prajāpati had emitted the living beings, his joints were disjointed. Now Prajāpati is certainly the Year, and his joints are the two joinings of day and night (that is, dawn and twilight), the full moon and the new moon, and the beginnings of the seasons. He was unable to rise with his joints loosened; and the gods cured him by (the ritual of) the *agnihotra*, strengthening his joints" (*Śat. Br.* 1. 6. 3.

17. Other texts state that heaven proceeded from his head, the atmosphere from his chest, and the earth from his feet (see Gonda, *Les religions de l'Inde*, vol. 1, p. 226). There is certainly influence here from the sacrifice of Puruṣa—but it confirms the structural analogy of these two gods.

18. Similar conceptions are known to be characteristic of the archaic cultures, especially those of the paleocultivators.

35–36). In other terms, the reconstitution and rearticulation of Prajāpati's cosmic body are effected by sacrifice, that is, by building a sacrificial altar in order to celebrate the *agnicayana* (§ 72). The same work (10. 4. 2. 2) adds that "This Prajāpati, the Year, is made up of 720 days and nights; that is why the altar comprises 360 enclosing stones and 360 bricks." "This Prajāpati who became disjointed is (now) the same fire altar built formerly." The priests restore Prajāpati, "reassemble" (*saṃskri*) him, by laying the courses of bricks that make up the altar. In short, *every sacrifice repeats the primordial act of creation and guarantees the continuity of the world for the following year.*

This is the original sense of sacrifice in the *Brāhmaṇas*: to recreate the cosmos that has been "disjointed," "exhausted" by cyclic time (the year). Through sacrifice—that is, by the continued activity of the priests—the world is kept alive, well integrated, and fertile. It is a new application of the archaic idea that demands the annual (or periodical) repetition of the cosmogony. It is also the justification for the pride of the Brahmans, convinced of the decisive importance of rites. For "the sun would not rise if the priest, at dawn, did not offer the oblation of fire" (*Śat. Br.* 2. 3. 1. 5). In the *Brāhmaṇas* the Vedic gods are ignored or are subordinated to the magical and creative powers of sacrifice. It is proclaimed that, in the beginning, the gods were mortal (*Taitt. Saṃ.* 8. 4. 2. 1; etc.); they became divine and immortal through sacrifice (ibid. 6. 3. 4. 7; 6. 3. 10. 2; etc.). From then on, everything is concentrated in the mysterious power of rite: the origin and essence of the gods, sacred power, knowledge, well-being in this world, and "nondeath" in the other. But sacrifice must be performed correctly and with faith; the least doubt of its efficacy can have disastrous consequences. In order to illustrate this ritual doctrine, which is at once a cosmogony, a theogony, and a soteriology, the authors of the *Brāhmaṇas* multiply myths or fragments of myths, reinterpreting them in accordance with the new point of view or inventing new ones on the basis of some fanciful etymology, a learned allusion, or an enigma.

77. Eschatology: Identification with Prajāpati through sacrifice

Yet a new idea very soon appears: sacrifice not only restores Prajāpati and insures the perpetuation of the world but is capable of creating a spiritual and indestructible being, the "person," the *ātman*. Sacrifice has not only a cosmogonic intent and an eschatological function but makes it possible to obtain a new mode of being. In building the fire altar (*agnicayana*) the sacrificer identifies himself with Prajāpati; more precisely, Prajāpati and the sacrificer are identified in the ritual act itself: the altar *is* Prajāpati, and, at the same time, the sacrificer *becomes* the altar. By the magical power of the rite, the sacrificer builds a new body for himself, ascends to heaven, where he is born a second time (*Śat. Br.* 7. 3. 1. 12), and obtains "immortality" (10. 2. 6. 8). This means that after death he will return to life, to "nondeath," a modality of existence that goes beyond time. What is of the first importance—and this is the purpose of the rite—is to be "complete" (*sarva*), "integral," and to preserve this condition after death.[19]

By "reassembling" (*samdhā, samskri*) Prajāpati, the sacrificer performs the same operation of integration and unification on his own person; in other words, he becomes "complete." Just as, through the sacrifice, the god recovers his person (*ātman*), the sacrificer builds his own self, his *ātman*, for himself (*Kauṣītaki Brāhmaṇa* 3. 8). The "fabrication" of the *ātman* resembles in some sense the reunification of Prajāpati, scattered and exhausted by his cosmogonic labor. The totality of ritual acts (*karma*), when it is achieved and well integrated, constitutes the "person," the *ātman*. This means that, through ritual activity, the psychophysiological functions of the sacrificer are brought together and unified; their sum constitutes the *ātman* (*Aitareya Br.* 2. 40. 1–7); it is by virtue of his *ātman* that the sacrificer becomes "immortal." The gods, too, attained to immortality by sacrifice, obtaining *brahman* (*Śat. Br.* 11. 2. 3. 6). Consequently, *brahman* and *ātman* are implicitly identified, even as early as the period of the *Brāhmaṇas*.[20] This is confirmed by another series of identifications: both Prajāpati and the fire altar are assimilated to the Rig Veda, and the syllables of the Rig are identified with the bricks of the altar. But since *brahman* is, itself, also assimilated to the 432,000 syllables of the Rig, it follows that it is also identified with Prajāpati and, in the last analysis, with the sacrificer, that is, with his *ātman*.[21]

19. See J. Gonda, *Les religions de l'Inde*, vol. 1, pp. 236 ff.
20. See Lilian Silburn, *Instant et cause*, pp. 74 ff.
21. Another text of the *Śatapatha Brāhmaṇa* (10. 6. 3. 2) describes the

If Prajāpati (*Brahman*) and *ātman* are identical, it is because they are the result of one and the same activity ("reconstruction," unification), though the materials are different: the bricks of the altar for Prajāpati-*Brahman*, the organic and psychomental functions for the *ātman*.[22] But it is important to emphasize that *it is a cosmogonic myth that, in the last analysis, constitutes the paradigmatic model for the "construction" of the ātman*. The various Yogic techniques apply the same principle: "concentration" and "unification" of the bodily positions, of the breaths, of psychomental activity.

The discovery of the identity of the self (*ātman*) and *brahman* will be tirelessly exploited and variously valorized in the Upanishads (§ 80). For the moment we will add that, in the *Brāhmaṇas*, *brahman* designates the process of the cosmic sacrifice and, by extension, the mysterious power that maintains the universe. But already in the Vedas *brahman* was thought to be, and was expressly called, the imperishable, the immutable, the foundation, the principle of all existence. It is significant that in several hymns of the Atharva Veda (e.g., 10. 7. 8) *brahman* is identified with the *skambha* (literally, "stay, support, pillar"); in other words, *brahman* sustains the world, for it is at once cosmic axis and ontological foundation. "In the *skambha* is all that is possessed by the spirit (*atmanvat*), all that breathes" (Atharva Veda 7. 8. 2). "He who knows the *brahman* in man knows the supreme being (*parameṣthin*, the Lord), and he who knows the supreme being knows the *skambha*" (ibid. 10. 8. 43). We perceive the effort to isolate the ultimate reality: *brahman* is recognized as the "pillar of the universe," the support, the base; and the term *pratiṣṭhā*, which expresses all these notions, is already frequently used in the Vedic texts. The Brahman is identified with *brahman* because he knows the structure and origin of the universe, because he knows the Word that expresses all that; for Vāc, the Logos, can transform any person into a Brahman (already Rig Veda 10. 124. 5). "The birth of

---

"golden Puruṣa" in the heart of man as a grain of rice or millet—adding, however, that it is greater than heaven, greater than the ether, than the earth, and than all things: "this self of the Spirit is my self; when I die, I shall obtain this self." The text is important, since, on the one hand, Puruṣa is identified with *brahman* (neuter), and, on the other, the equation *ātman-brahman* is already assured.

22. See Silburn, *Instant et cause*, pp. 104 ff.

the Brahman is an eternal incarnation of the *dharma*" (Manu 1. 98).[23]

A particular category of works, the *Araṇyakas* (literally, "of the forest"), allows us to follow the transition of the sacrificial system (*karma-kaṇḍa*) of the *Brāhmaṇas* to the primacy of metaphysical knowledge (*jñāna-kaṇḍa*) proclaimed by the Upanishads. The *Araṇyakas* were taught in secret, far from villages, in the forest. Their doctrines emphasize the self, subject of the sacrifice, instead of the concrete reality of the rites. According to the *Araṇyakas*, the gods are hidden in man; in other words, the correlation macrocosm-microcosm, the basis of Vedic speculation, now reveals the homology between the cosmic divinities and those present in the human body (see *Aitareya Araṇyaka* 1. 3. 8; 2. 1. 2; 3. 1. 1; etc. *Śāṅkhāyana Araṇyaka* 7. 2 ff.; etc.). Consequently, the "interiorization of sacrifice" (cf. § 78) makes it possible to direct the offerings at once to the "interior" and the "exterior" gods. The ultimate aim is union (*saṃhitā*) between the different theocosmic planes and the organs and psychophysiological functions of man. After a number of homologizations and identifications, the conclusion is reached that "consciousness of self (*prajñātman*) is one and the same thing as the Sun" (*Ait. Ar.* 3. 2. 3; *Śāṅkh. Ar.* 8. 3–7). This daring equation will be elaborated and articulated by the authors of the Upanishads.

78. *Tapas:* Technique and dialectic of austerities

We have several times referred to asceticism, *tapas*, for it is impossible to discuss the most important Indian gods, myths, and rites without mentioning this ritual "heating," this "warmth" or "ardor" obtained through austerities. The term *tapas*, from the root *tap*, "to heat," "to be boiling," is clearly documented in the Rig Veda (see, for example, 8. 59. 6; 10. 136. 2; 154. 2. 4; 167. 1; 109. 4; etc.). The concept belongs to an Indo-European tradition, for, in a parallel context, "extreme heat" or "rage" (*menos, furor, ferg, wut*) plays a part in rituals of the heroic type.[24] We add that "heating" by

23. See Eliade, *Yoga*, pp. 115 ff.; other texts will be found in J. Gonda, *Notes on Brahman*, p. 52.
24. See Eliade, *Yoga*, p. 107, n. 28.

various psychophysiological techniques, and even by a highly spiced diet, is documented among the medicine men and magicians of primitive cultures.[25] Obtaining magico-religious "power" is accompanied by a strong inner heat; this power itself is expressed by terms that mean "heat," "burning," "very hot," etc.

We have cited these facts in order to bring out the archaism and the considerable dissemination of austerities of the *tapas* type. This in no way implies a non-Āryan origin of Indian asceticism. The Indo-Europeans, and especially the Vedic Indians, had inherited prehistoric techniques, which they had valorized in different ways. But it must be made clear at this point that ritual "heating" nowhere else obtained the scope that *tapas* was to acquire in India, from the most ancient times down to our own day.

Ascetic "heating" has its model, or its homologue, in the images, symbols, and myths connected with the heat that "cooks" crops and broods eggs to insure their hatching, with sexual excitement, especially the ardor of orgasm, and with fire lighted by rubbing two sticks together. *Tapas* is "creative" on several planes: cosmogonic, religious, metaphysical. Prajāpati, as we saw, creates the world by "heating" himself through *tapas*, and the exhaustion that follows is assimilable to sexual fatigue (§ 76). On the plane of ritual, *tapas* makes "rebirth" possible—that is, passage from this world into the world of the gods, from the sphere of the "profane" to that of the "sacred." In addition, asceticism helps the contemplative to "brood" the mysteries of esoteric knowledge and gives him a revelation of profound truths. (Agni gives the *tapasvin* "heat of the head," thus making him clairvoyant.)

Asceticism radically modifies the mode of being of the practitioner, for it bestows on him a superhuman "power" that can become terrible and in certain cases "demonic."[26] The preliminaries for the most important sacrifices, the initiation ceremony, the *brahmacārin*'s apprenticeship all involved *tapas*. Essentially, *tapas* is produced by fasting, by keeping watch before a fire, by standing in the sun, or, more rarely, by absorbing intoxicating substances. But "heating" is

25. See some examples in our *Shamanism*, pp. 474 ff.

26. The term *śānti*, which in Sanskrit designates tranquillity, peace of soul, absence of passion, relief from sufferings, derives from the root *śam*, which originally included the meaning of "extinguishing" fire, anger, fever—in the last analysis the heat provoked by demonic powers; see D. J. Hoens, *Śānti*, esp. pp. 177 ff.

also obtained by holding the breath, which opens the way for a daring homologization of the Vedic ritual with the practices of Yoga. This homologization was made possible principally by the speculations on sacrifice in the *Brāhmaṇas*.

Sacrifice was early assimilated to *tapas*. It is proclaimed that the gods obtained immortality not only through sacrifice (§ 76) but also through asceticism. If in the Vedic cult the gods are offered *soma*, melted butter, and the sacred fire, in ascetic practice they are offered an "inner sacrifice," in which the physiological functions take the place of libations and ritual objects. Respiration is often identified with an "uninterrupted libation." [27] There is mention of the *prāṇāgni-hotra*, that is, of "the oblation to fire accomplished by respiration" (*Vaikhānasasmārtasūtra* 2. 18). The conception of this inner sacrifice is an innovation fraught with consequences; it will permit even the most eccentric ascetics and mystics to remain in the fold of Brahmanism and, later, of Hinduism. But then, too, the same inner sacrifice will be practiced by the Brahmans who are "dwellers in the forest," that is, by those who live as ascetics (*sannyāsi*) without thereby losing their social identity of "householders." [28]

In short, *tapas* is integrated into a series of homologizations effected on different planes. On the one hand—and in conformity with the distinctive tendency of the Indian spirit—the cosmic structures and phenomena are assimilated to the organs and functions of the human body and, in addition, to the elements of sacrifice (altar, fire, oblations, ritual instruments, liturgical formulas, etc.). On the other hand, asceticism—which implied (already in prehistoric times) a whole system of micro-macrocosmic correspondences (the breaths assimilated to the winds, etc.)—is homologized to the sacrifice. Certain forms of asceticism, for example holding the

27. In fact, "as long as he speaks, man cannot breathe, and then he offers his breathing to speech; as long as he breathes, he cannot speak, and then he offers his speech to breathing. These are the two continual and immortal oblations; in waking and in sleep, man offers them uninterruptedly. All other oblations have an end and share in the nature of the act (*karman*). The men of old, knowing this true sacrifice, did not offer the *agnihotra*" (*Kauṣītāki-Brāhmaṇa Upaniṣad* 2. 5). According to the *Chāndogya Up.* 5. 19–24, the true sacrifice consists in the oblations to the breaths: "he who offers the *agnihotra* without knowing this is like him who ... should make the offering in the ashes" (5. 24. 1).

28. Their religious position is reflected (though rather obscurely) in the *Araṇyaka* treatises.

breath, are even considered superior to sacrifice; their results are declared to be more precious than the "fruits" of sacrifice. But all these homologizations and assimilations are valid, that is, become real and religiously efficacious, only if the dialectic that has revealed them is understood.

In the last analysis, we have to do with a number of systems that are, on the one hand, homologized and, on the other hand, classified in a variable hierarchical series. *Sacrifice* is assimilated to *asceticism,* but, after a certain moment, what counts most is *understanding* the principle that justifies such assimilations. Very soon, with the Upanishads, comprehension, knowledge (*jñāna*), will be raised to a preeminent rank, and the sacrificial system, with the mythological theology that it implied, will lose its primacy in religion. But this system too, based on the superiority of "comprehension," will fail to maintain its supremacy, at least for certain segments of society. The yogins, for example, will accord decisive importance to asceticism and experimentation with mystical states; certain ecstatics or partisans of devotion of the theistic type (*bhakti*) will reject, wholly or in part, not only Brahmanic ritualism and the metaphysical speculation of the Upanishads but also asceticism (*tapas*) and the technique of Yoga.

This dialectic, with its capability of discovering countless homologies, assimilations, and correspondences on the different planes of human experience (physiology, psychology, ritual activity, symbolization, mystical experimentation, etc.), was at work from the Vedic period, if not from Indo-European protohistory, and it will be called upon to play a considerable role in later periods. As we shall see, the dialectic of homologization reveals its creative possibilities especially at moments of religious and metaphysical crisis, that is, when a traditional system ends by losing its validity, and its world of values collapses.

79. Ascetics and ecstatics: *Muni, vrātya*

If ritual austerities form an integral part of the Vedic cult, we must not lose sight of the presence of other kinds of ascetics and ecstatics, scarcely mentioned in the ancient texts. Some of these ascetics and ecstatics lived on the margin of the Āryan society without therefore being considered "heretics"; but there were others who can be regarded as "foreigners," though it is practically impossible to decide if they belonged to the aboriginal strata or simply reflect the religious conceptions of certain Āryan tribes that evolved on the margin of the Vedic tradition.

Thus a hymn of the Rig Veda (10. 136) tells of an ascetic (*muni*) with long hair (*keśin*), clad in "brown filth," "girdled with wind" (that is, naked), and into whom "the gods enter." He exclaims: "In the intoxication of ecstasy, we are mounted on the winds. You, mortals, can perceive only our body" (strophe 3). The *muni* flies through the air: he is the horse of the wind element (*Vāta*) and the friend of Vāyu (the god of wind). He dwells by the two oceans, that of the rising and that of the setting sun (str. 5; cf. Ath. Veda 11. 5. 6; etc.). "He follows the tracks of the Apsarases, the Gandharvas, and wild beasts, and understands their thoughts" (str. 6). He "drinks with Rudra from the cup of poison" (str. 7). This is a typical example of ecstasy: the *muni*'s spirit forsakes his body, he divines the thought of semidivine beings and wild animals, he inhabits the "two oceans." The allusions to the horse of the wind and to the gods whom he incorporates indicate a shamanizing technique.

The Vedas also describe other supranormal experiences in connection with mythical personages (Ekavrātya, Brahmacārin, Vena, etc.), who probably represent the divinized models of certain ascetics and magicians. For the "man-god" remains a dominant motif in the spiritual history of India. Ekavrātya is probably the archetype of that mysterious group, the *vrātyas*, in whom various scholars have sought to see Śivaite ascetics, "mystics," forerunners of the yogins, or representatives of a non-Āryan population. A whole book of the Atharva Veda (15) is devoted to them, but the text is obscure. It shows, nevertheless, that the *vrātyas* practice asceticism (they remain standing for a year, etc.), are acquainted with a discipline of the breaths (assimilated to the various cosmic regions: AV 15. 14. 15 ff.), homologize their body to the macrocosm (18. 1 ff.). Yet this confraternity was important, for a special sacrifice, the *vrātyastoma*, had been established to reincorporate its members into Brahmanic society.[29] During the *vrātyastoma*, other personages were present,

29. The Vrātyas wore a turban, dressed in black, and carried over their shoulders two ram skins, one black and the other white; as emblems they had a pointed stick, an ornament around the neck, and an unstrung bow. A cart drawn by a horse and a mule served them as their place of sacrifice.

the chief of these being a *māgadha*, who filled the role of chanter, and a prostitute (AV 15. 2). On the occasion of a solstitial rite (*mahāvrata*) she copulated ritually with the *māgadha* or with a *brahmacārin*.[30]

The Brahmacārin, too, is conceived as a personage on the cosmic scale. Initiated, clad in black antelope skins, with a long beard, he journeys from the eastern ocean to the northern ocean and "creates the worlds"; he is extolled as "an embryo in the bosom of immortality"; dressed in red, he practices *tapas* (AV 11. 5. 6–7). But, as often happens in India, his earthly "representative," the *brahmacārin* (whose first vow is chastity), had ritual intercourse with the prostitute.

Sexual union played a part in certain Vedic rituals (cf. the *aśva-medha*). It is important to distinguish between conjugal union regarded as a hierogamy[31] and sexual union of the orgiastic type, whose purpose is either universal fecundity or the creation of a "magical defense."[32] In both cases, however, it is a matter of rites, one could say of "sacraments," performed in view of a resacralization of the human person or of life. Later, Tantrism will elaborate a whole technique aiming at a sacramental transmutation of sexuality.

As for the different classes of ascetics, magicians, and ecstatics who lived on the margin of the Āryan society, but the majority of whom ended by being integrated into Hinduism, we have but little information. The richest sources are late; this, however, does not lessen their interest, for they certainly reflect an earlier situation. Thus, the *Vaikhānasasmārtasūtra* gives a long list of ascetics and hermits; some of them are distinguished by their hair and their garments, either torn or made from tree bark; others live naked, feed on urine and cow dung, inhabit graveyards, etc.; still others practice Yoga or a form of proto-Tantrism.[33]

To summarize: from the earliest times there are documents for different forms of asceticism, ecstatic experiences, and magico-religious techniques. It is possible to recognize austerities of the "classic" type and certain shamanizing motifs side by side with

30. See the references to the texts and the bibliography in Eliade, *Yoga*, pp. 103 ff.

31. "I am Heaven, thou art Earth!" says the husband to the wife (*Bṛhad. Up.* 6. 4. 20). Conception is accomplished in the name of the gods: "May Viṣṇu prepare the womb; may Tvaṣṭri shape the forms!" etc. (ibid. 6. 4. 21).

32. See Eliade, *Yoga*, pp. 254 ff. In this last case, we have to do with customs universally disseminated in the agricultural societies.

33. See ibid., pp. 138 ff.

ecstatic experiences typical of numerous other cultures and with some rudimentary Yogic practices. The heterogeneity and complexity of the behavior patterns, the techniques, and the soteriologies defended by those who had forsaken the world will continue to increase in later periods. Briefly, we can say that the ecstatic methods depend upon and continue the exalting experience of absorbing *soma* or other intoxicating substances and at the same time anticipate certain forms of mystical devotion, whereas the ascetic austerities and disciplines prepare the elaboration of the techniques of Yoga.

It must be added that, from the period of the Upanishads, there is an increase in the custom of forsaking social life and settling in the "forest" in order to be able to devote oneself entirely to meditation. This habit long since became paradigmatic, and it is still practiced in modern India. But retreat to the "forest" on the part of people who were neither ecstatics nor ascetics nor yogins by vocation was probably a rather surprising novelty in the beginning. At bottom, abandoning social life revealed a profound crisis in the traditional religion. Very probably this crisis had come on as the result of Brahmanic speculations on the subject of sacrifice.

80. The Upanishads and the quest of the *ṛṣis*: How can deliverance from the "fruits" of one's own acts be obtained?

In the *Brāhmaṇas* the Vedic gods were radically devalorized, to the advantage of Prajāpati. The authors of the Upanishads continue and complete this process. But they go further: they do not hesitate to devalorize the all-powerful sacrifice itself. Certain Upanishadic texts affirm that, without a *meditation* on the *ātman*, sacrifice is not complete (*Maitri. Up.* 1. 1). The *Chāndogya Upaniṣad* (8. 1. 6) affirms that even as the "world gained by acts (*karman*)" perishes, so will the world obtained by sacrifice. According to the *Maitri Upaniṣad* (1. 2. 9–10), those who deceive themselves concerning the importance of sacrifice are to be pitied; for, after having enjoyed, in the heavens, the high place gained by their good works, they will return to earth or descend to a lower world. Neither the gods nor the rites are of any more account for a true *ṛṣi*. His ideal is admirably expressed in the prayer transmitted by the earliest of the Upanishads, the *Bṛhadāraṇyaka* (1. 3. 28): "From nonbeing (*asat*) lead me to being (*sat*), from darkness lead me to light, from death lead me to immortality!"

The spiritual crisis that finds vent in the Upanishads seems to have been brought on by meditation on the "powers" of sacrifice. We have seen that, just as Prajāpati was reconstituted and recovered his "person" (*ātman*) by the virtue of sacrifice, so the sacrificer, by means of ritual acts (*karman*), "unified" his psychophysiological functions and built up his "self" (§ 77). In the *Brāhmaṇas* the term *karman* denotes ritual activity and its beneficial consequences (since, after his death, the sacrificer attained to the world of the gods). But reflection on the *ritual* process of "cause and effect" inevitably led to the discovery that every *act*, by the mere fact that it obtained a *result*, became an integral part of an endless series of causes and effects. Once the law of universal causality was recognized in *karman*, the certainty founded on the salutary effects of sacrifice was destroyed. For the postexistence of the soul in heaven was the outcome of the sacrificer's ritual activity; but where was it that the products of all his *other* acts, performed during his whole lifetime, were "realized"? So the blissful postexistence that was the reward for a correct ritual activity must have an end. But then what happened to the disincarnated soul (*ātman*)? In no case could it disappear definitively. There remained of it a countless number of acts performed during life, and these constituted so many causes that *must* have effects—that must, in other words, be "realized" in a new existence, whether here on earth or in another world. The conclusion was inescapable: after experiencing a blissful or an unhappy postexistence in an extraterrestrial world, the soul was bound to be reincarnated. This is the law of transmigration, *saṃsāra*, which, once discovered, dominated Indian religious and philosophical thought, both "orthodox" and heterodox (Buddhism and Jainism).

The term *saṃsāra* appears only in the Upanishads. As for the doctrine, its "origin" is not known. The attempt has been made—but without success—to explain the belief in the transmigration of souls by the influence of non-Āryan elements. However that may be, this discovery imposed a pessimistic view of existence. The ideal of the Vedic man—to live for a century, etc.—proves to be outworn. In itself, life does not necessarily represent "evil," on condition that it is used as a means of deliverance from the bonds of *karman*. The only goal worthy of a wise man is obtaining deliverance, *mokṣa*—

another term that, with its equivalents (*mukti*, etc.), takes its place among the key words of Indian thought.

Since every act (*karman*), religious or profane, strengthens and perpetuates transmigration (*saṃsāra*), deliverance can be gained neither by sacrifice nor by close relations with the gods nor even by asceticism or charity. In their hermitages the *ṛṣis* sought other means of freeing themselves. An important discovery was made by meditating on the soteriological value of knowledge, already praised in the Vedas and the *Brāhmaṇas*. Obviously, the authors of the *Brāhmaṇas* were referring to (esoteric) knowledge of the homologies implicit in the ritual operation. It was ignorance of the sacrificial mysteries that, according to the *Brāhmaṇas*, condemned men to a "second death." But the *ṛṣis* went further: they dissociated esoteric knowledge from its ritual and theological context; gnosis is now held to be capable of grasping absolute truth, by revealing the deep structures of the real. Such a "science" ends by literally destroying "ignorance" (*avidya*), which seems to be the lot of human beings (the "uninitiated" of the *Brāhmaṇas*). Certainly, this is an ignorance of a metaphysical kind, for it refers to the ultimate reality and not to the empirical realities of everyday experience.

It is in this sense of "metaphysical ignorance" that the term *avidya* took its place in the Indian philosophical vocabulary. *Avidya* concealed the ultimate reality; "wisdom" (gnosis) revealed truth, hence the real. From a certain point of view this "nescience" was "creative": it created the structures and the dynamism of human existence. Perforce of *avidya*, on the other hand, men lived an irresponsible existence, not knowing the consequences of their acts (*karman*). After impassioned searchings and long hesitations, sometimes dispelled by sudden illuminations, the *ṛṣis* identified in *avidya* the "first cause" of *karman* and hence the origin and dynamism of transmigration. The circle was now complete: ignorance (*avidya*) created or reinforced the law of cause and effect (*karman*) that, in its turn, inflicted the unbroken series of reincarnations (*saṃsāra*). Fortunately, liberation (*mokṣa*) from this infernal circle was possible, above all by virtue of gnosis (*jñāna, vidya*). As we shall see, other groups or schools also proclaimed the liberating virtues of Yoga techniques or mystical devotion. Indian thought early set itself to homologizing the different "ways" (*marga*) leading to deliverance. The effort culminated some centuries later in the famous synthesis proclaimed in the *Bhagavad-Gītā* (fourth century B.C.). But it is important to point out now that the discovery of the fatal sequence *avidya-karman-saṃsāra*, and of its remedy, deliverance (*mokṣa*) by means of gnosis, of metaphysical knowledge (*jñāna, vidyā*)—a discovery made, though imperfectly systematized, in the time of the Upanishads—constitutes the essence of later Indian philosophy. The most important developments concern the means of deliverance and, paradoxically, the person (or the "agent") who is held to enjoy this deliverance.

81. The identity *ātman-Brahman* and the experience of "inner light"

We have purposely simplified, in order to grasp the aim and the originality of the *ṛṣis* at once. In the earliest Upanishads,[34] several approaches are distinguished. Yet we must not overemphasize these differences, for the system of assimilations and homologies that is predominant in the *Brāhmaṇas* remains valid in the Upanishads too. The central problem is present, explicitly or implicitly, in every text. It is a matter of grasping and comprehending the first Being, the One/ All, which alone is capable of explaining the world, life, and the destiny of man. From the time of the Rig Veda it had been identified in the *tad ekam*—"the One" (neuter)—of the celebrated hymn 10. 129. The *Brāhmaṇas* call it Prajāpati or Brahman, but in these scholastic treatises the first Being was related to cosmic sacrifice and ritual sacrality. The *ṛṣis* bent their every effort to apprehending it by means of a meditation guided by gnosis.[35]

The first Being is, obviously, unthinkable, limitless, eternal; it is at once the One and the All, "creator" and "lord" of the world. Some even identified it with the universe; others sought it in the "person" (*puruṣa*) present in the sun, the moon, the word, etc., still others in the "limitless" that sustains the world, life, and consciousness.

34. That is, the Upanishads in prose, the *Bṛhadāraṇyaka*, the *Chāndogya*, the *Aitareya*, the *Kauṣitāki*, the *Taittirīya*. They were probably composed between 800 and 500 B.C.

35. However, it must not be forgotten that the *ṛṣis* of the Upanishads are the successors of the "seers" and the poet-philosophers of the Vedic period. From a certain point of view it can be said that the central intuitions of the Upanishads are already found, in a nonsystematized form, in the Vedas. Thus, for example, the equation "spirit" = "god" = "real" = "light." Cf. Gonda, *The Vision of the Vedic Poets*, pp. 40 ff., 272 ff.

Among the names of the first Being, the one that took precedence from the beginning was Brahman. In a famous passage of the *Chāndogya Upaniṣad* (3. 14. 2–4), Brahman is described as being "the whole world" and yet spiritual in nature; "life is his body, his form is light, his soul is space," and he encloses in himself all acts, desires, odors, tastes, etc. But he is at the same time "my *ātman* in the heart, smaller than a grain of barley, than a mustard seed," and yet "greater than the earth, greater than the atmosphere, greater than these worlds." "Containing all acts, all desires . . . , containing this whole world . . . , this is my *ātman* in the heart; this is Brahman. When I depart this life, I shall enter into him."[36] Yājñavalkya, too, speaks of him "who dwells in the earth, yet the earth knows him not, whose body is the earth and controls the earth from within," and identifies him with the "*ātman*, the inner controller, the immortal" (*Bṛhadāraṇyaka Up.* 3. 7. 3).

Like the Puruṣa of Rig Veda 10. 90, Brahman reveals himself to be at once immanent ("this world") and transcendent, distinct from the cosmos and yet omnipresent in the cosmic realities. In addition, as *ātman*, he inhabits the heart of man, which implies identity between the true "self" and the universal Being. And indeed, at death the *ātman* of "him who knows" is united with the Brahman; the souls of the others, the unilluminated, will obey the law of trans-migration (*saṃsāra*). There are several theories concerning post-existence without return to earth. According to some, those who have understood the esoteric symbolism of the "five fires"[37] travel through the different cosmic regions until they reach the "world of lightning." It is there that they meet with a "spiritual person," (*puruṣa mānasah*, that is, "born of the spirit"), who conducts them to the worlds of Brahman, where they will live for a long time and not return again. Modified, this theory will be taken up again by various devotional schools. According to other interpretations, how-

36. In another passage of the same Upanishad (*Chāndogya Up.* 6. 1–15), a master explains to his son, Śvetaketu, the creation of the universe and man by the primordial Being: after the creation, the Being impregnates the cosmic regions and the human body, where it is present like a grain of salt dissolved in water. The *ātman* represents the divine essence in man. And the teaching ends with the famous formula: "Thou art that (*tat tvam asi*), Śvetaketu!"

37. The sacrificial fires are homologized with the structures of the other world, of Parjanya, of this world, of man, and of woman (see *Bṛh. Up.* 6. 2. 9–15; *Chānd. Up.* 5. 4. 1–10. 2).

ever, union after death between the *ātman* and the universal Being (*Brahman*) constitutes a kind of "impersonal immortality"; the Self is merged into its original source, Brahman.

It is important to point out that meditations on the identity *ātman-Brahman* constitute a spiritual exercise, not a chain of reasoning. Grasping one's own Self is accompanied by an experience of "inner light" (*antaḥ-jyoti*), and light is supremely the image of both the *ātman* and the *Brahman*. We here have, of course, an ancient tradition, since from Vedic times the sun or light are regarded as epiphanies of Being, of Spirit, of immortality and procreation. According to the Rig Veda 1. 115. 1, the sun is the life or the *ātman*— the Self—of all things.[38] Those who have drunk *soma* become immortal, attain to light, and find the gods (RV 8. 48. 3). Now, the *Chāndogya Upaniṣad* 3. 13. 7 says: "The light that shines beyond this Heaven, beyond all, in the highest worlds beyond which there are none higher, is truly the same light that shines within man (*antaḥ puruṣa*)."[39] The *Bṛhadāraṇyaka Upaniṣad* (4. 3. 7) also identifies the *ātman* with the person that is in the heart of man, in the form of a "light in the heart." "That serene being, rising from its body and attaining the highest light, appears in its proper form. That being is the *ātman*. That is the immortal, the fearless. That is Brahman" (*Chāndogya Up.* 8. 3. 4).[40]

82. The two modalities of the Brahman and the mystery of the *ātman* "captive" in matter

The identity *ātman-Brahman*, perceived experientially in the "inner light," helps the *ṛṣi* to decipher the mystery of creation and at the

38. "Light is procreation" (*jyotir prajanaman*) says the *Śatapatha Br.* 8. 7. 2. 16–17. It "is the procreative power" (*Taitt. Saṃ.* 7. 1. 1. 1). Cf. Eliade, *The Two and the One*, p. 26, and "Spirit, Light, and Seed," pp. 3 ff.

39. The *Chāndogya Up.* 3. 17. 7 quotes two verses from the Rig Veda that speak of contemplating "the Light that shines higher than Heaven," and adds: "By contemplating (this) most High Light, beyond Darkness, we attain to the Sun, god among the gods." Becoming conscious of the identity between the inner light and the transcosmic light is accompanied by two well-known phenomena of "subtle physiology": heating of the body and hearing mystical sounds (ibid. 3. 13. 8).

40. So, too, in the *Muṇḍaka Up.* 2. 2. 10, the Brahman is "pure, light of lights." See other examples in our study "Spirit, Light, and Seed," pp. 4 ff., and in J. Gonda, *The Vision of the Vedic Poets*, pp. 270 ff.

same time of his own mode of being. Because he knows that man is a captive of *karman* and yet possesses an immortal Self, he perceives in Brahman a comparable situation. In other words, he recognizes in Brahman two seemingly incompatible modes of being: "absolute" and "relative," "spiritual" and "material," "personal" and "impersonal," etc. In the *Bṛhadāraṇyaka Upaniṣad* (2. 3. 3), Brahman is apprehended in two forms: corporeal (and mortal) and immortal. The Upanishads of the middle period[41] give a more systematic development to this tendency—already documented in the Rig Veda —to reduce the cosmic totality and consciousness to a single principle. The *Kāṭha Upaniṣad* (especially 3. 11 f.) presents a cosmological ontology of considerable originality: the universal Spirit (*puruṣa*) is at the summit; below it is the "nonmanifested" (*avyakta*), which seems to share in both the spiritual and the material; still lower is the Great Self (*mahān ātmā*), the Spirit manifested in matter, followed, on progressively descending planes, by other forms of consciousness —by the sense organs, etc. According to the *Śvetāśvatara Upaniṣad* 5. 1, hidden in the imperishable and infinite Brahman are knowledge (which insures immortality) and ignorance, assimilated to mortality.

This new system of homologies implies a reinterpretation of the old analogy between macrocosm and microcosm. This time it is the *ṛṣi*'s part to understand his existential situation by meditating on the paradoxical structure of the Brahman. Reflection proceeds on two parallel planes. On the one hand, the discovery is made that not only sensations and perceptions but also psychomental activity form part of the category of natural phenomena. (This discovery, outlined in the *Maitri Upaniṣad*, will be chiefly elaborated by the Saṃkhya and Yoga philosophies.) On the other hand, there is an increasing emphasis on the tendency (already documented in Rig Veda 10. 90. 3) to see in spirit and nature (*prakṛti*) two modalities of the primordial Being, the All/One.[42] Consequently, the cosmos and life represent the joint activity of these two modalities of the primordial Being.

Essentially, deliverance consists in comprehending this "mystery": once the paradoxical manifestation of the All/One is disclosed, it

41. The most important are *Kāṭha, Praśna, Maitri, Māṇḍūkya, Śvetāśvatara,* and *Muṇḍaka*. The period when they were composed is difficult to determine; it was probably between 500 and 200 B.C.

42. This has been well brought out by H. von Glasenapp, *La philosophie indienne*, p. 131.

becomes possible to free oneself from the wheels of the cosmic process. From different points of view, this cosmic process can be regarded as divine "play" (*lilā*), an "illusion" (*māyā*), due to non-knowing, or a "trial" forcing man to seek absolute freedom (*mokṣa*).[43] What is of the first importance is that the paradoxical coexistence of two contradictory modalities in the primordial Being makes it possible to give a meaning to human existence (itself no less para-doxical, because ruled by the law of *karman* though "containing" an *ātman*) and, in addition, makes deliverance possible. Indeed, by understanding the analogy between Brahman and his manifestation, the material creation, and the *ātman* caught in the net of trans-migration, *one discovers the fortuitous and impermanent character of the terrible sequence avidya-karman-saṃsāra.*

Certainly, the Upanishads of the middle period exploit these new discoveries differently. The two modalities of the Brahman are some-times interpreted as representing a personal god, superior to matter (his impersonal mode of being); it is in this sense that we may understand the *Kāṭha Upaniṣad* 1. 3. 11, which sets the personal principle (*puruṣa*) above its "impersonal" (*avyakta*, literally "non-manifested") modalities.[44] The *Śvetāśvatara* is even more significant, since it associates speculation on the absolute Being (Brahman) with devotion to a personal god, Rudra-Śiva. The "Threefold Brahman" (1. 12), God immanent in all nature and in all the forms of life (2. 16–17), is identified with Rudra, creator but also destroyer of the worlds (3. 2). As for nature (*prakṛti*), it is the *māyā* of the Lord (Rudra-Śiva), the creative "magic" that chains all individual beings (4. 9–10). Consequently, the cosmic creation can be understood either as a divine emanation or as "play" (*lilā*), in which, blinded by ignorance, human beings let themselves be caught. Deliverance is obtained by Sāṃkhya and Yoga, that is, by philosophical comprehension and the psychophysiological techniques of meditation (6. 13).[45]

It is important to emphasize the advancement of Yoga practices to the rank of a way of deliverance, side by side with gnosis, the preponderant method in the early Upanishads. The *Kāṭha Upaniṣad*

43. All these interpretations will become popular later.
44. Similarly in *Muṇḍaka* 2. 1. 2, the place of the *puruṣa* is above that of the *akṣara*, the "immutable," that is, of *prakṛti;* see Glasenapp, p. 123.
45. The distinctive characteristic of the *Śvetāśvatara Up.* is, however, devotion to Śiva; see Eliade, *Yoga*, pp. 121–22.

also presents Yoga practice side by side with meditation of the gnostic type (3. 13). Certain Yogic techniques are set forth in greater detail in the *Śvetāśvatara*, the *Māṇḍūkya*, and expecially the *Maitri* Upanishads.

Thus we see how the researches and discoveries recorded in the earliest Upanishads developed. On the one hand, there was an effort to separate the spiritual principle (*ātman*) from organic and psycho-mental life, dynamisms that were progressively devalorized by being included in the drives of nature (*prakṛti*). It is only the Self purified from psychomental experiences that was identified with Brahman and hence could be considered immortal. On the other hand, there was an effort to decipher and analyze the relations between the total Being (Brahman) and nature. Ascetic techniques and methods of meditation, both aiming at the dissociation of the Self from psycho-mental experience, will be elaborated and articulated in the earliest Yoga treatises. Rigorous analysis of the mode of being of the Self (*ātman, puruṣa*) and of the structures and dynamisms of nature (*prakṛti*) constitute the objective of the Sāṃkhya philosophy.

10 Zeus and the Greek Religion

83. Theogony and struggles between divine generations

The very name of Zeus proclaims his nature: he is, preeminently, an Indo-European celestial god (cf. § 62). Theocritus (4. 43) could still write that Zeus sometimes shines and sometimes comes down in rain. According to Homer, the portion received by Zeus "is the broad heaven amid the air and the clouds" (*Iliad* 15. 192). A number of his titles emphasize his structure as a god of the atmosphere: Ombrios and Hyetios (Rainy), Ourios (He who sends favorable winds), Astrapios (He who hurls the lightning), Brontōn (He who thunders), etc. But Zeus is far more than a personification of the sky as a cosmic phenomenon. His uranian character is confirmed by his sovereignty and by his countless hierogamies with various chthonian goddesses.

However, except for his name and his sovereignty (which he won only after hard fighting), Zeus does not resemble the ancient Indo-European sky gods, such, for example, as the Vedic Dyaus. Not only is he not the creator of the universe, he does not even belong to the group of Greek primordial divinities.

Indeed, according to Hesiod, in the beginning there existed only Chaos (Abyss), whence arose "broad-flanked" Gaea (Gaia, Earth), and Eros. Then Gaea "bore a being equal to herself, able to cover her entirely, starry Uranus (Heaven)" (*Theogony* 118 ff., after the translation by Mazon). Hesiod describes Uranus, "all avid for love and bringing with him night, approaching and enveloping the Earth" (*Theog.* 176 ff.). From this cosmic hierogamy[1] there came into the world a second divine generation, that of the Uranides: the

1. But, before the hierogamy, Gaea had, all by herself, borne the Mountains, the Nymphs, and the barren Sea (Pontus) (Hesiod, *Theogony* 129 ff.).

six Titans (the first, Oceanus, the last, Kronos) and the six Titanides (among them Rhea, Themis, Mnemosyne), the three one-eyed Cyclopes, and the three Hundred-armed Giants.

This inordinate and sometimes monstrous fecundity is typical of primordial periods. But Uranus hated his children "from the first day," and he hid them in Gaea's body. Furious, the goddess produced a great sickle and addressed her children: "Sons sprung from me and a raging father, . . . we will punish the criminal outrage of a father, your father though he be, since he was the first to think of shameful things." But, terrorized, "not one of them spoke a word" except Kronos, who undertook the task. And when Uranus approached, "drunken to penetrate the body of Earth" (Aeschylus, frag. 44 Nauck), Kronos castrated him with his sickle. From the blood that flowed upon Gaea there came into the world the three Erinyes, goddesses of vengeance, the giants, and the nymphs of ash trees. From the sexual organs of Uranus, thrown into the sea, Aphrodite was born.

This episode represents an especially violent version of the archaic myth of the separation of heaven and earth. As we have already observed (§ 47), it is a widely disseminated myth, documented on various levels of culture. The castration of Uranus puts an end to an uninterrupted procreation,[2] which was also, in the last analysis, useless, for the father "hid" the newborn infants in the earth. The mutilation of a cosmocrator god by his son, who thus becomes his successor, is the dominant theme of the Hurrian, Hittite, and Canaanite cosmogonies (§§ 46 ff.). In all likelihood, Hesiod knew these Oriental traditions,[3] for his *Theogony* is centered around the conflict between the divine generations and the struggle for universal sovereignty. And in fact, after reducing his father to impotence, Kronos took his place. He married his sister Rhea and had five children: Hestia, Demeter, Hera, Hades, Poseidon. But since he had learned from Gaea and Uranus that he was destined to "succumb one day under the blows of his own son" (*Theog.* 463 ff.), Kronos swallowed his children as soon as they came into the world. Frustrated, Rhea then followed Gaea's advice: on the day when she was

2. The *otiositas* of Uranus after his castration illustrates, though brutally, the tendency of creator gods to retire to the sky and become *dii otiosi* after achieving their cosmogonic work; see Eliade, *Patterns in Comparative Religion*, §§ 14 ff.

3. See, most recently, M. L. West, *Hesiod's Theogony*, pp. 18 ff.; P. Walcot, *Hesiod and the Near East*, pp. 27 ff.

to give birth to Zeus, she went to Crete and hid the infant in an inaccessible cave. Then she wrapped a great stone in swaddling clothes and gave it to Kronos, who swallowed it (*Theog.* 478 ff.).

When he grew up, Zeus forced Kronos to disgorge his brothers and sisters. He then freed his father's brothers, whom Uranus had chained. In token of gratitude, they offered him thunder and lightning. Furnished with such weapons, Zeus can thenceforth command "both mortals and immortals" (*Theog.* 493–506). But Kronos and the Titans must first be conquered. The war had continued indecisively for ten years when Zeus and the young gods, advised by Gaea, went to fetch the three Hundred-armed Giants, imprisoned by Uranus in the subterranean depths. Soon afterward the Titans were utterly defeated and imprisoned underground in Tartarus, under the guard of the Hundred-armed Giants (*Theog.* 617–720).

The description of the Titanomachy (especially 700 ff.) gives the impression of a regression to the precosmogonic stage. The triumph of Zeus over the Titans—incarnation of inordinate strength and violence—is consequently equivalent to a new organization of the universe. In a certain sense, Zeus creates the world anew (cf. Indra, § 68). However, this creation was dangerously threatened on two or more occasions. In a passage that was long considered to be an interpolation (lines 820–80), but whose genuineness has been demonstrated by the most recent editor of the *Theogony*,[4] a monstrous being, Typhon, son of Gaea and Tartarus, rises against Zeus. "From his shoulders came a hundred snake heads, frightful dragons, thrusting out blackish tongues; and from his eyes . . . flared a light like fire," etc. (*Theog.* 824 ff.). Zeus struck him with his thunderbolts and cast him down into Tartarus.[5] Finally, according to the Gigantomachy, an episode unknown to Homer and Hesiod and mentioned for the first time by Pindar (*First Nemean* 1. 67), the giants born of Gaea fecundated by the blood of Uranus rose against Zeus and his brothers. Apollodorus adds that it was to avenge the Titans that Gaea bore the giants and that it was after the overthrow of the giants that she procreated Typhon (*Bibl.* 1. 6. 1–3).

4. West, *Hesiod's Theogony*, pp. 379 ff.
5. Apollodorus, *Bibl.* 1. 6. 3, relates that, before being overthrown, Typhon succeeded in stealing Zeus's tendons, a motif that is reminiscent of an episode in the Hittite myth of the combat between the storm god and the dragon Illuyankas; cf. § 45. However, see West, *Hesiod's Theogony*, p. 392.

Gaea's machinations against the supremacy of Zeus are an expression of the obstructive efforts of a primordial divinity in regard to the work of cosmogony or the installation of a new order (cf. the Mesopotamian theomachy, § 21).[6] And yet it is due to Gaea and Uranus that Zeus is able to keep his sovereignty, thus putting a final end to the violent succession of divine dynasties.

84. Triumph and sovereignty of Zeus

And in fact, after overwhelming Typhon, Zeus parcels out dominion over the three cosmic zones by drawing lots. The ocean falls to Poseidon, the subterranean world to Hades, and the sky to Zeus, while the earth and Olympus belong to them in common (*Iliad* 15. 197 ff.). Zeus then undertakes a series of marriages. His first wife was Metis (Prudence). However, when she was pregnant with Athena, Zeus swallowed her; for he had listened to the advice of Gaea and Uranus when they had predicted to him the eventual birth of a "violent-hearted son, who should be king of men and gods" (*Theog.* 886 ff.). So it is due to the warning from the primordial couple that the sovereignty of Zeus was definitely insured. In addition, he incorporated Prudence into himself forever.[7] As for Athena, a blow from an ax brought her forth from her father's forehead (*Theog.* 924).

Zeus then marries the Titaness Themis (Order), Eurynome, Mnemosyne (who bore him the nine Muses), and finally Hera (*Theog.* 901 ff.). But before marrying Hera, he had loved Demeter, who bore Persephone, and Leto, mother of the divine twins Apollo and Artemis (910 ff.). He also had numerous liaisons with other goddesses, most of them chthonian in structure (Dia, Europa, Semele, etc.). These unions reflect the hierogamies of the storm god with the divinities of the earth. The meaning of these many marriages and erotic adventures is at once religious and political. By thus appropriating the pre-Hellenic local goddesses, venerated from time immemorial, Zeus replaces them and, in so doing, begins the process of symbiosis and unification that will give Greek religion its most specific characteristic.

6. But Gaea's anger can also be interpreted as a reaction against the violence and cruelty of Zeus.

7. On the mythological plane, this episode explains the later transformation of Zeus, the source of his "wisdom."

The triumph of Zeus and the Olympians did not find expression in the disappearance of the archaic divinities and cults, some of them pre-Hellenic in origin. On the contrary, a part of the immemorial heritage ended by being incorporated into the Olympian religious system. We have just noted the role of the primordial couple in the destiny of Zeus. We shall cite other examples. For the moment, we will refer to the episode of Zeus's birth and infancy in Crete.[8] We here undoubtedly have an Aegean mythico-ritual scenario, centered on the divine Infant, son and lover of a Great Goddess. According to the Greek tradition, the infant's cries were concealed by the noise made by the Curetes' clashing their shields together (mythological projection of the initiatory groups of young men performing their armed dance). The Palaikastro hymn (fourth to third centuries B.C.) praises the leaps of Zeus, "the greatest of the Curetes."[9] (The reference is probably to an archaic fertility ritual.) What is more, the cult of Zeus Idaeus, celebrated in a cave on Mount Ida, had the structure of an initiation into the Mysteries.[10] Now Zeus was in no way a god of the Mysteries. And it is also in Crete that the tomb of Zeus was later shown; so the great Olympian god was assimilated to one of the gods of the Mysteries, who die and return to life.

Aegean influences persist even in the classical period; they are to be found, for example, in the statues that show Zeus as young and beardless. But these are survivals that were tolerated, if not encouraged, by the immense and inexhaustible process of syncretism.[11] For already in Homer Zeus recovers the splendors and powers of a true Indo-European sovereign god. He is more than a god of the "vast sky," he is "the father of gods and men" (*Iliad* 1. 544). And in a fragment of his *Heliades* (frag. 70 Nauck), Aeschylus proclaims: "Zeus is the ether, Zeus is the earth, Zeus is the sky. Yes, Zeus is all that is above all." Master of atmospheric phenomena, he governs the fertility of the soil, and he is invoked as Zeus Chthonios when agricultural work is begun (Hesiod, *Works and Days* 465). By the

8. On Zeus Cretagenes, see Charles Picard, *Les religions pré-helléniques*, pp. 117 ff.

9. See H. Jeanmaire, *Couroï et Courètes*, pp. 427 ff.

10. Euripides, fragment of a lost tragedy, *The Cretans* (frag. 472 Nauck).

11. In the eastern Mediterranean this process will allow the incorporation of the Roman, Hellenistic, and Iranian heritage into the structure of the Byzantine Empire and, later, the preservation of Byzantine institutions by the Ottomans. See the third volume of the present work.

name of Ctesius he is protector of the house and symbol of plenty. He also watches over the duties and rights of the family, insures respect for the laws, and, as Polieus, defends the city. At an earlier period he was the god of purification, Zeus Katharsios, and also god of prophecy, especially at Dodona, in Epirus, where divination was performed by "the divine foliage of the great oak of Zeus" (*Odyssey* 14. 327 ff.; 19. 296 ff.).

Thus, despite the fact that he is the creator of neither the world nor life nor man, Zeus proves to be the uncontested chief of the gods and absolute master of the universe. The multitude of sanctuaries dedicated to Zeus prove his Panhellenic character.[12] Consciousness of his omnipotence is admirably illustrated in the famous scene in the *Iliad* (8. 17 ff.) in which Zeus makes this challenge to the Olympians: "Then [you] will see how far I am strongest of all the immortals. Come, you gods, make this endeavor, that you all may learn this. Let down out of the sky a cord of gold; lay hold of it all you who are gods and all who are goddesses, yet not even so can you drag down Zeus from the sky to the ground, not Zeus the high lord of counsel, though you try until you grow weary. Yet whenever I might strongly be minded to pull you, I could drag you up, earth and all and sea and all with you, then fetch the golden rope about the horn of Olympos and make it fast, so that all once more should dangle in mid air. So much stronger am I than the gods, and stronger than mortals" (trans. Richmond Lattimore, *The Iliad of Homer* [Chicago, 1951]).

The mythical theme of the golden cord (or chain) has given rise to countless interpretations, from Plato, through Pseudo-Dionysius, down to the eighteenth century.[13] But what concerns our purpose is that, according to an Orphic poem, the *Rhapsodic Theogony*, Zeus asks the primordial goddess Nyx (Night) how to establish his "proud empire over the immortals" and, especially, how to organize the cosmos so that "the whole shall be one and the parts distinct." Night teaches him the fundamentals of cosmology and then tells him of the golden cord that he must fasten to the ether.[14] To be sure, this

12. Zeus was worshiped everywhere in Greece, especially on the highest mountains; important sites of his cult were at Olympia and Athens in mainland Greece, and in Crete, Asia Minor, and the West.

13. On this theme, see our study, "Ropes and Puppets," in *The Two and the One*, pp. 160–88, esp. pp. 179 ff.

14. See the translation and commentary in P. Leveque, *Aurea Catena Homeri*, pp. 14 ff.

is a late text, but the tradition that it reports is old. *Iliad* 14. 258 ff. presents Night as a comparatively powerful goddess: Zeus himself avoids angering her. It is significant that the most celebrated proclamation of the omnipotence of Zeus should have connections with the interview that the supreme master asked a primordial goddess to grant him. Night's cosmological directives in a sense repeat the revelation of Gaea and Uranus that puts an end to the struggles for sovereignty.

As we have already observed, certain primordial divinities have survived the triumph of the Olympians. First of them all was Night, whose power and prestige we have just recalled. Then came Pontus (the Barren Sea); Styx, who took part in the battle against the Titans; Hecate, honored by Zeus and the other Olympians; Oceanus, the firstborn of the children of Gaea and Uranus. Each of them still played a part—modest, obscure, marginal—in the economy of the universe. When Zeus felt that his authority was definitely assured, he freed Kronos, his father, from his underground prison and made him the king of a fabulous land—the Isles of the Blessed in the farthest West.

85. The myth of the first races: Prometheus, Pandora

We shall never know the "history" of Kronos. He is certainly an archaic god, almost without a cult. His only important myth makes up an episode in the theomachy. However, Kronos is mentioned in connection with the first human race, the "race of gold." This indication is important: it shows us the beginnings and the first phase of the relations between men and the gods. According to Hesiod, "Gods and mortals have the same origin" (*Works and Days* 108). For men are born from the earth (*gēgeneis*), just as the earliest gods were born by Gaea. In short, the world and the gods came into being by an initial scission, followed by a process of procreation. And just as there were several divine generations, so there were five races of men: the races of gold, silver, and bronze, the race of heroes, and the race of iron (*Works* 109 ff.).

Now the first race lived under the reign of Kronos (*Works* 111), that is, before Zeus. This humanity of the age of gold, exclusively masculine, dwelt with the gods, "their powerful brothers." Men "lived like gods, their hearts free from cares, safe from pains and miseries" (*Works* 112 ff.). They did not work, for the soil offered them everything that they needed. Their life was spent in dancing, festivals, and all kinds of delights. They knew neither illness nor old age, and when they died it was as if they were overcome by sleep (*Works* 113 ff.). But this paradisal period—parallels to which are found in many traditions—was ended by the fall of Kronos.[15]

Hesiod then relates that the men of the race of gold "were covered by the earth," and the gods produced a less noble race, the men of the age of silver. Because of their sins, and also because they would not sacrifice to the gods, Zeus decided to destroy them. He then made the third race, that of bronze: a violent and warlike people who ended by killing one another, down to the last man. Zeus created a new generation, that of the heroes; they became famous through the grandiose battles before Thebes and Troy. Many of them suffered death, but the others were placed by Zeus at the ends of the earth, in the Isles of the Blessed, and Kronos reigned over them (*Works* 140–69). Hesiod says nothing of the fifth race, that of iron. But he laments that it was given him to be born into that period (*Works* 176 ff.).

The traditions reported by Hesiod raise many problems, but not all of them are directly concerned with our purpose. The myth of the "perfection of the beginnings" and of primordial bliss, both lost as the result of an accident or a "sin," is comparatively widespread. The variant Hesiod presents states that the decadence takes place progressively, in four stages, which is reminiscent of the Indian doctrine of the four *yugas*. But though their colors are given—white, red, yellow, and black—the *yugas* are not associated with metals. On the other hand, metals as specific signs of historical epochs are found in the dream of Nebuchadnezzar (Daniel 2:32–33) and in some late

---

15. It may appear paradoxical that the "savage" god who, according to the *Theogony*, swallowed his children as soon as they were born, reigned, still according to Hesiod (*Works* 111), during the Edenic period of humanity. But it must not be forgotten that the Kronos of the *Theogony* reflects strong Oriental influences. It is also surprising that the gods are presented as the "powerful brothers" of men. Such an assertion contradicts the general opinion that emphasizes the radical ontological difference between gods and men. Yet it should be pointed out that the fundamental distinction already existed at the period of the golden race: men enjoyed the bliss and the friendship of the gods, but not *immortality*. Besides, the gods belonged to the second divine generation, that of the Titans; in other words, the structures of the world and the modalities of existence were not yet strictly defined.

Iranian texts. But in the first case the reference is to dynasties, and in the second the succession of empires is projected into the future.

Hesiod had to insert the age of the heroes between the races of bronze and iron because the mythicized memory of the fabulous heroic period was too strong for him to ignore it. The age of the heroes interrupts—and quite inexplicably—the process of progressive degradation begun by the appearance of the silver race. However, the privileged destiny of the heroes poorly conceals an eschatology: they do not die, but enjoy a blissful existence in the Isles of the Blessed, the Elysium where Kronos now rules. In other words, the heroes to a certain extent recover the existence of the men of the golden age under the reign of Kronos. This eschatology will be greatly elaborated later, especially under the influence of Orphism. Elysium will no longer be the exclusive privilege of heroes but will become accessible to the souls of the pious and to the "initiated." This is a process of considerable frequency in the history of religions (cf. Egypt, § 30; India; etc.).

It must be added that the myth of successive ages does not represent the unanimous opinion concerning the origin of mankind. Indeed, the problem of the anthropogony seems not to have occupied the Greeks. They were more interested in the origin of some particular ethnic group, of a city, of a dynasty. Many families considered themselves descended from a hero who, in turn, had sprung from the union of a divinity with a mortal. One people, the Myrmidons, were descended from ants, another from ash trees. After the flood, Deucalion repeopled the earth with "his mother's bones," that is, with stones. Finally, according to a late tradition (fourth century), it was Prometheus who fashioned men from clay.

For reasons that we do not know, gods and men decided to part amicably at Mekone (*Theog.* 535). Men offered the first sacrifice in order definitively to settle their relations with the gods. It is on this occasion that Prometheus first plays a role.[16] He sacrificed an ox and divided it into two portions. But, wanting to protect men and, at the same time, to dupe Zeus, Prometheus covered the bones with a layer of fat and covered the flesh and entrails with the paunch. Attracted by the fat, Zeus chose the poorer portion for the gods, leaving the flesh and entrails for men. This, adds Hesiod, is why since then men burn the bones as an offering to the immortal gods (*Theog.* 556).

16. Prometheus' name does not appear in Homer.

This cunning division of the sacrifice had great consequences for humanity. On the one hand, it raised the carnivorous diet, as a paradigmatic religious act, to the position of highest homage offered to the gods; but, in the last analysis, this implied abandoning the vegetarian regime followed during the age of gold. On the other hand, Prometheus' trick angered Zeus against humankind, and he deprived them of the use of fire.[17] But the wily Prometheus brought fire down from heaven, hiding it in a hollow fennel-stalk (*Theog.* 567; *Works* 52). Furious, Zeus decided to punish men and their protector together. Prometheus was chained, and an eagle daily ate his "immortal liver," which was renewed again overnight (*Theog.* 521 ff.; *Works* 56). One day he will be set free by Heracles, son of Zeus, to the increase of the hero's glory.

As for human beings, Zeus sent them woman, that "beautiful evil" (*Theog.* 585), in the form of Pandora (the "present from all the gods," *Works* 81 ff.). "Snare from which there is no escaping, destined for mankind," Hesiod denounces her; "for it is from her that there came the race, the accursed tribe of woman, that terrible plague set among mortal men" (*Theog.* 592 ff.).[18]

86. The consequences of the primordial sacrifice

All in all, far from being a benefactor of humanity, Prometheus is responsible for its present fallen state. At Mekone he instigated the separation between men and gods. Then, by stealing fire, he exasperated Zeus and thus caused the invention of Pandora, that is, the appearance of woman and, in consequence, the propagation of all

17. Deprivation of the use of fire annulled the benefits of the division; for, obliged to eat raw flesh, and unable to sacrifice to the gods, men reentered the condition of wild animals.

18. Prometheus had vainly instructed his brother to accept nothing from Zeus. The naïve Epimetheus receives Pandora and marries her. Not long afterward, she opens the mysterious jar, from which all the evils escape and spread over the world. When Pandora replaces the cover, only Hope still remains at the bottom of the jar. As Séchan and Lévêque observe, "This is precisely what the angry Zeus wanted, to constrain man eternally to 'hard toil' (Hes., *Works* 91), and that is why he made Hope, 'who feeds the vain efforts of man' (Simonides 1. 6), enter the vessel" (*Les grandes divinités de la Grèce*, p. 54).

kinds of cares, tribulations, and misfortunes. For Hesiod, the myth of Prometheus explains the sudden coming of evil into the world; in the last analysis, "evil" represents the vengeance of Zeus.[19]

But this pessimistic view of human history, doomed by the double-dealing of a Titan, did not definitively impose itself. For Aeschylus, who substitutes the theme of progress for the myth of the primordial golden age, Prometheus is the greatest civilizing hero. The first men, Prometheus affirms, lived "underground, deep in caverns closed to the sun"; they did not even know the succession of the seasons or the domestication of animals or agriculture; it was he, Prometheus, who taught them all arts and all sciences (*Prometheus Bound* 442 ff.). It is he who gave them fire[20] and freed them from the fear of death (line 248). Jealous because he was not the author of this humanity, Zeus wanted to destroy it and create another (233). Prometheus alone dared to oppose this plan of the master of the world. To explain the anger of Zeus and Prometheus' intransigence, Aeschylus took from Pindar (or from his source) a dramatic detail: Prometheus possesses a terrible weapon, in the form of the secret told him by his mother, Themis. This secret concerned the ineluctable fall of Zeus[21] in a more or less distant future (522, 764 ff.). The Titan emphatically declared that Zeus has but one way to avoid this catastrophe: to free him (Prometheus) from his chains (769–70). Since the two other parts of the *Prometheus* trilogy have not been preserved, we do not know how the antagonism between the two divine figures was ended by their reconciliation. But in fifth-century Athens, Prometheus already had his annual festival; he was, in addition, associated with Hephaestus and Athena. In any case, perhaps under the influence of certain spiritual movements that were eagerly followed both by the intellectual elite and by the man in the street (see vol. 2 of this work), there had for some time been a marked emphasis on the wisdom and benignity of Zeus. Not only had the supreme master repented, by

19. Hesiod is categorical: from the day when Zeus sees himself "duped by Prometheus of knavish thoughts, from that day he prepares sad cares" (*Works* 47 ff.).

20. He does not give it back to them, as in Hesiod, by bringing it from heaven. "Aeschylus omitted the episode of Mekone, which was not in harmony with the tone of tragedy and might have diminished the prestige of his hero" (L. Séchan, *Le mythe de Prométhée*, p. 102, n. 62).

21. On the origin and development of this motif, see Séchan, ibid., pp. 23 ff., 42 ff., and J. P. Vernant, "Métis et les mythes de souveraineté."

setting Kronos up as king in Elysium; he had also forgiven the Titans. Pindar proclaims that "Zeus, the Immortal, had freed the Titans" (*Fourth Pythian* 291) and, in the *Prometheus Unbound*, the chorus is made up of the Titans freed from their chains.[22]

The division of the first sacrificial victim at Mekone shows its effects, on the one hand, in the break between gods and men and, on the other, in the condemnation of Prometheus. Yet Zeus's indignation seems excessive; for as Karl Meuli has shown,[23] this ritual division corresponds to the sacrifices offered to the celestial gods by the primitive hunters of Siberia and the herders of Central Asia—in fact, the latter present the uranian supreme beings with the animal's bones and head. In other words, what, at an archaic stage of culture, was considered the most fitting homage to a celestial god had become, in the act of Prometheus, a crime of lèse-majesté against Zeus, the supreme god. We do not know at what moment this warping of the original ritual meaning occurred. It seems, however, that Zeus's rage was provoked, not by the division in itself, but by the fact that it was arranged by Prometheus, in other words by a Titan, a member of the divine "old generation," who, to make matters worse, had sided with men against the Olympians. The example set by Prometheus could have unfortunate consequences; encouraged by this first success, men might go even further than the Titan had done. But Zeus would not tolerate a powerful and proud humanity. Men must never forget that their existential status was precarious and ephemeral. Hence they must keep their distance.

Indeed, later on, Deucalion, son of Prometheus, and the only survivor of the flood brought on by Zeus, offers him a sacrifice like the one at Mekone, and it is accepted. "Zeus receives Deucalion's demand favorably, but the myth indicates that he consents precisely insofar as distance is maintained."[24] From then on the most common sacrifice, the *thysia*, repeats this mythical model: part of the victim, the fat, is burned on the altar, and the other part is eaten by the sacrificers and their companions.[25] But the gods are also present:

22. See Séchan, p. 44.
23. K. Meuli, *Griechische Opferbräuche* (1946). See also W. Burkert, *Homo Necans*, pp. 20 ff.
24. J. Rudhardt, "Les mythes grecques relatifs à l'instauration du sacrifice," p. 14. Besides, Zeus does not answer Deucalion directly; he sends Hermes to learn what he wants (Apollodorus, *Bibl.* 1. 7. 2).
25. The closest analogue is the *zèbah* of the Hebrews (see § 57).

they feed on the sacrifices (*Iliad* 1. 423–24; 8. 548–52, etc.) or on the smoke that rises from the burning fat (*Il.* 1. 66–67; etc.).

The break brought on at Mekone is in some sense mended, and precisely by Deucalion. The son of Prometheus reestablishes the gods in the conditions that were agreeable to Zeus. (Besides, the humanity contemporary with the fatal division had perished in the flood.) It is significant that, after Aeschylus, Prometheus plays a comparatively small and unobtrusive part. Possibly the very success of the *Prometheus* trilogy contributed to this situation. For if Aeschylus had praised the unique greatness of this civilizing hero, protector of men, he had also illustrated the benignity of Zeus and the spiritual value of the final reconciliation, raised to the rank of paradigmatic model for human wisdom. Prometheus will not recover his sublime stature as eternal victim of tyranny until the age of European Romanticism.

In India, speculations on sacrifice find expression in a particular cosmogony and open the way to the metaphysics and techniques of Yoga (§§ 76–78). Among the Hebrews, blood sacrifices will be continually reinterpreted and revalorized, even after the criticisms of the prophets. As for Christianity, it was founded on the voluntary immolation of Christ. Orphism and Pythagoreanism, by emphasizing the virtues of a vegetarian diet, implicitly recognized the "sin" committed by men in accepting the division made at Mekone (see vol. 2). However, the punishment of Prometheus played only a secondary role in reflections on the "justice" of Zeus. Now the problem of divine "justice," with its corollary, human "destiny," exercised Greek thought from Homer on.

87. Man and destiny: The meaning of the "joy of life"

Judged from the Judeo-Christian point of view, Greek religion seems to take form under the sign of pessimism: human existence is by definition ephemeral and burdened with cares. Homer compares man to the "leaves that the wind scatters on the ground" (*Il.* 6. 146 ff.). The comparison is taken up again by the poet Mimnermus of Colophon (seventh century) in his long enumeration of evils: poverty, disease, mourning, old age, etc. "He is not a man to whom Zeus does not send a thousand ills." For his contemporary, Simonides, men are "creatures of a day," living like cattle, "not knowing by what road god will lead each of us to our destiny."[26] A mother prayed to Apollo to reward her piety by bestowing on her two children the greatest gift in his power; the god consented, and the children immediately died without pain (Herodotus 1. 31. 1 ff.). Theognis, Pindar, Sophocles proclaim that the best fate for human beings would be not to be born or, once born, to die as soon as possible.[27]

Yet death resolves nothing, since it does not bring total and final extinction. For Homer's contemporaries death was a diminished and humiliating postexistence in the underground darkness of Hades, peopled by pallid shadows, without strength and without memory. (Achilles, whose ghost Ulysses succeeds in calling up, declares that he would choose to be on earth, the slave of a poor man, "rather than to reign over all the dead.")[28] Besides, good done on earth was not rewarded, and evil was not punished. Of all the dead, only Ixion, Tantalus, and Sisyphus were condemned to eternal torment, for they had offended Zeus in person. And if Menelaus did not go down to Hades but was transported to Elysium, it was because, by marrying Helen, he had become Zeus's son-in-law. According to the tradition transmitted by Hesiod (cf. § 85), other heroes enjoy the same destiny. But they were privileged beings.

This pessimistic conception imposed itself when the Greeks became aware of the precariousness of the human condition. On the one hand, man is not, stricto sensu, the "creature" of a divinity (an idea held by many archaic traditions and by the three mono-theisms); hence he does not dare to hope that his prayers can establish a certain intimacy with the gods. On the other hand, he knows that his life is already decided by destiny, moira or aisa, the "lot" or "portion" granted to him—in short, the time allowed him until his death.[29] Consequently, death was decided at the moment of

26. The Ionian poets seem to be terrorized by misery, sicknesses, and old age. The only possible consolations are war and glory, or the enjoyments procured by wealth.

27. Theognis 425–28; Pindar, frag. 157; Sophocles, Oedipus at Colonus 1219 ff.

28. Odyssey 11. 489–91—a statement that became famous, but that will later be mercilessly criticized by Socrates; see Plato, Republic 3. 386a–387b; 387d–388b.

29. The meaning of the terms moira and aisa varied after Homer. These almost demonic powers, which drove men to madness, were later personified

birth; the duration of life was symbolized by the thread spun by the divinity.[30] However, certain expressions such as *"moira* of the gods" (*Od.* 3. 261) or *"aisa* of Zeus" (*Il.* 17. 322; *Od.* 9. 52) give us to understand that it is Zeus himself who determines fates. In principle, he can alter destiny, as he was preparing to do on behalf of his son Sarpedon (*Il.* 16. 433 ff.) at the moment when the latter's life had just reached its term. But Hera points out to him that such an act will result in annulling the laws of the universe—that is, of justice (*dikē*)— and Zeus admits that she is right.

This example shows that Zeus himself recognizes the supremacy of justice; besides, *dikē* is only the concrete manifestation, in human society, of the universal order, in other words, of the divine Law (*themis*). Hesiod declares that Zeus bestowed justice on men so that they would not behave like wild beasts. The first duty of man is to be just and to show honor (*timē*) to the gods, especially by offering them sacrifices. Certainly, the term *dikē* evolved in the course of the centuries that separate Homer from Euripides. The latter does not hesitate to write: "If the gods do anything that is ugly (or: base), they are not the gods!" (frag. 292, from *Bellerophon*). Before Euripides, Aeschylus had declared that Zeus does not punish the innocent (*Agamemnon* 750 ff.). But already in the *Iliad* Zeus can be recognized as the protector of *dikē*, since it is he who guarantees oaths and protects strangers, guests, and suppliants.[31]

In short, the gods do not strike men without reason, as long as mortals do not go beyond the limits prescribed by their own mode of existence. But it is difficult not to go beyond the imposed limits, for man's ideal is "excellence" (*aretē*). Now, excessive excellence runs the risk of arousing inordinate pride and insolence (*hybris*). This

---

and became three goddesses. The three Moirai appear for the first time in Hesiod, *Theog.* 900 ff.; they are the daughters of Zeus and Themis.

30. At first the "spinning" was done either by "the gods" (*Od.* 20. 196; etc.) or "the *daimon*" (*Od.* 16. 64), or by *moira* (*Il.* 24. 209) or *aisa* (*Il.* 20. 128). But finally, as in other Indo-European (but also Oriental) traditions, the "spinning" of destinies became the attribute of the Spinners (*Klothes*) or the Moirai. Cf. *Volospā*, str. 20; Eliade, *Patterns in Comparative Religion*, § 58. To "spin" someone's destiny is equivalent to "binding" him, in other words to immobilizing him in a "situation" that cannot be changed.

31. H. Lloyd-Jones, *The Justice of Zeus*, p. 6 (against the interpretation advanced by Dodds, *The Greeks and the Irrational*, p. 52, n. 18). Zeus is also the model for a king: as responsible for the well-being of his subjects, the

happened, for example, to Ajax, when he boasted that he had escaped death despite the gods and so was destroyed by Poseidon (*Od.* 4. 499–511). *Hybris* brings on a temporary madness (*atē*), which blinds the victim and leads him to disaster.[32] This is as much as to say that *hybris* and its result, *atē*, are the means that in certain cases (heroes, kings, adventurers, etc.) bring about the realization of *moira*, the portion of life allotted at birth to such mortals, whether they are overambitious or are simply misled by the ideal of excellence.

In the last analysis, man has nothing to work with except his own limitations, those which are assigned to him by his human condition and, particularly, by his *moira*. Wisdom begins with consciousness of the finiteness and precariousness of every human life. So the thing to do is to take advantage of everything that can be offered by the *present*: youth, health, physical pleasures, or occasions for displaying the virtues. This is Homer's lesson: to live wholly, but nobly, *in the present*. Certainly, this "ideal" born of despair will undergo changes: we shall examine the most important of them further on (see vol. 2). But consciousness of the predestined limits and the fragility of existence was never obliterated. Far from inhibiting the creative forces of the Greek religious genius, this tragic vision led to a paradoxical revalorization of the human condition. Since the gods had forced him not to go beyond his limits, man ended by realizing the *perfection* and, consequently, the *sacrality of the human condition.* In other words, he rediscovered and brought to the full the religious sense of the "joy of life," the sacramental value of erotic experience and of the beauty of the human body, the religious function of every organized collective occasion for rejoicing—processions, games, dances, singing, sports competitions, spectacles, banquets, etc. The religious sense of the *perfection of the human body*—physical beauty, harmonious movements, calm, serenity—inspired the artistic canon. The anthropomorphism of the Greek gods, as it is perceptible in the myths and, later, will be savagely criticized by the philosophers, finds its religious meaning again in the divine statuary. Paradoxically, a

---

basileus is necessarily the protector of traditional rights and customs, the *themistes*; in other words, he is bound to respect a certain *dikē*.

32. When Herodotus (1. 32) makes Solon say, "I know that the divinity is subject to envy and instability," he is chiefly criticizing the unintelligence of those who forget their human condition and let themselves be led astray by *hybris*.

religion that proclaims the irreducible distance between the divine world and the world of mortals makes the perfection of the human body the most adequate representation of the gods.

But it is above all the religious valorization of the present that requires emphasizing. The simple fact of *existing*, of *living in time*, can comprise a religious dimension. This dimension is not always obvious, since sacrality is in a sense camouflaged in the immediate, in the "natural" and the everyday. The joy of life discovered by the Greeks is not a profane type of enjoyment: it reveals the bliss of existing, of sharing—even fugitively—in the spontaneity of life and the majesty of the world. Like so many others before and after them, the Greeks learned that the surest way to escape from time is to exploit the wealth, at first sight impossible to suspect, of the lived instant.

The sacralization of human finitude and of the banality of an ordinary existence is a comparatively frequent phenomenon in the history of religions. But it is especially in China and Japan of the first millennium of our era that the sacralization of "limits" and "circumstances"—of whatever nature—achieved excellence and profoundly influenced the respective cultures. Just as in ancient Greece, this transmutation of the "natural datum" also found expression in the emergence of a particular esthetic.[33]

33. See the third volume of the present work.

11 The Olympians and the Heroes

88. The fallen great god and the smith-magician: Poseidon and Hephaestus

Poseidon is an ancient great god who for many reasons lost his original universal sovereignty.[1] Traces of his former majesty are found everywhere, beginning with his name, which Wilamowitz correctly explained as meaning "husband of Earth" (*Posis Das*). In the *Iliad* (15. 204) Zeus is his elder, but Hesiod certainly reflects an earlier tradition by presenting Zeus as the younger (*Theogony* 456). In any case, only Poseidon dares to protest against Zeus's abuse of power, reminding him that his proper domain is limited to heaven.[2] We can detect in this detail the memory of a former sovereign god's resistance to the rise of a younger and more fortunate deity. By receiving, at the division of the universe, sovereignty over the seas, Poseidon became a true Homeric god; in view of the importance of the sea for the Hellenes, he was certain never to lose his religious actuality. However, his original structure was radically altered, and the northern mythico-religious heritage that he had brought to Greece was almost entirely dispersed or reinterpreted.

Indeed, the Indo-European people who worshiped Poseidon did not know the sea until they arrived in southern Greece. A number of Poseidon's characteristics have nothing to do with the sea. As Poseidon Hippios he is the god of horses, and in several places, especially Arcadia, he was worshiped in the form of a horse. It is in Arcadia that Poseidon met with Demeter wandering in search of

1. At Pylos, in the Achaean period, Poseidon enjoyed a religious position definitely superior to that of Zeus.
2. *Iliad* 15. 195. In *Iliad* 1. 400 ff. it is stated that Poseidon had once plotted with other gods to chain his brother.

Persephone. To escape him, the goddess changed herself into a mare, but Poseidon, in the form of a stallion, succeeded in possessing her. From their union were born a daughter and the steed Arion (Antimachus, in Pausanias 8. 25. 9). In the large number of his amorous adventures Poseidon is close to Zeus; at the same time, they bring out his original structure as "husband of Earth" and as "earth-shaker." According to Hesiod, he married Medusa, she too an ancient earth goddess. Another tradition recounts that Antaeus issued from his union with Ge.

His relations with the horse indicate that animal's importance for the Indo-European invaders. Poseidon is presented as the creator, the father, or the bestower of horses. Now the horse is connected with the infernal world, and this again brings out the god's character as "master of the Earth." His primordial power is also indicated by the gigantic or monstrous forms of his children: Orion, Polyphemus, Triton, Antaeus, the Harpies, etc. As *Posis Das*, the male spirit of the fertility inhabiting the earth, as Wilamowitz conceived him, the god whom the Indo-Europeans brought with them could be compared to the sovereign and fecundating gods, "masters of the Earth," of the Mediterranean and Oriental religions.[3] By becoming exclusively a marine god, Poseidon could retain only such of his original attributes as depended on the sea: capricious power and mastery over the fates of navigators.

Hephaestus enjoys a unique situation in Greek religion and mythology. His birth was peculiar: according to Hesiod, Hera engendered him "without a love union, in anger and spite against her husband."[4] In addition, Hephaestus differs from all the other Olympians by his ugliness and infirmity. He is lame in both feet, crooked or bandy-legged, and needs a support to walk. This infirmity was the result of his fall onto the island of Lemnos; Zeus had thrown him down from the top of Olympus because he had sided with his mother, Hera (*Iliad* 1. 500 ff.). According to another version, it was Hera who threw him into the sea at the moment of his birth, ashamed of his deformity (*Iliad* 18. 394 ff.). Two Nereids, Thetis and Eurynome, received him in a deep cave in the middle of the ocean. It is there that, for nine years, Hephaestus served his apprenticeship as smith and artisan.

3. See Leonard Palmer, *Mycenaeans and Minoans*, pp. 127 ff.
4. *Theogony* 927; cf. Apollodorus, *Bibl.* 1. 3. 5–6. But in *Iliad* 1. 578 Hephaestus affirms the paternity of Zeus.

The analogies with the themes of the "persecuted child" and the "maleficent infant" have been pointed out; in both cases the child emerges from the ordeal victorious. This undoubtedly represents an initiatory ordeal,[5] comparable to Dionysus' or Theseus' leaps into the waves.[6] But it is initiation of the magical and shamanic type that explains Hephaestus' mutilation. Marie Delcourt has compared Hephaestus' cut tendons or backward-turned feet to the initiatory tortures of the future shaman.[7] Like other magician-gods, Hephaestus paid for his knowledge of the smith's and the artisan's trades by his physical mutilation.

His works are at once masterpieces of art and magical wonders. Along with brooches, bracelets, rosettes (*Iliad* 18. 400–401), he makes the famous shield of Achilles (18. 369 ff.), the gold and silver dogs that flank the door of Alcinous' palace (*Odyssey* 7. 92), the shining houses of the gods, and automata, the most famous of which are the golden tripods that move by themselves and the two "handmaidens of gold" (*Il.* 18. 417 ff.) that resemble young girls and support him when he walks. At Zeus's bidding he fashions Pandora from clay and animates her. But Hephaestus is, above all, a master "binder." With his works—thrones, chains, nets—he binds gods and goddesses, as well as the Titan Prometheus. He gives Hera a golden throne, whose invisible bonds hold the goddess captive once she is seated in it. Since no god could free her from it, Dionysus was sent; he succeeded in intoxicating Hephaestus and brought him back to Olympus, where he finally set his mother free (Pausanias 1. 20. 2). His most celebrated exploit is also the most comic: Hephaestus imprisons Ares and his mistress, Aphrodite, in an invisible net and invites the Olympians to look at their guilty union (*Od.* 8. 266 ff.). The gods burst out laughing, but they are at the same time intimidated by this piece of handiwork, whose author proves, rather than a great artisan, to be a dangerous magician.

As a god-magician, Hephaestus is at once binder and looser and hence god-midwife (it is he who delivers Zeus of Athena). Nowhere

5. See Marie Delcourt, *Héphaistos ou la légende du magicien*, pp. 42 ff.

6. Indeed, it is by diving into the sea that Theseus obtains the ring and the magical crown—products of Hephaestus' art—which will enable him to enter and leave the labyrinth; see Delcourt, p. 119.

7. Delcourt, pp. 110 ff. Another element peculiar to shamanic traditions and to those of the smith-magicians is that Hephaestus learns his art in the cave of Eurynome (Death) or in the underground forge of Cedalion.

else is the equivalence of magic and technological perfection better brought out than in the mythology of Hephaestus. Certain sovereign gods (Varuṇa, Zeus) are masters of bonds. But the power to bind and loose is shared by other divine or demonic figures (for example, in India, Vṛtra, Yama, Nirrti). Knots, nets, laces, cords, strings are among the vivid images that express the magico-religious power necessary to command, govern, punish, paralyze, strike dead; in short, "subtle" expressions, paradoxically delicate, of a terrible, inordinate, supernatural power.[8] The mythology of Hephaestus associates the source of such a magical power with the trade secrets of metallurgists, smiths, and artisans—in short, to technological and craftsmanly perfection. But all techniques have their origin and their point of support in the mastery of fire, the apanage of shamans and magicians before it becomes the secret of potters, metallurgists, and smiths.

The "origins" of Hephaestus are unknown. Attempts to explain him by the pre-Hellenic heritage or by Indo-European traditions have failed. His archaic structure is obvious. More than a god of fire, he must have been a patron god of the various kinds of work that imply mastery of fire, in other words, a particular, and rather rare, form of magic.

89. Apollo: Contradictions reconciled

It may seem paradoxical that the name of the god considered to be the most perfect incarnation of the Hellenic genius does not have a Greek etymology. No less paradoxical is the fact that his most famous mythical exploits do not bear witness to the virtues that have come to be called "Apollonian": serenity, respect for law and order, divine harmony. The god often lets himself be carried away by vengeance, jealousy, and even spite. But these weaknesses will soon lose their anthropomorphic character and will end by revealing one of the many dimensions of divinity as it was understood by the Greeks.

He who, after Zeus, most radically illustrates the distance that separates man from the gods suffered the fate of the lowest of mortals: he was even refused the right to be born. Pregnant by Zeus, the

8. See our study "The 'God Who Binds' and the Symbolism of Knots," in *Images and Symbols*, pp. 92–124.

Titaness Leto sought in vain for a place to bear her child. No country dared to receive her for fear of Hera, who, in addition, had incited Python, the dragon of Delphi, to pursue her. Finally, the island of Delos accepted the Titaness, and she gave birth to twins, Artemis and Apollo. One of the infant's first acts was to punish Python. According to another, and earlier, version, Apollo traveled to Delphi, his future home. The road being blocked by a female dragon, Python, Apollo killed it with his arrows.[9] This is an exploit that can be justified, as it is possible to justify the execution of the giant Tityos, who had tried to violate his mother. But Apollo, again with his arrows, slaughtered the seven sons of Niobe (while Artemis killed the seven daughters) because the proud mother had humiliated Leto by boasting of her numerous progeny. He killed his sweetheart Coronis, who had deceived him with a mortal.[10] He also killed, but by mistake, his favorite, the beautiful youth Hyacinthus.

This aggressive mythology, which for many centuries inspired literature and the plastic arts, has its parallel in the history of Apollo's penetration into Greece. Briefly, it is the history of his replacing, more or less brutally, many pre-Hellenic local divinities, a process that is characteristic of Greek religion as a whole. In Boeotia the god was associated with Ptoös, as Apollo Ptoös, but in about the fourth century Ptoös became his son or his grandson. At Thebes he took the place of Ismenius. But the most famous example is his installation at Delphi, after he had killed the former master of the holy site, the Python. This mythical exploit was of considerable importance, and not only for Apollo. The victory of a god-champion over the Dragon, symbol at once of "autochthony" and of the primordial sovereignty of the telluric powers, is one of the most widespread myths (cf. § 45). What is peculiar to Apollo is, on the one hand, that he had to expiate this murder, thus becoming the unrivaled god of purifications, and, on the other hand, his installation

---

9. *Homeric Hymn to Apollo* 300 ff.; Apollodorus, *Bibl.* 1. 4. 1 ff.

10. But Apollo saved the child that she was about to bear, Asclepius. The latter became a famous physician; indeed, his power to heal was so great that once, in response to Artemis' pleas, he even restored Hippolytus to life. This miracle contravened the laws established by Zeus, and the king of the gods smote Asclepius with a thunderbolt. Apollo avenged himself by slaughtering the Cyclopes who had forged the thunderbolt. Guilty of a crime against his own clan (the Cyclopes were Titans, like Leto), Apollo was banished among mortals for a year; he worked as a slave in the household of Admetus.

at Delphi. Now it is as the Pythian Apollo that he obtained his position of Panhellenic eminence. The process was already accomplished in the eighth century.[11]

As for his "origin," it has been sought in the northern regions of Eurasia or in Asia Minor. The first hypothesis depends chiefly on his relations with the Hyperboreans, whom the Greeks considered to be the inhabitants of a country "bcyond Boreas," that is, beyond the North Wind. According to the Delphic myth,[12] Zeus had decided that Apollo should reside at Delphi and bring laws to the Hellenes. But the young god flew away, on a chariot drawn by swans, to the country of the Hyperboreans, where he spent a whole year. However, since the Delphians never ceased to invoke him with songs and dances, the god returned. After that, he spent the three months of winter among the Hyperboreans and returned at the beginning of summer. During his absence, Dionysus reigned at Delphi as master of the oracle.

According to Pindar, "no one could discover, either by land or by sea, the wonderful road that leads to the games of the Hyperboreans" (*Tenth Pythian* 29 ff.). In other words, the country and its inhabitants belong to mythical geography. It is a holy race, free from sickness and old age. It is Pindar again (frag. 272 Bowra) who declares that the Hyperboreans can live for a thousand years; they know neither work nor warfare and spend their time dancing and playing the lyre and the flute. Bacchylides (3. 58) recounts that, to reward "their piety," Apollo carried Cressus and his daughters to the land of the Hyperboreans. So we have to do with a paradisal place, comparable to the Isles of the Blessed, to which the souls of heroes go.

Herodotus (4. 32–35) reports the information given by the Delians concerning the offerings that Apollo received from the Hyperboreans: certain objects wrapped in wheat straw were handed over to the people of the neighboring country, who in their turn conveyed them to the country nearest by, and so on as far as Delos. It would be useless to look for a possible historical recollection in this tradition, which, among other things, placed the olive, especially the tree of the Mediterranean, in the country of the Hyperboreans.

11. See Wilamowitz, *Der Glaube der Hellenen*, vol. 2, p. 34; Marie Delcourt, *L'oracle de Delphes*, pp. 215 ff.

12. The earliest reference occurs in a poem of Alcaeus (ca. 600 B.C.), summarized by a late rhetorician, Himerius (fourth century A.D.).

Yet the northern regions—from Thrace to the country of the Scythians and the Issedones—had an important place in the fabulous traditions linked with Apollo. Some of his legendary disciples (Abaris, Aristeas) were "Hyperboreans," and Orpheus was always connected with Thrace. But this is a North which, though being gradually discovered and explored, retained a mythological aura. It is especially this imaginary North that inspired and fed mythological creativity.

In favor of Apollo's Asiatic origin, the fact is cited that his greatest places of worship were in Asia: Patara in Lycia, Didymas in Caria, Claros in Ionia, etc. Like so many other Olympian gods, he seems a newcomer in his holy places in continental Greece. In addition, in a Hittite inscription found near an Anatolian village, it has been possible to decipher the name Apulunas, "god of gates," which, as Nilsson reminds us, Apollo was in classical Greece.[13]

But the "genesis" of a god is interesting only insofar as it helps us to grasp the religious genius of his worshipers. Like the Greek people itself, its gods are the result of a grandiose synthesis. It is by virtue of this long process of confrontation, symbiosis, coalescence, and synthesis that the Greek divine forms were able to reveal all their virtualities.

90. Oracles and purification

Scarcely born, Apollo cries out: "Give me my lyre and my curved bow; I will declare to men the inflexible will of Zeus" (*Homeric Hymn to Apollo* 132). In the *Eumenides* of Aeschylus, he tells the Furies that he has "never delivered an oracle on man, woman, or city that was not an order from Zeus" (lines 616–19). This veneration for the father of the Olympians explains Apollo's connections with the ideas of order and law. In the classical period he represents especially the legal aspects of religion. Plato calls him the "national exegete" (*patrios exēgētēs; Rep.* 4. 427b). He imparts his counsel by the oracles at Delphi and, at Athens and Sparta, by his *exēgētai*, who transmit and explain the measures decided on by the god concerning the temple liturgies and, above all, the purifications made necessary

13. See Martin Nilsson, *Greek Folk Religion*, p. 79; Guthrie, *The Greeks and Their Gods*, p. 86, n. 1.

by homicides. For if Apollo became the god who keeps away evil (*apotropaios*) and the unrivaled purifier (*katharsios*), it is because he himself had to be purified after murdering the Python. Every crime of homicide produced a maleficent pollution, a power almost physical in nature, the *miasma*, a fearful scourge that threatened entire communities. Apollo contributed considerably to making the archaic customs concerning homicides more humane.[14] It is he who succeeded in getting Orestes acquitted of the crime of matricide (see Aeschylus' *Eumenides*).

Delphi had a prehistory as an oracular site long before Apollo. Whatever its etymology may have been, the Greeks connected the name with *delphys*, "womb."[15] The mysterious cavity was a mouth, a *stomion*, a term that also designates the vagina. The *omphalos* of Delphi was also documented from the pre-Hellenic period. Symbol of the navel, it was laden with genital meaning,[16] but it was above all a "center of the world." According to the legend, two eagles loosed by Zeus at the opposite ends of the world met on the *omphalos*. This venerable oracular site, where from ancient times the sacrality and the powers of Mother Earth were manifested, received a new religious orientation under the reign of Apollo.

Oracles were obtained by the Pythia (the priestess) and by the prophet who took part in the consultation. In the beginning, consultations took place once a year (on the god's anniversary), then once a month, and, finally, several times a month, except during the winter, when Apollo was away. The operation included the preliminary sacrifice of a goat. Usually the consultants put their questions in an alternative form: that is, was it better to do one thing or another. The Pythia gave the answer by drawing lots in the form of white or black beans.[17]

14. Custom demanded that the perpetrator of even involuntary murder should be killed by the victim's family; this was the only possible way to appease the soul of the victim and get rid of the pollution (*miasma*) produced by the crime. Draco's code introduces the authority of the state in place of the vendetta; the city tribunal now judged the crime and handed the culprit over to the victim's family.

15. The female snake Delphyne, born of the Earth, gives place to the male snake Python.

16. Discussed by Delcourt, *L'oracle de Delphes*, pp. 145 ff.

17. Antique divination, so simple in appearance, had a venerable model: Zeus chose among the destinies laid on his knees and bestowed each one as pleased him.

In the most serious cases the Pythia, inspired by Apollo, prophesied in the crypt of the temple. The term "Pythic delirium" has been used, but nothing indicates either hysterical trances or "possessions" of the Dionysiac type. Plato compared the delirium (*mania*) of the Pythia to poetic inspiration bestowed by the Muses and to the amorous transports of Aphrodite. According to Plutarch: "The god contents himself with putting in the Pythia visions and the light that illuminates the future; it is in this that enthusiasm consists."[18] On the figured monuments the Pythia is calm, serene, concentrated— like the god who inspires her.

By what means she attained this second state remains a mystery. The Pythia, chosen among the peasant women of Delphi, prophesied on set dates. The laurel leaves that she chewed, fumigations with laurel, the water from the spring Cassotis that she drank have no intoxicating properties and do not explain the trance. According to tradition, her oracular tripod was placed over a cleft (*chasma*) in the ground from which vapors with supernatural virtues rose. Excavations, however, have brought to light neither a fissure in the ground nor the cavern into which the Pythia descended (but it may be admitted that they might have disappeared as the result of earthquakes). The conclusion has been reached, a little too quickly, that the whole apparatus—*chasma* with vapors, descent of the Pythia into the corridor (the *adyton*)—is a comparatively recent mythical image.[19] Yet the *adyton* existed, and, as Marie Delcourt shows (*L'oracle de Delphes*, pp. 227 ff.), the antiquity and telluric structure of Delphi implied a ritual "descent" into the underground regions. Since no natural cause that could bring on the trance has been found, autosuggestion by the Pythia or suggestions at a distance by the prophet have been supposed. But the fact is that we know nothing about it.

91.   From "vision" to knowledge

The Apollonian "ecstasy," though sometimes brought on by inspiration (that is, possession) by the god, did not, however, imply the communion effected by Dionysian *enthousiasmos* (cf. §124). The

18. Plutarch, *Pythia* 7. 397c; cf. *Oracles* 40. 432d; Delcourt, p. 227.
19. The earliest testimonies to the fissure date from the first century B.C.

ecstatics inspired or possessed by Apollo were known especially for their cathartic and oracular powers. (On the contrary, initiates into the mysteries of Dionysus, the *bakchoi*, never show any prophetic powers.) The shamanic character of certain semimythical personages, reputed to be, above all, worshipers of Apollo, has been observed. The Hyperborean Abaris, priest of Apollo, was endowed with oracular and magical powers (for example, bilocation). Herodotus (4. 36) writes that he "carried his famous arrow over the whole earth, fasting," but from the time of Heraclides (frag. 51c) it was held that Abaris flew on an arrow. Now the arrow, which plays a certain role in the mythology and religion of the Scythians, is present in Siberian shamanic ceremonies;[20] it is also preeminently the weapon of Apollo. Similar legends—involving ecstatic trances that can be confused with death, bilocation, metamorphoses, descents to the underworld, etc.—circulated in connection with other fabulous personages: Aristeas of Proconnesus, Hermotimus of Clazomenae, Epimenides of Crete, Pythagoras. As for Orpheus, the famous "prophet" of Apollo, his mythology abounded in shamanic exploits (see volume 2).

As the Greeks knew him from the time of Homer, Apollo was, to be sure, much more than a patron god of ecstatics. Yet it is possible to discern a significant continuity between the two vocations—the shamanic and the Apollonian. Shamans are held to discover what is hidden and to know the future; visions, preeminently gifts of Apollo, bestow the same high powers on the god's worshipers. Just as in certain Siberian shamanic traditions, the visions given by Apollo stimulate the intelligence and incline to meditation; in the last analysis they lead to "wisdom." Walter Otto observed that obtaining any of the forms of occult knowledge "is always associated with a spiritual exaltation,"[21] and this is true especially for shamanic ecstasy. This explains the capital importance of music and poetry in the two traditions. Shamans prepare for their trance by singing and drumming; the earliest Central Asian and Polynesian epic poetry had as its model the adventures of shamans on their ecstatic journeys. Apollo's principal attribute is the lyre; when he plays, he charms the gods, wild beasts, and even stones (Euripides, *Alcestis* 579 ff.; Apollonius of Rhodes 1. 740).

20. See the references in our *Zalmoxis*, p. 36, nn. 42–43.
21. W. Otto, *The Homeric Gods*, p. 72.

The bow, Apollo's second attribute, also forms part of the shamanic paraphernalia, but its ritual use goes beyond the sphere of shamanism; the symbolism of the bow is universally disseminated. Apollo is "he who darts from afar"; yet the same epithet is applied to Rāma, the Buddha, and other heroes and fabulous personages. But the Greek genius brilliantly revalorized this archaic theme, just as it transfigured both the techniques of shamanism and its world of symbols. Thanks to Apollo, the symbolism of the bow and of archery reveals other spiritual situations: mastery over distance (and hence detachment from the "immediate," from the viscosity of the concrete), the calm and serenity implied by every effort of intellectual concentration. In short, Apollo represents a new theophany, the expression of a religious knowledge of the world and human existence that is specifically Greek and unrepeatable.

Heraclitus declared that "harmony is the result of a tension between contraries, like that of the bow and the lyre" (frag. 51). In Apollo the contraries are assumed and integrated into a new configuration, broader and more complex. His reconciliation with Dionysus forms part of the same process of integration that made him the patron of purifications as the consequence of his murder of Python. Apollo reveals to humankind the way that leads from divinatory "vision" to thought. The demonic element, implicit in all knowledge of the occult, is exorcised. The supreme Apollonian lesson is expressed in the famous Delphic formula "Know thyself!" Intelligence, knowledge, wisdom are regarded as divine models, bestowed by the gods, first of all by Apollo. Apollonian serenity becomes, for the Greek, the emblem of spiritual perfection and hence of the spirit. But it is significant that the discovery of the spirit completes a long series of conflicts followed by reconciliations and the mastery of the ecstatic and oracular techniques.

92. Hermes, "the companion of man"

Son of Zeus and the nymph Maia, Hermes is the least Olympian of the gods. He still retains certain attributes characteristic of the pre-Homeric divinities: he is still represented in ithyphallic form; he possesses a "magical rod," the caduceus, and the hat that confers invisibility; to immunize Odysseus against Circe's spells, he gives him the magical herb *moly* (*Odyssey* 10. 302–6). What is more, Hermes loves to mingle with men. As Zeus puts it, "his dearest occupation is to be the companion of man" (*Iliad* 24. 334 ff.). But in his relations with human beings he behaves at once as a god, a "trickster," and a master artisan. He is the unrivaled giver of good things (*Od.* 8. 335): every lucky chance is said to be a gift of Hermes. On the other hand, he is the incarnation of everything implied by ruse and double-dealing. He is scarcely born before he steals the cattle of his brother, Apollo; that is why he became the companion and protector of thieves. Euripides calls him "Lord of those who go about their business by night" (*Rhesus* 216 ff.).

But if he patronizes thefts and nocturnal amorous adventures, he is nonetheless the protector of flocks and herds and of travelers belated on the roads. "There is not another god who shows such solicitude for herds and their growth," writes Pausanias (2. 3. 4). He is the god of roads, and it is from one of the heaps of stones (*hermaion*) found on the edges of traveled ways, that he received his name; every passerby threw a stone on the pile.[22] In the beginning Hermes was probably a god who protected the nomadic herders, perhaps even a Master of Animals. But the Greeks interpreted the archaic attributes and powers of Hermes in a deeper sense. He rules the roads because he walks quickly (he has "golden sandals"), and he does not go astray at night because he knows the way. This is why he is at once guide and protector of herds and patron of thieves. It is also the reason for his becoming the messenger of the gods.

It is probably the same attributes that made Hermes a psycho-pompos: he guides the dead in the beyond because he knows the way and can orient himself in the dark. But he is not a god of the dead, though the dying say that they are seized by Hermes. He does not hesitate to move about freely through the three cosmic levels, and he comes to no harm from it. If he accompanies souls to Hades, it is he, too, who brings them back to earth, as he did Persephone, Eurydice, or, in the *Persians* of Aeschylus (629), the soul of the Great King. Hermes' relations with the souls of the dead are also explained by his "spiritual" faculties. For his astuteness and his practical intelligence, his inventiveness (it is he who discovers fire), his ability to make

22. The custom is still documented among numerous peoples and always in connection with travel.

himself invisible and to travel everywhere in the twinkling of an eye already announce the marvelous accomplishments bestowed by wisdom, especially mastery of the occult branches of knowledge, which later, during the Hellenistic period, will become the particular characteristics of Hermes. He who finds his way in the dark, guides the souls of the dead, and moves about with the speed of lightning, both visibly and invisibly, reflects, in the last analysis, a modality of spirit: not only intelligence and guile but also gnosis and magic.

After brilliantly analyzing Hermes' marvelous powers, W. Otto recognizes that "his world is not a heroic world" and concludes that "if his world is not noble . . . , it is far from being vulgar and repugnant."[23] This is true but inadequate. For what characterizes the figure of Hermes, already in the classical period, are his relations with the world of men, a world that is by definition open, constantly in process of being formed, that is, of being improved and exceeded. His first attributes—artfulness and inventiveness, mastery over darkness, interest in the activity of men, soul-guiding—will be continually reinterpreted and will end by making Hermes an ever more complex figure, at once civilizing hero, patron of knowledge, and paradigmatic image of the occult gnoses.

Hermes is one of the few Olympian gods who will not lose his religious quality after the crisis of the "classical" religion and will not disappear with the triumph of Christianity. Assimilated to Thoth and Mercurius, he will enjoy a new popularity during the Hellenistic period and, as Hermes Trismegistus, will survive, through alchemy and hermeticism, into the seventeenth century. The Greek philosophers will already see in Hermes the *logios*, the personification of thought. He will be regarded as possessing all forms of knowledge, especially the secret gnosis; this will make him "the chief of all magicians," victorious over the powers of darkness, for "he knows all things and can do all things."[24] The episode in the *Odyssey* involving the marvelous herb *moly* will be continually allegorized, both by the Greeks and by Christian authors. In this plant, which saves Odysseus from the fate of his companions, changed into swine by Circe, there will be seen spirit in opposition to instinct, or the education that purifies the soul. And Hermes, identified by the

23. Otto, *The Homeric Gods*, pp. 122 ff.
24. See the sources cited by Hugo Rahner, *Greek Myths and Christian Mystery*, pp. 191–92. See also volume 2 of the present work.

philosophers with the Logos, will be compared to Christ by the Church Fathers, in anticipation of the countless homologies and identifications made by the alchemists of the Renaissance (see volume 3).

93. The goddesses. I: Hera, Artemis

The privileged position accorded to Hera owes much to Homer, who emphasized the fact that she was consort to Zeus. Originally, Hera was the goddess of Argos; it is from there that her cult spread through the whole of Greece. Wilamowitz explains her name as the femine form of *hērōs* and as having the meaning *despoina*, "Our Lady."[25] It is difficult to decide whether the Achaeans brought the goddess with them or only her name. They were very probably impressed by the power and majesty of the Lady of Argos and so raised her to the rank of wife to their chief god,[26] and perhaps it is for this reason that Hera became the symbol and patroness of the institution of marriage. Zeus's countless infidelities aroused her jealousy and brought on quarrels that are related at length by the poets and mythographers. Zeus behaved toward Hera as no Achaean chief would ever have dared to behave to his wife: he beat her and once even hung her up with a great weight tied to her feet, a torture later practiced on slaves.[27]

According to Hesiod (*Theogony* 923–24), Hera gave Zeus three children, Hebe, Ares, and Eileithyia, and engendered Hephaestus all by herself (ibid. 926). Parthenogenesis, the power of self-fecundation, emphasizes the fact that even the most Olympian of the goddesses still retained her specifically Mediterranean and Asian character. It is difficult to determine the original meaning of the tradition according to which Hera renewed her virginity every year

25. Wilamowitz, *Glaube der Griechen*, vol. 1, p. 237.
26. Rose, *Handbook*, p. 52; Guthrie, *The Greeks and Their Gods*, p. 72.
27. *Iliad* 1. 567, 587; 15. 18 ff. Cf. Plautus, *Asinaria* 303–4; Rose, *Handbook*, p. 106 and n. 15. So far as it is possible to read the memory of historical realities in such scenes, the reference here is certainly to a comparatively early period, preceding the arrival of the Achaeans in the peninsula. What is significant is the fact that Homer and his audience could be amused by such brawls.

by bathing in the spring Canthus.[28] Is it a symbol bound up with the patriarchal conception of marriage (for we know that virginity was highly esteemed in societies of the patriarchal type)? However this may be, the Greeks radically transformed the goddess of Argos. Yet it is still possible to make out some of her original characteristics. Like the majority of Aegean and Asian goddesses, Hera was a divinity not merely of marriage but of universal fecundity. Though the hypothesis of a Hera–Mother Goddess has been rejected by some scholars, it is difficult otherwise to explain the fact that there was mention of a *hieros gamos* with Zeus (mythical or reactualized in rituals) at a number of places (Plataea, Euboea, Athens, Samos, etc.). This is the typical image of the union between a fecundating storm god and Mother Earth. In addition, Hera was worshiped at Argos as the "goddess of the yoke" and "rich in oxen." (In the *Iliad* Homer describes her as "ox-eyed.") Finally, she was considered to be the mother of terrifying monsters, such as the Hydra of Lerna. Now, giving birth to monsters is characteristic of telluric goddesses. Indeed, we have seen that, according to Hesiod, the mother of Typhon was Ge (Earth). But all these chthonian attributes and powers were gradually forgotten, and, from the time of Homer, Hera revealed herself as what she remained to the end: preeminently the goddess of marriage.

The name of Artemis, documented in the form Artimis in an inscription found in Lydia, indicates her Oriental origin. The goddess's archaic character is obvious: she is above all, and uniquely, the Mistress of Wild Beasts (*potnia therōn*, as she is called in *Iliad* 21. 470 ff.); that is, she is at once an impassioned devotee of the hunt and the protector of wild animals. Homer also calls her Agrotera, "She of the Wild Beasts," and Aeschylus (frag. 342) "the Lady of Wild Mountains." She especially loves to hunt at night. The lion and the bear are her favorite and heraldic animals; this recalls the Asian prototypes. Homer (*Iliad* 5. 49) tells how Artemis taught Scamandrius the art of hunting every kind of game. But she becomes indignant when two eagles tear up and devour a hare still carrying her young (Aeschylus, *Agamemnon* 133 ff.).

Artemis is preeminently the virgin goddess. Originally this could

28. Pausanias 2. 36. 2; he also mentions the secret cults of Hera at Argos, which appears exceptional to Rose (*Handbook*, p. 128, n. 11). But see Jeanmaire, *Dionysos*, pp. 208 ff.

be understood as meaning that she was free from the yoke of matrimony. But the Greeks saw in her perpetual virginity indifference to love. The *Homeric Hymn to Aphrodite* (1. 17) recognizes the latter goddess's powerlessness. In Euripides' tragedy *Hippolytus* (line 1301) Artemis herself openly declares her hatred for Aphrodite.

Yet she presents several elements of a mother goddess. In Arcadia, in her oldest cult site, she was associated with Demeter and Persephone. Herodotus (2. 156) states that Aeschylus regarded Artemis as the daughter of Demeter, that is, identified her with Persephone. Some Greek authors declare that in Crete she was called Britomartis,[29] which indicates her connections with the Minoan goddess. It is probable that among her names in other languages mention must be made of Cybele in Thrace and Ma in Cappadocia. It is not known when and in what region she began to be known as Artemis. At Ephesus the maternal function was represented plastically—so grotesquely that we hesitate to recognize a Greek divinity in it. Artemis was venerated by women as Locheia, goddess of childbirth. She was also *kourotrophos*, "nurse" and teacher of boys. In some of her rituals, documented in the historical period, it is possible to decipher the heritage of the female initiation ceremonies of the Aegean societies of the second millennium. The dance in honor of Artemis of the Alpheus, like the dances in honor of the goddess throughout the Peloponnesus, were orgiastic in character. A proverb said: "Where has not Artemis danced?" In other words: where are there not dances for Artemis?[30]

Under her many and sometimes contradictory aspects we divine the plurality of the archaic divine forms revalorized and integrated into a vast structure by the Greek religious genius. The ancient Lady of Mountains and Mistress of Wild Beasts of Mediterranean prehistory very soon assimilated the attributes and the revered powers of the mother goddesses, but without thereby losing her more archaic and more specific characteristics: patroness at once of hunters, wild animals, and girls. From the time of Homer her profile begins to define itself: Artemis governs the sacrality of wild life, which knows fertility and maternity but not love and marriage. She has always retained a paradoxical character, illustrated, above all, by the coexistence of contradictory themes (e.g., virginity-maternity).

29. See the references in Rose, *Handbook*, p. 131, n. 59.
30. Jeanmaire, *Dionysos*, pp. 212 ff.

The creative imagination of the Greek poets, mythographers, and theologians divined that such a coexistence of contraries can suggest one of the mysteries of divinity.

94.   The goddesses. II: Athena, Aphrodite

Athena is certainly the most important Greek goddess after Hera. It has not been possible to explain her name by Greek. As for her origin, Nilsson's hypothesis, accepted by the majority of scholars, appears to be reasonably convincing: Athena was a Lady of the Palace, protectress of the fortified palaces of the Mycenaean princes; though a domestic goddess, connected with the occupations of men and women, her presence in the citadel during a period of wars and pillage gave her the attributes and powers of a martial goddess. She springs from the head of Zeus clad in her armor, brandishing her lance, and giving her war cry. Many of her titles proclaim this martial character: Promachos (the Championess), Stheneia (the Powerful), Areia (the Warlike), etc.

However, as so many episodes of the *Iliad* show, Athena is the implacable enemy of Ares, whom she crushes in the famous battle of the gods in book 21 (390 ff.).[31] On the contrary, she admires Heracles, the true model of the hero. She helps him in his super-human ordeals and finally guides him to heaven (Pausanias 3. 18. 11, etc.). Athena likewise admired Tydeus and even wanted to make him immortal; but when she saw the hero, gravely wounded, split the skull of his enemy and swallow his brains, the goddess departed in disgust.[32] It is she again who, by her presence, restrains Achilles, ready, with his hand on his sword, to reply with it to Agamemnon's insults (*Iliad* 1. 194 ff.).

Even in an epic composed for an audience that admired feats of arms, Athena reveals herself as other than a martial goddess. It is because war is preeminently a male activity that she takes part in it. For, as she says herself: "In all things my heart leans toward the

31. It is true that Ares is detested by all the gods, who call him "mad" because he does not know "what is just" (*Iliad* 5. 761). Zeus himself recognizes that "no Olympian is so hated," for "he thinks only of wars and battles" (*Il.* 5. 890).

32. Bacchylides, frag. 41; Apollodorus, *Bibl.* 3. 6. 8. 3.

male, except for marriage" (Aeschylus, *Eumenides* 736). The *Homeric Hymn to Aphrodite* (1. 7–11) recognizes that the goddess of love has no power over Athena. Homer and Hesiod call her Pallas, "the Maiden," and at Athens she is "the Virgin" (Parthenos). But she is a different type of virgin goddess from Artemis: she does not avoid men, does not keep them at a distance. Athena becomes the friend and protector of Odysseus, whom she admires for his strong personality and his wisdom: he is the man "of many counsels" (*polymētis*), who alone can be compared with Zeus (*Iliad* 2. 169, 407, 636). In the *Theogony* (896) Hesiod considers her "equal to her father in strength and prudent wisdom." Athena is the only Olympian who has no mother. The *Homeric Hymn to Athena* (lines 4–5) briefly recalls that Zeus bore her from his own head, but it is Hesiod who recounts the whole myth: Zeus swallowed Metis, the goddess of intelligence, when she was already pregnant, and Athena came into the world by emerging through her father's skull (*Theogony* 886 ff.; cf. § 84). This episode has been considered a late addition; the original myth would simply have described the appearance of Athena on the summit of Mount Olympus. But Otto rightly emphasizes the archaic and "savage" nature of the swallowing theme.[33]

Whatever her origin may be, the myth of Athena's miraculous birth illustrates and confirms her very intimate relations with Zeus. "I am entirely on the father's side," she admits in the *Eumenides* (736). In the *Odyssey* (13. 297), she confides to Odysseus: "Among all the gods, I boast of my intelligence (*mētis*) and my skill." And indeed *mētis*, practical intelligence, is her most characteristic attribute. Athena is not only the patroness of the typically feminine arts of spinning and weaving. She is above all a "polytechnician," the inspirer and teacher of all kinds of specialized workers. It is from her that the smith learns to make the plowshare, and the potters invoke her: "Come to us, Athena, hold thy hand above our kiln!"[34] It is she, the tamer of horses, who invents the bit and teaches the use of chariots. When it comes to navigation, a domain properly ruled by Poseidon, Athena reveals the complexity, and at the same time the unity, of her *mētis*. First she intervenes in the many technical

33. See Otto, *Homeric Gods*, p. 51. Homer does not allude to this myth (as he also says nothing of the story of Kronos), but he calls Athena "the daughter of the powerful father" (*obrimopatrē*).
34. Cf. the Homeric epigram cited by Otto, *Homeric Gods*, p. 58.

operations involved in building a ship. But she also helps the pilot "rightly to steer" his vessel.[35]

It is unusual to find an example of what we might call the sacrality of technical invention and the mythology of intelligence. Other divinities illustrate the countless forms of the sacrality of life, fertility, death, social institutions, etc. Athena reveals the sacred character or divine origin of certain crafts and vocations that involve not only intelligence, technical skill, practical invention but also self-mastery, serenity under trials, confidence in the consistency, and hence the intelligibility, of the world. It is not hard to understand how the patroness of *mētis* will, in the period of the philosophers, become the symbol of divine knowledge and human wisdom.

Aphrodite represents a no less remarkable creation of the Greek genius, even though it is on an entirely different level. The goddess is certainly of Oriental origin, as the tradition persistently indicates (Herodotus, 1. 105; Pausanias, 1. 14. 7). In the *Iliad*, Aphrodite protects the Trojans. In addition, she shows analogies with divinities of the type of Ishtar. However, it is at Cyprus, millennial center of Aegeo-Asian syncretism, that her characteristic figure begins to define itself (*Odyssey* 8. 362 ff.). The process of Hellenization is quite advanced in the *Iliad* (5. 365), where Homer announces that she is the daughter of Zeus and Dione and the wife of Hephaestus.[36] But Hesiod preserved a more archaic version of her birth: the goddess issued from the foamy (*aphros*) semen that came from Uranus' sexual organs when they were thrown into the sea. Now, as we have seen (§ 46), the theme of the castration of a great god is of Oriental origin.

In her cult, certain Asiatic elements (for example, hierodules) can be distinguished, side by side with Mediterranean elements (the dove). On the other hand, the *Homeric Hymn to Aphrodite* presents her as a true Mistress of Wild Beasts: "after her came gray wolves, fawning on her, and grim-eyed lions, and bears, and fleet leopards, ravenous for deer." But a new feature, peculiar to Aphrodite, is added: the goddess "put desire in their breasts, so that they all mated, two together, about the shadowy coombes" (trans. H. G. Evelyn-

35. See M. Detienne, "Le navire d'Athéna."
36. It is not until later that Ares, god of war, becomes her husband; in *Odyssey* 8. 266–366 he is her lover.

White, *Hesiod, the Homeric Hymns, and Homerica,* Loeb Library ed. [Cambridge, Mass.: Harvard University Press, 1936]). Aphrodite "puts desire" into animals as well as into men and gods. She leads astray "even the reason of Zeus"; it is she who "easily makes him mate with mortal women, unknown to Hera" (ibid., lines 36, 40). Thus the *Homeric Hymn to Aphrodite* identifies in the sexual urge the element of unity common to the three modes of existence: animal, human, and divine. On the other hand, by emphasizing the irreducible and irrational character of concupiscence, the *Hymn* justifies the amorous adventures of Zeus (which will, furthermore, be indefinitely repeated by gods, heroes, and men). In short, there is here a *religious* justification of sexuality; for, incited by Aphrodite, even sexual excesses and outrages must be recognized as of divine origin.

Since she reigns on the three cosmic levels, Aphrodite is at once celestial (Asteria, Urania), maritime (Anadyomene, "risen from the sea"),[37] and terrestrial (under her feet the roads are covered with flowers, and it is she who is the "first cause" of vegetable fertility [Aeschylus, *Danaides* frag. 44]). But Aphrodite will never become the preeminent goddess of fertility. It is physical love, fleshly union, that she inspires, praises, and defends. In this sense it may be said that, thanks to Aphrodite, the Greeks rediscovered the sacred nature of the original sexual urge. The vast spiritual resources of love will be ruled by other divine figures, first of all by Eros. Now it is precisely this irrational and irreducible sexuality that will be exploited by writers and plastic artists, and to such an extent that, in the Hellenistic period, the "Charms of Aphrodite" will become literary clichés. We are almost tempted to see, in this artistic flowering under the sign of Aphrodite, the radical desacralization of physical love. But in fact it is a camouflage, inimitable and rich in meanings, such as is found in so many other creations of the Greek genius. Under the appearance of a frivolous divinity is hidden one of the most profound sources of religious experience: the revelation of sexuality as transcendence and mystery. We shall meet with other forms of this type of camouflage when we analyze the process of desacralization of the modern world (see volume 3).

37. The shell, a symbol that is at once aquatic and sexual, is among her sacred objects.

95. The heroes

Pindar distinguished three categories of beings: gods, heroes, and men (*Second Olympian* 1). For the historian of religions, the category of heroes raises certain important problems: what is the origin and ontological structure of the Greek heroes, and to what extent are they comparable to other types of beings intermediate between gods and men? In accordance with the belief of the ancients, Rohde held that the heroes "are closely related, on the one hand, to the chthonian gods, and, on the other, to dead men. In fact, they are nothing but the spirits of dead men, who live inside the earth, who live there eternally like the gods, and who came close to the latter in their power."[38] Like the gods, the heroes were honored by sacrifices, but the names and the procedures of these two categories of rites were different (see p. 287, below). On the other hand, in his work *Götternamen* (1896), published three years after Rohde's *Psyche*, Usener maintained the divine origin of the heroes: like the demons, the heroes proceed from "momentary" or "particular" divinities (*Sondergötter*), that is, from divine beings specialized in specific functions.

In 1921 Farnell proposed a compromise theory, which still has a certain reputation. According to this author, the heroes do not all have the same origin; he distinguishes seven categories of them: heroes of divine or ritual origin, personages who really lived (warriors or priests), heroes invented by poets or scholars, etc. Finally, in a rich and penetrating book, *Gli eroi greci* (1958), Brelich describes the "morphological structure" of the heroes as follows: they are personages whose death has something striking about it and who are closely connected with combats, athletic contests, prophecy and medicine, puberty initiations, and the Mysteries; they found cities, and their cult has a civic character; they are ancestors of consanguineous groups and are the "prototypical representatives" of certain fundamental human activities. The heroes are further characterized by singular, even monstrous, features and by an eccentric behavior that betrays their superhuman nature.[39]

In a summary formulation, it could be said that the Greek heroes

38. Erwin Rohde, *Psyche* (Eng. trans.), p. 117.
39. A. Brelich, *Gli eroi greci*, p. 313. The following pages owe much to Brelich's analyses.

share in an existential modality that is *sui generis* (superhuman, but not divine) and act in a primordial period—precisely, the period that follows the cosmogony and the triumph of Zeus (cf. §§ 83–84). Their activity takes place after the appearance of men but in a period of "beginnings," when structures were not always fixed and norms not yet duly established. Their own mode of being is an expression of the incomplete and contradictory character of the time of "origins."

The birth and childhood of the heroes are different from the ordinary. They descend from the gods but are sometimes held to have a twofold paternity (thus Heracles is the son of both Zeus and Amphitryon; Theseus, of Poseidon and Aegeus), or their birth is irregular (Aegisthus is the fruit of the incest between Thyestes and his own daughter). They are abandoned soon after birth (Oedipus, Perseus, Rhesus, etc.) and are nursed by animals,[40] spend their youth traveling in distant countries, make themselves conspicuous by countless adventures (especially athletic and martial exploits), and contract divine marriages (among the most famous, those of Peleus and Thetis, Niobe and Amphion, Jason and Medea).

The heroes are characterized by a specific form of creativity, comparable to that of the civilizing heroes of the archaic societies. Just like the Australian mythical ancestors, they alter the landscape, are believed to be autochthons (i.e., the first inhabitants of certain regions) and the ancestors of races, peoples, or families (the Argives descend from Argos, the Arcadians from Arcas, etc.). They invent—that is, "found," "reveal"—many human institutions: the laws of the city and the rules of urban life, monogamy, metallurgy, song, writing, tactics, etc., and are the first to practice certain crafts. They are preeminently founders of cities, and the historical personages who found colonies become heroes after death.[41] In addition, the heroes establish athletic games, and one of the characteristic forms of their cult is the athletic contest. According to one tradition, the four great Panhellenic games were consecrated to the heroes before they belonged to Zeus. (The agonistic cult at Olympia, for example, was celebrated in honor of Pelops.) This explains the heroization of victorious and famous athletes.[42]

40. Paris is nursed by a bear, Aegisthus by a goat, Hippothous by a mare, etc. This initiatory motif is, of course, extremely widespread; cf. §105.
41. Brelich, *Gli eroi greci*, pp. 129–85.
42. As was Cleomedes in the Olympic Games of 496 (Pausanias 6. 9. 6).

Certain heroes (Achilles, Theseus, etc.) are associated with initiation rites for adolescents, and the heroic cult is often performed by youths. Several episodes in the saga of Theseus are, in fact, initiatory ordeals; for example, his ritual dive into the sea (an ordeal equivalent to a journey into the beyond) and precisely into the submarine palace of the Nereids, fairies who are preeminently *kourotrophoi*; such, too, is Theseus' penetration of the labyrinth and his combat with the monster (the Minotaur)—a paradigmatic theme of heroic initiations; such, finally, was his abduction of Ariadne (one of the many epiphanies of Aphrodite), in which Theseus completes his initiation by a hierogamy. According to Jeanmaire, the ceremonies that made up the Theseia came out of archaic rituals that at an earlier period had marked the return of the adolescents to the city after their initiatory stay in the bush.[43] Similarly, certain moments in the legend of Achilles can be interpreted as initiatory ordeals: he was brought up by the Centaurs, that is, he was initiated in the bush by Masters who were masked or who showed themselves in animal forms; he underwent passing through fire and water, classic initiatory ordeals; and he even lived for a time among girls, dressed as a girl, in accordance with a custom typical of certain archaic puberty initiations.[44]

The heroes are also associated with the Mysteries: Triptolemus has a sanctuary, and Eumolpus his tomb, at Eleusis (Pausanias, 1. 38. and 1. 38. 2). In addition, the cult of heroes is bound up with oracles, especially with rites of incubation to effect a cure (Calchas, Amphiaraus, Mopsus, etc.); hence certain heroes (first of all, Asclepius) have relations with medicine.[45]

A characteristic feature of heroes is the manner of their death. Exceptionally, certain heroes are transported to the Isles of the Blessed (Menelaus), to the mythical island of Leuce (Achilles), to Olympus (Ganymede), or disappear underground (Trophonius, Amphiaraus). But the immense majority suffer a violent death in war (like the heroes of whom Hesiod tells, fallen before Thebes or Troy), in single combat, or by treachery (Agamemnon murdered by Clytemnestra, Laius by Oedipus, etc.). Often their death is singularly

43. H. Jeanmaire, *Couroï et Courètes*, pp. 323 ff., 338 ff., and passim; Eliade, *Birth and Rebirth*, p. 109; see also Brelich, pp. 124 ff.
44. See *Birth and Rebirth*, p. 109.
45. See the documentation in Brelich, pp. 106 ff.

dramatic: Orpheus and Pentheus are torn to pieces, Actaeon is killed by dogs, Glaucus, Diomedes, Hippolytus by horses; or they are devoured, or struck dead by Zeus, or bitten by a snake (Orestes, Mopsus, etc.).[46]

Yet it is their death that confirms and proclaims their superhuman condition. If they are not immortal like the gods, the heroes differ from men by the fact that they continue to act after their death. The remains of heroes are laden with redoubtable magico-religious powers. Their tombs, their relics, even their cenotaphs operated on the living for long centuries. In a sense it could be said that heroes approach the divine condition by virtue of their death: they enjoy an unlimited postexistence, which is neither larval nor purely spiritual but consists in a survival *sui generis*, since it depends on the remains, the traces, or the symbols of their bodies.

Indeed, contrary to the general custom, the remains of heroes were buried inside the city; they were even admitted into the sanctuaries (Pelops in the temple of Zeus at Olympia, Neoptolemus in that of Apollo at Delphi). Their tombs and cenotaphs formed the center of the heroic cult, involving sacrifices accompanied by ritual laments, mourning rites, tragic choruses. (The sacrifices offered to heroes were like those performed for the chthonian gods, and differed from the sacrifices offered to the Olympians. Victims were slaughtered with their throats toward the sky for the Olympians, with their throats bent toward the earth for the chthonian gods and the heroes. For the Olympians the victim had to be white, but it was black for the heroes and the chthonians, and the sacrificed victim was burned entirely—no living man must eat of it. The type of the altars to the Olympians was the classic temple, above ground and sometimes on an elevation; for the heroes and the chthonians it was a low hearth, an underground cave, or an *adyton*, which perhaps represented a tomb. The sacrifices for the Olympians were performed during the sunny morning, those for the heroes and the chthonians in the evening or the middle of the night.)[47]

All these facts bring out the religious value of the heroic death and the remains of the hero. By dying, the hero becomes a tutelary genius who protects the city from invasions, epidemics, and all kinds of

46. The sources are cited by Brelich, p. 89.
47. Rohde, *Psyche*, pp. 116–17; see also Guthrie, *The Greeks and Their Gods*, pp. 221–22.

calamities. At Marathon, Theseus was seen fighting at the head of the Athenians (Plutarch, *Theseus* 35. 5; see other examples in Brelich, *Gli eroi greci*, pp. 91 ff.). But the hero also enjoys an immortality of a spiritual order, the immortality conferred by *glory*, the perpetuity of his *name*. He thus becomes a paradigmatic model for all those who strive to exceed the ephemeral condition of the mortal, to save their names from final oblivion, to survive in the memory of men. The heroization of real persons—the kings of Sparta, the fallen at Marathon or Plataea, the Tyrannicides—is explained by their unusual exploits, which separate them from the rest of mortals and project them into the category of heroes.[48]

Classical Greece, and especially the Hellenistic period, left us a "sublime" vision of the heroes. In reality their nature is exceptional and ambivalent, even aberrant. The heroes prove to be at once good and bad and accumulate contradictory attributes. They are invulnerable (Achilles) and yet end by being slain; they are distinguished by their strength and beauty but also by monstrous characteristics (gigantic stature—Heracles, Achilles, Orestes, Pelops—but also stature much shorter than the average);[49] or they are theriomorphic (Lycaon, the "wolf") or able to change themselves into animals. They are androgynous (Cecrops), or change their sex (Teiresias), or dress like women (Heracles). In addition, the heroes are characterized by numerous anomalies (acephaly or polycephaly; Heracles has three rows of teeth); they are apt to be lame, one-eyed, or blind. Heroes often fall victim to insanity (Orestes, Bellerophon, even the exceptional Heracles, when he slaughtered his sons by Megara). As for their sexual behavior, it is excessive or aberrant: Heracles impregnates the fifty daughters of Thespius in one night; Theseus is famous for his numerous rapes (Helen, Ariadne, etc.); Achilles ravishes Stratonice. The heroes commit incest with their daughters or their mothers and indulge in massacres from envy or anger or often for no reason at all: they even slaughter their fathers and mothers or their relatives.

All these ambivalent and monstrous characteristics, these aberrant forms of behavior, suggest the fluidity of the time of "origins," when the "world of men" was not yet created. In this primordial period, irregularities and abuses of all kinds (that is, everything that will later be denounced as monstrosity, sin, or crime) directly or in-

48. See also Eliade, *Cosmos and History*, chap. 1.
49. Even Heracles; see the sources in Brelich, pp. 235 ff.

directly spur on the work of creation. However, it is after the heroes' creations—institutions, laws, techniques, arts—are effected that there arises the "world of men," where infractions and excesses will be forbidden. After the age of the heroes, in the new "world of men," the creative age, the *illud tempus* of the myths, is definitely ended.

The excesses of the heroes have no limits. They dare to violate even goddesses (Orion and Actaeon assail Artemis, Ixion attacks Hera, etc.) and do not stop short of sacrilege (Ajax assaults Cassandra near the altar of Athena, Achilles kills Troilus in the temple of Apollo). These offenses and sacrileges denote an inordinate *hybris*, a specific characteristic of the heroic nature (see § 87). The heroes confront the gods as if they were their equals, but their *hybris* is always, and cruelly, punished by the Olympians. Only Heracles manifests his *hybris* with impunity (when he threatens the gods Helios and Oceanus with his weapons). But Heracles is the perfect hero, the "hero-god," as Pindar calls him (*Third Nemean* 22). Indeed, he is the only hero whose tomb and relics are unknown; he conquers immortality by his suicide-apotheosis on the pyre, he is adopted by Hera and becomes a god, sitting among the other divinities on Olympus. It could be said that Heracles obtained his divine condition in consequence of a series of initiatory ordeals from which he emerged victorious, unlike Gilgamesh (cf. § 32) and certain Greek heroes, who, despite their limitless *hybris*, failed in their efforts at immortalization.

Figures comparable to the Greek heroes are also found in other religions. But it is only in Greece that the religious structure of the hero received so perfect an expression; it is only in Greece that the heroes enjoyed a considerable religious prestige, nourished imagination and reflection, and inspired literary and artistic creativity.[50]

50. The later metamorphoses of the hero, from the Middle Ages to Romanticism, will be analyzed in the third volume of the present work.

12 The Eleusinian Mysteries

96. The myth: Persephone in Hades

"Happy is he among men upon earth who has seen these mysteries!" exclaims the author of the *Homeric Hymn to Demeter*. "But he who is uninitiate and who has no part in them, never has lot of like good things once he is dead, down in the darkness and gloom" (lines 480–82; trans. H. G. Evelyn-White, *Hesiod, The Homeric Hymns, and Homerica* [Cambridge, Mass.: Harvard University Press, 1936]).

The *Hymn to Demeter* relates both the central myth of the two goddesses and the founding of the Eleusinian Mysteries. While she was gathering flowers on the plain of Nysa, Kore (Persephone), Demeter's daughter, was carried off by Pluto (Hades), god of the underworld. Nine days Demeter searched for her, and during all that time she did not touch ambrosia. Finally, Helios told her the truth: it was Zeus who had decided to marry Kore to his brother Pluto. Overcome with grief, and infuriated with the king of the gods, Demeter did not go back to Olympus. In the guise of an old woman she traveled to Eleusis and sat down by the Well of the Maidens. Questioned by the king's daughters, she said that her name was Doso and that she had just escaped from pirates, who had carried her off from Crete by force. She accepted their invitation to bring up the infant son of the queen, Metaneira, and demanded *kykeōn*, a mixture made from meal, water, and pennyroyal.

Demeter did not nurse Demophoön but rubbed him with ambrosia and at night hid him "like a brand" in the fire. The child became more and more like a god, for in fact Demeter wanted to make him immortal and eternally young. But one night Metaneira found her son in the fire and began to lament. "Witless are you mortals, and dull to foresee your lot, whether of good or of evil!" Demeter exclaims (line 256). Henceforth, Demophoön can no longer escape death. Then the goddess reveals herself in all her splendor, a brilliant light shining from her body. She demands that "a great temple and an altar below it" be built for her, where she will teach her rites to human beings (304 ff.). Then she leaves the palace.

As soon as the sanctuary was built, Demeter retired inside it, wasting away with yearning for her daughter. It was then that she brought on a terrible drought, which ravaged the earth (304 ff.). Zeus vainly sent messengers begging her to return among the gods. Demeter answered that she would not set foot on Olympus, and would not let vegetation grow, until she had seen her daughter again. Zeus had to ask Pluto to bring Persephone back, and the lord of Hades submitted. However, he succeeded in putting a pomegranate seed into her mouth and making her swallow it: this ensured Persephone's annual return to her husband for four months.[1] After recovering her daughter, Demeter consented to rejoin the gods, and the earth was miraculously covered with verdure. But before she returned to Olympus, the goddess revealed her rites and taught all her mysteries to Triptolemus, Diocles, Eumolpus, and Celeus—"awful mysteries which no one may in any way transgress or pry into or utter, for deep awe of the gods checks the voice" (478 ff.).

The *Hymn to Demeter* reports two types of initiations; more precisely, the text explains the foundation of the Eleusinian Mysteries both by the reunion of the two goddesses and as a result of the failure of the attempt to immortalize Demophoön. The history of Demophoön can be compared with the ancient myths relating the tragic error that, at a certain moment of primordial history, annulled the possibility of man's immortalization. But in this case there is neither error nor "sin" on the part of a mythical ancestor, who thereby loses his original immortal condition for himself and his descendants. Demophoön was not a primordial personage; he was the last-born son of a king. And Demeter's decision to immortalize him can be interpreted as her desire to adopt a child (who will console her for the loss of Persephone) and, at the same time, as her revenge against Zeus and the Olympians. Demeter was in the process of transforming a man into a god. Goddesses had this power of granting immortality

1. It is a widely disseminated mythical theme that whoever tastes the food of the otherworld cannot return to the world of the living.

to human beings, and fire, the "cooking" of the neophyte, was reckoned among the most effective means. Surprised by Metaneira, Demeter did not hide her disappointment at the stupidity of men. But the hymn makes no reference to the possible later generalizing of this technique of immortalization, that is, the establishment of an initiation capable of transforming men into gods by means of fire.

It was after the failure of her attempt to immortalize Demophoön that Demeter revealed her identity and demanded that a sanctuary be built for her. And it was not until after she had found her daughter again that she taught her secret rites. Initiation of the "mystery" type differs radically from the initiation interrupted by Metaneira. The initiate into the Eleusinian Mysteries did not obtain immortality. At a certain moment a great fire lit up the sanctuary of Eleusis. But though some examples of cremation are known, it is not probable that fire played a direct part in the initiations.

The little that we know about the secret ceremonies indicates that the central mystery involved the presence of the two goddesses. Through the initiation, the human condition was modified, but in a different way from the unsuccessful transmutation of Demophoön. The few ancient texts that refer directly to the Mysteries emphasize the postmortem bliss of the initiated. The expression "Happy is he among men . . ." of the *Hymn to Demeter* returns like a leitmotiv. "Happy he who has seen this before descending underground!" exclaims Pindar. "He knows the end of life! He also knows its beginning!" (*Threnoi*, frag. 10). "Thrice happy those among mortals who, having seen those Mysteries, will go down to Hades; only they can have true life there; for the rest, all there is evil" (Sophocles, frag. 719 Dindorf, 348 Didot). In other words, as the result of the things *seen* at Eleusis, the soul of the initiate will enjoy a blissful existence after death; it will not become the mournful fallen shade, without memory and strength, so feared by the Homeric heroes.

The only reference to agriculture in the *Hymn to Demeter* is the statement that Triptolemus was the first initiate into the Mysteries. Now according to the tradition, Demeter sent Triptolemus to teach agriculture to the Greeks. Some authors have explained the terrible drought as a consequence of the descent to Hades of Persephone, goddess of vegetation. But the hymn states that the drought was brought on by Demeter much later, precisely when she retired into the sanctuary which had been built for her at Eleusis. We may suppose, with Walter Otto, that the original myth told of the disappearance of vegetation but not of wheat; for before Persephone was carried off, wheat was not known. Numerous texts and figurative monuments bear witness to the fact that wheat was procured by Demeter *after* the drama of Persephone. So we can here decipher the archaic myth that explains the creation of cereals by the "death" of a divinity (§11). But, sharing the condition of the Olympian immortals, Persephone could no longer "die," like the divinities of the *dema* or Hainuwele type (cf. §12) or the gods of vegetation. The old mythico-ritual scenario, continued and developed by the Eleusinian Mysteries, proclaimed the mystical solidarity between the *hieros gamos*, violent death, agriculture, and the hope of a happy existence beyond the grave.[2]

In the last analysis, the rape—that is, the symbolic death—of Persephone had great consequences for humanity. As the result of it, an Olympian and benevolent goddess temporarily inhabited the kingdom of the dead. She had annulled the unbridgeable distance between Hades and Olympus. Mediatrix between the two divine worlds, she could thereafter intervene in the destiny of mortals. Using a favorite expression of Christian theology, we could say: *felix culpa!* Just so, the failed immortalization of Demophoön brought on the shining epiphany of Demeter and the foundation of the Mysteries.

97. The initiations: Public ceremonies and secret rituals

According to tradition, the first inhabitants of Eleusis were Thracians. The most recent archeological excavations have made it possible to reconstruct a great part of the history of the sanctuary. Eleusis appears to have been colonized about 1580–1500, but the first sanctuary (a chamber with two interior pillars supporting the roof) was built in the fifteenth century; and it is in the fifteenth century, too, that the Mysteries were inaugurated (Mylonas, *Eleusis*, p. 41).

2. When, in the fourth century B.C., Isocrates wanted to praise the merits of the Athenians, he reminded his hearers that it was in their country that Demeter had granted her most important gifts: agriculture, by which "man rises above the beasts," and initiation, which brings hope in regard to "the end of life and all eternity" (*Panegyricus* 28).

The Mysteries were celebrated at Eleusis for nearly two thousand years; probably certain ceremonies were altered in the course of time. The constructions and reconstructions made from the time of Pisistratus indicate the vigor and growing prestige of the cult. The nearness and protection of Athens certainly contributed to placing Eleusis at the very center of Panhellenic religious life. The literary and figurative documentation refers more particularly to the first stages of the initiation, which did not demand secrecy. Thus artists could represent Eleusinian scenes on vases and bas-reliefs, and Aristophanes (*Frogs* 324 ff.) allowed himself to allude to some aspects of the initiation.[3] This comprised several degrees. There were the Lesser Mysteries, the rites of the Greater Mysteries (the *teletai*), and the final experience, the *epopteia*. The true secrets of the *teletai* and the *epopteia* have never been divulged.

The Lesser Mysteries were usually celebrated once a year, in spring, during the month of Anthesterion. The ceremonies took place at Agrae, a suburb of Athens, and included a series of rites (fasts, purifications, sacrifices) performed under the direction of a mystagogue. Probably certain episodes of the myth of the two goddesses were reactualized by the aspirants to initiation. The Great Mysteries were also celebrated once a year, in the month of Boedromion (September–October). The ceremonies continued for eight days, and "all those who had pure hands" and spoke Greek, including women and slaves, had the right to take part, provided they had gone through the preliminary rites at Agrae in the spring.

On the first day, the festival took place in the precinct of the Eleusinium of Athens, to which, the evening before, the sacred objects (*hiera*) had been solemnly brought from Eleusis. On the second day, the procession went to the sea. Each aspirant, accompanied by his teacher, carried with him a young pig, which he washed in the sea and sacrificed on his return to Athens. On the next day, in the presence of the people of Athens and other cities, the king-archon (*archon basileus*) and his wife performed the great sacrifice. The fifth day marked the culminating point of the public ceremonies. An enormous procession set out from Athens at dawn. The neophytes, their teachers,

---

3. But Aristotle (*Nicomachean Ethics* 3. 1. 17) states that Aeschylus was in danger of losing his life because the Athenians thought that he had revealed certain secrets in his tragedies (the *Archers*, the *Priestesses*, *Iphigenia*, and *Sisyphus* were cited).

and many Athenians accompanied the priestesses who carried back the *hiera*. Toward the end of the afternoon the procession crossed a bridge over the Cephissus, where masked men hurled insults at the most important citizens.[4] At nightfall, with lighted torches, the pilgrims entered the outer court of the sanctuary. Part of the night was devoted to dances and songs in honor of the goddesses. On the following day the aspirants fasted and offered sacrifices, but as for the secret rites (the *teletai*) we are reduced to hypotheses. The ceremonies that took place in front of and inside the telesterion were probably connected with the myth of the two goddesses (Mylonas, *Eleusis*, pp. 262 ff.). We know that the mystai, torch in hand, imitated the wanderings of Demeter in search of Kore by torch-light.[5]

We shall presently discuss the efforts made to penetrate the secret of the *teletai*. We will add that certain ceremonies included the *legomena*, brief liturgical formulas and invocations whose content we do not know but which were of considerable importance; this is why initiation was forbidden to those who did not speak Greek. We know almost nothing about the rites performed during the second day spent at Eleusis. Probably that night brought the culminating act of the initiation, the supreme vision, the *epopteia*, accessible only to those who had been initiates for a year. The next day was devoted especially to rites and libations for the dead, and on the day after that—the ninth and last day—the mystai returned to Athens.

98. Can the Mysteries be known?

In their efforts to pierce the secrecy of the *teletai* and the *epopteia*, scholars have made use not only of the references found in the authors of antiquity but also of some information transmitted by Christian apologists. The data supplied by the latter must be examined with caution; however, they cannot be ignored. Since Foucart, much has often been made of a passage of Themistius, cited by Plutarch and preserved by Stobaeus, in which the experiences

4. The meaning of these *gephyrismoi* is disputed. Scholars have emphasized especially the apotropaic function of obscene expressions.

5. Seneca, *Herc. fur.* 364–66; *Hippol.* 105–7; see also Minucius Felix, *Octavius* 22. 2, etc.

of the soul immediately after death are compared to the ordeals of the initiate in the Greater Mysteries: at first, he wanders in darkness and undergoes all sorts of terrors; then, suddenly, he is struck by a marvelous light and discovers pure regions and meadows, hears voices, and sees dances. The mystes, a crown on his head, joins the "pure and holy men"; he beholds the uninitiated, huddled together in mud and fog, sunk in their wretchedness through fear of death and mistrust of bliss in the beyond (Stobaeus 4, p. 107 Meineke). Foucart considered that the rituals (*drōmena,* "things done") similarly involved a peregrination in darkness, various terrifying apparitions, and the sudden entrance of the mystes into a lighted meadow. But the testimony of Themistius is late and reflects Orphic conceptions.[6] Excavations of the sanctuary of Demeter and of the telesterion have shown that there were no underground chambers in which the mystai could ritually descend to Hades.[7]

There have also been attempts to reconstruct the initiation ritual on the basis of the secret formula, the *synthēma* or password of the mystai, transmitted by Clement of Alexandria (*Protrepticus* 2. 21. 2): "I fasted, I drank the *kykeōn*; I took from the chest [*kistē*]; after manipulating, I placed in the basket, then, removing from the basket, I replaced in the chest." Some authors hold that only the first two propositions belong to the Eleusinian formula. And indeed, they refer to well-known episodes: Demeter's fast and her drinking the *kykeōn*. The rest of the *synthēma* is enigmatic. Several scholars have believed that they have identified as the contents of the chest and basket a replica of the womb, or a phallus, or a snake, or cakes in the shape of genital organs. No hypothesis is convincing. It is possible that the receptacles contained objects that were relics from archaic times, bound up with a sexual symbolism characteristic of agricultural societies. But at Eleusis Demeter revealed a different religious dimension from those manifested in her public cult. Moreover, it is difficult to admit that such a ritual was also performed by the children who were being initiated. Then too, if the ritual to

6. Foucart, *Mystères*, pp. 392 ff. In *Phaedo* 69c Plato maintains that the punishments of sinners in Hades and the image of the meadow of the righteous were introduced by Orpheus, who had been inspired by Egyptian funerary customs.

7. This does not exclude the presence of infernal symbolism, for there was a cave—a temple of Pluto—which designated the entrance to the otherworld, and there was probably an omphalos there; see Kerényi, *Eleusis*, p. 80.

which the *synthēma* refers is interpreted by the symbolism of a mystical birth or rebirth, the initiation ought to have been completed at that moment. In that case, it is hard to understand the meaning, and the necessity, of the final experience, the *epopteia*. In any event, the testimonies concerning the *hiera* hidden in the receptacles indicate their *solemn presentation*, not their manipulation. So it is probable, as G. II. Pringshcim, Nilsson, and Mylonas maintain, that the *synthēma* refers to ceremonies documented very much later, during the Hellenistic period, in honor of Demeter (see Mylonas, *Eleusis*, pp. 300 ff. and note 39).

It has been supposed that the mystai partook of a sacramental meal, which is plausible. In that case, the meal took place at the beginning, after the drinking of the *kykeōn*, that is, before the *teletē* proper. Another ritual has been deduced from an indication by Proclus (*Ad Timaeum* 293c): the mystai looked skyward and cried "Rain!", they looked toward the earth and exclaimed "Conceive!" Hippolytus (*Philosophumena* 5. 7. 34) states that these two words constituted the great secret of the Mysteries. We certainly have here a ritual formula connected with the *hieros gamos* typical of the vegetation cults; but if it was uttered at Eleusis, it was not secret, for the same words appear in the inscription for a well near the Dipylon gate of Athens.

A quite surprising piece of information has been transmitted to us by Bishop Asterius. He lived about 440, when Christianity had become the official religion of the empire, which is to say that the author no longer feared denials on the part of pagan writers. Asterius speaks of an underground passage, wrapped in darkness, where the solemn meeting between the hierophant and the priestess took place, of torches extinguished, and of the "vast crowd who believe that their salvation depends on what those two do in the darkness."[8] But no underground chamber (*katabasion*) has been found in the telesterion, though the excavations have everywhere reached the rock. It is more likely that Asterius was referring to the Mysteries performed in the Hellenistic period in the Eleusinium at Alexandria. In any case, if the *hieros gamos* really existed, it is difficult to understand why Clement—after speaking of Eleusis—called Christ "the true hierophant."

8. *Encomium to the Holy Martyrs*, in *Patrologia graeca*, vol. 40, cols. 321–24.

In the third century Hippolytus added two other pieces of information to the dossier (*Philosophumena* 5. 38–41). He states that the *epoptai* were shown, "in solemn silence," an ear of wheat. Hippolytus adds that "during the night, in the midst of a brilliant fire celebrating the great and inexpressible Mysteries, the hierophant cries out: 'Holy Brimo has borne a sacred child, Brimos!' that is: the Powerful One [feminine] has given birth to the Powerful One [masculine]." The solemn presentation of an ear of wheat seems doubtful, since the mystai were supposed to bring ears of wheat with them and especially since ears of wheat are engraved on numerous monuments at Eleusis itself. Certainly, Demeter was the goddess of wheat, and Triptolemus was present in the mythico-ritual scenario of Eleusis. But it is difficult to believe that the revelation of a fresh ear constituted one of the great secrets of the *epopteia*, unless we accept the interpretation of Walter Otto, who speaks of a "miracle" peculiar to the Eleusinian Mysteries: "The ear of wheat growing and maturing with a supernatural suddenness is just as much a part of the mysteries of Demeter as the vine growing in a few hours is part of the revels of Dionysus" (*The Homeric Gods*, p. 25). Yet Hippolytus states that the cut ear was regarded by the Phrygians as a mystery that was later borrowed by the Athenians. So it is possible that the Christian author transposed to Eleusis what he knew about the Mysteries of Attis (a god whom, according to Hippolytus, the Phrygians called "the fresh ear of wheat").

As for the vocables "Brimo" and "Brimos," they are probably of Thracian origin. Brimo especially designates the queen of the dead; hence her name can be applied to Kore and Hecate as well as to Demeter. According to Kerényi, the hierophant proclaimed that the goddess of death had borne a son in the fire.[9] In any case, it is known that the final vision, the *epopteia*, took place in a dazzling light. Several ancient authors speak of the fire that burned in the small building, the Anactoron, the flames and smoke from which, escaping through an opening in the roof, were visible from a distance. In a papyrus from the time of Hadrian, Heracles addresses an initiate: "I was initiated long ago [or: elsewhere] . . . [I have beheld] the fire . . . [and] I have seen Kore" (see Kerényi, pp. 83–84). According

9. Other similar cases are known: for example, Dionysus or Asclepius, born in the funeral pyre of Coronis and taken from his mother's body by Apollo; see Kerényi, *Eleusis*, pp. 92 ff.

to Apollodorus of Athens, when the hierophant invoked Kore he struck a bronze gong, and the context implies that the kingdom of the dead burst open (Otto, *The Homeric Gods*, p. 27).

99. "Secrets" and "Mysteries"

It may be accepted that the epiphany of Persephone and her reunion with her mother constituted the central episode of the *epopteia* and that the decisive religious experience was inspired precisely by the presence of the goddesses. We do not know how this reunion was realized or what took place afterward. Nor do we know why such a vision was believed to make a radical change in the postmortem situation of the initiates. But there can be no doubt that the epoptes perceived a divine secret, which made him "familiar" to the goddesses; he was in some way "adopted" by the Eleusinian divinities.[10] The initiation revealed both closeness to the divine world and continuity between life and death. These are certainly ideas shared by all archaic religions of the agricultural type but suppressed by the Olympian religion. The "revelation" of the mysterious continuity between life and death reconciled the epoptes to the ineluctability of his own death.

The initiates into the Eleusinian Mysteries do not form a "church" or a secret association comparable to the Mysteries of the Hellenistic period. When they returned home, the mystai and the epoptai continued to take part in the public cults. In fact, it is not until after death that the initiates come together again, separated from the crowd of the uninitiated. From this point of view, the Eleusinian Mysteries, after Pisistratus, can be regarded as a religious system that complemented the Olympian religion and the public cults without, however, opposing the traditional religious institutions of the city. The chief contribution of Eleusis was soteriological in nature, and that is why the Mysteries were accepted and very soon patronized by Athens.

10. Guthrie (*The Greeks and Their Gods*, pp. 292–93) refers to an episode in the *Axiochus*, a dialogue wrongly attributed to Plato, in which Socrates assures Axiochus that he must not fear death; on the contrary, since he has been initiated into the Eleusinian Mysteries, he has become a relative (*gennētēs*) of the gods. Guthrie regards this text as proof of divine adoption. But the term *gennētēs* rather indicates fidelity, i.e., "thou who art one of the goddesses' faithful followers." But this, of course, does not exclude the idea of spiritual kinship.

Demeter was the most popular among the goddesses worshiped in all the regions of Greece and the Greek colonies. She was also the oldest; morphologically, she continued the Great Goddesses of the Neolithic. Antiquity also knew other Mysteries of Demeter, the most famous being those of Andania and Lycosura. We will add that Samothrace (initiation center for the northern countries—Thrace, Macedonia, Epirus) was famed for the Mysteries of the Cabiri and that, from the fifth century, Athens saw the celebration of the Mysteries of the Thraco-Phrygian god Sabazius, the first of the Oriental cults to make its way into the West. In other words, the Eleusinian Mysteries, despite their incomparable prestige, were not a unique creation of the Greek religious genius; they found their place in a larger system, concerning which we are, unfortunately, poorly informed. For these Mysteries, like those of the Hellenistic period too, presupposed initiations that had to remain secret.

The religious and, in general, the cultural value of "secrecy" has as yet been inadequately studied. All the great discoveries and inventions—agriculture, metallurgy, various techniques, arts, etc.— implied, in the beginning, secrecy, for it was only those "initiated" into the secrets of the craft who were believed able to guarantee the success of the operation. With time, initiation into the arcana of certain archaic techniques became accessible to the whole community. However, the various techniques did not entirely lose their sacred character. The example of agriculture is especially instructive; some millennia after its dissemination in Europe, agriculture still preserved a ritual structure, but the "craft secrets," that is, the ceremonies intended to insure an abundant harvest, were now universally accessible by means of an elementary "initiation."

It may be admitted that the Eleusinian Mysteries were bound up with an agricultural mystique, and it is probable that the sacrality of sexual activity, vegetable fertility, and food at least partly shaped the initiatory scenario. In this case we must suppose the implicit presence of half-forgotten *sacraments*, which had lost their original meaning. If the Eleusinian initiation made possible such primordial experiences, which revealed the mystery and the sacrality of food, sex, procreation, ritual death, Eleusis rightly deserved its fame as a holy place and a source of miracles. However, it is difficult to believe that the supreme initiation was confined to an anamnesis of archaic sacraments. Eleusis had certainly discovered a new religious dimension. The Mysteries were famous above all for certain "revelations" concerning the two goddesses.

Now such revelations demanded secrecy as a condition *sine qua non*. The procedure was the same in the various initiations documented in archaic societies. What is unique about the Eleusinian secrecy is the fact that it became a paradigmatic model for Mystery cults. The religious value of secrecy will be extolled in the Hellenistic period. The mythologization of initiatory secrets and their hermeneutics will later encourage countless speculations, which will end by shaping the style of a whole period. "Secrecy even increases the value of what is learned," writes Plutarch (*On the Life and Poetry of Homer* 92). Medicine and philosophy are both held to possess initiatory secrets, which different authors compare to aspects of Eleusis.[11] In the days of the Neo-Pythagoreans and Neo-Platonists, one of the clichés most employed was precisely the enigmatic style of the great philosophers, the idea that the masters revealed their true doctrine only to initiates.

This current of ideas finds its best support in the secrecy of Eleusis. The majority of modern critics allow little importance to the allegorical or hermeneutic interpretations proposed by many authors of late antiquity. Yet despite their anachronism, such interpretations are not without philosophical and religious interest; in fact, they continue the efforts of earlier authors to interpret the Eleusinian Mysteries without, at the same time, betraying their secret.

In the last analysis, besides the central role that the Eleusinian Mysteries played in the history of Greek religiosity, they indirectly made a significant contribution to the history of European culture, and notably to interpretations of initiatory secrecy. Its unique prestige ended by making Eleusis a symbol of pagan religiosity. The burning of the sanctuary and the suppression of the Mysteries mark the official end of paganism (see volume 2). This, of course, does not imply the disappearance of paganism but merely its occultation. As for the "secret" of Eleusis, it continues to haunt the imagination of seekers.

11. See, for example, Galen, *De usu partium* 7. 14; Plotinus, *Enneads* 6. 9. 11, etc.

13 Zarathustra and the Iranian Religion

100. The enigmas

The study of Iranian religion is full of surprises, even of disappointments. We approach the subject with the most lively interest, for we have learned beforehand of the Iranian contribution to the religious formation of the West. If the conception of linear time, replacing the notion of cyclical time, was already familiar to the Hebrews, a number of other religious ideas were discovered, revalorized, or systematized in Iran. To mention only the most important: the articulation of several dualistic systems (cosmological, ethical, religious dualisms); the myth of the savior; the elaboration of an optimistic eschatology, proclaiming the final triumph of Good and universal salvation; the doctrine of the resurrection of bodies; very probably, certain Gnostic myths; finally, the mythology of the Magus, reelaborated during the Renaissance, both by the Italian Neo-Platonists and by Paracelsus or John Dee.

However, as soon as the nonspecialist reader approaches the sources, he is disappointed and thwarted. Three-fourths of the old Avesta is lost. Among the texts that have been preserved, only the *gāthās*, presumably composed by Zarathustra, have the power to fascinate the nonspecialist. But an understanding of these enigmatic poems has not yet been attained with certainty. The rest of the present Avesta, and especially the Pahlavi books redacted between the fourth and ninth centuries, are characterized by their dryness, their disheartening monotony, and their platitude. Readers of the Vedas and the Upanishads, even readers of the *Brāhmaṇas*, cannot fail to be disappointed.

Yet the *ideas* that can occasionally be deciphered in the *gāthās*, or that are found, elaborated and systematized, in the later scriptures, are absorbing. But they are buried in a hodgepodge of ritual texts and commentaries. Except for the *gāthās*—the reading of which, despite their obscurities, is always rewarding—one is seldom seized by the power of the language, the originality of the images, the revelation of a profound and unexpected meaning.

As for the personal contribution of Zarathustra to the invention or revalorization of these religious conceptions, the opinions of Iranianists differ and tend to be mutually exclusive. Essentially, it is a matter of two historiographic points of view. According to the one, Zarathustra is a historical personage, a reformer of the traditional ethnic religion, that is, the religion that was shared by the Indo-Iranians in the second millennium B.C. According to the other, the religion of Zarathustra represents only one aspect of the Iranian religion, i.e., Mazdaism, whose center is the worship of Ahura Mazdā, and the authors who take this methodological position not only hold that there was no "reform" by the "prophet" Zarathustra; they deny even his historicity.

As we shall see in a moment, the problem of the historicity of Zarathustra ought not to constitute a difficulty. It was normal for the historical personage Zarathustra to be transformed into a paradigmatic model for the believers who made up the "Mazdean religion." After a few generations the collective memory can no longer preserve the authentic biography of an eminent personage; he ends by becoming an archetype, that is, he expresses only the virtues of his vocation, illustrated by paradigmatic events typical of the model he incarnates. This is true not only of Gautama Buddha or Jesus Christ but also of far less influential personages, such as Marko Kraljevic or Dieudonné de Gozon. But there are times when the *gāthās*, regarded by most scholars as the work of Zarathustra, contain some autobiographical details that confirm their author's historicity. They are, furthermore, the only such details; they survived the process of mythicization, active throughout the Mazdean tradition, because they were an integral part of the hymns composed by Zarathustra.

It is proper to use these few biographical details for a preliminary sketch of Zarathustra's life and religious activity. We will later give the corrections and supplements that seem to be required by the results of recent research.

It has been proposed that Zarathustra's activity should be placed between 1000 and 600 B.C. If the Mazdean tradition, which speaks of "258 years before Alexander," is accepted, Zarathustra's life can be placed between 628 and 551 B.C.[1] The earlier dates have been proposed in view of the archaic character of the language of the *gāthās*, especially of its analogies with the Vedas. Linguistic analysis allows the conclusion that the prophet lived in the eastern part of Iran, probably in Chorasmia or Bactria.[2]

According to tradition, he was a *zaotar* (Yašt 33. 16), that is, a sacrificing priest and chanter (cf. Sanskrit *hotṛ*), and his *gāthās* take their place in an old Indo-European tradition of sacred poetry. He belonged to the clan named Spitāma ("of the brilliant attack"), breeders of horses; his father's name was Pouruśaspa ("of the spotted horse"). Zarathustra was married, and the names of his two children are known, the younger being his daughter Pouručistā (*Yasna* 53. 3). He was poor. When, in a famous *gāthā*, he begs for the help and protection of Ahura Mazdā, he exclaims: "I know, O Wise One, why I am powerless: it is for my few flocks and because I have few men" (*Yasna* 46. 2).

The community to which he addressed his message was made up of sedentary herders with chiefs, called *kavi*, and priests called *karapan*, "murmurer," and *usig*, "sacrificer." It is these priests, guardians of the traditional Āryan religion, whom Zarathustra did not hesitate to attack in the name of Ahura Mazdā. The reaction soon made itself felt, and the prophet had to flee. "To what land shall I flee?" he exclaims. "Where flee, where go? I am separated from my tribe and my family; neither the village nor the wicked chiefs of the land are favorable to me" (*Yasna* 46. 1). He took refuge with Vishtaspa, chief of the Fryāna tribe, whom he succeeded in

1. Very probably the formula "258 years before Alexander" refers to the conquest of Persepolis (330 B.C.), which put an end to the empire of the Achaemenids. Zarathustra's first success, the conversion of King Vishtaspa, took place when the prophet was forty years of age. The traditional chronology ("258 years before Alexander"), accepted by the majority of investigators (see W. B. Henning, *Zoroaster, Politician or Witch-Doctor?* pp. 38 ff.; J. Duchesne-Guillemin, *La religion de l'Iran ancien*, pp. 136 ff. [Eng. trans., pp. 99 ff.]), has been rejected by M. Molé (*Culte, mythe et cosmologie dans l'Iran ancien*, p. 531) and G. Gnoli ("Politica religiosa e concezione della regalità," pp. 9 ff.).

2. See J. Duchesne-Guillemin, *La religion de l'Iran*, pp. 138–40; G. Widengren, *Les religions de l'Iran*, pp. 79–90 (Eng. trans., pp. 100–102). We cite the *gāthās* in accordance with the translation by J. Duchesne-Guillemin, *Zoroastre* (1948; Eng. trans. by M. Henning, *The Hymns of Zarathustra* [1952]).

converting, and who became his friend and protector (46. 14; 15. 16). Yet the resistance did not weaken, and in the *gāthās* Zarathustra publicly denounces some of his personal enemies: Bandva, who "is always the chief obstacle" (49. 1–2), and "the little prince Vaēpya," who "at the Bridge of Winter offended Zarathustra Spitāma by refusing him a halting place, him and his draught animals shivering with cold when they came to his house" (51. 12).

It is possible to decipher in the *gāthās* a few indications of Zarathustra's missionary activity. The prophet is surrounded by a group of friends and disciples, variously called the "poor" (*drigu*), the "friends" (*frya*), the "knowing" (*vīdva*), the "confederates" (*urvatha*).[3] He urges his companions to "take arms to drive away" the enemies, the "wicked one" (*Yasna* 31. 18). This Zarathustrian cohort is opposed by the "men's societies," with their device *aēšma*, "fury." It has been possible to show the equivalence of these Iranian secret societies with the groups of young Indian warriors, the Maruts, whose leader, Indra, is called *adhrigu*, that is "not-*dhrigu*" ("he who *is not* poor").[4] Zarathustra violently attacks those who sacrifice bovines (32. 12, 14; 44. 20; 48. 10); such blood rituals were characteristic of the cult of the men's societies.

101. The life of Zarathustra: History and myth

These indications, few and allusive as they are, fall far short of constituting the elements of a biography. Marjan Molé has attempted to show that even these scattered references to apparently real persons and events do not necessarily reflect historical realities; Vishtaspa, for example, represents the model of the initiate. Yet the historicity of Zarathustra appears not only from the allusions to concrete persons and events (the little prince Vaēpya, who, "at the Bridge of Winter," refused him shelter, etc.), but also from the authentic and passionate nature of the *gāthās*. We are struck, furthermore, by the urgency and existential tension with which Zarathustra questions his Lord: he asks him to teach him the secrets of the

3. After citing the Indian equivalents of these terms, Widengren shows that such an institution is probably as old as the Indo-Iranian community.
4. Stig Wikander, *Der arische Männerbund*, pp. 50 ff.

cosmogony, to reveal his future to him, but also the fate of certain persecutors and of all the wicked. Each strophe of the celebrated *Yasna* 44 is introduced by the same formula: "This is what I ask you, Lord—answer me well!" Zarathustra wants to know "who assigned their road to the sun and the stars" (3), "who fixed the earth below, and the sky of clouds, so that it does not fall" (4); and his questions concerning the Creation follow one another in an ever faster rhythm. But he wants to know, too, how his soul, "arrived at the Good, will be ravished?" (8), and "how shall we get rid of evil" (13), "how shall I deliver evil into the hands of justice?" (14). He demands that "visible marks" shall be given him (16) and, above all, that he shall be united with Ahura Mazdā and that his "word shall be efficacious" (17). But he adds: "Shall I obtain in payment, through Justice (*Arta*), ten mares, with a stallion, and a camel that have been promised me, O Wise One?" (18). He does not forget to question the Lord about an immediate punishment of "him who does not give his wage to him who has deserved it," for he already knows the punishment "that awaits him in the end" (19).

The punishment of the wicked, the rewarding of the virtuous, obsess Zarathustra. In another hymn he asks, "What penalty is provided for him who procures empire (*khshathra*, 'power, potency') for the wicked evildoer?" (*Yasna* 31. 15). Elsewhere he exclaims: "When shall I learn if you have power, O Wise One (Mazdā) with Justice (*Arta*), over each of those who threaten me with destruction?" (48. 9). He is impatient at seeing the members of the men's societies continuing to sacrifice bovines and consume *haoma* with impunity: "When wilt thou strike this filthy liquid?" (48. 10). He hopes that he can renew "*this* life" (30. 9) and asks Ahura Mazdā if the just will conquer the wicked *now* (48. 2; see further on). Sometimes we feel that he is hesitant, troubled, humble, wanting to know the Lord's will more concretely: "What dost thou command? What wouldst thou have as praise, as worship?" (34. 12).

It would be difficult to justify the presence, in the most venerable part of the Avesta, of so many concrete details if they did not represent recollections of a historical personage. It is true that mythological elements abound in the later legendary biographies of the Prophet, but, as we have just recalled, this is a well-known process: the transformation of an important historical personage into a paradigmatic model. One hymn (*Yašt* 13) extols the birth of the

Prophet in messianic terms: "At his birth and during his growth water and plants rejoiced, at his birth and during his growth water and plants grew" (13. 93 ff.). And it announces: "Henceforth the good Mazdean religion will spread over the seven continents" (13. 95).[5]

The late texts dwell at length on Zarathustra's celestial pre-existence. He was born at the "midpoint of history" and at the "center of the world." When his mother received the *xvarenah* of Zarathustra, she was enveloped in a great light. "For three nights the sides of the house appeared as if made of fire."[6] As for the substance of his body, created in heaven, it fell with the rain and brought forth the plants eaten by the two heifers belonging to the Prophet's parents; the substance passed into their milk, which, mixed with *haoma*, was drunk by his parents: they united for the first time, and Zarathustra was conceived.[7] Before his birth Ahriman and the *dēvs* (= *daēvas*) tried in vain to cause his death. Three days before he came into the world, the village shone so brightly that the Spitāmides, thinking it was on fire, abandoned it. On their return, they found a child radiating light. According to tradition, Zarathustra came into the world laughing. He was scarcely born before he was attacked by the *dēvs*, but he routed them by uttering the sacred formula of Mazdaism. He emerged victorious from the four ordeals, whose initiatory character is obvious (he was thrown on a pyre, into a den of wolves, etc.).[8]

It would serve no purpose to continue. Zarathustra's ordeals, victories, and miracles follow the paradigmatic scenario of the savior in the process of being divinized. To be stressed is the insistent repetition of the two motifs characteristic of Mazdaism: supernatural light and combats against demons. The experience of mystical light and ecstatic "vision" are also documented in ancient India, where they will have a great future. As for the combats with demons, that is to say, against the forces of evil, it constitutes, as we shall see, the essential duty of every Mazdean.

5. Cf. Widengren, *Les religions de l'Iran*, pp. 120 ff.; J. Duchesne-Guillemin, *La religion de l'Iran*, pp. 338 ff. (Eng. trans., pp. 226 ff.).
6. *Zātspram* 5, trans. Molé, *Culte, mythe et cosmologie*, p. 184. On the *xvarenah*, see note 23, below.
7. *Dēnkart*, 7. 2. 48 ff., trans. Molé, pp. 285–86.
8. Texts cited by Molé, pp. 298 ff., 301 ff. See also Widengren, *Les religions de l'Iran*, pp. 122 ff.

102. Shamanic ecstasy?

To return to Zarathustra's original message, a question at once arises: is it to be sought only in the *gāthās*, or is it permissible to use the later Avestan scriptures? There is no way to prove that the *gāthās* have brought us Zarathustra's whole doctrine. In addition, a number of later texts, even quite late ones, refer directly, though developing them, to concepts expressed in the *gāthās*. And it is well known that the elaboration of a religious idea first documented in late texts does not necessarily imply that the concept is a new one.

What is essential is to elucidate the type of religious experience characteristic of Zarathustra. Nyberg believed that he could compare it to the typical ecstasy of the Central Asian shamans. His hypothesis was rejected by the majority of scholars, but Widengren has recently presented it in more moderate and more convincing terms.[9] He cites the traditions according to which Vishtaspa used hemp (*bhang*) to obtain ecstasy: while his body lay asleep, his soul traveled to paradise. In addition, in the Avestan tradition, Zarathustra himself was believed to "give himself over to ecstasy." It is in trance that he would have had his visions and heard the word of Ahura Mazdā.[10] On the other hand, it is probable that song played an important part in the cult, if we take the name of paradise, *garô demânâ*, to mean "house of song." It is known that some shamans reach ecstasy by singing for a long time, yet not every cult system employing song is to be considered shamanic. It is also possible to see parashamanistic elements in the scenario elaborated around the Činvat Bridge (see below, §111) and also the shamanic structure of Artay Virāf's journey to heaven and hell.[11] However, the few allusions to a specifically shamanic initiation—involving dismemberment of the body and renewing the viscera—are found only in late texts that may reflect foreign influences (Central Asian, or deriving from Hellenistic syncretism, especially the Mystery religions).[12]

9. Widengren, pp. 88 ff.

10. See the sources cited by Widengren, p. 91. Trance brought on by narcotics was also known in ancient India; see Rig Veda 10. 136. 7 and the commentary in Eliade, *Shamanism*, pp. 407 ff.

11. See the references to the works by Nyberg and Widengren in *Shamanism*, pp. 396 ff.

12. Thus, for example, in the *Zātspram* there is mention of the initiation of Zarathustra by the Ahmarspand (Avestan Amesha Spentas); among other

It may be admitted that Zarathustra was familiar with the Indo-Iranian shamanic techniques (also known to the Scythians and the Indians of the Vedic period), and there seems to be no reason to suspect the tradition that explains Vishtaspa's ecstasy by hemp. But the ecstasies and visions documented in the *gāthās* and elsewhere in the Avesta do not show a shamanic structure. Zarathustra's visionary emotionality brings him close to other religious types. In addition, the Prophet's relations with his Lord, and the message that he never ceases to proclaim, have nothing of the "shamanic" style. In whatever religious milieu Zarathustra grew up, whatever the role of ecstasy in his conversion and that of his first disciples may have been, shamanic ecstasy does not play a central part in Mazdaism. As we shall very soon see, the Mazdean "mystical experience" is the result of a ritual practice illuminated by eschatological hope.

103. The revelation of Ahura Mazdā: Man is free to choose good or evil

Zarathustra receives the revelation of the new religion directly from Ahura Mazdā. By accepting it, he imitates the primordial act of the Lord—the choice of Good (see *Yasna* 32. 2), and he asks nothing else of his disciples. The essence of the Zoroastrian reform consists in an *imitatio dei*. Man is called to follow the example of Ahura Mazdā, but he is free in his choice. He does not feel that he is the slave or the servant of God (as the worshipers of Varuṇa, Yahweh, Allah admit themselves to be).

In the *gāthās* Ahura Mazdā holds the first place. He is good and holy (*spenta*). He created the world by thought (*Yasna* 31. 7. 11), which is equivalent to a *creatio ex nihilo*. Zarathustra declares that he "recognized" Ahura Mazdā "by thought," "as the first and the last" (31. 8), that is, as the beginning and the end. The Lord is accompanied by an escort of divine beings (the Amesha Spentas): Asha (Justice), Vohu Manah (Good Thought), Ārmaiti (Devotion),

---

ordeals, "molten metal was poured on his chest and grew cold there," and "his body was cut with knives, the interior of his belly appeared, blood flowed; but then he passed his hand over it and was healed" (*Zātspram*, 22. 12–13, trans. Molé, p. 334). These are specifically shamanic feats.

Xshathra (Kingdom, Power), Haurvatāt and Ameretāt (Integrity [health] and Immortality).[13] Zarathustra invokes and praises these Entities together with Ahura Mazdā, as in this *gāthā:* "Wise Lord most powerful, Devotion, Justice making the living prosper, Good Thought, Kingdom, hear me: Have pity on me when retribution comes to each" (33. 11; see also the following strophes).

Ahura Mazdā is the father of several Entities (Asha, Vohu Manah, Ārmaiti) and of one of the twin Spirits, Spenta Mainyu (the Beneficent Spirit). But this implies that he also engendered the other twin, Angra Mainyu (the Destroying Spirit). In the beginning, it is stated in a famous *gāthā* (*Yasna* 30), these two spirits chose, one of them good and life, the other evil and death. Spenta Mainyu declares, at the "beginning of existence," to the Destroying Spirit: "Neither our thoughts nor our doctrines, nor our mental powers; neither our choices, nor our words, nor our acts; neither our consciences, nor our souls are in agreement" (45. 2). This shows that the two spirits— the one holy, the other wicked—differ rather by *choice* than by *nature.*

Zarathustra's theology is not dualistic in the strict sense of the term, since Ahura Mazdā is not confronted by an anti-god; in the beginning, the opposition breaks out between the two Spirits. On the other hand, the unity between Ahura Mazdā and the Holy Spirit is several times implied (see *Yasna* 43. 3, etc.). In short, Good and Evil, the holy one and the destroying demon, proceed from Ahura Mazdā; but since Angra Mainyu freely chose his mode of being and his maleficent vocation, the Wise Lord cannot be considered responsible for the appearance of Evil. On the other hand, Ahura Mazdā, in his omniscience, knew from the beginning what choice the Destroying Spirit would make and nevertheless did not prevent it; this may mean either that God transcends all kinds of contradictions or that the existence of evil constitutes the preliminary condition for human freedom.

Where we are to look for the prehistory of such a theology is clear; it is in the different mythico-ritual systems of bipartitions and polarities, alternations and dualities, antithetical dyads and *coincidentia oppositorum*—systems that accounted at once for the cosmic rhythms and the negative aspects of reality and, first and foremost,

13. These Entities—or "Archangels," as they have also been called—are related to certain cosmic elements (fire, metal, earth, etc.).

for the existence of evil. But Zarathustra confers a new religious and moral meaning on this immemorial problem. It is in the few verses of the *gāthās* that there lie the seeds of the countless later elaborations that have given Iranian spirituality its specific characteristics.

The primordial separation between good and evil is the consequence of a choice, inaugurated by Ahura Mazdā and repeated by the Twin Spirits, who respectively chose Asha (Justice) and Drug (Deceit). Since the *daēvas*, the gods of the traditional Iranian religion, chose Deceit, Zarathustra demands that his disciples no longer worship them and, first of all, give up sacrificing bovines to them. Respect for the bovine plays a considerable part in the Mazdean religion. A reflection of the conflict between sedentary cultivators and nomads has been seen in this fact. But the antinomy proclaimed by Zarathustra goes beyond, at the same time that it includes, the social plane. It is a part of the Āryan national religious tradition that is rejected. Zarathustra places among the sinners Yima, son of Vivahvant, "who to flatter our people caused them to eat pieces of beef" (*Yasna* 32. 8). In addition, as we have just seen, the Prophet asked Ahura Mazdā when he would destroy those who practiced the *haoma* sacrifice (48. 10).

However, recent research has shown that the *haoma* ritual, together with the cult of Mithra, was not entirely condemned by Mazdaism, not even in the *gāthās*.[14] In addition, animal sacrifices were practiced without interruption, at least for the benefit of laymen.[15] It seems, therefore, that Zarathustra primarily opposed the excesses of the orgiastic rites, which involved countless blood sacrifices and the immoderate absorption of *haoma*. As for the epithet "herdsman" applied to Zarathustra, it does not refer, as has been maintained, to the duty of every Mazdean to protect and take good care of cattle. The metaphorical expressions "shepherds" and "flocks," documented throughout the ancient Near East and in ancient India, refer to chieftains and their subjects. The "cattle" of which Zarathustra is the "herdsman" means those men who practice the Good Religion.[16]

14. See the works by Molé, Zaehner, M. Boyce ("Haoma, Priest of the Sacrifice," etc.), and Gnoli (inter alia: "Lichtsymbolik in Alt-Iran").
15. Cf. M. Boyce, "Ātas-zohr and Ab-zohr"; Gnoli, "Questioni sull'-interpretazione della dottrina gathica," p. 350.
16. See G. G. Cameron, "Zoroaster, the Herdsman," passim; Gnoli, "Questioni," pp. 351 ff.

These corrections and revisions make possible a better understanding of the contribution made by Mazdaism to the religious
history of Iran. Indeed, it is known that, despite his "reform,"
Zarathustra accepted many traditional religious beliefs and ideas, at
the same time giving them new values. Thus, he takes up again the
Indo-Iranian tradition of the journey of the dead but stresses the
importance of the judgment: each will be judged by the choice that
he has made on earth. The just will be admitted into paradise, into
the "House of Song"; as for the sinners, they will remain "forever the
guests of the House of Evil" (*Yasna* 46. 11). The road to the beyond
passes over the Činvat Bridge, and it is there that the sorting of the
just from the wicked takes place. Zarathustra himself announces
the fateful crossing, when he will lead those who have worshiped
Ahura Mazdā: "With them all I shall cross the Bridge of the Sorter!"
(46. 10).

104. "Transfiguration" of the world

The Prophet does not doubt that the *daēvas* will be annihilated and
that the just will triumph over the wicked. But when will it take
place, this victory of Good that will radically renew the world? He
implores Ahura Mazdā: "Teach me that which thou knowest, Lord:
Even before the coming of the punishments that thou hast conceived,
O Wise One, will the just conquer the wicked? For it is in that, as
we know, that the reform of existence consists" (*Yasna* 48. 2). It is
the transfiguration of existence that Zarathustra awaits: "Give me
this sign: the total transformation of this existence. So that, worshiping you and praising you, I attain to the greatest joy" (34. 6).
"Make known the pattern that will cure existence!" he cries (44. 16).
He insists: "What retribution thou dost destine for the two sides,
O Wise One, by thy bright fire and by molten metal, give a sign of it
to souls, to bring harm to the wicked, advantage to the just" (51. 9).
    It is probable that Zarathustra had hoped for the imminent
"transfiguration" (*frašō-kereti*) of the world. "May we be those who
will renew this existence!" he exclaims (*Yasna* 30. 9).[17] Several times

17. Molé and Gnoli have cogently brought out the immediate renovation of
the world as the result of sacrifices (*yasna*) performed by the priests.

he calls himself *saošyant*, the "savior" (48. 8; 46. 3; 53. 2; etc.), a notion that will later give rise to a fabulous mythology. The eschatological ordeal by fire and molten metal that he announces (see also 30. 7; 32. 7) had as its objective both the punishment of the wicked and the regeneration of existence. As has happened more than once in history, the expectation of judgment and renewal of the world is progressively projected into an eschatological future that can be variously calculated. But it is important to emphasize the new interpretation given by Zarathustra to the idea of renewal. As we have seen (§ 21) and shall see again (§ 106), various mythico-ritual scenarios for the renovation of the world were known in the Near East, both by the Indo-Iranians and by other peoples. The ritual, which reiterated the cosmogony, was celebrated on the occasion of the New Year. But Zarathustra impugns this archaic scenario, whose purpose was the annual regeneration of the world, and announces a radical and definitive "transfiguration," effected once and for all. Furthermore, the renovation will no longer be obtained by performing a cosmogonic ritual but by the will of Ahura Mazdā. This renovation includes the judgment of each being and implies the punishment of the wicked and the rewarding of the just (§ 112). If the *gāthās* are the work of Zarathustra—and this is the nearly unanimous opinion of scholars—it is allowable to conclude that the Prophet did his utmost to abolish the archaic ideology of the cosmic cycle periodically regenerated, and proclaimed the imminent and irrevocable *eschaton*, decided and brought about by Ahura Mazdā.

In short, the point of departure for Zarathustra's preaching is the revelation of the omnipotence, holiness, and goodness of Ahura Mazdā. The Prophet receives the revelation directly from the Lord, but it does not found a monotheism. What Zarathustra proclaims, and gives as a model to his disciples, is the choice of God and the other divine Entities. By choosing Ahura Mazdā, the Mazdean chooses good over evil, the *true* religion over that of the *daēvas*. Hence every Mazdean must fight against evil. No toleration is allowed in respect to the demonic forces incarnated in the *daēvas*. This tension will very soon harden into dualism. The world will be divided into the good and the evil and will end by resembling a projection, on all cosmic and anthropological levels, of the opposition between the virtues and their contraries. Another opposition is barely indicated but will have a great future in Iranian speculation:

that between the spiritual and the material, between thought and the "bony world" (see *Yasna* 28. 2).

The spiritual, and in a sense "philosophical," nature of the religion of Zarathustra is striking.[18] The transmutation of the most important Āryan divinities into Amesha Spentas (the Blessed Holy Ones), who make up Ahura Mazdā's escort, and the fact that each of these Entities comprises an abstract value (Order, Power, Devotion, etc.) at the same time that it governs a cosmic element (fire, metal, earth, etc.), denote at once creative imagination and a capacity for rigorous reflection. By associating the Amesha Spentas with him, Zarathustra succeeds in defining the way in which Ahura Mazdā intervenes in the world and also makes it clear how the Lord, through his "archangels," can help and support his worshipers. The fact that the Prophet calls his God "wise," that he magnifies the importance of "truth," that he continually extols "good thought," only accentuates the newness of his message: he emphasizes the function and religious value of wisdom, that is, of science, of accurate and useful knowledge. To be sure, it is not a matter of abstract science in the modern sense of the term but of a creative thought that discovers and at the same time creates the structures of the world and the universe of values that is their correlative. From this point of view, Zarathustra's speculative effort may be compared with the meditations and discoveries of the sages depicted in the Upanishads, who radically transformed the Vedic conception of the world and human existence (§ 80).

But the comparison with the *ṛṣis* of the Upanishads becomes still more convincing when we observe the initiatory and eschatological character of Mazdean "wisdom." Certainly, being a private religion (like Vedism and Brahmanism), Mazdaism allowed the development of an esoteric dimension, which, though not forbidden, was nevertheless not accessible to all believers. *Yasna* 48. 3 mentions "secret doctrines." The initiatory and eschatological character is evident in the cult that Zarathustra proposes in place of the traditional sanguinary and frantic rites. The cult is so spiritual that even the term "sacrifice" (*yasna*) is equivalent, in the *gāthās*, to the term

18. This aspect of the religion of Zarathustra also corresponds to the image that Greek antiquity conceived of him: philosopher (according to Aristoxenes, Pythagoras was his disciple), Magus, master of initiation, author of Hermetic and alchemical treatises.

"thought."[19] When Ahura Mazdā approached him "as Good Thought" and asked him, "To whom would you address your worship?" Zarathustra replied, "To thy fire!"; and he added, "By making it the offering of veneration, I desire to think as much as I can of Justice!" (*Yasna* 43. 9). Sacrifice is the occasion, or more precisely the "support," of a theological meditation. And whatever interpretations were given later by the priests, it is significant that the fire altar became, and remained, the religious center of Mazdaism. As for the eschatological fire as Zarathustra conceived it, despite its retributive function, it purifies and spiritualizes the world.

But the function of the cult is still greater. According to a recent interpretation,[20] by means of the rite (*yasna*) the officiant acquires the condition of *maga*; that is, he enjoys an ecstatic experience that brings illumination (*čisti*). During this illumination the priest-sacrificer succeeds in separating his spiritual essence (*mēnōk*) from his corporal nature (*gētīk*); in other words, he recovers the condition of purity and innocence that preceded the "mixing" of the two essences. Now, this mixing took place as the result of Ahriman's attack. Hence the sacrificer contributes to the restoration of the primordial situation, to the transfiguration (*frašō-kereti*) of the world, the work of redemption inaugurated by the paradigmatic priest Zarathustra. It could even be said that the sacrificer already shares in the transfigured world.[21]

The state of *maga* is obtained primarily by the *haoma* sacrifice, the sacrifice of the "drink of immortality," which the priest imbibes during the ceremony.[22] Now *haoma* is rich in *xvarenah*, the sacred fluid, at once igneous, luminous, vivifying, and spermatic. Ahura Mazdā is preeminently the possessor of *xvarenah*, but this divine "flame" also springs from the forehead of Mithra (*Yašt* 10. 127) and, like a solar light, emanates from the heads of sovereigns.[23] However,

19. Meillet, *Trois conférences sur les Gātha*, p. 56; Duchesne-Guillemin, *Zoroastre*, p. 151.

20. See the works by Gnoli, especially "Lo stato di 'maga'" and "La gnosi iranica," pp. 287 ff.

21. Cf. Gnoli, "Questioni sull'interpretazione," pp. 349 ff. We shall later analyze (see volume 2) the meaning of *mēnōk* and *gētīk*.

22. Cf. M. Boyce, "Haoma, Priest of the Sacrifice"; Gnoli, "Lo stato di 'maga'," pp. 114–15, and "Questioni," p. 366.

23. See Duchesne-Guillemin, "Le *xvarenah*," and the bibliographical references given in our study "Spirit, Light, and Seed," pp. 13 ff. Mention should here be made of the Mesopotamian concept of "flaming splendor," *melammu*; cf. § 20 ("Present Position of Studies").

every human being possesses his *xvarenah*, and on the day of transfiguration, i.e., of the final Renovation, "the great light seeming to come from the body will burn continually on this earth."[24] By ritually absorbing *haoma* the sacrificer surpasses his human condition, comes close to Ahura Mazdā, and anticipates *in concreto* the universal Renovation.

It is difficult to determine if this eschatological conception of the cult was already completely formulated in Zarathustra's time. But it was certainly implicit in the function of sacrifice among the Indo-Iranians. From their particular point of view, the authors of the *Brāhmaṇas* shared a similar conception: the world was periodically restored, i.e., "re-created," by the unlimited power of sacrifice. But the eschatological function of the cult in Mazdaism unites, so to speak, the supreme exaltation of sacrifice, realized by the *Brāhmaṇas*, with the initiatory gnosis and visionary "illumination" of the Upanishads. In Iran, as in Brahmanic India, sacrificial technique and eschatological gnosis were cultivated by a religious élite and constituted an esoteric tradition. Insofar as the few episodes concerning the use of hemp by Zarathustra's disciples corresponded to a real situation,[25] they can be compared to the situation in ancient India, for there, too, we find a number of ecstatics using certain stupefacients, side by side with ascetics, visionaries, yogins, and contemplatives (see §§ 78 ff.). But the trances and ecstasies brought on by stupefacients played a small part in the Indian religions. Similarly, the earliest Zoroastrianism, so imperfectly reflected by the *gāthās*, seems to give first place to "wisdom," to inner "illumination" in the presence of the sacrificial fire.

According to tradition, Zarathustra was killed at the age of seventy-seven by the Turanian Brātvarxsh in a fire temple. A late source adds that the murderers were disguised as wolves.[26] The legend admirably expresses the meaning of Zarathustra's destiny, for the "wolves" were the members of the Āryan men's societies, so courageously stigmatized by the Prophet.

But the process of mythicization continued for at least fifteen

24. *Zātspram*, trans. Molé, *Culte, mythe et cosmogonie*, p. 98; see also ibid., p. 475, and other examples in Gnoli, "Questioni," pp. 367–68.

25. Cf. Widengren, *Les religions de l'Iran*, pp. 88 ff.

26. The Pahlavi *Rivāyat* 47. 23, cited by Jean de Menasce, *Anthropos*, vol. 35/36, p. 452 (cf. Duchesne-Guillemin, *La religion de l'Iran ancien*, p. 341, n. 3; Eng. trans., p. 228, n. 4).

centuries. We mentioned above some examples of the apotheosis of Zarathustra in the Mazdean tradition (§101). In the Hellenistic world Zoroaster is exalted as the paradigmatic Magus, and it is always as "Magus" that he is evoked by the philosophers of the Italian Renaissance. Finally, reflections of his most beautiful myth are found in Goethe's *Faust*.

105. The religion of the Achaemenids

The opposition between Ahura Mazdā and the *daēvas* was already taking shape in the Indo-Iranian period, since Vedic India opposed the *devas* to the *asuras*. But there is a difference; in India the religious values of the two groups evolved in a direction contrary to that in Iran: the *devas* became the "true gods," triumphing over the class of more archaic divinities, the *asuras*, who in the Vedic texts are regarded as "demonic" figures (§ 65). A similar process, though inversely oriented, took place in Iran; there the ancient gods, the *daēvas*, were demonized (§ 65). We can define the direction in which this transmutation took place: it was above all the gods of the warrior's function—Indra, Saurva, Vāyu—who became *daēvas*. None of the *asura* gods was demonized. What corresponded in Iran to the great proto-Indian *asura*, Varuṇa, became Ahura Mazdā.

Zarathustra probably played a part in this process. But the advancement of Ahura Mazdā to an exalted position is not Zarathustra's doing. Considered Supreme God, or simply a Great God among other great gods, Ahura Mazdā was venerated in the Iranian countries before Zarathustra. He is found under that name in inscriptions of the Achaemenid kings.

For years an intense controversy has divided scholars on the subject of the Zoroastrianism of Darius and his successors. Against the Zoroastrianism of the Great Kings, the following arguments, among others, are brought forward: Zarathustra is not named in any inscription; terms and names as important as *spenta*, Angra Mainyu, and the Amesha Spentas (except Arta) are absent; then too, the religion of the Persians at the time of the Achaemenids, as described by Herodotus, has nothing Zoroastrian about it. In favor of the Zoroastrianism of the Achaemenids, the name of the great god Ahuramazdā, glorified in the inscriptions, is cited, together with the fact that when, under Artaxerxes I (465–425), the new calendar was introduced, featuring the names of the Zoroastrian Entities, the reform aroused no opposition.[27]

However this may be, if the Achaemenids were not Zoroastrians, their theology was on the same plane as that of the *gāthās*: it abounds in abstract expressions, comparable to those of the *gāthās*, and it is "laden with moral considerations."[28] In addition, as Marjan Molé points out, we must not expect of a king the actions and formulas of priests; he does not perform a liturgy but accomplishes concrete acts; now this accomplishment is *fraša*, a term that expresses "what is good, what constitutes man's happiness, what allows the king to exercise his faculties."[29] In the first inscription that Darius causes to be engraved at Naqš-i-Rustam, near Persepolis, Ahuramazdā is extolled as "a great god, who created this earth, who created yonder sky, who created man, who created happiness for man, who made Darius king, one king of many, one lord of many."[30] The inscription dwells on the creativity of Ahuramazdā and—it might almost be said in consequence—on the religious responsibility of the sovereign. It is to maintain the creation of Ahuramazdā and to insure "happiness for man" that Darius was made king.

This privileged religious situation is justified by the myth of the founding of the Achaemenid dynasty. According to Herodotus 1. 107–17, after two dreams, which the Magi interpreted as bad omens for his throne, Astyages, king of the Medes, married his daughter to a Persian (hence a man of inferior race) named Cambyses, and when she bore a son, Cyrus, Astyages ordered that he be killed. But the child was saved and brought up by the wife of a herdsman,

27. See Duchesne-Guillemin, p. 167 (Eng. trans., p. 118); but this author has recently stated (in *Historia Religionum*, vol. 1, p. 326) that, as the result of an article by Bickerman, the argument from the "Zoroastrian calendar" must be abandoned.

28. G. Dumézil, *Naissances d'archanges*, pp. 62 ff. See also Zaehner, *Dawn and Twilight*, pp. 157 ff.

29. Molé, *Culte, mythe et cosmologie*, p. 35. Gnoli ("Considerazioni sulla religione degli Achemenidi," pp. 246 ff.) observes that, in the inscriptions, *fraša* means "excellent" and has no religious value; however, religious value is implicit in the "excellence" of every royal act.

30. R. G. Kent, *Old Persian*, p. 138 (translation); cf. Widengren, *Rel. de l'Iran*, p. 140, n. 1. The formula may be of Median origin (Nyberg, *Die Religionen des alten Irans*, p. 349), and Widengren (p. 140) believes it was influenced by Semitic conceptions of the Creator God.

Mithradates.[31] Cyrus grew up to adolescence among the young herdsmen, but his princely bearing betrayed him and his identity was discovered. Finally, after many adventures, he triumphed over the Medes, dethroned his grandfather, and founded the Achaemenid empire.

The mythical theme of the exposed and persecuted hero is found among many peoples. For our purpose, the following motifs are important: (a) the ordeals undergone by Cyrus, beginning with his exposure, are equivalent to an initiation of the military type; (b) symbolically, the future king is—or becomes—the son of the god Mithra (Mithradates, his adoptive father's name, means "gift of Mithra"); (c) after his victory over the king of the Medes, Cyrus founds an empire and a new dynasty; (d) this is as much as to say that he created a new world and inaugurated a new era—in other words, he accomplished a microcosmogony; (e) since the cosmogony was ritually repeated on the occasion of the New Year, it is legitimate to suppose that the mythico-ritual scenario of the foundation of the dynasty was made part of the Nawrōz ceremonies.

106. The Iranian king and the New Year festival

Darius conceived and built Persepolis as a sacred capital, reserved for the celebration of the New Year festival, the Nawrōz.[32] In fact, Persepolis was not a political capital, had no strategic importance, and, unlike Pasargadae, Ecbatana, Susa, and Babylon, is not mentioned in any Western or Eastern source.[33] The Nawrōz, like every ritual scenario of the New Year, renewed the world by symbolic repetition of the cosmogony. The conception was familiar to the Indo-Iranians; however, it is probable that, under the Achaemenids,

31. According to Justin 1. 4, the herdsman found the exposed infant being suckled by a bitch (a characteristic feature of myths of sovereign heroes). Now Herodotus reports that Mithradates' wife was named Spako, that is, in the Median language, "bitch"; cf. Widengren, "La légende royale," p. 226.

32. R. Girshman, "A propos de Persépolis," pp. 265, 277; see also A. U. Pope, "Persepolis, a Ritual City."

33. Not even Ctesias, who had spent thirty years at the court of the Great King, mentions Persepolis, which indicates the esoteric value of that sacred city; cf. K. Erdmann, "Persepolis," pp. 46–47. In fact, the Western world did not learn of the existence of Persepolis until the city was destroyed by Alexander the Great.

the scenario had also undergone Mesopotamian influences.[34] In any case, the New Year festival took place under the aegis of Ahura-mazdā, hieratically represented on several gates at Persepolis.

In a wide geographical zone, and from a certain historical moment, the cosmogony (and, indeed, all other forms of "creation" and "foundation") involved the victorious combat of a god or a mythical hero with a marine monster or a dragon (cf., for example, Indra-Vṛtra, Baal-Yam, Zeus-Typhon, etc.). It has been possible to show that a similar scenario existed among the Vedic Indians and in ancient Iran,[35] though in this last case the sources are late and present the myth in strongly historicized form. And in fact the fight of the hero Thraētona against the dragon Aži Dahāka, to which the Avesta refers (Yašt 9. 145; 5. 34; 19. 92 ff.), is recounted by Firdausi as the struggle of King Farîdûn (< Frêtôn < Thraētona) against a foreign usurper, the dragon Aždâhâk, who had captured and married the two sisters of the legitimate sovereign, Jamšed (< Yima Xšaêta). Farîdûn—like Thraētona—emerges victorious, kills the dragon, and delivers (and in turn marries) the two captive princesses. Now late traditions add that it was on New Year's Day that the king conquered Aždâhâk.[36] The Iranian heroes and kings are credited with having killed dragons (cf., for example, the legend of Ardashir), a motif that is, in any case, very widespread and to which we shall return. We add that, in Iran as elsewhere, the process of historiciza-tion of mythical themes and personages is counterbalanced by a contrary process: the real adversaries of the nation or the empire are imagined as monsters, and especially as dragons.[37]

What it is important to bear in mind for the moment is the fact that the Iranian king was responsible for the preservation and regeneration of the world, in other words, that on the plane proper to him he fought against the forces of evil and death and contributed to the triumph of life, fecundity, and Good. Zarathustra looked for universal regeneration by means of the Good Religion. In the last analysis, every Zoroastrian priest believed that by his sacrifices he anticipated the eschatological transfiguration. What the kings

34. See Gnoli, "Politica religiosa e concezione della regalità sotto i Sas-sanidi," pp. 23 ff.

35. See Wikander, Vayu, pp. 128 ff.; G. Widengren, Stand und Aufgabe, pp. 51 ff., and Les religions de l'Iran, pp. 58 ff.

36. Widengren, Rel. de l'Iran, p. 66.

37. Eliade, Cosmos and History, pp. 37 ff.

accomplished, *in the beginning* and annually, the priest hoped to realize annually—and the Saoshyant will effect it definitively at the time of the final Renovation. We do not know if, in the period of the Achaemenids, there was a conflict or a secret tension between the two religious ideologies, royal and sacerdotal. King Vishtaspa's friendship for the Prophet could constitute a paradigmatic model. But the confrontation will become explicit later, under the Sassanids. The phenomenon is also known elsewhere: Prince Siddharta became the Buddha, and his soteriology replaced that of the Brahmans.

107. The problem of the Magi. The Scythians

As it spread westward, Zoroastrianism encountered other types of religion and underwent their influences. Similarly, the Mazdaism of the Achaemenids did not remain unchanged. Xerxes, son of Darius, forbade the cult of the *daēvas* throughout his kingdom—which brings him still closer to the religion of Zarathustra. But later, and precisely from the time of the inscriptions of Artaxerxes II (405–359), Mithra and Anāhitā appear beside Ahuramazdā. Now, as we shall see, a similar syncretism manifests itself in the late Avesta, where the same gods' names are cited beside Ahura Mazdā and the Amesha Spentas.[38]

No less the subject of controversy is the problem of the Magi and their relations with Zoroastrianism. They have been regarded, for example, as an aboriginal tribe of sorcerers and necromancers, responsible for the degradation of Zoroastrianism or, on the contrary, as the true disciples of Zarathustra and his missionaries in western Iran. During the period of the Median Empire (seventh century) they seem to have been a hereditary caste of Median priests, comparable to the Levites and the Brahmans.[39] Under the Achaemenids they are the preeminent representatives of the sacerdotal class. According to the information transmitted by Herodotus, they interpreted dreams (1. 107 ff.), prophesied in connection with sacrifices of white horses (7. 13), and during the sacrifices chanted a "genealogy of the gods" (1. 132), which indicates that they were the guardians of a tradition

38. Widengren considers, however, that Mithra enjoyed a cult of no small proportions in Persia, even as early as the reign of Darius I (*Rel. de l'Iran*, p. 148).

39. Cf. Zaehner, *Dawn and Twilight*, p. 163.

of religious poetry.[40] In any case, the Magi had adopted a number of Zoroastrian rites and customs and ended by being regarded as disciples of Zarathustra; indeed, certain Greek writers considered him a Magus.

It is still Herodotus to whom we owe the most valuable pieces of information concerning the Iranians of the north, especially the Scythians. Among their deities we find the sky god (Papaios), Mithra (Helios-Apollo), "Ares," god of war, the Earth Goddess, and Aphrodite Urania (4. 59). Herodotus also reports a national legend concerning the origin of the Scythian tribes and the royal power (4. 5 ff.). The myth is explained by the tripartite ideology of the Indo-Europeans, and it survives in the popular epic of the Ossets of the Caucasus, descendants of the Scythians and the Alans.

The Greek historian declares (4. 59) that the Scythians had no temples, altars, or statues. However, they annually sacrificed horses and sheep, as well as 1 percent of their prisoners of war, to "Ares"; the god was represented by an iron sword raised on an artificial mound. Sacrifices of human beings (a concubine, a number of servants) and of horses accompanied the burial of kings (4. 71 ff.). Finally, it is important to note the shamanic character of one rite: the Scythians threw hemp seeds on red-hot stones and, adds Herodotus, who had not understood that a religious act was involved, the smoke made them "so happy that they howled in joy" (4. 75). In all probability, we here have an ecstatic experience, parallels to which can be found in the Zoroastrian tradition (§ 102).

108. New aspects of Mazdaism: The cult of Haoma

The *Yasna with Seven Chapters*, written in prose and making up *gāthās* 35–42, reflects the beginning of a comparatively complex process of adaptation and integration. To begin with, certain significant innovations are observable in vocabulary; the Amesha Spentas are mentioned for the first time as a group, and we find the term *yazata* ("gods"), which will become important in later Mazdaism. We distinguish a certain tendency toward resacralization of the cosmic realities. Fire is identified with the Holy Spirit, Spenta Maiyu

---

40. Widengren, *Rel. de l'Iran*, p. 139; see also pp. 135 ff.

(*Yasna* 36. 3); together with the sun, fire is associated with Ahura Mazdā.[41] The sun is the visible form of the Lord, "the highest of the highest" (36. 6). Asha, Truth, is likewise associated with light. Then too, the preeminence of Asha in the *Yasna with Seven Chapters* has been noted: Asha is invoked with Ahura Mazdā, and the union of the Lord with Truth "forever" is proclaimed (40. 2; 41. 6). Asha now signifies more than Truth, Justice, Order; it is a personification whose structure is both cosmic and spiritual;[42] it is called "the most propitious, beneficient, immortal, made of light" (37. 4). Vohu Manah, which inspired Zarathustra in the *gāthās*, is reduced to a subordinate position.

Still more surprisingly, there is mention of the "good wives" of Ahurā (the Ahurānīs), who are the Waters: "We venerate the Ahurānīs, the Waters" (*Yasna* 38. 3).[43] And Haoma acquires an important place in the cult: "We worship the glorious Haoma of gold, we worship the shining Haoma that makes life prosper, we venerate the Haoma from which death flees" (42. 5). A number of authors have interpreted this exaltation of Haoma as a proof of syncretism, after the death of Zarathustra, between the Prophet's message and the traditional religion. However, if it is true that Zarathustra in fact accepted the cult of Haoma, though at the same time stigmatizing its excesses, there is no question of syncretism but rather of a solemn elevation of the values of the old Indo-Iranian cosmic religion.

Zarathustra's *gāthās* and the *Gāthā with Seven Chapters* form part of the sacramental liturgy, the *yasna*, a great deal of which consists of monotonous invocations of the divine beings. The *Yašts*, on the other hand, are hymns addressed, separately, to various divinities. These are a number of gods whom Zarathustra had ignored—for example, Mithra—but also divine personages or personifications of religious realities, such as Haoma. The *Hóm-yašt* (*Yašt* 20) justifies the cult of *haoma* by a daring origin myth: while Zarathustra was

41. In the later *Yasnas*—1. 11; 3. 13; 7. 13—the sun will be called the eye of Ahura Mazdā, which indicates the reactualization of an archaic Indo-Iranian idea, for the sun is already the eye of Varuṇa in Rig Veda 1. 50. 6.

42. Zaehner, *Dawn*, p. 64.

43. As Zaehner observes (*Dawn*, p. 65), in the later texts the Waters are forgotten; Ahura Mazdā's wife will be Armaiti, the Good Thought of the *gāthās*, later identified with the Earth. This is certainly a relic of the traditional Iranian religion.

blessing the fire and reciting the *gāthās*, *haoma* approached him and invited him to gather and squeeze it. Questioning it, the Prophet learned that Vivahvant was the first to squeeze *haoma* and had obtained as reward the birth of a son, King Yima, "the most religious of human beings" (*Yašt* 20. 45).

We shall return to the meaning and prehistory of this mythico-ritual scenario: offspring obtained after, and by the power of, a sacrifice (see volume 2). It is to be noted that Yima and the *haoma* rite are extolled in Mazdaism jointly with blood sacrifices (*Yašt* 11. 4–7). Such an elevation of the Indo-Iranian heritage obviously occasioned strong resistance; indeed, blood sacrifices were later definitively suppressed, and *haoma* disappeared as an intoxicating drink, being replaced by a mixture of plant juices, water, and milk.[44]

109. Exaltation of the god Mithra

Still more surprising, and more important for the history of Mazdaism, is the *Mihr Yašt* (*Yašt* 10), the long hymn in honor of Mithra. "When I created Mithra of the broad pastures," Ahura Mazdā declares, "I made him as worthy of veneration and reverence as myself" (*Yašt* 10. 1). In other words, all the greatness, power, and creativity of Mithra are the work of the Wise Lord. In this prologue we recognize the effort of Mazdean theology to reconfirm the omnipotence of one supreme god. In fact, the *Mihr Yašt* relates and justifies the elevation of Mithra to the eminence that was his before Zarathustra's reform. When, at the end of the hymn, the two gods are united, the author uses the formula *Mithra-Ahurā* (*Yt.* 10. 145), a replica of the well-known Vedic binomial *Mitra-Varuṇa*.[45]

However, the god exalted in the *Mihr Yašt* was not reintegrated into Mazdaism without some changes. We can decipher in the hymn itself the different moments of a discrete theogony: a series of acts and gestures by Ahura Mazdā is directed precisely to the glorification and advancement of Mithra. The first thing to be emphasized is his multivalence. He is, to be sure, the god of contracts, and by promising to worship him (*Yašt* 10. 4–6) the believer undertakes no longer to

44. Widengren, *Rel. de l'Iran*, p. 131; cf. Duchesne-Guillemin, *La religion de l'Iran*, pp. 96 ff. (Eng. trans., pp. 74 ff.).

45. Dumézil has shown that Mithra's place was taken, in the *gāthās*, by Vohu Manan; see also Widengren, *Rel. de l'Iran*, p. 31.

break contracts. But he is also the god of war and shows himself to be violent and cruel (he furiously massacres the *daēvas* and the impious with his mace, *vazra*, a characteristic that brings him close to Indra). He is also a solar god, associated with Light (10. 142). He has a thousand ears and ten thousand eyes (10. 141), that is, he is all-seeing and omniscient, like any sovereign god; but he is also the universal provider, who insures the fertility of fields and flocks (10. 61 ff.). The phenomenon is current in the history of religions: a divinity is given a multiplicity of powers and attributes that are sometimes contradictory in order to obtain a "totality" necessary to his elevation, whether momentary or permanent, to the rank of the great gods.

Ahura Mazdā and the Amesha Spentas built a house for him above Mount Harā, that is, in the spiritual world that lies beyond the celestial vault (*Yašt* 10. 49–52).[46] Nevertheless, Mithra complains to the Lord that, though he is the protector of all creatures, he is not worshiped with prayers, as the other gods are (10. 54). Presumably he receives the cult that he demands, for later in the hymn we see Mithra on a chariot drawn by white horses (62 ff.) or, accompanied by Sraosha and Rashnu, traveling through the earth by night and exterminating the *daēvas* (95–101) or pursuing those who do not respect contracts (104–11). Still more significant are the stages of Mithra's elevation to the rank of supreme god. First Ahura Mazdā consecrates Haoma as priest of Mithra, and Haoma worships him (88), that is, offers him sacrifices. Then Ahura Mazdā prescribes the proper rite for the cult of Mithra (119–22) and performs it himself in paradise, in the House of Song (124). After this apotheosis, Mithra returns to earth to fight the *daēvas*, while Ahura Mazdā remains in the House of Song. The reunion of Ahura Mazdā and Mithra seals the fate of the *daēvas*. Mithra is worshiped as the light that lights the whole world (142–44). And the hymn ends with these words: "by the plant *barsom* we worship Mithra and Ahura, the glorious Lords of Truth, free forever from corruption: we worship the stars, the moon, and the sun. We worship Mithra, the Lord of all lands" (145).

46. The meaning of this mythical motif is well known: the building of a temple, in heaven, by the members of the pantheon salutes the victory (often of the cosmogonic type; cf. Marduk) of a god and consecrates his elevation to supreme rank (cf. Baal). Obviously, this mythological episode finds expression, on earth, in the building of a sanctuary in honor of the god (cf. § 50).

Mithra was advanced in Mazdaism especially as the god-champion in the struggle against the *daēvas* and the impious. The fact that Ahura Mazdā abandons this function entirely to him indicates a certain tendency to *otiositas* in the latter; but because the fight against the forces of evil is the principal obligation of Mazdaism, the hymn can be interpreted as a "conversion" of Mithra, hence as a victory of the Lord.

110. Ahura Mazdā and the eschatological sacrifice

The process of syncretism between the old ethnic religion and the message of Zarathustra can be deciphered in other hymns. Thus, for example, in *Yašt* 8, dedicated to the *yazata* Tištrya (personification of the star Sirius), Tištrya laments that he has not succeeded in vanquishing the demon Apaoša—who held back the Waters and threatened to ruin all Creation—because men ignored him in their rites. Then Ahura Mazdā venerates Tištrya, offering him a sacrifice (*yasna*); in consequence, Tištrya emerges victorious from his fight with the *daēva* and insures the fertility of the earth. Ahura Mazdā likewise sacrifices to Anāhitā and asks her "to grant him this favor: 'May I induce the pious Zarathustra to think, speak, and act according to the Good Religion?'" (*Yašt* 5. 17–19). In addition, the Wise Lord sacrifices to Vayu and begs him "to grant him this favor," that he may kill the creatures of Angra Mainyu (15. 3). No less unexpected is Ahura Mazdā's declaration that, without the help he received from the Fravashis—which are the preexisting souls of men —humanity and the animals would have disappeared and the material world have fallen under the empire of Falsehood (13. 12).

Zaehner[47] understands these texts as a contradiction to the doctrine of Zarathustra, that is, the self-humiliation of Ahura Mazdā, who not only venerates subordinate beings but asks for their help. And indeed the decisive importance attributed to the help of the Fravashis is reminiscent of a certain type of *deus otiosus*, when the Creator appears to suffer from a "mental fatigue" that obliges him to appeal to certain animals and even to his adversary.[48] But the fact that Ahura Mazdā venerates (*yaz-*) one or another god by

47. Zaehner, *Dawn and Twilight*, p. 81.
48. This is a case of a "dualistic" cosmogonic motif, comparatively well known in the folklore of eastern Europe, Central Asia, and Siberia, but also documented in Zervanism; see Eliade, "The Devil and God," *Zalmoxis*, pp. 79 ff.

consecrating sacrifices (*yasna*) to him does not necessarily imply that he places himself in a subordinate situation. The *Yašts* emphasize the creative power of the rites and the liturgy and present Ahura Mazdā in his sacerdotal function.[49] By offering him a sacrifice, Ahura Mazdā increases by tenfold the magico-religious power of the recipient of it. What is apparent from the hymns is especially the exceptional importance of sacrifice—a conception that is certainly Indo-Iranian but that is developed particularly in the *Brāhmaṇas* and will become increasingly central in Mazdaism.

As among the other Indo-Europeans, the ritual fire plays the capital role. *Yasna* "is essentially a sacrifice of *haoma* performed before the fire" (Duchesne-Guillemin, *La religion de l'Iran ancien*, p. 71). The maintenance, purification, and foundation of the sacred fires took on, in Mazdaism, proportions unknown elsewhere. For every Mazdean king, the supreme religious act consisted in founding a fire, that is, building a temple, endowing it with revenues, and appointing priests to it.[50] Though Zarathustra condemned certain blood sacrifices, it is not certain that he rejected them all. In any case, animal sacrifices are known in the Avesta (*Yasna* 11. 4; *Yašt* 8. 58). In addition, they are abundantly documented under the Achaemenids in the Parthian period, and under the Sassanids.[51]

We have seen (§ 104) in what sense Zarathustra—who himself designates himself Saoshyant and exclaims: "May we be those who will renew this existence" (*Yasna* 30. 9)—revalorized the old mythico-ritual scenario that insured the renewal of the world by ritual repetition of the cosmogony. In Zoroastrianism the eschatological intention of the sacrifice is continually reinforced, though its cosmic value is not thereby obliterated. We can discern a process analogous to the "historicization" of the cosmic rhythms and phenomena in Yahwism (§ 57). The combat against monsters and other traditional heroic themes are interpreted as moments in the Mazdean eschatological drama, that is, the struggle against the *daēvas*, the waiting and preparation for universal Renewal (*frašō-kereti*). Since the world was symbolically re-created and time itself was renewed by the New Year rite, the eschatological Renovation was finally given a place in the

49. See Gnoli, "Note su Yasht VIII," pp. 95 ff.
50. Duchesne-Guillemin, *La religion de l'Iran*, p. 84, n. 1 (Eng. trans., p. 64, n. 2) (bibliography).
51. Ibid., pp. 100 ff. (Eng. trans., pp. 76 ff.). See also above, § 103.

same scenario. The sacrifice performed by the Zoroastrian priest anticipates the final sacrifice by which Saoshyant will effect the Renovation. Consequently the officiant identifies himself with Saoshyant and, implicitly, with Zarathustra.[52]

Later the two intentions of the sacrifice—eschatological and cosmogonic—are again brought together. The traditions preserved in the Pahlavi texts emphasize a series of sacrifices by which Ahura Mazdā created the cosmos, the primordial man, and Zarathustra.[53] The eschatological Renovation will take place during the New Year festival, and then the dead will return to life, be judged, and, finally, "immortalized." It should be noted that the universal renewal, just like the original creation, will be the result of a sacrifice. The Pahlavi texts describe in great detail the final sacrifice, to be performed by Saoshyant and his assistants, in which Ohrmazd and the Amesha Spentas will take part, and after which men will return to life and become immortal and the whole universe will be radically regenerated.[54]

We see in what sense Zoroastrianism made use of the archaic values of sacrifice. Zarathustra had proclaimed a "holy war" against the forces of evil, and each of the faithful, by choosing the Good Religion, was summoned to combat the daēvas, to "purge" the world of demons; in other words, he took part in the universal work of cleansing performed by Ahura Mazdā and his archangels. The redeeming function of the Good Religion was progressively strengthened by glorification of the creative power of rite. Since the ultimate goal was universal regeneration, the fundamental, cosmogonic value of sacrifice was valorized; indeed, the eschatological Renovation not only "saves" humanity but creates it anew, by effecting the resurrection of the body. This implies a new Creation, indestructible, incorruptible. As Yašt 19. 90 announces: "The material world will no longer die away. . . . Falsehood will perish."

111. The soul's journey after death

Funerary rites, mythologies of death, conceptions concerning the postexistence of the soul change slowly, in spite of reforms and conversions. This is as much as to say that much of the data supplied

52. Molé, Culte, mythe et cosmologie, p. 134. The Saoshyant is the final Savior, identified with Zarathustra and, according to some late traditions, descended from the seed of the Prophet miraculously preserved in Lake Kasaoya.

53. The Pahlavi Rivayāt 16 B, fragment translated by Molé, pp. 126 ff.

54. See the texts translated by Molé, pp. 87 ff., 90, 126 ff., etc.

by the Avestan and Pahlavi texts are also valid for the pre-Zarathus-tran period. The rite documented in western Iran, specifically the burning of the body and burying the ashes in an urn, spread to other regions with Zoroastrianism. Still more archaic was a custom typical of the steppes of Central Asia: exposing the body in a place designated for the purpose, where it was eaten by vultures and dogs.[55] The Iranians of the East performed ritual lamentations and inflicted blows on themselves, even going as far as suicide. But Zoroastrianism drastically forbids "tears and lamentations," declaring them to be the invention of Angra Mainyu.[56]

As for the soul's experiences after death, we find certain familiar motifs—crossing a bridge, ascent to heaven, judgment—but also the theme of meeting with one's own Self. A poem that formed part of the *Hādōxt Nask* (*Yašt* 21–22) relates that the soul (*urvan*) of the just man remains close to his body for three days. Toward the end of the third night a perfumed wind rises from the South, and the *dāenā* of the deceased appears "in the form of a beautiful young girl, shining, white-armed, vigorous, of beautiful appearance, straight-bodied, tall, with upward-pointing breasts . . . fifteen years old" (*Hādōxt Nask* 9). Revealing her identity, the *dāenā* adds: "Lovable as I was, thou didst make me more lovable by thy good thoughts, thy good words, thy good deeds, thy good religion; beautiful, thou madest me still more beautiful; desirable, still more desirable" (ibid., 14). Then, in four strides, the soul traverses the three celestial spheres,[57] and reaches "the Lights without beginning" (15) that is, paradise. One of the dead asks how he passed "from corporeal existence to spiritual existence, from existence full of dangers to existence without danger" (16), but Ahura Mazdā intervenes: "Do not question him, for you remind him of the horrible, dangerous road, linked to separation, by which he passed, and which consists in a separation from the body and consciousness" (17)—a reference to the dramatic ordeals of the journey.[58] Ahura Mazdā orders that he be offered

55. Nyberg, *Die Religionen des alten Irans*, p. 310; Widengren, *Les religions de l'Iran*, p. 53.

56. Nyberg, pp. 316 ff.

57. These are the spheres of the stars, the moon, and the sun, designated in the text as "Good Thought," "Good Word," and "Good Deed"; see Widengren, p. 125, referring to Bossuet, "Die Himmelsreise der Seele," pp. 25 ff.

58. We are better informed concerning these ordeals by late texts, such as *Mēnōk i Xrat* 2. 115–17 and 151–53; see also Soederblom, *La vie future d'après le mazdéisme*, pp. 91 ff.; Pavry, *Doctrine*, pp. 19, 62 ff.

"spring butter," [59] which is, for the just man, his "nourishment after death" (18). On the contrary, the soul of the wicked man meets in the North Wind a frightful termagant and arrives at the zone of Darkness-without-a-Beginning, where Angra Mainyu demands that he be given poison (20–35).

Let us single out the characteristic features: (1) the soul meets its *dāenā*, that is, its own Self, [60] which preexists it ("lovable though I was") but which is at the same time the result of its religious activity on earth ("thou didst make me more lovable"); (2) the *dāenā* presents itself under an archetypized female form, at the same time preserving a concrete appearance; (3) we certainly have here an Indo-Iranian conception, since it is found in the *Kauṣītaki-Upaniṣad* 1. 3–6: the soul of him who sets out on the "road of the gods" (*devayāna*) is welcomed, among other divinities, by Mānāsi (the "Intelligent" [fem.]) and Cākshushī (the "Clairvoyant" [fem.]); it then crosses a lake and a stream, enters a city, and arrives before Brahman, who asks it: "Who art thou?" [61]

There is no reference to the Činvat Bridge in the *Hādōxt Nask*. However, Zarathustra speaks of it at length (§ 103). It represents an Indo-Iranian conception, known to other Indo-European peoples and documented elsewhere in the history of religions. The classic description [62] tells how the *dāenā* arrives with its dogs and guides the soul of the just man on the Činvat Bridge, over the Hara Berezaiti, the cosmic mountain (in fact, the bridge—which is at the "center of the world"—connects earth with heaven). Received by Vohu Manah, the souls pass before Ahura Mazdā and the Amesha Spentas. The separation of the good from the wicked takes place either before the bridge or at its entrance. As for the judgment of the soul, of which the Pahlavi texts speak and where the judge is Mithra, assisted by Sraosha and Rashnu (with a pair of scales), it is unknown in the

59. On the religious meaning of "spring butter," see Widengren, p. 126.

60. On the *dāenā*, see Gnoli, "Questioni sull'interpretazione," pp. 361 ff.

61. See Wikander, *Vayu*, pp. 47 ff. Widengren (pp. 57–59) mentions that the *Dātistān i Denik* 24. 5 calls the young girl the "treasurer [fem.] of good works," just as, according to the Buddhist text *Dhammapada* 219 ff., the virtuous "are received by their good works as if they were their dear kinsmen." The celestial journey of the deceased is in every respect like the ecstatic ascent of the soul through the stellar, lunar, and solar spheres before reaching Paradise (*garōdmān*), an ascent described in the late work *Ardai Virāz Nāmak*.

62. *Vīdēvdāt* 19. 28–32; Soederblom, *La vie future*, pp. 89–90. According to *Vīdēvdāt* 13. 19, the dogs guard the bridge; cf. Yama's dogs.

gāthās. In any case, it is superfluous in the scenario: crossing the bridge, comparable to an initiatory ordeal, in itself constitutes the judgment; for according to a widespread conception, the bridge widens under the feet of the just and becomes like a razor's edge when the impious approach it.

112. The resurrection of the body

Still more superficially Zoroastrianized are the eschatological myths and beliefs crystallized around Yima. Whereas in India Yama chiefly inspired the mythology of the First of the Dead, in Iran Yima became the First King and the model for the perfect sovereign. For the purpose of this chapter it will suffice to recall that the Iranian tradition associates the original paradise with the reign of Yima: for a thousand years death and suffering did not exist, and men remained ever young.[63] But when Yima began to tell lies, his *xvarenah* forsook him, and finally he, too, lost immortality.[64]

Another eschatological myth, originally independent, was integrated by Zoroastrian theology into the mythology of Yima. Ahura Mazdā warns Yima that a winter three years long will destroy all life on earth; he then asks Yima to build an enclosure (*vara*) in which he will save the best of men and the germs of all the animal species. The *vara* was imagined as an underground dwelling, for neither sun, moon, nor stars shine there.[65] This is an archaic eschatology, perhaps Indo-European (cf. the winter Fimbul in the Germanic tradition), but which in no way corresponds with the Zoroastrian vision. Yet it is understandable why Yima was introduced into this mythological scenario of the end of the world: he was the king of the fabled Golden Age, and in the *vara* were preserved, or, more precisely, "saved," the germs of a future humanity, ready to experience, after the eschatological catastrophe, the paradisal existence of the "beginnings."

63. *Yasna* 9. 4 ff. See other references in Soederblom, *La vie future*, pp. 175 ff., and A. Christensen, *Les Types du premier homme*, vol. 2, pp. 16 ff.

64. See Christensen, passim, and G. Dumézil, *Mythe et Epopée*, vol. 2, pp. 282 ff. (Eng. trans., *The Destiny of a King*, pp. 38 ff.).

65. *Vidēvdāt* 2. 20–32; cf. Soederblom, *La vie future*, pp. 172 ff. See also *Bundahišn* 39. 14; *Mēnōk i Xrat* 62. 15; Dumézil, *Mythe et Epopée*, vol. 2, pp. 247 ff.

Another eschatological idea is added, that of the resurrection of the body. The belief appears to be comparatively old, but it is expressly proclaimed in *Yašt* 19. 11 and 89 (see also 13. 129), which speaks of the "resurrection of the dead," in connection with the arrival of the "Living One," that is, of the Saoshyant announced by Zarathustra. So the Resurrection forms part of the final Renovation, which also implies the universal judgment. Several ideas, some of them comparatively old, now find expression in a grandiose eschatological vision: the radically and completely renewed world in fact represents a new Creation that will no longer be vitiated by the attacks of the demons; the resurrection of the dead—actually the re-creation of bodies—is equivalent to a cosmogony by virtue of the microcosmos-macrocosmos parallel, an archaic conception common to several Indo-European peoples, but which had a considerable development in India and Iran.

As we saw (§ 104), the final Renovation, already prefigured in the liturgy performed by Zarathustra, is anticipated in the rituals of the New Year (*Nawrōz*). The tradition ends by placing close to the New Year the three decisive events of the cosmic and human drama: the Creation, the revelation of the "Religion," and the eschatological Renovation.[66] But since the year is, figuratively, the totality of cosmic time, the last ten days of each year in a way anticipate the eschatological drama. It is the fabulous interval during which souls return to earth: one *Yašt* (13. 49–52) invokes the Fravashis,[67] who move about freely during the last ten days of the year. This belief is universally disseminated, but the Zoroastrians, like other theologians before and after them, place it in a much larger system: according to the Pahlavi tradition, Ohrmazd completed the creation of man during these last ten days of the year; consequently, the Fravashis arrive on earth at the moment of the creation of man and return at the end of time, that is, at the resurrection of bodies.[68]

The late texts develop the parallelism between the New Year festival and the eschatological Renovation, when the resurrection

66. Cf. Molé, *Culte, mythe et cosmologie*, p. 120.

67. The *fravashis* are the souls of the just and at the same time their celestial archetypes. As guardian angels of the faithful, the *fravashis* combat the incarnations of evil; but late sources describe them as armed horsemen protecting heaven; see Widengren, *Rel. de l'Iran*, p. 39. The complex figure of the *fravashis* appears to be the result of a long process of religious syncretism.

68. See the texts cited by Molé, *Culte, mythe et cosmologie*, p. 109.

will occur. On the occasion of each New Year, gifts of new clothing are received, and, at the end of time, Ohrmazd will give glorious garments to the resuscitated.[69] As we saw (§ 104), it is after the sacrifice accomplished by Saoshyant, whether or not assisted by Ahura Mazdā, that the universal Renovation and the resurrection of bodies will occur. This eschatological sacrifice in a way repeats the cosmogonic sacrifice; this is why it is similarly "creative." The resurrection, with its corollary, the indestructibility of bodies, represents a daring development of Zarathustra's eschatological thought; indeed, it represents a new conception of immortality.[70]

69. *Saddar Bundeheš* 32–37, trans. Molé, p. 111.
70. The two creations—spiritual (*mēnōk*) and material (*gētik*)—as well as the mythology of the primordial man (Gayomart) will be discussed in the second volume of the present work.

14

The Religion of Israel in the Period of the Kings and the Prophets

113. Kingship and the monarchy: The apogee of syncretism

"When Samual grew old, he appointed his two sons as judges over Israel." But his sons did not follow his example, and then the leaders came to him and said: "Give us a king to rule over us, like the other nations" (1 Sam. 8:1–5). Kingship, then, was a foreign institution. Some opponents of the idea did not spare their criticism, for in their eyes Yahweh was sole king of Israel. However, from the beginning the monarchy was regarded as pleasing to Yahweh. After being anointed by Samuel, Saul received the "spirit of Yahweh" (1 Sam. 10:6). For the king was the "anointed" (*mâśiah*) of God (1 Sam. 24:7, 11; 26:9, 11, 16, 23, etc.); he was adopted by Yahweh, became in a sense his son: "I will be a father to him and he a son to me" (2 Sam. 7:14). But the king is not engendered by Yahweh; he is only recognized, "legitimated," by a special declaration.[1] Yahweh grants him universal domination (Psalm 72:8), and the king sits on his throne beside God (Ps. 110:1 and 5; 1 Chron. 28:5; 29:23; etc.). The king is Yahweh's representative; hence he belongs to the divine sphere. But the unique position of Yahweh makes the "divinization" of the king impossible;[2] the latter is preeminently the "servant" of Yahweh (the word is applied to David sixty times).

The coronation ceremony includes, together with other rites, anointing, proclamation of kingship, and enthronement.[3] As repre-

1. See G. Fohrer, *History of Israelite Religion*, p. 147. The people of Israel was also a "son" of Yahweh (Fohrer, pp. 185 ff.).

2. Even in texts so closely connected with the monarchy as the Psalms, it is Yahweh, not the king, who is given the central role (Fohrer, p. 150).

3. See the texts cited and discussed by Ringgren, *La religion d'Israël*, pp. 236 ff. (Eng. trans., pp. 221 ff.); Fohrer, pp. 142 ff.

sentative of Yahweh, the king of Israel, exactly like the sovereigns of the ancient East, must maintain cosmic order (Ps. 2:10–12), impose justice, defend the weak (Ps. 72:1 ff.), insure the fertility of the land: "He will come down like rain on the aftercrop. . . . Grain everywhere in the country, even on the mountaintops" (Ps. 72:16, 6). We recognize the traditional images of a paradisal reign, images that the Messianic prophets will brilliantly refurbish. (Besides, the expectation of the ideal king, the *Messiah*, is bound up with the ideology of kingship.) The monarchy was interpreted as a new covenant between Yahweh and the dynasty of David, a continuation of the covenant of Sinai. It is in this *valorization of a foreign institution as a new act of sacred history* that we can appreciate the originality of the Israelite ideology of kingship.[4]

Solomon builds the Temple at Jerusalem, close to the royal palace; he thus associates the cult of the sanctuary with the hereditary monarchy. The Temple becomes Yahweh's residence among the Israelites. The Ark of the Covenant, which until then accompanied the Israelite armies, is set up in the darkness of the Holy of Holies (*debir*). But from this sanctuary the holiness of Yahweh radiates on the city and out over the whole earth (Ps. 15:1; 24:3; 46:5; Isaiah 31:4; 48:2; etc.). Mount Zion, on which the Temple was built, is a "center of the world."[5] The Temple of Jerusalem becomes the national sanctuary, and the royal cult is identified with the state religion. The office consists of propitiatory and expiatory rituals for the whole community, but it also includes public prayers for the king, for his glory, and for the exercise of his justice, which insures "the peace of the people" and universal prosperity (Pss. 20 and 72). In the last analysis, *the liturgical practice renews the structures of the world.*

Just as the Temple was built after a foreign model, the cult borrowed Canaanite forms. Syncretism attained proportions thitherto unknown, for the monarchy encouraged the fusion of the religious ideas and practices shared by the two strata of the population, the Israelites and the Canaanites. In addition, Solomon accepted the cults of his foreign wives and allowed the building of sanctuaries in honor of their gods (1 Kings 11:6–7). The kings regarded themselves

4. Von Rad, *Old Testament Theology*, vol. 1, pp. 319 ff.; Ringgren, p. 252.
5. On the importance of this symbolism for later speculation, see Eliade, *Cosmos and History*, chap. 1.

as heads of the state religion, but we are poorly informed concerning their sacerdotal function. When the Ark was transported to Jerusalem, David acted like a priest: he danced before the Ark, offered "holocausts before Yahweh . . . and blessed the people in the name of Yahweh Sabaoth" (2 Sam. 6:16–18). So, too, Solomon blessed the assemblage at the consecration of the Temple (1 Kings 8:14). And Psalm 110:4 proclaims the king "a priest of the order of Melchizedek for ever." But on other occasions the kings were criticized because they had performed rites reserved for the priests. Very probably the king played a part in the expiatory ceremonies at the New Year. On the other hand, certain Psalms seem to refer to a ritual of the symbolic death and resurrection of the king. So we may suppose a relation between the New Year festival—including a symbolic reactualization of the Creation—and the ritual of the king's "death and resurrection."[6]

At Solomon's death the kingdom split into two: that of the North, or Israel, and the kingdom of the South, or Judah. Since the Ark had remained at Jerusalem and the northern tribes no longer had access to the common sanctuary, Jeroboam, the first king of Israel, established two sanctuaries, at Bethel and at Dan, where Yahweh was worshiped in the form of two golden calves (1 Kings 12:28–29). It is possible that these tauromorphic statues served as the seat of the invisible God. However, there is here a Canaanite influence that violated the prohibition against images, and this innovation, bordering on apostasy, aggravated the misunderstanding between the two kingdoms.[7]

114. Yahweh and the creature

A whole group of Psalms, the "Psalms of Enthronement," exalt Yahweh as king. He is "a greater King than all other gods" (95:3); "Yahweh is king, the nations tremble . . . . You are a king who loves justice, insisting on honesty, justice, virtue" (99:1, 5). But the idea of

6. See G. Ahlström, *Psalm 89: Eine Liturgie aus dem Ritual des leidenden Königs*, pp. 143 ff.; Widengren, *Sakrales Königtum*, pp. 15 ff.; Ringgren, pp. 249 ff.; Fohrer, pp. 142 ff.

7. It is important to remember that, whereas in the south the hereditary monarchy of the Davidic dynasty continued, kingship in the north was more or less charismatic; see Ringgren, pp. 76 ff.

divine kingship does not depend on the institution of the monarchy. The conception is archaic: God is master of the world because it is he who created it. Yahweh conquered the primordial monster (Rahab, Leviathan, Tannin the Dragon), symbol of chaos. As cosmocrator, God resides in heaven and manifests his presence or his will in meteorological phenomena—lightning, thunder, rain. We have already mentioned his contradictory attributes (§ 59), a well-known formula for "totality." Yahweh dispenses good and evil, he gives death and life, he humbles and exalts (1 Sam. 2:6 ff.). His wrath is terrible, but he is also merciful. Yahweh is, above all, holy (*qâdoš*), which means that he is both inaccessible and dangerous and also brings salvation.[8]

Creator and king of the world, Yahweh is also the judge of his creation. "At the moment I decide, I will dispense strict justice" (Ps. 75:3). He judges justly (Ps. 96:10). His "justice," at once moral, cosmic, and social, constitutes the fundamental norm of the universe.[9] Yahweh is the "Living God," in other words, he differs both from idols, which "do not speak" and "must be carried, for they do not walk" (Jer. 10:5), and from men, who are "like the grass that springs up" (Ps. 10:5). Man, too, is a living being (*nèfèš*), for God breathed "breath" or "spirit" (*rûah*) into him; but his existence is short. In addition, whereas God is spirit, man is flesh (*basar*). This opposition does not imply a religious disapproval of the body; it emphasizes the precariousness and ephemerality of human existence in contrast to the omnipotence and eternity of God. The incommensurable distance between these two modes of being is explained by the fact that man is a creature of God. Yet he differs from the other creations, for *he was formed in God's image*, and he reigns over nature.

Man's mortality is the consequence of original sin, particularly of Adam's desire to make himself like God (§ 59). The biblical texts dwell on the futility of the human condition. Man was made from dust and will return to dust (Gen. 3:19). A long life is his greatest good. As in so many other traditional cultures, death is degrading: it reduces man to a larval postexistence in the grave or in *sheol*, a dark and terrifying region in the depths of the earth. Since death is essentially the negation of his work, Yahweh does not reign over

8. Ringgren, *La religion d'Israël*, p. 86.
9. "Justice" is comparable to the Babylonian *māsuru* and the Egyptian *ma^cat*; see Ringgren, *Word and Wisdom*, pp. 49 ff., 58.

sheol. Hence, the deceased is deprived of relations with God, which, for the believer, is the most terrible of trials. Yet Yahweh is stronger than death: if he wanted to, he could raise man from the grave. Certain Psalms refer to this prodigy: "You have brought my soul up from Sheol, of all those who go down to the Pit you have revived me" (30:4); "No, I shall not die, I shall live . . . ; though Yahweh has punished me often, he has not abandoned me to Death" (118:17). These are the only references to the resurrection of the dead before the Babylonian Captivity (587–538 B.C.), when part of the population will be exposed to the influence of the Iranian eschatology (see volume 2).[10]

"Slave" or "servant" of Yahweh, man must live in the fear of his God. Obedience is the perfect religious act. On the contrary, sin is disobedience, breaking the Commandments. However, consciousness of precariousness does not exclude confidence in Yahweh or the joy engendered by the divine blessing. But the relations between God and man do not go beyond this stage; the *unio mystica* of the soul with its creator is unthinkable for the theology of the Old Testament. By recognizing him as the creator and absolute sovereign, man arrives at knowing at least certain predicates of God. Since the Law (*torah*) proclaims in detail the divine will, the essential thing is to obey the Commandments, that is, to behave in accordance with right or justice (*sedhek*). Man's religious ideal is to be "just," to know and respect the Law, the divine order. As the Prophet Micah reminds his hearers (6:8): "What is good has been explained to you, man; this is what Yahweh asks of you: only this, to act justly, to love tenderly, to walk humbly with your God." Sin brings loss of the blessing (*berâkhâh*). But since sin is part of the human condition, and because Yahweh, despite his strictness, is merciful, punishment is never final.

115. Job, the just man tried

One exegete has held that "the meeting of power and goodness summarizes the way in which the Old Testament conceives God."[11]

10. But the idea of resurrection was already prepared by theology (Yahweh's omnipotence) and by certain Canaanite beliefs and rites; see H. Riesenfeld, *The Resurrection in Ez. XXXVII*, pp. 5 ff.; Widengren, *Sakrales Königtum*, p. 46; Ringgren, *La religion d'Israël*, p. 261 (Eng. trans., p. 247).

11. A. Weiser, *Die Psalmen* (1950), p. 308, cited by Ringgren, *La religion d'Israel*, p. 137 (Eng. trans., p. 126).

It may be doubted if all readers of the Book of Job subscribe to this opinion. The story is tragically simple:[12] its subject is the affliction of a just man, of whom Yahweh was very proud. "Did you notice my servant Job?" God asks Satan, the celestial "accuser." "There is no one like him on earth: a sound and honest man who fears God and shuns evil" (Job 1:8). But Satan replies that Job's devotion is explained by his prosperity, that is, by the divine blessing. And Yahweh then allows the "accuser" to put his most faithful servant to the test. Job loses his children and his wealth, and, prostrated by "malignant ulcers from the sole of his foot to the top of his head," he sits down among the ashes. He laments, cursing the day he was born, but he does not revolt against God. Three friends come to him and in long speeches try to convince him that the simple fact that he *suffers*—hence, is being *punished*—proves his guilt. So he must recognize and confess his "sins." But Job rejects the explanation of his misfortune by the doctrine of retribution. He knows that man "cannot be in the right against God" (9:2), that Yahweh "destroys innocent and guilty alike" (9:22); yet, addressing God, he dares to say: "You know very well that I am innocent and that no one can rescue me from your hand" (10:7). He does not understand why God pursues his own creature so relentlessly (10:8–22), for Job has no doubt of the paltriness of every human existence: "Will you intimidate a wind-blown leaf, will you chase the dried-up chaff?" (13:25). But he is unable to identify the nature of his crime: "How many faults and crimes have I committed? What law have I transgressed, or in what have I offended?" (13:23).[13]

One of his friends blames him for using such language, for the creature is guilty by definition: "How can any man be clean? Born of woman, can he ever be good? In his own Holy Ones God puts no trust, and the heavens themselves are not, in his eyes, clean" (15:14–15). But Job repeats that, in his case, there has been a personal

12. The date of the redaction of the Book of Job is uncertain. Though the text as we know it seems to be postexilic, the content is old.

13. His inability to understand his guilt is the central theme of Job's laments. "Yet have I ever laid a hand on the poor when they cried out for justice in calamity? Have I not wept for all whose life is hard, felt pity for the penniless?" (30:24–25). "Have I been a fellow traveler with falsehood, or hastened my steps towards deceit?" (31:5). "Have I been insensible to poor men's needs, or let a widow's eyes grow dim? Or taken my share of bread alone, not giving a share to the orphan?" (31:16–17; cf. 31:19–34).

decision on the part of Yahweh, whose purpose escapes him (19:6–7). When another friend speaks to him of the punishment of sinners, Job reminds him that the wicked, who do not serve God, "live on" and prosper (21:7–16). If he knew how to reach him, he would argue the case before Yahweh, tell him of evil deeds left unpunished; but the Lord is far away, absent, invisible (23, 24). It is precisely because he does not abandon his faith and his confidence in God that Job declares: "I will maintain my innocence to my dying day. I take my stand on my integrity, I will not stir: my conscience gives me no cause to blush for my life" (27:5–6). Yet Job cries out to a God who does not answer: "I stand before you, but you take no notice. You have grown cruel in your dealings with me" (30:20–21).

A fourth friend, Elihu, "still young," breaks in violently. He is indignant that Job could have said: "I am clean, and sinless, I am pure, free of all fault" (33:9). For, Elihu declares, "God never does wrong, does not deflect the course of right" (34:12); he does not spurn the blameless man (36:5). After Elihu's long speech,[14] Yahweh's answer is disappointing in its impersonality. God speaks "from the heart of the tempest" (38:1), in a veritable theophany, but he ignores Job's questions. Yahweh contents himself with reminding Job of his omnipotence, his cosmic work, the complexity of the universe, the infinite variety of the manifestations of life. After calling to witness the great cosmic structures and the laws that govern the heavens and the earth, God speaks to him of the lions and wild goats and other creatures whose life and proliferation he insures, after having fashioned them, each with its particular form and characteristic behavior. And he concludes by apostrophizing him: "Has God's critic thought up an answer?" (40:2). Job vainly tries to take refuge in silence: "My words have been frivolous: what can I reply? I had better lay my finger on my lips" (40:4).

In a second speech, Yahweh describes to him at length the beast Behemoth and the monster Leviathan. In answer Job shows that he has understood the secret meaning of Yahweh's lesson: the very existence of the universe is a miracle, the Creator's mode of being defies comprehension, the purpose of his acts remains impenetrable. "I know that you are all powerful. . . . I am the man who obscured your designs with my empty-headed words. I have been holding

14. This speech appears to be an interpolation.

forth on matters I cannot understand, on marvels beyond me and my knowledge. . . . I knew you only by hearsay, but now, having seen you with my own eyes, I retract all I have said, and in dust and ashes I repent" (42:1–6). In the last analysis Job recognized that he was guilty toward God. Yahweh immediately restored him to his former situation and, indeed, doubled all his possessions, and Job lived on until he was a hundred and forty years old (42:7–17).

After three millennia this febrile, enigmatic, and disquieting book continues to fascinate. The fact that God allowed himself to be tempted by Satan still troubles many naïvely religious souls. However, Job understood the lesson well: if *everything* depends upon God, and if God is impenetrable, it is impossible to judge his acts, hence impossible to judge his attitude toward Satan. Yahweh's secret lesson goes beyond "the case of Job." It is addressed to all those who are unable to understand the presence—and the triumph—of evil in the world. In short, for the believer, the Book of Job *is* an explanation of evil and injustice, of imperfection and terror. Since everything is willed and governed by God, whatever befalls the believer is charged with religious meaning. But it would be vain—and at the same time impious—to believe that, without God's help, man is capable of grasping the "mystery of iniquity."

116. The time of the prophets

"A man who is now called a 'prophet' (*nâbî*) was formerly called a 'seer'" (1 Sam. 9:9). And in fact the institution of the "seer" (*rōʿêh*) of the nomadic period was modified, after the conquest, under the influence of the *nâbîim*, whom the Israelites had found in Palestine. About 1000 B.C., Yahwistic "seers" (such as Nathan) and the *nâbîim* still coexisted (1 Sam. 10:5). Gradually the two institutions fused, and the result was classic Old Testament prophecy. Like the *nâbîim*, the prophets were associated with sanctuaries and the cult and had ecstatic experiences.

Elijah and Elisha illustrate the period of transition, but their religious vocations and activities already announce classic prophecy. Elijah makes his appearance in the Northern Kingdom, under kings Ahab and Ahazias (874–850 B.C.). He revolts against Ahab's policy. Ahab wanted to integrate the Israelites and the Canaanites by giving them equal rights and encouraging religious syncretism with the cult of Baal or Malkart, a cult protected by Queen Jezebel, a native of Tyre. Elijah proclaims Yahweh sole sovereign in Israel. It is Yahweh, not Baal, who dispenses rain and insures the fertility of the country. In the famous episode on Mount Carmel, when he competes with the prophets of Baal to end a three-year drought, Elijah shows that the Canaanite god is powerless to light the sacrificial altar and hence to bring rain.[15] In addition, Elijah fulminates against King Ahab, who killed one of his subjects in order to get possession of his vineyard, and he predicts that he will die by violence (1 Kings 21). Elijah's posthumous fame brings him close to Moses. Legend has Yahweh snatch him up to heaven in a chariot of fire (2 Kings 2:2 ff.). The biography of Elisha, disciple and successor of Elijah, is full of marvelous episodes (see 2 Kings 2:19 ff., etc.). Unlike Elijah, Elisha assembled a group of prophets around him. But like Elijah, he took an active part in political life, communicated oracles to the king, and even went with him to war (2 Kings 3:11).

Aside from wandering diviners and visionaries, two categories of prophets are distinguished. The first group comprises the cult prophets. They live near the temples, take part in the rites with the priests,[16] and are court prophets, connected with the royal sanctuaries. Very often they predict a desired victory to the king (see, for example, 1 Kings 22). This category of professional prophets, whose numbers are large, also includes those who are considered false prophets in the Old Testament.

More important in the religious history of Israel is the second group, made up of the great prophets of Scripture, from Amos to the "Second Isaiah." These do not proclaim their message as members of a profession but as having a special vocation. They do not represent certain clans or certain sanctuaries or the king but declare themselves to be messengers of God.[17] Their vocation is decided by a direct call from Yahweh. As Jeremiah tells it: "the word of Yahweh was

---

15. The contest forms part of a religious war: just as Jezebel had ordered the massacre of the prophets of Yahweh, Elijah, after his victory, demands that the people seize the 450 prophets of Baal. He "took them down to the wadi Kishon, and he slaughtered them there" (1 Kings 18:40).

16. Examples of their discourses are found in Psalms 2, 21, 81, 110, and 132 and in the books of the prophets Nahum and Habakkuk.

17. See G. Fohrer, *History of the Israelite Religion*, pp. 237 ff., and the bibliographies given on pages 235 and 238, n. 2.

addressed to me, saying, 'Before I formed you in the womb I knew you; before you came to birth I consecrated you; I have appointed you as a prophet to the nations'" (Jer. 1:4 ff.). Isaiah, for his part, one day saw in the Temple "the Lord Yahweh seated on a high throne," surrounded by seraphim, and he heard his voice, saying: "Whom shall I send? Who will be our messenger?" Isaiah answered: "Here I am, send me." And God dictated to him what he was to say to the people (Isa. 6:1–10). The summons is obeyed, despite the opposition of audiences (Hos. 9:7; Ezek. 12:21 ff.), but sometimes the preaching is interrupted by force (Amos 7:10 ff.) or by the prophet himself, when he feels that he has failed in his mission (Isa. 8:16–18).

All the great prophets are sincerely and passionately convinced of the genuineness of their vocation and the urgency of their message. They do not doubt that they are proclaiming the very word of God, for they have felt Yahweh's hand, or his spirit (*rūaḥ*), upon them.[18] Their divine possession is sometimes manifested by ecstasy, though exaltation or an ecstatic trance do not seem to be indispensable.[19] Certain prophets were even accused of "madness" (like Hosea: "the prophet is mad, this inspired fellow is raving" [Hos. 9:7]), but we cannot speak of a true psychopathological disease. Rather, there are emotional shocks, brought on by the terrifying presence of God and the gravity of the mission the prophet has just assumed. The phenomenon is well known, from the "initiatory maladies" of shamans to the "madnesses" of the great mystics of all religions. In addition, like the "specialists in the sacred" of archaic and traditional societies, the prophets are endowed with faculties of divination[20] and display marvelous powers that are magical in nature: they restore the dead to life, feed multitudes with very small quantities of foodstuffs, make certain persons fall ill, etc.[21] A number of the acts performed by the prophets have a symbolic value: Elijah throws his

18. See S. Mowinckel, "The 'Spirit' and the 'Word' in the Pre-exilic Reforming Prophets"; A. Haldar, *Associations of Cult Prophets among the Ancient Semites*, pp. 115 ff.

19. See the bibliographies given by Ringgren, *La religion d'Israël*, p. 268, n. 1 (Eng. trans., p. 254, n. 19), and by Fohrer, p. 234, n. 17. Ecstasy was more frequent among the *nâbîim* (Fohrer, p. 234).

20. Elijah foresees the imminent death of King Ahaziah (2 Kings 3:16–17) and knows that the king has ordered him killed (2 Kings 6:32); he knows the words spoken by the king of Damascus in his bedchamber (ibid.).

21. See the examples cited by Fohrer, p. 233.

cloak over Elisha (1 Kings 19:19–21); obeying Yahweh's order, Jeremiah breaks an earthenware jug to illustrate the coming ruin of Israel (Jer. 19:10 ff.); he wears a yoke to persuade the people to submit to the king of Babylon (Jer. 27).[22]

But whatever the source of their inspiration was (dream, vision, audition, miraculous knowledge, etc.), it was always the word of Yahweh that the prophets received. These direct, personal revelations were obviously interpreted in the light of their profound faith and transmitted in accordance with certain traditional models. The preexilic prophets have it in common that they announce above all God's judgment against Israel: Yahweh will send ruthless conquerors to destroy it; the Lord will use the great military empires as instruments of punishment against his own people, which had betrayed him. It is possible also to decipher a promise of hope in this terrible judgment? Old Testament prophecy has been thought to represent a variant of the alternation, well known in the Near East, between times of misfortune and times of good fortune, but this schema does not seem to apply to all the cases alleged.[23] As we shall see (§ 118), the only hope lies in the "remnant" of the chosen people that will survive the catastrophe. It is with this remnant that Yahweh will make a new covenant.

117.   Amos the shepherd. Hosea the ill-loved

Amos was active as a preacher under the reign of Jeroboam II (782/780–753/46 B.C.). He was not a professional *nâbî*: "I was a shepherd, and looked after sycamores: but it was Yahweh who took me from herding the flock, and Yahweh who said, 'Go, prophesy to my people Israel'" (Amos 7:14–15). He announces that God will judge the neighboring peoples—Damascus, Gaza, and Philistia, Tyre and Phoenicia—who have sinned against morality. This implies that all nations are under the jurisdiction of Yahweh. However, Amos fulminates especially against Israel, the Kingdom of the North, against its social injustices and its religious infidelity. The rich "have sold the virtuous man for silver ... and trample on the heads of

22. Cf. G. Fohrer, *Die symbolische Handlungen der Propheten.*
23. See Ringgren, p. 271 (Eng. trans., p. 257).

ordinary people" (2:6–7). But their wealth will be destroyed (4:7–11). Vainly do these surfeited sinners multiply sacrifices. Amos hears and repeats Yahweh's words: "I hate and despise your feasts. I take no pleasure in your solemn festivals. When you offer me holocausts, I reject your oblations" (5:21 ff.). It is integrity and justice that God expects of his worshipers (5:24–25).

Then, too, the cult had been corrupted by the introduction of Canaanite orgiastic elements (5:26; 8:14). A mere outward show of veneration for the holy places is useless: "Go to Bethel, and sin, to Gilgal, and sin your hardest!" (4:4). Only a return to the faith can save: "Seek good and not evil so that you may live, and that Yahweh, God of Sabaoth, may really be with you. It may be that Yahweh will take pity on the remnant of Joseph" (5:14–15).[24]

Like Amos, Hosea, his younger contemporary, preaches in the Kingdom of the North. His vocation and the meaning of his prophetic message seem to be linked with the vicissitudes of his marriage. But the interpretation of some allusions in the text of his discourses is very much in dispute. According to his first account (Hosea 1:2–9), Yahweh ordered him to marry a "woman given to prostitution," who bore children to whom he gave symbolic names—"Unloved" and "No-People-of-Mine"—in order publicly to proclaim that Yahweh no longer loved Israel and that Israel was no longer his people. According to the second account (3:1–5), Yahweh told him to contract another marriage, this time with a "woman loved by her husband but an adulteress in spite of it, just as Yahweh gives his love to the children of Israel though they turn to other gods." Probably the first wife was a woman who had taken part in Canaanite fertility rites. As for the second, chosen despite her unsavory past, she would indicate the benevolent attitude of Yahweh, ready to forgive Israel.

In any case, Hosea's proclamation is dominated by God's bitterness over his betrayal by his people. Israel was the spouse of Yahweh, but she was unfaithful to him; she has become "prostituted," in other words, has abandoned herself to the Canaanite fertility gods.

24. The oracles of restoration and paradisal fecundity that end the work (Amos 9:11–15) contrast so strongly with the oft-repeated condemnation that their genuineness may be doubted; see Ringgren, *La religion d'Israël*, p. 280: however, von Rad considers them authentic (*Old Testament Theology*, vol. 2, p. 138).

Israel does not know that fertility is a gift from Yahweh. "She said: 'I am going to court my lovers who give me my bread and water, my wool, my flax, my oil and my drink.' She would not acknowledge, not she, that I was the one who was giving her the corn, the wine, the oil, and who freely gave her that silver and gold of which they have made Baals" (2:7–10). We find again, now exacerbated, the irreducible conflict between Baal and Yahweh, between a religion that is cosmic in structure and fidelity to one God, creator of the world and master of history.

Tirelessly, Hosea attacks the syncretism Baal-Yahweh. "They renounce their God to play the whore. They offer sacrifice on the mountain tops, burn their offerings on the hills, under oak and pine and terebinth" (4:12–13). Israel has forgotten its history: "When Israel was a child I loved him, and I called my son out of Egypt. But the more I called to them, the further they went from me" (11:1–2). The anger provoked by this incorrigible ingratitude bursts out. The punishment will be terrible: "Very well, I will be a lion to-them, a leopard lurking by the way; like a bear robbed of her cubs I will pounce on them, and tear the flesh round their hearts; the dogs shall eat their flesh, and wild beasts tear them to pieces" (13:7–9).

The purely external cult is useless, "since what I want is love, not sacrifice; knowledge of God, not holocausts" (6:6). The high places, where the syncretistic ceremonies are celebrated, will be destroyed (10:8). The only salvation is a sincere return to Yahweh. "Israel, come back to Yahweh your God; your iniquity was the cause of your downfall. Say to him, 'Take all iniquity away so that we may have happiness again'" (14:2–3). Hosea is conscious of the fact that their fall does not allow sinners to "return to their God" (5:4). However, Yahweh's love is stronger than his anger. "I will not give rein to my fierce anger ... for I am God, not man: I am the Holy One in your midst and have no wish to destroy" (11:9). He wants to lead Israel "into the wilderness and speak to her heart. . . . There she will respond to me as she did when she was young, as she did when she came out of the land of Egypt. When that day comes . . . , she will call me 'My husband' . . . I will betroth you to myself for ever, betroth you with integrity and justice, with tenderness and love" (2:16–21). It will be a return to the beginnings of the mystical marriage of Yahweh and Israel. This conjugal love already announces belief in redemption: the grace of God does not wait for man's conversion but precedes it.[25] We add that this conjugal symbolism will be used by all the great prophets after Hosea.

118.   Isaiah: "A remnant of Israel" will return

Despite the similarity of their vocations, each of the great prophets of Scripture is distinguished by his style of existence, by the way in which he assumes his destiny. Isaiah saw and heard God in the Temple of Jerusalem in 746 or 740. His wife was also a prophetess, and, like the professional *nâbîim*, he had disciples.[26] He gave his last discourse in 701.

At first, Isaiah chiefly criticizes the moral and social situation of the kingdoms of Judah and Israel. He does not hesitate to attack even the king and the high officials (Isaiah 3:12–15). He announces that the judgment of God will spare no one (2:12–17). Like his predecessors, he declares that the cult does not suffice: "What are your endless sacrifices to me? says Yahweh. I am sick of holocausts of rams and the fat of calves. The blood of bulls and of goats revolts me" (1:11). Prayer is vain, for "your hands are covered with blood" (1:15). The only true devotion consists in practicing justice and doing good: "Learn to do good, search for justice, be just to the orphan, plead for the widow" (1:17).

The Assyrian attack on Syria and Palestine introduces a new element into Isaiah's preaching. The prophet sees in these grave military and political events the intervention of Yahweh in history:

25. Cf. Fohrer, *History of the Israelite Religion*, p. 250 and note 17 (bibliography). Paradoxically, the conjugal imagery used by Hosea draws upon the Canaanite fertility cult that he opposes; see Ringgren, p. 283 (Eng. trans., p. 269). But see André Neher, *L'essence du prophétisme*, pp. 247 ff., on the "existential" meaning of conjugal symbolism in Hebraic religious thought. Translation of mystical experience into terms of conjugal union will be taken up again in the Jewish and Christian interpretations of the Song of Songs and, especially, in the mystical theology of the Counter Reformation. In contrast, in Vaiṣṇava mysticism the mystical union between the soul and God is illustrated by the adulterous love between Rādhā and Kṛṣṇa.

26. It is important to point out that only the first thirty-nine chapters of the book that bears his name belong to him. The rest is made up of various oracles that are not earlier than the sixth century; the most important of them are the "Deutero-Isaiah" (chaps. 40–55) and the "Trito-Isaiah" (chaps. 56–66). A certain number of fragments were introduced into the Book of Isaiah still later (for example, the apocalypse of chaps. 24–27).

Assyria is only his instrument. For Isaiah, it is a case of divine vengeance; Yahweh is punishing the religious infidelity that has flowed like a torrent from social injustice and the collapse of moral values. This is why he opposes the king's foreign policy. Coalitions and political maneuvers are chimerical. There is but one hope: faith and confidence in Yahweh. "If you do not stand by me, you will not stand at all" (7:9b). It is faith in Yahweh, and not Egypt, that can help (31:1–3). To encourage the king, Isaiah announces a "sign from the Lord" : "The maiden is with child and soon will give birth to a son whom she will call Immanuel" (7:14). Before the child "knows how to refuse evil and choose good," Yahweh will perform many prodigies (7:16 ff.). This oracle has inspired countless interpretations.[27] Christian theological speculation has seen in the child's name, Immanuel ("God with us"), the announcement of the birth of Christ. In any case, the messianic meaning is obvious: Yahweh will raise up in the line of David a just king who will be victorious and whose descendants will reign forever.

When the king of Assur invades Palestine, Isaiah declares that he is no longer Yahweh's instrument but simply a tyrant with an insatiable lust for power (10:5–15). Consequently, he too will be destroyed (14:24–25). The prophet returns tirelessly to the power and sovereignty of God, and he announces the "day of Yahweh," when the Lord will judge the world (2:12–17). This is why he condemns not only the arrogance of the king of Assur but also the social and political sins of Judah—oppression of the poor (3:12–15), luxury (3:16–24), and debauchery (5:11–13), injustice (5:1–7, 23), the stealing of fields (5:8–10)—sins which he regards as so many acts of rebellion against Yahweh (1:2–3). He also condemns bad rulers (28:14–22) and the priests and cult prophets who mock him (28:7–13).

Isaiah believes in the invulnerability of Zion: the holy mountain has been and will be protected by Yahweh against the assaults of all enemies (14:24–32; 17:2–14; 29:1–8; etc.). He also keeps the hope of "a remnant of Israel" that "will return to the mighty God" (10:20–21).[28] But the essence of his message was not obeyed, and the

---

27. The essential bibliography is in Ringgren, *La religion d'Israël*, p. 286, n. 1 (Eng. trans., p. 272, n. 74); to this, add A. Neher, *L'essence du prophétisme*, pp. 228 ff.

28. Isaiah gives his first son the name Shear-jashub, "a remnant will return."

prophet does not hide his disillusion. His last discourse predicts the ruin of "the pleasant fields, the fruitful vine"; on "all the happy houses, on the gay city," thorns and briars will grow, "for the palace has been abandoned and the noisy city deserted" (32:9-14).

119. The promise made to Jeremiah

Descended from a priestly family, Jeremiah assumed his vocation in 626 and pursued it, with interruptions, for four decades. In a famous passage he relates the circumstances of his election (Jer. 1:1 ff.). Hesitating before the task laid upon him, he pleaded his youth: "I do not know how to speak: I am a child" (1:6). But the Lord touched his mouth and strengthened him (1:9 ff.). Jeremiah's first discourses are dominated by a particularly dramatic theme: the imminent catastrophe caused by "a people coming from the land of the North": "They are armed with bow and spear, they are cruel and pitiless" (6:22-23). It would be useless to seek for the historical model for these savage horsemen. The "people coming from the land of the North" takes its place among the mythological images of total destruction. For the invasion will bring the final ruin of the country: "I looked to the earth, to see a formless waste; to the heavens, and their light had gone" (4:23). Reduction to chaos will be the divine punishment for religious infidelity; yet it prepares a new creation, the New Covenant that Jeremiah will later proclaim. For Yahweh is merciful, and the prophet transmits his summons: "Come back, disloyal sons, I want to heal your disloyalty" (3:22; cf. 4:1 ff.).

On the death of King Josiah in 609, his son Jehoiakim succeeded him on the throne. He proved to be an odious despot, and Jeremiah did not hesitate to attack him. Standing at the gate of the Temple, he fulminates against all those—priests, prophets, people—who let themselves be deceived by the illusory security of their religious activity (7:1-15; 26:1 ff.). "Put no trust in delusive words like these: This is the sanctuary of Yahweh" (7:5). It is in vain that those who have stolen, killed, committed adultery, perjured themselves, burned incense to Baal run to the Temple, saying: "Now we are safe!", since they are ready to "go on committing these abominations." For Yahweh is not blind (7:9-11). The Lord reminds them of the fate of the sanctuary of Shiloh, destroyed by the Philistines: there "at first I gave my name a home; see what I have done to it because of the wickedness of my people Israel!" (7:12–13). Jeremiah was arrested, and, but for the protection of certain high officials, he would probably have been condemned to death (26:10 ff.). For a long time the prophet could not speak in public.[29]

The last stage of Jeremiah's preaching began in 595, when Nebuchadnezzar conquered Jerusalem and deported part of the Judean elite. While the new king, Zedekiah, was preparing a revolt with the help of Egypt, Jeremiah attempted to calm the people. Arrested and imprisoned as a traitor, he was later freed by the Babylonians. Soon afterward he left for Egypt with a group of fellow countrymen who were expatriating themselves (chaps. 37–39). He addressed his last discourse to "all the Jews living in the land of Egypt" (44:1). Through his prophet, the Lord rehearsed all the recent catastrophes: "You have seen all the misery I have brought down on Jerusalem and the towns of Judah; today they lie in ruins and uninhabited" (44:2). Vainly did God send his "servants the prophets"; the people persevered in their wickedness (44:4 ff.). To conclude, Yahweh announces yet another destruction: the "remnant of Judah," who had settled in Egypt, will likewise be annihilated (44:12 ff.).

One of the characteristics of Jeremiah's message is the large number of confessions and references to his personal feelings.[30] He dares to say to God: "Do you mean to be for me a deceptive stream with inconstant waters?" (15:18). Like Job, he asks: "Why is it that the wicked live so prosperously? Why do scoundrels enjoy peace?" (12:1). He wants to understand the ways of the Lord.[31] Yet despite the catastrophes that he predicts, and which in fact occur, Jeremiah does not lose confidence in redemption, even in a new Creation. Like a potter, Yahweh can destroy his work, but he is able to make a new one and a better (18:6 ff.). And indeed, through his prophet,

29. At Yahweh's bidding, Jeremiah consigned his prophecies of misfortune to a book. One day his servant, Baruch, wanted to read some parts of it in the Temple, but he was arrested and taken before the king, who burned the scroll. However, Jeremiah dictated a new book (Jer. 36).

30. See, especially, Jer. 11:18–23, 12:1–6, 15:10–12, 17:12–18, 18:18–23, and 20:7–18. See also Ringgren, *La religion d'Israël*, p. 295 and the bibliographies in notes 2 and 3 (Eng. trans., p. 281 and nn. 97–98).

31. Cf. von Rad, *Old Testament Theology*, vol. 2, pp. 203 ff.

God announces a New Covenant: "See, the days are coming when I will make a new covenant with the House of Israel (and the House of Judah). . . . Deep within them I will plant my Law, writing it on their hearts. Then I will be their God and they shall be my people" (31:31, 33).

Amos expected the redemption from a new act of love on the part of God which would make it possible for Israel to return "to the days of its youth." Jeremiah dares to hope for a radical regeneration of man. For, "Well you know, Yahweh, the course of man is not in his control" (10:23). That is why the Lord promises the coming regeneration of his people. "I will give them a different heart and a different behavior so that they will always fear me, for the good of themselves, and their children after them. I will make an everlasting covenant with them; I will not cease in my efforts for their good" (32:39–40). This is equivalent to a new creation of man, an idea which will have considerable consequences (among others, the Christian conception of a New Covenant revealed in the New Testament).[32]

120. The fall of Jerusalem. The mission of Ezekiel

"The kings of the earth never believed, nor did all the inhabitants of the world, that oppressor and enemy would ever penetrate the gates of Jerusalem" (Lamentations 4:12). So exclaims the anonymous author of Lamentations, who witnessed the fall of Jerusalem in 587. "Look, Yahweh, and consider: whom have you ever treated like this? Why, women have eaten their little ones, the children they have nursed in their arms! Why, priest and prophet have been slaughtered in the sanctuary of Yahweh!" (2:20). The catastrophe had decisive consequences for the history of Israel and for the development of Yahwism. The fall of the political and religious capital meant the disappearance of the state and the end of the Davidic monarchy. The Temple was burned and ruined, which entailed the cessation of sacrifices. A large part of the population was deported. But Babylon was an impure country, where the cult could

32. The expectation of an ideal king forms part of the same hope for a New Covenant: "I will let him come freely into my presence and he can come close to me" (Jer. 20:21).

not be practiced. The place of the Temple was taken by the religious school, which, in the course of time, will become the synagogue; here the community gathered periodically for prayers, hymns, and homilies. But the destruction of the Temple was a constant reminder of the disappearance of the nation. That is why prayer for the restoration of national independence was inseparable from prayer for the rebuilding of the Temple.[33]

Many were those who, at Jerusalem or in exile, doubted the power of Yahweh and adopted the gods of the conquerors. Some even doubted Yahweh's existence. But for others the catastrophe was the supreme proof of the Lord's wrath, tirelessly foretold by the prophets. There was an indignant reaction against "optimistic prophets." On the other hand, the great Scriptural prophets gained the esteem and admiration of which they had been deprived in their lifetimes. However, the elite that had been deported to Babylon will look elsewhere in the religious tradition for the support capable of safeguarding Israel (see volume 2).

It was in Babylon, where he arrived with a first group of deportees in 597, that the last great prophet, Ezekiel, carried out his ministry until 571. He was a priest, which explains the importance he attached to ritual purity. For Ezekiel, sins—and first of all idolatry—had made Israel unclean. Yahweh would bring about the redemption of his people by cleansing them with "clean water" (Ezek. 36:25).[34] In the beginning Ezekiel considered his task an ungrateful but indispensable work of demystification: it was necessary to destroy the hopes that the first Judean deportees held for the invulnerability of Jerusalem and, later, to comfort them after the destruction of the holy city.[35] In this first period of his preaching, Ezekiel announced the coming end of Jerusalem, the ineluctable consequence of Israel's infidelity. An allegorical story (chap. 23) compares Israel and Samaria (Judah) to two sisters who, though they were loved by Yahweh, "became prostitutes in Egypt when they were but girls" and continued their infidelities with the Assyrians and the Babylonians.

33. The author of Psalm 51 implores God to cleanse and free him and, at the same time, to "rebuild the walls of Jerusalem." "Then there will be proper sacrifice to please you" (Ps. 51:20–21).

34. Von Rad, *Old Test. Theol.*, vol. 2, pp. 224 ff.; Ringgren, *La religion d'Israël*, p. 300 (Eng. trans., p. 284).

35. See Fohrer, *Die Hauptprobleme des Buches Ezechiel*, passim, and his *History of the Israelite Religion*, pp. 317 ff.

Ezekiel constantly returns to the theme of the unfaithful woman whom Yahweh nevertheless was slow to abandon out of respect for his name (see, e.g., Ezek. 20). Israel's privileged situation is in no way due to merit; it is Yahweh's choice that has singled Israel out among other peoples. But more significant than the interpretation of the historical catastrophe as a crisis in the conjugal union of God and Israel is the idea of Yahweh's omnipresence. The presence of God is not confined to a certain privileged space. Hence it matters little if the believer worships Yahweh in his native country or in a strange land. What matters is his inner life and his conduct to his fellow men. More than any other prophet, Ezekiel addresses the individual.[36]

The fall of Jerusalem sees the beginning of a new period in Ezekiel's preaching, characterized by hope for the redemption of Israel. For God, nothing is impossible. In ecstasy, Ezekiel sees a "valley full of bones"; touched by the spirit, the skeletons "returned to life and stood up on their feet." So will the Lord do with the House of Israel (37:1–14). In other words, though Israel was dead, it could be resuscitated by a divine prodigy. In another oracle (chap. 36) Yahweh promises the return of the deportees, the reconstruction and proliferation of the people. But above all he announces the redemption of Israel: "I shall pour clean water over you and you will be cleansed. . . . I shall give you a new heart, and put a new spirit in you. . . . I shall make you keep my laws and sincerely respect my observances. You will live in the land which I gave your ancestors. You shall be my people and I will be your God" (36:25–28). As Jeremiah, too, held, there will be a New Covenant, and in fact a new creation. But since the dispersal of Israel raised a question of the Lord's omnipotence and honor, Ezekiel explains this new creation by Yahweh's desire to sanctify his "holy name, which the House of Israel has profaned among the nations" (36:21). David, prince and shepherd, exemplary "servant" of God, will reign over the new Israel (37:25 ff.; 34:23 ff.). And in the last chapters (40–48), Ezekiel gives a detailed description of the future Temple (whose image he sees in ecstasy) and of the cult as it is to be celebrated in the new Israel.[37]

36. Cf. Fohrer, *History*, p. 319, and the bibliography given in his note 4.
37. Ezekiel's ecstatic vision constitutes the starting point for the "theology of the Temple," which will have a magnificent development in both Judaism and Christianity.

121.   Religious valorization of the "terror of history"

The prophets do not disappear in the last years of the Exile and the postexilic period (see volume 2). But their message develops what could be called the "theology of salvation" outlined by Jeremiah. So it is legitimate at this point to estimate the role of prophecy in the religious history of Israel.

What strikes us first about the prophets is their criticism of the cult and the ferocity with which they attack syncretism, that is, Canaanite influences, what they call "prostitution." But this "prostitution," against which they never cease to fulminate, represents one of the most widespread forms of cosmic religiosity. Specifically characteristic of agriculturalists, cosmic religiosity continued the most elementary dialectic of the sacred, especially the belief that the divine is incarnated, or manifests itself, in cosmic objects and rhythms. Now such a belief was denounced by the adherents of Yahweh as the worst possible idolatry, and this ever since the Israelites' entrance into Palestine. But never was cosmic religiosity so savagely attacked. The prophets finally succeeded in emptying nature of any divine presence. Whole sectors of the natural world—the "high places," stones, springs, trees, certain crops, certain flowers—will be denounced as unclean because they were polluted by the cult of the Canaanite divinities of fertility.[38] The preeminently clean and holy region is the desert alone, for it is there that Israel remained faithful to its God. The sacred dimension of vegetation and, in general, of the exuberant epiphanies of nature will be rediscovered only late, in medieval Judaism.

The cult, and first of all blood sacrifices, was also criticized; not only was it corrupted by Canaanite elements, but priests and people alike considered ritual activity to be the perfect form of worship. But, the prophets proclaimed, it is in vain to seek Yahweh in sanctuaries; God scorns sacrifices, festivals, and ceremonies (see, inter alia, Amos 5:4–6, 14–15, 21–23); he demands uprightness and justice (5:24). The preexilic prophets never defined what the cult activity of the believer should be. The problem did not even arise so long as the people did not return to Yahweh. The prophets did not pursue

38. For the same reason, the Christian missionaries in India admitted into their churches only flowers that were not used in Hindu ceremonies, that is, the least beautiful flowers.

the reform of the cult but the transformation of men.[39] It is not until after the fall of Jerusalem that Ezekiel proposes a revised divine office.

Desacralization of nature, devalorization of cult activity, in short, the violent and total rejection of cosmic religiosity, and, above all, the decisive importance attributed to spiritual regeneration of the individual by a definitive return to Yahweh were the response of the prophets to the historical crises that threatened the very existence of the two Jewish kingdoms. The danger was great and immediate. The "joy in life" that is bound up with every cosmic religion was not only an apostasy, it was illusory, bound to disappear in the imminent national catastrophe. The traditional forms of cosmic religion, i.e., the mystery of fertility, the dialectic solidarity between life and death, henceforth offered only a false security. Indeed, cosmic religion encouraged the illusion that life does not cease to go on and hence that the nation and the state can survive, despite the gravity of historical crises. In other words, not only the people and the high officials but also the priests and the optimistic prophets tended to assimilate adversities on the historical plane with natural catastrophes (droughts, floods, epidemics, earthquakes, etc.). Now such catastrophes are never total or final. But the preexilic prophets announced not only the ruin of the country and the disappearance of the state; they also proclaimed the danger of total annihilation of the nation.

The prophets reacted against the official political optimism and attacked the Davidic monarchy for having encouraged syncretism instead of setting up Yahwism as the state religion. The "future" that they announced was in fact imminent. The prophets never ceased to predict it, in order to change the present by bringing about an inner transformation of the faithful. Their passionate interest in contemporary politics was religious in nature. In fact, the march of events was capable of forcing the sincere conversion of the nation and hence its "salvation," the only possibility for the survival of Israel in history. Fulfillment of the predictions uttered by the prophets confirmed their message and, particularly, the conception that historical events were the work of Yahweh. In other words, historical events acquired a religious meaning, were transformed into "negative theophanies," into the "wrath" of Yahweh. In this way they

39. See Fohrer, *History of the Israelite Religion*, p. 278.

unveiled an inner consistency by proving to be the concrete expression of a single divine will.

Thus, for the first time, the prophets *valorized history*. Historical events will thenceforth have a value in themselves, since they are determined by the will of God. Historical facts thus become "situations" of man face to face with God and, as such, acquire a religious value that nothing thitherto could bestow on them. Hence it is true to say that the Hebrews were the first to discover the meaning of history as an epiphany of God, and this conception, as was to be expected, was taken up again and amplified by Christianity.[40] But we must add that the discovery of history as theophany was not immediately and wholly accepted by the Jewish people; the ancient conceptions will survive for a very long time.

40. See Eliade, *Cosmos and History*, pp. 102 ff. On the "salvation" of time, its "valorization" in the framework of Israelite sacred history, see ibid., pp. 104 ff.

15 Dionysus, or Bliss Recovered

122. Epiphanies and occultations of a "twice-born" god

After more than a century of research, Dionysus still remains an enigma. By his origin, by his particular mode of being, by the type of religious experience that he inaugurates, he stands apart from the other great Greek gods. According to the myth, he is the son of Zeus and a princess, Semele, daughter of Cadmus, king of Thebes. Jealous, Hera sets a trap for her—and Semele demands of Zeus that he let her see him in his true form of a celestial god. The presumptuous princess is struck by Zeus's thunderbolt and gives birth prematurely. But Zeus sews the infant into his thigh, and, after some months, Dionysus comes into the world. So he is, indeed, the "twice-born." Numerous origin myths make the founders of royal families spring from the union of gods with mortal women. But Dionysus is born for the second time from Zeus. It is for this reason that, among the offspring of such unions, he alone is a god.[1]

Kretschmer attempted to explain the name Semele by the Thraco-Phrygian word designating the earth goddess, and this etymology has been accepted by such eminent scholars as Nilsson and Wilamowitz. Correct or not, the etymology does not help toward understanding the myth. In the first place, it is hard to conceive a *hieros gamos* between the celestial god and Mother Earth that ends in the destruction of the latter by fire. On the other hand, and this is essential, the earliest mythological traditions emphasize this fact: *a mortal woman*,[2] Semele, gave birth to a *god*. It was this paradoxical

1. Pindar, frag. 85; Herodotus 2. 146; Euripides, *Bacchae* 92 ff.; Apollodorus, *Bibl.* 3. 4. 3, etc.
2. *Iliad* 14. 323 calls her "a woman of Thebes," and Hesiod, *Theogony* 940 ff., a "mortal woman."

duality of Dionysus that interested the Greeks, for it alone could explain the paradox of his particular mode of being.

Born of a mortal woman, Dionysus did not by right belong to the pantheon of the Olympians; yet he succeeded in getting himself accepted and, in the end, also introduced his mother, Semele. As many references show, Homer knew him, but neither he nor his audience was interested in the "foreign" god, so different from the Olympians. Yet it is to Homer that we owe the earliest testimony concerning Dionysus. The *Iliad* (6. 128–40) refers to a celebrated episode: the Thracian hero Lycurgus pursues the nursing mothers of Dionysus, "and, all together, they threw the instruments of their cult to the ground," while the god, "filled with terror, leaped into the waves of the sea, and Thetis received him in her bosom trembling: for terrible dread had seized him when the warriors shouted." But Lycurgus "drew down on himself the wrath of the gods," and Zeus blinded him, and he did not live long, for he "was hated of all the immortal gods."

In this episode, which includes a pursuit by a "man-wolf" and a dive into the sea, we can decipher the memory of an ancient initiatory scenario.[3] However, at the time when Homer evokes it, the meaning and intention of the myth are different. It shows us one of the specific characteristics of Dionysus' destiny: his "persecution" by antagonistic personages. But the myth further testifies to the fact that Dionysus is recognized to be a member of the divine family, for not only Zeus, his father, but all the other gods feel offended by Lycurgus' action.

This "persecution" dramatically expresses the resistance against the god's mode of being and his religious message. Perseus advanced with his army against Dionysus and the "sea-women" who accompanied him; according to one tradition, he threw the god into the bottom of the Lernaean lake (Plutarch, *De Iside* 35). We shall encounter the theme of persecution again when we analyze the *Bacchae* of Euripides. There have been attempts to interpret such episodes as mythicized recollections of the opposition encountered by the Dionysiac cult. The underlying theory presupposes that Dionysus arrived in Greece comparatively late—that he is, by implication, a "foreign" god. After Erwin Rohde, the majority

3. See H. Jeanmaire, *Dionysos*, p. 76; on Lycurgus and puberty initiations, see Jeanmaire, *Couroï et Courètes*, pp. 463 ff.

of scholars regarded Dionysus as a Thracian god, introduced into Greece either directly from Thrace or from Phrygia. But Walter Otto emphasized the archaic and Panhellenic character of Dionysus, and the fact that his name—*di-wo-nu-so-jo*—is found in a Mycenaean inscription[4] seems to confirm his hypothesis. It is nevertheless true that Herodotus considered that Dionysus was "introduced late"; and in Euripides' *Bacchae* (line 219) Pentheus speaks of "this late-come god, whoever he may be."

Whatever the history of the penetration of the Dionysiac cult into Greece may have been, the myths and mythological fragments that refer to the opposition it encountered have a more profound meaning: they inform us concerning both the Dionysiac religious experience and the particular structure of the god. Dionysus was bound to incite resistance and persecution, for the religious experience that he inspired threatened an entire life-style and a universe of values. There was certainly a threat to the supremacy of the Olympian religion and its institutions. But the opposition was also the expression of a more intimate drama, and one that is abundantly documented in the history of religions: resistance to every *absolute* religious experience, because such experience can be realized only by denying *everything else* (by whatever term this may be designated: equilibrium, personality, consciousness, reason, etc.).

Walter Otto has well perceived the solidarity between the theme of the "persecution" of Dionysus and the typology of his many and various epiphanies. Dionysus is a god who shows himself suddenly and then disappears mysteriously. At the Agriona festivals of Chaeronea, the women sought him in vain and came back with the news that the god had gone to the home of the Muses, who had hidden him (Otto, *Dionysos*, p. 79). He disappears by diving to the bottom of Lerna or into the sea, and he reappears—as in the Anthesteria festival—in a ship on the waves. Allusions to his "awakening" in his cradle (Otto, pp. 82 ff.) point to the same mythical theme. These periodical epiphanies and occultations place Dionysus among the gods of vegetation.[5] And in fact he shows a

4. On a fragment in Linear B from Pylos (X a O 6).
5. Attempts have been made to see in Dionysus a tree god or a god of grain or the vine, and the myth of his dismemberment has been interpreted as illustrating the "passion" of cereals or the preparation of wine (already in the mythographers cited by Diodorus Siculus 3. 62).

certain solidarity with the life of plants: ivy and the pine became almost his attributes, and his most popular festivals coincide with the agricultural calendar. But Dionysus is related to the totality of life, as is shown by his relations with water and germination, blood or sperm, and by the excess of vitality manifested in his animal epiphanies (bull, lion, goat).[6] His unexpected manifestations and disappearances in a way reflect the appearance and occultation of life—that is, the alternation of life and death and, in the last analysis, their unity. But this is no "objective" observation of that cosmic phenomenon, whose banality could inspire no religious idea and produce no myth. By his epiphanies and his occultations, Dionysus reveals the mystery, and the sacrality, of the conjunction of life and death. This revelation is religious in nature, since it is effected by the actual presence of the god. For these appearances and disappearances are not always connected with the seasons. Dionysus shows himself in winter, and he disappears at the same spring festival at which he has his most triumphant epiphany.

Disappearance, occultation are mythological expressions of the descent to Hades, hence of death. And indeed, the tomb of Dionysus was shown at Delphi; he was also said to have died at Argos. Then too, when, in the Argive ritual, Dionysus is called up from the depths of the sea (Plutarch, *De Iside* 35), it is from the land of the dead that he rises. According to an Orphic hymn (no. 53), when Dionysus is absent, he is considered to be with Persephone. Finally, the myth of Zagreus-Dionysus, which we shall discuss further on, relates the violent death of the god, killed, dismembered, and devoured by the Titans.

These various but complementary aspects of Dionysus are still perceptible in his public rituals, despite their inevitable "purifications" and reinterpretations.

123. The archaism of some public festivals

From the time of Pisistratus, four festivals in honor of Dionysus were celebrated at Athens.[7] The Rural Dionysia, which took place

6. See the texts and references discussed by W. Otto, *Dionysos*, pp. 162–64.
7. The fact that two of these festivals bear the names of the months that correspond to them—Lenaeon and Anthesterion—proves their archaism and their panhellenic character.

in December, were village festivals. A large phallus was carried in procession, a numerous crowd accompanying it with songs. Essentially an archaic ceremony, and widely disseminated throughout the world, the phallophoria certainly preceded the cult of Dionysus. Other ritual diversions included competitions and contests and, above all, parades of maskers or persons disguised as animals. Here too the rites preceded Dionysus, but it is understandable how the god of wine came to lead the procession of maskers.

We are much less well informed concerning the Lenaea, celebrated in midwinter. A quotation from Heraclitus states that the word *Lenai* and the verb "to perform the *Lenai*" were used as equivalents to "Bacchants" and "to play the Bacchant." The god was invoked with the assistance of the *daidouchos*. According to a gloss on a verse of Aristophanes, the Eleusinian priest, "torch in hand, utters: 'Call the god!' and the hearers cry: 'Son of Semele, Iacchus,[8] giver of riches!'"

The Anthesteria were celebrated in approximately February/ March, and the Greater Dionysia, instituted later, in March/April. Thucydides (2. 15. 4) regarded the Anthesteria as the earliest festival of Dionysus. It was also the most important. The first day was called Pithoegia, the opening of the earthenware jars (*pithoi*) in which the wine had been kept since the autumn harvest. The casks were conveyed to the sanctuary of Dionysus in the Marsh to make libations to the god, and then the new wine was tasted. The second day (called Choës, the "jugs") saw a contest of drinkers: they were supplied with a jug full of wine and at a given signal swallowed the contents as fast as possible. Like certain competitions at the Rural Dionysia (for example, the *askoliasmos*, in which young men tried to keep their balance as long as possible on an oiled wineskin), this competition also fits into the well-known scenario of competitions and jousts of every kind (in sports, oratory, etc.) that promote the renovation of life.[9] But euphoria and intoxication in a way anticipate life in a beyond that does not resemble the gloomy Homeric other-world.

8. The genius of the processions of the Eleusinian Mysteries, Iacchus, was assimilated to Dionysus; the sources are discussed by W. Otto, *Dionysos*, p. 80; cf. Jeanmaire, *Dionysos*, p. 47.

9. This is, of course, an extremely archaic scenario that is universally disseminated; one of the most important inheritances from prehistory, it still holds a privileged place in all types of societies.

The day of the Choës was also the occasion for a procession representing the god's entrance into the city. Since he was believed to arrive from the sea, the procession included a boat borne on four chariot wheels and carrying Dionysus holding a vine and, with him, two satyrs playing flutes. The procession, made up of numerous participants, probably disguised, and a sacrificial bull, preceded by a flute-player and garland-bearers, made its way to the Lenaeum, an ancient sanctuary open only on that day. There various ceremonies took place, in which the *basilinna*, "the queen," that is, the wife of the king-archon, and four ladies-in-waiting took part. From this moment, the basilinna, heiress of the city's ancient queens, was regarded as the spouse of Dionysus. She rode beside him in the cart, and a new procession, of the nuptial type, made its way to the Boucoleum, the old royal residence. Aristotle states that it is in the boucoleum (literally, "ox stable") that the hierogamy between the god and the queen was consummated (*Ath. Pol.* 3. 5). The choice of the Boucoleum indicates that the taurine epiphany of Dionysus was still familiar.

Attempts have been made to interpret this union in a symbolic sense, and the god has been supposed to have been impersonated by the archon. But Walter Otto rightly emphasizes the importance of Aristotle's testimony.[10] The basilinna receives the god in the house of her husband, heir to the kings—and Dionysus reveals himself as a king. Probably this union symbolizes the marriage of the god to the entire city, with the auspicious consequences that can be imagined. But it is an act characteristic of Dionysus, a divinity whose epiphanies are brutal and who demands that his supremacy be publicly proclaimed. We know of no other Greek cult in which a god is believed to unite himself with the queen.

But the three days of the Anthesteria, especially the second day, that of Dionysus' triumph, are days of ill omen, for the souls of the dead return and, with them, the *kēres*, bearers of maleficent influences from the infernal world. In addition, the last day of the Anthesteria was dedicated to them. Prayers were offered for the dead, a *pan-*

10. The union is completely different from the one, for example, of Bel at Babylon (the company of a hierodule when the god came to stay in the temple), or that of the priestess who had to sleep in the temple of Apollo, at Patara, in order to receive directly from the god the wisdom that she was to reveal through the oracle; see Otto, p. 84.

spermia, a gruel made from various grains, was prepared and had to be consumed before dark. And at nightfall there was a general cry: "To the gate, *kēres*! The Anthesteria are over!" This ritual scenario is well known and is documented almost everywhere in agricultural civilizations. The dead and the powers of the otherworld govern fertility and riches and are their bestowers. "It is from the dead," the author of a Hippocratic treatise writes, "that food, growth, and seeds come to us." In all the ceremonies consecrated to him, Dionysus reveals himself as at once the god of fertility and of death. Heraclitus (frag. 15) already said that "Hades and Dionysus [are] one and the same."

We referred above to Dionysus' connections with water, humidity, vegetable sap. The "miracles" that accompany or foretell his epiphanies must also be mentioned: water springing from rock, rivers filled with milk and honey. At Teos a spring of wine gushes out on the day of his festival (Diodorus Siculus, 3. 66. 2). At Elis, three empty bowls, left overnight in a sealed room, are found to be full of wine the next morning (Pausanias, 6. 2. 6. 1–2). Similar "miracles" are documented elsewhere. The most famous was the "vines of a day," which flowered and produced grapes in a few hours; this occurred in various places, for a number of authors mention it.[11]

124. Euripides and Dionysiac orgiasm

Such "miracles" are distinctive of the frantic and ecstatic cult of Dionysus, which reflects the most original and in all probability the most archaic element of the god. In Euripides' *Bacchae* we have inestimable testimony to what the encounter between the Greek genius and Dionysiac orgiasm may have been. Dionysus himself is the protagonist of the *Bacchae*, which is something unprecedented in ancient Greek drama. Outraged that his cult is still unrecognized in Greece, Dionysus arrives from Asia with a troop of maenads and stops at Thebes, his mother's birthplace. The three daughters of King Cadmus deny that their sister Semele had been loved by Zeus and had given birth to a god. Dionysus smites them with "madness," and his aunts, together with the other Theban women, rush away to

11. Sophocles, *Thyestes* (frag. 234), and the other sources cited by Otto, pp. 98–99.

the mountains, where they celebrate orgiastic rites. Pentheus, who had succeeded to the throne of his grandfather Cadmus, had forbidden the cult, and, despite the advice he had received, he persisted in his intransigence. Disguised as an officiant of his own cult, Dionysus is captured and imprisoned by Pentheus. But he escapes miraculously and even succeeds in persuading Pentheus to go and spy on the women during their orgiastic ceremonies. Discovered by the maenads, Pentheus is torn to pieces; his own mother, Agave, brings back his head in triumph, believing it to be the head of a lion.[12]

Whatever Euripides' intention may have been when, at the end of his life, he wrote the *Bacchae*, this masterpiece of Greek tragedy is also the most important document concerning the Dionysiac cult. The theme "resistance, persecution, and triumph" here finds its most brilliant illustration.[13] Pentheus opposes Dionysus because he is a "foreigner, a preacher, a sorcerer ... with beautiful perfumed blond curls, rosy cheeks, and in his eyes the grace of Aphrodite. Under the pretext of teaching the sweet and charming practices of the *evoe*, he corrupts girls" (*Bacch.* 233 ff.). Women are inspired to forsake their houses and run about the mountains by night, dancing to the music of tabors and flutes. And Pentheus principally fears the power of wine, for "with women, as soon as the juice of the grape figures in the feast, everything is unwholesome in these devotions" (260–62).

However, it is not wine that brings on the ecstasy of the bacchantes. One of Pentheus' servants, who had come upon them on Cithaeron at dawn, describes them as dressed in fawnskins, crowned with ivy, girdled with snakes, carrying in their arms and giving suck to fawns or wild wolf-cubs (695 ff.). Specifically Dionysiac miracles abound: the bacchantes strike the rocks with their thyrsi, and water or wine flows out; they scratch the ground, and milk bubbles up from it; and the ivy-wreathed thyrsi drip honey. "Certainly," the servant goes on,

---

12. There are other examples of "madness" brought on by Dionysus when he was not recognized as a god, e.g., the women of Argos (Apollodorus 2. 2. 2; 3. 5. 2) and the daughters of Minyas at Orchomenos, who tore to pieces and devoured the son of one of them (Plutarch, *Quaest. gr.* 38. 299e).

13. In the fifth century, Thebes had become the center of the cult, for it was there that Dionysus had been conceived, and there, too, was Semele's tomb. Nevertheless, the resistance of the earlier times had not been forgotten, and one of the lessons of the *Bacchae* was certainly this: that a god must not be rejected because he is considered "new."

"if you had been there, you would have been converted to this god whom you scorn, and addressed your prayers to him after such a sight" (712–14).

Discovered by Agave, the servant and his companions come near to being torn to pieces. The bacchantes then fling themselves on the animals grazing in the field and, "with no sword in hand," tear them to shreds. "Under the effect of a thousand girls' hands," threatening bulls are torn to pieces in the twinkling of an eye. The maenads then sweep down on the plains. "They caught up infants from their houses. Whatever they put on their shoulders stays there unbound, without falling into the mud, even bronze, even iron. On their hair fire darts, but without burning. Furious at being pillaged by the bacchae, the people rush to arms. And this is the miracle that was to be seen, lord: the javelins thrown at them drew no blood, and they, darting their thyrsi, wound the folk" (754–63).

It would serve no purpose to emphasize the difference between these frantic and savage nocturnal rites and the public Dionysiac festivals that we discussed above (§ 123). Euripides presents us with a secret cult, specifically characteristic of the Mysteries. "These mysteries, according to thee, what are they?" Pentheus asks. And Dionysus replies: "Their secrecy forbids communicating them to those who are not bacchants." "What use are they to those who celebrate them?" "It is not permitted thee to learn that, but they are things worthy to be known" (470–74).

The mystery consisted in the participation of the bacchantes in the total epiphany of Dionysus. The rites are celebrated at night, far from cities, in the mountains and forests. Through the sacrifice of the victim by tearing it to pieces (*sparagmos*) and the consumption of the raw flesh (*ōmophagia*), communion with the god is realized. For the animals that are torn apart and devoured are epiphanies, or incarnations, of Dionysus. All the other experiences—exceptional physical strength, invulnerability to fire and weapons, the prodigies (water, wine, milk, springing from the ground), "familiarity" with snakes and the young of wild beasts—are made possible by enthusiasm, by identification with the god. The Dionysiac ecstasy means, above all, surpassing the human condition, the discovery of total deliverance, obtaining a freedom and spontaneity inaccessible to human beings. That among these freedoms there also figured deliverance from prohibitions, rules, and conventions of an ethical and social order appears to be certain—which explains, in part, the mass adherence of women.[14] But the Dionysiac experience touched the deepest levels. The bacchantes who devoured raw flesh reintegrated a behavior that had been suppressed for tens of thousands of years; such frenzies revealed a communion with vital and cosmic forces that could be interpreted only as a divine possession. That the possession was confused with "madness," *mania*, was to be expected. Dionysus himself had experienced "madness," and the bacchante only shared in the ordeals and passion of the god; in the last analysis, it was one of the surest methods of communicating with him.

The Greeks knew other cases of *mania* brought on by gods. In Euripides' tragedy *Heracles*, the hero's madness is the work of Hera; in Sophocles' *Ajax*, it is Athena who produces the insanity. Corybantism, which the ancients compared with Dionysiac orgiasm, was a *mania* brought on by possession by the Corybantes, and the treatment of it ended in nothing short of an initiation. But what distinguishes Dionysus and his cult is not these psychopathic crises *but the fact that they were valorized as religious experience*, whether as a punishment or as a favor from the god.[15] In the last analysis, the interest of comparisons with apparently similar rites or collective movements—for example, certain convulsive dances of the Middle Ages or the ritual omophagy of the Aissawa, a mystical brotherhood of North Africa[16]—lies precisely in the fact that they reveal the originality of the Dionysian religion.

It is very seldom that there suddenly appears in the historic period a god so laden with an archaic heritage: rites involving theriomorphic masks, phallophoria, *sparagmos*, omophagy, anthropophagy, *mania*,

---

14. Teiresias, however, defends the god: "Dionysus does not oblige women to be chaste. Chastity depends on character, and the woman who is naturally chaste will take part in his orgies without being corrupted" (*Bacch.* 314 ff.).

15. What separates a shaman from a psychopath is that he succeeds in curing himself and ends by possessing a stronger and more creative personality than the rest of the community.

16. Rohde compared the spread of the ecstatic religion of Dionysus with the epidemics of convulsive dances in the Middle Ages. R. Eisler drew attention to the Aissawa (ʿIsāwiyya), who practice ritual omophagy (called *frissa*, from the verb *farassa*, "to tear"). Mystically identified with carnivores, whose names they bear (jackalls, panthers, lions, cats, dogs), the adepts tear up, disembowel, and eat bovines, wolves, rams, sheep, and goats. The chewing of the raw flesh is followed by a frantic dance of jubilation, "in order savagely to enjoy ecstasy and communicate with the divinity" (R. Brunel).

enthousiasmos. Most remarkable of all is the fact that, while still preserving this heritage, a residue from prehistory, the cult of Dionysus, once it was integrated into the spiritual universe of the Greeks, never ceased to create new religious values. Indeed, the frenzy brought on by divine possession—"madness"—interested many authors and often provoked irony and derision. Herodotus (4. 78–80) relates the adventure of a Scythian king, Skyles, who at Olbia, on the Borysthenes (Dnieper), had himself "initiated into the rites of Dionysus Baccheus." During the ceremony (*teletē*), possessed by the god, he played "the bacchant and the madman." In all probability this refers to a procession in which the initiates, "under the empire of the god," let themselves be carried away by a frenzy which the onlookers, as well as those who were possessed, considered to be "madness" (*mania*).

Herodotus was satisfied to recount a story that had been told to him at Olbia. Demosthenes, in a famous passage (*De corona* 259), while attempting to ridicule his adversary, Aeschines, in fact reveals to us certain rites celebrated by *thiasoi* (private religious organizations) at Athens in the fourth century in honor of Sabazius, a Thracian god homologous with Dionysus. (The ancients regarded him as the Thracian Dionysus under his indigenous name.)[17] Demosthenes refers to rites followed by readings from "books" (probably a written text, containing *hieroi logoi*); he speaks of "nebrizing" (reference to the fawnskin, *nēbris*; possibly what was involved was a sacrifice including the eating of the raw animal), of "craterizing" (the *kratēr* was the vessel in which wine and water, the "mystical beverage," were mixed), of "purification" (*katharmos*), consisting principally of rubbing the initiate with clay and flour. Finally, the acolyte raised the initiate, prostrated or lying on the ground, and the initiate repeated the formula: "I have escaped from evil and found better." And the whole assemblage burst out in loud cries (*ololygē*). The next morning saw the procession of the initiates, crowned with fennel and branches of white poplar. Aeschines marched at the head of it, brandishing snakes and shouting: "Evoe, mysteries of Sabazius!" and dancing to cries of "Hyes, Attes, Attes, Hyes." Demosthenes also mentions a basket in the shape of a fan,

17. According to the ancient glosses, the term *saboi* (or *sabaioi*) was the equivalent, in the Phrygian language, of the Greek *bacchos*; see Jeanmaire, *Dionysos*, pp. 95–97.

the *liknon*, the "mystical winnowing fan," the original cradle of the infant Dionysus.

At the center of the Dionysiac ritual, we always find, in one form or another, an ecstatic experience of a more or less violent frenzy: *mania*. This "madness" was in a way the proof that the initiate was *entheos*, "filled with the god." The experience was certainly unforgettable, for there was a sharing in the creative spontaneity and intoxicating freedom, in the superhuman force and invulnerability of Dionysus. Communion with the god shattered the human condition for a time, but it did not succeed in transmuting it. There is no reference to immortality in the *Bacchae* or in so late a work as the *Dionysiaca* of Nonnus. This suffices to distinguish Dionysus from Zalmoxis, with whom he has been compared, and sometimes confused, since Rohde; for that god of the Getae "immortalized" the initiates into his mysteries. But the Greeks did not yet dare to bridge the infinite distance that, in their eyes, separated divinity from the human condition.

125. When the Greeks rediscover the presence of the God

The initiatory and secret character of the private *thiasoi* seems to be certain (see *Bacchae* 470–74),[18] even though at least a part of the ceremonies (for example, the processions) were public. It is hard to determine when, and under what circumstances, the secret and initiatory Dionysiac rites assumed the particular function of the Mystery religions. Highly esteemed scholars (Nilsson, Festugière) deny the existence of a Dionysiac Mystery on the ground of the complete lack of definite references to any eschatological hope. But, especially in the ancient period, we are very poorly informed concerning secret rites, to say nothing of their esoteric meaning (which must have existed, since esoteric meanings of secret and initiatory rites are documented all over the world and on all levels of culture).

In addition, the morphology of the eschatological hope must not be limited to the expressions made familiar by Orphism or the Mysteries of the Hellenistic period. The occultation and epiphany

18. It should be remembered in this connection that during the festival of the Anthesteria certain rites were performed only by women, and in the strictest secrecy.

of Dionysus, his descents to Hades (comparable to a death followed by a resurrection), and, above all, the cult of the Infant Dionysus,[19] with rites celebrating his "awakening"—even leaving aside the mythico-ritual theme of Dionysus-Zagreus, which we shall emphasize in a moment—indicate the will, and the hope, for a spiritual renewal. Everywhere in the world the divine infant is charged with an initiatory symbolism revealing the mystery of a "rebirth" of a mystical nature. (For religious experience, it matters very little whether such symbolism is understood intellectually or not.) It must be recalled that the cult of Sabazius, identified with Dionysus, already presented the structure of a mystery ("I have escaped from evil!"). To be sure, the *Bacchae* does not mention immortality; however, communion, even provisional, with the god was not without consequences for the postmortem condition of the *bacchos*. The presence of Dionysus in the Eleusinian Mysteries permits us to suspect the eschatological meaning of at least certain orgiastic experiences.

But it is especially from the time of Dionysus-Zagreus that the Mystery character of the cult becomes definite. The myth of the dismemberment of the infant Dionysus-Zagreus is known to us chiefly through Christian authors.[20] As was to be expected, they present it euhemerized, incomplete, and with malevolence. But precisely because they were free from the prohibition against speaking openly of sacred and secret things, the Christian writers have transmitted a number of precious details. Hera sends the Titans, who first attract the infant Dionysus-Zagreus with certain playthings (rattles, *crepundia*, a mirror, knucklebones, a ball, a top, a bull-roarer) and then slaughter him and cut him to pieces. They boil the pieces in a kettle and, according to some authorities, eat them. A goddess—Athena, Rhea, or Demeter—receives, or saves, the heart and puts it in a coffer. Informed of the crime, Zeus destroys the Titans with his thunderbolt. The Christian authors do not mention the resurrection of Dionysus, but this episode was known to the ancients. The Epicurean Philodemus, a contemporary of Cicero, speaks of the three births of Dionysus, "the first from his mother,

19. The cult of the Infant Dionysus was known in Boeotia and in Crete, but it ended by also spreading into all of Greece.
20. Firmicus Maternus, *De errore prof. relig.* 6; Clement of Alexandria, *Protrept.* 2. 17. 2; 18. 2; Arnobius, *Adv. Nat.* 5. 19; the texts are reproduced in Kern, *Orphica fragmenta*, pp. 110–11.

the second from the thigh, and the third when, after his dismemberment by the Titans, Rhea gathered together his limbs and he came to life again."[21] Firmicus Maternus ends by adding that in Crete (where he localizes his euhemerized story) the murder was commemorated by yearly rites, which repeated what "the child had done and suffered at the moment of his death": "in the depths of the forests, by the strange cries they utter, they feign the madness of a raging soul," giving it out that the crime was committed through madness, and "they tear a living bull with their teeth."

The mythico-ritual theme of the passion and resurrection of the infant Dionysus-Zagreus has given rise to endless controversies, especially because of its "Orphic" interpretations. For our purpose, it will suffice to point out that the information transmitted by the Christian authors is corroborated by earlier documents. The name of Zagreus is mentioned for the first time in an epic poem of the Theban cycle, *Alcmaeonis* (sixth century B.C.):[22] it means "great hunter," which corresponds with the savage, orgiastic character of Dionysus. As for the crime of the Titans, Pausanias (8. 37. 5) has provided us with a piece of information that, despite the skepticism of Wilamowitz and other scholars, remains precious. He reports that Onomacritus, who lived in Athens in the sixth century B.C., in the period of the Pisistratids, wrote a poem on this subject: "Having taken the name of the Titans from Homer, he founded *orgia* of Dionysus, making the Titans the authors of the god's sufferings." According to this myth, the Titans, when they approached the divine infant, were powdered with plaster, so as not to be recognized. Now in the mysteries of Sabazius, celebrated at Athens, one of the initiation rites consisted in dusting the candidates with a powder or with plaster.[23] The two facts have been connected since antiquity (cf. Nonnus, *Dionys.* 27. 228 ff.). But what we have here is a form of archaic initiation ritual, well known in primitive societies: the

21. Philodemus, *De piet.* 44; Jeanmaire, *Dionysos*, p. 382.
22. Frag. 3 Kinkel, vol. 1, p. 77; see also Euripides, frag. 472; for Callimachus (frag. 171) Zagreus is a special name of Dionysus; see other examples, in Otto, *Dionysos*, pp. 191 ff.
23. Demosthenes, *De corona* 259. When they took part in the Dionysiac festivals, the Argives covered their faces with chalk or plaster. The relations between chalk (*titanos*) and the Titans (*Titanes*) have been emphasized. But this mythico-ritual complex was occasioned by confusion between the two terms (see Farnell, *Cults*, vol. 5, p. 172).

novices rub their faces with powder or ashes in order to resemble ghosts; in other words, they undergo a ritual death. As for "mystical playthings," they have long been known; a papyrus of the third century B.C., found at Faiyum and unfortunately mutilated, mentions the top, the bull-roarer, knucklebones, and the mirror (*Orph. Frag.* 31).

The most dramatic episode of the myth—especially the fact that, after dismembering the infant, the Titans threw his limbs into a caldron, where they boiled them and then roasted them—was known, with all its details, in the fourth century B.C.; what is more, all these details were rehearsed in connection with "the celebration of the mysteries." [24] Jeanmaire has cogently pointed out that boiling in a caldron or passing through fire are initiation rites that confer immortality (cf. the episode of Demeter and Demophoön) or rejuvenation (the daughters of Pelias cut up their father and boiled him in a caldron).[25] Add that the two rites—dismemberment and boiling or passing through fire—are characteristic of shamanic initiations.

So we can recognize in the "crime of the Titans" an ancient initiatory scenario whose original meaning had been forgotten. For the Titans behave like Masters of Initiation, that is to say, they "kill" the novice in order to cause him to be "reborn" to a higher mode of existence (in our example, we could say that they confer divinity and immortality on the infant Dionysus). But in a religion that proclaimed the absolute supremacy of Zeus, the Titans could play only a demonic role, and they were incinerated by Zeus's thunderbolt. According to some variants, men were created from their ashes, and this myth played a considerable role in Orphism.

The initiatory character of the Dionysiac rites can also be perceived at Delphi, when the women celebrated the god's rebirth; for the Delphic winnowing fan "contained a dismembered Dionysus ready to be reborn, a Zagreus," as Plutarch testifies (*De Iside* 35), and this Dionysus, "who was reborn as Zagreus, was at the same time the Theban Dionysus, son of Zeus and Semele." [26]

24. Cf. the "problem" attributed to Aristotle (Didot, *Aristote* 4. 331. 15), discussed, after Salomon Reinach, by Moulinier, *Orphée et l'orphisme*, p. 51. In the third century, Euphorion knew a similar tradition (ibid., p. 53).

25. Jeanmaire, *Dionysos*, p. 387. See other examples in Marie Delcourt, *L'oracle de Delphes*, pp. 153 ff.

26. Delcourt, pp. 155, 200. Plutarch, after speaking of the dismemberment of Osiris and his resurrection, addresses his friend Clea, the leader of the

Diodorus Siculus seems to refer to the Dionysiac mysteries when he writes that "Orpheus transmitted in the ceremonies of the mysteries the tearing-to-pieces of Dionysus" (5. 75. 4). And in another passage Diodorus presents Orpheus as a reformer of the Dionysiac mysteries: "This is why the initiations due to Dionysus are called Orphic" (3. 65. 6). The tradition transmitted by Diodorus is valuable insofar as it confirms the existence of Dionysiac mysteries. But it is probable that, as early as the fifth century B.C., these mysteries had already borrowed certain "Orphic" elements. And in fact Orpheus was then proclaimed "prophet of Dionysus" and "founder of all initiations" (see chap. 19 of vol. 2).

More than the other Greek gods, Dionysus astonishes by the multiplicity and novelty of his epiphanies, by the variety of his transformations. He is always in motion; he makes his way everywhere, into all countries, among all peoples, into every religious milieu, ready to associate himself with various divinities (even with such antagonistic deities as Demeter and Apollo). He is certainly the only Greek god who, revealing himself under different aspects, dazzles and attracts both peasants and the intellectual elite, politicians and contemplatives, orgiastics and ascetics. Intoxication, eroticism, universal fertility, but also the unforgettable experiences inspired by the periodic arrival of the dead, or by *mania*, by immersion in animal unconsciousness, or by the ecstasy of *enthousiasmos*—all these terrors and revelations spring from a single source: *the presence of the god*. His mode of being expresses the paradoxical unity of life and death. This is why Dionysus constitutes a type of divinity radically different from the Olympians. Was he *nearer* to human beings than the other gods? In any case, one could approach him, could even incorporate him; and the ecstasy of *mania* proved that the human condition could be surpassed.

These rituals were capable of unexpected developments. The dithyramb, tragedy, the satyr play are, more or less directly, Dionysiac creations. It is absorbing to follow the transformation of a collective rite, the *dithyrambos*, involving ecstatic frenzy, into a

---

maenads at Delphi: "That Osiris is the same as Dionysus, who could know better than you who govern the Thyiades, you who were initiated by your father into the mysteries of Osiris?"

spectacle and finally into a literary form.[27] If, on the one hand, certain public liturgies became spectacles and made Dionysus the god of the theater, other rituals, secret and initiatory, developed into Mysteries. At least indirectly, Orphism is indebted to the Dionysiac traditions. More than any other Olympian, this *young god* will not cease to gratify his worshipers with new epiphanies, unexpected messages, and eschatological hopes.

27. The dithyramb, "a round dance intended, at the sacrifice of a victim, to bring on collective ecstasy with the help of rhythmical movements and ritual acclamations and vociferations was able—and precisely during the period (seventh–sixth centuries) in which the great genre of the choral lyric was developing in the Greek world—to evolve into a literary form by the increasing importance of the parts sung by the *exarchōn*, by the insertion of lyric passages on themes more or less adapted to the circumstance and to the person of Dionysus" (Jeanmaire, *Dionysos*, pp. 248–49).

Abbreviations

ANET	J. B. Pritchard, *Ancient Near Eastern Texts Relating to the Old Testament* (Princeton, 1950; 2d ed., 1955)
Ar Or	*Archiv Orientálni* (Prague)
ARW	*Archiv für Religionswissenschaft* (Freiburg and Leipzig)
BEFEO	*Bulletin de l'Ecole française d'Extrême-Orient* (Hanoi)
BJRL	*Bulletin of the John Rylands Library* (Manchester)
BSOAS	*Bulletin of the School of Oriental and African Studies* (London)
CA	*Current Anthropology* (Chicago)
ERE	*Encyclopaedia of Religion and Ethics*, ed. James Hastings
HJAS	*Harvard Journal of Asiatic Studies*
HR	*History of Religions* (Chicago)
IIJ	*Indo-Iranian Journal* (The Hague)
JA	*Journal Asiatique* (Paris)
JAOS	*Journal of the American Oriental Society* (Baltimore)
JAS	*Journal of the Asiatic Society, Bombay Branch*
JIES	*Journal of Indo-European Studies* (Montana)
JNES	*Journal of Near Eastern Studies* (Chicago)
JRAS	*Journal of the Royal Asiatic Society* (London)
JSS	*Journal of Semitic Studies* (Manchester)
OLZ	*Orientalische Literaturzeitung* (Berlin and Leipzig)
RB	*Revue Biblique* (Paris)

REG	*Revue des Etudes Grecques* (Paris)
RHPR	*Revue d'Histoire et de Philosophie religieuses* (Strasbourg)
RHR	*Revue de l'Histoire des Religions* (Paris)
SMSR	*Studi e Materiali di Storia delle Religioni* (Rome)
VT	*Vetus Testamentum* (Leiden)
WdM	*Wörterbuch der Mythologie* (Stuttgart)
ZDMG	*Zeitschrift der deutschen morgenländischen Gesellschaft* (Leipzig)

Present Position
of Studies:
Problems and Progress.
Critical Bibliographies

1. For a rapid initiation into universal prehistory, see Grahame Clark, *World Prehistory* (Cambridge, 1962); Grahame Clark and Stuart Piggott, *Prehistoric Societies* (London, 1965) (this work contains a rich bibliography); H. Breuil and R. Lantier, *Les hommes de la pierre ancienne; paléolithique et mésolithique*, rev. ed. (Payot, 1959) (Eng. trans., *The Men of the Old Stone Age [Palaeolithic and Mesolithic]*, trans. B. B. Rafter [London, 1965]).

A more complete documentation will be found in H. Müller-Karpe, *Handbuch der Vorgeschichte*, vol. 1: *Altsteinzeit* (Munich, 1966), and in the first volume published under the editorship of Karl J. Narr, *Handbuch der Urgeschichte* (Bern and Munich, 1967). Karl Narr has provided an excellent summary, completed by an extensive bibliography, in *Abriss der Vorgeschichte* (Munich, 1957), pp. 8–41. See also his *Urgeschichte der Kultur* (Stuttgart, 1961); F. Bordes, *Old Stone Age* (New York, 1968), and *La préhistoire: Problèmes et tendances*, Éditions du CNRS (Paris, 1968).

An analysis of recent hypotheses on the origins of language and society can be found in Frank B. Livingstone, "Genetics, Ecology and the Origins of Incest and Exogamy," *CA* 10 (February 1969): 45–61 (bibliography, pp. 60–61). On the origin of language we follow Morris Swadesh, *The Origin and Diversification of Language* (Chicago, 1971).

In several of his studies Karl Narr has examined the hypotheses put forward concerning the "hominization" of the primates and has attempted to present a probable picture of the Paleanthropians; see, inter alia, "Approaches to the Social Life of Earliest Man," *Anthropos* 57 (1962): 604–20; "Das Individuum in der Urgeschichte: Möglichkeiten seiner Erfassung," *Saeculum* 23 (1972): 252–65.

On the problems raised by the peopling of America, see E. F. Greenman, "The Upper Paleolithic and the New World," *CA* 4 (1963): 41–91; Allan Bryan, "Early Man in America and the Late Pleistocene Chronology of Western Canada and Alaska," ibid. 10 (1969): 339–65; Jesse D. Jennings and Edward Norbeck, eds., *Prehistoric Man in the New World* (Chicago, 1964); Gordon R. Willey, *An Introduction to American Archaeology* (Englewood Cliffs, N.J., 1966), vol. 1, pp. 2–72 and passim.

See also Frederick D. McCarthy, "Recent Development and Problems in the Prehistory of Australia," *Paideuma* 14 (1968): 1–17; Peter Bellwood, "The Prehistory of Oceania," *CA* 16 (1975): 9–28.

During tens of millennia the sequence of the Paleolithic culture is the same in Europe, Africa, and Asia. The same sequence is found in Australia and in North and South America, though the temporal horizon is much shorter. For the period 20,000–10,000 B.C. it cannot be said that any one region obtained a decisive technological advance over the others. To be sure, there are variations in the structure of tools, but these variations presumably reflect local adaptations and not a technological progress; see Marvin Harris, *Culture, Man, and Nature* (New York, 1971), p. 169. This *cultural unity* of the Paleolithics constitutes the common source of the traditions inherited by later cultures; in addition, it permits comparison with contemporary hunting societies. For an admirable analysis of Paleolithic "survivals" in certain Greek myths and rites, see Walter Burkert, *Homo Necans* (Berlin, 1972). On the hunting cultures, see the symposium *Man the Hunter*, edited by Richard B. Lee and Irven Devore (Chicago, 1968).

2. In order to understand why scholars have hesitated to admit the possibility of a consistent and complex religiosity among the Paleanthropians, it is necessary to remember that, in the second half of the nineteenth century, the term "religion" had a decidedly limited application, the rest being designated by various pejorative terms: "magic," "superstition," "savagery," etc. Some writers referred to "men without religion," because they had found nothing in certain tribes that could be compared to the familiar polytheisms and "fetishistic systems." The supporters of "religiosity" were accused of idealizing the Paleanthropians, because "religion" was taken to mean an ideological complex comparable to Judeo-Christianity, Hinduism, or the pantheons of the ancient Near East.

Nothing would be gained by citing all the works devoted to prehistoric religions; most of them retain only a bibliographical interest. The following may be consulted for their documentations or their advanced hypotheses: T. Mainage, *Les religions de la préhistoire* (Paris, 1921); G. H. Luquet, *L'art et la religion des hommes fossiles* (Paris, 1926); C. Clemen, *Urgeschichtliche Religion*, 2 vols. (Bonn, 1932–33); E. O. James, *Prehistoric Religion* (London and New York, 1957). See also Emmanuel Anati, ed., *Symposium international sur les religions de la préhistoire—Valcamonica,*

18–23 septembre 1972 (Brescia, 1975), and our observations in *HR* 16 (1976): 178–82.

Fuller discussions will be found in some more recent publications: Johannes Maringer, *The Gods of Prehistoric Man* (New York, 1960); Étienne Patte, *Les hommes préhistoriques et la religion* (Paris, 1960); André Leroi-Gourhan, *Les religions de la préhistoire: Paléolithique* (Paris, 1964); Karl J. Narr, *Kultur, Umwelt und Leiblichkeit der Eiszeitmenschen* (Stuttgart, 1963); Narr, "Approaches to the Religion of Early Paleolithic Man," *HR* 4 (1964): 1–29; Narr, "Religion und Magie in der jüngeren Altsteinzeit," in *Handbuch der Urgeschichte* (1966), vol. 1, pp. 298–320. Useful for its critical bibliography of recent works is Narr's article "Wege zum Verständnis prähistorischer Religionsformen," *Kairos* 3 (1963): 179–88.

Mythologies that can develop from the making of tools have as yet been insufficiently studied. We have analyzed the symbolism and some mythological themes of the arrow in "Notes on the Symbolism of the Arrow," in *Religions in Antiquity: Essays in Memory of E. R. Goodenough*, edited by Joseph Neusner (Leiden, 1968), pp. 463–75.

3. The essential data for the funerary practices of the Paleolithics are clearly presented by J. Maringer, *The Gods of Prehistoric Man* (New York, 1960), pp. 14–37, 74–89. Still useful for the documentation available before 1940 is E. O. James, *Prehistoric Religion: A Study in Prehistoric Archaeology* (London, 1957), pp. 17–34. See also Grahame Clark, *The Stone Age Hunters* (London, 1967), pp. 41 ff. For a critical discussion, see Leroi-Gourhan, *Les religions de la préhistoire*, pp. 37–64.

For more elaborate analyses, see H. Breuil, "Pratiques religieuses chez les humanités quaternaires," *Scienza e Civiltà* (1951), pp. 45–75; A. Glory and R. Robert, "Le culte des crânes humains aux époques préhistoriques," *Bulletin de la Société d'Anthropologie de Paris* (1948), pp. 114–33; H. L. Movius, Jr., "The Mousterian Cave of Teshik-Tash, Southeastern Uzbekistan, Central Asia," *American School of Prehistoric Research*, bull. no. 17 (1953), pp. 11–71; P. Wernert, "Cultes des crânes: Représentation des esprits des défunts et des ancêtres," in M. Gorce and R. Mortier, eds., *L'histoire générale des religions* (Paris, 1948), vol. 1, pp. 51–102.

On the meaning of the skull exhumed at Circeo, see A. C. Blanc, "I Paleantropi di Saccopastore e del Circeo," *Quartär* (1942), pp. 1–37.

Raymond A. Dart has demonstrated the antiquity of the exploitation of ocher mines in South Africa and elsewhere; see his "The Multimillennial Prehistory of Ochre Mining," *NADA* (1967), pp. 7–13, and "The Birth of Symbology," *African Studies* 27 (1968): 15–27. These two articles contain many bibliographical references.

On burial "as an embryo," see G. van der Leeuw, "Das Sogenannte Hockerbegräbnis und der ägyptische *Tjknw*," *SMSR* 14 (1938): 150–67.

4. Emil Bachler reported on the results of his excavations in *Das alpine Paläolithikum der Schweiz* (Basel, 1940).

For other discoveries, see K. Hoermann, *Die Petershöhle bei Velden in Mittelfranken: Eine altpaläolithische Station* (Nuremberg, 1933); K. Ehrenberg, "Dreissig Jahre paläobiologischer Forschung in österreichischen Höhlen," *Quartär* (1951), pp. 93–108; Ehrenberg, "Die paläontologische, prähistorische, und paläoethnologische Bedeutung der Salzofenhöhle im Lichte der letzten Forschungen," *Quartär* (1954), pp. 19–58. See also Lothar Zotz, "Die altsteinzeitliche Besiedlung der Alpen und deren geistigen und wirtschaftliche Hintergründe," *Sitzungsberichte der Physikalischmedizinische Sozietät zu Erlangen* 78 (1955–57): 76–101, and, especially, Müller-Karpe, *Altsteinzeit*, pp. 205, 224–26.

Comparison with the offerings characteristic of certain Arctic peoples has been made by A. Gahs, "Kopf-, Schädel-, und Langknochenopfer bei Rentiervölkern," *Festschrift für P. W. Schmidt* (Vienna, 1928), pp. 231–68. For his part, Wilhelm Schmidt has returned to this problem several times; see, inter alia, "Die älteste Opferstelle des altpaläolithischen Menschen in den Schweizer Alpen," *Acta Pontificiae Academiae Scientiarum* 6 (Vatican City, 1942): 269–72; "Das Primitialopfer in der Urkultur," *Corona Amicorum: Festgabe für Emil Bächler* (Saint Gall, 1948), pp. 81–92. See also J. Maringer, "Das Blut in Kult und Glauben der vorgeschichtlichen Menschen," *Anthropos* 71 (1976): 226–53.

Karl Meuli has presented his interpretation of bone deposits in "Griechische Opferbräuche," *Phyllobolia für Peter von der Mühll* (Basel, 1945), pp. 185–288, esp. pp. 283–87.

On the problem of "sacrifices" in the Paleolithic, see Oswald Menghin, "Der Nachweis des Opfers im altpaläolithikum," *Wiener Prähistorische Zeitschrift* 13 (1926): 14–19; H. C. Bandi, "Zur Frage eines Bären- oder Opferkultes im ausgehenden Altpaläolithikum der Alpinen Zone," *Helvetia Antiqua, Festschrift Emil Vogt* (Zurich, 1966), pp. 1–8; S. Grodar, "Zur Frage der Höhlenbärenjagd und des Höhlenbärenkult in den paläolithischen Fundstellen Jugoslawien," *Quartär* 9 (1957): 147–59; W. Wust, "Die paläolithisch-ethnographischen Bärenriten und das Altindogermanische," *Quartär* 7–8 (1956): 154–65; Mirko Malez, "Das Paläolithikum der Veternicahöhle und der Bärenkult," *Quartär* 10–11 (1958/59): 171–88. See also I. Paulson, "Die rituelle Erhebung des Bärenschädels bei arktischen und subarktischen Völker," *Temenos* 1 (1965): 150–73.

F. E. Koby has raised doubts concerning the existence of deposits of skulls and the bear cult; see his "L'ours des cavernes et les Paléolithiques,"

L'Anthropologie 55 (1951): 304–8; "Les Paléolithiques ont-ils chassé l'ours des cavernes?" *Actes de la Société Jurassienne d'émulation* 57 (1953): 157–204); "Grottes autrichiennes avec culte de l'ours?" *Bull. de la Soc. Préhist. française* 48 (1951): 8–9. Leroi-Gourhan is of the same opinion; see his *Les Religions de la préhistoire*, pp. 31 ff.

For a full critical discussion, see Johannes Maringer, "Die Opfer der paläolithischen Menschen," *Anthropica* (St. Augustin bei Bonn, 1968), pp. 249–71.

W. Koppers has suggested some interesting ethnological parallels; see his "Der Bärenkult in ethnologischer und prähistorischer Beleuchtung," *Paleobiologica* (1933), pp. 47–64; "Künstlicher Zahnschift am Bären im Altpaläolithikum und bei den Ainu auf Sachalin," *Quartär* (1938): 97–103. The rituals are analyzed by Alexander Slawik, "Zum Problem des Bärenfestes der Ainu und Giliaken," *Kultur und Sprache* (Vienna, 1952), pp. 189–203.

The relations between the bear ceremonial and shamanism in the European Paleolithic have been studied by Karl Narr, "Bärenzeremoniell und Schamanismus in der älteren Steinzeit Europas," *Saeculum* 10 (1959): 233–72.

On the characteristic beliefs of hunters that the animal can be reborn from its bones, see Eliade, *Shamanism: Archaic Techniques of Ecstasy*, trans. Willard R. Trask, Bollingen Series 76 (New York, 1964), pp. 160 ff. The prohibition against breaking the bones of game or domestic animals has been analyzed in the light of recent research by Joseph Henninger, "Neuere Forschungen zum Verbot des Knochenzerbrechens," *Studia Ethnografica et Folkloristica in honorem Béla Gunda* (Debrecen, 1971), pp. 673–702. I. Paulson's study, "Die Tierknochen im Jagdritual der nordeurasiatische Völker," *Zeitschrift für Ethnologie* 84 (1959): 270–92, deserves special mention.

5. There is an extensive bibliography on prehistoric caves and rock art. See, in particular, H. Breuil, *Quatre cent siècles d'art pariétal* (Montignac, 1951) (Eng. trans., *Four Hundred Centuries of Cave Art*, trans. Mary Boyle [Montignac, 1952]); J. Maringer and H. Bandi, *Art in the Ice Age* (London, 1953); Paolo Graziosi, *Palaeolithic Art* (London, 1960); A. Leroi-Gourhan, *Préhistoire de l'art occidental* (Paris, 1965) (Eng. trans., *Treasures of Prehistoric Art* [New York, 1967]); A. Laming, *Lascaux: Paintings and Engravings* (Harmondsworth, Eng., 1959); Laming, *La signification de l'art rupestre paléolithique* (Paris, 1962), with an extensive critical bibliography; R. F. Heizer and M. A. Baumhoff, *Prehistoric Rock Art of Nevada and Eastern California* (Berkeley and Los Angeles, 1962); Peter J. Ucko and Andrée Rosenfeld, *Palaeolithic Cave Art* (New York, 1967). See also

Simposio de arte rupestre, Barcelona, 1966 (Barcelona, 1968), especially the studies by P. Graziosi, "L'art paléo-épipaléolithique de la Province méditerranéenne et ses nouveaux documents d'Afrique du Nord et du Proche-Orient" (pp. 265 ff.), Emmanuel Anati, "El arte rupestre galaico-portuguès" (pp. 195 ff.), and Henri Lhote, "Données récentes sur les gravures et les peintures rupestres du Sahara" (pp. 273 ff.). The conditions for valid comparisons between the artistic creations of prehistory and those of peoples on the ethnological level have been examined by Karl Narr, "Interpretation altsteinzeitlicher Kunstwerke durch völkerkundliche Parallelen," *Anthropos* 50 (1955): 513–45. See now Narr's more recent article, "Zum Sinngehalt der altsteinzeitlichen Höhlenbilder," *Symbolon*, n.s. 2 (1974): 105–22. A Marxist interpretation has been presented by G. Charrière, *Les significations des représentations érotiques dans les arts sauvages et préhistoriques* (Paris, 1970).

Leroi-Gourhan distinguishes, stylistically and chronologically, five periods in Paleolithic art: (1) developed Mousterian (about 50,000 B.C.), in which bones and "small stone slabs bearing regularly spaced incisions" are documented but no figurative works yet appear; (2) the Primitive period (Aurignacian, about 30,000 B.C.), which has yielded engraved or painted figures, on calcareous slabs, "of very abstract and very crude figures, representing heads or foreparts of usually unidentifiable animals mingled with genital representations," and, later (about 25,000–20,000 B.C.), human figures complying with a very similar stylization: "the central part of the body is enormous in comparison with the head and the extremities, which has given rise to the idea of particularly steatopygous Paleolithic women"; (3) the Archaic period (late Solutrean, about 30,000–25,000 B.C.), including several sites of the greatest importance (Lascaux, La Pasiega) ("Technical mastery is now complete, and the paintings, sculptures, or engravings display an extraordinary quality of execution"); (4) the Classic period (Magdalenian, about 15,000–11,000 B.C.), when the decorated caves attain their maximum in geographic extension: realism of forms is carried very far; (5) and the Late period (late Magdalenian, about 10,000 B.C.), in which caves are no longer decorated and the art is essentially mobiliary: "The figures have lost the last traces of the antique styles, the animals are integrated into a realism in which precision of form and movement is striking. This mobiliary art now extends northward to Great Britain, Belgium, and Switzerland. About 9000 B.C. a rather sudden decline marks the end of the Upper Paleolithic; the few examples from the closing Magdalenian dissolve into crudity and schematism" (*Les religions de la préhistoire*, pp. 87–88).

The *Simposio de arte rupestre* contains two articles by Henri Lhote which criticize the method of Leroi-Gourhan and Laming: "La plaquette dite de 'La Femme au Renne,' de Laugerie-Basse, et son interprétation zoologique" (pp. 79–97), and "Le bison gravé de Ségriés, Moustiers-Ste-Marie" (pp. 99–108). A critical discussion of Leroi-Gourhan's interpretation will be found in Ucko and Rosenfeld, *Palaeolithic Cave Art*, pp. 195–221.

Suggestive observations on the symbolism of prehistoric art and its stylistic expressions will be found in the studies by Herbert Kühn, "Das Symbol in der Vorzeit Europas," *Symbolon* 2 (1961): 160–84, and by Walther Matthes, "Die Darstellung von Tier und Mensch in der Plastik des älteren Paläolithikum," ibid. 4 (1964): 244–76. The publications by H. Bégouen, N. Casteret, and J. Charet on the Montespan and Tuc d'Aubert caves are discussed by Ucko and Rosenfeld, *Palaeolithic Cave Art*, pp. 188–98, 177–78.

The engraved slate slab from Lourdes is reproduced by Maringer, *The Gods of Prehistoric Man*, fig. 27. It has been suggested that the scene engraved on a bone excavated in the La Vache cave (Ariège) should be interpreted as indicating an initiation ceremony; see Louis-René Nougier and Romain Robert, "Scène d'initiation de la grotte de la Vache à Alliat (Ariège)," *Bull. de la Soc. de l'Ariège* 23 (1968): 13–98. A clear reproduction of the design will be found in Alexander Marshak, *The Roots of Civilization* (New York, 1972), p. 275, fig. 154.

Horst Kirchner has proposed a shamanic interpretation of the famous cave painting from Lascaux in his study "Ein archäologischer Beitrag zur Urgeschichte des Schamanismus," *Anthropos* 47 (1952): 244–86. This interpretation has been accepted by Karl Narr, "Bärenzeremoniell und Schamanismus in der älteren Steinzeit Europas," *Saeculum* 10 (1959): 233–72, esp. p. 271. See also Eliade, *Shamanism*, pp. 502 ff.; A. Marshak, *The Roots of Civilization*, pp. 277 ff.

J. Makkay has given the same interpretation to the "Great Magician" in the Trois Frères cave in "An Important Proof to the Prehistory of Shamanism," *Alba Regia* 2/3 (Székesfehérvár, 1963): 5–10.

See also E. Burgstaller, "Schamanistische Motive unter den Felsbildern in den österreichischen Alpenländern," *Forschungen und Fortschritte* 41 (1967): 105–10, 144–58; H. Miyakawa and A. Kollantz, "Zur Ur- und Vorgeschichte des Schamanismus," *Zeitschrift für Ethnologie* 91 (1960): 161–93 (useful for its Japanese documentation).

6. On the female statuettes, see the documentation collected by E. Saccasyn-Della Santa, *Les figures humaines du paléolithique supérieur eurasiatique* (Antwerp, 1947), to be supplemented by later discoveries, recorded in the bibliography by Karl J. Narr, *Antaios* 2 (1960): 155, n. 2. For the interpretation, cf. F. Hančar, "Zum Problem der Venusstatuetten im eurasiatischen Jungpaläolithikum," *Prähistorische Zeitschrift* 30/31 (1939/40): 85–156; Karl J. Narr, "Weibliche Symbol-Plastik der älteren Steinzeit," *Antaios* 2 (1960): 131–57; Karl Jettmar, in I. Paulson, A. Hultkrantz, and K. Jettmar, *Les religions arctiques et finnoises* (French translation, 1965), pp. 292–99 (summarizing Gerasimov's excavations at Malᶜta). See also J. Maringer, *The Gods of Prehistoric Man*, pp. 153 ff.; A. Leroi-Gourhan, *Les religions de la préhistoire*, pp. 87 ff. This art of figurines ("Kleinplastik," as Narr terms it) is believed to be the result of influences from the eastern Mediterranean; a comparatively naturalistic style is dominant in the Franco-Cantabrian region, while geometric schematization became the rule in the East and Northeast. But it is now accepted that the Late Paleolithic of Siberia was influenced by the cultures of Mongolia and Southeast Asia; see Jettmar, *Les religions arctiques et finnoises*, p. 292.

Leroi-Gourhan's interpretation has been criticized by Ucko and Rosenfeld, *Palaeolithic Cave Art*, pp. 195 ff., and by Henri Lhote, "La Plaquette dite de 'La Femme au Renne,'" in *Simposio de arte rupestre*, pp. 80–97 (cf. ibid., pp. 98–108, a critique by Maning).

On the so-called X-ray style and its relations with shamanism, see Andreas Lommel, *Shamanism: The Beginnings of Art* (New York and Toronto, n.d.), pp. 129 ff. The book was discussed by several authors in *Current Anthropology* 11 (1970): 39–48.

7. Alexander Marshak presented his discovery for the first time in "Lunar Notation on Upper Paleolithic Remains," *Scientia* 146 (1964): 743–45. This short article was followed by a series of more detailed contributions: "New Techniques in the Analysis and Interpretation of Mesolithic Notations and Symbolic Art," in *Actes du symposium international*, ed. Emmanuel Anati (Valcamonica, 1970), pp. 479–94; *Notations dans les gravures du paléolithique supérieur: Nouvelles méthodes d'analyse*, Mémoire no. 8 of the Institut de préhistoire de l'Université de Bordeaux (Bordeaux, 1970); "Le bâton de commandement de Montgandier (Charente): Réexamen au microscope et interprétation nouvelle," *L'Anthropologie* 74 (1970): 321–52; "Cognitive Aspects of Upper Paleolithic Notation and Symbol," *Scientia* 178 (1972): 817–28. The results of these researches are analyzed in his book *The Roots of Civilization: The Cognitive Beginnings of Man's First Art, Symbol, and Notation* (New York, 1972); cf. our review: "On Prehistoric Religions," *HR* 14 (1974): 140–47, esp. 140–43.

The study "The Meander as System: The Analysis and Recognition of Iconographic Units in Upper Paleolithic Compositions" was presented at the Colloquium of the Australian Institute of Aboriginal Studies in

Canberra, May 1974. The author has kindly made the manuscript of this important contribution available to us.

For a comparative study of circular dances, see Evel Gasparini, "La danza circolare degli Slavi," *Ricerche Slavistiche* 1 (1952): 67–92, and his *Il Matriarcaio Slavo: Antropologia Culturale dei Protoslavi* (Florence, 1973), pp. 665 ff. Cf. our review in *HR* 14 (1974:) 74–78.

The secret myth of the Peul shepherds, communicated by Amadou Hampaté Bâ (who was himself initiated), has been published by Germaine Dieterlen, *Koumen*, Cahiers de l'Homme (Paris, 1961); it is on the basis of this myth that Henri Lhote was able to interpret certain rock paintings of the Hoggar and the Tassili; see his "Données récentes sur les gravures et les peintures rupestres du Sahara," in *Simposio de Arte Rupestre*, pp. 273–90, esp. pp. 282 ff.

H. von Sicard holds that the African Luwe still reflects the belief in a Supreme God of the Eurafrican hunters before 8000 B.C.; cf. "*Luwe* und verwandte mythische Gestalten," *Anthropos* 63/64 (1968/69): 665–737, esp. 720 ff.

The myths of the "cosmogonic dive" are documented in eastern Europe, in central and northern Asia, in aboriginal (pre-Āryan) India, in Indonesia, and in North America; see Eliade, *Zalmoxis: The Vanishing God*, trans. Willard R. Trask (Chicago, 1972), chap. 3: "The Devil and God" (pp. 76–130).

W. Gaerte's study, "Kosmische Vorstellungen im Bilde prähistorischer Zeit: Erdberg, Himmelsberg, Erdnabel und Weltströme," *Anthropos* 9 (1914): 956–79, is out of date but is still useful for its iconographic documents.

Benjamin Ray has provided a brilliant analysis of the magico-religious power of the word among the Dinkas and the Dogons: "'Performative Utterances' in African Rituals," *HR* 13 (1973): 16–35. (The term "performative utterances" was coined by the English philosopher J. L. Austin.)

8. A. Rust has published several works on the excavations carried on at Meiendorf, Stellmoor, and Ahrensburg-Hopfenbach over a period of forty years; the most important are *Die alt- und mittlesteinzeitlichen Funde von Stellmoor* (Neumünster in Holstein, 1934); *Das altsteinzeitliche Rentierjägerlager Meiendorf* (Neumünster, 1937); *Die Jungpaläolitischen Zeltanlagen von Ahrensburg* (1958); *Vor 20,000 Jahren* (Neumünster, 1962).

On the religious meanings of these discoveries, see A. Rust, "Neue endglaziale Funde von kultische-religiöser Bedeutung," *Ur-Schweiz* 12 (1948): 68–71; Rust, "Eine endpaläolitische hölzerne Götzenfigur aus Ahrensburg," *Rom. Germ. Kom. d. deutsch. Arch. Inst.* (Berlin, 1958), pp. 25–26; H. Pohlhausen, "Zum Motiv der Rentierversenkung der Hamburger und Ahrensburger Stufe des niederdeutschen Flachlandmagda-lenien," *Anthropos* 48 (1953): 987–90; H. Müller-Karpe, *Handbuch der Vorgeschichte*, vol. 1, p. 225; vol. 2, p. 496 (no. 347); J. Maringer, "Die Opfer der paläolitischen Menschen," *Anthropica* (St. Augustin bei Bonn, 1968), pp. 249–72, esp. 266–70.

On sacrifice by immersion, see Alois Closs, "Das Versenkungsopfer," *Wiener Beiträge zur Kulturgeschichte und Linguistik* 9 (1952): 66–107.

On the problem of the religious meanings of the rock art of eastern Spain, see H. Obermaier, *Fossil Man in Spain* (New Haven, 1924); J. Maringer, *The Gods of Prehistoric Man*, pp. 176–86.

9. The best and most complete presentation of the problem of the pre-historic art of Palestine is the study by J. Perrot, "Préhistoire palestinienne," in *Dictionnaire de la Bible*, supplement to vol. 8 (1968), cols. 286–446. See also R. de Vaux, *Histoire ancienne d'Israël* (Paris, 1971), vol. 1, pp. 41–59. On the Natufian culture, see D. A. E. Garrod, "The Natufian Culture: The Life and Economy of a Mesolithic People in the Near East," *Proceedings of the British Academy* 43 (1957): 211–27; E. Anati, *Palestine before the Hebrews* (New York, 1963), pp. 146–78; H. Müller-Karpe, *Handbuch der Vorgeschichte*, vol. 2: *Jungsteinzeit* (Munich, 1968), pp. 73 ff. On the Natufian religion, see most recently Jacques Cauvin, *Religions néolithiques de Syro-Palestine* (Paris, 1972), pp. 19–31.

On the religious significations of skulls and on ritual cannibalism, see Müller-Karpe, *Handbuch*, vol. 1, pp. 239 ff.; Walter Dostal, "Ein Beitrag zur Frage des religiösen Weltbildes der frühesten Bodenbauer Vordera-siens," *Archiv für Völkerkunde* 12 (1957): 53–109, esp. 75–76 (with bibliog-raphy); R. B. Onians, *The Origins of European Thought* (Cambridge, 1951; 2d ed. 1954), pp. 107 ff., 530 ff.

10. On the "ritual hunt" in Africa, see Helmut Straube, *Die Tierverklei-dungen der afrikanischen Naturvölker* (Wiesbaden, 1955), pp. 83 ff., 198 ff., and passim. On the resemblances between the techniques of war and the hunt among the Assyrians, the Iranians, and the Turko-Mongols, see Karl Meuli, "Ein altpersischer Kriegsbrauch," *Westöstliche Abhandlungen: Festschrift für Rudolph Tchudi* (Wiesbaden, 1954), pp. 63–86.

We add that the hunt has given rise to other themes in mythology and folklore. To cite only one example: the pursuit of a species of deer leads the hero into the otherworld or into a world of enchantment and magic, or, finally, the hunter meets Christ or the Bodhisattva, etc.; cf. Eliade, *Zalmoxis*, pp. 131–63. In a large number of myths concerning the conquest of a territory, founding a city, crossing a river or a swamp, etc., it is the animal that finds the solution to an apparently hopeless situation; see Eliade, *Zalmoxis*, pp. 135 ff., 162.

11. On the domestication of plants and animals, see Müller-Karpe, *Handbuch der Vorgeschichte*, vol. 2, pp. 240–56; Peter J. Ucko and G. W. Dimbley, eds., *The Domestication and Exploitation of Plants and Animals* (Chicago, 1969); Gary A. Wright, "Origins of Food Production in Southwestern Asia: A Survey of Ideas," *Current Anthropology* 12 (October–December, 1971): 447–79.

For a comparative study, see F. Herrmann, "Die Entwicklung des Pflanzenanbaues als ethnologisches Problem," *Studium Generale* 11 (1958): 352–63; Herrmann, "Die religiösgeistige Welt des Bauerntums in ethnologischer Sicht," ibid., pp. 434–41.

Robert Braidwood distinguishes four phases of primitive agricultural activity: people inhabiting villages and practicing an elementary cultivation ("primary village farming"), agriculture of fixed villages ("settled village farming"), "incipient cultivation," and, finally, "intensified village farming"; see R. Braidwood and L. Braidwood, "Earliest Village Communities of South West Asia," *Journal of World History* 1 (1953): 278–310; R. Braidwood, "Near Eastern Prehistory: The Swing from Food-Gathering Cultures to Village-Farming Communities Is Still Imperfectly Understood," *Science* 127 (1958): 1419–30; cf. R. Braidwood, "Prelude to Civilization," in *City Invincible: A Symposium on Urbanization and Cultural Development in the Ancient Near East*, ed. Carl H. Kraeling and Robert M. Adams (Chicago, 1960), pp. 297–313; Carl O. Sauer, *Agricultural Origins and Dispersals* (New York, 1952); Edgar Anderson, *Plants, Man, and Life* (Boston, 1952).

On myths of the Hainuwele type and their religious and cultural meaning, see A. E. Jensen, *Das religiöse Weltbild einer frühen Kultur* (Stuttgart, 1948), pp. 35 ff.; Jensen, *Myth and Cult among Primitive Peoples* (English trans., Chicago, 1963), [German ed., Wiesbaden, 1951]), pp. 166 ff.; Carl A. Schmitz, "Die Problematik der Mythologeme 'Hainuwele' und 'Prometheus,'" *Anthropos* 55 (1960): 215–38; Eliade, *Myth and Reality*, trans. Willard R. Trask (New York, 1963), pp. 103 ff.; T. Mabuchi, "Tales concerning the Origin of Grain in the Insular Areas of Eastern-Southeastern Asia," *Asian Folklore Studies* 23 (1964): 1–92; Atsuhiko Yoshida, "Les excrétions de la Déesse et l'origine de l'agriculture," *Annales* 21 (July–August 1966): 717–28.

Ileana Chirasi has recently identified in Greek mythology certain mythico-ritual complexes of the Hainuwele type, which seem to belong to the "precereal" phase (*Elementi di culture precereali nei miti e riti greci* [Rome, 1968]).

According to the German ethnologist Kunz Dittmer, the cultivation of roots and bulbs would already have begun, in Southeast Asia, during the Upper Paleolithic. Women had the responsibility for planting and harvesting; they wove baskets and, later, made pottery. In consequence, the cultivated fields became the women's property. The husband came to live in his wife's house, and descent was matrilinear. The men, in addition to hunting and fishing, undertook the task of clearing land. This type of civilization, which Dittmer defines as a combination of hunting and planting ("Jäger-Pflanzer") spread into tropical Africa, Melanesia, and the two Americas.

Still in Southeast Asia, there later appeared the cultivation of tubers and horticulture; it is during this period that the domestication of the pig and of poultry occurred. This civilization is characterized by an organization of the matriarchal type, by male secret societies (to terrorize the women), age groups, the economic and religious importance of woman, lunar mythologies, orgiastic fertility cults, head-hunting, and the cult of skulls. The regeneration of life was accomplished by human sacrifices. The cult of ancestors was justified by their role in fertility. Further characteristic elements: shamanism and the development of art (music, cult drama, masks of the secret societies, plastic representations of ancestors). This type of civilization (or cultural cycle) had already spread, during the Mesolithic period, into Southeast Asia (it is still found today among certain primitive peoples of Outer India and Indochina), Equatorial Africa, and the Pacific, with the exception of Polynesia.

Dittmer explains the cultivation of cereals as a substitute (*Ersatz*) for vegeculture, made necessary by the spread of the practice into the steppe zones. The passage from vegeculture to the cultivation of cereals took place in India; it is there that the most ancient cereal—millet—was cultivated. From India the new technique spread into western Asia, where the wild species of several graminaceae were domesticated. Dittmer distinguishes two specific cultural circles in the cultivation of cereals: (*a*) cultivation of the "extensive" type, in the regions enjoying a sufficient quantity of rain, and (*b*) "intensive" cultivation, that is, employing terraces, irrigation, and gardening. Each of these cultural cycles has its own corresponding sociological, economic, and religious structures (see Kunz Dittmer, *Allgemeine Völkerkunde* [Braunschweig, 1954], pp. 163–90).

H. Baumann, on the contrary, considers that the cultivation of tubers was invented by imitating and readapting the technique of cereal cultivation; see his *Das doppelte Geschlecht* (Berlin, 1955), pp. 289 ff.

12. On the mystical equivalence woman:cultivated ground, see Eliade, *Patterns in Comparative Religion*, trans. Rosemary Sheed (New York,

1958), pp. 239–64, 331–66; and Eliade, *Myths, Dreams, and Mysteries*, trans. Philip Mairet (London, 1960), pp. 156–92.

Against Albert Dieterich's hasty generalizations (*Mutter Erde*, 3d ed. [Berlin, 1925]), see Olof Pettersson, *Mother Earth: An Analysis of the Mother-Earth Concepts according to Albert Dieterich* (Lund, 1967), and the critical remarks of R. Turcan in *RHR* 175 (1969): 70–79. See also P. J. Ucko, *Anthropomorphic Figurines* (London, 1968), and Andrew Fleming, "The Myth of the Mother-Goddess," *World Archaeology* 1 (1969): 247–61.

On the parthenogenesis of Greek and Mediterranean goddesses, see Uberto Pestalozza, *Religione mediterranea: Vechi e nuovi studi* (Milan, 1951), pp. 191 ff.

On the periodic renewal of the world, cf. Eliade, *Cosmos and History: The Myth of the Eternal Return*, trans. Willard R. Trask (New York, 1959), pp. 62 ff., and *Myth and Reality*, pp. 39 ff.

On the symbolism of the Cosmic Tree, see the documents and bibliographies given in Eliade, *Shamanism*, pp. 39 ff., 168 ff., 194 ff., 282 ff.

On circular time and the cosmic cycle, see *Cosmos and History*, pp. 49 ff.

On the religious valorization of space, see *Patterns in Comparative Religion*, pp. 367 ff.

On the symbolism of habitations in the Neolithic culture of Yang-chao, see R. A. Stein, "Architecture et pensée religieuse en Extrême-Orient," *Arts Asiatiques* 4 (1957): 177 ff.; see also Eliade, *Shamanism*, pp. 261 ff.

On classificatory and ritual dichotomy, and the different kinds of antagonisms and polarities, see Eliade, *The Quest: History and Meaning in Religion* (Chicago, 1969), pp. 127–75.

13. On the archeological documents of Jericho and their interpretation, see Kathleen Kenyon, *Digging Up Jericho* (London, 1957); Kenyon, *Archaeology in the Holy Land* (London, 1960); J. Garstang and J. B. E. Garstang, *The Story of Jericho* (London, 1948); E. Anati, *Palestine before the Hebrews*, pp. 273 ff.; and R. de Vaux, *Histoire ancienne d'Israël*, pp. 41 ff.

On the Neolithic religions of Syria and Palestine, see, most recently, J. Cauvin, *Religions néolithiques de Syro-Palestine*, pp. 43 ff. (excavations at Jericho, Munhata, Beidha, Tell Ramad), and pp. 67 ff. (for Ras Shamra, Byblos, etc.); see also Müller-Karpe, *Handbuch der Vorgeschichte*, vol. 2, pp. 335 ff., 349 ff.

Mellaart considered that the preceramic culture of Jericho (phase B, 6500–5500 B.C.) was derived from the Hacilar culture (7000–6000 B.C.); see his "Hacilar: A Neolithic Village Site," *Scientific American* 205 (August, 1961): 90. But in *Earliest Civilization of the Near East* (London and New

York, 1965), p. 45, he cites the new radiocarbon dates for Jericho (phase B): 6968 and 6918 B.C.; in other words, the two cultures appear to be contemporary.

As for Çatal Hüyük, it represents the largest Neolithic city in the Near East. Though incompletely excavated (one quarter of the surface in 1965), Çatal Hüyük has revealed a surprising degree of civilization: a developed agricultural (several species of grains and vegetables), stock-rearing, commerce, and numerous richly decorated temples. See James Mellaart, *Çatal Hüyük: A Neolithic Town of Anatolia* (New York, 1967). See also Walter Dostal, "Zum Problem der Stadt- und Hochkultur im Vorderen Orient: Ethnologische Marginalien," *Anthropos* 63 (1968): 227–60.

On Tell Halaf, the essential bibliography is given by Müller-Karpe, *Handbuch*, vol. 2, pp. 59 ff., 427–28.

On the Obeid culture, see Müller-Karpe, ibid., pp. 61 ff., 339, 351, 423 (bibliography of the excavations), and 425 ff. (the White Temple, the ziggurat). Cf. M. E. L. Mallowan, *Early Mesopotamia and Iran* (1965), pp. 36 ff.

Another sanctuary deserves mention at this point: the "Eye Temple," excavated by Mallowan at Brak, in the valley of Habur (1,000 kilometers north of Uruk), and dated by him at about 3000 B.C. Among the finds were several thousand "idols" in black and white alabaster, characterized by one pair, or several pairs, of eyes. According to Mallowan, they represent ex-votos offered to an all-seeing divinity, protectress of the city; see his *Early Mesopotamia*, pp. 48 ff. and figs. 38–40. The temple was consecrated to the goddess Inanna. In his book *The Eye Goddess* (1957), O. G. S. Crawford studies the dissemination of this iconographic type as far as to England and Ireland, but a number of the examples that he cites are not convincing.

The religious symbolism of the figurines and other objects of Mesopotamian prehistory has been studied by B. L. Goff, *Symbols of Prehistoric Mesopotamia* (New Haven and London, 1963); see esp. pp. 10–48 (Tell Halaf and Obeid periods), and figs. 58–234.

14. On the earliest European civilization, see Marija Gimbutas, "Old Europe, c. 7000–3000 B.C.: The Earliest European Civilization before the Infiltration of the Indo-European Peoples," *Journal of Indo-European Studies* 1 (1973): 1–20.

On the religious ideas and cults, see Marija Gimbutas, *The Gods and Goddesses of Old Europe, 7000–3500 B.C.: Myths, Legends, and Cult Images* (Berkeley and Los Angeles, 1974); J. Maringer, "Priests and Priestesses in Prehistoric Europe," *HR* 17 (1977): 101–20.

On the sanctuary of Căscioarele, see Vladimir Dumitrescu, "Edifice destiné au culte découvert dans la couche Boian-Spantov de la station-*tell* de Căscioarele," *Dacia* n.s. 14 (1970): 5–24.

On the temple model, see Hortensia Dumitrescu, "Un modèle de sanctuaire découvert dans la station énéolithique de Căscioarele," *Dacia* n.s. 12 (1968): 381–94.

15. On the discovery of metals and the development of metallurgical techniques, see T. A. Rickard, *Man and Metals: A History of Mining in Relation to the Development of Civilization* (New York, 1932); R. I. Forbes, *Metallurgy in Antiquity* (Leiden, 1950); Charles Singer, E. Y. Holmyard, and A. R. Hall, *A History of Technology* (Oxford, 1955), vol. 1. See the bibliographies in Eliade, *The Forge and the Crucible*, trans. Stephen Corrin (New York, 1962), pp. 179–81, and "The Forge and the Crucible: A Postscript" (*HR* 8 [1968]: 74–88), p. 77.

On miners and smiths, see *The Forge and the Crucible*, pp. 53–86; "A Postscript," pp. 78–80. On divine smiths and civilizing heroes, see *The Forge and the Crucible*, pp. 87–108. On the "origins" of alchemy, see A. M. Leicester, *The Historical Background of Chemistry* (New York, 1956), vol. 1; I. R. Partington, *History of Chemistry* (London, 1961), vol. 1; Allen G. Debus, "The Significance of the History of Early Chemistry," *Cahiers d'histoire mondiale* 9 (1965): 39–58; Robert P. Multhauf, *The Origins of Chemistry* (London, 1966).

16. For a general introduction to Sumerian history, culture, and religion, see A. Parrot, *Sumer* (Paris, 1952), and especially the following works by S. N. Kramer: *The Sumerians: Their History, Culture, and Character* (Chicago, 1963); *From the Tablets of Sumer* (Indian Hills, 1956), republished under the title *History Begins at Sumer* (New York, 1959); "Mythology of Sumer and Akkad," in S. N. Kramer, ed., *Mythologies of the Ancient World* (New York, 1961), pp. 93–137; and *Sumerian Mythology* (Philadelphia, 1944; rev. ed., 1961). All these works contain numerous almost complete translations of Sumerian texts. See also Adam Falkenstein and W. von Soden, *Sumerische und akkadische Hymnen und Gebeten* (Zurich, 1953), and G. R. Castellino, *Mitologia sumero-accadica* (Turin, 1967). The monograph by Charles F. Jean, *La religion sumérienne* (Paris, 1931), is still useful. A noteworthy synthesis has been presented by Raymond Jestin, "La religion sumérienne," in *Histoire des religions*, ed. Henri Charles Puech (Paris, 1970), vol. 1, pp. 154–202. See also Thorkild Jacobsen, "Formative Tendencies in Sumerian Religion," in Ernest Wright, ed., *The Bible and the Ancient Near East* (New York, 1961), pp. 267–78; Jacobsen, "Early Mesopotamian Religion: The Central Concerns," *Proc. Amer. Philos. Soc.* 107 (1963): 473–84.

The Sumerian religion is treated, together with the Akkadian, in Edouard Dhorme, *Les religions de Babylonie et d'Assyrie*, coll. "Mana" (Paris, 1954), pp. 1–330 (rich critical bibliographies). See also V. Christian, "Die Herkunft der Sumerer," *Sitzungsberichte der Akademie in Wien* 236, no. 1 (1961); A. Falkenstein, "La cité-temple sumérienne," *Cahiers d'histoire mondiale* 1 (1954): 784–814; F. R. Kraus, "Le rôle des temples depuis la troisième dynastie d'Ur jusqu'à la première dynastie de Babylone," ibid., pp. 518–45; A. Sjöberg and E. Bergmann, *Sumerian Temple Hymns* (1969). See also J. van Dijk, "Les contacts ethniques dans la Mésopotamie et les syncrétismes de la religion sumérienne," in *Syncretism*, edited by Sven S. Hartman (Stockholm, 1969), pp. 171–206.

As early as 1944 B. Landsberger had shown that the Sumerian cultural terminology (i.e., words related to agriculture, metallurgy, trades), as well as the names of rivers and cities, are of pre-Sumerian origin. Cf. Kramer, *The Sumerians*, pp. 41 ff.

Before settling in lower Mesopotamia, the Sumerians worshiped the same divinities in common; among the most important were An, En-lil, En-ki, Inanna. But later each city had its divine patron; for example, En-lil was the god of Nippur, En-ki reigned at Eridu, Nanna at Ur, etc.

The myth of Dilmun has been translated by Kramer in *ANET*, pp. 34–41, and in *From the Tablets of Sumer*, pp. 169–75; by Maurice Lambert in "La naissance du monde à Sumer," *Naissance du Monde: Sources orientales* (Paris, 1959), vol. 1, pp. 103 ff.; and recently by Castellino in *Mitologia sumero-accadica*, pp. 50 ff.

On An, see Dhorme, *Religions*, pp. 22–26, 45–48; see also D. O. Edzard, "Die Mythologie der Sumerer und Akkader," *WdM*, vol. 1, pp. 40–41.

On En-ki, see Dhorme, *Religions*, pp. 31–38, 50–51; J. Bottéro, "Les divinités sémitiques en Mésopotamie ancienne," *Studi Semitici* 1 (Rome, 1958): 17–63, esp. 36–38.

17. For a comparative presentation of the myths concerning the creation of man, see Theodor Gaster, *Myth, Legend, and Custom in the Old Testament* (New York, 1969), pp. 8 ff. The Mesopotamian texts are translated by Alexander Heidel, *The Babylonian Genesis* (Chicago, 1942), pp. 62–72.

According to a tradition transmitted by Berossus (third century B.C.), it is Bel (= Marduk) who ordered the gods to cut off his head and fashion man from earth mixed with his blood (Heidel, *Babylonian Genesis*, pp. 77–78). If this tradition is genuine, man's body would be made up of a divine and a "demonic" substance (for the earth derives from Tiamat).

In the myth known as the "Creation of the Spade," En-lil separates Heaven from Earth in order that men can "arise from the soil"; trans. Castellino, *Mitologia sumero-accadica*, pp. 55 ff.

On the meanings of the term *me*, see B. Landsberger, *Islamica* 2 (1926): 369; T. Jacobsen, *JNES* 5 (1946): 139, n. 20; J. van Dijk, *La sagesse suméro-akkadienne* (Leiden, 1953), p. 19; and K. Oberhuber, *Der numinose Begriff ME in Sumerischen* (Innsbruck, 1963). See also Yvonne Rosengarten, *Sumer et le sacré: Le jeu des* prescriptions (me), *des dieux, et des destins* (Paris, 1977).

On the rite of sacred marriage between the sovereign and Inanna, see S. N. Kramer, *The Sacred Marriage Rite: Aspects of Faith, Myth, and Ritual in Ancient Sumer* (Bloomington, Ind., 1969), and his "Le Rite du Mariage sacré Dumuzi-Inanna," *RHR* 181 (1972): 121–46.

On the concept of celestial models of cities and temples, see Eliade, *Cosmos and History*, pp. 6 ff.

The importance of the "king list" has been shown by Thorkild Jacobsen, *The Sumerian King List* (Chicago, 1939). A new translation has been provided by Kramer, *The Sumerians*, pp. 328–31. The tradition that the earliest kings descended from heaven—and ascended there after death—is preserved in Tibet, where the kings used a miraculous rope; cf. some examples in Eliade, *The Two and the One*, trans. J. M. Cohen (London, 1965), pp. 166 ff. (also published under the title *Mephistopheles and the Androgyne: Studies in Religious Myth and Symbol*). See also Erik Haarh, *The Yar-Lum Dynasty* (Copenhagen, 1969), pp. 138 ff. The myth of the king-messiah descended from heaven will attain great popularity in the Hellenistic period.

18. The essential bibliography on myths of the flood will be found in T. Gaster, *Myth, Legend, and Custom*, p. 353, to be supplemented by Eliade, *Myth and Reality*, pp. 54 ff.

The Sumerian fragments have been translated by Kramer, *ANET*, pp. 42–43.

On the flood myth in the *Epic of Gilgamesh*, see Alexander Heidel, *The Gilgamesh Epic and the Old Testament Parallels* (Chicago, 1946), pp. 224 ff.; A. Schott and W. von Soden, *Das Gilgamesch-Epos* (Stuttgart, 1958), pp. 86–99; W. G. Lambert, *JSS* 5 (1960): 113–23; E. Sollberger, *The Babylonian Legend of the Flood* (London, 1962); Ruth E. Simoons-Vermeer, "The Mesopotamian Flood-Stories: A Comparison and Interpretation," *Numen* 21 (1974): 17–34. For the version given by Berossus, see P. Schnabel, *Berossus und die hellenistische Literatur* (1923), pp. 164 ff., and Heidel, *The Gilgamesh Epic*, pp. 116 ff.

According to a passage in the *Epic of Gilgamesh* (tab. XI, line 14), "their heart led the great gods to produce a flood." According to Ea's words to En-lil (XI, 179 ff.), it can be understood that "sinners" existed, but no particulars are given. A fragment of the work known as the "Epic of Atrahasis" explains En-lil's anger by the uproar made by men, who had "become prosperous"; cf. Heidel, *The Gilgamesh Epic*, pp. 107 and 225 ff. According to recently published texts, the flood was regarded as a divine punishment: men had rebelled against their "destiny," which was to serve the gods by labor and worship; cf. G. Pettinato, "Die Bestrafung des Menschengeschlects durch die Sintflut," *Orientalia* n.s. 37 (1968): 156–200; W. G. Lambert, *Atrahasīs: The Story of the Flood* (Oxford, 1969).

19. There is a large bibliography on Inanna; the essential works are listed by E. O. Edzard in *WdM*, vol. 1, pp. 81–89. See also W. W. Hallo and J. van Dijk, *The Exaltation of Inanna* (New Haven and London, 1968); Wolfgang Helck, *Betrachtungen zur Grossen Göttin und den ihr verbundenen Gottheiten* (Munich, 1971), pp. 71–89; and the recent works by S. N. Kramer, *The Sacred Marriage Rite* (1969) and "Le Rite du Mariage sacré Dumuzi-Inanna," *RHR* 181 (1972): 121–46.

On Ishtar as hermaphrodite, see J. Bottéro, "Les divinités sémitiques," *Studi Semitici* 1 (1958): 40 ff. On Ishtar as goddess of war, see M. T. Barrelet, "Les déesses armées et ailées: Inanna-Ishtar," *Syria* 32 (1955): 222–60.

On Dumuzi-Tammuz, see the bibliography in *WdM*, vol. 1, pp. 51–53. The most important recent contributions are by Louis van den Berghe, "Réflexions critiques sur la nature de Dumuzi-Tammuz," *La Nouvelle Clio* 6 (1954): 298–321; T. Jacobsen, "Toward the Image of Tammuz," *HR* 1 (1961): 189–213; and O. R. Gurney, "Tammuz Reconsidered: Some Recent Developments," *JSS* 7 (1962): 147–60.

On the role of Geshtinanna in Dumuzi's "return," see A. Falkenstein in *Bibliotheca Orientalis*, vol. 22, pp. 281 ff. The differences between the Akkadian and Sumerian versions are analyzed in the study by A. Falkenstein, "Der sumerische und der akkadische Mythos von Inannas Gang zur Unterwelt," in *Festschrift W. Caskel* (1968), pp. 96 ff., and by Jean Bottéro, in *Annuaire de l'École des Hautes Études*, 1971–72, sec. IV, pp. 81–97. The most significant differences are these: the Sumerian version has no detailed description of the underworld (it knows the "Great Below" as antipodal to heaven, the "Great Above"; Bottéro, p. 86); in the Akkadian version Ishtar threatens, if she is not admitted to the underworld immediately, to demolish its gates and free the dead, who "will devour the living" (Bottéro, p. 86); in the Sumerian version the "water of life" is found in the underworld itself (in the "wineskin" that contained the drink of the infernal gods; Bottéro, p. 89); in the Akkadian version, it appears to be Ereshkigal who orders her messenger to wash Tammuz, anoint him with perfume, and clothe him in a "splendid dress"; so it is she who is responsible for Ishtar's indignation and, in the last analysis, for the ruin of Tammuz (Bottéro, pp. 91 ff.).

In his book *Tammuz: Der Unsterblichkeitsglaube der altorientalischen Bildkunst* (Berlin, 1949), Anton Moortgat proposed a new interpretation of Dumuzi-Tammuz on the basis of the iconographic documentation, but very few figures can be identified with certainty; cf. van den Berghe, "Réflexions critiques."

20. An excellent presentation of Babylonian religion has been provided by J. Nougayrol in *Histoire des religions* (Paris, 1970), vol. 1, pp. 203–49. See also J. Bottéro, *La religion babylonienne* (Paris, 1952), and his "Les divinités sémitiques anciennes en Mesopotamie," in S. Moscati, ed., *Le antiche divinità semitiche* (= *Studi Semitici* 1 [Rome, 1958]), pp. 17–63. G. Furlani, who had published a work in two volumes in 1928–29 (*La religione babilonese e assira*), has synthesized his researches in "La religione dei Babilonesi e Assiri," in *Le Civiltà dell'Oriente* (Rome, 1958), vol. 3, pp. 73–112. See also R. Follet, "Les aspects du divin et des dieux dans la Mésopotamie antique," *Recherches des sciences religieuses* 38 (1952): 189–209. A. L. Oppenheim's skepticism ("Why a 'Mesopotamian Religion' Should Not Be Written," *Ancient Mesopotamia: Portrait of a Dead Civilization* [Chicago, 1964], pp. 172 ff.) does not appear to be shared by his colleagues. See also M. David, *Les dieux et le destin en Babylonie* (Paris, 1949), and the illuminating synthesis by Thorkild Jacobsen, *The Treasures of Darkness: A History of Mesopotamian Religion* (New Haven, 1976).

On Ereshkigal and Nergal, see Dhorme, *Les Religions de Babylonie et d'Assyrie*, pp. 39–43, 51–52.

On Marduk, see Dhorme, pp. 139–50, 168–70; W. von Soden, in *Zeitschrift für Assyriologie* n.s. 17 (1955): 130–66. On the god Assur, see G. van Driel, *The Cult of Assur* (Assen, 1969).

On the temples, see Dhorme, pp. 174–97; H. J. Lenzen, "Mesopotamische Tempelanlagen von der Frühzeit bis zum zweiten Jahrtausend," *Zeitschrift für Assyriologie* n.s. 17 (1955): 1–36; G. Widengren, "Aspetti simbolici dei templi e luoghi di culto del vecino Oriente antico," *Numen* 7 (1960): 1–25; A. L. Oppenheim, *Ancient Mesopotamia*, pp. 106 ff., 129 ff.

For the rites, see G. Furlani, "Il sacrificio nella religione dei Semiti di Babilonia e Assiria," *Memorie della Accademia dei Lincei* 6, no. 3 (1932): 105–370; Furlani, *Riti babilonese e assiri* (Udine, 1940); F. Thureau-Dangin, *Rituels akkadiens* (Paris, 1921); and, for a general exposition, with a rich bibliography, see Dhorme, pp. 220–57. For the intercessory gods, who serve as intermediaries between the worshiper and the deity whom he invokes, see Dhorme, pp. 249–50. For prayers, see A. Falkenstein and W. von Soden, *Sumerische und akkadische Hymnen und Gebeten* (Stuttgart, 1953), and Dhorme, pp. 247 ff.

On the confession of sins, see R. Pettazzoni, *La confesione dei paccati* (Bologna, 1935), vol. 2, pp. 69–139.

On the luminosity of the gods, see A. L. Oppenheim, "Akkadian *pul(u)h(t)u* and *melammu*," *JAOS* 63 (1943): 31–34; Oppenheim, "The Golden Garments of the Gods," *JNES* 8 (1949): 172–93; and especially Elena Cassin, *La splendeur divine* (Paris and The Hague, 1968), pp. 12 ff. (critique of Oppenheim's hypothesis); pp. 26 ff. (light and chaos; divine sovereignty); and pp. 65 ff. (the *melammu* and the royal function). Cf. § 104, above, on the Iranian *xvarenah*.

On magic, see Meissner, *Babylonien und Assyrien*, vol. 2, pp. 198 ff.; Dhorme, pp. 259 ff.; G. Contenau, *La Magie chez les Assyriens et les Babyloniens* (Paris, 1947); Erica Reiner, "La magie babylonienne," in *Le monde du sorcier*, Sources Orientales no. 7 (Paris, 1966), pp. 67–98; J. Nougayrol, "La religion babylonienne," pp. 231–34. We quote a few lines from Nougayrol's conclusion (p. 234): "The Babylonian imagination, which had turned a little aside from the Sumerian 'stories of gods,' seems to delight in 'stories of devils.' In these very numerous and very long compositions by magicians, there may well be an element of literature intended to dazzle the profane. . . . But there is also undeniably present a substratum of anxiety, of which that concerning 'atomic war' can give us an idea. . . . More than any other people, it seems, the people of Mesopotamia, surrounded by 'barbarians' who constantly threatened it and periodically invaded its soil, had the feeling that civilization and the 'good life' are fragile and constantly called into question."

21. The *Enuma elish* has been frequently translated. The most recent versions are those by R. Labat, *Le poème babylonien de la création* (Paris, 1935) and *Les religions du Proche-Orient asiatique*, pp. 36–70; E. A. Speiser, "The Creation Epic," *ANET*, pp. 60–72; A. Heidel, *The Babylonian Genesis* (Chicago, 1942; 2d rev. ed., 1951); and Paul Garelli and Marcel Leibovici, "La naissance du monde selon Akkad," in *La naissance du monde*, Sources Orientales no. 1 (Paris, 1960), pp. 132–45.

Heidel's book also contains translations of other Babylonian cosmogonic texts and a study comparing them with the cosmogony in the Old Testament. See also W. von Soden in *Zeitschrift für Assyriologie* 47 (1954): i ff.; F. M. T. de Liagre, *Opera minora* (Groningen, 1953), pp. 282, 504 ff.; W. G. Lambert and P. Walcot, "A New Babylonian Theogony and Hesiod," *Kadmos* 4 (1965): 64–72 (see also the present work, chap. 6, § 47).

An analysis of the *Enuma elish* as an expression of Mesopotamian thought will be found in T. Jacobsen, "The Cosmos as a State," in H. Frankfort et al., *Before Philosophy: The Intellectual Adventure of Ancient Man* (Chicago, 1946; Penguin Books, 1949), pp. 137 ff., esp. pp. 182–99.

In a number of studies Jacobsen has brought out the "democratic" character of the Sumerian government and, by extension, of the Babylonian pantheon (for example, as the *Enuma elish* shows, Marduk is raised to the rank of supreme god by the assembly of all the divinities); see Jacobsen, "Early Political Development in Mesopotamia," *Zeitschrift für Assyriologie* 52 (1957): 91–140, and his article in *JNES* 2, pp. 159 ff. See also "The Battle between Marduk and Tiamat," *JAOS* 88 (1968): 104–8.

The sacred character of royalty in the ancient Near East has occasioned a long controversy. Some scholars have seen in the king, representative of the god, the center of a mythico-ritual system typical of all the religions of the ancient Near East. This methodological orientation, known as the "myth-and-ritual school" or "patternism," has inspired a large number of works, among which it will suffice to cite the two volumes published by S. H. Hooke, *Myth and Ritual* (1933) and *The Labyrinth* (1935), and the works of I. Engnell and G. Widengren. "Patternism" has been criticized, especially by H. Frankfort in *The Problem of Similarity in Ancient Near Eastern Religions*, Frazer Lecture (Oxford, 1951). This eminent scholar maintained that the differences between the relevant forms were more important than the similarities. For example, he drew attention to the fact that the pharaoh was considered to be a god or became a god, whereas in Mesopotamia the king was only the god's representative. In any case, it is obvious that the differences and similarities are equally important when we are dealing with *historically related cultures*. See also S. H. Hooke, "Myth and Ritual: Past and Present," in Hooke, ed., *Myth, Ritual, and Kingship* (Oxford, 1958), pp. 1–21; S. G. F. Brandon, "The Myth-and-Ritual Position Critically Considered," ibid., pp. 261–91 (this study contains a rich critical bibliography down to 1955).

22. On the *akitu*, see H. Zimmern, *Zum babylonischen Neujahrsfest*, 2 vols. (Leipzig, 1906, 1918); S. A. Pallis, *The Babylonian* akitu *Festival* (Copenhagen, 1926) (cf. the critique of this by H. S. Nyburg, *Le monde orientale* 23 [1929]: 204–11); R. Labat, *Le caractère religieux de la royauté assyro-babylonienne* (Paris, 1939), pp. 95 ff.} H. Frankfort, *Kingship and the Gods* (Chicago, 1948), pp. 313 ff.; W. G. Lambert, in *JSS*, vol. 13, pp. 106 ff. (Marduk's victory was reactualized at every New Year festival.) On the New Year festival considered as repetition of the cosmogony see A. J. Wensinck, "The Semitic New Year and the Origin of Eschatology," *Acta Orientalia* 1 (1923): 158–99; Eliade, *Cosmos and History*, pp. 62–73.

On the festival of the destinies, see Dhorme, *Les religions de Babylonie*, pp. 244 ff., 255 ff.

On the sacred character of Mesopotamian royalty see R. Labat, *Le caractère religieux de la royauté assyro-babylonienne;* Dhorme, *Les religions de Babylonie*, p. 20 (divinization of kings); H. Frankfort, *Kingship and the Gods*, pp. 215 ff.; I. Engnell, *Studies in Divine Kingship in the Ancient Near East* (Uppsala, 1943), pp. 18 ff.; G. Widengren, *The King and the Tree of Life in Ancient Near Eastern Religion* (Uppsala, 1951); Sidney Smith, "The Practice of Kingship in Early Semitic Kingdoms," in S. H. Hooke, ed., *Myth, Ritual, and Kingship*, pp. 22–73; A. L. Oppenheim, *Ancient Mesopotamia*, pp. 98 ff.; J. Zandee, "Le Messie: Conceptions de la royauté dans les religions du Proche-Orient ancien," *RHR* 180 (1971): 3–28. See also *Rencontre Assyriologique Internationale: Le palais et la royauté*, edited by P. Garelli (Paris, 1974).

23. We have used the translations by G. Contenau, *L'Epopée de Gilgamesh* (Paris, 1939); Alexander Heidel, *The Gilgamesh Epic and Old Testament Parallels* (Chicago, 1946); E. A. Speiser, *ANET*, pp. 72–99; and A. Schott and W. v. Soden, *Das Gilgamesch Epos* (Stuttgart, 1958). Now see Labat, *Les religions du Proche-Orient*, pp. 149–226.

At present, six episodes of the legend of Gilgamesh are known in Sumerian versions: (1) the expedition to the cedar forest and the victory over Huwawa (trans. Kramer, *From the Tablets*, pp. 204–7; Kramer, *The Sumerians*, pp. 192–97); (2) Gilgamesh and the Heavenly Bull; (3) the flood and the immortalization of Zisudra; (4) the death of Gilgamesh (*ANET*, pp. 50–52), an episode lacking in the Babylonian version; (5) Gilgamesh and Agga (translated in *Tablets*, pp. 29–30; *The Sumerians*, pp. 197–200), one of the shortest Sumerian epic texts (115 lines), no trace of which has been found in the Babylonian Epic (but some authors hold that this episode has a historical foundation and hence ought not to be included among the mythological texts); (6) Gilgamesh, Enkidu, and the otherworld (translated in *Tablets*, pp. 224–25; *The Sumerians*, 197–205).

This last episode makes up the contents of tablet XII of the *Epic of Gilgamesh* (see above, chap. 3, p. 92, n. 50). Gilgamesh cuts down a gigantic tree and gives the trunk to Inanna-Ishtar to make into a throne and a couch. From its roots and its crown he makes two magic objects for himself, the *pukku* and the *mekku*, whose interpretation is still disputed; probably they are musical instruments (drum and drumsticks?). As the result of a ritual error these objects fall into the world below. Touched by his master's despair, Enkidu offers to go and look for them. But, since he fails to follow the instructions that Gilgamesh has given him to avoid irritating the spirits, Enkidu cannot come up again. In his sorrow Gilgamesh prays to the gods, and Nergal, the sovereign of the underworld, allows Enkidu's spirit to return to earth for a few moments. Gilgamesh questions him concerning the fate of the dead. His companion hesitates: "If I told thee the law of the netherworld which I know, I should see thee sit down and weep!" (col. IV, lines 1–5). But Gilgamesh insists, and Enkidu gives him a short and depressing description: "All that is deep in dust. . . ."

See the following publications by S. N. Kramer: *Gilgamesh and the Huluppu-Tree* (Assyriological Study no. 8, Oriental Institute of Chicago); "Gilgamesh: Some New Sumerian Data," in P. Garelli, ed., *Gilgamesh et sa légende* (Paris, 1960), pp. 59–68; "The Epic of Gilgamesh and Its Sumerian Sources," *JAOS* 64 (1944): 7–22; and "Sumerian Epic Literature," in *La Poesia epica e la sua formazione* (Accad. Naz. dei Lincei, 1970), pp. 825–37. See also A. Schaffer, *Sumerian Sources of Tablet XII of the Epic Gilgamesh*, Dissertation, Department of Oriental Studies, University of Pennsylvania, Philadelphia, 1962. According to A. Falkenstein, the name of the hero was read in Sumerian as Bilgameš; cf. *Reallexicon der Assyriologie* (Berlin and Leipzig, 1932——), vol. 3 (1968), pp. 357 ff.

There is an immense bibliography on the *Epic of Gilgamesh* (in which P. Jensen saw the chief source of universal literature; see his *Das Gilgamesh-Epos in der Weltliteratur*, vol. 1 [Strasbourg, 1906]). The most important contributions are listed in the translations by Contenau, Heidel, Kramer, and A. Schott and W. v. Soden. See also the studies collected by P. Garelli, *Gilgamesh et sa légende* (pp. 7–30, bibliography) and the articles by A. Falkenstein et al. in *Reallexikon der Assyriologie*, vol. 3 (1968), pp. 357–75, by W. v. Soden in *Zeitschrift der Assyr.*, vol. 53, pp. 209 ff., and by J. Nougayrol, "L'Epopée Babylonienne," in *La poesia epica e la sua formazione*, pp. 839–58. Recently Kurt Jaritz has interpreted a certain number of episodes (the drum, the dreams, the cedar forest, etc.) as illustrating shamanic ideas and practices; see his "Schamanistisches im Gilgameš-Epos," *Beiträge zu Geschichte, Kultur und Religion des alten Orients* (Baden-Baden, 1971), pp. 75–87. A similar interpretation has been proposed by E. A. S. Butterworth, *The Tree at the Navel of the Earth* (Berlin, 1970), pp. 138 ff.

The myth of Adapa represents another unsuccessful attempt at immortalization, but in this case the responsibility does not fall on the hero. Adapa was created by Ea as intelligent but mortal. Once, because the South Wind had overturned his boat, Adapa broke its wings. This was a violation of the cosmic order, and Anu summoned him to judgment. Before his departure, Ea gave him precise instructions as to his behavior in heaven, and especially warned him not to accept the "bread of death" and the "waters of death" that would be offered him. Adapa did not hide the fact that he had broken the Wind's wings in revenge. Impressed by his sincerity, Anu offered him the "bread of life" and the "waters of life." But Adapa refused them, thus losing the opportunity to become immortal.

Indirectly, this mythical episode seems to reflect a tension between Anu and Ea, the reasons for which we do not know. See the new translation, with commentary, by Labat, *Les religions du Proche-Orient asiatique*, pp. 290–94.

On concepts related to death and the beyond, see B. Meissner, *Babylonien und Assyrien*, vol. 2, pp. 143 ff.; A. Heidel, *The Gilgamesh Epic*, pp. 137 ff.; J. M. Aynard, "Le jugement des morts chez les Assyrobabyloniens," in *Le Jugement des Morts*, Sources Orientales no. 4 (Paris, 1961), pp. 81–102.

24. For the wisdom literature, we have followed the translations by Robert H. Pfeifer published in *ANET*, pp. 343–440. Other translations have been provided by W. G. Lambert, *Babylonian Wisdom Literature* (Oxford, 1960), pp. 21–62 ff.; by G. R. Castellino, *Sapienza babilonese* (Turin, 1962); and by R. Labat, *Les religions du Proche-Orient*, pp. 320 ff. See also J. J. A. van Dijk, *La sagesse suméro-akkadienne* (Leiden, 1953); J. Nougayrol, "Une version ancienne du 'Juste Souffrant,'" *RB* 59 (1952): 239–50; and the recent bibliography given in O. Eissfeldt, *The Old Testament: An Introduction* (1963), p. 83, n. 3.

For Babylonian divination, see A. L. Oppenheim, *Ancient Mesopotamia*, pp. 206–27. See also *La divination en Mésopotamie et dans les régions voisines*, Travaux du Centre d'Études supérieures spécialisé d'Histoire des Religions de Strasbourg (1966), in which the most noteworthy contributions are those by A. Falkenstein, "'Wahrsagung' in der Sumerischen Überlieferung"; A. Finet, "La place du devin dans la société de Mari"; J. Nougayrol, "Trente ans de recherches sur la divination babylonienne, 1935–1963"; and A. L. Oppenheim, "Perspectives on Mesopotamian Divination." A recent addition is Jean Nougayrol, "La divination babylonienne," in *La Divination*, ed. André Caquot and Marcel Leibovici (Paris, 1968), vol. 1, pp. 25–81. These works provide rich bibliographies.

On Babylonian oneiromancy, see A. L. Oppenheim, *The Interpretation of Dreams in the Ancient Near East, with a Translation of an Assyrian Dream Book* (Philadelphia, 1956); Marcel Leibovici, "Les songes et leur interprétation à Babylone," in *Les songes et leur intérpretation*, Sources Orientales no. 2 (Paris, 1959), pp. 65–85.

On horoscopes, see A. Sachs, "Babylonian Horoscopes," *Journal of Cuneiform Studies* 6 (1952): 49–75. On astrology, see Nougayrol, "La divination babylonienne," pp. 45–51 (bibliography, p. 78), and A. L. Oppenheim, *Ancient Mesopotamia*, pp. 308 ff.

On scientific discoveries, see O. Neugebauer, *The Exact Sciences in Antiquity*, 2d ed. (Providence, 1957); Neugebauer, "The Survival of Babylonian Methods in the Exact Science of Antiquity and the Middle

Ages," *Proceedings of the American Philosophical Society* 107 (1963): 528–35; A. L. Oppenheim, *Ancient Mesopotamia*, pp. 288–310.

On the influence of Mesopotamian ideas, see Oppenheim, pp. 67 ff. (bibliography, p. 356, n. 26); on the influences documented in the Old Testament, see the bibliography in W. H. P. Römer, *Historia Religionum* (Leiden, 1969), vol. 1, pp. 181–82.

25. For the general history of Egypt, see E. Drioton and J. Vandier, *L'Egypte*, 2d ed. (Paris, 1946); John A. Wilson, *The Culture of Ancient Egypt* (= *The Burden of Egypt*) (Chicago, 1951; 5th ed., 1958); William C. Hayes, *The Sceptre of Egypt*, vol. 1: *From the Earliest Times to the End of the Middle Kingdom* (New York, 1953); Joachim Spiegel, *Das Werden der altägyptischen Hochkultur* (Heidelberg, 1953); F. Daumas, *La civilisation de l'Egypte pharaonique* (Paris, 1965). There are excellent recent summaries in the work published under the editorship of J. R. Harris, *The Legacy of Egypt* (Oxford, 1971).

On the prehistoric cultures of Egypt, see: E. J. Baumgartel, *The Cultures of Prehistoric Egypt* (London, 1955); H. Frankfort, *The Birth of Civilization in the Near East* (London, 1951), pp. 41 ff., 100 ff.; Wilson, *The Culture of Ancient Egypt*, pp. 18 ff.; W. B. Emery, *Archaic Egypt* (Harmondsworth: Pelican Books, 1963).

It is not yet known how agriculture made its way into Egypt. It is probable that it spread from Palestine, for traces of a Neolithic culture (ca. 4500 B.C.) have been excavated at Merimdeh, near the Delta. The dead were buried in the houses, but without offerings of funeral objects. The Upper Egyptian culture called "Badarian" (from the name of the site, Badari), knows, in addition to agriculture and stock-raising, a black-and-red pottery. The dead were buried in a bent posture; domestic animals were also buried, wrapped in textiles. In comparison with Tell Halaf and Warka, the Neolithic Egyptian cultures appear poor and marginal.

With the appearance of the Amratian culture (Early Predynastic) we witness the first attempts toward exploiting the natural irrigation of the Nile Valley. Stone and copper are worked, but the pottery is coarser than that of the Badarian period (probably because stone vessels were beginning to be made; see Clark, *World Prehistory*, p. 104). Food offerings and clay figurines have been found in the burials. It was only during the Late Predynastic (Nakada II) that metallurgy was introduced, a thousand years after its rise in the Near East. A number of other cultural elements were borrowed from Asia, but only after a considerable lapse of time. Wheeled vehicles, long known in Mesopotamia, were introduced into Egypt only under the Empire (ca. 1570 B.C.). The greatness of Egyptian civilization begins with the uniting of the two lands, Upper and Lower Egypt. As for the beginnings of urban civilization, which are of considerable interest for any comparative study, their archeological traces are buried under the mud of the Nile. On the Badarian and Amratian cultures, see Müller-Karpe, *Handbuch der Vorgeschichte*, vol. 2, pp. 28–55, 339–45, 353–61.

The bibliography down to 1948 is listed by Jacques Vandier, *La religion égyptienne*, 2d ed. (Paris, 1949), pp. 3–10; see also (ibid., pp. 24–29) Vandier's critical exposition of the opinions of K. Sethe (*Urgeschichte u. älteste Religion der Ägypter* [Leipzig, 1930]) and of H. Kees (*Der Götterglaube im alten Ägypten* [Leipzig, 1941; 2d ed., Berlin, 1956]) on the primitive religions of Egypt. Cf. R. Weill, "Notes sur l'histoire primitive des grandes religions égyptiennes," *Bulletin de l'Institut Français d'Archéologie Orientale* 47 (1948): 59–150.

Among general studies on the religions of Egypt we mention: Adolf Erman, *Die Religion der Ägypter* (Berlin and Leipzig, 1934); Herman Junker, *Pyramidenzeit: Das Werden der altägyptische Religion* (Einsiedeln, 1949); J. Garnot Sainte-Fare, *Religions de l'Egypte* (Paris, 1951); S. Donadoni, *La religione dell'Egitto antico* (Milan, 1955); H. Frankfort, *Ancient Egyptian Religion* (New York, 1948); Frankfort, *Kingship and the Gods: A Study of Ancient Near Eastern Religion as the Integration of Society and Nature* (Chicago, 1948); R. T. Rundle Clark, *Myth and Symbol in Ancient Egypt* (London, 1959). The book by S. Morenz, *Egyptian Religion*, trans. Ann Keep (Ithaca, N.Y., 1973), is at once an updating and an admirable synthesis undertaken from the viewpoint of the general history of religions. See also C. J. Bleeker, "The Religion of Ancient Egypt," *Historia Religionum* (Leiden, 1969), vol. 1, pp. 40–114; Bleeker, *Hathor and Thoth: Two Key Figures of the Ancient Egyptian Religion* (Leiden, 1973), pp. 10 ff., 159 ff.; P. Derchain, "La religion égyptienne," *Histoire des religions*, ed. H. C. Puech (1970), vol. 1, pp. 63–140.

Indispensable for its rich documentation and bibliographical references is Hans Bonnet, *Reallexicon der ägyptischen Religionsgeschichte* (Berlin, 1952). Gunther Roeder has recently published a rich collection of texts, with admirable illustrations, in *Die ägyptische Religion in Text und Bild:* vol. 1, *Die ägyptische Götterwelt;* vol. 2, *Mythen und Lengenden um ägyptischen Gottheiten und Pharaonen;* vol. 3, *Kulte, Orakel und Naturverehrung im alten Aegypten;* vol. 4, *Der Ausklang der ägyptische Religion, mit Reformation, Zauberei und Jenseitsglaube* (Zurich, 1959–61).

The historical documents are accessible in the translation by J. H. Breasted, *Ancient Records of Egypt*, 5 vols. (Chicago, 1906–7). The *Pyramid Texts* have been translated into German by Sethe, into French by Speleers, and into English by Mercer; we follow the translation by R. O. Faulkner, *The Ancient Egyptian Pyramid Texts* (Oxford, 1969), but we have also used the fragments translated by Breasted, Weill, Clark, Sauneron, and Yoyotte.

On the religious vocabulary, see C. J. Bleeker, "Einige Bemerkungen zur religiösen Terminologie der alten Aegypten," in *Travels in the World of the Old Testament: Studies Presented to Professor M. A. Beek* (Assen, 1974), pp. 12–26.

26. A systematic exposition of the Egyptian cosmogonies, supplemented by annotated translations of the texts, has been furnished by S. Sauneron and J. Yoyotte, "La naissance du monde selon l'Egypte ancienne," in *La naissance du monde* (Paris, 1959), pp. 19–91. See also the translations by J. Wilson, *ANET*, pp. 3–10.

The various cosmogonic doctrines are discussed by Vandier, *La religion égyptienne*, pp. 57 ff. Cf. the analysis by Rundle Clark, *Myth and Symbol*, pp. 35 ff., and especially Morenz, *Egyptian Religion*, pp. 159 ff. On the Hermopolis cosmogony, see S. Morenz and J. Schubert, *Der Gott auf der Blume: Eine ägyptische Kosmogonie und ihre weltweite Bildwirkung* (Ascona, 1954). On the creative value of the word, see J. Zandee, "Das Schöpferwort im alten Aegypten," *Verbum, Studia Theologica Rheno-Traiectina* 6 (1964): 33 ff. See also R. B. Finnestad, "Ptah, Creator of the Gods," *Numen* 23 (1976): 81–113.

The importance of Thebes from the end of the third millennium brought its god Amon (who was opportunely associated with Re) to the forefront. But the cosmogony accomplished by Amon is borrowed from the systems of Heliopolis, Hermopolis, and Memphis; see the texts translated, with annotations by Wilson, *ANET*, pp. 8–10; Sauneron and Yoyotte, pp. 67 ff.

On the symbolism of the primordial hill and sacred space, see Hellmut Brunner, "Zum Raumbegriff der Aegypter," *Studium Generale* 10 (1957): 610 ff.; A. Saleh, "The So-Called 'Primeval Hill' and Other Related Elevations in Ancient Egyptian Mythology," *Mitteilungen des Deutschen Archäologischen Instituts* (Abt. Cairo) 25 (1969): 110–20; I. E. S. Edwards, *The Pyramids of Egypt* (Harmondsworth: Pelican Books, 1961); J. Leclant, "Espace et temps, ordre et chaos dans l'Egypte pharaonique," *Revue de Synthèse* 90 (1969); Othmar Keel, *Die Welt der altorientalischen Bildsymbolik und das Alte Testament* (Zurich and Neukirchen, 1972), pp. 100 ff. (comparative study, admirably illustrated).

There were several myths concerning the origin of man; according to one version, Ptah had shaped his body from clay, on the potter's wheel (see Bonnet, *Reallexicon*, p. 617); in Upper Egypt the demiurge was Khnum (ibid., p. 137). No myth on the origin of death is known; a brief allusion (*Pyr.* 1466) refers to the mythical time "before death existed."

The myth concerning the destruction of men is comparatively old; see the bibliography in Vandier, *Rel. égypt.*, p. 53. See *The Book of the Divine Cow*, translated by Alexandre Piankoff in *The Shrines of Tut-Ankh-Amon*

(New York, 1955), p. 27. When Re realized that Hathor was ready to destroy the human race, he caused beer the color of blood to be poured during the night; when Hathor, the next morning, prepared to continue the slaughter, she drank so much of it that she succumbed to intoxication.

Men had decided to revolt because Re had grown too old. And in fact, after the episode just related, Re decided to renounce the sovereignty of the world. Admitting in the presence of the gods that his body was as weak as it has been during the primordial period, he asked his daughter, Nut, to carry him up to heaven (*Book of the Divine Cow*, trans. Piankoff, in *Shrines*, p. 29). His successor was Shu or Geb. Re's "old age" and impotence, and above all his retirement to the distant sky, are mythical elements that are abundantly documented: the transformation of a celestial god, creator and cosmocrator, into a *deus otiosus*. The fact that, in the Egyptian version, it is a *solar* god who becomes a *deus otiosus* shows reinterpretation by theologians.

27. On the divinity of the Egyptian kings, see: A. Moret, *Du caractère religieux de la royauté pharaonique* (Paris, 1902) (largely outdated); H. Jacobsohn, *Die dogmatische Stellung des Königs in der Theologie der alten Ägypter* (Gluckstadt, 1939); H. Frankfort, *Kingship and the Gods*, pp. 15–215; G. Posener, *De la divinité du pharaon* (Paris, 1960); H. Goedicke, *Die Stellung des Königs im Alten Reich* (Wiesbaden, 1960); H. Brunner, *Die Geburt des Gottkönigs* (Wiesbaden, 1964).

On "Menes" as creator of a united Egypt, see Frankfort, *Kingship and the Gods*, pp. 17 ff. Royalty already appears at the end of the predynastic period. Frankfort emphasizes the ideological origin of the "dual monarchy" (i.e., the shared sovereignty of Upper and Lower Egypt). This political formula expressed the tendency of the Egyptian mind "to understand the world in dualistic terms as a series of pairs of contrasts balanced in unchanging equilibrium" (*Kingship*, p. 19). "The dualistic forms of Egyptian kingship did not result from historical incidents. They embody the peculiarly Egyptian thought that a totality comprises opposites" (ibid.).

Frankfort cites some African parallels that may explain the origin of this dualistic ideology (p. 16). We shall meet with other examples of dyads and polarities; see, for the moment, Eliade, *The Quest*, pp. 127 ff. ("Prolegomenon to Religious Dualism").

On the meanings of *maᶜat*, see Bonnet, *Reallexicon*, pp. 430–34; Frankfort, *Ancient Egypt. Rel.*, pp. 53 ff., 62 ff.; Posener, *Littérature et politique dans l'Egypte de la XIIᵉ Dynastie* (Paris, 1956); Morenz, *Egyptian Religion*, pp. 113–30 (with bibliography).

On the tendency to impersonality, see A. de Buck, *Het Typische en het Individueele by de Egyptenaren* (Leiden, 1929); Ludlow Bull, "Ancient

Egypt," in *The Idea of History in the Ancient Near East*, ed. Robert C. Dentan (New Haven, 1955), pp. 1–34.

On cults and festivals, see Vandier, *La rel. égypt.*, pp. 165–203, and Morenz, *Egyptian Religion*, pp. 81–109 (excellent comparative discussion, with recent bibliography). The work by Moret, *Le rituel du culte divin journalier en Egypte* (Paris, 1902) can still be used. See also H. Kees, *Das Priestertum im ägyptischen Staat vom NR bis zur Spätzeit* (Leiden, 1953); J. Garnot Sainte-Fare, *L'hommage aux dieux dans l'ancien Empire égyptien d'après les textes des Pyramides* (Paris, 1954); S. Sauneron, *Les prêtres de l'ancienne Egypte* (Paris, 1967) (Eng. trans. by Ann Morrisett, *The Priests of Ancient Egypt* [New York, 1960]).

On the *sed* festival, the essential can be found in Vandier, pp. 200–202; there is an excellent analysis, with references to the literary and iconographic sources, in Frankfort, *Kingship*, pp. 79 ff.

On the festival of Min, see H. Gauthier, *Les fêtes du dieu Min* (Cairo, 1931); Vandier, pp. 202–3; Frankfort, *Kingship*, 186 ff.

28. The pharaoh's ascent to heaven as recounted in the *Pyramid Texts* has been described by J. H. Breasted, *Development of Religion and Thought in Ancient Egypt* (New York, 1912), pp. 70–141, and by R. Weill, *Le champ des roseaux et le champ des offrandes dans la religion funéraire et la religion générale* (Paris, 1936).

It is not certain that the epithet *maa-kheru* ("just of voice"), "which is placed after the name of every deceased person from the time of the Middle Kingdom," should be translated by "blessed, beatified." Rather, it expresses "the idea that the deceased has had the benefit of the Osirian rites" (J. Yoyotte, "Le jugement des morts dans l'Egypte ancienne," p. 37) (see the bibliographical references for § 33).

29. There is an extensive literature on Osiris. We mention only the essential studies: Bonnet, *Reallexicon*, pp. 568–76; Vandier, *La rel. égypt.*, pp. 58 ff., 81 ff., 134 ff.; Frankfort, *Kingship*, pp. 181 ff.; Rundle Clark, *Myth and Symbol*, pp. 97 ff.; E. Otto and M. Hirner, *Osiris und Amun* (Munich, 1960). See also A. Scharff, *Die Ausbreitung des Osiriskulte in der Frühzeit und während des Alten Reiches* (Munich, 1948); J. G. Griffiths, *The Origins of Osiris*, Münchener Aegyptologische Studien no. 9 (Berlin, 1966). The work by E. A. Wallis Budge, *Osiris: The Egyptian Religion of Resurrection*, 2 vols. (London, 1911; rev. ed., New York, 1961) is still useful for its documents, iconography, and African parallels. During the fashion launched by Frazer, Osiris was seen as exclusively an agrarian god; this interpretation, defended in France by A. Moret, has been criticized and rejected by, among others, Emile Chassinat, in his posthumous work *Le Mystère d'Osiris au mois de Khoiac* (Cairo, 1966), vol. 1, pp. 30 ff. What seems certain is the complex character of Osiris; he is at once a cosmic and a funerary god, representative of both universal fertility and kingship, master of the judgment of the dead, and, later, a divinity of the "Mysteries."

The myths of Osiris in the Middle Kingdom and the Empire are summarized by Vandier, *La rel. égypt.*, pp. 48–51.

The *Coffin Texts* have been edited by A. de Buck, *The Egyptian Coffin Texts*, 6 vols. (Chicago, 1935–50). They are in the course of being translated by R. O. Faulkner; volume 1, *The Ancient Egyptian Coffin Texts*, has been published (Warminster, 1974).

On the cult of Osiris, see the two volumes by Chassinat, *Le Mystère d'Osiris au mois de Khoiac*; Rundle Clark, *Myth and Symbol*, pp. 132 ff. (the erection of the *djed* pillar, symbol of the god's spine), pp. 157 ff.; Frankfort, *Kingship*, pp. 181 ff.

On Horus and Seth, see Bonnet, *Reallexicon*, pp. 307–18, 702–15, with the essential bibliography. Also see H. de Velde, *Seth, God of Confusion* (1967).

30. On the First Intermediate Period, see H. Stock, *Die erste Zwischenzeit Aegyptens* (Rome, 1949); Wilson, *The Culture of Ancient Egypt*, p. 104–24; Drioton and Vandier, *L'Egypte*, pp. 213 ff.

The literary compositions discussed in the text have been translated by Adolf Erman, *The Literature of the Ancient Egyptians*, trans. A. M. Blackman (London, 1927; republished as a Harper Torchbook [New York, 1966] under the title *The Ancient Egyptians*, with an important introduction by W. K. Simpson); pp. 75 ff.: "The Instruction for King Meri-ka-Re"; pp. 92 ff: "Ipuwer"; pp. 132 ff.: "Song of the Harper"; pp. 86 ff.: "Dispute of a Man Weary of Life." We have chiefly followed the translations by Wilson, *ANET*, pp. 405 ff., 441 ff., 467. R. O. Faulkner has provided a new translation of "The Dispute of a Man Weary of Life" in the *Journal of Egyptian Archeology* 42 (1956): 21–40 ("The Man Who Was Tired of Life"). R. J. Williams has examined the recent literature on the same text, ibid., 48 (1962): 49–56. Several studies have been published on the *Admonitions of Ipu-wer*; see the bibliography in W. K. Simpson's introduction to the Harper Torchbooks edition of Erman's book, pp. xxix–xxx; also see ibid., p. xxviii, for an analysis of recent studies on the *Instruction for King Meri-ka-Re* (this last text is long and not always intelligible).

On the literature of the Intermediate Period of the Twelfth Dynasty, see G. Posener, *Littérature et politique dans l'Egypte de la XIIe dynastie* (Paris, 1956).

31. On the Middle Kingdom, see H. E. Winlock, *The Rise and Fall of the Middle Kingdom in Thebes* (New York, 1947); Wilson, *The Culture of Ancient Egypt*, pp. 124–53; Drioton and Vandier, *L'Egypte*, pp. 234 ff. The pharaohs undertook works of considerable magnitude (they added 27,000 acres of arable land near Faiyum, etc.). Though not following a policy of conquest, Egypt was respected and feared in the Mediterranean, the Aegean, and the Near East.

On the Hyksos, see Robert M. Engberg, *The Hyksos Reconsidered* (Chicago, 1939); Winlock, the last two chapters; Wilson, pp. 154–65; T. Säve-Söderbergh, "The Hyksos Rule in Egypt," *Journal of Egyptian Archeology* 37 (1951): 53–72; Theodore Burton-Brown, *Early Mediterranean Migrations* (Manchester, 1959), pp. 63 ff. As for the xenophobia of the Egyptians, it must be borne in mind that for a long time they did not recognize the "humanity" of foreigners; it is for this reason that they were sacrificed (Wilson, pp. 139 ff.). On this problem see also F. Jesi, "Rapport sur les recherches relatives à quelques figurations du sacrifice humain dans l'Egypte pharaonique," *JNES* 17 (1958): 194–203. As early as the First Intermediate Period the "Asiatics" were accused of having fomented anarchy, although their number was insignificant at the time (Wilson, pp. 110 ff.). It was not until after the Hyksos conquest that "Asiatics" settled in great numbers in the Delta region.

On the role of the high priest of Amon, see G. Lefebvre, *Histoire des Grands Prêtres d'Amon de Karnak jusqu'à la XXIᵉ Dynastie* (Paris, 1929); Vandier, *La relig. égypt.*, pp. 170 ff.; Wilson, *Culture*, pp. 169 ff.

The great hymn to Amon-Re has been translated several times: see Wilson, *ANET*, pp. 365–67; Erman, *The Ancient Egyptians*, pp. 283–87. The hymn is inspired by the Memphite theology (Erman, *Die Religion der Ägypter*, p. 119), which illustrates the tendency of Egyptian religiosity to return to and reinterpret traditional doctrines. Equally important is what has been called a "Universalist Hymn to the Sun," published and translated by A. Varille, in *Bulletin de l'Institut français d'archéologie orientale* no. 41 (Cairo, 1942), pp. 25–30; see also the translation by Wilson, *ANET*, pp. 367–69.

32. On the "Amarna revolution," see J. D. S. Pendlebury, *Tell-el-Amarna* (London, 1935); Drioton and Vandier, *L'Egypte*, pp. 86 ff., 334 ff.; Wilson, *The Culture of Ancient Egypt*, pp. 212 ff.; Rudolph Anthes, *Die Maat des Echnaton von Amarna*, *JAOS*, suppl. no. 14 (1952); Cyril Aldred, *New Kingdom Art in Ancient Egypt during the Eighteenth Dynasty* (London, 1951), esp. pp. 22 ff.

The great hymn to Aton has been translated in Erman, *The Ancient*

Egyptians, pp. 288–91; Breasted, *The Dawn of Conscience* (New York, 1953), pp. 281–86; and Wilson, *ANET*, pp. 369–71.

On the continuity Amon(-Re)–Aton, see Alexandre Piankoff, *The Shrines of Tut-Ankh-Amon* (New York, 1955), pp. 4 ff.

33. What Edouard Naville called the "Litany of the Sun" constitutes one of the most important texts of the Empire. We follow the translation by Piankoff, *The Litany of Re* (New York, 1964), pp. 22–43. See also the texts translated by the same author in his work *The Tomb of Ramesses VI* (New York, 1954).

There are several translations of the *Book of the Dead*; we follow the most recent one, by T. C. Allen, *The Book of the Dead, or Going Forth by Day* (Chicago, 1974). On the other funerary books (*The Book of What Is in the Beyond; The Book of Gates; The Book of Night*), see Vandier, *La relig. égypt.*, pp. 107 ff., 128–29. For the *Book of the Two Roads* we have used the translation by Piankoff, *The Wandering of the Soul* (Princeton, 1974), pp. 12–37. See also S. Morenz, *Altägyptischer Jenseitsführer: Papyrus Berlin 3127* (Frankfurt a. M., 1966).

The subterranean world of the dead, *duat*, is already documented in the *Pyramid Texts*; see the examples cited by Breasted, *Development of Religion and Thought in Ancient Egypt*, p. 144, n. 2. On the representations of the Hells, see Erik Hornung, *Altägyptische Höllenvorstellungen* (Berlin, 1968). For a description and translation of the texts, see the work by E. A. Wallis Budge, *The Egyptian Heaven and Hell*, 3 vols. (reprinted in one volume, London, 1925). The "negative" elements of death, considered as man's supreme enemy, are minutely analyzed by J. Zandee, *Death as an Enemy according to Ancient Egyptian Conceptions* (Leiden, 1960), pp. 5–31 (general presentation) and pp. 45–111 (the vocabulary expressing the various aspects of death: total destruction, decomposition, prison, etc.). The book by H. Kees, *Totenglauben und Jenseitsvorstellungen der alten Aegypter* (1926; 2d ed., Berlin, 1956), remains the best comprehensive study, despite certain too-personal interpretations. For the essential data on the cult of the dead (mummification, funerals, tombs, the *mastaba*, the pyramid, the hypogeum) see Vandier, *La relig. égypt.*, pp. 111–30 (with an extensive bibliography).

For the Egyptians, as for other peoples of antiquity (India, China, Greece, etc.), death not only effected the separation of the soul from the body; it also revealed the distinction among the three spiritual principles: the *akh*, the *ba*, and the *ka*. The first "essentially designates divine force, supernatural force" (Vandier, p. 131). The meaning of the word— "shining, glorious"—indicates the celestial nature of the dead. (In fact, when the dead are called *akhu*, they are regarded as supernatural beings, inhabitants of heaven; cf. Frankfort, *Kingship*, p. 64.) The *ba*, represented, like the *akh*, in the form of a bird, constitutes the "soul" properly speaking. "The *Ba* required the corpse, or at least a statue, in order to retain its identity. It was thought to return to the body in the grave after roaming through the fields and groves" (Frankfort, *Kingship*, p. 64; cf. Frankfort, *Ancient Egyptian Religion*, pp. 96 ff.). The *ba* is the deceased himself under a certain aspect. The *ka*, on the other hand, is not individualized and, except in the case of the pharaoh, is never depicted; the term can be translated as "vital force." The *ka* belongs to the individual during his lifetime but also follows him into the beyond (Frankfort, *Kingship*, p. 63). Only the king's *ka* figures on the monuments. "Born with the king as his twin, it accompanies him through life as a protective genius; it acts as his twin and as his protector in death" (ibid., p. 69).

It is important to note that the Old Kingdom texts speak only of the *ba* of the pharaohs. "In other words, in the early period Egyptians apparently did not possess a *ba*" (Morenz, *Egyptian Religion*, p. 206). It is only from the First Intermediate Period that possessing a *ba* becomes general. Obviously, this is merely a *literary* situation; we do not know what the historical reality was. But it is significant that, in this case too, the "example" of the pharaoh constitutes the model increasingly imitated by the less privileged. See also L. Greven, *Der Ka in Theologie und Königskult der Ägypter des Alten Reiches* (Glückstadt, 1952), and Louis Zabkar, *A Study of the Ba Concept in Ancient Egyptian Texts* (Chicago, 1968).

On the Judgment, see E. Drioton, *Le jugement des âmes dans l'ancienne Egypte* (Cairo, 1949); Vandier, *La relig. égypt.*, pp. 134 ff.; J. Spiegel, *Die Idee vom Totengericht in der aegyptischen Religion* (Glückstadt, 1935); J. Yoyotte, "Le jugement des morts dans l'Egypte ancienne," in *Le jugement des morts*, Sources Orientales no. 4 (Paris, 1961), pp. 16–80 (translations of texts, commentaries, and bibliography). See also M. Guilmot, "L'espoir en l'immortalité dans l'Egypte ancienne du Moyen Empire à la basse époque," *RHR* 166 (1964): 1–20.

On the declaration of innocence, see E. Drioton, "Contribution à l'étude du chapitre CXXV du Livre des Morts: Les confessions négatives," *Recueil d'études égyptiennes dédiées à la mémoire de J. F. Champollion* (Paris, 1922), pp. 545–64. Certain ideas and beliefs expressed in chapter 125 are very ancient: they "go back at least to the pyramid period. Of the negative and positive 'code of ethics' included in chapter 125, we have traces from as early as the Fifth and Sixth Dynasties" (Yoyotte, "Le jugement," p. 63). R. Pettazzoni has pointed out some ethnographic parallels to the negative confession; see his *La confessione dei peccati* (Bologna, 1935), vol. 2, pp. 21, 56–57.

The funerary work *The Book of the Divine Cow* emphasizes the magical value of its contents. He who shall know this text, it is written, "will not have to bend in the tribunal . . . and all the robberies he may have committed on earth will not be counted" (trans. Yoyotte, p. 66; see the complete translation of *The Book of the Divine Cow* in Piankoff, *Shrines of Tut-Ankh-Amon*, pp. 27–34). The exaltation of "knowledge" above morality is a leitmotiv of Indian thought from the *Brāhmaṇas* and the Upanishads to Tantrism.

34. There is an extensive bibliography on the megalithic cultures. We have analyzed the most important contributions in a study soon to be published, "Megaliths and History of Religions."

An excellent introduction has been provided by Glyn Daniel, *The Megalith Builders of Western Europe* (London, 1958); the second edition (Pelican Books, 1962) contains an addendum (pp. 143–46) which presents the new chronology established on the basis of carbon 14 analyses; indeed, the new chronology largely vitiates the author's thesis; see, further on, § 36. See also Fernand Niel, *La civilisation des mégalithes* (Paris, 1970) and the bibliographies given by Glyn Daniel and J. D. Evans in the *Cambridge Ancient History*, vol. 2: *The Western Mediterranean* (1967), chap. 37, pp. 63–72.

The megaliths of Spain and Portugal have been exhaustively studied by Georg and Vera Leisner, *Die Megalithgräber der Iberischen Halbinsel: Der Süden* (Berlin, 1943), and *Der Westen*, 3 vols. (Berlin, 1956, 1959, 1960). See also L. Pericot, ed., *Corpus de sepulcros megalíticos*, fascs. 1 and 2 (Barcelona, 1961); fasc. 3 (Gerona, 1964); L. Pericot, *Los sepulcros megalíticos Catalanes y la cultura pirinaica*, 2d ed. (Barcelona, 1951).

On the megaliths of France, see Z. Le Rouzic, *Carnac* (Rennes, 1909); Le Rouzic, *Les monuments mégalithiques de Carnac et de Locmariaquer* (Carnac, 1907–53); Glyn Daniel, *The Prehistoric Chamber Tombs of France* (London, 1960); Daniel, *The Megalith Builders*, pp. 95–111; E. Octobon, "Statues-menhirs, stèles gravées, dalles sculptées," *Revue Anthropologique* (1931), pp. 291–579; M. and J. Pequart and Z. Le Rouzic, *Corpus des signes gravés des monuments mégalithiques du Morbihan* (Paris, 1927). On the megalithic cultures of the British Isles, see G. Daniel, *The Prehistoric Chamber Tombs of England and Wales* (1950), and *The Megalith Builders*, pp. 112–27; see also the bibliography given below for § 35.

Sibylle von Cles-Reden has provided a popular presentation, illustrated by a large number of excellent photographs, in *The Realm of the Great Goddess: The Story of the Megalith Builders* (London, 1961) (translation of *Die Spur der Zykopen*, 1960).

Dominik Wolfel has devoted a large part of his study "Die Religionen des vorindogermanischen Europa" (in *Christus und die Religionen der Erde*, vol. 1 [1950], pp. 161–537), to the religion of the megalith builders (pp. 163–253, and passim). It should be consulted with caution. There is a succinct presentation, but composed before the carbon 14 analyses, in J. Maringer, *The Gods of Prehistoric Man*, pp. 227–55.

On the menhirs, Horst Kircher has published a very learned work, "Die Menhire in Mitteleuropa und der Menhirgedanke," *Abhandlungen der Akademie in Mainz, Geistes- und Sozialwissenschaftliche Klasse* (1935), pp. 609–816.

35. From the vast literature on Stonehenge, we will mention a few recent studies: R. J. C. Atkinson, *Stonehenge* (Harmondsworth: Penguin, 1960); A. Thom, *Megalithic Sites in Britain* (Oxford, 1967); G. S. Hawkins, *Stonehenge Decoded* (London, 1966) (but see the critique by R. I. C. Atkinson, *Nature* 210 [1966]: 1320 ff.); Colin Renfrew, *Before Civilization* (London and New York, 1973), pp. 120 ff., 214 ff.

It is worth mentioning that an enormous number of megalithic tombs (three thousand!) have been identified in southern France—more than six hundred in the Département de l'Aveyron alone. This is more than twice as many as have been found in England and Wales. See Daniel and Evans, *The Western Mediterranean*, p. 38. The dolmens in the Département de l'Hérault have been exhaustively studied by J. Arnal, *Préhistoire* 15 (1963). It is also in southern France that the only menhir statues so far known are found.

On the prehistory of Malta, see J. D. Evans, *Malta* (London, 1959); Evans, *Prehistoric Antiquities of the Maltese Islands* (London, 1971); Gunther Zuntz, *Persephone: Three Essays on Religion and Thought in Magna Graecia* (Oxford, 1971), pp. 3–58; Colin Renfrew, *Before Civilization*, pp. 147 ff.

Zuntz (pp. 25 ff.) has demonstrated the importance of the symbolism of the spiral in the decoration of the Maltese temples and has identified Danubian influences (the Cîrna figurines).

36. Gordon Childe has summarized his views on the diffusion of the "megalithic religion" in his latest book, *The Prehistory of European Society* (Pelican Books, 1958), pp. 124–34: "Missionaries of the Megalithic Religion."

According to Glyn Daniel, the beginning of construction of the megalithic type is directly connected with the arrival of the Minoans or the Aegeans in the central and western Mediterranean (*The Megalith Builders of Western Europe*, p. 135). The phenomenon is one of a commercial and colonial thrust, but the colonization was the work of a people possessing a strong religious belief and quite complicated funerary practices. Daniel asks why the megalithic monuments contain so few objects made of metal, despite the fact that their builders exploited mines and were chiefly engaged in trade in metals. He holds that the immigrants purposely refrained from burying metal tools and buried stone replicas instead (p. 137).

The subtitle of Colin Renfrew's book *Before Civilization* is significant: *The Radiocarbon Revolution and Prehistoric Europe.* See also, by the same author, "Wessex without Mycenae," *Annual of the British School of Archaeology at Athens* 63 (1968): 277–85; "Malta and the Calibrated Radiocarbon Chronology," *Antiquity* 46 (1972): 141–45; and "New Configurations in Old World Chronology," *World Archaeology* 2 (1970): 199–211.

37. Several authors, reacting against the inhibition provoked by the extravagances of G. Elliot Smith and W. J. Perry, have examined the ensemble of the megalithic cultures of protohistory; see, for example, A. Serner, *On "Dyss" Burial and Beliefs about the Dead during the Stone Age, with Special Regard to South Scandinavia* (Lund, 1938); H. G. Bandi, "La répartition des tombes mégalithiques," *Archives Suisses d'Anthropologie Générale* 12 (1946): 39–51; V. Gordon Childe, "Megaliths," *Ancient India,* no. 4 (1947/48), pp. 4–13. Aside from R. Heine-Geldern, only one scholar has made a joint study of the two groups of megalithic cultures, i.e., those of prehistory and those at the ethnographic stage, though he confined his study to the menhirs; we refer to Joseph Röder, *Pfahl und Menhir: Eine vergleichend vorgeschichtliche volks- und völkerkundliche Studie* (= *Studien zur westeuropäischen Altertumskunde,* vol. 1 [Neuwied am Rhein, 1949]).

As for the contributions by R. Heine-Geldern, the most important are: "Die Megalithen Südostasiens und ihre Bedeutung für die Klärung der Megalithenfrage in Europa und Polynesien," *Anthropos* 13 (1928): 276–315; "Prehistoric Research in the Netherlands Indies," in *Science and Scientists in the Netherlands Indies,* ed. P. Honig and F. Verdoorn (Cambridge, Mass., 1945), pp. 129–67; "Zwei alte Weltanschauungen und ihre kulturgeschichtliche Bedeutung," *Anzeiger der phil.-hist. Klasse der Oesterreichischen Akademie der Wissenschaften* 94 (1957): 251–62; "Das Megalithproblem," in *Beiträge Oesterreichs zur Erforschung der Vergangenheit und Kulturgeschichte der Menschheit—Symposion 1958* (1959), pp. 162–82. The bibliography of Heine-Geldern is listed and analyzed by H. H. E. Loofs, *Elements of the Megalithic Complex in Southeast Asia: An Annotated Bibliography* (Canberra, 1967), pp. 3–4, 14–15, 41–42, 48, 94.

Heine-Geldern's hypothesis and the objections raised by his critics are discussed in our study "Megaliths and History of Religions."

38. For a summary bibliography on Harappa and Mohenjo-daro, see Eliade, *Yoga: Immortality and Freedom*, trans. Willard R. Trask, Bollingen Series 56 (New York, 1958), pp. 430 f. The essential treatment still remains Sir John Marshall's book, *Mohenjo-daro and the Indus Culture*, 3 vols. (London, 1931), but it should be supplemented by some recent studies that present the results of excavations undertaken after 1930. See E. J. Mackay, *The Indus Civilization* (London, 1935); Mackay, *Further Excavations at Mohenjo-daro* (Delhi, 1938); Mackay, *Chanhudaro Excavations 1935–36* (New Haven, 1943); M. S. Vats, *Excavations at Harappa* (Delhi, 1940); S. Piggott, *Prehistoric India* (Pelican Books, 1950); J. M. Casal, *La civilisation de l'Indus et ses énigmes* (Paris, 1969) (on this, see Maurizio Tosi's observations, *East and West* 21 [1971]: 407 ff.); Bridget and Raymond Allchin, *The Birth of Indian Civilization* (Pelican Books, 1968) (contains a rich critical bibliography); Sir Mortimer Wheeler, *The Indus Civilization*, 3d ed. (Cambridge, 1968) (this is a completely revised edition of the book published in 1953); Walter A. Fairservis, *The Roots of Ancient India: The Archaeology of Early Indian Civilization* (New York, 1971); in this synthetic study Fairservis also summarizes the results of his excavations in western Pakistan, and especially in the Quetta Valley, the Zhob and Loralai region, and the Seistan basin. See also D. H. Gordon, *The Prehistoric Background of Indian Culture* (Bombay, 1960); Ahmad Hasan Dani, *Prehistory and Protohistory of Eastern India* (Calcutta, 1960); and Robert H. Brunswig, "Radiocarbon Dating and Indus Civilization: Calibration and Chronology," *East and West* 25 (1975): 111–45.

In his important book *The Pivot of the Four Quarters: A Preliminary Inquiry into the Origins and Character of the Ancient Chinese City* (Chicago, 1971), Paul Wheatley has also studied the Harappan ceremonial centers (pp. 230 ff.).

On the symbolism of the "center of the world," see Eliade, *Cosmos and History*, pp. 12 ff., and "Centre du Monde, Temple, Maison," in *Le symbolisme cosmique des monuments religieux* (Rome, 1957), pp. 57–82.

On the cosmological symbolism of traditional cities, see Werner Müller, *Die heilige Stadt: Roma quadrata, himmlisches Jerusalem und der Mythe vom Weltnabel* (Stuttgart, 1961).

39. On the Indus religion, see Eliade, *Yoga*, pp. 353 ff.; Sir John Marshall, *Mohenjo-daro*, vol. 1, pp. 50 ff.; Piggott, *Prehistoric India*, pp. 200 ff.; Wheeler, *The Indus Civilization*, pp. 108 ff.; Allchin, *The Birth of Indian Civilization*, 311 ff.; Fairservis, *The Roots of Ancient India*, pp. 292 ff. All these authors recognize the "Hinduistic" character of the Harappan religion and emphasize the continuity of certain cult objects, symbols, and divine figures, from protohistory down to the present. This unanimity is significant, for these archeologists have directed excavations in India; in other words, their scientific competence is happily supplemented by first-hand knowledge of the country.

"Continuity" has also been confirmed by the researches of Mario Cappieri, "Ist die Induskultur und ihre Bevölkerung wirklich verschwunden?" *Anthropos* 60 (1965): 719–62. W. Koppers has noted some exact analogies between certain fertility rites practiced in Central India and the Harappan iconography; see his "Zentralindische Fruchtbarkeits-riten und ihre Beziehungen zur Induskultur," *Geographica Helvetica* 1 (1946): 165–77. For his part, Josef Haekel has studied the ceremonies connected with Gardens of Adonis in certain villages of Gujarat. The Austrian scholar explains the presence of this specifically Mediterranean ritual by the fact that the authors of the Indus civilization were pre-Āryan cultivators arrived from Iran; hence they shared in the protohistorical civilization of the Near East and the Mediterranean; see his "'Adonis-gärtchen' im Zeremonialwesen der Rathwa in Gujarat (Zentralindien): Vergleich und Problematik," *Ethnologische Zeitschrift Zurich* 1 (1972): 167–75.

Continuity is disputed by (among others) H. P. Sullivan, "A Re-examination of the Religion of the Indus Civilization," *HR* 4 (1964): 115–25, and J. Gonda, *Change and Continuity in Indian Religion* (The Hague, 1965), pp. 19–37.

R. L. Raikes has emphasized the decisive role of seismic movements and floods in the ruin of Mohenjo-daro; see his "The Mohenjo-daro Floods," *Antiquity* 39 (1965): 196–203; "The End of the Ancient Cities of the Indus Civilization," *American Anthropologist* 65 (1963): 655–59, and 66 (1964): 284–99; and, especially, *Water, Weather and Archaeology* (London, 1967). The incontestable lowering of the economic and cultural level in the final phases of Mohenjo-daro was certainly aggravated by the demoralization consequent upon repeated floods. But the death blow seems to have been struck by the invaders from the East, probably Āryan-speaking immi-grants. Excavations have revealed traces of a final massacre, after which Mohenjo-daro ceased to exist; see Wheeler, *Indus Civilization*, pp. 129 ff., and the bibliography given below, § 64.

40. The fundamental work on the prehistory and protohistory of Crete remains Sir Arthur Evans' *The Palace of Minos*, 5 vols. (London, 1921–50); see also A. J. Evans and J. L. Myres, *Scripta Minoa*, vol. 2 (1952); P. Demargne, *La Crète dédalique* (Paris, 1947); L. Cottrell, *The Bull of Minos* (1956); L. R. Palmer, *Mycenaeans and Minoans* (London, 1961); R. W. Hutchinson, *Prehistoric Crete* (Baltimore, 1962) (with a rich bibliography, pp. 355–68); and J. W. Graham, *The Palaces of Crete* (Princeton, 1962).

On the Cretan religions, see especially Charles Picard, *Les religions préhelléniques: Crète et Mycènes* (Paris, 1948) (excellent bibliographies), and M. P. Nilsson, *The Minoan-Mycenaean Religion and Its Survival in Greek Religion*, 2d ed. (Lund, 1950). See also A. W. Persson, *Religion of Greece in Prehistoric Times* (Berkeley, 1950); M. Ventris and J. Chadwick, *Documents in Mycenaean Greek* (Cambridge, 1956); L. A. Stella, "La religione greca nei testi micenei," *Numen* 5 (1958): 18–57; S. Luria, "Vorgriechische Kulte," *Minos* 5 (1957): 41–52; M. Lejeune, "Prêtres et prêtresses dans les documents mycéniens," *Hommages à Georges Dumézil* (Brussels, 1960), pp. 129–39; R. F. Willetts, *Cretan Cults and Festivals* (New York, 1962); H. van Effenterre, "Politique et religion dans la Crète minoenne," *Revue historique* 229 (1963): 1–18.

On the sacred caves, see note 42 and P. Faure, "Spéléologie crétoise et humanisme," *Bulletin de l'Association Guillaume Budé* (1958), pp. 27–50; Faure, *Fonction des cavernes crétoises* (Paris, 1964), pp. 162 ff., on the Skotino cave as a site of initiations.

On the labyrinth and its initiatory function, see W. A. Matthews, *Mazes and Labyrinths: A General Account of Their History and Development* (London, 1922); W. F. Jackson Knight, *Cumaean Gates: A Reference of the Sixth Aeneid to the Initiation Pattern* (Oxford, 1936); K. Kerényi, *Labyrinth-Studien* (Zurich, 1950); Oswald F. A. Menghin, "Labirinthe, Vulvenbilder und Figurenrapporte in der Alten und Neuen Welt: Beiträge zur Interpretation prähistorisches Felsgraphik," in *Beiträge zur Alten Geschichte und deren Nachleben: Festschrift Franz Altheim* (Berlin, 1969), vol. 1, pp. 1–13; Philippe Borgeaud, "The Open Entrance to the Closed Palace of the King: The Greek Labyrinth in Context," *HR* 14 (1974): 1–27.

It is important to note the complete absence of buildings resembling what will later be the classic temple. The single example of a public sanctuary is the one at Gournia, but it too, according to Nilsson, derives from the domestic cult. Even rituals of the agrarian type were performed in palace courtyards.

41. On the naked goddesses, see Picard, *Rel. préhel.*, pp. 48 ff., 111 ff.; Nilsson, *Minoan-Mycenaean Religion*, pp. 397 ff.

On the vegetation cults, cf. Persson, *Religion of Greece*, pp. 25 ff.; Picard, *Rel. préhel.*, pp. 191 ff.

On the religious role of the bull and the sacred bullfights, see Persson, pp. 93 ff., and the critical bibliography in Picard, p. 199, to which add J. W. Graham, *The Palaces of Crete*, pp. 73 ff.

On the double ax, see Picard, pp. 200–201; Hutchinson, *Prehistoric Crete*, pp. 225 ff.

On the tomb of the priest-king of Cnossus, see C. F. Lehman-Haupt, "Das Tempel-Grab des Priesterkönigs zu Knossos," *Klio* 25 (1932): 175–76; Picard, p. 173.

On the Hagia Triada sarcophagus, see R. Paribeni, "Il sarcofagio dipinto di Haghia Triada," *Monumenti Antichi publicati per cura della reale Accademia dei Lincei*, vol. 19, pp. 5–86, pls. I–III, and the reproductions in J. Harrison, *Themis* (Cambridge, 1912; 2d ed., 1927), pp. 159, 161–77, figs. 31–38; F. von Duhn, "Der Sarkophage aus H. Triada," *ARW* 12 (1909): 161–85; Nilsson, *Minoan-Mycenaean Religion*, pp. 426–43; Picard, pp. 107 ff., 168 ff.

42. On the continuity of pre-Hellenic structures, see Charles Picard, *Rel. préhel.*, pp. 201 ff., 221 ff.; Nilsson, *Minoan-Mycenaean Religion*, pp. 447 ff.; Hutchinson, *Prehistoric Crete*, pp. 199 ff.

"In general, we witness a more or less conservative prolongation . . . of the Minoan pantheon, and of the world of supernatural beings anterior to the Mycenaean period" (Picard, p. 252). The eminent archeologist remarks that the arrangement of "mystery" temples was derived from the installations documented in pre-Hellenic Crete: "there are barriers, portions to which access is reserved, *abata*, *adyta*; the cists (still sunk into the ground) of the 'temple-repositories' of Cnossus were the prelude to the Eleusinian *kistai*: sacred coffers that have become portable but on which the two goddesses sometimes appear together. At Malia a large circular *kernos*, with cupules for offerings, is already set into the flagging of a room in the palace, in direct contact with the earth. The analogy of such arrangements with those of the princely metropolis of Malia itself has been particularly noted; there we have the essential instruments of a cult that is at once agrarian and funerary, the sacred furniture of ceremonies that appear to be mystical, in honor of a Mother Earth who is the guardian at once of the living and the dead" (p. 142). Cf. §§ 97–99.

P. Faure considers Britomartis to be the patron goddess of Skoteino; thus it is possible to "account for the facts of the cult that is documented there, including the modern facts, such as the celebration of the Parasceve" ("Spéléologie crétoise et humanisme," p. 40). On Britomartis, see also Willetts, *Cretan Cult and Festivals*, pp. 179 ff.

On Egyptian influences (psychistasis, partial mummification of bodies, adoption of gold masks, etc.), see Picard, pp. 228 ff., 279 ff. The gold masks were intended to transform the dead person into a supernatural being with incorruptible features, like the statues of the immortals (Picard, p. 262).

43. On the history and culture of the Hittites, see A. Goetze, *Kleinasien*,

2d ed. (1957); O. R. Gurney, *The Hittites* (Harmondsworth, 1952; 2d ed., 1954; latest printing, 1972).

On the Hurrians, see E. A. Speiser, "The Hurrian Participation in the Civilisation of Mesopotamia, Syria, and Palestine," *Cahiers d'Histoire Mondiale* 1 (1953): 311–27; F. Imparati, *I Hurriti* (Florence, 1964); R. de Vaux, "Les Hurrites de l'histoire et les Horites de la Bible," *Revue Biblique* 74, pp. 481–503.

For the Hittite cuneiform texts and their translations down to 1958, see E. Laroche, "Catalogue des textes hittites," *Revue Hittite et Asianique* 14 (1956): 33–38, 69–116; 15 (1957): 30–89; 16 (1958): 18–64.

The most important texts have been translated by A. Goetze, *ANET*, pp. 120–28, 201–11, 346–64, 393–404, and by H. Güterbock, E. Laroche, H. Otten, M. Vieyra, and other authors, whose bibliography will be found in Gurney, *The Hittites*, p. 224. The most recent French translation is the one by Maurice Vieyra, in the work *Les religions du Proche-Orient: Textes et traditions sacrés babyloniens, ougaritiques, hittites*, ed. R. Labat (Paris, 1970), pp. 525–66.

Among the general presentations of the Hittite religion, we mention especially R. Dussaud, "La religion des Hittites et des Hourites," in E. Dhorme and R. Dussaud, *La religion de Babylonie*, pp. 333–53; H. Güterbock, "Hittite Religion," in *Forgotten Religions*, ed. V. Ferm (New York, 1950), pp. 81–109; Güterbock, "Hittite Mythology," in *Mythologies of the Ancient World*, ed. S. N. Kramer (1961), pp. 141–79; H. Otten, "Die Religionen des alten Kleinasien," in *Handbuch der Orientalistik* (1964), vol. 8, pp. 92–116; Maurice Vieyra, "La religion de l'Anatolie antique," in A. Puech, ed., *Histoire des religions*, vol. 1, pp. 258–306. The book by Giuseppe Furlani, *La religione degli Hittiti* (Bologna, 1936) is still useful, though the author—according to Güterbock ("Hittite Religion," p. 109)—had access only to translations of Hittite texts, of which very few had been translated at the time he was writing. See, now, O. R. Gurney, *Some Aspects of Hittite Religion*, 1976 Schweich Lectures of the British Academy (Oxford, 1976), with a rich bibliography.

See also the following publications of E. Laroche: *Recherches sur les noms des dieux hittites* (Paris, 1947); "Teššub, Hebat et leur cour," *Journal of Cuneiform Studies* 2 (1948): 113–36; and "Le panthéon de Yazilikaya," ibid. 6 (1952): 115–23.

For a brief presentation of the Hittite gods and myths, see Einar von Schuler, *WdM*, vol. 1, pp. 172–76 (gods and goddesses), 196–201 (solar divinities), 208–13 (storm gods).

On the religious role of the king, see O. R. Gurney, "Hittite Kingship," in *Myth, Ritual and Kingship*, ed. S. H. Hooke (Oxford, 1958), pp. 105–21.

On the rituals, see B. Schwartz, "The Hittite and Luwian Ritual of

Zarpia of Kizzuwatna," *JAOS* 58 (1938): 334–53; M. Vieyra, "Rites de purification hittites," *RHR* 119 (1939): 121–53; H. Otten, *Hethitische Totenrituale* (Berlin, 1958). On the New Year festival (*purulli*), see Volkert Haas, *Der Kult von Nerik: Ein Beitrag zur hethitischen Religionsgeschichte* (Rome, 1970), pp. 43 ff.

A purification ritual for an army after a defeat is remarkable for its archaism; it involves the sacrifice of a man, a goat, a puppy, and a little pig. These victims are cut in two, and the army passes between the separated halves. See O. Masson, "A propos d'un rituel hittite pour la lustration d'une armée," *RHR* 137 (1950): 5–25; Gurney, *The Hittites*, p. 151. The analogy with the sacrifice ordered by Yahweh when he concluded his covenant with Abraham (Gen. 15:9–18) has been noted. Ritual passing between the two halves of victims is known to numerous peoples; see Frazer, *Folk-lore in the Old Testament* (London, 1919), vol. 1, pp. 393–425, and see T. Gaster, *Myth, Legend, and Custom in the Old Testament* (New York, 1969), pp. 363 ff., for bibliographical supplements. See also J. Henninger, "Was bedeutet die rituelle Teilung eines Tieres in zwei Hälften?" *Biblica* 34 (1953): 344–53; A. E. Jensen, "Beziehungen zwischen dem Alten Testament und der nilotischen Kultur in Afrika," *Culture in History*, ed. S. Diamond (New York, 1960), pp. 449–66. On prayer, see O. R. Gurney, *Hittite Prayers* (1940), and the detailed observations made by E. Laroche, "La prière hittite: Vocabulaire et typologie," *Annuaire, École Pratique des Hautes Études, Ve Section*, 72 (1964–65): 3–29.

44. The various versions of the myth are analyzed by H. Otten, *Die Ueberlieferungen des Telepinu-Mythus, Mitteilungen der Vorderasiatisch-aegyptischen Gesellschaft* 46 (Leipzig, 1943). There is a comparative commentary in T. Gaster, *Thespis*, 2d rev. ed. (New York, 1961), pp. 295 ff. See also the analysis by Güterbock, "Gedanken über das Werden des Gottes Telepinu," *Festschrift Johannes Friedrich* (Heidelberg, 1959), pp. 207–11, and Güterbock, "Hittite Mythology," pp. 144–48 in Samuel N. Kramer, ed., *Mythologies of the Ancient World* (Garden City, N.Y., 1961).

According to the version in which the protagonist is the storm god, the great solar god invites the "thousand divinities" to the banquet; but, though they eat and drink, they can satisfy neither their hunger nor their thirst. After the failure of the first messengers, the father of the storm god goes to find his own father and asks him, "Who sinned so that the seed perished and everything dried up?" The great father answers him: "No one sinned, but you alone sinned!" (Güterbock, "Hittite Mythology," pp. 145–46).

Gaster has brought out several common elements in the mythico-ritual scenarios of Telepinus and the gods of fertility; see his *Thespis*, pp. 304 ff.

45. On Illuyankas, see, most recently, A. Goetze, *Kleinasien*, pp. 139 ff., and E. v. Schuler, *WdM*, vol. 1, pp. 177–78.

The text that recounts the myth is preceded by the following instruction: "Such are the words of Kellas, the anointed (= the priest) of (the city of) Nerik: what follows is the recital of the festival of the *purulli* of the god of the storm of the sky: When the moment has come to utter words (that is, when the festival is to be celebrated): 'May the land develop and prosper, may the land be protected; and if then it develops and prospers, the festival of the *purulli* is celebrated'" (trans. M. Vieyra, "Les religions de l'Anatolie," p. 288; cf. Goetze, *ANET*, p. 125).

There is a comparative commentary in Gaster, *Thespis*, pp. 256 ff.

46. On Kumarbi, see H. G. Güterbock, "The Hittite Version of the Hurrian Kumarbi Myths: Oriental Forerunners of Hesiod," *American Journal of Archaeology* 52 (1948): 123–24; Güterbock, "Hittite Mythology," pp. 155–72; H. Otten, *Mythen vom Gotte Kumarbi* (Berlin, 1950); P. Meriggi, "I miti di Kumarbi, il Kronos Hurrico," *Athenaeum* n.s. 31 (Pavia, 1953): 101–15; C. Scott Littleton, "The 'Kingship in Heaven' Theme," in *Myth and Law among the Indo-Europeans*, ed. Jaan Puhvel (Berkeley, 1970), pp. 93–100.

On Ullikummi, see H. G. Güterbock, *The Song of Ullikummi* (New Haven, 1952).

In his rich but confused book, *Das doppelte Geschlecht* (Berlin, 1955), H. Baumann has noted the relations between the megalithic traditions, androgynism, and the cosmogonic theme of the separation of heaven and earth.

On the myth of men born from the earth, see the bibliography in Eliade, *Patterns in Comparative Religion*, p. 237. This theme is abundantly documented, especially in the Caucasus; see A. von Löwis of Menar, "Nordkaukasische Steingeburtsagen," *ARW* 13 (1901): 509–24. On the myths narrating the birth of divine beings from a *petra genetrix* (= Great Goddess = *matrix mundi*), see R. Eisler, *Weltmantel und Himmelszelt* (Munich, 1910), vol. 2, pp. 411, 727 ff.; Eliade, *The Forge and the Crucible*, pp. 43 ff., 186.

47. The fragments of Philo of Byblos' *Phoenician History* which deal with religion have been translated, with commentaries, by Carl Clemen, *Die phönikische Religion nach Philo von Byblos* (Leipzig, 1939). A cuneiform text published and translated by W. G. Lambert describes the blood-stained succession of five generations of gods; the sons kill their fathers and mothers, marry their mothers and sisters, and successively usurp the sovereignty. Some similarities with Hesiod's *Theogony* have been noted; cf. W. G. Lambert and P. Walcot, "A New Babylonian Theogony and

Hesiod," *Kadmos* 4 (1965): 64–72; see also C. Scott Littleton, "The 'Kingship in Heaven' Theme," in Puhvel, *Myth and Law*, pp. 112–14.

Stig Wikander has brought out an Iranian parallel to the Hittite and Greek myths of the divine generations. The source is recent (it is the *Shahnameh*, the epic by Firdausi written about A.D. 976), but the heroes— Jamshid, Zohak, and Feridun—in some sense represent historicized versions of the mythological personages Yima, Aži, Dahāka, Thraētaona. Hence the myth of divine sovereignty can be considered an integral part of the Indo-European tradition (Wikander, "Histoire des Ouranides," *Cahiers du Sud* 36 [1952]: 8–17). But this myth is not documented among other Indo-European peoples. Scott Littleton tends to see in the Babylonian traditions (*Enuma-elish* and the fragment translated by Lambert) the ultimate source of all the myths of divine generations (Littleton, "The 'Kingship in Heaven' Theme," pp. 109 ff.).

48. For the history of Palestine after the Early Bronze Age, see P. Garelli, *Le Proche-Orient asiatique, des origines aux invasions des Peuples de la Mer* (Paris, 1969), pp. 45 ff.; B. Mazar, "The Middle Bronze Age in Palestine," in *Israel Exploration Journal* [Jerusalem] 18 (1968): 65–97; R. de Vaux, *Histoire ancienne d'Israël, des origines à l'installation en Canaan* (Paris, 1971), pp. 61–121 (excellent bibliographies).

On the Amorites, see S. Moscati, *I predecessori d'Israele: Studi sulle più antiche genti semitiche in Siria e Palestina* (Rome, 1956); I. J. Gelb, "The Early History of the West Semitic Peoples," *Journal of Cuneiform Studies* 15 (1961): 27–47; K. M. Kenyon, *Amorites and Canaanites* (London, 1966); R. de Vaux, *Histoire ancienne d'Israël*, pp. 64 ff.

The excavations at Tell Hariri, the ancient Mari, have brought to light thousands of tablets written in the "Old Babylonian" dialect of Akkadian. They supply the names of a certain number of gods, principally ʿAnat, Dagan, Addu. But because mythological texts are lacking we do not know the fundamental religious beliefs and conceptions.

Amurru, the eponymous god of the Amorites, "is a man who does not know how to bend his knees (to cultivate the ground), who eats raw meat, who owns no house during his lifetime and is not buried after his death" (text cited by de Vaux, p. 64). Similar sterotypes will be used, throughout the three following centuries, in regard to the "barbarians" (Germans, Avars, Huns, Mongols, Tatars) who endanger the great urban civilizations, from the Roman Empire to China.

It must be understood that these Amorites have nothing to do with the Amorites mentioned in the Bible. "The Bible applied to a part of the pre-Israelite population of Palestine the name of Amurru" (de Vaux, p. 68).

On the Canaanite religion and civilization, see J. Gray, *The Canaanites*

(London, 1964); Gray, *The Legacy of Canaan*, 2d ed. (Leiden, 1965); Margaret S. Drower, "Ugarit," *Cambridge Ancient History*, vol. 2 (1968), chap. 21b (excellent bibliographies); R. de Vaux, *Histoire*, pp. 123 ff.; Marvin H. Pope and Wolfgang Rolling, "Die Mythologie der Ugariter und Phönizier," in *WdM*, vol. 1, pp. 219–312; O. Eissfeldt, "Kanaanäisch-ugaritische Religion," in *Handbuch der Orientalistik* (Leiden, 1964), vol. 8, pt. 1, pp. 76–91; A. Jirku, *Der Mythus der Kanaanäer* (Bonn, 1966); J. C. De Moor, "The Semitic Pantheon of Ugarit," *Ugarit-Forschungen* 2 (1970): 187–228; H. Gese, in H. Gese, Maria Hofner, K. Rudolph, *Die Religion Altsyriens, Altarabiens, und der Mandäer* (Stuttgart, 1970), pp. 1–232; F. M. Cross, *Canaanite Myth and Hebrew Epic* (Cambridge, Mass., 1973).

The Ugaritic texts edited up to 1965 have been published in transcription by C. H. Gordon, *Ugaritic Text-book* (Rome, 1954); see also Gordon's *Ugaritic Literature: A Comprehensive Translation of the Poems and Prose Texts* (Rome, 1949), and "Canaanite Mythology," in *Mythologies of the Ancient World*, ed. S. N. Kramer, pp. 183–215. Other translations consulted are H. L. Ginsberg, "Ugaritic Myths, Epics, and Legends," *ANET*, pp. 129–55; G. R. Driver, *Canaanite Myths and Legends* (Edinburgh, 1956); A. Jirku, *Kanaanäische Mythen und Epen aus Ras Schamra-Ugarit* (Güttersloh, 1962); A. Caquot and M. Sznycer, "Textes Ougaritiques," in *Les religions du Proche-Orient: Textes et traditions sacrés babyloniens, ougaritiques, hittites*, ed. R. Labat (Paris, 1970), pp. 350–458.

There is already a considerable literature on Ugaritic religion and mythology. The essential bibliography is given by M. H. Pope and W. Rolling, "Mythologie"; H. H. Rowley, *Worship in Ancient Israel: Its Forms and Meaning* (London, 1967), pp. 11 ff.; Georg Fohrer, *History of Israelite Religion* (1968; English trans., New York, 1972), pp. 42–43; R. de Vaux, *Histoire*, pp. 136 ff. See also L. R. Fischer, ed., *Ras Shamra Parallels: The Texts from Ugarit and the Bible* (Rome, 1975), vol. 2.

On El and his role in the pantheon, see O. Eissfeldt, *El im ugaritischen Pantheon* (Leipzig, 1951); M. Pope, *El in the Ugaritic Texts* (Leiden, 1955); Ulf Oldenburg, *The Conflict between El and Baʾal in Canaanite Religion* (Leiden, 1969), esp. pp. 15–45, 101–20, 164–70. Now see F. M. Cross, *Canaanite Myth and Hebrew Epic*, pp. 20 ff. (there is a critique of Oldenburg's thesis in n. 51).

See also C. F. A. Schaeffer, *The Cuneiform Texts of Ras-Shamra-Ugarit* (London, 1939), pp. 60 ff.; Schaeffer, "Nouveaux témoignages du culte de El et de Baal à Ras Shamra-Ugarit et ailleurs en Syrie-Palestine," *Syria* 43 (1966): 1–19 (figurines of bulls as attribute of El, found in the excavations). On *Il* (*el*) as a divine name, see J. J. M. Roberts, *The Earliest Semitic Pantheon* (Baltimore and London, 1972), pp. 31 ff.: "The picture, then, that the Old Akkadian name gives of Il is a portrait of a high but gracious god, who is interested in man's welfare, and who is particularly active in the giving of children. This characterization corresponds in great part to what we know of ʿEl in the rest of the Semitic World" (p. 34).

On Dagan, see E. Dhorme, "Les avatars du dieu Dagon," *RHR* 138 (1950): 129–44; Ulf Oldenburg, *The Conflict*, pp. 47–57.

49. On Baal, see Arvid S. Kapelrud, *Baal in the Ras Shamra Texts* (Copenhagen, 1952); Hassan S. Haddad, "Baal-Hadad: A Study of the Syrian Storm-God," Ph.D. diss., University of Chicago, 1960; U. Cassuto, "Baal and Môt in the Ugaritic Texts," *Israel Exploration Journal* 12 (1962): 77–86; W. Schmidt, "Baals Tod und Auferstehung," *ZRGG* 15 (1963): 1–13; Ulf Oldenburg, *The Conflict*, pp. 57–100, 122–42, 176–77; M. Pope and W. Rolling in *WdM*, vol. 1, pp. 253–69 (with bibliography of the principal translated texts and their interpretation, pp. 268–69); J. C. de Moor, *The Seasonal Pattern in the Ugaritic Myth of Baʿlu* (= *Alter Orient und Altes Testament*, vol. 16) (Neukirchen-Vluyn, 1971); and, especially, F. M. Cross, *Canaanite Myth and Hebrew Epic*, pp. 112 ff. (Baal and Anath), pp. 147 ff. (theophanies of Baal and Yahweh).

The separation of the first divine couple, as the result of Baal's carrying Asherah away, seems to be indicated by the following scene: When Baal sends Asherah to El to demand a palace from him, El "opens his mouth and laughs" and asks: "Why has the Procreatress of the Gods come? . . . Does the love of El the King stir you?" But Asherah answers, scornfully: "Our King is ʾAlʾiyân Baʿal, our Judge, and there is none above him" (*Ugaritic Manual*, no. 51; trans. Oldenburg, p. 118). It is not until later, when Baal kills Asherah's 77 sons (*Ugaritic Manual*, no. 75; Oldenburg, p. 117) that the goddess approaches El and urges him to take vengeance.

Yam is identical with the ophidian dragon (*tannin*) Lotan, the Leviathan of the Old Testament. Cf. Psalm 74:14: "You crushed Leviathan's heads." The Apocalypse (12:3 ff.) describes "a huge red dragon, which had seven heads." On Yam, see, among others, Gray, *The Legacy of Canaan*, pp. 26 ff., 86 ff.; Oldenburg, *Conflict*, pp. 32–34, 134–37, and the comparative study in T. Gaster, *Thespis*, pp. 114 ff.

On Koshar-wa-Hasis, see Gaster's commentaries, *Thespis*, pp. 161 ff.

50. On the goddess Anath, see, in addition to the works on Baal, Arvid S. Kapelrud, *The Violent Goddess Anat in the Ras Shamra Texts* (Oslo, 1969); M. Pope, *WdM*, vol. 1, pp. 235–41; Wolfgang Helck, *Betrachtungen zur grossen Göttin und den ihr verbundenen Gottheiten* (Munich and Vienna, 1971), pp. 152 ff., 200 ff.; Joseph Henninger, "Zum Problem der Venussterngottheit bei den Semiten," *Anthropos* 71 (1976): 129–68.

On the analogies between Anath and Durgā, see Walter Dostal, "Ein Beitrag zur Frage des religiösen Weltbildes des frühesten Bodenbauer Vorderasiens," *Archiv für Völkerkunde* 12 (1957): 74 ff.

On Anath's "cannibalism" (she eats Baal's corpse), see Charles Virolleaud, "Un nouvel épisode du myth ugaritique de Baal," *Comptes-rendus de l'Académie des Inscriptions et Belles-Lettres*, 1960, pp. 180–86, and the observations by Michael C. Astour, "Un texte d'Ugarit récemment découvert et ses rapports avec l'origine des cultes bacchiques grecs," *RHR* 154 (1963): 1–15; Astour, *Hellenosemitica* (Leiden, 1964; rev. ed., 1967), pp. 170 ff.; W. F. Albright, *Yahveh and the Gods of Canaan* (New York, 1968), pp. 131 ff.

On the relations between Anath and Ashtarte, see J. J. M. Roberts, *The Earliest Semitic Pantheon*, pp. 37 ff.; Wolfgang Helck, *Betrachtungen*, pp. 155 ff. The goddess Ashtarte seems to be a double of Anath and plays almost no role. "A new mythological text has restored her importance and emphasizes her warlike character and her role as protector of justice and right" (R. de Vaux, *Histoire ancienne d'Israël*, p. 145, referring to a text published by Charles Virolleaud, *Le Palais Royal d'Ugarit*, vol. 5, and to the commentary by W. Herrmann, "Aštart," *Mitt. für Orientforschung* 15 [1969]: 6–55).

On the cosmological symbolism of the palace-temple, see Eliade, *Cosmos and History*, pp. 14 ff.; Eliade, "Centre du Monde, Temple, Maison," in *Le symbolisme cosmique des monuments religieux*, Serie Orientale Roma, no. 14 (Rome, 1957), pp. 57–82; Ananda Coomaraswamy, "The Symbolism of the Dome," *Indian Historical Quarterly* 14 (1938): 1–56; Loren R. Fisher, "Creation at Ugarit and in the Old Testament," *Vetus Testamentum* 15 (1965): 313–24; see also U. Cassuto, "Il palazzo di Baʾal nella tavola II AB di Ras Shamra," *Orientalia* n.s. 7 (1938): 265–90; A. S. Kapelrud, "Temple Building, a Task for Gods and Kings," *Orientalia* 32 (1963): 56–62.

51. On Mot, see, most recently, Oldenburg, *The Conflict*, pp. 35–39; M. Pope, in *WdM*, vol. 1, pp. 300–302; Cross, *Canaanite Myth*, pp. 116 ff. See also U. Cassuto, "Baal and Môt in the Ugaritic Texts," *Israel Exploration Journal* 12 (1962): 77–86.

On Athtar, cf. J. Gray, "The Desert God ʿAttr in the Literature and Religion of Canaan," *JNES* 8 (1949): 72–83; A. Caquot, "Le dieu ʿAthtar et les textes de Ras Shamra," *Syria* 35 (1958): 45–60; Oldenburg, *Conflict*, pp. 39–45.

52. On the cult of Baal at Ugarit, see Kapelrud, *Baal in the Ras Shamra Texts*, pp. 18 ff.; Kapelrud, *The Ras Shamra Discoveries and the Old*

Testament (Norman, Okla., 1963). See also J. Gray, "Sacral Kingship in Ugarit," *Ugaritica* (Paris, 1969), vol. 6, pp. 289–302. Archaic elements typical of fertility cults abound: stone phalli, images of the naked goddess, tauromorphic images of Baal, animal masks and horns worn by certain priests (see Schaeffer, *Cuneiform Texts*, p. 64, pl. X, fig. 2).

On the public sacrifice offered by men and women (and by the king and queen) to expiate confessed sins, see A. Caquot, "Un sacrifice expiatoire à Ras Shamra," *RHPR* 42 (1962): 201–11.

As R. de Vaux observes (*Histoire*, p. 146), the Canaanite sacrifices and the Israelite sacrifices "had a common ritual; for example, the holocaust of the prophets of Baal and that of Elijah on Mount Carmel are prepared in the same way (I Kings 18)."

On the Canaanite cult, see now Fohrer, *History of Israelite Religion*, pp. 57 ff., with recent bibliographical references.

On the conflict between Yahweh and Baal, see the bibliography given below, § 60.

On the epic poems of Keret and Aqhat-Daniel, and their Greek parallels, see Cyrus A. Gordon, *The Common Background of Greek and Hebrew Civilizations* (New York, 1965), pp. 128 ff. This author sees in the poem of Keret "the earliest known example of the Helen of Troy motif," a motif of Indo-European origin, documented in India and Greece but unknown in Mesopotamia and Egypt (Gordon, pp. 132 ff.). On this problem, see also Michael C. Astour, *Hellenosemitica*, 2d ed. (1967), who explains the reciprocal borrowings and analogies between the Syro-Palestinian and Greek worlds by their geographical situations and their political idiosyncrasies: "Both were broken, geographically dismembered territories without a central axis. This brought about similar state formations and internal orders. . . . The Greek and the West-Semitic worlds formed a common circle of small states, incapable of unification and centralization, unless if conquered by some outside empire" (pp. 358–59).

53. For the ancient history of Israel, we have used especially M. Noth, *Geschichte Israels* (Göttingen, 1950; 2d rev. ed., 1954) (Eng. trans. by S. Godman, *The History of Israel* [London, 1958]); J. Bright, *A History of Israel* (Philadelphia, 1959); and R. de Vaux, *Histoire ancienne d'Israël: Des origines à l'installation en Canaan* (Paris, 1971). This last work contains admirable critical bibliographies. See also W. F. Albright, *Archaeology and the Religion of Israel*, 2d ed. (Baltimore, 1946); Albright, *The Biblical Period from Abraham to Ezra* (New York, 1963); R. de Vaux, *Les institutions de l'Ancien Testament*, 2 vols., 2d ed. (Paris, 1961, 1967) (Eng. trans. by John McHugh, *Ancient Israel: Its Life and Institutions* [New York, 1961]); Otto Eissfeldt, *The Old Testament: An Introduction* (New

York, 1965) (translated from the 3d German ed., 1964, with supplementary bibliographies, pp. 722–85); J. Pedersen, *Israel: Its Life and Culture*, 4 vols. (Copenhagen, 1926, 1940); G. von Rad, *Old Testament Theology*, vol. 1 (New York, 1962) (the German original was published in 1957); M. Noth, *Die Ursprünge des alten Israel im Lichte neuer Quellen* (Cologne and Opladen, 1961); *The Bible and the Ancient Near East: Essays in Honor of W. F. Albright*, ed. C. Ernest Wright (New York, 1968), pp. 85–139 (on the archeology of Palestine, by E. Wright); pp. 265–99 (on problems of chronology).

There is a large number of books on the religious history of Israel; the most useful, among books published during the past dozen years, are T. Kaufmann, *The Religion of Israel*, translated from the Hebrew and abridged by M. Greenberg (Chicago, 1960); H. Ringgren, *La religion d'Israël* (Paris, 1966; German ed., Stuttgart, 1963; Eng. trans. by David E. Green, *Israelite Religion* [Philadelphia, 1966]); W. Eichrodt, *Religionsgeschichte Israels* (1969); G. Fohrer, *History of Israelite Religion* (Nashville, 1972; German ed., 1968).

The cosmogonic texts have been translated, with commentary, by Jean Bottéro, in "La naissance du monde selon Israel," *Sources Orientales*, no. 1, pp. 187–234 (= *La naissance du monde*, Paris, 1959). On the biblical cosmology, see H. Gunkel, *Schöpfung und Chaos in Urzeit und Endzeit*, 2d ed. (Göttingen, 1921), esp. pp. 29 ff.; V. Maag, "Jahwäs Begegnung mit der Kanaanäische Kosmologie," *Asiatische Studien/Etudes Asiatiques* 18–19 (1965): 252–69.

Among the most recent translations of Genesis, with commentary, the most accessible for nonspecialists is E. A. Speiser, *Genesis* (New York, 1964).

For the myths on the creation of man, see the bibliography given above, § 17.

54. On Eden and myths of Paradise, see P. Humbert, *Etudes sur le récit du Paradis et de la chute dans la Genèse* (1940); W. Andrae, "Der kultische Garten," *Die Welt des Orients* 6 (1952): 485–94; G. Widengren, *The King and the Tree of Life in Ancient Near Eastern Religion* (1951); A. Dammron, *La mythologie sumérienne et les premiers chapitres de la Genèse* (1959); Theodor H. Gaster, *Myth, Legend, and Custom in the Old Testament* (1969), pp. 24–37, 332–34 (bibliography); F. F. Hvidberg, "The Canaanite Background of Genesis I–III," *Vetus Testamentum* 10 (1960): 285 ff.; J. Coppens, *La connaissance du bien et du mal et le péché du Paradis*, Analecta Lovanesis Biblica et Orientalia (1958).

On the Tree of Life and the Tree of Knowledge, see Eliade, *Patterns in Comparative Religion*, pp. 287 ff.; Gaster, *Myth, Legend, and Custom*, pp. 337–38.

On Cain and Abel, see Gaster, pp. 51–55 (bibliography, pp. 341–42). On metallurgical rituals and symbolisms, see Eliade, *The Forge and the Crucible*, pp. 53 ff.; on the social organization and magical powers of smiths, see ibid., pp. 81 ff.

On the "sign of Cain" (Gen. 4:15), see the comparative material cited by Frazer and Gaster in Gaster, *Myth, Legend, and Custom*, pp. 55–65 (bibliography, pp. 344–45).

55. On the union of the "sons of God" with the "daughters of men," see C. E. Closen, *Die Sünde der "Sohne Gottes" (Gen. VI, 1–4)* (Rome, 1939); Gaster, pp. 351–52 (bibliography); B. S. Childs, *Myth and Reality in the Old Testament* (Naperville, Ill., 1960), pp. 49 ff.; G. A. Cooke, "The Sons of (the) God(s)," *Zeitschrift für die Alttestamentliche Wissenschaft* 76 (1964): 22–47.

On the Flood, see the notes to § 18; Gaster, p. 352 (bibliography); A. Parrot, *Déluge et Arche de Noé* (1952); C. Lambert, "Il n'y aura jamais de déluge (Genèse IX:11)," *Nouvelle Revue Théologique* 77 (1955): 581–601, 693–724.

On the Tower of Babel, see Gaster, pp. 360–61 (bibliography), and A. Parrot, *La Tour de Babel* (1953). On the symbolism of the ziggurat, see Eliade, *Cosmos and History*, pp. 13 ff.; G. Widengren, "Aspetti simbolici dei templi e luoghi di culto del vecino Oriente antico," *Numen* 7 (1960): 1–25. On myths of ascent to heaven, see Eliade, *Australian Religions*, pp. 29 ff., and Eliade, "Notes on the Symbolism of the Arrow," pp. 468 ff., in *Religion in Antiquity: Essay in Memory of Erwin R. Goodenough*, edited by Jacob Neusner (Leiden, 1968).

The book by A. Borst, *Der Turmbau von Babel: Geschichte der Meinungen über Ursprung und Vielfalt der Sprache und Völker*, 6 vols. (Stuttgart, 1957–63), is an extremely erudite encyclopedia of the genealogical legends of Western history.

56. On the nomadic Semites of the second millennium, see Joseph Henninger, "Zum Frühsemitischen Nomadentum," in *Viehwirtschaft und Hirtenkultur: Ethnographische Studien* (Budapest, 1969), pp. 33–68, esp. 44–50 (the patriarchs); 50–53 (nomads in the Mari texts).

On the Habiru and their relations with the Hebrews, see the summary of research and recent bibliography in R. de Vaux, *Histoire ancienne d'Israël*, pp. 202–8 ("Habiru-ᶜApiru was an ethnic term designating one of the Semitic groups of the west, 'Amorites' or 'Proto-Aramaeans,' with whom we have connected the patriarchs," p. 208). See also Albright, *From the Stone Age*, pp. 238 ff.; Albright, *Yahweh and the Gods of Canaan*, pp. 75 ff.; Fohrer, *History of Israelite Religion*, p. 30 (notes 8–10 contain bibliographies).

On the date of the patriarchs, see R. de Vaux, *Histoire*, pp. 245–53. On the "god of the father," see Albrecht Alt, *Der Gott der Väter* (1929; = *Kleine Schriften zur Geschichte des Volkes Israel* [1953], vol. 1, pp. 1–78); also available in an English translation: *Essays on Old Testament History and Religion*, trans. R. A. Wilson (New York, 1968) (see pp. 1–100). Alt's theses are discussed in Fohrer, pp. 36 ff.; de Vaux, pp. 256 ff.; Ringgren, *La religion d'Israël*, pp. 29 ff. The relations between the "god of the father" and El, and between El and Yahweh, have recently been analyzed from a new viewpoint by R. M. Cross, *Canaanite Myth and Hebrew Epic* (Cambridge, Mass., 1973), pp. 1–76.

The interpretation of the name El Shaddaï is still in dispute. It has been proposed to derive it from a word related to the Akkadian *šadū*, "mountain": it would be "(El) of the Mountains"; cf. Ringgren, pp. 34–35. But since it would be preferable to find an etymology for it in the Semitic of the Northwest, the Hebrew *šaday/šadèh* has recently been proposed: this would be "El of the Plain, or of the Fields, or of the Steppe" (de Vaux, p. 264, with bibliography).

It is noteworthy that the patriarchal narratives that know El do not mention Baal. This indicates that the ancestors of the Israelites, entering Canaan before the period of the Hyksos, did not find the cult of Baal; that god acquired his importance toward the middle of the second millennium, or perhaps a little earlier, at Ugarit: see de Vaux, p. 266. However, as we have already observed (p. 152, n. 26), there was probably a local god of storms and agricultural fertility whose name was forgotten after Baal was introduced.

There is no sign of the cult of "idols" among the patriarchs. But when Rachel is ready to leave the house of her father, Laban, she steals from him the *teraphim*, the domestic idols (Gen. 31:19) that Laban calls "my gods" (31:30). On the meaning of the *teraphim*, see A. R. Johnson, *The Cultic Prophet in Ancient Israel*, 2d ed. (1962), pp. 32 ff., and Rowley, *Worship in Ancient Israel*, pp. 19 ff. In any case, Rachel's act cannot be an indication of the religion of Jacob. See also Ringgren, pp. 38–39.

As for circumcision, it was probably practiced in the time of the patriarchs. Its origin is unknown; see R. de Vaux, *Les Institutions de l'Ancien Testament*, 2d ed. (Paris, 1961), pp. 78–82; Eng. trans., pp. 46–48; E. Isaac, "Circumcision as a Covenant Rite," *Anthropos* 59 (1964): 444–56. It has been maintained that circumcision was borrowed from the Egyptians, but it was not universally practiced in Egypt. On the other hand, the custom is documented in northern Syria from the beginning of the third millennium. Hence the ancestors of the Israelites could have known it before they arrived in Canaan. "At that time it had its primitive meaning as an initiation into marriage and the common life of the clan, as it still has in Gen. 34:14–16; it is only later that it became the sign of the covenant between God and his people, which the sacerdotal author of Gen. 17 refers to the time of Abraham" (de Vaux, *Histoire ancienne d'Israël*, vol. 1, p. 273; the recent bibliography is given in notes 94 and 96). On circumcision as an initiation rite in archaic societies, see Eliade, *Birth and Rebirth: The Religious Meanings of Initiation in Human Culture*, trans. Willard R. Trask (New York, 1958), pp. 21 ff. (paperback title, *Rites and Symbols of Initiation*).

57. On blood sacrifices, see R. de Vaux, *Les sacrifices de l'Ancien Testament* (Paris, 1964), pp. 7–27 (Eng. trans., *Studies in Old Testament Sacrifice* [Cardiff, 1964], chap. 1); de Vaux, *Histoire ancienne d'Israël*, pp. 270 ff. On the Central Arabian customs, see J. Henninger, "La religion bédouine préislamique," in *L'antica società beduina*, ed. F. Gabrieli (Rome, 1959), pp. 135–36, and his "Les fêtes de printemps chez les Arabes et leurs implications historiques," *Revista do Museu Paulista* (Sao Paulo), n.s. 4 (1950): 389–432. See also Henninger's recent book, *Les fêtes de printemps chez les Sémites et la Pâque israélite* (Paris, 1975) (copious bibliographies).

58. The figure of Moses has recently given rise to some rather original interpretations; see E. Auerbach, *Moses* (Amsterdam, 1953); H. Cazelles, *Moïse, l'homme de l'Alliance* (1955); H. H. Rowley, *From Joseph to Joshua* (Oxford, 1950); Rowley, "Moses and the Decalogue," *BJRL* 34 (1951): 81–118. See also R. Smend, *Das Mosebild von Heinrich Ewald bis Martin Noth* (1959). On Moses' mission, see de Vaux, *Histoire ancienne*, pp. 305 ff. On the various traditions concerning the departure from Egypt and the Passover, see Fohrer, *History of Israelite Religion*, pp. 68 ff.; R. de Vaux, *Institutions*, vol. 2, pp. 383–94 (bibliography, pp. 467–68) (Eng. trans., pp. 484–93, 550–51); de Vaux, *Les sacrifices de l'Ancien Testament*, pp. 7 ff. (Eng. trans. chap. 1).

The influence of Passover on the tradition recorded in Exodus 1–15 has been especially emphasized by J. Pedersen, *Israel: Its Life and Culture* (1940), vol. 3, pp. 384–415; vol. 4, pp. 728–37; his theory has been criticized and modified by G. von Rad and S. Mowinckel; see Fohrer, *History*, pp. 68 ff.

As we have already observed (p. 179), the celebration of Passover, originally a pastoral spring festival, was explained as the ritual commemoration of the departure from Egypt; in other words, a periodical ceremony expressing cosmic religiosity ends by being historicized. On the other hand, the fabulous events of the Exodus, i.e., the passage of the Sea of Reeds and the destruction of the Egyptian army, received, as time passed, two different interpretations. In the oldest documentation (Exodus 15:1–

10), pharaoh's troops are buried under waves raised by the breath of Yahweh. It is only later, in the Psalms, that the parting of the sea is mentioned: "Dividing the sea, bringing them through, making the waters stand up like dikes" (Ps. 78:13; cf. Ps. 77:17–20).

In this case the miracle of the Sea of Reeds is put into relation with the Creation, that is, with Yahweh's victory over the marine monster Rahab and Leviathan: "Did you not split Rahab in two and pierce the dragon through? Did you not dry up the sea, the waters of the great Abyss, to make the seabed a road for the redeemed to cross?" (Isaiah 51:9–10). The Exodus, as well as the conquest of Canaan (and, later, the return of the exiles, announced by the text of Deutero-Isaiah that we have just quoted), in some sort constitutes a repetition of the cosmogonic work (see Cross, *Canaanite Myth and Hebrew Epic*, pp. 100 ff.). But in the last analysis the two viewpoints—historic and cosmological—are complementary; the conquest of Canaan, most certainly a historical event, is equally a divine work, for it is Yahweh who insures the victory of the Israelites.

59. In his book *Law and Covenant in Israel and the Ancient Near East* (Pittsburgh, 1955), B. E. Mendenhall has compared the Code of the Covenant with the treaties that the Hittite kings concluded with their vassals in Asia Minor. Such a treaty contains, after a preamble (stating the king's name and titles and summarizing the existent relations between the two parties), the stipulations imposed on the vassal, instructions for the preservation of the document in a temple and its solemn periodical reading, the list of the witnessing gods, and, finally, formulas of malediction and benediction. Albright, who accepts the thesis, stresses the necessity of treaties and contracts for the primitive Hebrews, the majority of whom were caravaners; see his *Yahweh and the Gods of Canaan*, pp. 107 ff., with bibliographies. Mendenhall's thesis is criticized in R. de Vaux, *Histoire*, p. 410, n. 141. De Vaux asks how the seminomadic group led by Moses could have known the contracts of the Hittite kings. Then, too, there are differences in the structures of the two texts; for example, in the Code of the Covenant the closing maledictions and benedictions are lacking. In addition, whereas the "stipulations" are usually expressed in the form of conditions—"If it happens that . . . "—but the Covenant employs apodeictic formulas. De Vaux observes that the Hittite kings' treaties with semibarbarous peoples do not follow the classic formula. Hence there are several types of "covenant formula" (De Vaux, p. 413).

On the role of the oasis of Kadesh Barnea in the constitution of the Yahwistic traditions, see T. J. Meek, *Hebrew Origins* (New York, 1936; reprint, 1960), pp. 119 ff.; R. de Vaux, *Les Institutions de l'Ancien Testament*, vol. 2, pp. 228 ff. (Eng. trans., pp. 369 ff.); Ringgren, pp. 49 ff. (Eng.

trans., pp. 30 ff.). The volcanic elements of Yahweh's manifestation on Sinai have been analyzed by J. Koenig, "Le Sinaï, montagne de feu," *RHR* 167 (1964): 129–55; Koenig, "Aux origines des théophanies iahvistes," *RHR* 169 (1966): 1–36. But Cross has shown that the "revelation on Sinai" is a "theophany through storm," comparable to that of Baal; see his *Canaanite Myth and Hebrew Epic*, pp. 147 ff. See also G. E. Mendenhall, *The Tenth Generation: The Origins of the Biblical Traditions* (Baltimore, 1973), pp. 56 ff., and also p. 105 (on the incident at Baalpeor).

60. Some recent theories concerning the settling of the Israelites in Canaan (especially those of Y. Kaufmann, A. Alt, M. Noth, W. F. Albright, and G. E. Mendenhall) are analyzed by R. de Vaux, *Histoire ancienne*, pp. 444–54. See also R. Smend, *Jahvekrieg und Strämmebund* (Göttingen, 1963) (Eng. trans. by Max G. Rogers, *Yahweh War and Tribal Confederation* [Nashville, Tenn., 1970]).

On the conflict between Yahwism and the Canaanite religion, see R. Hillman, *Wasser und Berg: Kosmische Verbindungslinien zwischen dem Kanaanäischen Wettergott und Jahve* (Diss., Halle, 1965); J. Maier, "Die Gottesvorstellung Altisraels und die Kanaanäische Religion," in *Bibel und Zeitgemässer Glaube* (1965), vol. 1, pp. 135–58; T. Worden, "The Literary Influence of the Ugaritic Fertility Myth on the Old Testament," *VT* 3 (1953): 273–97; Fohrer, *History*, pp. 103 ff.; de Vaux, *Histoire*, p. 147 (n. 99 has bibliography). On syncretism, see G. W. Ahlström, *Aspects of Syncretism in Israelite Religion* (Lund, 1963).

The work by R. Dussaud, *Les Origines cananéennes du sacrifice israélite*, 2d ed. (1921; rev. ed., 1941) is still very useful. See also Rowley, *Worship in Ancient Israel*, pp. 61 ff., and the bibliography given on p. 65, n. 1. Human sacrifice was never accepted by the Israelites; the sacrifices of children attested in the seventh century represent an outside influence; see de Vaux and also Eissfeldt, summarized by Rowley, p. 65, n. 1.

On prophecy in the ancient Near East and among the Israelites, see A. Haldar, *Association of Cult Prophets among the Ancient Semites* (Uppsala, 1945); J. Lindblom, *Prophecy in Ancient Israel* (Philadelphia, 1965); these two works contain rich bibliographies. See also J. Pedersen, "The Role Played by Inspired Persons among the Israelites and the Arabs," *Studies in Old Testament Prophecy* (Robinson Festschrift) (1950), pp. 127–42; A. Lods, "Une tablette inédite de Mari, intéressante pour l'histoire ancienne du prophétisme sémitique," ibid., pp. 103–10; A. Malamat, "Prophetic Revelation in New Documents from Mari and the Bible," *Vetus Testamentum*, suppl., 15 (1966): 207–27; G. Fohrer, *Studien zur alttestamentlichen Prophetie, 1949–1965* (1967).

61. The history of studies—in particular the history of the hypotheses concerning the original homeland of the Indo-Europeans and their migrations—is summarized by P. Bosch-Gimpera, *Les Indo-Européens*, trans. R. Lantier (Paris, 1961), pp. 21–96, and by G. Devoto, *Origini indeuropee* (Florence, 1962), pp. 8–194. These two works contain important bibliographies. The work by O. Schrader, *Reallexicon der indogermanische Altertumskunde*, 2d ed. (Berlin and Leipzig, 1917–32), has not been replaced. See also A. Nehring, "Studien zur indogermanischen Kultur und Urheimat," in W. Koppers et al., *Die Indogermanen- und German-enfrage* (Salzburg and Leipzig, 1936), pp. 7–229.

Accounts of the most recent archeological excavations will be found in some works by Marija Gimbutas: *The Prehistory of Eastern Europe* (1956); *Bronze Age Cultures in Central and Eastern Europe* (The Hague, 1965); "Proto-Indo-European Culture: The Kurgan Culture during the Fifth, Fourth and Third Millennia B.C.," in George Cordona, ed., *Indo-European and Indo-Europeans* (Philadelphia, 1970), pp. 155–97; "The Beginning of the Bronze Age in Europe and the Indo-Europeans: 3500–2500 B.C.," *JIES* 1 (1973): 163–214; and "The Destruction of Aegean and East Mediterranean Urban Civilization around 2500 B.C.," in R. Crossland and A. Birchall, eds., *Bronze Age Migrations in the Aegean* (1973), pp. 129–39. Homer L. Thomas, in "New Evidence for Dating the Indo-European Dispersal in Europe" (*Indo-European and Indo-Europeans*, pp. 199–251), proposes to carry back the dates of the expansion of the Indo-Europeans (radiocarbon analysis shows their presence in Holland ca. 2470 or 2600 B.C.). Ward H. Goodenough, in "The Evolution of Pastoralism and Indo-European Origins" (ibid., pp. 253–65) places the homeland of the Indo-Europeans in the eastern regions of Poland and in the western Ukraine. See also Paul Friedrich, "Proto-Indo-European Trees," ibid., pp. 11–34; T. Burrow, "The Proto-Indoaryans," *JRAS* (1973): 123–40; M. M. Winn, "Thoughts on the Question of Indo-European Movements into Anatolia and Iran," *JIES* 2 (1974): 117–42 (on the Indo-European groups living in Anatolia and Iran ca. 3000 B.C.). For a critical bibliography on the Indo-Europeans in Hither Asia, see M. Mayrhofer, *Die Indo-Arier im Alten Vorderasien* (Wiesbaden, 1966); cf. Mayrhofer in *IIJ* 7 (1964): 208 ff., and in *Die Arien im Vorderen Orient—Ein Mythos?* (Vienna, 1974). The religious function of the tumuli (*kurgan*) indicates a strong ancestor cult, comparable to that of the megalithic civilizations (cf. § 35). See also R. Ghirshman, *L'Iran et la migration des Indo-Aryens et des Iraniens* (Leiden, 1977).

62. On Max Müller's theories, see Richard M. Dorson, "The Eclipse of Solar Mythology," in *Myth: A Symposium*, ed. Thomas A. Sebeok

(Philadelphia, 1955), pp. 15–38. The work by Leopold von Schröder, *Arische Religion*, 2 vols. (Leipzig, 1914, 1916), can still be used. In the first volume the author presents the Indo-European supreme beings, in the second the cosmic divinities (Earth, Sun, Fire, etc.). A third volume would have studied the notion of the soul and the ancestor cult. Of the vast literature directly or indirectly inspired by National Socialist ideology, we may cite, as an example, Friedrich Cornelius, *Indogermanische Religions-geschichte* (Munich, 1942). The first volume (the only one published) of *Glaubensgeschichte der Indogermanen* (Stuttgart, 1937) by J. W. Hauer is really made up of a series of independent studies. A critique of the racist interpretation of Indo-European spirituality will be found in the various contributions brought together under the title *Die Indogermanen- und Germanenfrage*, published by W. Koppers in the series Wiener Beiträge zur Kulturgeschichte und Linguistik (Salzburg and Leipzig, 1936), and in the third volume of *Rassen und Völker im Vorgeschichte und Geschichte des Abendlandes* (Lucerne, 1946), by Wilhelm Schmidt (esp. pp. 275–318).

On the Indo-European religious vocabulary, see G. Devoto, *Origini indeuropee*, pp. 295 ff., and the second volume of E. Benveniste, *Le vocabulaire des institutions indo-européennes* (Paris, 1969). For a penetrating analysis of the term *theos*, see G. Gallavotti, "Morfologia di *theos*," *SMSR* 33 (1962): 25–43. On the Iranian divinity of fire, see Stig Wikander, *Der arische Männerbund* (Lund, 1938), pp. 76 ff., and § 104 above.

Eric Hamp (against Benveniste, vol. 2, pp. 223 ff.) has recently demonstrated the existence of a common Indo-European term for "sacrifice"; see his "Religion and Law from Iguvium," *JIES* 1 (1973): 322.

A late development associates divine energy with the souls of the dead, especially among the Germans, where the original root GHAV, GHUTO, which designated the "evoked," ends by expressing the idea of god. Equally late in appearing, it seems, is the term WELO, "soul," which signifies "he who frees himself into the air," that is to say, is set free by cremation; see Devoto, *Origini*, pp. 295–316.

It is important to point out a characteristic difference between the Indo-Europeans and the Semites: the value attributed to writing. Herodotus 1. 136 reports that the Persians teach their sons only three things: to ride, to shoot with the bow, and to tell the truth. According to a passage in the annals of the Assyrian king Assurbanipal V, the Semitic sovereign learns to ride (and to drive the chariot), to shoot with the bow, and "the wisdom of Nabu and the art of writing in accordance with the traditions of the masters"; see G. Widengren, *Numen* 1 (1954): 63, n. 311; Widengren, *Religionsphänomenologie* (Berlin, 1969), pp. 570 ff. See also G. Dumézil, "La tradition druidique et l'écriture: Le Vivant et le Mort," *RHR* 122

(1940): 125–33. This radical difference between the Indo-European religions, based on oral tradition, and the "religions of the Book," where the scribes enjoyed great prestige, created difficulties when the Zoroastrian clergy decided to publish its sacred book, the *Avesta*, for even in the Sassanian period (third–seventh centuries), writing was considered a work of the demons; see A. Bausani, *Persia religiosa* (Milan, 1959), pp. 20 ff. See also G. Widengren, "Holy Book and Holy Tradition in Iran: The Problem of the Sassanid Avesta," in F. F. Bruce and E. G. Rupp, eds., *Holy Book and Holy Tradition* (Manchester, 1968), pp. 36–53.

63. The most convenient introduction to the work of Georges Dumézil is *L'Idéologie tripartie des Indo-Européens* (Brussels, 1958). The bibliography of his work down to 1960 is given in *Hommages à Georges Dumézil* (Brussels, 1960), pp. xi–xxiii. For a chronological presentation of Dumézil's studies and an analysis of the criticisms that have been directed against him, see C. Scott Littleton, *The New Comparative Mythology: An Anthropological Assessment of the Theories of Georges Dumézil* (Berkeley and Los Angeles, 1966). A certain number of studies of Dumézil's concepts have been published in the volumes *Myth and Law among the Indo-Europeans*, ed. Jaan Puhvel (Berkeley and Los Angeles, 1970), and *Myth in Indo-European Antiquity*, ed. G. I. Larson (Berkeley and Los Angeles, 1974). See also the articles by J. F. Richards, Alf Hiltebeitel, J. Gonda, C. Scott Littleton, and David M. Knipe in *Journal of Asian Studies* 34 (1974): 127–68. Richard Bodéus, "Société athénienne, sagesse grecque et idéal indo-européen," *L'Antiquité Classique* 41 (1972): 453–86, has brilliantly examined Dumézil's concept of tripartition in the light of the Greek data.

While waiting for the new edition of the three volumes of Dumézil's *Jupiter, Mars, Quirinus* (Paris, 1941–45) and of *Mitra-Varuṇa: Essai sur deux représentations indo-européennes de la souveraineté* (1940; 2d ed., 1948), one may read *Heur et malheur du guerrier* (Paris, 1969), a recasting of *Aspects de la fonction guerrière chez les Indo-Européens* (1956) (Eng. trans. by Alf Hiltebeitel, *The Destiny of the Warrior* [Chicago, 1970]); *L'héritage indo-européen à Rome* (Paris, 1949); *Servius et la Fortune* (Paris, 1943); and *Mythe et Epopée*, 3 vols. (Paris, 1968–73) (Eng. trans. of vol. 2, pt. 3, by Alf Hiltebeitel, *The Destiny of a King* [Chicago, 1973]). In the first volume of *Mythe et Epopée* (pp. 31–257), Dumézil develops Stig Wikander's demonstration regarding the existence of the tripartite schema in the *Mahābhārata*. Wikander's article, "La légende des Pandava et le fond mythique du Mahābhārata" (in Swedish, in *Religion och Bibel*, vol. 6, pp. 27–39) was translated by Dumézil in *Jupiter, Mars, Quirinus* (1948), supplementary vol. 4, pp. 37–53. On the gods of the Mitanni, see G. Dumézil, "Les 'trois fonctions' dans le Rig Veda et les dieux indiens de

Mitani," Académie royale de Belgique, *Bulletin de la Classe des Lettres*, 5th ser. 47 (1961): 265–98.

According to V. M. Apte, from the time of the redaction of the first nine books of the Rig Veda, "the society was thought of as composed of priests, warriors, and stock-breeders; and if these groups were not yet called by their names of *brāhmana, kṣatriya*, and *vaiśya*, the abstract substantives—names of notions—of which these names of persons are only derivatives, were already formed into a hierarchical system that distributively defined the principles of the three activities: *brāhman* (neuter), 'knowledge and use of the mystical correlations among the parts of the real, visible or invisible'; *kṣatra*, 'power'; and *viś*, at once 'peasantry' and 'organized habitat' and, in the plural, *viśaḥ*, 'ensemble of the people in its local and social groupings'" (Dumézil, *L'idéologie tripartie*, p. 8, summarizing V. M. Apte, "Were Castes Formulated in the Age of the Rig Veda?" *Bulletin of the Deccan College Research Institute*, no. 2, pp. 34–46). Dumézil finds the tripartite schema recurring in the succession of the first Roman kings: (1) Romulus, redoubtable sovereign (type Varuṇa); (2) Numa the Wise, founder of cults and laws (type Mitra); (3) Tullus Hostilius, exclusively a warrior (Indra; Mars); and (4) Ancus Marcius, a pacific king, under whom the Roman masses and wealth developed (Quirinus) (Dumézil, *Heur et malheur du guerrier*, pp. 15 ff.) (*The Destiny of the Warrior*, pp. 7 ff.).

64. On the Āryan penetration into India, see K. Jettmar, "Zur Wanderungsgeschichte der Iranier," *Die Wiener Schule der Völkerkunde, Festschrift zum 25 jährigen Bestand* (Vienna, 1956), pp. 327–49; P. Bosch-Gimpera, "The Migration Route of the Indo-Aryans," *JIES* 1 (1973): 513–17. See also *East and West* 21 (1971): 14 ff.

The earliest Āryan culture in India is examined in the work of R. C. Majumdar in *The Vedic Age*, vol. 1 of *History and Culture of the Indian People* (London, 1951) (excellent bibliographies).

The role of the Āryans in the final destruction of the Indus civilization is discussed by Sir Mortimer Wheeler, *The Indus Civilization*, 3d ed. (Cambridge, 1968), pp. 132 ff.; R. Heine-Geldern, "The Coming of the Aryans and the End of the Harappa Culture," *Man* 56 (1956): 136–40; Bridget and Raymond Allchin, *The Birth of Indian Civilization* (Baltimore, 1968), pp. 154 ff.; Walter A. Fairservis, Jr., *The Roots of Ancient India* (New York, 1971), pp. 345 ff. See also G. D. Kumar, "The Ethnic Components of the Builders of the Indus Valley Civilization and the Advent of the Aryans," *JIES* 1 (1973): 66–80.

For rites connected with the occupation of territories, see Ananda Coomaraswamy, *The Rig Veda as Land-náma-Bók* (London, 1935).

The relative chronology of the hymns, the schools, and the recensions of the four collections—Rig Veda, Yajur-Veda, Sāmaveda, Atharva Veda —are concisely presented by L. Renou, *L'Inde classique* (Paris, 1947), vol. 1, pp. 270 ff. The translations of the different Vedic texts are listed by Nurvin J. Hein in Charles J. Adams, ed., *A Reader's Guide to the Great Religions* (New York and London, 1965), pp. 49–50 (2d ed., 1977, pp. 110–11). The French translations are mentioned by Jean Varenne, *Le Véda, premier livre sacré de l'Inde* (Paris, 1967), vol. 1, pp. 36–38. The most important are those by Louis Renou, *Hymnes et prières du Véda* (1938); *La poésie religieuse de l'Inde antique* (1942); *Hymnes spéculatifs du Véda* (1956), and the translations by Jean Varenne, published in *Le Véda*, vols. 1 and 2. See also Victor Henry, *Les livres VII à XII de l'Atharva Véda* (Paris, 1892–96); P. E. Dumont, *L'agnihotra* (Baltimore, 1939).

Indispensable is the translation by K. F. Geldner, *Der Rig-Veda*, 3 vols. (Cambridge, Mass., 1951).

For a history of interpretations of the Vedic religion, see L. Renou, *Religions of Ancient India* (London, 1953), pp. 7 ff. The work by A. Bergaigne, *La religion védique d'après les hymnes du Rigvéda*, 3 vols. (Paris, 1878–97) is still unequaled. Also deserving of consultation are Maurice Bloomfield, *The Religion of the Veda* (New York, 1908); A. A. Macdonell, *Vedic Mythology* (Strasbourg, 1897); H. Oldenberg, *La religion du Véda* (French trans., 1903); A. Hillebrandt, *Vedische Mythologie*, 2d ed. (Breslau, 1929); A. B. Keith, *The Religion and Philosophy of the Veda and Upanishads*, 2 vols. (Cambridge, Mass., 1925); G. Fussman, "Pour une problématique des religions indiennes anciennes," *JA* 265 (1977): 21–70.

Louis Renou has presented a concise history of Vedism in *Religions of Ancient India*, pp. 1–45. See also, by the same author, *L'Inde classique*, pp. 314–72 (this section translated by Philip Spratt as *Vedic India* [Calcutta, 1957]); *Le destin du Véda dans l'Inde* (= *Etudes védiques*, vol. 6, 1960; Eng. trans. by Dev Raj Chanana, *The Destiny of the Veda in India* [Delhi, 1965]).

The most recent work, with a very rich bibliography, is the one by J. Gonda, *Les religions de l'Inde*, vol. 1: *Védisme et hindouisme ancien* (French trans., Paris, 1962). See also J. Gonda, *The Vision of the Vedic Poets* (The Hague, 1965); Gonda, *Loka: World and Heaven in the Veda* (Amsterdam, 1966); P. Horsch, *Die vedische Gāthā- und Sloka-Literatur* (Bern, 1966).

65. On the *devas* and *asuras* in the Vedic period, the study by T. Segerstedt, "Les Asuras dans la religion védique," *RHR* 55 (1908): 157–203, 293–316, can still be consulted; but its general thesis—the identification of the Asuras with the primitive inhabitants of India—is debatable. See also P. von Bradke, *Dyāus Asura, Ahura Mazdā, und die Asuras* (Halle, 1885).

According to von Bradke, the word *asura* appears 71 times in the Rig Veda (57 times in the singular, 4 in the dual, and 10 in the plural); of the 10 times that the word appears in the plural, it has a meaning hostile to the *devas* 8 times; in contrast, in the singular the word has this hostile meaning only 4 times (von Bradke, p. 22). See also Herman Güntert, *Der arische Weltkönig und Heiland* (Halle, 1923), pp. 101 ff.

The conflict between Devas and Asuras for universal sovereignty is presented in detail for the first time in the *Brāhmaṇas*; see Sylvain Levi, *La doctrine du sacrifice dans les Brāhmanas* (Paris, 1898), pp. 27–61.

On the cosmogonic meaning of the Devas-Asuras conflict, see F. B. J. Kuiper, "Basic Concept of Vedic Religion," *HR* 15 (1975): 107–20. On the identification Varuṇa-Vṛtra, see Bergaigne, *Rel. védique*, vol. 3, pp. 113, 128, 147. For a metaphysical interpretation of the pair *devas-asuras*, see A. K. Coomaraswamy, "Angel and Titan: An Essay in Vedic Ontology," *JAOS* 55 (1935): 373–419.

66. On Varuṇa, see the bibliographies given in Eliade, *Patterns in Comparative Religion*, pp. 66 ff., 117, and *Images and Symbols*, pp. 95–99; to these add G. Dumézil, *Mitra-Varuṇa*, 2d ed. (1948), esp. pp. 83 ff., 116 ff.; J. Gonda, *Les religions de l'Inde*, vol. 1, pp. 93–106; H. Lüders, *Varuṇa* (Göttingen, 1951–59), esp. vol. 2: *Varuṇa und das Ṛta*. On *ṛta*, see the recent bibliography in Gonda, *Les religions de l'Inde*, vol. 4, p. 98, n. 3. *Ṛta* is opposed, on the ethical plane, by *anṛta*, "disorder," "falsehood," and on the cosmic plane by *nirṛti*, "dissolution." See also H. de Glasenapp, *La philosophie indienne* (French trans., Paris, 1951), p. 33.

On Varuṇa's "retreat" before the popularity of Indra, see L. Renou, *Religions of Ancient India*, pp. 20 ff.

On *māyā* in the Vedic period, see G. Dumézil, "Ordre, fantaisie, changement dans les pensées archaïques de l'Inde et de Rome," *Rev. Etudes Latines* 32 (1954): 139–62, esp. pp. 142–50, with a rich documentation. Add J. Gonda, *Four Studies in the Language of the Veda* (The Hague, 1959), pp. 119–94, and Gonda, *Change and Continuity in Indian Religion* (1965), pp. 164–97. A. Bergaigne, *Le religion védique*, vol. 3, pp. 80 ff., has studied the other divine beings that possess their *māyā*: Agni, Soma, Tvaṣṭri, etc.; see also Eliade, *Images and Symbols*, pp. 99 ff.

On the mythical origin of *dharma*, see Paul Horsh, "Vom Schöpfungs-mythos zum Weltgesetz," *Asiatische Studien* 21 (1967): 31–61.

On the structural solidarity Varuṇa-Vṛtra and, in general, the con-substantiality gods-serpents, see *Images and Symbols*, pp. 98 ff.; *The Two and the One*, pp. 91 ff.; A. Coomaraswamy, "Angel and Titan: An Essay in Vedic Ontology," *JAOS* 55 (1935): 373–419. Kuiper has shown that in the Rig Veda, where he is conceived as supporting heaven and earth by a cosmic axis, Varuṇa performs the function that will later be attributed to the serpent Śeṣa; see *IIJ* 8 (1964): 108, 116, 118. On the assimilation of Varuṇa to serpents in the *Mahābhārata*, see Gösta Johnsen, "Varuṇa and Dhrtarāstra," *IIJ* 9 (1966): 245–65, esp. 260–61.

67. The ambivalence of Varuṇa is not exceptional; see L. Renou, "L'ambiguïté du vocabulaire du Rgveda," *JA* 231 (1939): 161–235; Renou, *Religions of Ancient India*, pp. 20 ff. On the ambivalence of Soma, see Eliade, *The Two and the One*, pp. 89–90. See, further on, § 68, on the "fraternity" Indra-Vṛtra.

On Mitra, see H. Güntert, *Der arische Weltkönig und Heiland* (Halle, 1923), pp. 49 ff., 120 ff.; G. Dumézil, *Mitra-Varuṇa*, pp. 79 ff., with bibliography; J. Gonda, *Les religions de l'Inde*, vol. 1, pp. 103 ff. with bibliography; Gonda, *The Vedic God Mitra* (Leiden, 1972).

On Aryaman, see P. Thieme, *Der Fremdling im Ṛg Veda* (1938); Thieme, "Mitra and Aryaman," *Transactions of the Connecticut Academy of Arts and Sciences* 41 (1957): 1–96; and the following works by G. Dumézil: *Le troisième souverain: Essai sur le dieu indo-iranien Aryaman* (Paris, 1949); *Les dieux des Indo-Européens* (1952), pp. 40–59; and *L'idéologie tripartie des Indo-Européens* (Brussels, 1958), pp. 68, 108–18.

On Aditi and the Adityas, see G. Dumézil, *Déesses latines et mythes védiques* (1956), pp. 90 ff.; J. Gonda, *Some Observations on the Relations between "Gods" and "Powers" in the Veda* (The Hague, 1957), pp. 76 ff.; Gonda, *Les religions de l'Inde*, vol. 1, pp. 104 ff., with bibliography.

68. For a brief exposition on the subject of Indra, see J. Gonda, *Les religions de l'Inde*, vol. 1, pp. 70–81 (with bibliography); H. Lommel, *Der arische Kriegsgott* (Frankfurt, a.M., 1939); G. Dumézil, *Heur et malheur du guerrier* (1969), esp. pp. 63 ff., 112 ff. (*Destiny of the Warrior*, pp. 65, 123 ff.); E. Benveniste and L. Renou, *Vṛtra et Vṛthragna, étude de mythologie indo-iranienne* (1934).

On the cosmogonic role of Indra, see Norman W. Brown, "The Creation Myth of the Rig Veda," *JAOS* 62 (1942): 85–98; Eliade, *Cosmos and History*, pp. 19 ff.; Stella Kramrisch, "The Triple Structure of Creation in the Rg Veda," *HR* 2 (1960): 140–75, 256–85, esp. pp. 140–48; F. B. J. Kuiper, "Cosmogony and Conception: A Query," *HR* 10 (1970): 91–138, esp. pp. 98–110.

On the combat between a god-champion and the dragon, see Eliade, *Cosmos and History*, pp. 54 ff.; Theodor H. Gaster, *Thespis* (New York, 1950), p. 141 ff.; J. Fontenrose, *Python* (Berkeley and Los Angeles, 1959); F. R. Schröder, "Indra, Thor, und Herakles," *Zeitschrift für deutsche Philologie* 76 (1957): 1–41; V. Ivanov and V. Toporov, "Le mythe indo-européen du dieu de l'orage poursuivant le serpent: Reconstruction du schéma." *Exchange et communication: Mélanges C. Lévi-Strauss* (Paris, 1969).

On the paradigmatic function of the combat Indra-Vṛtra, see F. B. J. Kuiper, "The Ancient Aryan Verbal Contest," *IIJ* 4 (1960): 217–81. On the Maruts, see Stig Wikander, *Der arische Männerbund* (Lund, 1938), pp. 75 ff. On the "fecundating" aspect of Indra, see J. J. Meyer, *Trilogie altindischer Mächte und Feste der Vegetation* (Zurich, 1937), esp. vol. 3, pp. 154 ff. (late developments); J. Gonda, "The Indra Festival according to the Atharvavedins," *JAOS* 87 (1967): 413–29.

We have not discussed certain parallel myths that oppose Indra to the Three-headed One (son to Tvaṣṭṛ) or to Namuci. Dumézil finds the same scenario among the Romans, in Greece, and in Scandinavia; see his *Heur et malheur du guerrier*, pp. 33 ff., 63 ff. (*Destiny of the Warrior*, pp. 29 ff., 65 ff.). The paradigmatic combat between Indra and Vrtra later gave rise to a daring interpretation, though one that had been prepared for by the Vedic conception of divine ambivalence and bipolarity. The god-champion becomes the "brother" of the dragon, since the latter was created by Tvaṣṭṛ, Indra's father. According to the myth, Tvastr had failed to invite his son to a *soma* sacrifice. But Indra, succeeding in approaching the sacrifice, seized the *soma* by force. Furious, his father threw what was left of the divine liquid into the fire, exclaiming: "Grow, and become Indra's enemy!" From this remaining portion of *soma*, poured into the fire, Vṛtra was born (*Taitt. Saṃ.* 2. 4. 12 and 5. 1 ff.; *Kauśitaki Br.* 15. 2–3). But the latter quickly swallowed the gods Agni and Soma, and the other divinities took fright. Alarmed, Tvaṣṭṛ gave lightning to Indra, thus insuring his final victory. *Śatapatha Brāhmaṇa* 1. 6. 3 gives a highly significant detail: conquered, Vṛtra addresses Indra in these terms: "Strike me not, for thou art now what I was."

Such myths, and their theological exegesis,

reveal a less well known, because less obvious, aspect of divine history. One might almost say that this is a "secret history" of the divinity, which is intelligible only to initiates, that is to say, to those who know the tradition and understand the doctrine. The "secret" Vedic history reveals, on the one hand, the blood brotherhood of the Devas and Asuras, the fact that these two classes of superhuman beings sprang from one and the same principle; and on the other, it makes clear the *coincidentia oppositorum* in the deep nature of the divinities, who are by turns, or simultaneously, benevolent and terrible, creative and destructive, solar and ophidian (that is, manifest and virtual), etc. One recognizes the effort of the Indian spirit to discover a single principle which will explain the world, to reach a standpoint from which contraries are resolved and contradictions abolished (Eliade, *The Two and the One*, pp. 93–94).

On this problem see also Conrado Pensa, "Considerazioni sul tema della bipolarità nelle religioni indiane," *Gururājamañjarikā: Studi in onore di Giuseppe Tucci* (Naples, 1974), pp. 379–409.

69. The hymns addressed to Agni have been translated, with commentaries, by L. Renou, *Études védiques et pāniniennes*, vols. 12–14 (Paris, 1964–65). On Agni, the respective chapters in the works by Bergaigne, Oldenberg, Hillebrandt, A. B. Keith, Macdonell (*Vedic Mythology*), and Gonda should be consulted.

On Indo-European conceptions of the sacrality of the domestic fire, see Schrader-Nehring, *Reallexicon*, vol. 1, pp. 495 ff.; vol. 2, pp. 239 ff., 475 ff.

On the cult of the sacred fire among the Indo-Iranians, see Stig Wikander, *Feuerpriester in Kleinasien und Iran* (Lund, 1946).

On Agni as "erotic fire," especially in the post-Vedic period, see Wendy Doniger O'Flaherty, *Asceticism and Eroticism in the Mythology of Śiva* (Oxford, 1973), pp. 90–110.

70. The hymns devoted to Soma have been translated, with commentaries, by L. Renou, *Etudes védiques et pāniniennes*, vols. 8 and 9 (Paris, 1961). See also S. S. Bhawe, *The Soma-Hymns of the Ṛgveda*, 2 vols. (Baroda, 1957–60). All the information concerning the plant *soma*, from the Rig Veda to recent studies, is to be found in Hillebrandt, *Vedische Mythologie*, 2d ed., vol. 1, pp. 193–498; see also Wendy Doniger O'Flaherty, "The Post-Vedic History of the Soma Plant," in R. Gordon Wasson, *Soma: Divine Mushroom of Immortality* (New York, 1968), pp. 95–147. In this work R. G. Wasson attempts to prove that the original *soma* plant was the mushroom *Amanita muscaria*; see the review by F. B. J. Kuiper, in *IIJ* 12 (1970): 279–85, and Wasson's reply, ibid., pp. 286–98. See also the critique by John Brough, "Soma and Amanita muscaria," *BSOAS* 34 (1971): 331–62, and the article by Paul Demiéville in *T'oung-Pao* 56 (1970): 298–302, on the data concerning the dissemination of *soma* in pre-Buddhist China.

On the god Soma, see the relevant chapters in the works by Bergaigne, Oldenberg, A. B. Keith, and Gonda. See also N. J. Shende, "Soma in the Brāhmanas of the Rgveda," *JAS* (Bombay) 38 (1963): 122 ff.; J. Gonda, "Soma, amṛta and the Moon," in *Change and Continuity in Indian Religion* (The Hague, 1965), pp. 38–70.

On the theft of *soma*, see David M. Knipe, "The Heroic Theft: Myths from Ṛg Veda IV and the Ancient Near East," *HR* 6 (1967): 328–60, with a rich bibliography. See also Ulrich Schneider, *Der Somaraub des Manu: Mythus und Ritual* (Wiesbaden, 1971).

On the common character of the Indo-Iranian liturgy of *soma/haoma*, see the study by V. Henri, "Esquisse d'une liturgie indo-iranienne," in Caland, *Agniṣṭoma* (1907), pp. 469 ff.; J. Duchesne-Guillemin, *La religion de l'Iran ancien* (1962), pp. 95 ff. (Eng. trans., *Religion of Ancient Iran* [Bombay, 1973], pp. 73 ff.); Duchesne-Guillemin, *Symbols and Values in Zoroastrianism* (New York, 1966), pp. 84 ff.

A. E. Jensen has compared the sacrificial murder of Soma by the other gods to the immolation of a divinity of the *Dema* type by his companions, a preeminently creative sacrifice; see his *Myth and Cult among Primitive Peoples* (Eng. trans., Chicago, 1963), pp. 175 ff.

71. On Uṣas, see L. Renou, *Etudes védiques et pāniniennes*, vol. 3: *Les hymnes à l'Aurore du Rgveda* (Paris, 1957); A. K. Coomaraswamy, *The Darker Side of Dawn*, Smithsonian Miscellaneous Collections, vol. 94, no. 1 (Washington, D.C., 1935), pp. 4 ff.; G. Montesi, "Il valore cosmico dell'Aurora nel pensiero mitologico del Rig-Veda," *SMSR* 24–25 (1955): 111–32.

On Vāyu, see Stig Wikander, *Vayu* (Uppsala and Leipzig, 1941).

On Sūrya and the Aśvins, see D. P. Pandey, *Sūrya* (thesis, Leiden, 1939); Gonda, *Rel. de l'Inde*, vol. 1, pp. 116 ff.

On Rudra, see E. Arbman, *Rudra* (Uppsala, 1922); J. W. Hauer, *Glaubensgeschichte der Indo-Germanen*, vol. 1, pp. 174–298; W. Wust, *Rudra* (Munich, 1955); Gonda, *Rel. de l'Inde*, vol. 1, pp. 106–12; Gonda, *Viṣṇuism and Śivaism: A Comparison* (London, 1920), pp. 1–17.

On Viṣṇu in the Vedic period, see J. Gonda, *Aspects of Early Viṣṇuism* (Utrecht, 1954); Gonda, *Rel. de l'Inde*, vol. 1, pp. 112 ff.; F. B. J. Kuiper, "The Three Strides of Viṣṇu," *Indological Studies in Honor of W. Norman Brown* (New Haven, 1962), pp. 137–51. In his article "Viṣṇu et les Maruts à travers la réforme zoroastrienne," *JA* 241 (1953): 1–25, Dumézil brings out the correspondences between Viṣṇu and the Iranian deity Rašnu, on the one hand, and between the Maruts and the Fravashis, on the other. On Aryaman, see Dumézil, *Le troisième souverain* (Paris, 1949).

72. A clear and concise description of the Vedic rituals is available in L. Renou and J. Filliozat, *L'Inde classique* (1949), vol. 1, pp. 345–72. More elaborate treatments will be found in A. Bergaigne, *La religion*, vol. 1, pp. 121 ff.; A. B. Keith, *Religion and Philosophy of the Veda* (1925), vol. 1, pp. 252–379; J. Gonda, *Les religions de l'Inde* (1962), vol. 1, pp. 129–209. The book by Albert Hillebrandt, *Ritualliteratur* (Strasbourg, 1897) still remains indispensable. See also K. R. Potdar, *Sacrifice in the Rig-Veda* (Bombay, 1953), and especially R. N. Dandekar, ed., *Śrautokoṣa: Encyclopedia of Vedic Sacrificial Ritual* (Poona, 1962). See also Ganesh Umakant Thite, *Sacrifice in the Brāhmaṇa Texts* (Poona, 1975); Madeleine

Biardeau and Charles Malamoud, *Le sacrifice dans l'Inde ancienne* (Paris, 1976). On the *soma* sacrifice, see W. Caland and V. Henry, *L'Agnistoma*, 2 vols. (Paris, 1906–7). On the sacrifice of animals, see E. Mayrhofer and Passler, "Haustieropfer bei den Indo-iraniern und den anderen indo-germanischen Völkern," *Ar Or* 21 (1953): 182–205.

On the *pravargya*, see J. A. B. van Buitenen, *Pravargya, an Ancient Indian Iconic Ritual* (Poona, 1968).

On the *upanayana* ceremony in modern Hinduism, see J. Gonda, *Change and Continuity*, pp. 264 ff., 459 ff.

By examining a certain number of analogies between the *agnicayana* ritual and the indigenous culture characterized by black-and-red ceramics (construction of an altar with 10,800 bricks, although the Āryans of the Vedic period did not use bricks; cooking technique; references to "Orientals" assimilated to the Asuras; etc.), H. S. Converse concludes that this species of sacrifice was non-Āryan in origin; see his "The *agnicayana* Rite: Indigenous Origin?" *HR* 14 (1974): 81–95.

The domestic rites (*grhya*) already present the structure of the Hinduistic cult; their "Vedic" character is comparatively superficial (L. Renou, *Religions of Ancient India*, p. 39).

On *dākṣiṇās*, sacrificial gifts offered to priests, see J. C. Heesterman, "Reflections on the Significance of the *dākṣiṇā*," *IIJ* 3 (1959): 241–58. Heesterman remarks (p. 257) that "the *dākṣiṇā* is the material manifestation of the cyclical course of the universe as it is represented in the ritual." See also J. Gonda, "Gifts and Giving in the Ṛgveda," *Vishvesh Varanand Indological Journal* 2 (1964): 21–30, and, for the Iranian homologue, H. Lommel, "Zarathustras Priesterlohn," in *Festschrift für Willibald Kirfel* (Bonn, 1955), pp. 187–96.

73. On the *aśvamedha*, see P. E. Dumont, *L'Aśvamedha: Description du sacrifice solennel du cheval dans le culte védique* (Paris, 1927); J. Gonda, *Les rel. de l'Inde*, vol. 1, pp. 203 ff.; Gonda, *Ancient Indian Kingship from the Religious Point of View* (Leiden, 1966; first published in *Numen* 3–4 [1956–57]: 110 ff.); C. D. d'Onofrio, "Le 'nozze sacre' della regina col cavallo," *SMSR* 24–25 (1953–54): 133–62, esp. 153 ff.

On the horse sacrifice among the Indo-Europeans, see W. Koppers, "Pferdeopfer und Pferdekult der Indo-Germanen," *Wiener Beiträge zur Kulturgeschichte und Linguistik* 4 (1936): 279–409; Jaan Puhvel, "Aspects of Equine Functionality," in Puhvel, ed., *Myth and Law among the Indo-Europeans* (Berkeley, 1970), pp. 159–72.

On *puruṣamedha*, see W. Kirfel, *Der Aśvamedha und der Puruṣamedha, Festschrift W. Schumbring* (Hamburg, 1951), pp. 39–50; James L. Sauvé, "The Divine Victim: Aspects of Human Sacrifice in Viking Scandinavia and Vedic India," in J. Puhvel, ed., *Myth and Law among the Indo-Europeans*, pp. 173–91.

74. On the initiatory symbolism of the *dīkṣā*, see Eliade, *Birth and Rebirth*, pp. 53 ff.

For a description of the ceremony, see A. Hillebrandt, *Ritualliteratur*, pp. 157 ff.; A. B. Keith, *The Religion and Philosophy of the Veda and Upanishads*, vol. 1, pp. 300 ff. J. Gonda provides an excellent analysis of the *dīkṣā*, from the Vedic period on into modern Hinduism, in his book *Change and Continuity in Indian Religion* (The Hague, 1965), pp. 315–462.

On the *rājasūya*, see A. Hillebrandt, *Ritualliteratur*, pp. 143 ff.; A. B. Keith, *Rel. and Phil.*, vol. 1, pp. 340 ff.; P. V. Kane, *History of Dharma-śāstra* (Poona, 1941), vol. 2, pp. 1214 ff.; J. Gonda, *Ancient Indian Kingship from the Religious Point of View*, pp. 79 ff.; and, especially, J. C. Heesterman, *The Ancient Indian Royal Consecration* (The Hague, 1957). In proto-historic times the *rājasūya* was probably annual and was celebrated to regenerate the cosmos. Its structure resembles that of the Indian seasonal festivities, *utsava*. It is also probable that, in ancient times, the people played a more important part in it.

The study by Ananda Coomaraswamy, "Atmayajña: Self-Sacrifice," *HJAS* 6 (1942): 358–98, deserves to be consulted for the author's courageous and profound exegesis.

75. In India the myth of the cosmogonic dive was preserved in a comparatively archaic form, since it is a Great God who descends to the bottom of the primordial waters and brings up the earth. In the *Brāhmaṇas*, it is Prajāpati who dives, transformed into a boar. In the *Rāmayana*, the role is transferred to Brahmā; in the *Viṣṇu-Purāṇa*, the boar is Brahmā-Viṣṇu, and in the *Bhāgavata Purāṇa* it is an *avatāra* of Viṣṇu (see the references in Eliade, *Zalmoxis*, pp. 115–17). But it is only from the period of the epic and the Purāṇas that this cosmogonic myth becomes popular. It is probable, furthermore, that it contains pre-Āryan elements, either Munda or proto-Munda; see *Zalmoxis*, pp. 117 ff.

From the abundant literature on the Indian cosmogonies, we mention some recent publications: Norman W. Brown, "The Creation Myth of the Rig Veda," *JAOS* 62 (1942): 85–98; Stella Kramrisch, "The Triple Structure of Creation in the Rig Veda," *HR* 2 (1962–63): 140–75, 256–91; F. B. J. Kuiper, "Cosmogony and Conception: A Query," *HR* 10 (1970): 91–138; Hans Penner, "Cosmogony as Myth in the Vishnu Purāna," *HR* 5 (1966): 283–99. See also the selection of Sanskrit texts, translated, with commentaries, by Anne Marie Esnoul, in *La naissance du monde* (Paris, 1959), pp. 331–65.

On the term *takṣ-*, "carpenter," on the plane of cosmogonic thought, see L. Renou, *Études sur le vocabulaire du Ṛgveda: Première série* (Pondicherry, 1958), pp. 23 ff.

On the *Puruṣasūkta*, see W. Norman Brown, "The Sources and Nature of *puruṣa* in the *Puruṣasūkta*," *JAOS* 51 (1931): 108–18; Ananda K. Coomaraswamy, "Rgveda 10, 90, 1: *aty atiṣṭhad daśāṅgulam*," *JAOS* 66 (1946): 145–61; A. W. Macdonald, "A propos de Prajāpati," *JA* 240 (1953): 323–38; Paul Mus, "Où finit Puruṣa?" *Mélanges d'Indianisme à la mémoire de Louis Renou* (Paris, 1968), pp. 539–63.

On *puruṣasūkta* as paradigmatic model, see J. Gonda, *Viṣṇuism and Śivaism* (London, 1970), p. 27.

On the Indo-European parallels, see Güntert, *Der arische Weltkönig und Heiland* (Halle, 1923), pp. 315–43; F. R. Schröder, "Germanische Schöpfungsmythen," *Germanisch-Romanisch Monatsschrift* 19 (1931): 1–26, 81–99; Bruce Lincoln, "The Indo-European Myth of Creation," *HR* 15 (1975): 121–45.

On the birth of the Vedic gods and the conquest of immortality, see A. B. Keith, *Religion and Philosophy*, pp. 82 ff. For a comparative study, see G. Dumézil, *Le Festin d'immortalité* (Paris, 1924).

On the origin of man and the mythical Ancestor, see Arthur Christensen, *Les types du premier homme et du premier roi dans l'histoire légendaire des Iraniens*, 2 vols. (1917, 1934); G. Dumézil, *Mythe et Epopée* (1971), vol. 2, pp. 234 ff.; O. Höfler, "Abstammungstraditionen," *Reallexicon der germanischen Altertumskunde*, vol. 1, pp. 18–29.

In India, the loss of immortality *in corpore*, for the benefit of a spiritual "nondeath," also had consequences in the relations between gods and men; according to certain traditions, in the beginning the gods descended and met with men in their corporeal forms (see *Taittirīya Saṃhitā* 3. 5. 2; *Kāthaka Saṃ.* 37. 17; *Pañcaviṃśa Br.* 15. 5. 24). This represents a rather widespread archaic conception.

76. According to another tradition, Prajāpati was himself the product of *tapas*: in the beginning, non-Being (*asat*) became "thought" (*manas*); growing hot (*atāpyata*), thought gave birth to smoke, light, fire, and finally to Prajāpati (*Taitt. Br.* 2. 2. 9. 1–10). In the *Śatapatha Br.* 11. 1. 6. 1 non-Being is represented by the primordial waters.

In Rig Veda 10. 61. 7, mention is made of the incest between the Sky Father and his daughter, the Dawn. In the *Brāhmaṇas*, it is Prajāpati who desires his daughter (*Śat. Br.* 1. 7. 4). He approached her in the form of a stag (*Aitt. Br.* 3. 33. 34); he even attempted to possess her, but the gods prevented him, and Prajāpati's semen, spilled on the ground, produced a lake (*Ait. Br.* 13. 1–10). On the importance of this mythical theme, see

Wendy D. O'Flaherty, "Asceticism and Sexuality in the Mythology of Śiva, Part II," *HR* 9 (1969): 9 ff.

The theme of the "exhaustion" and "disjointing" of Prajāpati after the creation can be compared with legends of southeastern European folklore that bring out the "weariness" of the god after his cosmogonic labor; see Eliade, *Zalmoxis*, pp. 88 ff.

On Prajāpati, see the texts cited and commented upon by Sukumari Bhattacharji, *The Indian Theogony* (Cambridge, 1970), pp. 322 ff., and Gonda's observations in *Les religions de l'Inde*, vol. 1, pp. 227 ff. For a comparative analysis of the myth, see A. W. Macdonald, "A propos de Prajāpati," *JA* 240 (1952): 323–38.

On sacrifice in the period of the *Brāhmaṇas*, the book by Sylvain Lévi, *La doctrine du sacrifice dans les Brāhmanas* (1898) remains indispensable. See also A. K. Coomaraswamy, *Hinduism and Buddhism* (New York, 1943), pp. 19 ff.

77. On Brahman, see L. Renou and L. Silburn, "Sur la notion du bráhman," *JA* 237 (1949): 7–46, and the bibliography listed in Eliade, *Yoga*, p. 388. Additional items for the bibliography are L. Renou, "Le passage des Brāhmana aux Upaniṣad," *JAOS* 73 (1953): 138–44; Lilian Silburn, *Instant et cause* (Paris, 1955), pp. 50 ff.; J. Gonda, *Notes on Brahman* (Ultrecht, 1950); Gonda, *Les religions de l'Inde*, vol. 1, pp. 45 ff., 237 ff.; and G. Tucci, *Storia della filosofia indiana* (Bari, 1957), pp. 279 ff.

On the notion of the Brahman in the history of Indian thought, the *History* volumes by Surendranath Dasgupta, S. Radhakrishnan, E. Frauenwalder, et al., may be consulted, as well as Karl H. Potter, *Bibliography of Indian Philosophies* (Delhi, Patna, and Varanasi, 1970).

On the *Araṇyakas*, see A. B. Keith, *Religion and Philosophy*, pp. 490 ff.; J. N. Farquhar, *An Outline of the Religious Literature of India* (Oxford, 1920), pp. 30 ff.; J. van Buitenen, "Vedic and Upanishadic Bases of Indian Civilization," in J. W. Elder, ed., *Chapters in Indian Civilization* (Dubuque, Iowa, 1970), vol. 1, pp. 6 ff.

78. On *tapas*, see Eliade, *Yoga*, pp. 106–11 and the bibliography listed on p. 385. To this add Chauncey Y. Blair, *Heat in the Rig Veda and Atharva Veda* (New Haven, 1961); D. J. Hoens, *Śānti: A Contribution to Ancient Indian Religious Terminology* (The Hague, 1951); Eliade, *Shamanism*, p. 412; J. Gonda, *Les Religions de l'Inde*, vol. 1, pp. 223 ff., 309 ff., 338 ff. (with bibliography); W. D. O'Flaherty, *Asceticism and Eroticism in the Mythology of Śiva* (London, 1973), pp. 40 ff.

79. On the ascetic (*muni*) wih long hair (*keśin*), see Eliade, *Yoga*, pp. 102

ff.; Gonda, *Religions*, vol. 1, pp. 223 ff.; W. Wust, *múni, PHMA: Mitteilungen zur indo-germanische, vornehmlich indo-iranische Wortkunde*, no. 7 (Munich, 1961): 24–65.

On the Vrātyas, see J. W. Hauer, *Der Vrātya: Untersuchungen über die nichtbrahmanische Religion altindien* (Stuttgart, 1927); Eliade, *Yoga*, pp. 103 ff.; W. Wust, *vratá-, PHMA*, pp. 66–73. Hauer believed that the Vrātyas represented a brotherhood, with secret initiation rites, belonging to the advance guard of the Āryans. According to J. C. Heesterman, the Vrātyas practiced a type of sacrifice that anticipated the *śrauta* rituals; see his "Vrātya and Sacrifice," *IIJ* 6 (1962–63): 1–37.

On ascetics in ancient and medieval India, see David N. Lorenzen, *The Kāpālikas and Kālāmukhas* (Berkeley and Los Angeles, 1972), pp. 187 ff.

80. A certain number of Upanishads have been translated into English. S. Radhakrishnan has, in *The Principal Upanishads* (New York, 1953), edited and translated, with commentaries, thirteen Upanishads, preceded by a long introduction of 145 pages. See also Robert Hume, trans., *The Thirteen Principal Upanishads* (London, 1931); Swami Nikhilānanda, *The Upanishads*, 4 vols. (New York, 1949–59); and J. A. B. Van Buitenen, *The Maitrāyaṇiya Upaniṣad* (The Hague, 1962). See, for French translations, the list in Jean Varenne, *Le Véda*, vol. 1, pp. 37–38. We mention, in particular, the translations by Emile Senart (*Bṛhadāraṇyaka*, 1930; *Chāndogya*, 1934), by Louis Renou (*Kāṭha, Kena, Īśa, Kauṣītaki*), by J. Maury (*Muṇḍaka*), E. Lesimple (*Māṇḍūkya, Taittirīya*), L. Silburn (*Aitareya, Śvetāśvatara*), J. Bousquet (*Praśna*), A. M. Esnoul (*Maitri*), B. Tubini (*Brahmabindu, Kaivalya*, etc.), J. Varenne (*Ganapati, Mahānārāyana, Prāṇāgnihotra*). There is a good selection in J. Varenne, *Le Véda*, vol. 2, pp. 614–704. The same author has published *Les Upanishads du Yoga*, translated from the Sanskrit with annotations (Paris, 1971).

The critical bibliography is given in Eliade, *Yoga*, pp. 388–89, and J. Gonda, *Les religions de l'Inde*, vol. 1, pp. 232, 239. Particularly useful are R. D. Ranade, *A Constructive Survey of Upanishadic Philosophy* (Poona, 1926); H. Oldenberg, *Die Lehre der Upanishaden und die Anfänge des Buddhismus* (Göttingen, 1915); S. N. Dasgupta, *Indian Idealism* (Cambridge, 1933), pp. 20 ff.; Walter Ruben, *Die Philosophen der Upanishaden* (Bern, 1947); and J. Gonda, *Les religions de l'Inde*, vol. 1, pp. 239 ff.

The Upanishads are considered to be annexes to the four Vedas; hence they form part of the "revelation" (*śruti*). To be sure, in the Rig Veda "knowledge" already possessed a magico-religious value. In the *Brāhmaṇas* the "science" of sacrifice insured immortality: the world of the gods "belongs only to those who know" (*Śat. Br.* 10. 5. 4. 16). But in the Upanishads, the "science" of sacrifice is replaced by the *knowledge of*

Brahman. For "sacrifices are like boats floating in the open sea, which can sink at any moment" (*Muṇḍaka Up.* 1. 2. 7).

81. The Vedic and Brahmanic conceptions concerning postexistence in the beyond are complex and confused. A famous hymn to Soma (RV 9. 113) reveals the desire of the soul to be placed "there where perpetual light shines, in the same world where the sun had its place. . . . There where Yama is . . . , where is the enclosure of the sky . . . , where the eternally young waters are, make me an immortal in that place, O Soma" (after the translation by Jean Varenne). The journey to the sky, the bridge that connects earth and sky, the two dogs that guard the bridge, the questioning of the soul are all motifs that are found in both ancient India and Iran; they probably go back to the period of Indo-Iranian unity (see § 111). Existence underground, where—according to another tradition that ended by becoming predominant—Yama reigns, is reserved for sinners of all kinds. "These worlds, whose name is 'The Sunless,' covered as they are with all kinds of blind darkness; to them, after their death, go those who have killed their soul" (*Īśa Up.* 1. 3). From the *Śatapatha Brāhmaṇa* on, the texts describe a certain number of tortures. In the course of time the descriptions of the twenty-one hells become increasingly dramatic. Sinners are eaten by wild beasts and snakes, they are elaborately roasted, cut to pieces with saws, tormented by thirst and hunger, boiled in oil or pounded in mortars, ground in stone or iron pots, etc. But after undergoing such sufferings, the victims are not at the end of their torments: they are still to experience the agonies that accompany their migration into various animal bodies.

The hells have their counterpart in the celestial paradises that correspond to them. The epics—the *Mahābhārata* and the *Rāmayana*—and the *Purāṇas* describe especially the five heavens of the five great gods. In ascending order, these are the Heaven of Indra, peopled by women dancers and musicians; the Heaven of Śiva, where the god and his family reign; the Heaven of Viṣṇu, made entirely of gold and dotted with pools covered with lotus flowers; the Heaven of Kṛṣṇa, with his dancing girls and his devotees; and finally the Heaven of Brahmā, where the souls enjoy the celestial nymphs. The palaces of gold and precious stones, the paradisal gardens, the musical instruments that accompany the songs and dances of ravishingly beautiful girls are tirelessly described. Some of these Hindu paradisal themes will be taken up again by Buddhist authors.

In the *Brāhmaṇas* the idea of a "new death" (*punarmṛtyu*) takes shape, that is, the "second death," which is final and awaits the souls of those who have not performed certain sacrifices. However, the notion of *karman* ends by assimilating this second death to the return to earth in the form of a new incarnation. According to the Upanishads, the souls of the dead depart by the "road of the Manes" (*pitryāna*), or the lunar road. Arrived on the moon, the souls undergo an interrogation of the initiatory type; those that are unable to answer fall back to earth, to be reborn there. "Those who know" make their way to the gods by the "road of the gods" (*devayāna*), also called the solar road. The *Kauṣītaki Up.* (1. 2–7) gives the following details: from the world of the gods the souls proceed to the world of the Brahman, where they are confronted with various initiatory ordeals. Brahman questions the newcomer: "Who art thou?" and the newcomer must answer: "What thou art, I am." Brahman says to him: "Then who am I?" "Truth," the soul must answer (1. 6). In the end Brahman says: "What has been my domain is henceforth thine" (1. 7). In short, the first road leads to a new reincarnation, while the second gives access to the world of the gods. But to reach the transcendental world of Brahman, the soul must undergo still more initiatory ordeals. In other words, after death, there are three possibilities: (1) the soul's return to earth, in a new incarnation; (2) a paradisal sojourn among the gods; (3) identification of the soul with Brahman. According to the authors of the Upanishads, the celestial paradise is provisional and, after a certain time, souls are obliged to return to earth and be reincarnated. Hence the only real possibility of deliverance is postmortem identification with Brahman, made possible by gnosis and contemplation.

On the "inner light," see Eliade, *The Two and the One*, pp. 26 ff.; Eliade, "Spirit, Light and Seed," *HR* 11 (1971): 1–30, esp. pp. 3–16 (now in *Occultism, Witchcraft, and Cultural Fashions* [Chicago, 1976]); J. Gonda, *The Vision of the Vedic Poets* (1963), pp. 268 ff.

82. On the two modalities of Brahman, cf. H. de Glasenapp, *La philosophie indienne*, French trans. (Paris, 1951), pp. 131 ff.

The paradox of the "corporeal" ("mortal") and "incorporeal" ("immortal") Brahman carries on the speculations concerning the ambivalence of certain Vedic gods and the coincidence of contraries that, for Indian thought, defines divinity; see, above, the supplementary notes to § 68.

On cosmic "play," see Ananda K. Coomaraswamy, "Līlā," *JAOS* (1941): 98–101.

83. The historical study and hermeneutic analysis of Greek religion make up one of the most fascinating chapters in the history of European culture. Since it is impossible to summarize the different interpretations in a few lines—from those of K. O. Müller or F. G. Welcker, in the mid-nineteenth century, to the most recent contributions by Brelich, Burkert, or Vernant and Detienne—we will give only the essentials of the bibliography. First to be mentioned are some synthetic works: Gilbert Murray, *The Five Stages of Greek Religion* (1925); M. P. Nilsson, *A History of Greek Religion* (1925; 2d ed., 1949); L. Gernet and A. Boulanger, *Le génie grec dans la religion* (1932); O. Kern, *Die religion der Griechen*, 3 vols. (1926–38); W. K. C. Guthrie, *The Greeks and Their Gods* (1950); R. Pettazzoni, *La religion dans la Grèce antique*, French trans. (Paris, 1953). Still to be read with profit are J. E. Harrison, *Prolegomena to the Study of Greek Religion* (Cambridge, 1903; 2d ed., 1922); H. J. Rose, *A Handbook of Greek Mythology* (London, 1928; 4th ed., 1950). Walter Otto has published an admirable, and very personal, interpretation of Greek religion and mythology under the title *Die Götter Griechenlands* (Frankfurt, 1928). The book by U. von Wilamowitz-Moellendorf, *Der Glaube der Hellenen*, 2 vols. (Berlin, 1931–32), represents the testament of the great German historian and philologist. Finally, the enormous work by M. P. Nilsson, *Geschichte der griechischen Religion*, 2 vols. (Munich, 1940; 3d ed., 1947, 1950), is a veritable summa, indispensable for the wealth of its documentation. The five volumes of L. R. Farnell, *The Cults of the Greek States* (Oxford, 1896–1909), are still useful for the materials collected and analyzed. The book by E. R. Dodds, *The Greeks and the Irrational* (Berkeley, 1951), enjoys an astonishing popularity; its success reflects certain tendencies of the contemporary *Zeitgeist*. See now the recent synthesis by Walter Burkert, *Griechische Religion der archaischen und klassischen Epochen* (Stuttgart, 1977).

On Zeus, A. B. Cook has published an extensive work, *Zeus*, 3 vols. (Cambridge, 1914–40); actually, it is rather a series of monographs on various aspects of the god and, in general, of Greek religion. There is no need to indicate the chapters devoted to Zeus in various general works. The essentials have been presented by Guthrie, *The Greeks and Their Gods*, pp. 49–81. See also M. P. Nilsson, "Vater Zeus," *ARW* 35 (1938): 156–71 (republished in *Opuscula Selecta* 2 [Lund, 1952]: 710–31), and especially Hugh Lloyd-Jones, *The Justice of Zeus* (Berkeley, 1971).

For the *Theogony*, we use the edition by M. L. West, *Hesiod's Theogony, edited with Prolegomena and Commentary* (Oxford, 1966). The parallels with the ancient Near East have been frequently discussed since 1940; see Peter Walcott, *Hesiod and the Near East* (Cardiff, 1966).

It was Gaea who advised Rhea to give birth in Crete. The two goddesses are the hypostases of Mother Earth; indeed, the etymology of Rhea is "the broad," i.e., the Earth.

When he was forced by Zeus to disgorge his brothers and sisters, Kronos first vomited up the stone; it was set up by Zeus at Delphi, at the foot of Parnassus (Pausanias 10. 24. 6); cf. West, *Hesiod's Theogony*, p. 303 (commentary on lines 498–500).

84. On Metis, his first wife, and the consequences of her being swallowed by Zeus, see J. P. Vernant, "Métis et les mythes de souveraineté," *RHR* 3 (1971): 29–76.

On Zeus Cretagenes, his infancy in Crete, and the relations with the Cretan male god, see Charles Picard, *Les religions préhélléniques* (Paris, 1948), pp. 115 ff.; H. Jeanmaire, *Couroï et Courètes* (Lille, 1939), pp. 427 ff.; Martin P. Nilsson, *The Minoan-Mycenaean Religion and Its Survival in Greek Religion*, 2d ed. (Lund, 1950), pp. 55 ff. West, *Hesiod's Theogony*, pp. 297 ff., has shown the antiquity of the tradition of the infancy in Crete (*Theog.* 477).

On the "golden cord" with which Zeus could draw all things to him, see Pierre Lévêque, *Aurea Catena Homeri* (Paris, 1959), and Eliade, *The Two and the One*, pp. 179 ff.

We add some particulars in regard to the primordial divinities who survived the triumph of the Olympians. Night gave birth, by herself, to a number of semidivine beings, rather indistinct and more nearly resembling personified abstractions: Death, Sleep, Sarcasm, Woe, Old Age, etc. (Hesiod, *Theog.* 211 ff.). But the Orphic texts present her as Mother and universal queen (see Kern, *Orph. fragm.*, nos. 24, 28, 28a, 65, etc.).

On the mythico-religious structure of Nyx and the meaning of her progeny, see Dario Sabbatucci, *Saggio sul misticismo greco* (Rome, 1965), pp. 95 ff.

Pontus (the Barren Sea) had, from his union with Gaea, his mother, a considerable progeny; see L. Séchan and P. Lévêque, *Les grandes divinitiés de la Grèce* (Paris, 1966), p. 49 (and the bibliographical notes, p. 64).

Because she had joined in the war against the Titans, Zeus proclaimed Styx "the great oath of the gods" (*Theog.* 399 ff.). See also Séchan and Lévêque, *Les grandes divinités de la Grèce*, p. 64, n. 68.

As for Hecate, she is preeminently a primordial goddess. Zeus did not touch the rights and privileges that she possessed as a Titaness (*Theog.* 423 ff.). Hecate will later become a goddess specializing in sorcery; see Diodorus, *Bibl.* 4. 45.

Oceanus, the first Titan, "whose course, never sleeping, rolls around the immense earth" (Aeschylus, *Prometheus* 138 ff.), married his sister Tethys. But there are certain traces of an archaic cosmogony, unknown to Hesiod and Homer, according to which Oceanus and Tethys incarnated the male and female principles in the primordial waters; in short, they represent the original couple, from which the gods and all reality descend; see Séchan and Lévêque, pp. 50, 51, 65, Sabbatucci, pp. 110–16, and especially the important study by J. P. Vernant, "Thétis et le poème cosmogonique d'Alcman," *Hommage à Marie Delcourt, Latomus* 114 (1970): 38–69, with a rich bibliography (see, e.g., p. 38, n. 2, 39, n. 8).

85. The literary sources for Kronos are brought together by Farnell, *Cults,* vol. 5, chap. 3. Certain scholars (Kern, Pohlenz) have seen in Kronos and the Titans divinities of the autochthonous population, conquered by the Āryan-speaking invaders. In other words, the conflict between the Olympians and the Titans would reflect certain historical events. But the Oriental parallels seem to invalidate this hypothesis.

On the Hesiodic myth of the five ages, see the sources edited, with commentaries, by Arthur O. Lovejoy and George Boas, *Primitivism and Related Ideas in Antiquity* (Baltimore, 1935), pp. 25 ff. The parallel Iranian versions (especially the *Bundahišn*) are translated and discussed by N. Söderblom, *ERE,* vol. 1, pp. 205–19. Ugo Bianchi compares the golden race in Elysium with the Iranian tradition concerning the first king, Yima, who became sovereign of Vara, a country underground but miraculously illuminated; see his "Razza aurea, mito delle cinque razze ed Elisio," *SMSR* 34 (1963): 143–210, esp. 187–89. Rejecting the general opinion of scholars (for example, that advanced by H. C. Baldry, "Who Invented the Golden Age?" *Classical Quarterly* n.s. 2 [1952]: 83–92), J. Gwyn Griffiths, in "Archaeology and Hesiod's Five Ages," *Journal of the History of Ideas* 17 (1956): 109–19, holds that the myth refers to the discovery and progressive use of metals; cf. Baldry's reply, *Journal of the History of Ideas* 17 (1956): 553–54. Among the best discussions of this problem are J. Kerschensteiner, *Platon und der Orient* (Stuttgart, 1945), pp. 161 ff. ("Der Metalmythos"); J. P. Vernant, "Le mythe hésiodique des races: Essai d'analyse structurale," *RHR* (1960): 21–54 (reprinted in the volume *Mythe et pensée chez les Grecs* [Paris, 1965], pp. 13–41); Vernant, "Le mythe hésiodique des races: Sur un essai de mise au point," *Revue de Philologie* (1966): 247–76 (republished in *Mythe et pensée,* pp. 42–79).

On Prometheus, see E. Vandvick, *The Prometheus of Hesiod and Aeschylus* (Oslo, 1943); Louis Séchan, *Le mythe de Prométhée* (Paris, 1951); Karl Kerényi, *Prometheus: Archetypal Image of Human Existence* (New York, 1963) (the German edition was published in 1946).

86. On Greek sacrifices see R. K. Yerkes, *Sacrifice in Greek and Roman Religions and Early Judaism* (New York, 1952), esp. pp. 88 ff., and, above all, Karl Meuli, "Griechische Opferbräuche," *Phyllobolia: Festschrift Peter von der Mühll* (Basel, 1946), pp. 185–288, and Walter Burkert, *Homo Necans* (Berlin, 1972), pp. 8–97 and passim (p. 9, n. 2, for bibliography). As Meuli writes, "The Olympian sacrifice is simply a ritual slaughter"

(p. 223). A receptacle filled with water and a basket containing barley are brought. The participants wash their hands and also sprinkle the victim. Then they take out the barley, as if they were preparing a vegetarian meal —but at the bottom of the basket the knife is found. Certain ritual acts follow: a moment of silence, a prayer, the sacrificing priest cutting a few hairs from the victim's forehead and throwing them on the fire; when he strikes, all the women cry out together. The blood is collected in a vessel and poured on the altar. Then the femurs are burned with fat and small pieces of meat. The entrails are broiled on the altar and eaten on the spot (Meuli, pp. 265 ff.; cf. Burkert, *Homo Necans*, pp. 10 ff.).

The festival of the Bouphonia (literally, the "murder of the ox"), celebrated at Athens, enables us to recover an interpretation of the blood sacrifice which contains archaic elements. "Taking advantage of his master's inattention, a plow ox approaches the altar of Zeus Polieus and begins eating the offerings laid on the altar, the cereals and cakes reserved for the god of the city. Seeing this sacrilege, the infuriated priest of Zeus seizes an ax, strikes the beast, and kills it. Terrified by the act he has committed, the 'murderer of the ox' flees posthaste, leaving the weapon of the crime on the spot. The second section of the ritual is played out in two parts. In the first, the case is judged at the Prytaneum before the proper tribunal for crimes of blood: the guilt of the ax is established, and it is expelled from Attic territory. In the second, the whole city ritually consumes the flesh of the victim, while the hide of the ox, stuffed with straw, is set up and harnessed to a plow in a simulacrum of work" (Marcel Detienne, *Les Jardins d'Adonis* [Paris, 1972], p. 106 [Eng. trans., *The Gardens of Adonis* (New York, 1976)]; for bibliography, see p. 105, n. 2; to this add Burkert, *Homo Necans*, pp. 154–61, and the article by U. Pestalozza, "Le origini della Buphonia ateniensi" [1956], now reprinted in *Nuovi saggi di religione mediterranea* [Florence, 1964], pp. 203–23).

The "comedy of innocence" (*Unschuldskomödie;* Meuli, pp. 224 ff.) is found again in the hunting rites of Siberian peoples (see inter alia, Eveline Lot-Falck, *Les rites de chasse* [Paris, 1953], pp. 170 ff.). M. Detienne cogently interprets the sacrilegious character of the blood sacrifice, as it was considered by the Greeks: "To offer the gods an animal victim is to shed blood, is to commit an actual murder. Animal sacrifice appears to the city to be a pollution; but it is an inevitable and necessary pollution, for killing the ox is an essential act in establishing the city's relations with the divine powers" (*Les Jardins d'Adonis*, pp. 106–7).

Like so many other peoples of protohistory, the Greeks also practiced human sacrifice, though for various reasons. The replacement of the man by the animal (e.g., Iphigenia; Isaac) has its parallel in sacrifices of human beings ritually identified with animal victims. Athamas kills his son

Learchus "like a stag" (Apollodorus, *Bibl.* 3. 4. 3); according to Lucian (*De dea Syr.* 58), at Bambyke, when children were sacrificed, those present cried, "They are calves!"

The possible relations between the sacrifice of goats and the origin of tragedy have been reexamined by W. Burkert, "Greek Tragedy and Sacrificial Ritual," *Greek, Roman and Byzantine Studies* 7 (1966): 87–121.

There are some differences between sacrifices for the Olympians and sacrifices offered to the chthonian divinities and the heroes; see § 95.

On Prometheus and Deucalion, see J. Rudhardt, "Les mythes grecs relatifs à l'instauration du sacrifice: Les rôles correlatifs de Prométhée et de son fils Daucalion," *Museum Helveticum* 27 (1970): 1–15.

On the *Prometheus* trilogy of Aeschylus, see Louis Séchan, *Le mythe de Prométhée*, pp. 4 ff.; H. Lloyd-Jones, *The Justice of Zeus*, pp. 95 ff.

On the Greek myth of the origin of men from an ash tree, see G. Bonfante, "Microcosmo e macrocosmo nel mito indoeuropeo," *Die Sprache* 5 (1959): 1–19.

87. On *moira* and *aisa*, see W. C. Greene, *Moira: Fate, Good, and Evil in Greek Thought* (Cambridge, Mass., 1944); Ugo Bianchi, *Dios Aisa: Destino, uomini e divinità nell'epos, nelle teogonie e nel culto dei Greci* (Rome, 1953); B. C. Dietrich, *Death, Fate, and the Gods* (London, 1967).

On the symbolism of spinning, see Eliade, *Patterns in Comparative Religion*, § 58; on the equivalence between "spinning" someone's destiny and "binding" him, see Eliade, *Images and Symbols*, chap. 3, "The God Who Binds and the Symbolism of Knots."

The history of the idea of justice, *dikē*, has recently been brilliantly presented by Hugh Lloyd-Jones, *The Justice of Zeus* (Berkeley, 1971). Ever since Nilsson, parallels have been drawn between the structure of the Homeric pantheon and that of the feudal Mycenaean royalty. "Justice" (*dikē*) can be compared to the will of the gods. Like the Mycenaean kings, the gods can be capricious and cruel, though they cannot descend to baseness. The only unforgiveable crime is disloyalty to the king or treachery. In Homer, *dikē* seems to mean both the "characteristic behavior" of a social class and the "right" that devolves upon the individuals belonging to that class. The structure, the history, and the crisis of the Mycenaean sovereignty are well discussed by J. P. Vernant, *Les origines de la pensée grecque* (Paris, 1962), pp. 13–39.

On *themis* and *themistes*, see Lloyd-Jones, *The Justice of Zeus*, pp. 6 ff., 167–68 (bibliography).

For the history of the idea of *hybris*, from antiquity to modern times, see the very personal work by Robert Payne, *Hubris: A Study of Pride* (London, 1951; rev. ed., New York, 1960).

88. On the etymology of Poseidon (*Posis Das*) see Wilamowitz, *Glaube der Hellenen*, vol. 1, pp. 212 ff. (discussed earlier by P. Kretschmer in *Glotta* 1 [1909]: 27 ff.; cf. also Cook, *Zeus*, vol. 2, pp. 583 ff.).

See also Guthrie, *The Greeks and Their Gods*, pp. 94–99; Louis Séchan and Pierre Lévêque, *Les grandes divinités de la Grèce*, pp. 99–116. F. Schachermeyr makes every effort to reconstruct the history of Poseidon: when, about 1900 B.C., the Indo-Europeans arrived in Greece, bringing with them the horse, they found a Mother Earth, a sovereign goddess accompanied by a male *paredros*; the conquerors identified this *paredros* with their horse god, master of the waters, of fertility, and of the infernal world. Poseidon—"husband of Da," Mother Earth—would be the result of this coalescence; see Schachermeyr, *Poseidon und die Entstehung des griechischen Götterglaubens* (Berne, 1950). See also Leonard Palmer, *Mycenaeans and Minoans* (London, 1961), pp. 127 ff.; C. Scott Littleton, "Poseidon as a Reflex of the Indo-European 'Source and Waters' God," *JIES* 1 (1973): 423–40.

Ileana Chirassi has brought out the differences between the Mycenaean Poseidon and the Olympian god (for example, the presence at Pylos of a goddess, Posideia, who probably reflects the archaic conception of primordial androgynous divinities, of the type of En-ki and Nin-ki, El and Elat, etc.); see Chirassi, "Poseidaon-Enesidaon nel pantheon miceno," *Atti e Memorie del I Congresso Internazionale di Micenologia* (Rome, 1968), pp. 945–91, esp. pp. 956 ff.

On the chthonian meanings of the horse, see J. M. Blasquez, "El caballo en las creencias griegas y en las de otros pueblos circum-mediterraneos," *Revue Belge de philologie et d'histoire* 45 (1967): 48–80.

On Hephaestus see Farnell, *Cults*, vol. 5, pp. 374 ff.; Nilsson, *Geschichte*, vol. 1, pp. 526 ff.; L. Malten, "Hephaistos," *Jahrbücher des deutschen archaeologischen Instituts* 27 (1912): 232 ff.; F. Brommer, "Die Rückführung des Hephaistos," ibid. 52 (1937): 198 ff.; and Marie Delcourt, *Héphaistos où la légende du magician* (Paris, 1957). A late tradition attempts to reconcile the two myths of the birth of Hephaestus: "Hera becomes pregnant by Zeus, but before their marriage. When Hephaestus is born, she declares, in order to save appearances, that she conceived him without a father" (Delcourt, p. 33). The episode with the golden throne that Hephaestus sent to Hera is not in Homer, but it soon became popular. Plato mentions it, disapprovingly, among the irresponsible legends current about the gods (*Republic* 2. 378). See Delcourt, pp. 78–79, 86–96, where she reports and analyzes the versions transmitted by Libanius and Hyginus.

On ritual mutilations of magicians, see Delcourt, pp. 110 ff.

On "masters of fire" and divine smiths, see Eliade, *The Forge and the Crucible*, pp. 79 ff.

On Hephaestus' connections with other related divine figures, see Delcourt, pp. 154 ff.

89. On Apollo, consult especially Farnell, *Cults of the Greek States*, vol. 4, pp. 98 ff.; Rose, *A Handbook of Greek Mythology*, pp. 135 ff.; A. B. Cook, *Zeus*, vol. 2, pp. 453–59 (for criticism of theories and controversies); Nilsson, *Geschichte*, vol. 1, 529 ff.; Guthrie, *The Greeks and Their Gods*, pp. 73 ff., 183 ff. Cf. also K. Kerényi, *Apollon* (Vienna, 1937; 2d ed., 1953).

On the substitution of Apollo for pre-Hellenic divinities, see Farnell, *Cults*, vol. 4, pp. 125 ff., 263 ff. The legend of Hyacinthus—whose etymology itself proves that he was an ancient Mediterranean god—is mentioned for the first time by Euripides (*Helen* 1470 ff.; cf. Apollodorus, *Bibl.* 3. 10. 3; Rose, *Handbook*, pp. 142, 160–61). The mythico-religious meanings of the metamorphosis of Hyacinthus into a flower are analyzed by Ileana Chirassi, *Elementi di culture precereali nei miti e riti greci* (Rome, 1968), pp. 159 ff. The festival of the Hyacinthia in Laconia was consecrated at once to Apollo and to his involuntary victim. At Ismenium, as at Delphi, Apollo is associated with Athena; at Tegyra, in northern Boeotia, he appears with Latona and Artemis; see Delcourt, *L'oracle de Delphes* (1955), pp. 216 ff. In other words, as god of Delphi, Apollo is a creation of Greek religiosity.

The two hypotheses concerning the origin of Apollo—northern or Anatolian—are discussed by Guthrie, pp. 75 ff.

On the legend of the Hyperboreans, see Cook, *Zeus*, vol. 2, pp. 459–501 (he identifies the itinerary with the Milky Way). Herodotus also speaks of two "Hyperborean virgins," who, long ago, came in person to Delos, bringing offerings, and did not return. The historian had described their tombs so accurately that they were discovered by the French excavations at the place indicated. But there is nothing "Hyperborean" about them: they are Cycladic burials of the Bronze Age. What is involved, then, is an archaic cult whose meaning had been forgotten, and the sacred nature of the tombs was associated with imaginary heroes. Cf. C. T. Seltman, cited by Guthrie, p. 77. See also Charles Picard, *Les religions préhelléniques*, p. 271, for other examples of cults of heroes attached to Mycenaean tombs of historical Greece.

Marie Delcourt (*L'oracle de Delphes*, p. 163) supposes that the *hiera* that the virgins brought to Delos, hidden in a sheaf of wheat, were images of the phallus, represented as a perforating weapon.

90. In the *Eumenides*, Aeschylus explains the religious meaning of Orestes' being acquitted of the crime of matricide. Orestes admits his crime and submits himself to the Areopagus to be judged. He is defended by Apollo and acquitted by Athena; what is more, the Erinyes (who, as symbols of the telluric and maternal forces, could not leave the most horrible of crimes, matricide, unavenged) are "converted" by Athena: they become the Eumenides—Kindly Goddesses—and are charged with nourishing and sustaining life. As for the pollution of the crime, it is washed away by the sacrifice of a pig (*Eumenides* 281 ff.). Though prescribed by Apollo, this is a sacrifice peculiar to the chthonian and infernal powers. This goes to show that, despite his Olympian structure, the god of Delphi takes into account complementary, and even antagonistic, religious realities.

On Delphi and the Delphic oracular traditions, see P. Amandry, *La mantique apollonienne à Delphes* (Paris, 1950); J. Defradas, *Les thèmes de la propagande delphique* (1954); and Marie Delcourt, *L'oracle de Delphes* (1955). The oracular texts have been edited by H. Parke and D. Wormell, *The Delphic Oracle*, 2 vols. (Oxford, 1956). See also K. Latte, "The Coming of the Pythia," *Harvard Theol. Rev.* 33 (1940): 9 ff.

On Dionysus at Delphi, see H. Jeanmaire, *Dionysos* (Paris, 1951), pp. 187–98, 492–93 (critical bibliography).

91. On Greek "shamanism," see my books: *Shamanism*, pp. 387 ff.; *Zalmoxis*, pp. 34 ff. (with bibliography). E. R. Dodds, *The Greeks and the Irrational* (Berkeley, 1951), pp. 141 ff., explains the dissemination of shamanic techniques and mythologies by contact between the Greek colonies of the Hellespont and the Black Sea and the Iranian populations (i.e., the Scythians). But Karl Meuli, who first brought out the shamanic structure of certain Scythian customs and showed their reflections in Greek traditions, has, in addition, identified shamanic elements in Greek epic poetry; see his "Scythica," *Hermes* 70 (1935): 121–76, esp. 164 ff. Walter Burkert considers the *goēs* the authentic Greek shaman, since he is connected with the cult of the dead ("Goēs: Zum griechischen 'Schamanismus,'" *Rheinisches Museum für Philologie* n.s. 105 [1962]: 35–55).

On some shamanic characteristics in the myth of Orpheus and the legends of Aristeas and other fabulous personages, see the second volume of the present work.

92. On Hermes, see Farnell, *Cults*, vol. 5, pp. 1 ff.; Nilsson, *Geschichte*, vol. 1, pp. 510 ff.; S. Eitrem, *Hermes und die Toten* (Christiania, 1909); P. Raingeard, *Hermès psychagogue* (Paris, 1935); K. Kerényi, *Hermes der Seelenführer* (Zurich, 1944) (Eng. trans., *Hermes, Guide of Souls*, 1974); N. O. Brown, *Hermes the Thief* (Madison, Wis., 1947); Walter Otto, *The Homeric Gods*, pp. 104–24; Jeanine J. Orgogozo, "L'Hermès des Achéens," *RHR* 136 (1949): 10–30, 139–79.

On *moly*, Hermes' herb, see Hugo Rahner, *Greek Myths and Christian Mystery* (New York and London, 1963), pp. 181 ff. See also the bibliographies on hermeticism in the second volume.

From a certain point of view, Ares, the god of war, constitutes an enigma. Homer does not hide the fact that he was detested by the gods: "Thou art the most hateful to me of all the immortals who inhabit Olympus! If thou wert born of some other god, destructive as thou art, thou wouldst long since have been in a place still lower than that of the sons of Uranus!" exclaims Hera, his mother (*Iliad* 5. 889 ff.). The Greeks celebrated him neither in cult nor in the plastic arts or literature, despite the fact that they "practiced war as much as, perhaps more than, any other people of antiquity" (Séchan and Lévêque, *Les grandes divinités de la Grèce*, p. 248). Compared to his Italic homologue, Mars, or to other Indo-European gods of war, Ares seems a minor divinity.

According to Homer, Ares came from Thrace (*Il.* 13. 301). And when he is freed from the net in which Hephaestus has shut him up with Aphrodite, Ares goes to Thrace (*Od.* 8. 361). Then too, Herodotus (5. 7) states that the Thracians worshiped only three gods: Ares, Dionysus, and Artemis. Was it because of his Thracian origin that this savage god— "mad one who knows no law" (*Il.* 5. 757)—never succeeded in becoming integrated into Greek religiosity?

93. According to W. H. Roscher, Hera must originally have been a moon goddess (*Lexikon*, I, II [1886–90], pp. 2087 ff.; cf. the criticism of this hypothesis in Farnell, *Cults*, vol. 1, pp. 180 ff.). For Rose, Hera was especially the goddess of women and their fecundity (but not of vegetable fertility); see his *Handbook*, p. 103. The idea maintained by Welcker (*Die griechische Götterlehre*, 3 vols. [1857–63]), that she was a Terra Mater, rejected by Farnell and Rose, has been revived in a more convincing form by Guthrie, *The Greeks and Their Gods*, pp. 68 ff.

On Hera's relations with the cow, see Farnell, *Cults*, vol. 1, pp. 181 ff.; Cook, *Zeus*, vol. 1, pp. 444 ff.

On the Aegean Hera, see C. Picard, *Les religions préhelléniques*, p. 243; U. Pestallozza, "Hera Pelasga," *Studi Etruschi* 2d ser. 25 (1957): 115–82 (reprinted in *Nuovi saggi di religione mediterranea*, pp. 225–56); Louis Séchan and Pierre Lévêque, *Les grandes divinités de la Grèce*, pp. 184–85. Ileana Chirassi has convincingly shown the continuity between the Mediterranean "goddess with the lily" and Hera in "Riflesi di una primitiva cultura precerealicola nel mondo miceneo," *Annali della Facoltà di Lettere e Filosofia dell'Università di Trieste* 3 (1966–67): 15–26.

A few words on the goddess Hestia will suffice. She has almost no myths, but she presents a certain ritual importance, since she protects hearths, domestic or public. Homer does not know her name, but Hesiod proclaims her the eldest daughter of Kronos and Rhea (*Theog.* 454). Hestia is preeminently a virgin and "sedentary" goddess: she never leaves "the high dwellings of the immortal gods." Etymologically connected with the Latin goddess Vesta, she incarnates the sacrality of fire; this probably explains her abstract character (cf. § 104). Her name has been derived from an Indo-European root meaning "to burn." But it is equally possible that the cult of Hestia continues a pre-Hellenic cult of the hearth; see C. Picard, *Les religions préhelléniques*, pp. 242 ff.

On Artemis, reference should be made to Farnell, *Cults*, vol. 2, pp. 425 ff.; Nilsson, *Geschichte*, vol. 1, pp. 481–500; K. Hoenn, *Artemis, Gestaltwandel einer Göttin* (Zurich, 1946); and the clear exposition by Guthrie, *The Greeks and Their Gods*, pp. 99–106. See also Ileana Chirassi, *Miti e culti arcaici di Artemis nel Peloponese e Grecia centrale* (Trieste, 1964).

An Illyrian origin of the name has been proposed by M. S. Ruiperez, *Emerita* 15 (1947): 1–60.

On the type of Artemis at Ephesus, see Charles Picard, *Éphèse et Claros* (Paris, 1922), pp. 474 ff.

On the Brauronia festival, involving the ritual transformation of young girls, followers of Artemis, into bear cubs (probably what took place was a bear dance), see H. Jeanmaire, *Couroï et Courètes* (Lille, 1939), pp. 237 ff.

From the seventh century on, Artemis was identified with Hecate, a lunar goddess, with the Thracian goddess Bendis, and with Cybele.

94. The interpretation of Athena as a pre-Greek goddess, protectress of Minoan or Mycenaean princes, proposed by Nilsson (*Minoan-Mycenaean Religion*, 2d ed., pp. 487 ff.), has been generally accepted. For A. B. Cook, Athena was a pre-Greek goddess, specifically the Mountain Mother localized in the rock of the Acropolis (*Zeus*, vol. 3, p. 749; cf. ibid., pp. 224 ff.).

For detailed expositions on the subject of Athena and her cults, see Farnell, *Cults*, vol. 1, pp. 184 ff.; Nilsson, *Geschichte d. Griech. Rel.*, vol. 1, pp. 433 ff. The chapter on Athena is among the best in the book by Walter Otto, *The Homeric Gods* (pp. 43–60). See also M. Guarducci, "Atena oraculare," *Parola di Passato* 6 (1951): 338–55; C. J. Herrington, *Athena Parthenos and Athena Polias: A Study in the Religion of Periclean Athens* (Manchester, 1955).

On the episode of Metis swallowed by Zeus (*Theogony* 886 ff.), see the commentary by M. L. West, *Hesiod: Theogony. Edited with Prolegomena and Commentary* (Oxford, 1966), pp. 401 ff. In two recent articles Marcel Detienne has brilliantly enriched the interpretation of Athena; see his "Le navire d'Athéna," *RHR* 178 (1970): 133–77, and "Athena and the

Mastery of the Horse," *HR* 11 (1971): 161–84. See also H. Jeanmaire, "La naissance d'Athéna et la royauté magique de Zeus," *Rev. archéologique* 48 (1956): 12–39.

On Aphrodite, see E. Simon, *Die Geburt der Aphrodite* (Berlin, 1959); M. P. Nilsson, *Griechische Feste* (1906), pp. 362–87; Nilsson, *Geschichte*, vol. 1, pp. 519 ff.; Farnell, *Cults*, vol. 2, pp. 618 ff.; R. Flacelière, *L'amour en Grèce* (Paris, 1960).

On the Oriental origin of the cult of Aphrodite, see H. Herter, in *Éléments orientaux dans la religion grecque ancienne* (Paris, 1960), pp. 61 ff. The Indo-European elements of Aphrodite have been brought out, but exaggeratedly, by K. Tumpel, in Pauly-Wissowa, *Real-Encyclopädie*, s.v.; see also M. Stubbs, "Who Was Aphrodite?" *Orpheus* (1954), pp. 170 ff.

95. Erwin Rohde made the heroes the subject of the fourth chapter of his *Psyche* (Tübingen and Leipzig, 1893; 2d ed., 1897); cf. the English translation, *Psyche: The Cult of Souls and Belief in Immortality among the Greeks* (New York, 1925), pp. 115–55. Three years later, in his work *Götternamen: Versuch einer Theorie der religiösen Begriffsbildung* (Bonn, 1896), Herman Usener developed the notion of the *Sondergötter*, especially criticizing H. Spencer's theory of the priority of the ancestor cult (pp. 253 ff.) and devoting a single polemic reference to Rohde (p. 248). Paul Foucart followed the general lines of Rohde's interpretation in *Le culte des héros chez les Grecs* (1918) (Mémoires de l'Institut Français, 1921); so, too, did S. Eitrem, in Pauly-Wissowa, *Real-Encyclopädie*, vol. 8, pt. 1 (1912), s.v. "Heroes," and F. Pfister, *Der Reliquienkult im Altertum* (Giessen, 1910–12).

The "compromise theory" presented by L. R. Farnell, in his *Greek Hero Cults and Ideas of Immortality* (Oxford, 1921), was widely accepted; cf., inter alia, M. P. Nilsson, *The Minoan-Mycenaean Religion*, 2d ed. (Lund, 1950), pp. 585 ff., and *Geschichte der Griechische Religion*, vol. 1, 2d ed. (Munich, 1955), p. 188.

Clear expositions and useful analyses will be found in the works of C. Robert, *Die Griechische Heldensage*, 2 vols. (Berlin, 1921–26); L. Rademacher, *Mythos und Sage bei den Griechen* (Munich, 1938); Marie Delcourt, *Légendes et cultes des héros en Grèce* (Paris, 1942); H. J. Rose, *Gods and Heroes of the Greeks* (London, 1957); and K. Kerényi, *Greek Heroes* (London, 1959).

An important contribution, undertaken from the point of view of the general history of religions, was made by Angelo Brelich, *Gli eroi greci: Un problema storico-religioso* (Rome, 1958). After alluding to the earlier interpretations, from Rohde to Nilsson, the author presents the role of the heroes in myth and cult (the hero and death, the hero and athletic contests, prophecy, initiations, etc.) and examines their relations with other mythical beings in order finally to isolate the specific structure of the Greek hero.

To the three categories of beings distinguished by Pindar (goás, heroes, men), Plato added a fourth, that of demons (*Cratylus* 397c ff.).

On puberty initiations in archaic Greece, see H. Jeanmaire, *Couroï et Courètes* (Lille, 1939); Eliade, *Birth and Rebirth*, pp. 108 ff.; Brelich, *Gli eroi greci*, pp. 124 ff.; Brelich, *Paides e Parthenoi* (Rome, 1969), vol. 1.

The difference between sacrifices performed for the Olympians, on the one hand, and for the chthonic gods and the heroes, on the other—a difference which Rohde emphasized (*Psyche*, Eng. trans., p. 116 ff.)—was also noted by Jane Harrison, Meuli, C. Picard, and Guthrie. Picard also referred to the difference in the ritual gestures: the hand was raised, palm toward the sky, for the Olympians; it was lowered, palm toward the ground, to invoke the powers of the soil (Picard, "Le geste de la prière funéraire en Grèce et en Étrurie," *RHR* [1936]: 137 ff.). However, A. D. Nock (*Harvard Theological Review* 37 [1944]: 141 ff.) and W. Burkert (*Homo Necans* [Berlin, 1972], pp. 16 ff. and note 41) have pointed out that this difference is not always documented; see also Brelich, *Gli eroi greci*, pp. 16–18.

96. The Greek term, used chiefly in the plural, *ta mystēria*, probably derives from an Indo-European root MU, the original meaning of which, "to shut the mouth," refers to "ritual silence." Cf. Gk. *myō* and *myeō*, "initiate into the Mystery," and *myēsis*, "initiation" (a term used only of initiations into Mysteries).

For the literary sources, see L. R. Farnell, *Cults of the Greek States* (Oxford, 1907), vol. 3, pp. 307–67. For the archeological explorations, see F. Noack, *Eleusis: Die baugeschichtliche Entwicklung des Heiligtums* (Berlin and Leipzig, 1927); K. Kuruniotis, "Das eleusinische Heiligtum von den Anfangen bis zur vorperikleische Zeit," *ARW* 33 (1935): 52–78; G. E. Mylonas, *The Hymn to Demeter and Her Sanctuary at Eleusis*, Washington Studies in Language and Literature 13 (Saint Louis, 1942); Mylonas, *Eleusis and the Eleusinian Mysteries* (Princeton, 1961), pp. 23–186; E. Simon, "Neue Deuting zweier eleusinischer Denkmäler des 4. Jh. v. Chr.," *Antike Kunst* 9 (1966): 72–92; H. Metzger, *Les représentations dans la céramique attique du IVᵉ siècle* (Paris, 1951), pp. 231–65; Metzger, *Recherches sur l'imagerie athénienne* (Paris, 1965), pp. 1–53.

On the Homeric hymn, see the edition by N. J. Richardson, *The Homeric Hymn to Demeter* (Oxford, 1973); see also K. Deichgräber, *Eleusinische Frömmigkeit und homerische Vorstellungswelt im Homerischen Demeterhymnus* (Mainz, 1950); Francis R. Walton, "Athens, Eleusis, and the Homeric Hymn to Demeter," *Harvard Theological Review* 45 (1952): 105–14; Ugo Bianchi, "Saggezza olimpica e mistica eleusina nell'inno omerico a Demeter," *SMSR* 35 (1964): 161–93; Mary L. Lord, "Withdrawal and Return in the *Homeric Hymn to Demeter* and the Homeric Poems," *Classical Journal* 62 (1967): 214–48.

From the immense literature devoted to the Eleusinian Mysteries, we single out L. R. Farnell, *Cults*, vol. 3, pp. 126–98; Paul Foucart, *Recherches sur l'origine et la nature des Mystères d'Éleusis* (Paris, 1895); Foucart, *Les Mystères d'Éleusis* (Paris, 1914); Martin P. Nilsson, *Minoan-Mycenaean Religion and Its Survival in Greek Religion* (Lund, 1927; 2d ed., rev. and enl., 1950), pp. 468 ff., 558 ff.; Nilsson, "Die eleusinischen Gottheiten," *ARW* 32 (1935): 79–141, republished in *Opuscula Selecta* (Lund, 1952), vol. 2, pp. 542–623; Nilsson, *Greek Popular Religion* (New York, 1940; new ed., 1961), pp. 42–64; S. Eitrem, "Eleusis: Les mystères et l'agriculture," *Simbolae Osloenses* 20 (1940): 133–51; Victor Magnien, *Les Mystères d'Éleusis: Leurs origines. Le rituel de leurs initiations* (Paris, 1938) (useful for the texts cited and translated); Walter F. Otto, "Der Sinn der eleusinischen Mysterien," *Eranos-Jahrbuch* 9 (1939): 83–112, republished as "The Meaning of the Eleusinian Mysteries" in *The Mysteries: Papers from the Eranos Yearbooks* no. 2 (New York, 1955), pp. 14–31; Momolina Marconi, "Sul misterio dei Misteri Eleusini," *SMSR* 22 (1949–50): 151–54; C. Kerényi, *Eleusis: Archetypal Image of Mother and Daughter* (New York, 1967); Georges Méautis, *Les Dieux de la Grèce et les Mystères d'Éleusis* (Paris, 1959); P. Boyancé, "Sur les Mystères d'Éleusis," *REG* 75 (1962): 460–82; Walter Burkert, *Homo Necans* (Berlin, 1972), pp. 274–327. See also the studies by A. Körte, O. Kern, A. Delatte, Charles Picard, et al., cited below.

Following the opinion of Herodotus (2. 49 ff., 146), Paul Foucart affirmed the Egyptian origin of the Eleusinian Mysteries. But Charles Picard observes that "nowhere as yet has any Egyptian object datable from the second half of the second millennium appeared, even isolatedly, in the hieron" ("Sur la patrie et les pérégrinations de Déméter," *REG* 40 [1927]: 321–30, esp. 325). Axel Persson ("Der Ursprung der eleusinischen Mysterien," *ARW* 21 [1922]: 287–309), and Charles Picard (*Les religions préhelléniques* [Paris, 1948], pp. 89, 111, 114 ff.) have suggested a Cretan origin for the Mysteries. However, recent excavations have invalidated the hypothesis of Cretan or Minoan influence on the buildings at Eleusis (see Mylonas, *Eleusis*, pp. 16 ff.; cf. ibid., pp. 49, 68, etc.). M. P. Nilsson has attempted to establish the Mycenaean origins of the mythico-ritual complex of Eleusis (*Minoan-Mycenaean Religion*, pp. 558 ff.; see also *Opuscula Selecta*, vol. 2, pp. 585 ff.). Mylonas points out that the traditions indicate, rather, a northern origin for the cult (*Eleusis*, pp. 19 ff.)—Thessaly or

Thrace. According to Pausanias 1. 38. 2–3, Eumolpus, the first hierophant and founder of the family of the Eumolpids, was supposed to be a native of Thrace. However, the name Eumolpus is pre-Hellenic (Nilsson, *Minoan-Mycen. Rel.*, pp. 520 ff.). In any case, whatever their origin, it is certain that the Mysteries are pre-Hellenic and that they continue a cult whose structure is archaic. From a second family, the Kerykes, the other officiants descended: the dadouchos, "bearer of the torch," the hierokeryx, "herald of the ceremonies," and the priest who officiated at the altar. Until the destruction of Eleusis by Alaric in 396, the hierophants and other officiants were all descended from these two families.

As for the "genesis" of the Mysteries, the majority of scholars have sought it in a mythico-ritual scenario bound up with agriculture. For Nilsson, Demeter is the Corn Mother, and Kore the Corn Maiden: they symbolize the old and new crops. Hence the reunion of the two goddesses would finally represent the meeting of the two crops (*Greek Popular Religion*, pp. 51 ff.). Nilsson states that, at Eleusis, "there were no doctrines, but only some simple, fundamental ideas about life and death as symbolized in the springing up of the new crop from the old" (ibid., p. 63). A similar explanation had already been put forward by R. M. Cornford in "The *aparchai* and the Eleusinian Mysteries," in *Essays and Studies presented to William Ridgeway* (Cambridge, 1913), pp. 153–66. We have criticized elsewhere, and precisely in discussing Nilsson's *Greek Popular Religion*, the inadequacy of such "genetic" pseudo-explanations of religious phenomena: see Eliade, "Mythologie et Histoire des religions," *Diogène* (January 1955): 108 ff. The relations of the Eleusinian Mysteries to agriculture are also analyzed by R. Pettazzoni in *I Misteri* (Bologna, 1924), pp. 45 ff., and *La religion dans la Grèce antique* (Paris, 1953), pp. 73 ff.

On the myths and rites of the pomegranate in the Mediterranean world, see Uberto Pestalozza "Iside e la Melagrana," in his *Religione Mediterranea* (Milan, 1951), pp. 1–70, and Ileana Chirassi, *Elementi di cultura precereali nel miti e riti greci* (Rome, 1968), pp. 73–90.

On consecration by fire, see J. G. Frazer, "Putting Children on the Fire," appendix 1 to his edition of Apollodorus, *The Library*, vol. 2, pp. 311–17; C. M. Edsman, *Ignis Divinus* (Lund, 1949); and especially Marie Delcourt, *Pyrrhos et Pyrrha: Recherches sur les valeurs du feu dans les légendes helléniques* (Paris, 1965), pp. 66 ff. What Demeter wanted to do for Demophoön Isis tried to do for Arsinoë's child, and Thetis for Achilles. But, stupidly interrupted by terrified mortals, none of these attempts succeeded. On "masters of fire," see Eliade, *Shamanism*, pp. 257 ff., 438 ff., 474 ff., and *The Forge and the Crucible*, pp. 79 ff.

On the episode of Baubo, see Charles Picard, "L'épisode de Baubô dans les Mystères d'Eleusis," *RHR* 95 (1927): 1–37; V. Magnien, *Les Mystères d'Eleusis*, pp. 86 ff.

According to what has been called the Orphic version of the myth of Demeter (see Malten, "Altorphische Demetersagen," *ARW* 5 [1909]: 417 ff.), there lived at Eleusis a poor peasant, Dysaules, and his wife Baubo; they had only a wretched hovel, for wheat had not yet been revealed by Demeter. According to the Attic tradition, Triptolemus was the son of Dysaules (Pausanias, 1. 14. 3). Another son, Eubuleus, was a swineherd, and his swine were swallowed up at the same time as Persephone. One Orphic hymn (41. 6) recounts that, when she ended her fast at Eleusis, Demeter went down to Hades following the instructions given her by Eubuleus (see also K. Kerényi, *Eleusis*, pp. 43, 171).

The ancients had connected Eleusis with Elysium, the realm of the Blessed (see A. B. Cook, *Zeus*, vol. 2, pp. 36 ff.).

97. Sterling Dow and Robert F. Healey, *A Sacred Calendar of Eleusis* (Cambridge, 1965), have reconstructed the calendar of ceremonies on the basis of an inscription of about 330 B.C.

On the Lesser Mysteries, see P. Roussel, "L'initiation préalable et le symbole Eleusinien," *Bulletin de correspondance hellénique* 54 (1930): 51–74; Mylonas, *Eleusis*, pp. 239–43. The sacrifice of pigs was characteristic of the cult of Demeter everywhere in Greece; see, most recently, W. Burkert, *Homo Necans*, pp. 284 ff. On the other hand, such sacrifices on the occasion of initiation ceremonies are fully documented among the cultivators of the Polynesian islands. Burkert (p. 286) points out that the Greek for "piglet" (*choiros*) meant, in vulgar parlance, the female sexual organ. Symbolically, the sacrifice of a young pig represented killing a girl.

On the *gephyrismoi*, see E. de Martino, "Gephyrismi," *SMSR* 10 (1934): 64–79.

On *kykeōn*, see A. Delatte, "Le cyceon, breuvage rituel des mystères d'Eleusis," *Bull. Classe des Lettres, Acad. Royale de Belgique*, 5th ser. 40 (1954): 690–752.

A large number of texts, of unequal value, referring to the initiations, are cited and translated by V. Magnien, *Les Mystères d'Eleusis*, pp. 198 ff. (to be consulted with caution). On the rituals, see Mylonas, *Eleusis*, pp. 243–85; Dario Sabbatucci, *Saggio sul misticismo greco* (Rome, 1965), pp. 127 ff. See also Charles Picard, "Le prétendu 'baptême d'initiation' élusinien et le formulaire des mystères des Deux-déesses," *RHR* 154 (1959): 129–45; Ugo Bianchi, *Ο ΣΥΜΠΑΣ ΑΙΩΝ*, in *Ex Orbe Religionum* (Leiden, 1972), vol. 1, pp. 277–86; H. Ludin Jansen, "Die Eleusinische Weihe," ibid., pp. 287–98. The sacrifices and rituals connected with the initiation were performed inside the enclosure of the sanctuary, which makes

Eleusis unique among Greek cults. The Olympian sacrifice was not performed in the temples but on altars, and these could be erected anywhere, as well in houses as in streets and fields.

On the cosmic and ritual meaning of the two vessels (*plēmochoai*), filled with water and overturned by the initiate while he repeated a formula (perhaps the famous formula of which Proclus speaks in *Ad Timaeum* 293c), see Edward L. Ochsenschlager, "The Cosmic Significance of the *plēmochoē*," *HR* 9 (1970): 316–37.

As for the revealing of secrets (see § 97, note 3), antiquity knew a few other examples. A rhetorical exercise that has come down to us under the name of Sopater presents the case of a young man who dreamed that he was initiated; he contemplated the *drōmena*, or "things done," but, since he did not hear the words spoken by the hierophant, he could not be considered an initiate. Andocides, on the other hand, was accused because he showed the *hiera* to noninitiates and repeated the words that must not be uttered (references in Mylonas, *Eleusis*, p. 272, nn. 194, 195). Alcibiades parodied the secret ceremonies and had to go into exile; some of his accomplices who were caught suffered the death penalty (Xenophon, *Hellenica* 1. 4. 14; etc.).

98. Synesius has preserved a short fragment from a youthful work by Aristotle concerning initiation into the Mysteries: "Aristotle is of the opinion that those who are initiated are not expected to learn something but to experience emotions and be put in certain dispositions, obviously after becoming open to receive them" (*Dio*, ed. Krabinger, vol. 1, pp. 271–72 = Aristotle, frag. 15 Rose; after the translation by Jeanne Croissant, *Aristote et les Mystères* [Paris, 1932], p. 137). A parallel text, transmitted by Psellus and published by J. Bidez, *Catalogue des manuscrits alchimiques grecs* (1928), vol. 6, p. 171, has been fully analyzed by Croissant, pp. 145 ff.

On the passage from Themistius, see, most recently, Mylonas, *Eleusis*, pp. 264 ff. There is an excellent analysis of the late sources by Farnell in his *Cults*, vol. 3, pp. 176 ff.

On the *synthēma*, or password, transmitted by Clement of Alexandria, see U. Pestalozza, *Religione Mediterranea: Vecchi e nuovi studi* (Milan, 1951), pp. 216–34 ("Ortaggi, frutti e paste nei Misteri Eleusini"); Mylonas, *Eleusis*, pp. 294–303; W. Burkert, *Homo Necans*, pp. 298 ff.

The identification of the objects hidden in the chest and the basket has given rise to a long controversy, which still continues. A. Körte held that the basket contained the replica of a womb (*kteis*); touching it, the mystes believed that he was reborn as a child of Demeter (*ARW* [1915]: 116 ff.). O. Kern went still further: the mystes united himself with the goddess by touching the *kteis* with his sexual organ (*Die griechische Mysterien der classischen Zeit* [1927], p. 10). For A. Dieterich, on the contrary, it was a phallus that the mystes found in the basket: by placing it on his chest, he was united with the goddess and became her child (*Eine Mythrasliturgie* [1903], p. 123; *Mutter Erde*, 3d ed. [1925], pp. 110 ff.). According to Charles Picard, the basket contained a phallus and the chest a womb: by manipulating them, the mystes achieved union with the goddesses ("L' épisode de Baubô," *RHR* 95 [1927]: pp. 237 ff.). S. Eitrem proposes a snake, a pomegranate, and cakes in the shape of a phallus and a womb ("Eleusinia," pp. 140 ff.). Such explanations have been rejected by many scholars: Maas, Farnell, Roussel, Deubner, Otto, Kerényi, and others (see also Mylonas, *Eleusis*, p. 296, n. 22). But it was worthwhile to mention these exercises in historico-religious exegesis: they contribute to an understanding of the Western *Zeitgeist* during the first third of the twentieth century.

As to the various data on initiation into the Mysteries reported by the Church Fathers, it is certain that they show a definite purpose: to attack and discredit paganism. However, the Fathers did not dare to invent, for they risked being triumphantly contradicted by pagan authors. But it must also be borne in mind that they were writing during the full tide of religious syncretism and that they referred primarily to the Hellenistic Mysteries. Indeed, just as numerous Neo-Platonic and Neo-Pythagorean authors proclaimed the unity of all the Mysteries, Christian authors, adopting their point of view, regarded as Eleusinian rituals that belonged to more recent Mysteries. In addition, these apologetes likewise shared the Hellenistic fashion for explanation by analogy, which makes their testimony still more dubious.

Fire and cremation at Eleusis. It is probable that certain mystai were incinerated on the terrace on which the temple stood, between 1110 and 700 B.C. (Kerényi, *Eleusis*, p. 93). On the other hand, we know the history of a Brahman, Zarmaros or Zarmanochegos, who, in 20 B.C., when Augustus was at Eleusis again, demanded to be initiated, and, after being present at the *epopteia*, entered the fire and was consumed (Dio Cassius, 54. 9. 10; Strabo, 15. 1. 73; cf. Kerényi, p. 100). May we read in these ritual cremations a memory of the "divinization" of Demophoön by fire? See also Marie Delcourt, *Pyrrhos et Pyrrha* (Paris, 1965), pp. 68 ff.

99. On the cult of Demeter, see Farnell, *Cults*, vol. 3, pp. 38 ff.; Nilsson, *Geschichte*, vol. 1, pp. 461 ff.

On the Mysteries of Demeter in the rest of Greece, see Nilsson, *Geschichte*, vol. 1, p. 478; R. Stiglitz, *Die grossen Göttinen Arkadiens* (Vienna, 1967), pp. 30 ff.; G. Zuntz, *Persephone* (Cambridge, 1971), pp. 75 ff.

In the first century B.C., Diodorus Siculus (5. 73. 3) reported the following tradition: the inhabitants of Crete affirm that the Mysteries were disseminated from their island, giving as proof the fact that the secrets imparted in the Eleusinian initiations, in the Mysteries of Samothrace, and in the cult founded by Orpheus were, in Crete, freely shared by all who wanted to know them. Insofar as Diodorus' information is correct, it probably refers to the rites, and especially to the mythologem, illustrative of the relations between the cycle of agriculture (disappearance of the seed underground, followed by appearance of the new harvest) and the rape of Persephone and her reunion with Demeter.

The role of Dionysus in the Mysteries is the subject of controversy. In the fourth century, Dionysus was identified with Iacchus, personification of the shout given (Herodotus, 8. 65) or of the hymn sung (scholiast on Aristophanes, *Frogs* 309) during the procession to Eleusis. According to Farnell, Sophocles (*Antigone* 1119–21, 1146–52) teaches that Iacchus is Dionysus in his Eleusinian hypostasis (*Cults*, vol. 3, p. 149). But Dionysus does not appear to have figured among the deities venerated in the Mysteries (Mylonas, *Eleusis*, p. 238). His presence at Eleusis is a consequence of syncretism, a movement that will become more accentuated in the Hellenistic period.

100. The history of studies in the field of the Iranian religions has been admirably presented by J. Duchesne-Guillemin, *The Western Response to Zoroaster* (Oxford, 1958). See also G. Widengren, "Stand und Aufgaben der iranischen Religionsgeschichte," *Numen* 1 (1954): 16–83; 2 (1955): 47–134, and Gherardo Gnoli, who, in "Problems and Prospects of the Studies on Persian Religion" (in *Problems and Methods of the History of Religions*, edited by U. Bianchi, C. J. Bleeker, and A. Bausani [Leiden, 1972], pp. 67–101), refers especially to works published after 1940. Still useful for their rich documentation are J. H. Moulton, *Early Zoroastrianism* (London, 1913), A. V. William Jackson, *Zoroastrian Studies* (New York, 1928), especially "The Iranian Religion" (pp. 3–215), and, above all, L. H. Gray, *The Foundations of Iranian Religions* (Bombay, 1929) (repertory of facts). New orientations in the interpretation of the Iranian religions begin to appear with the following: the little book by E. Benveniste, *The Persian Religion according to the Chief Greek Texts* (Paris, 1929); H. Lommel, *Die Religion Zarathustras nach dem Awesta dargestellt* (Tübingen, 1930); the very personal monograph by H. S. Nyberg, *Die Religionen des alten Iran* (Leipzig, 1938); G. Widengren, *Hochgottglaube im alten Iran* (Uppsala, 1938); G. Dumézil, *Naissances d'archanges* (Paris, 1945) (see also his *Tarpeia* [Paris, 1947], pp. 33–113); J. Duchesne-Guillemin, *Zoroastre* (Paris, 1948); and Duchesne-Guillemin, *Ormazd et*

Ahriman: L'aventure dualiste dans l'antiquité (Paris, 1953). Four works of synthesis have recently appeared: R. C. Zaehner, *The Dawn and Twilight of Zoroastrianism* (London, 1961) (see the critique by Duchesne-Guillemin, *IIJ* 7 [1964]: 196–207); J. Duchesne-Guillemin, *La religion de l'Iran ancien* (Paris, 1962) (Eng. trans., *Religion of Ancient Iran* [Bombay]); Marjan Molé, *Culte, mythe et cosmologie dans l'Iran ancien* (Paris, 1963); and G. Widengren, *Die Religionen Irans* (Stuttgart, 1965); French trans., *Les religions de L'Iran* (Paris, 1968). Duchesne-Guillemin's and Widengren's volumes contain excellent bibliographies. Molé's daring interpretation has given rise to controversies, but the book is valuable for the great number of texts translated. Supplementary bibliographical references will be found further on, in connection with particular subjects. Also see, now, Mary Boyce, *A History of Zoroastrianism*, vol. 1: *The Early Period* (Leiden and Cologne, 1975).

As for the texts: three-fourths of the Avesta is believed to be lost. See the summary of the extant sections in Duchesne-Guillemin, *La religion de l'Iran ancien*, pp. 32–40 (Eng. trans., pp. 22–29) (see ibid., pp. 40–50 [Eng. trans., pp. 29–36], for a very elaborate exposition of the constitution of the Avesta). The only complete translation of the Avestan text is that by J. Darmsteter, *Le Zend-Avesta*, 3 vols. (Paris, 1892–93; reprinted 1960). But "it is unusable for the *gāthās*" (Duchesne-Guillemin). Among the more recent translations of the *gāthās* (after that by C. Bartholomae, *Die Gāthās des Awesta* [Strasbourg, 1905], which remains indispensable), we mention Duchesne-Guillemin, *Zoroastre*, pp. 166–296 (it is this translation that is followed in the text) (this portion of the book has been translated into English by M. Henning in *The Hymns of Zarathustra* [London, 1952]); and H. Humbach, *Die Gāthās des Zarathustra*, 2 vols. (Heidelberg, 1959), with paraphrase and notes. See also Bernfried Schlerath, "Die Gāthās des Zarathustra," *Orientalistische Literatur-Zeitung* 57 (1962), cols. 565–89; a critical review of recent exegeses, partially reproduced in B. Schlerath, ed., *Zarathustra* (Darmstadt, 1970), pp. 336–59; and Wolfgang Lentz, *Yasna 28: Kommentierte Uebersetzung und Komposition-Analyse* (Mainz, 1955). On the *Yašts* and Pahlavi literature, see further on.

W. B. Henning, *Zoroaster, Politician or Witch-Doctor?* (Oxford, 1951), vigorously criticized the work by the archeologist E. Herzfeld, *Zoroaster and His World* (Princeton, 1947), and the book by H. S. Nyberg. (In the preface to the new edition of *Rel. d. alten Iran*, Nyberg replies to Henning's criticisms and defines his position.)

The traditional chronology of Zarathustra has been rejected by Molé, *Culte, mythe, et cosmologie*, pp. 530 ff., and by Gherardo Gnoli, most recently in "Politica religiosa e concezione della regalità sotto i Sassanidi," in *La Persia nel Medioevo* (Rome, 1971), pp. 1–27, esp. pp. 9 ff. A critical bibliography of the problem will be found in the article by O. Klima, "The Date of Zoroaster," *Ar. Or.* 27 (1959): 556–644.

On the Āryan "men's societies," see Stig Wikander, *Der arische Männerbund* (Lund, 1938), and G. Widengren, *Rel. de l'Iran*, pp. 39 ff. (with recent bibliography). Widengren's book contains a synthetic exposition of pre-Zoroastrian ideas and beliefs (pp. 23–78).

101.　On the transformation of a historical personage into an archetype, see the examples cited and commented upon in Eliade, *Cosmos and History*, pp. 37 ff. The elaboration of the legend of Zarathustra has been presented by Duchesne-Guillemin in *La religion*, pp. 337 ff. (Eng. trans., pp. 226 ff.).

In his work *Culte, mythe et cosmologie*, Marjan Molé attempts to reconstruct the image of Zarathustra in the nongathic Avesta. "He is praised above all for having offered correct sacrifices, for having uttered certain efficacious formulas, for having transmitted them to men, who from then on know how to protect cattle, water, and plants: not for having taught a new doctrine. This image suggests that of an Orpheus or a Zalmoxis rather than that of a Semitic prophet" (Molé, "Réponse à M. Duchesne-Guillemin," *Numen* [1961]: 53). Molé recognizes that he can say nothing concerning the historicity of Zarathustra (ibid., pp. 53 ff.; cf. *Culte, mythe et cosmologie*, pp. 530 ff.). In the entire Mazdean tradition, Zarathustra is the prototype of the priest, while Vishtaspa is the prototype of the initiate. However, none of this excludes the historicity of the personage known by the name of Zarathustra.

Gherardo Gnoli holds a similar position: the doctrine transmitted in the *gāthās* under the name of Zarathustra comprises only one aspect of Mazdaism, particularly its esoteric aspect, that is, the sacerdotal and initiatory tradition reserved for religious elites. In contrast, the Mazdaism practiced by the Achaemenids represents the public cult, celebrated for the state and the sovereign. See Gnoli, "Politica religiosa," pp. 17 ff., and his "La Religione persiana," in *Storia delle Religioni*, 6th ed. (Turin, 1971), pp. 235–92, esp. 247 ff.

A suggestive analysis of Zarathustra's religious vocation has been given by K. Rudolph, "Zarathustra—Priester und Prophet," *Numen* 8 (1961): 81–116.

102.　H. S. Nyberg was the first to insist on the "shamanic" ecstasy of Zarathustra; see his *Die Religionen des alten Irans*, pp. 177 ff. G. Widengren returned to the analysis of shamanic elements in Zoroastrianism in *Stand und Aufgaben*, pp. 90 ff., and *Les religions de l'Iran*, pp. 88 ff. See also Eliade, *Shamanism*, pp. 397–401. An excellent analysis and a considered interpretation of ecstatic elements in Zarathustra has been provided by Alessandro Bausani, *Persia religiosa* (Milan, 1959), pp. 38 ff.

103. Georges Dumézil has identified in the Amesha Spentas sublimated substitutes for the Indo-Iranian functional gods; see his *Naissance d'archanges* (Paris, 1945), chaps. 2–4; *Tarpeia* (1947), pp. 33–113; and *Idéologie tripartie des Indo-Européens* (Brussels, 1958), pp. 40 ff. See also Duchesne-Guillemin, *La rel. de l'Iran ancien*, pp. 171 ff., 193 ff. (Eng. trans., pp. 135 ff., 148 ff.); G. Widengren, *Les religions de l'Iran*, pp. 28 ff. Zaehner and Gnoli are among the Iranianists who reject Dumézil's hypothesis.

On Ahura Mazdā, see the relevant chapters in the works by Duchcsnc-Guillemin, Widengren, Zaehner, Molé, et al. F. B. J. Kuiper, "Avestan Mazda," *IIJ* 1 (1957): 86–95, has shown that the meaning of the name is "intelligent, informed Lord" ("he who knows"). See also I. Gershevitch, "Zoroaster's Own Contribution," *JNES* 23 (1964): 12–38.

On the creation, see G. Gnoli, "Osservazioni sulla dottrina mazdaica della creazione," *Annali dell'Istituto Orientale di Napoli* n.s. 13 (1963): 163–93.

Antoine Meillent has emphasized the social character of the Zoroastrian reform (contrast between the agriculturalist and the nomad, opposition of the warrior aristocrats to the cultivators); see *Trois conférences sur les Gathas de l'Avesta* (Paris, 1925).

On the celebrated "Complaint of the Soul of the Ox" (*Yasna* 29), see G. Dumézil's article in *Bulletin de l'Académie royale de Belgique, Classe des Lettres*, 1 (1965): 23–51. The author (pp. 33 ff.) rejects the interpretations proposed by some scholars (H. Lommel, M. Molé) according to which this "Complaint" would be bound up with a cosmogonic myth involving the immolation of a primordial ox. In fact, the subject is "the condition of bovines and the dangers perennially threatening them in societies still not fully settled, where, with their herder-and-farmer masters, they are exposed to the cruelties of other groups of men" (p. 36).

On the "crime of Yima" (flesh food), see Dumézil, *Mythe et Epopée* (1971), vol. 2, pp. 312 ff. (Eng. trans., *The Destiny of a King*, pp. 67 ff.).

As to the cult of *haoma*, it is probable that Zarathustra's attack (*Yasna* 33. 44) is aimcd rather at orgiastic excesses than at the sacrifice in itself. On haoma in the gathic and postgathic Avesta, see Zaehner, *Dawn and Twilight of Zoroastrianism*, pp. 85 ff.; Molé, *Culte, mythe, et cosmologie*, pp. 229 ff.; G. Gnoli, "Licht-Symbolik in Alt-Iran: Haoma Ritus und Erlöser-Mythos," *Antaios* 8 (1967): 528–49; Gnoli, "Problems and Prospects," pp. 74 ff., with a recent bibliography; M. Boyce, "Haoma,

Priest of the Sacrifice," *W. B. Henning Memorial Volume* (London, 1970), pp. 62–80.

On animal sacrifices performed for the benefit of laymen, see M. Boyce, "*Ātaš-zōhr and Āb-zōhr*," *JRAS* (1966): 100–118; Gnoli, "Questioni sull'-interpretazione della dottrina gathica," *Annali dell'Istituto Orientale di Napoli* 31 (1971): 341–70, esp. 350 ff.

On the qualificative "herdsman," see G. Cameron, "Zoroaster the Herdsman," *IIJ* 10 (1968): 261–81, and Gnoli's considerations, "Questioni sull'interpretazione," pp. 351 ff.

On the "Činvat Bridge," see below, § 111.

104. On the "Renovation" (*frašō-kereti*) of the world, see Molé, *Culte, mythe, et cosmologie*, s.v.

On the "philosophical" character of Zarathustra's message, see A. Pagliaro, "L'idealismo zarathustriano," *SMSR* 33 (1962): 3–23.

On the texts that describe the fire ritual, see Duchesne-Guillemin, *La religion*, pp. 79 ff. (Eng. trans., pp. 61 ff.); see also Stig Wikander, *Feuer-priester in Kleinasien und Iran* (Lund, 1967). There are classifications into two, three, or five sacred fires; the last distinguishes the fire that shines before the Lord, the fires that are found in the bodies of men and animals, in plants and clouds, and finally the fire that is used for work. The *Chāndogya Upaniṣad* also distinguishes three sacrificial fires and five natural fires; see Duchesne-Guillemin, "Heraclitus and Iran," *HR* 3 (1963): 34–49, esp. 38–39.

Gherardo Gnoli has presented his interpretation of the sacrifice (*yasna*) in several works: "Lo stato di 'maga,'" *Annali dell'Istituto Orientale di Napoli* n.s. 15 (1965): 105–17; "La gnosi iranica: Per una impostazione nuova del problema," in *Le Origine dello Gnosticismo*, ed. Ugo Bianchi (Leiden, 1967), pp. 281–90, esp. 187 ff.; "Questioni sull'interpretazione della dottrina gathica," pp. 358 ff.

On the *xvarenah*, see Duchesne-Guillemin, "Le *xvarenah*," *Annali dell'Istituto Orientale di Napoli, Sezione Linguistica* 5 (1963): 19–31; G. Gnoli, "Lichtsymbolik in Alt-Iran," pp. 99 ff.; Gnoli, "Un particolare aspetto del simbolismo della luce nel Mazdeismo e nel Manicheismo," *Annali . . . di Napoli* n.s. 12 (1962): 95–128; and Eliade, "Spirit, Light, and Seed," *HR* 11 (1971): 1–30, esp. pp. 13–16 (now in *Occultism, Witchcraft, and Cultural Fashions* [Chicago, 1976], pp. 93–119, 132–42).

105. On the demonization of the *daēvas*, see G. Widengren, *Les religions de l'Iran*, pp. 36 ff., 97, 137 ff.; Duchesne-Guillemin, *La religion*, pp. 189 ff. (Eng. trans., pp. 133 ff.). E. Benveniste had shown that the demonization of the *daēvas* was not typically Zoroastrian in his *The Persian Religion according to the Chief Greek Texts* (Paris, 1929), pp. 39 ff. See, most recently, Gnoli, "Problems and Prospects of the Studies on Persian Religion," pp. 75 ff.

On Iranian religious dualism, see Ugo Bianchi, *Zaman i Ohrmazd* (Turin, 1958). According to this author, "total dualism" must not be regarded as posterior to Zarathustra (p. 25).

On the relations between the religion of the Achaemenids and Zoroastrianism, see the history of the controversy in Duchesne-Guillemin, *The Western Response to Zoroaster*, pp. 52 ff., and *La Religion de l'Iran antique*, pp. 165 ff. (Eng. trans., pp. 119 ff.). The Zoroastrianism of the Achaemenids is admitted by, among others, Kaj Barr, G. Cameron, Ilya Gershevitch. See the critique of this position in Widengren, *Les religions de l'Iran*, pp. 166–74. Marjan Molé eliminates the problem of the Zoroastrianism of the Achaemenids; for him all the forms of Iranian religion coexisted in time (see his *Culte, mythe et cosmologie*, esp. pp. 26–36). Cf. G. Gnoli, "Considerazioni sulla religione degli Achemenidi alla luce di una recente teoria," *SMSR* 35 (1964): 239 ff. For criticism of the "Zoroastrian calendar," see E. Bickerman, "The 'Zoroastrian' Calendar," *Ar Or* 35 (1967): 197–207.

The best edition of the Achaemenian inscriptions, accompanied by a translation, is that by R. G. Kent, *Old Persian: Grammar, Texts, Lexicon*, 2d ed. (New Haven, 1953).

A new inscription of Xerxes I, discovered in 1967 near Persepolis, has been translated, with a commentary, by Manfred Mayrhofer, "Xerxes König der Könige," *Almanach der Oesterreichischen Akademie der Wissenschaften* 119 (1969): 158–70. See ibid., p. 163, n. 14, for a contribution to the bibliography of the Zoroastrianism of the Achaemenids. See also "Une statue de Darius découverte à Suse," *JA* (1972): 235–66—a study by several authors.

On the problem of Iranian royalty, see the following works by G. Widengren: "The Sacral Kingship in Iran," in *La regalità sacra* (Leiden, 1959), pp. 242–57; "La légende royale de l'Iran antique," in *Hommage à Georges Dumézil* (Brussels, 1960), pp. 225–37; and *Les religions de l'Iran*, pp. 73 ff., 117 ff., 266 ff. Mesopotamian influences on the Iranian concept of royalty, pointed out by Widengren and other scholars, are also brought up by Gnoli in *Ex Orbe Religionum, Studia Geo Widengren oblata* (Leiden, 1972), vol. 2, pp. 94 ff.

See also J. Wolski, "Les Achémenides et les Arsacides, contributions à la formation des traditions iraniennes," *Syria* 43 (1966): 65–89.

On the initiatory scenario that can be deciphered in the saga of Cyrus, see Gerhard Binder, *Die Aussetzung des Königskindes: Kyros und Romulus*, *Beiträge zur klassischen Philologie* no. 10 (Meisenheim am Glan, 1964), esp. pp. 17–39, 58 ff., 116 ff.

106. On the ritual function of Persepolis—the sacred city built by Darius for the celebration of the *Nawrōz*—see R. Ghirshman, "A propos de Persépolis," *Artibus Asiae* 20 (1957): 265–78; A. U. Pope, "Persepolis, a Ritual City," *Archeology* 10 (1957): 123–30; and K. Derdmann, "Persepolis: Daten und Deutungen," *Mitteilungen der deutschen Orient-Gesellschaft zu Berlin*, no. 29 (1960), pp. 21–47.

On the relations among the Indo-European myths of the "exposed infant" and ritual combat against dragons, the founding of cities, and the cosmogony, see Gerhard Binder, *Die Aussetzung des Königskindes*, pp. 58 ff.

On the *Nawrōz*, see Eliade, *Cosmos and History*, pp. 63 ff.; Widengren, *Rel. de l'Iran*, pp. 58 ff.

107. On the problem of the Magi and their relations with Zoroastrianism, see G. Messina, *Die Ursprung der Magier und die zarathustrische Religion* (Rome, 1930); Widengren, *Rel. de l'Iran*, pp. 134 ff., 147 ff., 156 ff., 221 ff.; Zaehner, *Dawn and Twilight*, pp. 160 ff., 189 ff. According to the opinion accepted by a number of scholars, the Magi were originally a sacerdotal caste of the Medes. After their "conversion" to Mazdaism, they emigrated to the western part of the Empire. According to Widengren (p. 136), the treatise *Vidēvdāt* (= *Vendidad*) reflects the ideas, beliefs, and ritual views of the Magi. The same author (pp. 175 ff.) holds that Zurvan (see volume 2) was a divinity worshiped by the Magi.

For a new presentation of the protohistory of the Scythians, see S. P. Tolstov, "Les Scythes de l'Aral et le Khorezm," *Iranica Antiqua* 1 (1961): 42–92.

On the tripartite ideology among the Scythians, see Dumézil, *Mythe et Epopée*, vol. 1, pp. 439–575 (synthesis of earlier works). On the shamanism of the Scythians, see Karl Meuli, "Scythica," *Hermes* 70 (1935): 121–79, and Eliade, *Shamanism*, pp. 394 ff.

108. Unlike Zarathustra's *gāthās* in verse, the *Yasna-with-Seven-Chapters* is written in prose. On this text, see O. G. von Wesendonk, *Die Religionsgeschichtliche Bedeutung des Yasna haptanhaiti* (Bonn, 1931); Nyberg, *Die Religionen des alten Irans*, pp. 275 ff.; Zaehner, *Dawn and Twilight*, pp. 62 ff.; Duchesne-Guillemin, *La religion*, pp. 215 ff. (Eng. trans., pp. 147 ff.).

The *Yašts* have been translated by H. Lommel, *Die Yäšts des Awesta* (Göttingen and Leipzig, 1927). The *Hom Yašt* has been translated by J. M. Unvala, *Neryosangh's Sanskrit Version of the Hōm Yast* (*Yasna IX–XI*), *with the Original Avesta and Its Pahlavi Version* (Vienna, 1924). In his book *Vayu* (Uppsala, 1941), vol. 1, pp. 1–95, Stig Wikander has provided a German translation of *Yašt* 15, followed by a historico-religious commentary.

109. *Yašt* 10 has been translated, with a full commentary, by I. Gershevitch, *The Avestan Hymn to Mithra* (Cambridge, 1959). Cf. F. B. J. Kuiper, "Remarks on the Avestan Hymn to Mithra," *IIJ* 5 (1961): 36–60, and Ugo Bianchi, "La stella Sirio e l'influenza dell'astrologia caldea nell' Iran antico," *SMSR* 34 (1963): 237 ff.

110. On the *yazata* Tištrya (personification of the star Sirius) and the sacrifice offered to it by Ahura Mazdā, see G. Gnoli, "Note sur Yasht VIII, 23–52," *SMSR* 34 (1963): 91–101.

111. The sources used in §§ 111 and 112 are for the most part composed in Pahlavi. It would serve no purpose to dwell on the still unsolved problems of the chronology. The reader will find a clear exposition in the book by Duchesne-Guillemin, *La religion de l'Iran ancien*, pp. 40 ff. (Eng. trans., pp. 21 ff.). A nearly complete translation of the Pahlavi books was published by E. W. West, *Pahlavi Texts*, vols. 5, 18, 24, 37, and 47 of *Sacred Books of the East* (Oxford, 1888–97). The translation is outdated, but there are more recent translations of the *Bundahisn*, of some parts of the *Denkart*, and of other Pahlavi books; see Zaehner, *Dawn and Twilight*, p. 342, and especially Duchesne-Guillemin, *La religion*, pp. 52–63 (Eng. trans., pp. 40–49), which gives a summary of each work and notes the editions and the fragments translated. See also the bibliography drawn up by Colpe, "Altiran: Einleitung," in *WdM* 12 (1974): 197 ff.

Beliefs concerning postexistence have been analyzed by Nathan Söderblom, *La vie future d'après le mazdéisme* (Paris, 1901), and J. D. C. Pavry, *The Zoroastrian Doctrine of a Future Life* (New York, 1926); see a recent restatement in Widengren, *Les religions de l'Iran*, pp. 52 ff., 124 ff., 192 ff. The study by W. Bousset, "Die Himmelsreise der Seele," *ARW* 4 (1910): 136–69, 229–73 (reprinted, 1960), remains indispensable.

The *Hādōxt Nask* has been several times translated and commented upon since Söderblom (see his *La vie future*, pp. 82–88). See, inter alia, Karl F. Geldner, *Die Zoroastrische Religion* (= *Religionsgeschichtliches Lesebuch* [Tübingen, 1926], vol. 1, pp. 42–44); Carsten Colpe, *Die religionsgeschichtliche Schule* (Göttingen, 1961), pp. 126–29; G. Widengren, *Iranische Geisteswelt* (Baden-Baden, 1961), pp. 171–77. In contradiction to Carsten Colpe's exceptions (*Die Religionsgeschichtliche Schule*, pp. 121 ff.), Widengren has shown (*OLZ*, cols. 533–48) that this is an ancient text, whose language is close to that of the *gāthās*; see also his "Les origines du gnosticisme et l'histoire des religions," in *Le Origini dello gnosticismo*, ed. Ugo Bianchi (Leiden, 1964), pp. 28–60, esp. 49 ff., and *Les religions de l'Iran*, pp. 124 ff.; also L. H. Gray, "A Suggested Restoration of the *Hadoxt Nask,*" *JAOS* 67 (1947): 14–23.

The interpretation of the *dāenā* has occasioned controversies; see Gnoli, "Questioni sull'interpretazione," pp. 361 ff. The term, which ended by designating "religion," probably derives from the root *dāy-*, "to see," and is to be compared to the Vedic *dhīh*, "vision"; see Humbach, *Die Gāthās des Zarathustra*, vol. 1, pp. 56–58; J. Gonda, *The Vision of the Vedic Poets* (The Hague, 1963), pp. 259–65. The original meaning is bound up with Indo-Iranian concepts of inner vision; see Gnoli, "Questioni," p. 363. In its individual sense, the *dāenā* is regarded as a faculty at once human and divine (personified in the *paredros* of Ahura Mazdā); the collective meaning indicates the sum of all the individual *dāenās*, that is, those of the faithful who share the same doctrines and practice the same rites, a spiritual "collective being," the "Mazdean religion" or "church," in the sense of a community of the faithful; see Gnoli, p. 365.

On the initiatory symbolism of the Činvat Bridge and the meaning of the *dāenā*, see H. Corbin, *Terre céleste et Corps de Résurrection* (Paris, 1960), pp. 68 ff.; M. Molé, "Dāenā, le pont Činvat et l'initiation dans le Mazdéisme," *RHR* 158 (1960): 155–85.

On parallels to the Činvat, see Eliade, *Shamanism*, pp. 482 ff. ("The Bridge and the 'Difficult Passage'"); cf. Duchesne-Guillemin, *Religion*, pp. 333 ff. (Eng. trans., pp. 223 ff.). The traditions of the Western Middle Ages are examined by Peter Dinzelbacher, *Die Jenseitsbrücke im Mittelalter*, diss., University of Vienna no. 104 (Vienna, 1973).

112. The myth of Yima's *vara* and the catastrophic winter has been studied by Söderblom, *La vie future*, pp. 169–82; A. Christensen, *Les types du premier Homme et du premier Roi dans l'histoire légendaire des Iraniens*, 2 vols. (Leiden and Uppsala, 1917–34), vol. 2, pp. 16 ff., and passim. See also Dumézil, *Mythe et Epopée*, vol. 2, pp. 246 ff., 282 ff. (Eng. trans., *The Destiny of a King*, pp. 4 ff., 38 ff.).

For a comparative study of the "end of the world," see A. Olrik, *Ragnarok* (German translation by W. Ranisch, 1922).

On the *fravashis*, see N. Söderblom, *Les Fravashis: Étude sur les traces dans le mazdéisme d'une ancienne conception sur la survivance des morts* (Paris, 1899) (extract from *RHR*, vol. 39). The term is not documented in the *gāthās* (which refer instead to the *dāenā*). The *fravashis* return to earth during the last days of the year; cf. *Yašt* 13. 49; al Bīrūnī, *Chronology of Ancient Nations*, trans. H. Sachau (London, 1879), p. 210; Windengren,

Religions, p. 38. The belief is archaic and universally disseminated; see Eliade, *Cosmos and History*, pp. 62 ff.

As for the warlike aspect of the *fravashis*, Dumézil has brought out certain analogies with the Maruts; see his "Viṣṇu et les Marut à travers la réforme zoroastrienne," *JA* 242 (1953): 1–25, esp. 21 ff.

But the *fravashis* are also the celestial "double" of the men of the past, the present, and the future (*Yasna* 24. 5); according to some sources (cf. *Yašt* 13. 82–84), the Amesha Spentas also have their *fravashis*. In a passage of the *Vidēvdāt* (19. 46–48), Zarathustra learns to evoke the *fravashi* of Ahura Mazdā. This is a daring and enigmatic conception; but, as Bausani observes (*La Persia religiosa*, p. 68), the idea has not been explored.

113. On Israelite kingship and the monarchy, see J. Pedersen, *Israel: Its Life and Culture*, 4 vols. (London and Copenhagen, 1926, 1940), vol. 1/2, pp. 41 ff.; G. von Rad, *Old Testament Theology* (New York, 1926), vol. 1, pp. 306 ff.; G. Fohrer, *History of Israelite Religion* (Nashville, 1972), pp. 122 ff. (with a rich bibliography, pp. 122–23, 139–40); H. Ringgren, *La religion d'Israël*, pp. 235 ff. (critical presentation of the "Uppsala School") (Eng. trans., pp. 220 ff.); J. de Fraine, *L'aspect religieux de la royauté israélite* (Rome, 1954); Geo Widengren, *Sakrales Königtum im Alten Testament und im Judentum* (Stuttgart, 1955); Widengren, "King and Covenant," *JSS* 2 (1957): 1–32; M. Noth, *Gott, König und Volk im Alten Testament* (= *Gesammelte Studien* [1957], pp. 188–229); G. von Rad, "Das judäische Königsritual," in *Gesammelts Schriften* (1958), pp. 205–13; R. de Vaux, "Le roi d'Israël, vassal de Yahvé," in *Mélanges E. Tisserant* (1964), vol. 1, pp. 119–33; A. R. Johnson, *Sacral Kingship in Ancient Israel*, 2d ed. (1967). For a comparative study, see Sidney Smith, "The Practice of Kingship in Early Semitic Kingdoms," in *Myth, Ritual, and Kingship*, ed. S. H. Hooke (Oxford, 1958), pp. 22–73; and especially K. H. Bernhardt, *Das Problem der altorientalischen Königsideologie im Alten Testament* (Leiden, 1961), and I. Seibert, *Hirt-Herde-König* (Berlin, 1969).

On David and Solomon, see Fohrer, *History of Israelite Religion*, pp. 125 ff.; R. A. Carlson, *David the Chosen King* (1965); and G. W. Ahlström, "Solomon the Chosen One," *HR* 8 (1968): 93–110.

On the symbolism of the Temple of Jerusalem and the importance of the royal cult, see N. Poulssen, *König und Tempel im Glaubenszeugnis des Alten Testament* (Stuttgart, 1967); G. W. Ahlström, *Psalm 89: Eine Liturgie aus dem Ritual des leidenden Königs* (Lund, 1959); T. A. Busink, *Der Tempel von Jerusalem. I: Der Tempel Salomos* (Leiden, 1970). See also J. Schreiner, *Sion-Jerusalem: Jahwes Königssitz* (Munich, 1963); F. Stolz, *Strukturen und Figuren im Kult von Jerusalem* (Berlin, 1970); E. L. Ehrlich, *Die Kultsymbolik im Alten Testament und im nachbiblischen Judentum*

(Stuttgart, 1959); H. J. Hermisson, *Sprache und Ritus im altisraelitischen Kult* (Neukirchen and Vluyn, 1965).

114. On the "Psalms of Enthronement," see S. Mowinckel, *Psalmenstudien*, vol. 2: *Das Thronbesteigungsfest Jahwäs und der Ursprung der Eschatologie* (Christiania, 1922). On the cult function of the Psalms, see S. Mowinckel, *The Psalms in Israel's Worship*, 2 vols. (New York and Oxford, 1962); H. Ringgren, *Faith of the Psalmist* (Philadelphia, 1963); H. Zirker, *Die kultische Vergegenwartigung der Vergangenheit in den Psalmen* (Bonn, 1964); C. Westermann, *The Praise of God in the Psalms* (Richmond, 1965). See also O. Keel, *Feinde und Gottesleugner: Studien zum Image des Widersacher in den Individualpsalmen* (Stuttgart, 1969).

On Yahweh as "living God," see H. Ringgren, *La religion d'Israël*, pp. 99 ff. (Eng. trans., pp. 87 ff.); Fohrer, *History*, pp. 164 ff. See also Ringgren, *World and Wisdom: Studies in the Hypostatization of Divine Qualities in the Ancient Near East* (Lund, 1947). On the Israelite conceptions of the living being and of "breath-spirit," see the works by von Rad, and see O. Eissfeldt, *The Old Testament*.

On the idea of the resurrection, see H. Riesenfeld, *The Resurrection in Ezekiel XXXVII and in the Dura-Europos Paintings* (Uppsala, 1948); Widengren, *Sakrales Königtum*, pp. 45 ff.

115. The Book of Job is made up of a prologue and epilogue in prose and a central part, in verse, comprising the dialogues between Job and his friends. There is a certain divergence between the parts in verse and those in prose.

From the enormous literature on Job, we single out O. Eissfeldt, *The Old Testament*, pp. 454 ff., 764 ff. (bibliography); G. Fohrer, *Studien zum Buche Hiob* (1963); S. Terrien, *Job* (Neuchâtel, 1963); J. Pedersen, "Scepticisme israëlite," *RHPR* 10 (1930): 317–70; P. Humbert, "Le modernisme de Job," *VT*, suppl. 3 (1955): 150–61; H. H. Rowley, "The Book of Job and Its Meaning" (= *From Moses to Qumran* [1963], pp. 141–83).

116. On Elijah, see G. von Rad, *Old Testament Theology*, vol. 2, pp. 14–31; G. Fohrer, *History of Israélite Religion*, pp. 230 ff. (n. 15, bibliography); L. Bronner, *The Stories of Elijah and Elisha as Polemics against Baal Worship* (1968), and the two volumes of the *Etudes Carmélitaines: Elie le Prophète*, vol. 1: *Selon les Ecritures et les traditions chrétiennes;* vol. 2: *Au Carmel, dans le Judaïsme et l'Islam* (Paris, 1956); see especially P. Marie-Joseph Stiassny, "Le Prophète Elie dans le Judaïsme," in vol. 2, pp. 199–255.

On the cult prophets, see A. Haldar, *Associations of Cult Prophets among the Ancient Semites* (Uppsala, 1945); H. H. Rowley, *Worship in Ancient Israel*, pp. 144–75; J. Jeremias, *Kultprophetie und Gerichtsverkundigung in der späteren Königzeit Israels* (Neukirchen and Vluyn, 1970).

On the relations between the kings and the cult prophets, see J. Petersen, *Israel*, vol. 1/2, pp. 124 ff.; F. M. Cross, *Canaanite Myth and Hebrew Epic*, pp. 217 ff., 237 ff.

The recent literature on Old Testament prophecy is analyzed in the studies by H. H. Rowley, "The Nature of Old Testament Prophecy in the Light of Recent Study," *Harvard Theological Review* 38 (1945): 1–38, and G. Fohrer, "Neuere Literatur zur Alttestamentlichen Prophetie," *Theologische Rundschau* (1951): 277–346; ibid. (1952): 192–97, 295–361; Fohrer, "Zehn Jahre Literatur zur altestamentlichen Prophetie," ibid. (1962): 1–75, 235–97, 301–74. For a brief exposition, see von Rad, *Theology*, vol. 2, pp. 50 ff.; Fohrer, *History of Israelite Religion*, pp. 230 ff. See also S. Mowinckel, "The 'Spirit' and the 'Word' in the Pre-Exilic Reforming Prophets," *Journal of Biblical Literature* 53 (1934): 199–227; André Neher, *L'essence du prophétisme* (Paris, 1955), pp. 85–178 (the Hebraic framework of prophecy), and 179–350 (the experience of prophecy); Claude Tresmontant, *La doctrine morale des prophètes d'Israël* (Paris, 1958).

On the symbolic meaning of acts performed by the prophets, see G. Fohrer, *Die symbolischen Handlungen der Propheten*, 2d ed. (1968).

117. On Amos and Hosea, see G. von Rad, *Theology*, vol. 2, pp. 129–46; Ringgren, *La religion d'Israël*, pp. 278 ff.; Fohrer, *History of Israelite Religion*, pp. 243–61; H. S. Nyberg, *Studien zum Hoseabuche* (Uppsala, 1935); A. Caquot, "Osée et la royauté," *RHPR* 41 (1961): 123–46; E. Jacob, "L'héritage cananéen dans le livre du prophète Osée," *RHPR* 43 (1963): 250–59.

118. On Isaiah, see O. Eissfeldt, *The Old Testament*, pp. 303–46 (bibliography, pp. 303–4); von Rad, *Theology*, vol. 2, pp. 147–69; Fohrer, *History*, pp. 251–57. Cf. also S. H. Blank, *Prophetic Faith in Isaiah* (1958). Micah of Moresheth, a younger contemporary of Isaiah, probably preached between 725 and 711. His eight discourses occur in the first three chapters of his book. Certain passages (1:16; 2:4–5, 10, 12–14), as well as other sections, are postexilic additions. Micah is not concerned with international policy but attacks the social iniquities and moral depravity of Judah. Punishment will not be long in coming. The country will be devastated (5:10; 6:16), and "Zion will become ploughland, Jerusalem a heap of rubble, and the mountain of the Temple a wooded height" (3:12). In the postexilic additions there is a Messianic pericope. Out of Bethlehem will be born "the one who is to rule over Israel"; then Assyria will be conquered, and the king "will extend his power to the ends of the land. He himself will be peace" (5:1–5). See Fohrer, *History*, p. 257, n. 20, for bibliography on Micah.

In the last third of the seventh century three "minor prophets" carry on their ministry: Zephaniah, Habakkuk, and Nahum. The first deserves attention for the vigor with which he announces the imminence of the "day of Yahweh": "The great day of Yahweh is near. . . . A day of wrath, that day, a day of distress and agony, a day of ruin and devastation," etc. (1:14 ff.).

119. On Jeremiah, see G. von Rad, *Theology*, vol. 2, pp. 188–99; Eissfeldt, *Old Testament*, pp. 346–64, 717–18 (with a rich bibliography); Fohrer, *History*, pp. 188–99.

120. On Ezekiel, see von Rad, vol. 2, pp. 230–37; Eissfeldt, pp. 365–81 (rich bibliography, pp. 365–69, 758); G. Fohrer, *Die Hauptprobleme des Buches Ezechiel* (1952); Fohrer, *History*, pp. 316–21. See also J. Steinmann, *Le prophète Ezéchiel et les débuts de l'exil* (1953); T. Chary, *Les prophètes et le culte à partir de l'exil* (1955).

121. On the concept of the "day of Yahweh," see G. von Rad, "The Origin of the Concept of the Day of Yahweh," *JSS* 4 (1959): 97–108, and his *Old Testament Theology*, vol. 2, 119–25.

On the King of the future, the Messiah, see S. Mowinckel, *He That Cometh* (New York, 1954), pp. 96 ff., 155 ff.

On the religious valorization of history in the prophets, see Eliade, *Cosmos and History*, pp. 102 ff.

122. The history of the interpretations of Dionysus is the subject of a still unpublished doctoral dissertation by Park McGinty, "Approaches to Dionysos: A Study of the Methodological Presuppositions in the Various Theories of Greek Religion as Illustrated in the Study of Dionysos" (University of Chicago, December 1972). McGinty discusses the interpretations of Friedrich Nietzsche (*Die Geburt der Tragödie*, 1871; Eng. trans. by Walter Kaufman, *The Birth of Tragedy* [New York, 1967]); Erwin Rohde (*Psyche*, 1894; Eng. trans., New York, 1925); Jane Harrison (*Prolegomena*, 1901; *Themis*, 1912); Martin P. Nilsson (especially *Geschichte der griechische Religion*, vol. 1, pp. 571 ff., and *The Minoan-Mycenaean Religion*, 1927; 2d ed., 1950); Walter Otto (*Dionysos*, 1933; English trans. by R. B. Palmer, *Dionysos: Myth and Cult* [Bloomington, Ind., 1965]); E. R. Dodds (*The Greeks and the Irrational*, 1951), and W. K. Guthrie. In

French there is the admirable work by H. Jeanmaire, *Dionysos: Histoire du culte de Bacchus* (Paris, 1951), with a rich bibliography (pp. 483–504).
On the etymology of Semele, see P. Kretschmer, *Aus der Anomia* (1890), pp. 17 ff. Kretschmer connected the Thraco-Phrygian vocable Semelô, documented in Phrygian funerary inscriptions from the imperial period and designating the Earth Goddess, with Slavic *zemljia*, "earth," and Zemnya, the Lithuanian name of the chthonian goddess. This etymology has been accepted by Nilsson (*Min.-Mycenaean Rel.*, p. 567) and Wilamowitz (*Der Glaube der Hellenen*, vol. 2, p. 60) but is rejected, among others, by Otto (*Dionysos*, pp. 69 ff.).

For a century scholars attempted to explain the "persecution" of Dionysus by the history of the penetration of his cult into Greece; implicitly, the god was considered a "foreigner," come from Thrace (e.g., Rohde) or from Phrygia (e.g., Nilsson). Since the discovery of his name in the Mycenaean inscriptions, a number of authors have defended the Cretan origin of Dionysus; see Karl Kerényi, "Die Herkunft der Dionysosreligion nach dem heutigen Stand der Forschung," in *Arbeitsgemeinschaft für Forschung des Landes Nordrhein Westfalen* (Cologne, 1956), pp. 5 ff.; Kerényi, *Der Frühe Dionysos* (1960). Cf. the remarks by Pestalozza, "Motivi matriarcali in Etolia ed Epiro," *Rendiconti Ist. Lomb. di Scienze e Lettere* 87 (Milan, 1957): 583–622; republished in *Nuovi saggi di religione mediterranea* [Florence, 1964], pp. 257–95, esp. 272–73, n. 3. See also T. B. L. Webster, "Some Thoughts on the Prehistory of Greek Drama," *Bull. Inst. Classical Studies, University of London* 5 (1958): 43–48; G. van Hoorn, "Dionysos et Ariadne," *Menemosyne* 12 (1959): 193–97, and especially J. Puhvel, "Eleuther and Oinoâtis," in *Mycenaean Studies*, ed. E. L. Bennett, Jr. (Madison, Wis., 1964), pp. 161–70.

123. The festivals in honor of Dionysus are analyzed by Jeanmaire, *Dionysos*, pp. 25 ff. (bibliography). See also, on the Lenaea, M. P. Nilsson, *Griechische Feste* (Leipzig, 1906), pp. 275 ff.; L. Deubner, *Attische Feste* (Berlin, 1932), pp. 125 ff. On the Anthesteria, see Jeanmaire, pp. 48–56 and 486 (bibliography).

On the religious function of contests and ritual combats, see Eliade, *The Quest*, pp. 163 ff.

On the mythico-ritual theme of the periodical return of the dead, see Eliade, *The Two and the One*, pp. 125 ff.; V. Lanternari, *La Grande Festa* (Milan, 1959), pp. 411 ff.

124. E. R. Dodds has analyzed, from a comparative viewpoint, certain specifically Dionysiac features described in the *Bacchae* (oreibasia ["roaming the mountains"], frantic dances, Maenadism, attacks on villages), showing that these are rites and customs documented everywhere in Greece, before and after Euripides; see his "Maenadism in the *Bacchae*," *Harvard Theological Review* 33 (1940): 155–76. Jeanmaire has pursued the inquiry beyond Greece in his *Dionysos*, pp. 119 ff. (the *zar* and the *buri* in North Africa, Arabia, and Abyssinia). In Greece, examples of *mania* brought on by other gods are known; see Jeanmaire, pp. 109 ff. Farnell (*Cults*, vol. 5, pp. 167–71) has brought together the references to human sacrifices and ritual cannibalism. On Corybantism, see Jeanmaire, pp. 123 ff., and the comparative study by Ernesto de Martino, *La Terra del rimorso* (Milan, 1961), pp. 220 ff. For a ritual interpretation of the episode of Pentheus, see Clara Gallini, "Il travestismo rituale di Penteo," *SMSR* 34 (1967): 211 ff.

The rites of tearing in pieces (*sparagmos*) and consuming raw flesh (*ōmophagia*) characterize the Muslim sect of the Aissawa ('Isāwiyya); see R. Eissler, "Nachleben dionysischen Mysterienritus," *ARW* (1928): 172–83, who was the first to use the book by René Brunel, *Essai sur la confrérie religieuse des Aissäoua au Maroc* (Paris, 1926); cf. also Eisler, *Man into Wolf* (London, 1951), pp. 112 ff.; Jeanmaire, *Dionysos*, pp. 259 ff.

On the survival of the bull sacrifice in Thrace, see C. A. Romaios, *Cultes populaires de la Thrace* (Athens, 1949), pp. 50 ff.

125. We shall return in volume 2 to the Dionysiac Mystery, in the chapter devoted to the religions of the Hellenistic period, and certain meanings of the myth of the dismemberment of the infant Dionysus-Zagreus will be discussed in the chapter on Orphism.

On the playthings with which the Titans attracted the infant Dionysus-Zagreus, see Jane Harrison, *Themis*, pp. 61 ff.; R. Pettazzoni, *I Misteri* (Bologna, 1924), pp. 19 ff.; Jeanmaire, *Dionysos*, p. 383 (on the papyrus from Faiyum). It is important to point out that certain details of this episode reflect archaic ideas and beliefs. One of the playthings in particular, the bull-roarer, is used in the puberty rites of primitives (see Eliade, *Birth and Rebirth*, pp. 22 ff.; O. Zerries, *Das Schwirrholz* [Stuttgart, 1942], pp. 84 ff., 188 ff.), and the practice of covering the face with chalk or gypsum (Harrison, *Prolegomena*, pp. 491 ff.; Pettazzoni, *La religion dans la Grèce antique*, pp. 120 ff.) is documented in many primitive secret societies.

Walter Otto (*Dionysos*, pp. 191 ff.) has shown that some of the data contained in comparatively late works derive from older sources.

On the "problem" attributed to Aristotle, see L. Moulinier, *Orphée et l'orphisme à l'époque classique* (Paris, 1955), pp. 51 ff.

The Mysteries of Dionysus have given rise to a lengthy controversy. We shall return to this problem in the second volume of the present work. See, for the moment, P. Boyancé, "L'antre dans les mystères de Dionysos," *Rendiconti della Pontificia Accademia di Archeologia* 33 (1962): 107–27; R. Turcan, "Du nouveau sur l'initiation dionysiaque," *Latomus* 24 (1965): 101–19; P. Boyancé, "Dionysiaca: A propos d'une étude récente sur l'initiation dionysiaque," *Revue des Etudes Anciennes* 68 (1966): 33–60.

Index